Correction Chart

This list of the most widely used correction symbols and abbreviations covers the most common errors in writing. The number following the explanation refers to the section of the *Handbook* to be consulted for a discussion of the error and for help in revising.

Ab   abbreviation incorrect or inappropriate   16.1

Abst   expression too abstract   23.4

Adj   incorrect adjective form   9

Adv   incorrect adverb form   9, 9.4

Agr   error in agreement
     subject-verb   5
     pronoun and antecedent   7.2

Amb   ambiguous expression

Apos   apostrophe incorrectly used or omitted   15.3
     with possessive of nouns   6.2
     with possessive pronouns   7.3

Awk   awkward expression

Big W   big word or stilted language   24.1

Cap   use capital letter   15.1

Case   wrong case form of pronoun   7.3

CF   comma fault   2.2

Coh   lacks coherence (continuity)
     between paragraphs   21.3
     within paragraphs   27.3

Comma   error in use of comma   11

Comp   mistake in comparison of adjective or adverb   9.7, 9.8

Dead   deadwood   25.4

Div   word division incorrect   22.2, 28.1

Dm   dangling modifier   4.4

Emph   ideas in sentence not emphasized correctly   26.4

Fig   ineffective or inappropriate figure of speech   24.4

Frag   fragmentary sentence   2.1

FS   fused sentence   2.3

Hyph   error in use of hyphen   15.2

Id   unidiomatic
     expression   8.5
     comparison   9.8

Inf   expression too informal   24.2

Ital   add italics (underline)   14.3

lc   use lower case letter   15.1

Mix   mixed construction   2.4

MM   misrelated modifier
     verbal phrase   4.3
     adverbial modifier   9.5

Mng   meaning not clear

MS   error in manuscript form   28.1

No Cap   no capital letter   15.1

Num   incorrect use of figures or words for numbers   16.2

Org   faulty organization   20

Par, ¶   paragraph   27

¶ Con   paragraph lacks continuity   27.3

¶ dev   paragraph poorly developed   27.1

Paral   elements should be parallel in form   26.3

Parens   parentheses used incorrectly or omitted   13.2

Pass   passive voice used ineffectively   8.3

Pl   incorrect plural form   6.1, 17.3

Pron   incorrect pronoun form   7

Punc   error in punctuation

No Punc   punctuation should be omitted

Punctuation Symbols

⊙   period   10.1

!   exclamation mark   10.3

?   question mark   10.2

⌄   comma   11
     with coordinate clauses   11.1
     after conjunctive
     adverbs   11.2
     after introductory
     elements   11.3
     with nonrestrictive
     modifiers   11.4
     with interrupting
     elements   11.5
     in a list or series   11.6
     for clarity   11.7
     conventional uses   11.8

No ⌄   omit comma   11.9

⌃   semicolon   12.1

colon   12.2

/--/   dash   13.1

(/)   parentheses   13.2

⌐/⌐   brackets   13.3

quotation marks   14.1

/.../   ellipses   14.2

/=/   hyphen   15.2

apostrophe   15.3

Ref   reference of pronoun unclear   7.1

Rep   careless repetition   25.5

Rest   error in punctuation of restrictive
or nonrestrictive modifier   11.4

Shift   shift (inconsistency)
     in pronoun form   7.6
     in verb tense   8.1

SL   sentence length ineffective   25.2

Sp   spelling error   17

Sub   faulty subordination   3.4, 3.5, 26.2

T   error in use of tense   8.1

Trans   needs better transition   21.3

Trite   trite expression   24.3

Var   ineffective or insufficient
sentence variety   26.1

Vb   error in verb form   8

Wdy   wordy   25.3

W W   wrong word   17.2, 23.3

//   elements should be parallel in form

⌒   close up space

separate with a space

∧   omission

X   careless error

✓   good

Handbook of Current English

Sixth Edition

Grammar and Usage

Punctuation and Other Conventions

Composition

Diction

Sentences and Paragraphs

Practical Writing Tasks

Handbook

of Current English

Sixth Edition

Jim W. Corder

Texas Christian University

Scott, Foresman and Company
Glenview, Illinois

Dallas, Tex.   Oakland, N.J.   Palo Alto, Cal.   Tucker, Ga.   London, England

Library of Congress Cataloging in Publication Data

Corder, Jimmie Wayne.
   Handbook of current English.

   Includes index.
   1. English language — Rhetoric. 2. English language —
   Grammar — 1950- I. Title.
PE1408.P4376 1981 808'.042 80 – 22879
ISBN 0-673-15425-4

Some of the material in this book was first published in *Contemporary Writing* by Jim
W. Corder. Copyright © 1979 Scott, Foresman and Company.

The instructor's guide may be obtained through a local Scott, Foresman representative or by writing to English Editor, College Division, Scott, Foresman and Company,
1900 East Lake Avenue, Glenview, IL 60025.

2   3   4   5 6-GBC-86 85 84 83 82 81

Acknowledgments

The sources of quotations used for illustrative purposes are indicated in the text. Special acknowledgment is due for permission to reprint the following selections:

Excerpts from *Desert Solitaire* by Edward Abbey. Copyright 1968 by Edward Abbey. Reprinted by permission of Harold Matson Co., Inc.

Reprinted by permission of the publishers and the Trustees of Amherst College from *The Poems of Emily Dickinson,* edited by Thomas H. Johnson, Cambridge, Mass.: The Belknap Press of Harvard University Press, Copyright © 1951, 1955 by the President and Fellows of Harvard College.

"On Morality" excerpted with the permission of Farrar, Straus & Giroux, Inc. and William Morris Agency, Inc. from *Slouching Toward Bethlehem* by Joan Didion. Copyright © 1965, 1968 by Joan Didion.

Excerpt from the *Fort Worth Star-Telegram,* January 26, 1977. Reprinted by permission.

Uwe George. *In the Deserts of This Earth.* Translated from the German by Richard and Clara Winston. New York: Harcourt Brace Jovanovich, Inc., 1977, p. 39.

Glamour Editorial. Courtesy *Glamour,* Copyright © 1979 by The Condé Nast Publications Inc.

From *The Lottery* by Shirley Jackson. Copyright 1948, 1949 by Shirley Jackson. Copyright renewed © 1976, 1977 by Laurence Hyman, Barry Hyman, Mrs. Sarah Webster and Mrs. Joanne Schnurer. Reprinted by permission of Farrar, Straus & Giroux, Inc. and Brandt & Brandt.

From *I Have a Dream* by Martin Luther King, Jr. Copyright © 1963 by Martin Luther King, Jr. Reprinted by permission of Joan Daves, Agent.

By permission. From *Webster's New Collegiate Dictionary* © 1980 by G. & C. Merriam Co., Publishers of the Merriam-Webster Dictionaries.

"Year-round roses" from "Observations" © 1977 Mobil Corporation.

From the Introduction to *The Way to Rainy Mountain* by N. Scott Momaday. The Introduction was first published in *The Reporter,* January 26, 1967, and was reprinted in *The Way to Rainy Mountain,* copyright 1969. The University of New Mexico Press.

Excerpt from *The Way to Rainy Mountain* by N. Scott Momaday. Copyright © 1969 by the University of New Mexico Press. Reprinted by permission.

Excerpt from "Marrakech" from *Such, Such Were the Joys* by George Orwell. Reprinted by permission of Harcourt Brace Jovanovich, Inc., Mrs. Sonia Brownell Orwell and Martin Secker & Warburg.

From "Sneer Words" by William Safire, *New York Times Magazine,* January 13, 1980. © 1980 by The New York Times Company. Reprinted by permission.

From "Strong Stuff" by William Safire, *New York Times Magazine,* January 27, 1980. © 1980 by The New York Times Company. Reprinted by permission.

Excerpt from "Human-Not-Quite Human" from *Unpopular Opinions* by Dorothy L. Sayers. Reprinted by permission of David Higham Associates Limited.

From "Money Need, Social Change Combine to Cut Apron Strings" by Philip Shabecoff, *New York Times,* May 7, 1978. © 1978 by The New York Times Company. Reprinted by permission.

From " 'Super Sell' Raked in Millions for CBS" by Tom Shales. © 1980, The Washington Post Company. Reprinted by permission.

Excerpts from "A Way of Writing" by William Stafford reprinted by permission of The University of Michigan Press from *Writing the Australian Crawl,* copyright © 1978 The University of Michigan. "A Way of Writing" first appeared in Field, Vol. 2, Spring 1970.

Letters to the editor of *Time,* June 27, 1977. Reprinted by permission. Copyright 1977 Time Inc. All rights reserved.

From "Dear Abby" by Abigail van Buren, *Fort Worth Star-Telegram,* January 23, 1980. Reprinted by permission.

E. B. White, "Democracy." From *The Wild Flag* (Houghton Mifflin); © 1943 E.B. White. Originally in *The New Yorker.* Reprinted by permission.

From pp. 192, 198, 248–249 in *One Man's Meat* by E.B. White. Copyright 1940, 1941 by E.B. White. Reprinted by permission of Harper & Row, Publishers, Inc.

Preface

The Sixth Edition of the *Handbook of Current English* perpetuates certain convictions that have marked the book from its beginning: that selective and thoughtful use of language is important in every part of everyone's life; that some forms of expression are more effective and more appropriate in given situations than others; that a "good" language is a language decently suited to its speaker or writer, to the subject at hand, to the audiences that receive the language, and to the context in which all come together. This edition has been revised to retain all the coverage of former editions, to expand some portions, and to add some new material. All changes, I hope, are in aid of clear, straightforward, and sufficient advice to students.

New material appears in various ways, though the organization of the book remains essentially the same as that of the Fifth Edition. Modest alterations and additions occur in the Introduction, slightly reorganized and now called "Using the Language." I have made few changes in the first half of the book (Sections 1–17) except for brief clarifications and for expansions of some exercises. In Section 18 the discussion of the relationship among writer, subject, and audience and the preliminary discussion of types of writing are both, I believe, appreciably improved. Section 19 has been reorganized for what I believe will be better and more natural use. Section 28, on revising and correcting papers, has been expanded. In former editions, this section focused too narrowly upon revising and correcting a paper *after* it has been completed or submitted. The new first part of the section concentrates on the need for revising while the writing of the paper is still in progress. Section 29 includes an expanded coverage of letter writing and a new part on report writing. In Section 30 I have eliminated the sample research paper used in the Fifth Edition and put in its place two somewhat shorter papers, which I believe clearly illustrate the various techniques that students need to practice. The conventions of written presentation of research have been updated to conform to those of the *MLA Handbook*. A new feature, at the end of Sections 18, 19, 20, 21, and 28, is an "essay in progress" in stages from the first rough notes to a revised complete version.

Throughout the revision, my purpose has been to make material accessible. I believe the present sequence is good and usable; at the same time, I believe that the sections can be rearranged according to the needs of particular teachers and particular classes, and that they can stand alone as reference sources.

The organization and features of *Handbook of Current English* are designed to make the text easy and effective to use, as the following discussion explains.

Introduction: Using the Language.   The introduction is a discussion of the English language; it includes an account of distinctions between speaking and writing and of some varieties of English and the ways they can be used. The introduction suggests some ways of moving among varieties of English according to the principle of appropriateness. Some recommendations made throughout the text may be clearer if students read this material at the start of the course.

Part One: Resources for Composition

Sections 1 through 9: Grammar and Usage.   These sections review the grammar of English sentences and the functions of various kinds of words and word groups.

Sections 10 through 17: Punctuation and Other Conventions. These sections discuss and illustrate the principles governing the use of punctuation, mechanics, and other conventions, as well as various customs for using capital letters, apostrophes, abbreviations, and numbers. The final section, Spelling, suggests ways to overcome various spelling problems.

The sections in this first half of the *Handbook* treat single, definite topics. Grammatical definitions are included where they are relevant and necessary to the discussion. Many particular matters of usage are discussed at the point where they relate to general principles, but many more are included in the Glossary of Usage.

Part Two: Practices in Composition

The second half of the *Handbook* serves as a brief rhetoric and as a practical guide to college writing.

Sections 18 through 21: Composition.   These beginning sections focus on the processes of discovering what can or should be written and on the first steps in giving shape and character to the writing. These four sections constitute a discussion of what might be called prewriting.

Sections 22 through 24: Diction.   These sections discuss the dictionary and deal with appropriate and effective uses of words.

Sections 25 through 27: Sentences and Paragraphs. These sections discuss means by which sentences and paragraphs can be managed and controlled to shape meaning; they show ways of using various sentence patterns and various patterns of paragraph construction to develop ideas.

Sections 28 through 30: Practical Writing Tasks. Problems of revising and practical matters in whole compositions are the chief concerns here. Section 28, on revising, suggests ways of altering emphasis, mood, tone, and direction to suit the needs of the writing at hand. Section 29 discusses and illustrates some particular kinds of writing, including answers to essay examinations, literary analyses, letters, and reports. The final section is devoted to the special problems of research writing. Two new sample research papers are included.

Glossary of Usage. The Glossary gives succinct advice about the words and constructions that most often cause confusion in college writing.

Exercises. Where possible, the exercises call for students to do some writing themselves, rather than to respond to another person's writing or to underline or to fill in blanks. The exercises characteristically appear, not bunched at the ends of sections, but within the sections, immediately following the pertinent material. Colored circles mark exercises wherever they occur within the section.

Marginal tabs and correction charts. The colored marginal thumb tabs correspond to each of the six main divisions discussed above. In the margin of each right-hand page is also the pertinent correction symbol or abbreviation to indicate the material on those pages.

Themes can be marked by using either the correction symbols or the section numbers; the two are coordinated in the correction chart on the inside front cover as well as on the marginal tabs. In the text itself, the handwritten correction symbols appear with specific suggestions for revision, printed in color. Students should study the text that follows each suggestion whenever they are not sure why revision is necessary.

Appearing on the inside back cover of the book is a checklist for revision; it should be helpful for students to go over their papers with those questions in mind before they hand in their themes.

Workbook, Exercisebook, and Diagnostic Tests. The *Handbook of Current English* consists of a total program. Along with the *Handbook* itself is *Workbook of Current English,* by William E. Mahaney, *Universal Supplementary Exercisebook,* by Kathleen Ruhl, and *Diagnostic Tests,* by Hugh Paschal and revised by Dorothy Strang. Keyed to the *Handbook,* the *Workbook* contains imaginative and varied exercises to give students further practice in identifying structures, correcting errors, and writing sentences and paragraphs using specific writing principles. Usable with any modern handbook, *Universal Supplemenary Exercisebook* provides twice as many exercises as most exercise books accompanying handbooks. The *Diagnostic Tests* are intended to test student's mastery of grammatical and rhetorical skills; they are available to schools that adopt the *Handbook* or *Workbook.*

Acknowledgments

I cannot list all of the teachers, scholars, and friends to whom I am indebted, but I want to mention some. In the text itself, as some will note, I have sometimes used plural pronouns, not because I think of myself as an editorial "we," but because I'm glad to remember Porter Perrin, who first conceived this handbook.

I want to thank many of the *Handbook's* users for valuable suggestions on the revision. I am especially grateful to Santi Buscemi, Middlesex County College; Helen Rothschild Ewald, Washburn University; Jenefer Giannasi, Northern Illinois University; Geraldine Lasch, SUNY Agricultural and Technical College at Alfred; Jo Ann Pevoto, College of the Mainland; John Ruszkiewicz, University of Texas; and Gina Williams, Hillsborough Community College, Ybor City Campus. I am grateful for the continuing friendship and aid of Richard D. Welna and Amanda Clark of Scott, Foresman and Company, and for new friends there, Harriett Prentiss, Jane Steinmann, and Meredith Hellestrae, who have been uncommonly kind and helpful to me and thoughtful of the book's potential readers.

And finally, inadequately but constantly, I thank Patsy.

Jim W. Corder

Contents

Introduction: Using the Language   1
The Language We Use   1
The Search for a "Good" Language   14
**Review: Some Versions of American English —
A Summary   15**
The Design of the Book and Its Focus on Writing   21

Part One: Resources for Composition

Grammar and Usage

1   Grammar of Sentences   24
1.1   Main Sentence Elements   25
1.2   Secondary Sentence Elements   29
Review: Main Sentence Elements   30
1.3   Phrases and Clauses   32
Review: Modifiers   33
1.4   Sentences Classified by Clause Structure   35
1.5   Sentences Classified by Purpose   38
1.6   Unorthodox Sentences   38

2   Common Sentence Errors   41
2.1   Fragmentary Sentences   41
2.2   Comma Faults   44
2.3   Fused Sentences   48
2.4   Mixed Constructions   49

3   Subordinate Clauses and Connectives   50
3.1   Adjective Clauses   50
3.2   Adverb Clauses   51
3.3   Noun Clauses   52
3.4   Subordination for Exact Statement   54
3.5   Faulty Subordination   57

4   Verbals   60
4.1   Using Verbal Phrases   61
    Review: Forms and Uses of Verbals   62
4.2   Idiomatic Use of Infinitives and Gerunds   64
4.3   Misrelated Modifiers   65
4.4   Dangling Modifiers   66
4.5   Absolute Modifiers   67

5   Agreement of Subject and Verb   69
5.1   Verbs with Compound Subjects   69
5.2   Verbs with Collective Nouns as Subjects   72
5.3   Blind Agreement   74

6   Nouns   78
6.1   Plurals of Nouns   78
    Review: Forms, Functions, and Classes of Nouns   79
6.2   Possessive (Genitive) Case   80
6.3   Use of *A* and *An* with Nouns   83
6.4   Noun Modifiers   83

7   Pronouns   85
7.1   Reference of Pronouns   85
    Review: Kinds of Pronouns   88
7.2   Agreement of Pronoun and Antecedent   91
7.3   Case of Pronouns   94
7.4   Reflexive and Intensive Pronouns   97
7.5   Choice of Personal Pronoun Form   98
7.6   Avoiding Shifts in Pronoun Form   99

8   Verbs   101
8.1   Tense   101
    Review: Most Frequently Used Verb Tenses   103
8.2   Irregular Verbs and Auxiliaries   105
    Review: Terms Used in Describing Verbs   111
8.3   Active and Passive Voice   113
8.4   Use of the Subjunctive Mood   115
8.5   Idioms with Verbs   116
    Review: Troublesome Idioms with Verbs   117

9   Adjectives and Adverbs   118
9.1   Position of Adjectives   118
9.2   Predicate Adjectives   119
9.3   Demonstrative Adjectives   120
9.4   Forms of Adverbs   121
9.5   Position of Adverbs   122
9.6   Double Negatives   125
9.7   Comparison of Adjectives and Adverbs   126
9.8   Making Comparisons Idiomatic   129
        Review: Parts of Speech   132

Punctuation and Other Conventions

10   End Punctuation   133
10.1   Periods   133
10.2   Question Marks   134
10.3   Exclamation Marks   135

11   Commas   137
11.1   Commas Between Coordinate Clauses   137
11.2   Commas After Conjunctive Adverbs   138
11.3   Commas After Long Introductory Elements   138
        Review: Commas   140
11.4   Commas with Nonrestrictive Modifiers   141
11.5   Commas to Set Off Interrupting and Parenthetical
        Elements   144
11.6   Commas to Separate Items in a Series   146
11.7   Commas to Separate for Clarity   148
11.8   Commas in Conventional Places   148
11.9   Misused Commas   150

12   Semicolons and Colons   153
12.1   Semicolons   153
12.2   Colons   156

13   Dashes, Parentheses, and Brackets   159
13.1   Dashes   159
13.2   Parentheses   160
13.3   Brackets   161

14 Quotation Marks, Ellipses, and Italics 164
14.1 Quotation Marks 164
14.2 Ellipses 170
14.3 Italics 171

15 Capital Letters, Hyphens, and Apostrophes 175
15.1 Capital Letters 175
15.2 Hyphens 180
15.3 Apostrophes 184

16 Abbreviations and Numbers 187
16.1 Abbreviations 187
16.2 Numbers 191

17 Spelling 196
17.1 Overcoming Spelling Problems 196
17.2 Common Spelling Errors 199
17.3 Spelling Troublesome Plurals 202
17.4 Some Principles of Spelling 203
17.5 Variant Spellings 206

Part Two: Practices in Composition

Composition

18 Discovering What You Have to Say 210
18.1 Finding and Exploring What You Have to Say 211
Review: Finding a Subject and Locating Material 219
18.2 The Meeting Place of Author, Subject, and Audience 224
• **An Essay in Progress, 1: First Notes 226**

19 Occasions and Opportunities in Writing   229

19.1 Exposition   233
19.2 Narration   236
19.3 Description   240
19.4 Argumentation   243
19.5 Other Ways to Study Writing   249
   • **An Essay in Progress, 2:   First Efforts at Development   251**

20 Organizing Your Material   252

20.1 The Outline in Relation to the Paper   252
20.2 Types of Outlines   254
20.3 Standard Outline Form   260
   • **An Essay in Progress, 3:   First efforts at Organization   265**

21 Writing the First Draft   266

21.1 Getting Started   267
21.2 Developing Your Material   268
21.3 Relating Paragraphs in Sequence   272
21.4 Opening Paragraphs   274
21.5 Closing Paragraphs   278
21.6 Writing a Title   281
   • **An Essay in Progress, 4:   The First Draft   283**

Diction

22 Using a Dictionary   285

22.1 Selecting a Dictionary   286
22.2 Learning to Use Your Dictionary   288

23 The Meaning of Words   297

23.1 Words in Context and Situation   297
23.2 Fair Words and Slanted Words   300
23.3 Choosing the Right Word   303
23.4 Concrete and Abstract Words   308

24   The Effect of Words   312
    24.1   Formal Words   312
    24.2   Informal Words   316
    24.3   Live Words and Death Masks   318
    24.4   Figures of Speech   321
            Review: Types of Figurative Language   322

Sentences and Paragraphs

25   Sentence Length and Economy   326
    25.1   Sentence Length as a Matter of Style   326
    25.2   Sentence Length and Meaning   329
    25.3   Avoiding Wordiness   333
    25.4   Removing Deadwood   334
    25.5   Avoiding Careless Repetition   337

26   Sentence Variety, Control, and Emphasis   341
    26.1   Sentence Variety   341
    26.2   Subordination to Control and Clarify
            Meaning   346
    26.3   Parallelism   347
    26.4   Sentence Emphasis   350

27   Paragraphs   355
    27.1   Paragraph Development and Length   355
    27.2   Patterns of Paragraph Development   364
    27.3   Paragraph Continuity   367

Practical Writing Tasks

28   Revising and Correcting a Paper   374
    28.1   Revising a Draft   374
            Review: A Checklist for Revising   376
    28.2   Manuscript Form   378
    28.3   Revising a Corrected Paper   382
            • **An Essay in Progress, 5:   A Revised Version   389**

29 Practical and Vocational Writing 392
29.1 Essay Examination Answers 393
29.2 Writing About Literature 398
29.3 Public Letters 402
  Review: Sample Letters 411
29.4 Reports 415
  Review: Sample Report 417

30 The Research Paper 422
30.1 Choosing a Topic 423
30.2 Locating Appropriate Source Material 425
  Review: Sample Library Catalog Cards 427
  Review: Sample Entries from the *Readers'*
  ***Guide* 429**
30.3 Preparing the Working Bibliography 432
  Review: Sample Bibliography Cards 434
30.4 Evaluating Your Material 435
30.5 Taking Notes 436
30.6 Planning the Paper 437
  Review: Sample Note Cards 438
  Review: An Original Source and Sample
  Notes 439
30.7 Writing the First Draft 441
30.8 Documenting the Paper 442
30.9 Assembling the Completed Paper 456
  Sample Paper, "The Agenda Setting Function of the
   News Media in the Gas Crisis of Spring and Fall,
   1979" 458
  Sample Paper, "The ABCs of Public
   Television" 469

Glossary of Usage 483

Index 499

- *An Essay in Progress, 1:* **First Notes 226**
- *An Essay in Progress, 2:* **First Efforts at Development 251**
- *An Essay in Progress, 3:* **First Efforts at Organization 265**
- *An Essay in Progress, 4:* **The First Draft 283**
- *An Essay in Progress, 5:* **A Revised Version 389**

Handbook

of Current English

Introduction: Using the Language

In reading and writing, there are none of those helpful accompaniments we count on in the actual practice of conversing, such as vocal intonation, facial expression, gesture. One of the writer's principal problems is to compensate for these losses, for most people are more convincing in person than on paper. That is why writing has to be learned; that is why books like this one are offered as helps for writers. Somehow the writer has to evoke, out of mere ink marks on paper, a character whose language the reader will trust, enjoy, profit from. — Walker Gibson,
PERSONA

The Language We Use

Everyone who will use this textbook speaks English. Assuming that we're native speakers of English, we know the language long before we study it. Well before we start school, we can understand sentences, even though we may have never heard words in precisely those combinations before. By the time we can talk, we can say sentences that we have never said or heard before. We can say sentences long before we know that there are such things as sentences. But even if we know English before we study it, there is still ample reason to study it in school and all our lives.

Paradoxically, English is both easy and difficult to study. Easy, because we do already know the language. Difficult, because English is varied and changing. When we speak, we don't all sound alike, and when we write, we don't all write in the same way. Each of us knows English in various versions, and each of us may use one version when talking to a close friend, say, and another when speaking to a forty-year-old English teacher. In the talk that we hear every day we understand many different ways of speaking; we can understand still other ways of speaking in print.

Yet using a language well depends on more than an awareness of our abilities to speak and understand different varieties. It is also more than writing "complete" sentences, using correct verb forms, making verbs agree with their subjects and pronouns with their antecedents. Beyond these forms and conventions, using a language well is a matter of choosing from the broad range of our language the words and constructions that will best convey our ideas to an unspecified or a particular audience, that will best enable us to present ourselves fully and honestly to others. But no one can make choices unless choices are available. To make good choices in language, we must recognize different versions of English and know the various ways English is used in contemporary writing and speaking.

The Elements of Language

Basically a language consists of a system of sounds, a collection of words, some changes in word forms, and some patterns into which the words fit to convey meaning. It may or may not have a system of writing and printing.

Sounds

English has between forty and fifty sounds (about twenty of them vowel sounds and the rest consonant) and variations in pause, pitch, and stress. Each sound is used with slight modifications in actual speech; for example, some people have a full *r* and others a very slight indication of the sound. The pronunciation of words varies considerably among the different regions in which English is used, so that we can easily identify some people as New Yorkers, others as Southerners, others as New Englanders.

Words

Counting everything from slang and local words to rarely used words and limited scientific terms, there are well over two million English words. Many of these are used in several different senses — one dictionary gives forty different meanings for the word *check*. An unabridged dictionary has about 500,000 entries; a college dictionary has about 150,000 entries; a college student probably uses or recognizes over 50,000 basic words, not counting forms made by changes in tense *(-ed)* or number *(-s)*. English forms many derivatives by adding prefixes *(in-, anti-, re-, super-)* and suffixes *(-er, -ish, -ship, -teria)*, and it makes compounds freely by putting two or more words together *(bookcase, streamlined)*.

Word Forms

Some languages are *inflected;* that is, their words change form to express grammatical relations in case, number, gender, person, tense, and the like. Latin and German, for example, are highly inflected. English uses very few changes in word forms: only a few endings, like the *-s* or *-es* of nouns *(boys, churches)*, the *-s, -ed, -ing* of verbs *(asks, asked, asking)*, *-er* and *-est* for comparing adverbs and adjectives *(hotter, hottest; nearer, nearest)*, and a few internal changes, like the changes in vowels in *man-men, sing-sang.*

Constructions

There are two basic ways to combine English words into groups: with phrases centered on nouns or their equivalents *(in the morning; crossing the street)* and with clauses centered on verbs *(he runs the forty-yard dash; when she saw the results)*. We interpret the meaning of these familiar patterns according to the order in which the words stand, an order that we pick up naturally as children and follow almost instinctively. Out of these simple word groups we build sentences of varying length and complexity. The study of the relationships between words and word groups in sentences is *syntax,* a large part of what we call *grammar.*

Intro

Writing Practices

English, which like other languages first developed in speech, is represented in writing and printing by the twenty-six letters of the alphabet, a dozen or so punctuation marks, and devices like capitals and italics. Our accepted habits of spelling, punctuation, capitalization, and other practices were developed mostly by printers and serve chiefly to represent the spoken language.

These are the *materials* of language. What we do with them is another matter. This book is about *current* English, which appears in many forms. The book uses — and usually recommends — edited American English, that is, the English you'd expect to hear from people who have spoken, heard, written, read, and examined English long enough to be familiar with its traditional characteristics and the ways it is habitually used in many books, magazines, classrooms, and meetings. Another way to describe edited American English is to say that if you use it, you generally accept judgments on usage made by many people over a long period of time.

There is good reason to do so. When you speak to people, you are usually with them; they can watch your face and your hands, whether you lean toward them or turn coolly away from them, whether you speak softly or boldly. Talking depends on the environment; a context already exists. Writing has to create its own context. When someone reads what you have written, you can't count on being there. More often than not, you are *not* there. Your readers may be diverse and unexpected, and you may want or need to give your readers a language whose characteristics you can expect them all to understand. Qualities that a language accumulates in many places over a period of some time will be clearer to readers, more accessible to them, than qualities that belong only to you and a close circle of friends.

Varieties of English Usage

Living languages undergo continual growth and change. Ordinarily the changes are slow and barely noticeable — slightly different pronunciations, new shadings in the meaning of words, and gradual shifts in grammatical constructions — but their cumulative effect can be dramatic. The works of Shakespeare, written four centuries ago, are difficult for the modern reader: many of the words are unfamiliar and the grammar occasionally seems strange. The works of Chaucer, written a few centuries earlier, are hard to read without a large glossary and a grammar guide. Still earlier works, like *Beowulf,* can be understood only by specialists who have studied Old English much as they would study a foreign language. Yet all these works are written in a language that can claim to be called English and have been admired by many generations of readers of English.

Obviously our language has changed a great deal in the course of its history, and it will go on changing. Not only does the language change as time passes; at any given moment in its history, it also shows many internal variations. The work and worry and play of everyday life include all kinds of activities and situations, and English, both spoken and written, must serve them all. There are differences in the words and constructions typically used in different kinds of publications, even within a range no wider than that from newspapers to textbooks, and we use different language in writing or speaking to different people and for different purposes. If in your writing you needed to say something about an object presented as something that it is not, you might use any one of the following words: *simulated, spurious, fraudulent, counterfeit, imitation, false, sham, pseudo, phony, bogus,* perhaps *put-on.* When you use one of the words, you may simply be using the word that you are most accustomed to. If you make a deliberate choice, however, the choice depends on many things — who you are, where you live, the people you spend most time with, the audience that will receive what you say or write, how much of your own personal language you are willing to use, and other factors. In most instances, you do have some choice among words when you write.

Since choices in vocabulary and construction are usually available, it seems foolish to trust what we already know about language and assume that the way in which we use words is always going to be sufficient. There is no one "right" kind of choice to make; no language should be forced into or kept in a neat mold. Until fairly recently, it was common for students of language to assume that "good" English was fixed, that departure from an inflexible set of rules governing its use was automatically "bad" English. This highly *prescriptive* approach to language study reflected the belief that there was some ideal form of English, orderly and uniform. Students had merely to learn the laws and apply them, just as they would in studying physics or chemistry. Although the prescriptive approach often produced good results, both practical experience and modern linguistic scholarship—called *descriptive* because it studies and describes the language as it *is*—have shown it to be less than satisfactory. No single system of conventions and rules can accurately describe a complex, changing language. Whether we like it or not, our language is changing and varied, and because it is, it offers choices.

But choices aren't choices unless we know what they are. There is no perfect way of describing or listing all the possible forms of spoken English. *One* way to catch the variety of spoken English is to start with highly personal language, and then see what happens to personal language in groups, in special times, in special places.

Intro

Idiolects

Everyone has a personal language. It may be remarkably different from the language of someone who lives two hundred miles away, or even next door; it may be scarcely distinguishable from another person's language. This personal language can be called an *idiolect*. The word is formed by a combination of two terms, the first of which *(idio)* originally meant something like *personal, separate,* or *one's own;* the second originally comes from a word meaning *to converse.* An idiolect is distinguishable in some way, even if the speaker only occasionally uses words that those around him do not use, or uses words in ways that others do not. An idiolect grows out of your own life, and it may change as your life changes. Each of the speakers in the passage that follows begins to be recognizable, even in a few lines. The second speaker's language, in particular, tells something about his age, his location, the manner of life he has led:

> Potter looked at his enemy. "I ain't got a gun on me, Scratchy," he said. "Honest, I ain't." He was stiffening and steadying, but yet somewhere at the back of his mind a vision of the Pullman floated: the seagreen figured velvet, the shining brass, silver, and glass, the wood that gleamed as darkly brilliant as the surface of a pool of oil—all the glory of the marriage, the environment of the new estate. "You know I fight when it comes to fighting, Scratchy Wilson; but I ain't got a gun on me. You'll have to do all the shootin' yourself."
>
> His enemy's face went livid. He stepped forward, and lashed his weapon to and from before Potter's chest. "Don't you tell me you ain't got no gun on you, you whelp. Don't tell me no lie like that. There ain't a man in Texas ever seen you without no gun. Don't take me for no kid." His eyes blazed with light, and his throat worked like a pump. —Stephen Crane, "The Bride Comes to Yellow Sky"

The writer of the passage below, however, uses a different language. It is a language that is both active (some fifteen verbs and a number of nouns or modifiers made from verbs — *spincasting, calling, shielded*) and easy, with familiar pronoun references and pleasantly varied sentences that range from six to fifty-seven words.

> Trotlines from shore to shore get you more fish and bigger ones, but they're also more labor. After I'd finished with the line I worked along the beach, spincasting bootlessly for bass. Four Canada geese came diagonally over the river, low, calling, and in a moment I heard a clamor at the head of the island, shielded from me by the island's duned fringe and by willows. I climbed up through them to look. At least 200 more honkers took off screaming from the sand bar at the upper end of the bare plain. The passenger ran barking after them. Calling him back, I squatted beside a drift pile, and in the rose half-light of dusk watched through the field glass as they came wheeling in again, timid but liking the place as I liked it, and settled by tens and twenties at the bar and in the shallows above it where the two channels split. — John Graves, *Goodbye to a River*

An idiolect is not necessarily restrictive. People can easily understand other people's idiolects, and almost everyone regularly shifts from one idiolect into another and then another. But it is possible for a personal language to be so uniquely personal as to be incomprehensible to a hearer or reader — as in forms of baby talk, or in some kinds of family lingo.

Dialects

When a community of speakers and writers uses idiolects that have much in common in pronunciation, grammar, and vocabulary, the combined idiolects are often referred to as a *dialect*. Usually we think of a dialect only as the language of a particular geographical region, but we can use the word to name any gathering of idiolects that share essential characteristics. A dialect is almost like a code: speakers and writers of a dialect can usually converse with and write to speakers of the general language, but they also know the special language of their group or region. When Paul Simon wrote and sang that he was "Lookin' for fun and feelin' groovy," his language linked him to people who used the language in a similar way. When another speaker says, "He's jis a good ole boy, tryin' to get along," he or she is using a dialect common in parts of the South and West. Dialects occur everywhere; people who grow food in the fields sometimes use distinguishable dialects, to be sure, and so do people who teach the third grade, and so do people whose language is often supposed to be remarkably proper.

Regional dialects.   There are, of course, many *regional dialects;* some of them are readily recognizable. Migration habits, work habits, geographical features, plant and animal life, and other characteristics of a particular region sometimes help to create a language for the region that is easily distinguishable from other dialects. A regional dialect may be marked by special words; people in the Southwest, for example, have more occasion to talk about *canyons* and *mesas* than people in Virginia do, both because of southwestern topography and because of their exposure to Spanish languages.

A regional dialect may be identified at times by special pronunciations of ordinary words. After the election of Jimmy Carter in 1976, newspapers often printed pieces on "how to speak Southern," with definitions — "bard" means *borrowed,* "gull" means *girl,* "stow" means *store,* "ahmoan" means *I am going to,* as in "Ahmoan go eat dinner."

A regional dialect may be marked, too, by characteristic constructions (in the following passage, *she'd 'a' scanted herself*), by pronunciations *(creatur, Squer'ls),* and by words not commonly used elsewhere *(bangeing)*:

> "Sylvia takes after him," the grandmother continued affectionately, after a moment's pause. "There ain't a foot o' ground she don't know her way over, and the wild creatur's counts her one o' themselves. Squer'ls she'll tame to come an' feed right out o' her hands, and all sorts o' birds. Last winter she got the jay-birds to bangeing here, and I believed she'd 'a' scanted herself of her own means to have plenty to throw out amongst 'em, if I hadn' kep' watch." — Sarah Orne Jewett, "A White Heron"

Temporal dialects.   Another kind of dialect might be called *temporal.* Language changes faster in some communities than in others; sometimes a group preserves usages or words while another group hurries into acceptance of new words, new usages, discarding the old. Martin Luther King's speech in Washington, D.C., on August 28, 1963, as the passage below will testify, gained a part of its power to move and to exhilarate from its recollection of rhythms, words, and constructions from the King James Bible:

> I have a dream that one day every valley shall be exalted, every hill and mountain shall be made low, the rough places will be made plane and crooked places will be made straight, and the glory of the Lord shall be revealed, and all flesh shall see it together.
> This is our hope. This is the faith that I go back to the South with. With this faith we will be able to hew out of the mountain of despair a stone of hope. With this faith we will be able to transform the jangling discords of our nation into a beautiful symphony of brotherhood. With

Intro

this faith we will be able to work together, to pray together, to struggle together, to go to jail together, to stand up for freedom together, knowing that we will be free one day.

Occupational dialects.   Professional languages, craft languages, and shoptalk may be called *occupational dialects.* A wide range of such dialects is before us a good part of the time. We frequently borrow words from occupations for use in conversation and, less frequently, in writing—for example, *feedback, input, bug, huddle, fade-in, fade-out, close-up,* or *program* (as used with computers). Occupational dialects, of course, occur most frequently in speech or writing connected to particular occupations, but as the words listed above may suggest, parts of some occupational dialects have come into common use and no longer seem to be only forms of dialects.

Occupational dialects occur in many ways. In professional journals and specialized books, for example, we may expect to find languages that are common to people within given occupations. The passage below, though it appeared in a popular magazine, *The Saturday Review,* depends heavily on a language taken from theological and psychological studies:

> The third dilemma I propose is that our highly vaunted sexual freedom has turned out to be a new form of puritanism. I define puritanism as a state of alienation from the body, separation of emotion from reason, and use of the body as a machine. These were the elements of moralistic puritanism in Victorian times; industrialism expressed these same characteristics of puritanism in economic guise. Our modern sexual attitudes have a new content, namely, full sexual expression, but in the same old puritan form—alienation from the body and feeling, and exploitation of the body as though it were a machine.— Rollo May, "Antidotes for the New Puritanism"

Public dialects.   We hear and read some special languages that we might call *public dialects.* Most of us hear, see, speak, read, and sometimes write words, phrases, and constructions that come from politics, television, magazines, motion pictures, and other forms of public communication. How many people said "At this point in time" instead of "now" during the Watergate hearings in the summer of 1973? How many people take over the language of Archie Bunker, or of *M.A.S.H.,* or of Steve Martin, or of Johnny Carson, or other popular television programs and characters? The public language of television and magazine advertisements is a fantasy language, never quite specific, always full of promise— "This is an unretouched photograph of Bonnie wearing Corn-silk—the makeup that gives you the look of innocence," or "There's a skin cleanser that leaves your skin the way nature intended," or "You're going to be beautiful . . . both of you, in Palm Beach Formals."

General English

Most of the language you hear or read in a week, however, probably doesn't belong to any one of these dialects, though the *public dialects* are extraordinarily pervasive. If we take into account all of the language you hear or read in a week, from television, classrooms, friends, overheard conversations, radio disc jockeys, newspapers, magazines, and elsewhere, a good part of it doesn't have the distinctive character of personal idiolect, regional dialect, occupational dialect, or even public dialect. Much of it is in that broad range of language so commonly used that it attracts no attention to itself, and of course there are varieties of language within that range. These varieties we might call *general dialects*. In writing, the vocabulary and sentence structure of the general dialects seem natural, and close to those of speech. Punctuation is usually relatively light, and sentences are likely to vary widely in length and complexity.

In the following passage the author talks about his people, the Kiowas, but the language he uses is community property:

> Once there was a lot of sound in my grandmother's house, a lot of coming and going, feasting and talk. The summers there were full of excitement and reunion. The Kiowas are a summer people; they abide the cold and keep to themselves, but when the season turns and the land becomes warm and vital they cannot hold still; an old love of going returns upon them. The aged visitors who came to my grandmother's house when I was a child were made of lean and leather, and they bore themselves upright. They wore great black hats and bright ample shirts that shook in the wind. They rubbed fat upon their hair and wound their braids with strips of colored cloth. Some of them painted their faces and carried the scars of old and cherished enmities. They were an old council of warlords, come to remind and be reminded of who they were. Their wives and daughters served them well. The women might indulge themselves; gossip was at once the mark and compensation of their servitude. They made loud and elaborate talk among themselves, full of jest and gesture, fright and false alarm. They went abroad in fringed and flowered shawls, bright beadwork and German silver. They were at home in the kitchen, and they prepared meals that were banquets. — N. Scott Momaday, *The Way to Rainy Mountain.*

General dialects are not limited to transmitting matters of general interest; they may also carry specialized information:

> Yet if our agriculture-based life depends on the soil, it is equally true that soil depends on life, its very origins and the maintenance of its true nature being intimately related to living plants and animals. For

soil is in part a creation of life, born of a marvelous interaction of life and nonlife long eons ago. The parent materials were gathered together as volcanoes poured them out in fiery streams, as waters running over the bare rocks of the continents wore away even the hardest granite, and as the chisels of frost and ice split and shattered the rocks. Then living things began to work their creative magic and little by little these inert materials became soil. Lichens, the rocks' first covering, aided the process of disintegration by their acid secretions and made a lodging place for other life. Mosses took hold in the little pockets of simple soil — soil formed by crumbling bits of lichens, by the husks of minute insect life, by the debris of a fauna beginning its emergence from the sea. — Rachel Carson, *Silent Spring*

While general English may sometimes be flat or uninteresting, it doesn't have to be. In this passage from a short story the language is a compressed form of what we all might say (except perhaps "the world leaps into proportion"), but it has the quality of feeling that we associate with literature:

The man who expected to be shot lay with his eyes open, staring at the upper left-hand corner of his cell. He was fairly well over his last beating, and they might come for him any time now. There was a yellow stain in the cell corner near the ceiling; he had liked it at first, then disliked it; now he was coming back to liking it again.

He could see it more clearly with his glasses on, but he only put on his glasses for special occasions now — the first thing in the morning, and when they brought the food in, and for interviews with the General. The lenses of the glasses had been cracked in a beating some months before, and it strained his eyes to wear them too long. Fortunately, in his present life he had very few occasions demanding clear vision. But, nevertheless, the accident to his glasses worried him, as it worries all near-sighted people. You put your glasses on the first thing in the morning and the world leaps into proportion; if it does not do so, something is wrong with the world. — Stephen Vincent Benét, "The Blood of the Martyrs," *Thirteen O'Clock*

Dialect Modifications

Most of the English that we hear, read, speak, and write falls within what we have called the *general dialects*. Some language within this range is far more casual and informal than others. Many of us, even if our speech or writing shows no other distinguishing marks (such as our occupation, or the place we live), use language that is breezy and often uncomplicated. Sentences are often short, and words and phrases may be more characteristic of speaking than of writing: *cop, deadpan, iffy, chancy, phony, peeve, whodunit* — words such as these may be called *colloquial* by some dictionaries, which means that they occur more often in speech than in writing.

When we are writing or speaking informally, we're likely to

make some use of *slang*, newly made words *(stagflation, shortfall, Koreagate)*, or old words with new meanings *(cool, straight, trip, far-out)*, or phrases conspicuously overused *(bottom line, positive stroking)*. A continual flow of usually short-lived words and phrases comes into the language, for many reasons. Sometimes we want to be different; sometimes we believe that we have to have new words to name new experiences; sometimes we want to separate ourselves from some other group (parents, for example) by acquiring our own language. Some slang proves useful and becomes a part of the general vocabulary.

When we are being informal, we are likely to use a good many *localisms*, words or phrases characteristic of a particular region, taken perhaps from a *regional dialect*. We often use regional names for common things *(coal oil* or *kerosene; fried cake, cruller, fatcake,* or *doughnut; sack, poke,* or *bag)*, special names for local occupations *(mule skinner, carhop)*, or special names for features of the landscape peculiar to a region *(canyon, coulee, gulley, hogback, arroyo, bayou)*. These words sometimes reflect the language of the early settlers of an area, as the Dutch in New York or the Spanish in the Southwest.

Nonstandard English
Some of the varieties of language mentioned above are *nonstandard* forms of English. A *standard* may be defined as an accepted measure of quality. If a measure of quality is accepted, that means it has wide use. Idiolects, dialects, and the various dialect modifications are associated with particular people, particular groups, particular places, particular times. In this special sense then, they are *nonstandard,* not languages for wide use.

Any language can be a nonstandard form. If major grammatical errors occur, if spelling is inconsistent, if punctuation is inadequate, if usage is not widely accepted, then a language may be called *nonstandard.* Indeed, you should know that perhaps the most common way of judging a language is by its propriety and consistency in grammar, spelling, punctuation, and usage.

But we should remember, too, that any language can be used to deceive, to betray, to oppress. Each of the varieties of language — those primarily spoken forms we have already mentioned and the primarily written forms discussed in the following sections — can, in a sense, be nonstandard English. Although nonstandard English is most often defined by its vocabulary, its sounds, or its grammatical construction, we might also count as nonstandard *any* language that violates itself, that fails in its purpose to communicate as effectively as possible.

Edited American English

No perfect system exists for classifying and naming all versions of the English language. The idiolects, dialects, and versions of language mentioned above are examples only. All of them are forms of spoken English. Some of them can also be written effectively.

For use in writing, however, almost any language has to be edited. When you write, you are ordinarily presenting your language publicly. That means that what you might ordinarily *say* may need to be corrected and prepared for presentation. *Edited American English* is a version of the language that you may associate with schools, good newspapers, good books, or good public speakers. It is an idiolect or dialect that has been modified to produce a uniformity in sound, a consistency with such grammatical standards as have traditionally been taught in English and American schools, and a vocabulary that can be shared by people in different places and at different times. Edited American English is produced by a kind of filtering process. In the filtering process, what separates people from each other linguistically is supposed to be trapped and discarded, while what binds people together linguistically is left free for use. Few people speak edited American English; many write it. What we should remember, it seems clear, is that edited American English is another variety of language available to us.

That doesn't mean that all forms of edited American English are alike. The forms of spoken English mentioned above, when edited for public presentation, can become appropriate edited American English. The language of our casual conversations, of our idiolects and dialects, can be the basis of a kind of *informal* edited American English. The general spoken English described earlier is a basis for *general* edited American English. Formal English, found chiefly in writing, is principally a development from *general* edited American English, but more fully edited and more complex. It is more influenced by the conventions built up by writers and editors in the past. It usually occurs in discussions of specialized topics and in writing addressed to somewhat limited audiences.

The vocabulary of formal English includes most of the general words and some from idiolects and dialects. Necessarily, formal English uses the specialized vocabulary of the subject matter being discussed; it also may use a good many abstract words. Its grammatical constructions tend to be fuller than those of general English, and ordinarily its sentences are somewhat longer and more complex. Formal writing tends to follow older practices in punctuation and to use *close* punctuation — more frequent marks than is typical in general English, and heavier ones, such as a semicolon where a comma might serve.

The formal English used in academic, scientific, technical, and scholarly writing is usually impersonal. Good formal writing, how-ever, is not stilted or dull. This account of the mapping of Switzer-land shows the single-minded attention to the subject, the compact and orderly statement of ideas, and the moderate use of technical terms that characterize good impersonal formal English:

> The heroic task of making a topographic survey and map of Swit-zerland fell to the lot of General Guillaume Henri Dufour (1787 – 1875). Under his personal supervision the work was begun in 1830 and the first sheet was published in 1842. Thirty-four years later the entire survey, on a scale of 1 : 100,000 was finished and the last of the 25 sheets came from the press. Soon after, the map appeared in atlas form, published at Berne. Far from being a pioneering effort that would require immediate revision, the Dufour atlas proved to be a model of accuracy and artistic delineation, not only for future map makers of Switzerland, but for cartographers at large. The sheets of the atlas were used as a basis for later surveys on different scales, and on the sheets of Switzerland's new survey references were made to the corresponding sections and subsections of the original Dufour map. The art work and conventional signs on the new map were al-most identical with those on the Dufour originals. The lettering and bench marks (figures denoting heights), prominent buildings, roads, boundaries and forests were printed in black. Small slopes and passes, ravines and narrow defiles that could not be shown by equally spaced contour lines were printed in brown hachures. Black hachures were used to indicate rocky prominences and precipices, the general effect being a pictorial representation by oblique lighting. Horizontal sur-veys were shown in bronze and water was indicated by shades of blue. – Lloyd A. Brown, *The Story of Maps*

Intro

A more personal type of formal English is shown in the following passage. Some of the words and phrases are formal – *inert knowl-edge, radical error,* and *delicate, receptive, responsive to stimulus.* The constructions are full: note the sentence beginning *Whoever was the originator* and the following sentence, beginning *But what-ever its weight of authority.* But some constructions (*I appeal to you, as practical teachers. So far, so good.*) carry an unmistakable personal emphasis and keep us aware that the writer is expressing himself as an individual.

> I appeal to you, as practical teachers. With good discipline, it is always possible to pump into the minds of a class a certain quantity of inert knowledge. You take a text-book and make them learn it. So far, so good. The child then knows how to solve a quadratic equation. But what is the point of teaching a child to solve a quadratic equation? There is a traditional answer to this question. It runs thus: The mind is an instrument, you first sharpen it, and then use it; the acquisition of the power of solving a quadratic equation is part of the process of sharpening the mind. Now there is just enough truth in this answer to

have made it live through the ages. But for all its half-truth, it embodies a radical error which bids fair to stifle the genius of the modern world. I do not know who was first responsible for this analogy of the mind to a dead instrument. For aught I know, it may have been one of the seven wise men of Greece, or a committee of the whole lot of them. Whoever was the originator, there can be no doubt of the authority which it has acquired by the continuous approval bestowed upon it by eminent persons. But whatever its weight of authority, whatever the high approval it can quote, I have no hesitation in denouncing it as one of the most fatal, erroneous, and dangerous concepts ever introduced into the theory of education. The mind is never passive; it is a perpetual activity, delicate, receptive, responsive to stimulus. You cannot postpone its life until you have sharpened it. Whatever interest attaches to your subject-matter must be evoked here and now; whatever powers you are strengthening in the pupil, must be exercised here and now; whatever possibilities of mental life your teaching should impart, must be exhibited here and now. That is the golden rule of education, and a very difficult rule to follow. — Alfred North Whitehead, *The Aims of Education*

These are some versions of our language — countless idiolects, many dialects — regional, occupational, general, public — edited American English, formal language. Each can be used to move or to inform; each can be warm, generous, and powerful; each can be used with precision.

The Search for a "Good" Language

A "good" language is not just a gathering of specific practices in vocabulary, grammar, and usage that you must invariably follow. Many languages are available, all equally reputable and, in certain circumstances, all equally "good." The objective in writing is not first to conform to some previously established system of usages, but to use the resources of the language in order to speak fully, precisely, and honestly. Good writing is not born of a system of rules and usages; systems of rules and usages are born of good writing.

Some Qualities of Good Language

A language can enable us to remember our experiences, put them in order and establish connections between them, speculate on them and draw conclusions from them. A language can enable us to praise or to blame. As the previous section suggests, many languages and dialects are available to serve these purposes, each

Review:

Some Versions of American English — A Summary

• *Spoken Language:*

IDIOLECT: an individual's personal language, influenced by environmental factors (geographical area, occupation) and personal characteristics (age, sex, personality).

DIALECT: the combined idiolects of a *community of speakers.* Dialects can overlap, but can be classified as being regional, temporal, occupational, public.

DIALECT MODIFICATIONS: slang, localisms, fad words.

GENERAL ENGLISH: includes the languages above. What might be called the dialect of the great majority of speakers of American English without the strong modifications of other dialectal factors.

NONSTANDARD ENGLISH: does not meet the accepted measure of quality in usage and grammar.

• *Written Language:*

Edited American English

INFORMAL ENGLISH: characterized by short sentences, "breezy" style; includes personal and journalistic writing.

GENERAL ENGLISH: characterized by the constructions and vocabulary of general English, with more attention paid to grammatical conventions; includes most books, magazines, etc.

FORMAL ENGLISH: characterized by full constructions and specialized vocabulary; generally impersonal and found mostly in academic, scientific, technical, scholarly, and other specialized forms of writing.

NONSTANDARD ENGLISH: see above.

Intro

suitable in particular circumstances. Each of these dialects may have its own distinct structure, and each can be written.

We are not usually there when someone reads what we have written. Our meaning and intention rest in the words on the page, and they are sometimes bare and skimpy. Any language we use is incomplete: a language won't let us say two things at once under normal circumstances; when we say one thing, we're *not* saying another. When we write, to complicate the problem, our written words must be able to stand alone. We are not there to explain, to modify, to fill in, to shift emphasis. We should, then, expect to give our greatest care to writing and insure if we can the precision and the fullness of our meaning. Readers are likely to be people much like ourselves. They have their own varied interests and preoccupations, their own thoughts, and they can't be expected to fill in gaps we leave out. Readers won't pay attention just because we've written something.

Writing is a kind of contract between writer and reader. The writer asks readers for the time they will spend in reading; to do so obliges the writer to give care to the writing. The reader requires of the writer some worth in what is written and owes the writer at least a little curiosity, patience, and willingness to listen. Any language that takes care to insure the precision and fullness of meaning and to promote this bond between reader and writer is likely to be a "good" language.

An Appropriate Language

This *Handbook* customarily recommends what we earlier called edited American English, for several reasons. In the first place, as we have already mentioned, no single handbook can fully describe all the versions of English; no book can describe any version of the language *fully*. As far as possible, however, this book sets out to describe and recommend the kind of language that appears most commonly in print, that is, the language of most books, newspapers, and magazines. Edited American English is valuable because it is widely used, and it is widely used because it is flexible and will serve many purposes. It is a language suited for use in sociological research and cookbooks, personal letters and political commentary. We recommend it, finally, because it is a language we can speak, hear, and read in common. Its widespread use in publications and in schools makes it accessible to many people. The language does not belong to any single person, group, or region. Edited American English is a language in which we can be together. We have not tried to *list* the hallmarks or characteristics of edited American English: the rest of this *Handbook* tries to *show* what edited usage is like. When we say, "Many writers prefer to . . ."

or "It's usually best to say . . ." or "Try to avoid . . ." we are recommending general American English edited for written use.

Any language you use can be a "good" language if it is used appropriately. Edited American English can also be governed by a standard of appropriateness, though it is crucial to know what *appropriateness* means in this context. Language is appropriate when it is honest — honest for the writer, honest about the subject, honest to the audience. Language is appropriate when the user treats evidence fairly, without falsification or manipulation. Language is appropriate when it arises from open motives, not from hidden motives. Language is appropriate when it rests upon a suitable history — that is to say, the writer or speaker has had the experience, acquired the evidence, and done the thinking implied in what he or she says. Language is appropriate when it works as nearly as possible without manipulation or coercion. Conversely, language is *inappropriate* when it is unnecessarily ambiguous or uninterpretable, when it denies hearers or readers access to information necessary for a full interpretation, when it tries to coerce audiences, when it is empty noise, or when it somehow violates the possibilities of expression and communication (see the section on "Nonstandard English"). When you write a language, the choice of vocabulary, usage, and construction is, in a way, not yours alone. Your subject makes certain demands. Your audience, which has certain expectations, deserves good treatment. We cannot use language solely as if it were our private toy. Nor can we use language solely to please others. If we are to use a language well, we must use it so that it is appropriate to us as speakers or writers, appropriate to its audience, appropriate to the particular situation in which we find ourselves.

Appropriateness to Speaker or Writer

As a writer, you dominate the writer-reader relationship. Your judgment controls the language you use. Whatever your purpose in writing, express your ideas in language that seems natural to you. Your writing should be an honest expression of your own character. Your language is what presents you to a reader; you cannot be everywhere your writing is, and only your language can bring a distant reader and you into any accord. The most fitting language for you is the language that gives you and your ideas the fullest expression.

That doesn't mean that you should necessarily rest content with the idiolect or dialect or language that you already speak. It means, rather, that you ought to make any language you use your own so that you understand it and feel comfortable using it. Start with your present language. How well do you understand the way you already speak and write? What is your present language like? Does it have special traits that other people won't understand? Are you sure of yourself in spelling, punctuation, sentence structure? When you write a paper for a college course, do you choose the best part of your natural language, or do you assume an entirely different sort of English? If you return to a paper that you wrote some time ago and read it aloud, does it sound at all like something you would or could say? If it doesn't, can you tell what happened to your language in the paper?

The suggestions and the pressures of teachers or critics may have some brief effect on the way you use language, but in the long run you set your own standard. The language you use is your responsibility. Good English is not primarily a matter of rules, but of judgment. You are not struggling under a series of *don'ts* but trying to discover among the wide resources of modern English the language that best suits your purpose, your audience, and yourself.

Appropriateness to Listener or Reader

If you are trying to reach particular types of readers, you may have to adjust your subject matter and your manner of expression to their expectations. You have to be more than merely understandable; you may have to meet your readers largely on their own ground. Your readers are as real as you are. If the language you use is not a language your readers can use and respond to, then your ideas won't reach them. It might make you feel good to know that you are right in what you say, but you shouldn't expect applause from readers who can't respond to your language. Meeting your readers on common ground, or on their ground, is often easy. You make some adjustments in your language almost automatically in letters, writing in somewhat different ways to different people. You don't have to abandon your natural language, but you need to focus on the intelligibility of what you are saying or writing.

Clarity.   Since your aim in writing is to communicate, use clear and exact words that your readers will understand. If the subject requires terms that may be unfamiliar, try to make them clear by the way you use them or add a tactful explanation. In some instances you may have to provide a formal definition. Clarity also calls for sentences that are not too long and that have a natural, direct movement—though you must remember the demands of your subject and situation, as well. Experienced readers can grasp more elaborate sentences than those who read little or read hurriedly. But anyone will be pleased with direct, straightforward sentences.

Careful attention to punctuation is also necessary if you are to make your statements clear to your readers. The various marks—

commas, semicolons, and periods—indicate the groups of words that are to be understood as units and often show the relationship between these units. Omissions or misused marks may force readers to go over a passage two or three times; superfluous marks may keep them from grouping words that belong together or may slow the speed of reading to the point of exasperation.

Correctness.   Part of a writer's concern for readers is meeting their expectations in language. This means avoiding careless and elementary errors. Elementary errors may indicate to some readers that you just can't be bothered, that you aren't doing as well as you easily could and should. When you finish writing a paper, take time to check it carefully for errors in spelling, punctuation, and other matters of usage.

Intro

Interest.   All readers will appreciate some liveliness in what they read, in the writer's expression as well as the choice of material. Too many students seem to feel that serious writing requires a flat and lifeless or a pompous sort of language. In striving for liveliness, you needn't try for novelty or use words that are out of the ordinary; draw on the vocabulary you might use in an intelligent, reasonably animated conversation. Avoid dragging and monotonous sentences; vary their length and pattern so as to please active, alert minds. Attract your readers' interest by referring, when appropriate, to things people have said and done, and use details to demonstrate your ideas.

One warning: In gearing your writing to your readers' background and expectations, don't underestimate their intelligence, compromising yourself and insulting them. Visualize them at their best and write for them as they are then.

Appropriateness to Purpose and Situation

The teacher in your composition class may be interested in seeing essays and other forms of writing that you do using a wide variety of languages and methods. Your composition teacher may be glad enough for you to try out your own idiolect, any dialects that you can control, and even some formal language. But most of your other teachers, perhaps all of them, probably expect what we have called edited American English in the papers they assign.

The standards of written usage in a composition course are about the same standards that would be expected in similar published material. This means that papers about personal experiences, college activities, or your own private reflections might be in general American English. It also means that papers required in other college courses, where your writing will usually carry less of your own character and attitudes and will usually focus with greater concentration on an impersonal subject, may have to meet other expectations and be more nearly formal English.

This expectation for college writing is not the result of an arbitrary decision. By acquiring the ability to use a more formal variety of language, you have won a larger vocabulary for yourself and probably a wider variety of sentence structures. The vocabulary and structure of formal language are often necessary if you wish to say anything about many academic subjects. Consider a single instance. Suppose that you are in a philosophy course; one of your assignments is to write a critique of a book on philosophy that will include an examination of the author's premises, the mode of his argument, and the style of his presentation. To complete the assignment means, among other things, that you must know what a *critique* is, and that you must command a language that will let you talk about *premises, modes of argument,* and *styles of presentation.*

The rather formal language that will enable you to discuss these things may not, however, be useful in a meditative reminiscence about the time you sat on a mesa at twilight among Comanche ghosts. If you pay attention to purpose and situation, you should be able to treat most subjects in the language they deserve. Inexperienced writers frequently use language that is too heavy to be appropriate to them or to their subjects. For example, a student who wanted to say that he had rebelled against his parents despite having come from a happy home wrote:

> Although my domestic environment was permissive and munificent and my sibling relationships were good, I found it necessary to express my generation's mores in reaction to paternal supervision.

The student may seriously have believed that this kind of writing was better than a simple statement. He would almost certainly object to being told that his sentence was bad English, worse perhaps than if it contained some inaccurate or illogical expressions. But inaccuracies can be quite easily corrected, whereas inflated and pompous language must be completely rewritten to be effective. The artificial "formality" of such language is not found in good formal writing, and it should be avoided in student papers.

Once you find the tone that is right for your situation, you should stay with it unless there is some special reason for changing. Although the lines between the varieties of usage cannot be drawn precisely, conspicuous shifts from one to another should ordinarily be avoided, as in the second of these two sentences:

> In the distant pines the rising wind whined as it played among the needles. And when the storm broke, the rain came down in buckets.

Superficial consistency is not so important as fundamental appropriateness, but ordinarily one variety of English should be used throughout a piece of writing.

Reading the work of practiced writers is one good way to increase your sensitivity to language and its various uses. Before attempting to write for an unfamiliar situation, read and study some good examples of writing done for a similar purpose. Don't try to write an article for a magazine that you have never read, and don't try to write a technical report or reference paper without ever having seen one. Try to learn what is typically done and follow the accepted practices unless you have a good reason for some other usage.

Intro

The Design of the Book and Its Focus on Writing

The first seventeen chapters of this book are about particular features of the English language — grammar, usage, punctuation, and other conventions. These sections describe the way edited American English typically behaves as a system of language. The remaining chapters are chiefly about the written uses of language. The first seventeen chapters are a kind of reference/guide to language; the rest are about the process of writing.

No perfect order exists for talking about language and writing. It is possible to start almost anywhere and find a useful way of exploring the subject. As the book is arranged, the first seventeen chapters may be used for study in their own right or as continuous reference for writing assignments. The remaining chapters reflect, to some extent at least, a sequence of events that many of us go through as we write, from discovering what is to be said, through the first efforts at planning and drafting, to concern about particular features of the writing, and on to completed works.

Much that is said throughout the book applies to both speaking and writing, but the focus here is upon writing. Most of us will go on talking, but there are fewer reasons to write. Telephones, computer-assisted communication, and increasingly sophisticated multiple-use television suggest that we will have many ways to communicate without writing.

Still, we need to write, for a variety of reasons. Some school and job assignments, of course, require it, but there are more compelling reasons for writing. Writing is almost inevitably a more conscious and deliberate act than speaking. Accordingly, writing gives us a chance to be more precise and more thorough than we are in speaking; we have in writing an opportunity to organize our thoughts and experiences deliberately, to establish connections carefully, to speculate and draw conclusions thoughtfully. Furthermore, writing is both portable and permanent; it can be taken easily to other times and other places. Through it we can remember what we have been and imagine what we will be. By its nature writing is an effort to go beyond the written structures that others have created, to seek what is still possible to say, to say what hasn't yet been said.

• *Exercises*

A good part of the time most of us take for granted the languages we use and hear regularly. We may not pay much attention to language differences unless we hear words or phrases that are new to us or startling in their context. One way to work toward using your language thoughtfully and well is to pay close attention to what you say and hear, becoming more conscious of the languages around you.

1. What are the identifying marks of the language used by your family and the people you were closest to in your early years? List words, expressions, special ways of saying things that you have heard from family and friends, but do not commonly hear elsewhere.

2. If you are in school, list new expressions and ways of saying things that you have heard since starting school. Which of them have you started using yourself?

3. Which words and expressions that you use or hear appear to have been popularized by their use on some television program?

4. Which words and expressions are used to express approval by your family? Your friends and associates now? Which words and expressions are used to express disapproval by your family? By your current friends and associates?

5. Which words and expressions seem to recur most frequently around you?

6. Which words and expressions that you use or hear seem to be associated with a particular region?

Part One
Resources for Composition

GRAMMAR AND USAGE

1   GRAMMAR OF SENTENCES

2   COMMON SENTENCE ERRORS

3   SUBORDINATE CLAUSES AND
    CONNECTIVES

4   VERBALS

5   AGREEMENT OF SUBJECT AND VERB

6   NOUNS

7   PRONOUNS

8   VERBS

9   ADJECTIVES AND ADVERBS

PUNCTUATION AND OTHER CONVENTIONS

10   END PUNCTUATION

11   COMMAS

12   SEMICOLONS AND COLONS

13   DASHES, PARENTHESES, AND BRACKETS

14   QUOTATION MARKS, ELLIPSES, AND ITALICS

15   CAPITAL LETTERS, HYPHENS, AND
     APOSTROPHES

16   ABBREVIATIONS AND NUMBERS

17   SPELLING

1   Grammar of Sentences

. . . the right to utter a sentence is one of the very greatest liberties; and we are entitled to little wonder that freedom of utterance should be, in every society, one of the most contentious and ill-defined rights. The liberty to impose this formal unity is a liberty to handle the world, to remake it, if only a little, and to hand it to others in a shape which may influence their actions. — Richard Weaver, THE ETHICS OF RHETORIC

The *sentence* is the primary constructed unit in edited American English and in all other forms of English. Indeed, a sentence form of some kind exists in most, if not all, languages.

What appears to happen in the English sentence form is that two or more kinds of experience are put together so as to make a new kind of statement or experience. You can know what *pants* are and what *tearing* is, but when you read the sentence, "My pants are torn," you can understand it without stopping to think about the separate things, *pants* and *tearing*. The sentence is something new and different from the kinds of experience that it includes. In the common sentence form the two (sometimes more) kinds of experience are stated, usually one as a subject, the other as a verb. Sometimes, however, one or the other or both of the experiences are not stated, but supplied by the context.

> He went to town yesterday. [In this sentence, the different kinds of experience or reality included are the person referred to as *He* and the act of *going.*]
>
> Why weren't you there? [In this sentence, the two are the person referred to as *you* and the idea of *being in some place.*]
>
> Please try to be on time. [In this sentence, one is omitted, but since we can understand that the speaker is talking directly to someone, we know that what is left out is *you.*]
>
> Why not? [Here all of the experiences are omitted from the sentence, and we would have to depend on the circumstances in which the words appear to know what the experiences are. They might, for example, be a shortened form of "Why can't I go to town?"]
>
> Good! [Here again we would have to depend on the circumstances in which the word appears to know what the statement is.]

All of these are sentences, though they may look remarkably different from each other. A written sentence is one or more words, punctuated as an independent unit, that say something. A sentence is made complete by its grammatical form and meaning or occasionally, in special circumstances, by the context in which it appears.

When you write, you often twist and turn sentences this way and that to get them to say what you want. It is useful to you in this work to understand different kinds of sentences and what each can do, the way the parts of a sentence fit each other, and the possibilities for altering and controlling your sentences. This section reviews the basic grammatical terms you may need to analyze and describe sentences and to discuss the relations between the words of which they are composed.

1.1

Gr

1.1 Main Sentence Elements

Most English sentences are made with a subject and a verb. You may see this pattern referred to as the "major" or "favorite" sentence type in English.

The Subject

The subject (s) of a sentence is a noun or noun equivalent (pronoun, noun clause, gerund, infinitive) that is the starting point of the sentence. The *simple subject* is a single word, like *students* in the first sentence below. The *complete subject* consists of the simple subject plus any words that modify it: *Hurried students*.

> s
> Hurried **students** often make careless mistakes. [noun]
> s
> **She** runs faster than her brother does. [pronoun]
> s
> **What he doesn't know** is that he talks too much. [noun clause]
> s
> **Talking** is his only exercise. [gerund]
> s
> **To listen** is to suffer. [infinitive]

The Verb

A verb (v) is a word that has forms like *ask, asks, asked, asking* or *sing, sang, sung, singing* and in a sentence agrees with the subject. In the typical sentence the verb follows the subject and, like the subject, is often a nucleus for modifying words. The verb may consist of one or more words:

            s   v
Hurried students often **make** careless mistakes.
    v   s   v
Does he **listen** to what she says?
        s   v
Leslie Jones **has driven** for twenty years without getting a ticket.
              s   v
Perhaps the defendant **should be given** the benefit of the doubt.

The *predicate* is the verb and whatever words are related to it, such as objects, complements, and modifiers. In the following sentences the complete predicate is in boldface type, the verb itself marked with a v:

            s   v
Hurried students **often make careless mistakes.**
        s   v
The doorbell **rang.** [The verb is the complete predicate.]
                  s   v
After finishing his second year, George **spent two long sessions talking with his advisor about his major.**

The Object

The *direct object* (o) of a verb is a noun or noun equivalent that completes the statement. It answers the question asked by adding "what" or "whom" after the verb. (Hurried students often make what? Careless mistakes.)

            s   v   o
Hurried students often make careless **mistakes.** [noun]
        s   v   o
The Sherwoods have decided **to buy a home.** [infinitive phrase]
  s   v   o
He wondered **what he should do.** [noun clause]

The *indirect object* (IO) is used with verbs of telling, asking, giving, receiving, and so on. It names the receiver of the message, gift, or whatever, answering the question "to whom or what" or "for whom or what." It comes *before* the direct object.

    s   v   IO   o
He gave the **church** a memorial window.

The same meaning can usually be expressed in a prepositional phrase placed *after* the direct object:

    s   v   o
He gave a memorial window **to the church.**

The Complement

A complement (c) is a noun or an adjective in the predicate which follows a linking verb (LV). In contrast to an object, a complement is related to the subject rather than to the verb, because a linking verb (sometimes called a *copula*) expresses a condition rather than direct action. A noun used as a complement is called a *predicate noun;* an adjective used as a complement is called a *predicate adjective:*

1.1

Grs

>   S   LV   C
> Mary Enderby is a skilled **architect.** [predicate noun]
>   S   LV   C
> The tenor sounded a little **flat.** [predicate adjective]

The most common linking verb is *be* in its various forms: *is, are, was, were, has been, might be.* Other linking verbs include *seem* and *appear* and, in some contexts, *feel, grow, act, look, smell, taste,* and *sound.*

    See also 9.2, Predicate Adjectives.

• *Exercises*

1. List both the main sentence elements (subject, verb, direct object, indirect object, complement) and the complete predicate of each sentence in the paragraph below.

> Year-round roses, in Minnesota no less. About 50 miles northwest of Minneapolis, a power company is piping some of its "waste" warm water through underground conduits to a half-acre greenhouse. Even when night-time temperatures get as low as 25 below zero, the greenhouses maintain a cozy 60 degrees, and the results are roses, snapdragons, tomatoes, lettuce, green peppers, and pine seedlings. Commercial growers are studying the demonstration project with an eye toward large-scale production. The warm water, incidentally, is piped to cooling towers anyhow, making the crops something of a technological bonus. — Mobil Corporation, "Observations"

2. List the main sentence elements (subject, verb, direct object, indirect object, complement) of each sentence of the paragraphs below.

> Certain words grab business namers by the throat. For a time, "organization" had a vogue — "The Lawrence Organization." Then the British "group" surfaced, giving the impression of a vast array of enterprises under one roof: "The Continental Group," "The Diebold Group." Recently, the pretentious "center" was examined here — "learning center" for school, or "vision center" for an eyeglasses shop.
>   Comes now "system." It all began, I think, when a gun manufacturer who liked complexity began calling his weapon a "weapons system," because it fit with other weapons, or wheels. Interconnec-

tion was the key: teachers like "school systems" like astronomers like "solar systems."—William Safire, "Strong Stuff," *New York Times Magazine,* January 27, 1980

Word Order

In English we identify the main sentence elements chiefly by their position in the sentence—by their word order. Although the form of the words is the same, it makes a great deal of difference whether you say "the ball hit the boy" or "the boy hit the ball."

Typical Word Order.   The typical order of the main elements is subject–verb–object (or subject–linking verb–complement). This is the order in which we make most statements and the means by which we understand them.

In "The class congratulated Rachel" we know through experience that *class* is the subject of *congratulated* because it comes before the verb, and that *Rachel* is the object because it follows the verb. When the verb is in the *passive voice* (a past participle following some form of the verb *be*), the order of sentence elements remains subject–verb: Rachel was congratulated by the class.

So familiar is this order that we recognize it even though the statement itself may be gibberish, or "jabberwocky," as in these lines by Lewis Carroll:

> . . . the slithy toves
> Did gyre and gimble in the wabe. . . .

Whatever the meaning, most people would agree that because of the order of the words, the subject is *toves* and the verbs are *did gyre* and *gimble.*

Inverted Order.   The typical order of sentence elements is reversed in questions, exclamations, and emphatic statements:

>   V   S   O
> QUESTION: Have you a minute to spare?
>   C   S   LV
> EXCLAMATION: How wasteful these meetings are!
>   O S   V
> EMPHATIC OBJECT: A better job I never had.

In sentences with *there* or *it* as an *anticipating subject* (AS) or *expletive,* the real subject comes after the verb:

> AS LV   C   S
> It is a difficult choice.
>   AS   LV   C   S
> There are several reasons for the difficulty.

When the usual order of elements is reversed, you can find the subject of the sentence by locating the verb and then seeing what word answers the question formed by putting "who" or "what" before it. Thus in the expression "A lot he knows about it," *knows* is the verb, and since the answer to "*Who* knows?" is obviously *he, he* (rather than *lot*) is the subject.

1.2

1.2 Secondary Sentence Elements

Gr

In addition to the main sentence elements (subject – verb – object or subject – linking verb – complement), most sentences also contain secondary elements. Secondary elements are typically used as modifiers (M) – they describe, limit, or make more exact the meaning of main elements. The table on page 33 shows the various ways in which modifiers – single words, phrases, and clauses – might be used to qualify or expand a simple statement.

Adjectives and Adverbs as Modifiers

Single words used as modifiers are ordinarily related to the element they modify by means of word order. *Adjectives* relate to nouns and usually stand before the words they modify, but sometimes they come immediately after; in both examples, *climb* is the word modified:

> M   M
> It was a **slow, dangerous** climb.

> M   M
> The steepness of the slope made the climb **slow** and **dangerous.**

Adverbs are more varied in position because often they relate to the sentence as a whole. However, when they modify a particular word (verb, adjective, or adverb) they usually stand close to it:

> M
> They **particularly** wanted to go. [modifies *wanted*]

> M
> He came home from the movies **quite** late. [modifies *late*]

See 9, Adjectives and Adverbs.

Other Words and Word Groups as Modifiers

In English a noun often modifies another noun: *glass* jar, *ski* pants, *dance* hall. Nouns used in this way are usually called *modifiers* (not adjectives) or, more exactly, *nouns used attributively.* (See 6.4, Noun Modifiers.)

Review: Main Sentence Elements

SUBJECT: Noun or noun equivalent that performs an action or is in a particular state of being; it usually appears before the verb and determines the number (singular or plural) of the verb.

VERB: A word that is inflected to show tense, person, and number. Signifies the action or state of being of the subject.

PREDICATE: The verb and all words related to it.

DIRECT OBJECT: Noun or noun equivalent that answers the question asked by adding *what?* or *whom?* to the verb.

INDIRECT OBJECT: Noun that names the receiver of some action, answering the question *to whom or what?* or *for whom or what?* added to the verb. It comes before the direct object.

COMPLEMENT: Noun or adjective in the predicate, following a *linking verb;* it refers to the subject rather than the verb, because a linking verb expresses a condition rather than direct action.

* *Examples:*

         S   V   DO
Careless drivers may injure pedestrians.
      S   V   IO   DO
Charity may give the needy financial aid.
         S   LV   C
Some drivers are often careless.
         S   LV   C
Charity is often the last resort of the needy.

Prepositional phrases function as modifiers in many English sentences:

>   M
> An apartment-dweller **in a large city** [modifies *apartment-dweller*]can
>   M   M
> live **in the same place** [modifies *can live*] **for a year** [modifies *can live*]
>   M
> and never speak **to his next-door neighbor.** [modifies *speak*]

1.2

Verbal phrases and subordinate clauses also can function as modifiers:

>   M
> **Finding no one at home,** he scribbled a note and left it under the front door. [participle phrase modifying *he*]
>   M
> He needed a way **to make money.** [infinitive phrase modifying *way*]
>   M
> People **who live in glass houses** shouldn't throw stones. [subordinate clause modifying *People*]

See 3, Subordinate Clauses, and 4, Verbals.

Appositives

An appositive (A) is a noun or noun equivalent placed beside another noun to supplement or complement its meaning. It has the same grammatical function as the noun to which it relates. In speech, it is marked by a pause and a change in pitch:

>   A
> Your lawyer, **Mr. Jenkins,** is on the telephone.
>   A
> The story takes place in Thebes, **a city in ancient Greece.**

See 11.4, Appositives.

Modifiers of Modifiers

Words, phrases, and clauses that modify the main sentence elements may themselves be modified. These expressions are called *modifiers of modifiers:*

>   MM   M   S   V   M   M   O
> The **local** high-school orchestra played several difficult selections
> MM   M
> **very** well.

• *Exercise*

Expand the following sentences using modifiers, to at least twelve words each:

1. Dogs bark.

2. This typewriter works well.

3. The car runs.

4. The house is old.

5. The people elected a new congressman.

1.3 Phrases and Clauses

English sentences are constructed of single words, phrases, and clauses. Main (or independent) clauses form the principal grammatical units of sentences; they express completed statements and can stand alone. Phrases and subordinate clauses, on the other hand, are dependent on other sentence elements and are used very much like single words.

Phrases

Phrases are groups of related words connected to a sentence or to one of the elements in it by means of a preposition or a verbal. A phrase has no subject or predicate and cannot stand alone.

Prepositional Phrases.   A prepositional phrase consists of a preposition (*at, from, by, in, of, under,* etc.) followed by a noun or noun equivalent, plus whatever modifiers it may have. It functions like an adjective or adverb, depending on what element it modifies:

> He came **from a small town** [modifies the verb *came*] **in northeastern Minnesota** [modifies the noun *town*].

Verbal Phrases.   A verbal phrase consists of a participle, gerund, or infinitive (none of which has full verb function) plus its object or complement and modifiers. A participle phrase functions as an adjective; a gerund phrase as a noun; and an infinitive phrase as either a noun, an adjective, or an adverb. (See 4, Verbals.)

> Sentences **containing several unrelated ideas** [participle phrase modifying *Sentences*] are seldom effective.

> **Containing the enemy** [gerund phrase used as subject] was their first objective.

Review: Modifiers

- ### *Modifiers of the Subject*

         M   S

A WORD: The **local** orchestra played a selection.

         S   M

A PHRASE: The orchestra, **consisting largely of amateurs,** played a selection.

         S   M

A CLAUSE: The orchestra, **which had practiced hard for several weeks,** played a selection.

- ### *Modifiers of the Verb*

         V   M

A WORD: The orchestra played the selection **badly.**

         V   M

A PHRASE: The orchestra played the selection **with more enthusiasm than technique.**

         V   M

A CLAUSE: The orchestra played the selection **as if they had never rehearsed together before.**

- ### *Modifiers of the Object*

         M   O

A WORD: The orchestra played a **difficult** selection.

         O   M

A PHRASE: The orchestra played a selection **of old folk tunes.**

         O   M

A CLAUSE: The orchestra played a selection **which no one in the audience had ever heard before.**

- ### *Modifiers of the Main Clause*

         M

A WORD: **Nevertheless,** the orchestra played the selection.

         M

A PHRASE: **Considering their lack of experience,** the orchestra played the selection fairly well.

         M

A CLAUSE: **Since there were no other requests,** the orchestra played the selection.

1.3

Grs

The easiest way **to understand grammatical construction** [infinitive phrase modifying *way*] is **to analyze your own sentences** [infinitive phrase used as complement].

Clauses

A *main* (or independent) clause contains a subject and predicate and is the grammatical core of a sentence. In the three sentences below, the main clauses are in boldface. Each is a complete expression and could stand alone as a sentence:

> S   V
> **I laughed** because I couldn't help myself.
>
> S   V   O   S   V   O
> **She hated English,** but **she needed one more course to graduate.**
>
>   S   V   O
> If I were you, **I would find a new job.**

A *subordinate* (or dependent) clause also has a subject and a predicate, but it functions as *part* of a sentence. It is related to the main clause by a connecting word that shows its subordinate relationship, either a relative pronoun *(who, which, that)* or a subordinating conjunction *(because, although, since, after, if, when,* etc.):

> I laughed **because I couldn't help myself.**

Subordinate clauses are used like nouns (as subjects, objects, or complements), like adjectives (modifying nouns or pronouns), or like adverbs (expressing relationships of time, cause, result, degree, contrast, and so forth). The subordinate clauses are emphasized in the following examples:

> He confessed **that he loved me.** [noun clause, object of *confessed*]
>
> Many of the criminals **whose cases crowded the docket each year** were third- or fourth-time offenders. [adjective clause modifying *criminals*]
>
> **After you plant the seeds,** you should water the garden right away. [adverb clause of time]
>
> The peas in his garden were stunted **because he did not water soon enough.** [adverb clause of cause]

See 3, Subordinate Clauses and Connectives.

• *Exercise*

Start with this sentence: *She walked.*

1. Add a *phrase* that tells where she walked.

2. Add a *phrase* that tells how she walked.

3. Add a *phrase* that tells when she walked.

4. Add a *phrase* that tells where she walked and a *clause* that tells why she walked there.

5. Add a *clause* that tells when she walked, a *phrase* that tells where she walked, and a *clause* that tells to what place she walked.

1.4 Sentences Classified by Clause Structure

1.4

Grs

Sentences may be classified according to the kind and number of clauses they contain as *simple, compound, complex,* or *compound–complex.*

Simple Sentences

A simple sentence contains one independent clause and no subordinate (dependent) clauses:

> The man went across the street.

Although simple sentences contain only one clause, they need not be limited to a small, simple idea. They may contain any number of modifiers, and either the subject or the predicate (or both) may be compound:

> For the first time in four billion years a living creature had contemplated himself and heard with a sudden, unaccountable loneliness, the whisper of the wind in the night reeds. [compound predicate]—Loren Eiseley, *The Immense Journey*

> Journalism professors, books, editors and reporters often explain news in terms of characteristics or values. [compound subject]—Ivan and Carol Doig, *News: A Consumer's Guide*

> Colleges and universities do not exist to impose duties but to reveal choices. [compound subject, compound object]—Archibald MacLeish, "Why Do We Teach Poetry," *The Atlantic Monthly*

Compound Sentences

Compound sentences contain two or more main clauses and no subordinate clauses:

> The nations of Asia and Africa are moving with jet-like speed toward gaining political independence [first main clause], but we still creep at horse-and-buggy pace toward gaining a cup of coffee at a lunch counter. — Martin Luther King, Jr., "Letter from Birmingham Jail"

Each clause in a compound sentence is independent and is *coordinate* (of equal rank) with the other clauses. The clauses may be joined (or separated) in one of three ways:

With Coordinating Conjunctions.   Independent clauses are most frequently linked by the coordinating conjunctions *and, but, or, nor, for, yet* or the correlatives *either . . . or, neither . . . nor, both . . . and, not only . . . but (also):*

> It rained all morning, **but** it cleared up for the picnic.
> **Either** you play to win **or** you don't play at all.

Without Connectives.   Independent clauses not joined by coordinating conjunctions are conventionally separated by semicolons:

> They are generous-minded; they hate shams and enjoy being indignant about them; they are valuable social reformers; they have no notion of confining books to a library shelf. — E. M. Forster, *Aspects of the Novel*

With Conjunctive Adverbs.   The clauses in a compound sentence are sometimes linked by a conjunctive adverb such as *accordingly, also, consequently, however, nevertheless, therefore, then.* However, the connective function of these adverbs is weak, and a semicolon should be used before them:

> The urban renewal program has many outspoken opponents; **nevertheless,** some land has already been cleared.

See 12.1, Semicolons.

Complex Sentences

A complex sentence consists of one main clause and one or more subordinate clauses:

> As far as I could determine [subordinate clause], Paris hadn't changed at all [main clause] since I last visited it ten years before [second subordinate clause].

In published writing today, complex sentences are used far more frequently than the other three types are. Often, as many as half of the sentences in a particular piece of writing are complex. Complex sentences offer more variety than simple sentences do; it is often possible, for example, to shift subordinate clauses around in the sentence in order to get different emphases or different rhythms. Look at the example above again. It could be changed in various ways, keeping essentially the same words but changing the emphasis:

> Since I last visited Paris ten years ago [subordinate clause], it hadn't changed at all [main clause], as far as I could determine [subordinate clause].

Or,

> Paris hadn't changed at all [main clause], as far as I could determine [subordinate clause], since I last visited it ten years ago [second subordinate clause].

The tone changes slightly in these examples: in the first example the idea emphasized is that Paris hadn't changed at all; the second sentence emphasizes the visit ten years before; and the third places more doubt on the idea of Paris not changing because *as far as I could determine* gets heavier emphasis. Complex sentences are often more precise than compound sentences are: a compound sentence treats two ideas equally, while a complex sentence establishes a more exact relationship.

1.4

Grs

Compound-Complex Sentences

A compound-complex sentence contains two or more main clauses and one or more subordinate clauses:

> When two men fight a duel [first subordinate clause], the matter is trivial [first main clause], but when 200 million people fight 200 million people [second subordinate clause], the matter is serious [second main clause]. — Bertrand Russell, *The Impact of Science on Society*

Compound-complex sentences occur far less frequently than the other types do.

• *Exercises*

1. Combine the short sentences in each group below into a single sentence by reducing some to phrases or subordinate clauses. Arrange the parts in any way necessary to create sentences.

   a. He left before sunrise. He reached his old country home by noon. He had time to look around a while. He went on to his aunt's house.
   b. The ball took a bad bounce. It hit the second base player in the eye. She picked it up anyway. She threw it to first base. The runner was out. The second base player fell to her knees.
   c. The wind died. It was sunset. The night was clear. The wisp of moon was not out yet. There were stars. It was still. The crackling of the fire was the only sound.

2. Write one sentence on each model shown below. An example of each is given.

   a. compound: main clause + conjunction + main clause
      He ate the squash, but he didn't like it.
   b. complex: subordinate clause + main clause
      When he had planted the beans, he marked the row with two stakes.

c. compound-complex: subordinate clause + main clause + conjunction + main clause
After he bought the car, he regretted his haste, but then it was too late.
d. complex: main clause + subordinate clause
He disliked the car because it used too much gas.
e. compound-complex: main clause + subordinate clause + conjunction + main clause + subordinate clause
He went to the country whenever he could, and he was sorry that he couldn't stay longer.

1.5 Sentences Classified by Purpose

Sentences are conventionally classified by meaning or purpose as follows:

Statements   (often called *declarative sentences*):

Jim laughed.
Most of the sentences we speak and write are declarative.

Questions:

At what temperature does water boil?
Why do you ask?

Commands   (including requests and instructions):

Write soon.
When the liquid boils, remove it from the heat.

Exclamations   (feelings, facts, or opinions expressed in an emphatic way):

How lucky you are!
He should be thrown out!

1.6 Unorthodox Sentences

While the great majority of written sentences contain both subjects and verbs, some do not. In speech, we may express ourselves by a single word ("Yes." "Oh?"), a phrase ("In a minute."), or a clause ("If you say so."). Similarly, we occasionally find single words, phrases, and subordinate clauses used as sentences in published material:

> And so on to Bangkok. Spit and hiss of water, the gramophone quiet. The lights out along the deck, nobody about. — Graham Greene, *The Shipwrecked*

We do not have to supply any "missing" words to get the author's meaning (such as "And so *the ship sailed* on to Bangkok."). Such statements are meaningful and complete as they stand. But they are minor types, exceptions to the typical English sentence pattern with subject and predicate. When they appear in print, they are used deliberately and for a special purpose — to imitate dialog, for example, or to create emphasis, or to avoid colorless, repetitious verbs.

1.6

Grs

Subjectless Sentences

Commands and requests generally do not have subjects:

> Don't let me hear you say that again.
> Please try.

The subject is sometimes omitted in informal writing (seldom in serious writing) when it is easily carried over from the preceding sentence by the context:

> They took no interest in civilized ways. Hadn't heard of them, probably. — Clarence Day, *Life with Father*

Verbless Sentences

Several types of sentences without a main verb are used in all levels of speaking and writing. The verbs are not left out; they are not thought, spoken, or written. The statements are complete and independent without them.

Exclamations.   *Ouch!, Oh!,* and similar words make complete exclamations, as do such phrases as *What luck!* and *How terrible!*

Answers to Questions.   Short answers without a main verb *(Yes. No. Not if I can help it.)* are considered complete sentences. Occasionally a writer may use a verbless construction to answer a question he has raised himself:

> What is a hero? **The exceptional individual.** How is he recognized, whether in life or in books? **By the degree of interest he arouses in the spectator or the reader.** — W. H. Auden, *The Enchaféd Flood*

Descriptive Details.   Descriptive details are sometimes set off in sentences by themselves for emphasis or to avoid colorless verbs like *is, are, has:*

> I was watching a bunch of men hold their fingers to their lips and shush each other to keep quiet. **Every one of them haw-hawing and tittering under their breath and pointing to a kid asleep on the floor.** He was about twenty. **Little white cap from the ten-cent store, a pair of old blue washed-out pants, shirt to match, a set of dirty heels caked over with the dust of many railroads, and a run-over pair of low-cut shoes.** — Woody Guthrie, *Bound for Glory*

Common Sentence Errors

Except for misspelled words, which sooner or later will attract someone's attention, probably the three most conspicuous errors in sentence construction are fragmentary sentences, comma faults, and fused sentences.

These three faults are common, but if they occur often in your writing they are considered serious because they suggest either that you are not recognizing and distinguishing between separate complete statements, or that you are not checking your writing carefully.

2.1 Fragmentary Sentences

Frag **Revise the fragment marked by joining it to another sentence, by making it into a complete sentence, or by rewriting the passage.**

A *fragmentary sentence* is an incomplete statement — a phrase or a subordinate clause — punctuated as a complete sentence. Fragmentary sentences occur frequently in our speech, and they often make good enough sense there, as responses to what someone else has said, for example, or as additions to what we have already said. When you write something down, however, you can't give it gestures and tone; a reader has only the written words as a guide to your meaning. A fragmentary sentence is likely to be a fragmentary idea that needs to be finished or added to another idea.

A sentence fragment can be corrected in various ways:

1. by joining it to another sentence;
2. by supplying a subject and a predicate;
3. by rewriting the passage in which it occurs.

Each of these ways is illustrated below. (See 1.6 for a discussion of the occasional effective use of fragmentary sentences.)

Joining a Fragment to Another Sentence

A fragmentary sentence usually should be part of the preceding sentence. If you read the passage aloud, you will notice that you pause only slightly before the sentence fragment and do not drop your voice as noticeably as you do at the end of complete sentences. This means that the fragment should be joined to the preceding sentence, usually with a comma. Sometimes it should also be rephrased.

> SENTENCE FRAGMENT: The next afternoon we made our way through the harbor of Okinawa. **That island, which had made history during World War II.**
>
> REVISED: The next afternoon we made our way through the harbor of Okinawa, the island which had made history during World War II.

Phrases as Fragments.   Phrases are subordinate sentence elements and should not be punctuated as complete sentences:

> FRAGMENT: I cite these examples to show you how interesting accounting can be. **And to give you an idea of the kind of problems an accountant has to solve.** [The fragment has no main subject and verb. It is an infinitive phrase — *to give* belongs in the first sentence parallel with *to show*.]
>
> REVISED: I cite these examples to show you how interesting accounting can be and to give you an idea of the kind of problems an accountant has to solve.
>
> FRAGMENT: For the past five years I have been contributing annually to the March of Dimes. **Without ever suspecting that one day a member of my own family might benefit from this foundation.** [prepositional phrase]
>
> REVISED: For the past five years I have been contributing a small amount annually to the March of Dimes, without ever suspecting that one day a member of my own family might benefit from this foundation.
>
> FRAGMENT: Professor Brown suddenly glanced up from his notes. **His eyes twinkling with suppressed laughter.** [*Twinkling* is a participle, not a full verb.]
>
> REVISED: Professor Brown suddenly glanced from his notes, his eyes twinkling with suppressed laughter.

Explanatory phrases beginning with *such as, for example, that is, namely,* and similar expressions belong in the same sentence as the statement they explain:

> FRAGMENT: Their mother had a hard time cooking for them because they disliked so many foods. **For example, squash, sweet potatoes, beets, okra, cabbage, apricots, and peaches.**
>
> REVISED: Their mother had a hard time cooking for them because they disliked so many foods, for example, squash, sweet potatoes, beets, okra, cabbage, apricots, and peaches.

Subordinate Clauses as Fragments.   *Subordinate clauses* are only parts of sentences and should not stand alone without a definite reason. A relative pronoun *(who, which, that)* or a subordinating conjunction (such as *although, because, if, when, while*) indicates that what follows is a subordinate clause and that it should be combined with a main clause.

> FRAGMENT: At the time, my old rowboat with its three-horsepower motor seemed a high-speed job to me. **Although it only attained a speed of about twelve miles an hour.** [adverb clause, beginning with *Although*]
>
> REVISED: At the time, my old rowboat with its three-horsepower motor seemed a high-speed job to me, although it only attained a speed of about twelve miles an hour.
>
> FRAGMENT: The whole area is honeycombed by caves. **Many of which are still unexplored.** [adjective clause, introduced by *which*]
>
> REVISED: The whole area is honeycombed by caves, many of which are still unexplored.

2.1

Frag

Making a Fragment into a Sentence

If the fragment deserves special emphasis, it can be made into a sentence by inserting a subject and a predicate:

> FRAGMENT: He talked for fifty minutes without taking his eyes off his notes. **Apparently not noticing that half the class was asleep.** [*Noticing* is a participle, not a verb.]
>
> REVISED: He talked for fifty minutes without taking his eyes off his notes. Apparently he did not notice that half the class was asleep. [The subject is *he;* the predicate is the verb *did notice* plus the words related to it.]
>
> FRAGMENT: National elections and student elections may be compared as closely as an object and its photograph. **The only difference being in size.** [*Being* is a participle, not a verb.]
>
> REVISED: National elections and student elections may be compared as closely as an object and its photograph. The only difference is in size. [*Is* is the verb, and *difference* is the subject.]

Rewriting a Fragment

Sometimes involved or hopelessly snarled sentence fragments have to be completely revised. The following long "sentence" has three phrases that seem to be subjects, but there is no *main* verb. A number of verbs appear, but each one is in a subordinate construction.

> FRAGMENT: **The people** who only said, "Oh, too bad," on seeing the lifeless puppy, **the small boy** who removed the dead puppy from the gutter, and the **middle-aged man** who kept saying that people were making a greater fuss about this incident than had been made over his own accident at this same corner a year ago, when he was almost run over by a taxi.
>
> REVISED: When the small boy removed the dead puppy from the gutter, some people only said, "Oh, too bad." But the middle-aged man

kept saying that people were making a greater fuss about this incident than they had made over his own accident at this same corner a year ago, when he was almost run over by a taxi.

• *Exercises*

1. Advertisements often use sentence fragments. The name of a product by itself is sometimes followed by a period to create emphasis. Short phrases punctuated as if they were sentences may seem more direct and to the point. When words and phrases are punctuated as sentences, they can be more readily moved around for purposes of design and visual effect. Find three advertisements that depend on fragments (Volkswagen advertisements are one good place to look) and rewrite the text with complete sentences. Be prepared to discuss which you think is more effective.

2. Rewrite the following sentences so that they contain no fragments.

   a. Statistics are not yet available to show the actual decrease in accidents. Since this program is still in the process of being completed and traffic has doubled in the past few months.
   b. The area thrives on competition since the same kinds of shops are all grouped together. An example of this being the three supermarkets, which are within a mile of each other.
   c. Public transportation will have to be subsidized by the government. Because it will be too expensive for people to ride otherwise.
   d. A popular person usually has three good personality traits. A good sense of humor, considerateness of others, and good grooming.
   e. The professor was obviously displeased with the performance of the class. His eyes looking as angry as lightning bolts.

2.2 Comma Faults

 Change the comma marked to a period or semicolon or revise the passage to make an acceptable sentence or sentences.

A comma fault (also called a *comma splice*) is two or more independent clauses not joined by a coordinating conjunction and written with only a comma between them. The result is that one clause is simply backed up against the other:

> The card catalog is the key to the books in the library, many large libraries have separate catalogs for certain collections of books.

Each of the two clauses joined here is a main clause that could stand alone as a simple sentence. The clauses should be separated by a period or joined into a compound sentence by a semicolon or an appropriate connective:

> The card catalog is the key to the books in the library; many large libraries have separate catalogs for certain collections of books.

> The card catalog is the key to the books in the library, and many large libraries have separate catalogs for certain collections of books.

2.2

CF

If you understand clause structure and are aware of when you use clauses, your writing probably won't have many comma faults. If you make this error often, review 1.4, Sentences Classified by Clause Structure. You may also find it helpful to read your papers aloud. If your voice drops or if you pause noticeably at a comma, check the sentence to see if it is actually two independent statements. For example, read this sentence aloud to see how much more marked the pause is at the comma following *past* (a comma fault) than at the comma following *five-thirty:*

> The long shopping days of Front and Market streets are a thing of the past, the stores now open for business at ten in the morning and close at five-thirty, including Saturdays.

The pause indicates that there are two separate statements here; a new sentence should begin after *past.*

Making Two Sentences

A comma fault may be removed by using a period instead of the comma, making two full sentences:

> COMMA FAULT: He took a couple of steps, stopped, reached out, and turned a valve, as he did so he told us the valves had to be checked daily.
> REPUNCTUATED: He took a couple of steps, stopped, reached out, and turned a valve. As he did so, he told us the valves had to be checked daily.

This is usually the best solution when the ideas are clearly distinct or when there are many commas in either or both statements. However, correcting a comma fault by putting a period between two very short, closely connected statements may result only in two weak sentences:

> I opened the door noisily, he didn't move. [Here joining the clauses by **but** is preferable to making each a separate sentence.]

Using a Semicolon

Comma faults may sometimes be corrected by substituting a semi-colon for the comma. This is appropriate when the ideas expressed in the two clauses are closely related:

> COMMA FAULT: Charley then crossed the room and threw a switch which started the motor, returning, he wiped the sweat from his forehead with the back of his hand.
>
> REPUNCTUATED: Charley then crossed the room and threw a switch which started the motor; returning, he wiped the sweat from his forehead with the back of his hand.

A great many comma faults in student papers occur with "conjunc-tive" adverbs such as *accordingly, consequently, however, there-fore.* When such adverbs appear at the junction of two independent clauses, the conventional punctuation is a semicolon. Although such words show the connection between ideas in the clauses, their connective function is weak.

> COMMA FAULT: The person with a college education has training far beyond that which can be obtained solely from books, **therefore** his or her chances for success may be greater than are those of a person without this education.
>
> REPUNCTUATED: The person with a college education has training far beyond that which can be obtained solely from books; therefore, his or her chances for success may be greater than are those of a person without this education.

Other uses of adverbs like *however* and *therefore* are discussed on page 154.

Revising the Passage

Often the best way to remove a comma fault is to revise the sen-tence, using a connective that will show the relation between the statements. The connective may be a coordinating conjunction (such as *and* or *but*), a subordinating conjunction (*although, be-cause, if, since, when*), or a relative pronoun (*who, which, that*) referring to a noun in the first statement. Sometimes one statement can be revised as a phrase, as in the third example:

> COMMA FAULT: It is a personal matter, everyone has to cope with it sooner or later.
>
> REVISED: It is a personal matter **that** everyone has to cope with sooner or later.
>
> COMMA FAULT: I enjoy being in the midst of a party, particularly if I feel some responsibility for its success, conversation is a stimulant more powerful than drugs.

> REVISED: I enjoy being in the midst of a party, particularly if I feel some responsibility for its success, **because** conversation is a stimulant more powerful than drugs.
>
> COMMON FAULT: Many companies are looking for experts in pollution control, this is a rapidly expanding field.
>
> REVISED: Many companies are looking for experts in pollution control, a rapidly expanding field.

2.2

CF

There are many ways of correcting comma faults. The method of revision you choose probably ought to depend as much as possible upon what you are trying to do in the passage where the fault occurs. Consider this comma fault:

> The war provided the setting for many novels, three of them were especially outstanding.

Suppose this occurs in the opening paragraph of a paper in which you intend to review a number of war novels very briefly and then focus at some length on three that you think are outstanding. You might revise the sentence as shown below, subordinating the first statement to show that the review of several novels is less significant in the paper than the close study of three (see 3 and 26.2):

> While the war provided the setting for many novels, three of them were especially outstanding.

If you intend in your paper to give equal time and attention to the review of several novels and to the close study of three, you might revise the fault in this way:

> The war provided the setting for many novels. Three of them were especially outstanding.

If the review of a number of novels is what is most important in your paper, and the three novels are simply being used as examples, then you might revise in this way:

> The war provided the setting for many novels, including three that were especially outstanding.

• *Exercise*

Comma faults can often be corrected in several different ways, as the example below suggests. Study the example, and then correct the following sentences in the way that you feel is most effective. Be prepared to discuss your revisions.

Comma fault: The Braves traded Hank Aaron, it was a big mistake.
Revised as a compound sentence: The Braves traded Hank Aaron; it was a big mistake.

Revised as two sentences: The Braves traded Hank Aaron. It was a big mistake.

Revised by rewriting: It was a big mistake for the Braves to trade Hank Aaron.

When the Braves traded Hank Aaron, they made a big mistake.

Trading Hank Aaron was a big mistake for the Braves.

1. I'd like to own a bigger car, I don't think I could afford the gas.

2. Bricklayers were hired on a contingency basis, that is, they weren't paid until the building was finished.

3. Jim hit a single down the right-field line, David scored from second base.

4. Julie is an excellent guitarist, she taught herself.

5. The electricity went off during the storm, we could not read or watch television.

2.3 Fused Sentences

 Use a period or semicolon between the two statements, or revise the passage to make an acceptable sentence or sentences.

A fused sentence (also called a run-on sentence) is the same kind of error as a comma fault, except that no punctuation at all appears between the main clauses. It should be corrected in the same way as a comma fault:

1. make two sentences of the fused sentence;
2. use a semicolon to separate the two main clauses;
3. rewrite the passage.

> FUSED SENTENCE: Two volumes of this work are now completed the first will be published next year.
> POSSIBLE REVISIONS: Two volumes of this work are now completed. The first will be published next year.
> Two volumes of this work are now completed, the first **of which** will be published next year.

• *Exercise*

Following the suggestions in the text, repair the fused sentences below.

1. The birds began to sing it was late in the afternoon.

2. The steak was very expensive lots of prices have been going up lately.

3. "What is the purpose in this?" he asked he did not believe in fraternity initiations.

2.4 Mixed Constructions

Mix Revise the mixed construction to make an acceptable sentence or sentences.

When several sentence faults are combined or when a construction is not one of the standard sentence types, the result is sometimes called a mixed construction. Repunctuating cannot correct errors of this kind; the whole passage must be rewritten into acceptable sentence units.

> MIXED CONSTRUCTION: I had always admired his novels, and when I had a chance to meet him, a real delight. [independent and subordinate clauses improperly joined by *and*]
> POSSIBLE REVISION: I had always admired his novels and was delighted when I had a chance to meet him.

> MIXED CONSTRUCTION: Charles was a hard worker, but I wondered how was he going to get everything finished on time? [shift from statement to question]
> POSSIBLE REVISION: Although Charles was a hard worker, I wondered how he was going to finish everything on time.

> MIXED CONSTRUCTION: Of course the Haitian diet is quite different from ours, this is obvious consisting largely of beans and rice. [a comma fault and a misplaced modifying phrase]
> POSSIBLE REVISION: Of course the Haitian diet, consisting largely of beans and rice, is quite different from ours.

Since mixed constructions usually involve a combination of errors, their variety is almost infinite. The only sure way to avoid them is to be sure you understand the principles of sentence construction.

3 Subordinate Clauses and Connectives

A subordinate clause has a subject and a predicate, but it is shown to be an incomplete statement—a subordinate part of the sentence—by a special kind of connective that relates it to the main clause. In the following sentence, *when* and *that* are the connectives; *few people thought* is the main clause:

> **When Truman ran for re-election in 1948,** few people thought **that he could win.**

Subordinate (dependent) clauses are used in sentences as modifiers, subjects, objects, or complements. Depending on the grammatical function they serve, they are classified as adjective clauses (3.1), adverb clauses (3.2), or noun clauses (3.3).

About half the sentences in most kinds of writing contain one or more subordinate clauses, for subordination shows the relationship between ideas more clearly than a series of simple or compound sentences. Effective use of subordinate clauses is discussed at the end of this section. For a discussion of subordination and style, see 26.2, Subordination to Control and to Clarify Meaning.

3.1 Adjective Clauses

A clause that modifies a noun or pronoun is an adjective clause. The relative pronouns *who, which,* and *that* (p. 89) are the words most frequently used to introduce adjective clauses; these pronouns also serve as subjects or objects within the clause:

> Some people **who buy modern paintings** are interested in them more as investments that as art. [*Who* is the subject of the clause, which modifies *people.*]

> The goals **for which he had fought all his life** no longer seemed important to him. [*Which* is the object of the preposition *for*; the clause modifies *goals.*]

> Many books **that are commercially successful** do not qualify as serious literature. [*That* is the subject of the clause, which modifies books.]

> He received a letter from an uncle **whom he had not seen for twenty years.** [*Whom* is the object of the verb *had seen;* the clause modifies *uncle.*]

50

Adjective clauses may also be introduced by the relative adverbs *when, where,* and *why:*

> It was a day **when everything went wrong.** [The clause modifies *day.*]
>
> She returned to the town **where she had lived as a girl.**[The clause modifies *town.*]
>
> The reason **why these early settlements disappeared** has never been explained satisfactorily. [The clause modifies *reason.*]

Clauses Without Relative Words

Sometimes an adjective clause is a restrictive modifier, a modifier that is essential to the sentence because it limits the meaning (see 11.4). In this case, the relative word is a pronoun or proper name:

> The only books [that] Alice read in high school were those [that] her teacher assigned.
>
> He is a person [whom] everyone admires.

These clauses without relatives (they are still subordinate clauses) have long been used in English and are acceptable in all varieties of writing.

And Which

And is sometimes needlessly used between an adjective clause and the rest of a sentence. The relative pronoun *who, which,* or *that* is the only connective needed; the use of *and* or *but* is superfluous and defeats the subordination:

> CARELESS: The sea anemone is a fascinating creature **and which** looks more like a plant than an animal.
>
> REVISED: The sea anemone is a fascinating creature which looks more like a plant than an animal.

3.2 Adverb Clauses

A subordinate clause that modifies a verb, adjective, adverb, or main clause is an adverb clause. It usually expresses a relationship of time, place, direction, cause, effect, condition, manner, or concession :

> He lived abroad for three years but returned to the United States **when war broke out.** [The clause modifies the verb *returned.*]
>
> During her husband's absence she managed the business better **than he had.** [The clause modifies the adverb *better.*]

3.2

Sub

He becomes very stubborn **when he meets opposition.** [The clause modifies the predicate adjective *stubborn*.]

Because she was a woman of principle, even her opponents respected her. [The clause modifies the main statement, *even her opponents respected her.*]

English has many connectives for expressing these adverb relationships. The following are among the most common:

after	because	since	unless
although	before	so	until
as	if	so that	when
as if	in order that	though	where
as long as	provided that	till	while

See also 3.4, page 55, Using Exact Connectives.

3.3 Noun Clauses

Because they function as nouns, subordinate clauses used as subjects, objects, complements, and appositives are called noun clauses. Most noun clauses are introduced by *that,* but *whatever, whoever, who, what, why, when, where,* and *whether* are also used.

As Objects

Noun clauses are most frequently used as direct objects:

The President said **that his meeting with the Arab heads of state had been fruitful.**

No one knows **why these early settlements disappeared.**
They wondered **what would happen next.**

Noun clauses also serve as objects of prepositions:

From **what you have told me,** I think he is making more money than he deserves.

There is a prize for **whoever gets there first.**

In the last sentence, *whoever* is the correct form rather than *whomever* because the pronoun is the subject of the clause.

As Appositives

Noun clauses are quite often used as appositives:

Most people still accept the myth **that progress is inevitable.**
The possibility **that he might lose** never occurred to him.

As Subjects

Sentences beginning with a subject clause introduced by *that* or *whether* sometimes seem rather stilted, especially if the clause is relatively long. In most kinds of writing, constructions of this kind can more easily appear *after* the verb:

> STILTED: **That he could raise his grade by studying harder** had never occurred to him.
>
> REVISED: It had never occurred to him **that he could raise his grade by studying harder.**
>
> STILTED: **Whether or not we should revise our foreign policy** was the principal topic of discussion.
>
> REVISED: The principal topic of discussion was **whether or not we should revise our foreign policy.**

3.3

Sub

Subject clauses introduced by other words are common in all levels of writing:

> **Whatever is worth doing at all** is worth doing well.
> **Where he disappeared** is a matter of conjecture.

As Complements

Noun clauses sometimes occur as complements, particularly in definitions and explanations. Such constructions are sometimes awkward, however, and it is often better to substitute a different wording:

> AWKWARD: Usually the winner is **whoever has the most endurance.**
> BETTER: The person with the most endurance usually wins.
> OR: Whoever has the most endurance usually wins.
>
> AWKWARD: Our materialism is **why some Europeans criticize us.**
> BETTER: Some Europeans criticize us for our materialism.

After "The reason *is* (or *was*) . . ." the preferred connective in formal and general writing is *that* rather than *because (because* means "the reason that"):

> The reason he lost the election was **that** [preferable to **because**] he lacked organized support.

• *Exercises*

1. Combine the following pairs of sentences by making one of the sentences into a subordinate clause.
   a. The hamster is a handsome animal. It looks like a bundle of fur.
   b. He was a strong man. He was feared and admired.
   c. The rain has fallen for two days. It has washed the bridge away.
   d. Those delegates are not here yet. They attended a big party last night.
   e. He was fourteen years old. He began to shave.

2. Combine each group of sentences below into a single sentence with one main or independent clause and at least one subordinate clause.
   a. Fort Phantom Hill is in ruins.
      It is twelve miles northeast of Abilene.
      I had never seen it before.
      I had erected the fort many times in my mind.
   b. Construction of the fort was authorized in November, 1851.
      Major General Smith gave the order.
      He commanded the 8th Military Department.
      The 8th Military Department included Texas.
   c. Major General Smith wanted a fort.
      He wanted it to be on the Clear Fork of the Brazos River.
      It would protect settlers on the upper Brazos.
   d. He had seen reports on the site.
      The reports were favorable.
      The site was "alive with deer, turkey, and bear."
   e. The troopers arrived on the site.
      There was no timber for construction.
      Water had to be hauled from four miles away.
   f. The fort took its name from a nervous sentry.
      He was on night duty.
      It was just after they had camped.
   g. He fired at something.
      He testified later.
      It was "an Indian on the Hill."
   h. They could not find the marauder.
      It was a phantom on the hill.
      They called it Fort Phantom Hill.

3.4 Subordination for Exact Statement

Sub   Show the intended relationship between ideas by using appropriate subordination, or correct the faulty subordination.

Ideas that deserve equal emphasis should be grammatically coordinate (as in *My son is in high school and my daughter is in college*). But an important part of writing is discriminating among ideas that do *not* deserve equal emphasis. Statements that describe or explain another statement or tell how, when, where, or why something happened should be expressed in subordinate constructions whenever the relationship is not immediately clear from the context. For example, there is no reason why three separate sentences should be made of these obviously related ideas:

> Mozart made his first trip to Italy in 1769. He was thirteen years old. His father went with him.

If the first statement is the one the writer wants to emphasize, it can stand as a main clause while the other two are reduced to a secondary level:

1. In 1769 Mozart made his first trip to Italy
    2. when he was thirteen years old
    2. accompanied by his father

Then the sentence would look like this:

3.4

> In 1769, **when he was thirteen years old** [subordinate clause], Mozart made his first trip to Italy [main clause], **accompanied by his father** [verbal phrase].

Sub

Showing the Relative Importance of Ideas

A subordinate clause usually indicates that the matter subordinated is less important to the subject being discussed than the main statement. To judge the rightness of subordination it is necessary to know what the emphasis of the passage is. For instance, in joining the two statements "The lightning struck the barn" and "Mother was setting the table for supper," the first would be the main statement in a general account of the event:

> The lightning struck the barn [main clause] just as Mother was setting the table for supper [subordinate clause].

But if the point to be emphasized is what Mother was doing when the lightning struck, the sentence would probably be written like this:

> When the lightning struck the barn [subordinate clause], Mother was setting the table for supper [main clause].

The paragraph would then probably go on to tell what Mother did in the crisis.

In revising sentences, then, it is important to see that the parts are related according to their relative importance.

Using Exact Connectives

Subordinate clauses are exact because their connectives show a precise and specific relationship to the main clause. Coordinating conjunctions, especially *and,* are much less definite in meaning than adverb connectives like *because, since, when, while* or the adjective connectives *who, which, that:*

> COORDINATE STATEMENT: Sandra was waiting for the bus and she saw a purse on the sidewalk.
>
> ONE STATEMENT SUBORDINATED: **While she was waiting for the bus,** Sandra saw a purse on the sidewalk.

COORDINATE STATEMENT: "I, Too, Sing America" is one of Langston Hughes' best-known poems, and it has been reprinted in many textbooks.

ONE STATEMENT SUBORDINATED: "I, Too, Sing America," **which is one of Langston Hughes' best-known poems,** has been reprinted in many textbooks.

In speaking we tend to rely on only a few of the conjunctions available for expressing adverb relationships (see 3.2), but in writing greater exactness is required. Particular care should be taken so that the common conjunctions *as* and *so* are not overused.

Using *as* and *so*.   The conjunction *as* may introduce various kinds of adverb clauses:

DEGREE OR MANNER: I went as fast **as I could go.**
TIME: Our guests arrived **as the clock struck nine.**
CAUSE: **As it was getting dark,** we made for home.
COMPARISON: Lettuce is not as fattening **as avocados are.**
ATTENDANT CIRCUMSTANCE: **As the fire spread,** the sky grew darker.

The variety of its meanings makes *as* a word to be watched in writing. In some instances it is the proper and only connective to use — to express comparisons, for example (We went as far *as the others did*), or in clauses of manner (*As Maine goes,* so goes the nation). But in many other constructions, *while, when, since,* or *because* would be more exact and emphatic:

While [not *as*] we were walking, he told us stories.
The war was almost over **when** [not *as*] he was drafted.

As is especially weak when used in place of *because*. To introduce clauses of reason, purpose, or result, *since* or *because* is better in most writing:

He refused to join in the square dancing **because** [not *as*] he was afraid of making a fool of himself.

Like *as,* the word *so* (or *and* so) is an overworked and often inexact connective. In most writing it should be replaced by a more definite word:

INEXACT: She couldn't find a job, **so** she decided to go to summer school.
REVISED: **Since** she couldn't find a job, she decided to go to summer school.

INEXACT: He was new to the neighborhood, **so** he had few friends.
REVISED: **Because** he was new to the neighborhood, he had few friends.

The inexact sentences are not wrong; in both, *so* means *therefore* or *consequently*. But the revised sentences are better; *since* and *because* are signals alerting the reader at the outset that cause-effect relationships occur in the sentences.

In clauses of purpose, *so that* is preferable to *so:*

> He went to New York **so that** [not *so*] he could find a job in publishing.

3.5

Sub

• *Exercise*

Combine the following pairs of sentences, choosing one of the statements to be the subordinate idea. Use a connective that accurately shows the relationship.

1. They pawned his big pocket watch. They needed money for groceries at the end of the month.

2. They knew what to expect of the weather. They had lived on the plains for forty years.

3. The Comanches had gathered and camped deep in Palo Duro Canyon. MacKenzie's troopers found them.

4. He got the garden planted by April 15. It cost him forty dollars for fertilizer, a new hoe, and a sore back.

5. I don't like the new address form for letters. It requires special abbreviations for state names.

6. These abbreviations all have just two letters (CA, NY, TX). They don't look like names or even like abbreviations.

7. Perhaps we'll forget the names. The names had lovely sounds — Nebraska, Wyoming, Montana, Kentucky.

8. The abbreviations are useful. A machine can read and sort the letters.

9. Machines can read and sort the letters. Humans are free to do less boring work.

3.5 Faulty Subordination

Faulty subordination usually results from a careless stringing together of ideas as they happen to come into the writer's mind. Consider, for example, the haphazard use of dependent constructions in the following sentence:

> Because her mother died when Barbara was five years old, and since her father lived a solitary life, Barbara had a very unhappy childhood, having no family to confide in.

The elements in this cluttered statement might be rearranged to establish a better sense of order and proportion:

> Barbara had a very unhappy childhood. She was five years old when her mother died, and since her father led a solitary life, she had no family to confide in.

When you go over the first draft of your papers, revise any subordinate elements that weaken your sentences or obscure their meaning.

Tandem Subordination

It is usually best to avoid statements in which a series of dependent clauses are strung together. Too many clauses beginning with similar connectives *(who, which, that; when, since, because)*, each built upon the preceding one, are called tandem subordination, or "house-that-Jack-built" constructions:

> TANDEM SUBORDINATION: He had carefully selected teachers **who** taught classes **that** had a slant **that** was specifically directed toward students **who** intended to go into business.
>
> REVISED: He had carefully selected teachers who specifically slanted their courses toward students intending to go into business.
>
> TANDEM SUBORDINATION: The recordings **which** I bought last week were scarce items **that** are essential to people **who** are making collections of folk music **which** comes from Spain.
>
> REVISED: Last week I bought some scarce recordings that are essential to collectors of Spanish folk music.

Sentences that begin and end with the same kind of subordinate clauses are awkward because of their seesaw effect:

> **When** he came home from work, Dad would always complain **when** the children weren't there to meet him.

Such constructions can be improved by changing one of the connectives. Usually it is possible to choose a connective that is more exact:

> When he came home from work, Dad would always complain **if** the children weren't there to meet him.

Inverted Subordination

Putting the main idea of a sentence in a subordinate clause or phrase ("inverting" the proper relationship between statements) may result in an awkward or incongruous statement:

> INVERTED: She was eighteen when her hands were severely burned, which meant that she had to give up her goal of becoming a concert pianist.

MORE ACCURATE: When she was eighteen, [main clause:] **her hands were severely burned.** As a result, [main clause:] **she had to give up her goal of becoming a concert pianist.**

Inverted or "upside-down" subordination frequently occurs in sentences that trail off into weak participle phrases:

The road was blocked, **causing us to make a twenty-mile detour.**

Such sentences can be improved by putting the less important statement in an adverb clause:

We had to make a twenty-mile detour **because the road was blocked.**

3.5

Sub

• *Exercise*

Practice further with subordination by rewriting the first three to five paragraphs of several newspaper articles. You should be able to combine some sentences by turning some short ones into subordinate clauses.

4 Verbals

Because *verbals* are forms of *verbs,* the two are sometimes confused. *Verbs* (see 8) are often described as finite, or limited, because one form only can be used to show time. *Verbals,* which are discussed in this section, are described as nonfinite, meaning that they do *not* change their form to indicate time or tense. It may help to get the distinction clear if we note differences between finite and nonfinite forms.

If we say, "Joe went to the movies this afternoon," or "Joe went to the movies yesterday," the verb *went* (a form of *go*) is finite. That means that we can tell from the form of the verb that the action took place at a particular time in the past. *Went* is finite because it can only be used to record past action. If we say, "Joe will go to the movies tomorrow," the verb *will go* is finite; it can only be used to tell of future action. Other forms of verbs are finite in similar ways.

Verbals are not limited in this way. We can say, "Joe has always liked *to go* to the movies" (in past time), or "Joe likes *to go* to the movies" (present time), or "Joe will always like *to go* to the movies" (future time). In each instance the infinitive *to go* keeps the same form because it is nonfinite.

Verbals, then, are nonfinite verb forms; they are used in sentences as nouns (subjects, objects, complements) or modifiers. They have many qualities of verbs: aided by auxiliary verbs, they can show tense, for example, and they can take objects, but they cannot serve as full, finite verbs to make sentences or clauses. In many sentences, however, verbal phrases function very much like subordinate clauses in showing the relationship between main and subordinate ideas:

> **When she graduated from college,** she went to New York in search of a job. [subordinate clause]

> **Having graduated from college,** she went to New York in search of a job. [verbal phrase, modifying *she*]

Verbals are classified by form and function as

1. **infinitives** *(to ask, to buy),* which can serve either as nouns or as modifiers;
2. **participles** *(asking, asked, buying, bought),* which modify nouns and pronouns; and

3. gerunds *(asking, buying),* which are verbal nouns.

Although the present participle and the gerund are identical in form, they can be distinguished by the way they are used in sentences:

> PARTICIPLE: a **dancing** figure [modifier]
> GERUND: **dancing** takes skill [noun]

The forms and principal uses of verbals are illustrated in the table on page 62. See also 8, Verbs.

4.1

Vbl

4.1 Using Verbal Phrases

Like full verbs, verbals can take objects, complements, and adverbial modifiers. In some constructions they also take a subject, if the meaning of that term is stretched a little.

> **Slowly weaving its way from twig to twig,** the spider built its nest. [*way* is the direct object of the participle *weaving,* which is modified by the adverb *slowly; way* is modified by the prepositional phrase *from twig to twig;* the entire participle phrase modifies *spider,* the subject of the sentence]
>
> He avoided the accident by **running his car onto the shoulder of the road.** [*car* is the direct object of the gerund *running,* which is modified by the phrase *onto the shoulder of the road;* the verbal phrase is the object of the preposition *by*]
>
> She wanted **to be an architect or industrial designer.** [*architect* and *designer* are complements of the infinitive *to be;* the verbal phrase serves as object of the verb *wanted*]

Subjects with Infinitives

An infinitive phrase often has an expressed subject:

> He wanted **the whole department** [subject of the infinitive] **to be reorganized.**

If the subject of an infinitive is a pronoun, it is in the object form:

> They asked **him** [subject of the infinitive] **to be chairman.**
> **Their mother told them** [subject of the infinitive] **to behave.**

Subjects with Gerunds

When a noun or pronoun precedes a gerund, serving as its "subject," some questions of usage arise: sometimes the possessive form is used, sometimes the common form. The writer must de-

Review: Forms and Uses of Verbals

- ## *Infinitives*

An infinitive is (1) the base form of a verb (with or without *to*) or (2) any verb phrase that can be used with *to* to function in a sentence as a noun, an adjective, or an adverb.

Forms:	Active	Passive
PRESENT	(to) ask, (to) be asking	(to) be asked
PAST	(to) have asked, (to) have been asking	(to) have been asked

Principal uses:

SUBJECT: *To be called* to the principal's office makes little boys nervous.

OBJECT: He does not like *to express his opinion.*

MODIFIER (**adjective**): I have plenty of work *to do.* (Modifies *work*)

MODIFIER (**adverbial**): The students came *to learn Russian.* (Modifies *came*)

ABSOLUTE PHRASE MODIFYING THE MAIN CLAUSE: *To tell the truth,* he is a bore.

- ## *Participles*

A participle is a verb form, typically ending in *-ing* or *-ed,* used as a modifier

Forms:	Active	Passive
PRESENT	asking	being asked
PAST	having asked	asked, having been asked

Principal uses:

MODIFIER OF A NOUN: a *smiling* candidate; a *clogged* drain

PARTICIPIAL PHRASE MODIFYING A NOUN: The candidate *getting a majority of the votes* will be nominated.

ABSOLUTE PHRASE MODIFYING THE MAIN CLAUSE: *Everything considered,* a portable typewriter seems the most practical gift.

- ## *Gerunds*

A gerund is a verb form, typically ending in *-ing* or *-ed,* used as a noun.

Forms:	Active	Passive
PRESENT	asking	being asked
PAST	having asked	having been asked

Principal uses:

GERUND AS SUBJECT: *Having been asked* made him happy.

GERUND PHRASE AS SUBJECT: *Taking anthropology* opened a whole new field.

GERUND AS OBJECT: She taught *dancing.*

GERUND AS COMPLEMENT: Seeing is *believing.* (*Seeing* is also a gerund.)

GERUND AS A MODIFIER OF A NOUN: the *dining* room, a *fishing* boat

GERUND AS APPOSITIVE: He had only one hobby, *collecting stamps.*

pend partly on the sound in choosing the form that seems more natural, but the following principles should serve as guides:

1. When the subject of a gerund is a personal pronoun or a proper noun, the possessive form is generally used:

> The less said about **his** singing, the better.
> They insisted on **Bob's** playing the piano.

4.1

Vbl

2. When the subject is stressed, the common form is usually preferred with nouns and the object form with pronouns:

> Did you hear about the **mayor** being arrested for speeding?
> I can't imagine **him** winning an award.

3. When the subject is a plural noun, the common form is usually preferred:

> The manager disapproves of **people** smoking in meetings.
> The staff will not tolerate **visitors** coming and going at will.

4. If the subject is abstract, the common form is used:

> It was a case of **panic** getting the upper hand.
> There is a danger of the **temperature** dropping suddenly.

5. When the subject is modified by other words, the common form is used:

> There was something suspicious about the **daughter** of the sponsor winning the $10,000 prize.

> At the outbreak of the Civil War no one in Washington foresaw the possibility of **Grant,** who had failed in so many undertakings, leading the Union forces.

6. With other noun forms, usage is divided. If you are writing a formal paper, it is usually best to use the possessive form, but the common form of the noun is widely used in general English:

> FORMAL: The neighbors complained about the **dog's** barking at night.
> GENERAL: The neighbors complained about the **dog** barking at night.

> FORMAL: Jones worried about his **secretary's** taking another job.
> GENERAL: Jones worried about his **secretary** taking another job.

• *Exercise*

Write sentences that include the terms shown below. Let the noun or pronoun be the subject of the gerund.

Example: Ricardo/strumming on his old guitar
Sentence: The dog howled at the sound of Ricardo's strumming on his old guitar.

1. the cousin of the senator/getting the contract for the bridge

2. orchestra/talking during rehearsal

3. pronoun referring to Ricardo/giving up

4. my mother/saying such things

5. fear/overcoming his sense of responsibility

4.2 Idiomatic Use of Infinitives and Gerunds

Sometimes we say things in a particular way, not because it is grammatically proper, but simply because it is a way of speaking or writing that has for a long time been customary. When we say that we *put up with* something, the expression doesn't make much sense grammatically, but we know that it means *tolerate* because it is an *idiom* that we are familiar with.

Some expressions are regularly completed by infinitives (privileged *to attend*), others by gerunds (the privilege *of attending*). When one form is substituted for the other, the result is an unidiomatic construction: for example, "eager *to join*" is a standard idiom, but "eager *of joining*" is not. Here are typical expressions, some that call for a gerund, others for an infinitive. You will find others in your dictionary under the key (main) word of the construction.

Gerund	Infinitive
cannot help going	compelled to do
capable of working	able to work
skilled in writing	the desire to write
the habit of giving	the tendency to give
successful in getting	manage to get
ignore saying	neglect to say
my object in paying	my obligation to pay
satisfaction of doing	satisfying to do

With many words, especially common ones, either a gerund or an infinitive is idiomatic: a way *of doing* it, a way *to do* it.

The and *of* in Gerund Phrases

Gerunds are more direct when they are not preceded by *the* and when they are completed by a direct object rather than an *of* phrase:

AWKWARD: In **the** revising **of** the first draft, writers should check their spelling.

DIRECT: In revising the first draft, writers should check their spelling.

To with Infinitives

Most infinitive constructions are introduced by *to*, "the sign of the infinitive":

> She needed time **to think.** They hoped **to get** home before dark. His efforts **to be promoted** failed.

To is not used, however, after auxiliary verbs (*can, may, must, shall, will*):

> I can **see.** You must **try** it. We may **go** to Europe next fall.

4.3

mm

With a few verbs (*do, dare, help, need,* etc.) usage varies:

> I did see him. It did me good **to see** him.
> I helped him [**to**] **learn** to drive.

Split Infinitives

If an adverb comes between *to* and an infinitive (I don't want *to ever see* him again) the phrase is called a *split infinitive.* A writer should avoid split infinitives that are obviously awkward or that call undue attention to themselves:

> AWKWARD: I will not describe the circumstances of our meeting, or even attempt **to physically describe her.**
> BETTER: I will not describe the circumstances of our meeting, or even attempt **to describe** her physically.

But constructions of this sort are not always awkward. When the normal position of the adverb is after the word *to,* a split infinitive is standard usage (The receptionist asked them *to please sit* down). Putting the adverb modifier immediately before or after the infinitive would be unnatural or misleading in some statements:

> UNNATURAL: Autumn is the time **really to see** Europe.
> BETTER: Autumn is the time **to really see** Europe.

4.3 Misrelated Modifiers

mm   Revise the sentence so that the expression marked is clearly related to the word or statement that it modifies.

Verbals, either as single words or in phrases, are most often used as modifiers of individual words:

> I first noticed him **sitting alone in a corner.** [present participle, modifying *him*]

> The town hall, **completely renovated four years ago,** always impresses visitors. [past participle, modifying *town hall*]

He still had three years **to serve in prison** before he would be eligible for parole. [infinitive, modifying *years*]

Like other modifiers, verbal modifiers should be clearly related to the words they modify. When a verbal construction seems to refer to a word that it cannot sensibly modify, it is said to be *misrelated*. Participle phrases usually give writers the most trouble:

MISRELATED: On the other side of the valley, **grazing peacefully like cattle,** we saw a herd of buffalo. [the phrase seems to refer to *we*]
REVISED: On the other side of the valley **we** saw a herd of buffalo, **grazing peacefully like cattle.** [the phrase clearly refers to *buffalo*]

Misrelated modifiers may be momentarily confusing to the reader (or unintentionally humorous) and should therefore be avoided. Sometimes the correction can be made by putting the modifier immediately before or after the word it is meant to modify, as in the example above, but often it is better to rewrite the sentence:

MISRELATED: One early-day western senator is said to have passed out compaign cards to the voters **pinned together with five-dollar bills.** [the participle phrase seems to refer to *voters*]
REVISED: One early-day western senator is said to have pinned five-dollar bills to the campaign cards he passed out to voters.

Occasionally modifiers are placed so that they seem to refer to either of two elements in the sentence. These constructions (sometimes called *squinting modifiers*) can be avoided by changing the position of the modifier or by otherwise revising the sentence:

SQUINTING: The woman who was standing in the doorway **to attract attention** dropped her purse.
REVISED: The woman who was standing in the doorway dropped her purse **to attract attention.**
OR: The woman, standing in the doorway **to attract attention,** dropped her purse.

Other types of misrelated modifiers are discussed in 9.5, Position of Adverbs.

4.4 Dangling Modifiers

 Revise the sentence to include the word to which the dangling modifier refers.

Dangling modifiers refer to a word that is implied rather than actually stated in the sentence. Like misrelated modifiers, they can make a sentence confusing or ludicrous:

> **Having moved at fifteen,** his hometown no longer seemed familiar.

This error often occurs when passive rather than active verbs are used:

> DANGLING: **In painting four of these pictures,** his wife was used as his model.
> REVISED: **In painting four of these pictures, he** used his wife as his model.
> DANGLING: **To find the needed information,** the whole book had to be read.
> REVISED: **To find the needed information, I** had to read the whole book.

4.5

abs m

Usually the easiest way to correct a dangling modifier is to name the agent or "doer" of the action immediately after the phrase, as in the revisions shown above. It is often better, however, to revise the sentence entirely, making the relationships more accurate by using other constructions. Changing the verbal phrase to a subordinate clause often improves the sentence:

> DANGLING: **Having been delayed by a train accident,** the leading role was played by a local actress.
> REVISED: **Because the leading lady was delayed by a train accident,** her role was played by a local actress.

4.5 Absolute Modifiers

A writer should distinguish clearly between verbal modifiers that obviously dangle, such as those cited above, and *absolute modifiers*—participle or infinitive phrases that modify the statement as a whole and thus do not need a specific reference word in the main clause. As the word *absolute* suggests, these modifiers are complete and independent; their form does not depend on anything else in the sentence.

A number of absolute constructions are common expressions:

> **Everything considered,** this plan seems best.
> **To make a long story short,** we bought the house.
> **Considering the cost of labor,** the price is reasonable.

Absolute modifiers can usually be converted easily into subordinate clauses: *When everything is considered,* this plan seems best.

An absolute phrase with a subject is sometimes called a *nominative absolute*. This construction is often used in descriptive and narrative prose for adding details or parenthetical material:

> He stalked like the specter of a soldier, **his eyes** [subject] **burning** [participle] with the power of a stare into the unknown.—Stephen Crane, *The Red Badge of Courage*

The Portuguese listened with his head cocked to one side, **his dark eyes** [subject] **ringed** [participle] with ash-gray circles, and now and then he wiped his damp veined dead-white hands on his stained apron. — Carson McCullers, *Member of the Wedding*

• *Exercise*

Some of the sentences below contain misrelated or dangling modifiers. Rewrite the sentences to make the relationships clear. The sentences with absolute modifiers need no revision. Notice that the sentences needing correction can be revised in more than one way. In the first revision below, the subject *their actions* is dominant; in the second revision, using *I* as the subject makes it dominant.

Example: Having grown tired of them, their actions no longer concerned me.

Revision: Because I had grown tired of them, their actions no longer concerned me.

Revision: Having grown tired of them, I felt that their actions no longer concerned me.

1. Being thoroughly persuaded of them myself, the beliefs I hold seem to me to be obviously true.

2. My spirits often sink in despair, however, trying to find ways to convince others of these truths.

3. After having convinced a friend against his will, both he and I find that our friendship is in doubt.

4. It does not really persuade anyone to accept my beliefs by citing authorities to prove my point.

5. To be honest about it, my friends have grown weary of my arguments and often try to avoid me.

6. After having satisfied my own mind in every detail of an argument, the decision I reach seems incontrovertible.

7. My position tends to harden very rapidly, my decision having been reached, and I am not likely to change my mind.

8. To be perfectly frank, it is unwise for you to pretend that you are convinced by what I say to be polite.

9. Above and beyond the call of mere friendship, being more important, truth is what matters.

10. To do justice to any friendship based on truth, it takes absolute candor on both sides.

5   Agreement of Subject and Verb

agr   **Make the verb marked agree in form with its subject.**

agr

In English, parts of speech that change form to show number, gender, or person should agree or correspond when they are related to each other. Pronouns agree with their antecedents (see 7.2) and verbs with their subject. Agreement or correspondence means, for example, that if a subject is plural, then its verb ought to be plural as well.

Agreement between subject and verb is not always a problem in general English because our verbs don't change form much. The verb *be,* of course, changes nearly every time you notice, but other verbs have only two forms in the present tense and only one form in the past tense. We say *I swim* and *you swim,* and then change the form for the third person singular, *he swims, she swims, it swims.* In the past tense, we would use the same form for all. There are some variations from this practice in some English dialects. Some, for example, consistently use only one form in the present tense: *I do, you do, he do, she do, it do.* See 8, Verbs, for a discussion of English verb forms.

Questions about agreement of subject and verb are most likely to arise when verbs have compound subjects or collective nouns as subjects, or when the number of the subject (whether it is singular or plural) is blurred by other words between the subject and verb. These problems are discussed in the following sections.

5.1 Verbs with Compound Subjects

A compound subject is made up of two or more words, phrases, or clauses joined by *and, or, nor.* The number of the verb depends on which conjunction is used and on the meaning of the subject.

Subjects Joined by *and*

The conjunction *and* is used to join coordinate items, to add them together. Thus subjects joined by *and* usually take a plural verb:

> **Bob, Ted,** and **Sandra swim** with the varsity team.

> The first **draft** of your paper and the **version** finally turned in might **differ** in several ways.

Exception: When the words of a compound subject refer to the same person or are considered together as a unit, the verb is usually singular:

> His warmest **admirer** and severest **critic was** his wife.
>
> **Law** and **order means** different things to people with different political opinions.

Subjects Joined by *or, nor*

Compound subjects joined by *or, nor, either . . . or, neither . . . nor* sometimes take singular verbs and sometimes plural. Here are some ways to tell the difference:

1. When both subjects are singular, the verb ordinarily is singular:

   > **One** or the **other is** certainly to blame.
   >
   > Neither **Senator Jackson** nor **Senator Kennedy has been invited** to debate the health-care bill.

Exceptions: In questions, where the verb precedes the subject, general usage tends to use a plural verb:

> **Are** [formal: *Is*] either **Stevenson** or **Percy** supporting the bill?

In general usage a plural verb may also follow two singular subjects if they are not considered as separate:

> Neither **radio** nor **television provide** [formal: **provides**] adequate news coverage.

2. When both subjects are plural, the verb is plural:

   > No artificial **colorings** or **preservatives are used.**

3. When one subject is singular and the other plural, usage varies. In formal writing the verb usually agrees with the nearer subject:

   > One major **accident** or several minor **ones seem** to occur at this corner every weekend.
   >
   > Neither the **revolutionists** nor their **leader was** to blame.

   In general usage a plural verb is often used even if the nearer subject is singular:

   > Neither the **revolutionists** nor their **leader were** to blame.

4. When the subjects are pronouns in different persons, formal usage requires that the verb agree in person and number with

the nearer subject. In general usage (and even in formal usage if the alternative is awkward) the verb is usually plural:

FORMAL: Either **you** or **she is** likely to be elected.
GENERAL: Either **you** or **she are** likely to be elected.

FORMAL AND GENERAL: Neither **you** nor **I are** trained for that job. [*Am* would sound unnatural.]

Such problems of agreement can usually be avoided by substituting a different, more natural construction:

One of you **is** likely to be elected.

Neither of us **is** trained for that job.

5.1

agr

Subjects Followed by *as well as*

In formal usage a singular subject followed by a phrase introduced by *as well as, together with, along with, in addition to* ordinarily takes a singular verb:

The **treasurer as well as the president was held** responsible for the mismanagement of the company.

But a plural verb is often used in these situations when the added phrase is clearly intended as a compound subject:

Both the **production** of small cars, **together with the supply** in the dealers' showrooms, **have been outstripped** by the demand.

A simple solution—and one that may make the statement more direct—is to use *and* wherever appropriate:

Both the **production** of small cars and the **supply** in the dealers' showrooms **have been outstripped** by the demand.

• *Exercise*

Write sentences using the subjects given below, making sure that the verb agrees with the subject.

Example: backaches, dizzy spells, and blinding headaches
Sentence: Backaches, dizzy spells, and blinding headaches *are* signals that you should see a doctor.

1. beer, wine, and champagne

2. neither aspirin nor sinus tablets

3. both alligators and crocodiles

4. neither drugs nor tobacco

5. the teacher together with the class

5.2 Verbs with Collective Nouns as Subjects

Words that refer to a group of people or objects but are singular in form are called collective nouns or group nouns: *army, audience, choir, committee, crowd, faculty, gang, group, government, jury, mob, orchestra, public, team.* Verbs and pronouns used with collective nouns are either singular or plural, depending upon the meaning of the group word.

Nouns Referring to the Group as a Unit

Singular verbs and singular pronouns are used with collective nouns that refer to the group as a unit:

> **Class is** dismissed.
>
> The **committee has** already held **its** first meeting of the year.
>
> The **audience is** requested to remain seated during intermission.

Nouns Referring to Individuals in a Group

When a collective noun refers to the members of the group, especially if it represents them as acting individually, a plural verb and plural reference words are used:

> The graduating **class have** all agreed to have **their** pictures taken.
>
> The **committee are** arguing among **themselves.**
>
> The **audience have** taken **their** seats.

Sentences like these often sound rather unnatural, and in most cases it is better to substitute a clearly plural subject (the committee *members,* the *members* of the audience).

Verbs with Measurements and Figures

Expressions signifying quantity or extent (*miles, liters, years, pounds*) take singular verbs when the amount is considered as a unit:

> **Five dollars is** too much to pay for a book in that condition.
>
> **Four quarts** of oil **is** all the crankcase holds.
>
> **Three months passes** in no time at all on a dude ranch.

When the amount is considered as a number of individual units, a plural verb is used:

> **Two more dollars are** missing from the till this morning.
>
> There **are three quarts** of milk in the refrigerator.
>
> The last **three months have been** the driest in California's history.

In expressions of addition and multiplication, usage is evenly divided:

> Five and seven **is** [or **are**] twelve.

> Five times seven **is** [or **are**] thirty-five.

A singular verb is used in expressions of subtraction and division:

> Twenty-five from thirty-one **leaves** six.

5.2

Verbs with *data, number, public*

agr

Data is a plural form and is generally so considered in formal, particularly scientific, writing; but since the singular *datum* is rarely used, *data* is often used for both singular and plural in general writing; agreement often depends on context:

> SINGULAR IDEA: The **data** the president needs **has been analyzed** by his assistant. [*data* refers to a body of facts]
>
> PLURAL IDEA: After the **data** [individual facts] **have been gathered** and **analyzed,** you can decide which elements are most essential to your study.

Number may be either singular or plural: preceded by *the*, it refers to the total sum and takes a singular verb; preceded by *a*, it refers to the individual units and takes a plural verb:

> **A number** of pages **are** badly torn.
>
> **The number** of pages assigned for daily reading **was** gradually increased to twelve.
>
> Physicians were disturbed to find that **an** alarming **number** of bacteria **were** developing a tolerance to penicillin.

Public takes a singular verb if the writer wishes to signify the whole group (The *public is* invited to attend); it takes a plural verb if the writer is considering the individual members (The *public are* invited to express their opinions).

Words Ending in *-ics*

Physics, mathematics, economics, civics, linguistics, and similar *-ics* words that refer to a science, art, or a body of knowledge are usually considered singular; other words ending in *-ics* that refer to physical activities or qualities *(athletics, acrobatics, tactics)* are generally treated as plurals.

> SINGULAR FORMS: **Physics was** my most difficult subject in high school. **Ballistics is** the study of the motion of projectiles.
>
> PLURAL FORMS: **Athletics have** been virtually abolished from some smaller schools.
> New **calisthenics are** designed for older people.

Some words ending in -*ics* (*ethics, politics, acoustics*) may be used in either a singular or plural sense:

> SINGULAR IDEA: In almost every group, **politics is** a controversial subject.
>
> PLURAL IDEA: Radical **politics were** offensive to the Federalists.
>
> SINGULAR IDEA: **Acoustics is** a branch of science that is growing fast.
>
> PLURAL IDEA: The **acoustics** in this room **are** not all they might be.

When you are in doubt about the number of a word ending in -*ics*, consult a dictionary.

5.3 Blind Agreement

Sometimes writers make a verb agree with a nearby expression rather than with its actual subject. Since this often occurs when a writer accepts the nearest convenient word or phrase that looks like a subject, it is frequently referred to as "blind agreement." The error usually occurs in the following situations:

Plural Nouns Between Subject and Verb

A singular subject followed by a phrase or clause containing plural nouns is still singular:

> Here and there a **man** [subject] such as Columbus, Galileo, and others **has** [not *have*] ventured into the unknown physical and intellectual worlds.
>
> The **lumberman** [subject] who previously sold only to carpenters and builders now **finds** [not *find*] hundreds of amateurs eager to build their own homes.
>
> I decided to see exactly how **one** of those new cars **is** [not *are*] put together.

one of those who

In formal English, the verb in clauses that begin *one of those who* (or *that*) is plural:

> He is one of those men who never **care** how they look. [The verb is plural because its subject *who* refers to *men*, not to *one*.]
>
> "The Lottery" is one of those stories that **leave** you more puzzled when you finish than when you began. [*Stories* is the antecedent of *that*.]

Although a singular verb is common in spoken English ("one of those girls who *plays* in the band") and in a good deal of published material, the plural verb is customarily used in formal English.

Exception: When *the only* precedes *one of those who* the verb is singular, since the pronoun *who* then refers to a single person or thing:

> She is the only one of those women who **plays** bridge well.

5.3

agr

there is, there are

When a sentence begins with the introductory (or "dummy") word *there* (sometimes referred to as an "anticipating subject"), the number of the verb is determined by the subject which follows:

> There **are** conflicting **opinions** [subject] about smoking in the classrooms.
>
> There **is** great narrative and dramatic **power** [subject] in the first part of this novel.
>
> At our camp there **were** at least a dozen **men** [subject] who were familiar with the mountain trail.

In this construction a singular verb is frequently used before a compound subject, especially if a plural verb would be unidiomatic, as in the second example below:

> There **is food** and **drink** enough for everyone.
>
> There **was nothing** he could do and **little** he could say.

But notice that starting a statement with *there is* or *there are* is often wasteful and wordy:

> WORDY: There is great narrative and dramatic power shown in the first part of this novel.
>
> REVISED: Great narrative and dramatic power show in the first part of this novel.
>
> WORDY: There were at least a dozen men at our camp who were familiar with the mountain trail.
>
> REVISED: At our camp at least a dozen men were familiar with the mountain trail.

Verb and Complement

A verb agrees with its subject and not with its complement or its object:

> Our chief **trouble** [subject] **was** [not *were*] the black flies that swarmed about us on the trip.
>
> The **black flies** [subject] that swarmed about us on our trip **were** [not *was*] our chief trouble.

The **material** [subject] that was most interesting to me when I worked on my reference paper **was** [not *were*] the books that stated the facts forcefully.

Inverted Word Order

When the word order is inverted, care must be taken to make the verb agree with its subject and not with some other word:

Throughout the story **appear** thinly disguised **references** [subject] to the author's own boyhood.

Is any **one** [subject] of these pictures for sale?

Accompanying the senator **were** her **secretary** and two **members** of her legal staff. [The verb has a compound subject.]

series, portion, part

Subjects like *series, portion, part, type* take singular verbs even when modified by a phrase with a plural noun:

A *series* of panel discussions *is* scheduled for the convention.

A substantial **portion** of the reports **is** missing.

The most interesting **part** of the investigations **was** the discovery and identification of the forged letters.

• *Exercises*

1. Find the subject of the italicized verbs in the following paragraph. If the subject is a pronoun, indicate what word or idea it refers to.

   Epidemics *have taken* a great toll of lives in past generations. Death in infancy and early childhood *was* frequent and there *were* few families who didn't lose a member of the family at an early age. Medicine has changed greatly in the last decades. Widespread vaccinations *have* practically eradicated many illnesses, at least in western Europe and the United States. The use of chemotherapy, especially the antibiotics, *has contributed* to an ever decreasing number of fatalities in infectious diseases. Better child care and education *has effected* a low morbidity and mortality among children. The many diseases that have taken an impressive toll among the young and middle-aged *have been conquered*. The number of old people *is* on the rise, and with this fact come the number of people with malignancies and chronic diseases associated more with old age. — Elisabeth Kubler-Ross, from *On Death and Dying*

2. Determine the subject of each of the following sentences and select the verb form that agrees with it. If there is any problem of agreement, explain your choice of verb in terms of the points made in this section.

a. The wages of sin (is, are) death.
b. All (is, are) well.
c. Comparison of things that are unlike and that, by their uniqueness (produces, produce) a sense of wonder in us, (show, shows) that the writer is just displaying his or her own cleverness.
d. Too many metaphors (is, are) a sign of a young writer.
e. "Patience and fortitude," though describing virtues, (is, are) a motto often used to counsel sloth.
f. These United States of ours (has, have) become a great nation.
g. He is one of those people who (is, are) always making trouble.
h. To have loved and lost (is, are) an experience most of humanity (has, have) suffered.
i. The bulk of our tax dollars (go, goes) to defense spending.
j. Neither metaphor nor simile (is, are) useful if the image is confused.

5.3

agr

3. Write sentences that include the following items:

a. *Three semesters,* meant as a single unit, used as the subject
b. The word *ethics* used as the subject in a plural sense
c. A singular subject followed by a phrase that includes a plural noun
d. *There are* at the beginning of the sentence
e. The expression *one of those who*
f. *A portion of the audience* used as the subject

6 Nouns

Nouns are words used in sentences chiefly as subjects of verbs, objects of verbs or prepositions, as complements following a linking verb, as appositives, or as modifiers of other words. They change their form to show number (by adding *-s, -es,* etc.) and possession (*'s, s'*). A noun may designate a person (*George Washington, child*), place (*Spain, home*), thing (*pencil, steak*), quality (*beauty, rage*), action (*hunting, logrolling*), or idea (*justice, reality*).

The table on page 79 shows the forms, functions, and customary ways of classifying nouns. The following sections focus on the common problems that writers may have with nouns: how to use plural and possessive forms conventionally, when to use *a* or *an* before nouns, and how to spot unidiomatic or clumsy noun modifiers.

6.1 Plurals of Nouns

 Change the noun marked to a standard plural form.

Most English nouns form the plural simply by adding *-s* to the singular form *(cats, girls, books, things)*. If the plural makes an extra syllable, *-es* is added to the singular form *(bushes, churches, kisses, Joneses)*.

A few nouns preserve older methods of forming the plural, adding *-en (children, oxen)* or changing the vowel *(feet, teeth, geese, mice)*. Some nouns have the same form for both singular and plural:

1. all words ending in *-ics*, such as *athletics, civics, mathematics;*
2. the names of some animals, such as *deer, fish, mink, sheep;*
3. a number of words rarely or never used in the singular, such as *barracks, headquarters, measles, pants, scissors.*

There are few hard-and-fast rules for troublesome plurals, however, and you should consult the dictionary whenever you are unsure of a plural form. If the plural of a noun is irregular, it will be shown under the entry for the singular form; if no plural is given, the plural is formed in the usual way, by adding *-s* or *-es.*

Review: Forms, Functions, and Classes of Nouns

• *Forms*

SINGULAR AND PLURAL FORMS
Singular: boy, mother, box, child, goose, hero, baby, phenomenon
Plural: boys, mothers, boxes, children, geese, heroes, babies, phenomena

COMPOUND NOUNS OR GROUP WORDS, two or more nouns (written as one word, as two words, or hyphened) that function as a single unit: bookcase, football; pine tree, high school; father-in-law, hangers-on

POSSESSIVE FORM: boy's, Harriet's, girls', cats'

GENDER. A few nouns in English have one form for the masculine, one for the feminine: actor, actress

6.1

Noun

• *Functions*

SUBJECT OF A VERB: The *tires* squealed as the *car* skidded around the corner.

OBJECT OF A VERB: The new company manufactured *toys.*

COMPLEMENT: A whale is a *mammal.* He became *president.*

OBJECT OF A PREPOSITION: The acrobats were performing inside the *tent.*

INDIRECT OBJECT: He gave the *church* a memorial window.

APPOSITIVE: Mr. McDermott, the insurance *agent,* is here.

MODIFIER OF A NOUN: He thought *cigarette* holders looked silly. *Mr. Tyler's* car was stolen.

MODIFIER OF A STATEMENT: *Each year* we make new resolutions.

• *Classes*

PROPER NOUNS, names of particular people, places, and things, written with capitals: Anne, George W. Loomis, London, Monday, Monroe Doctrine

COMMON NOUNS. In contrast with these proper nouns, all the other groups are common nouns and are written with lower-case letters

CONCRETE NOUNS, names of objects that can be seen and touched: leaf, leaves, road, panda, manufacturer

ABSTRACT NOUNS, names of qualities, actions, ideas that are perceived mentally: kindness, hate, idealism, fantasy, concept

COLLECTIVE NOUNS, names of groupings of individuals: fleet, army, company, committee, bevy

MASS NOUNS, names of material aggregates or masses not defined as individual units: food, money, intelligence, justice

COUNT NOUNS, names of things perceived as individual units: car, shelf, pencil, cow, vase

Since writers ordinarily know when a plural form is needed, the chief problems with noun plurals are spelling problems. Section 17.3, Spelling Troublesome Plurals, shows some groups of nouns whose plurals may cause spelling problems.

• *Exercise*

Write a sentence using the plural form of the following words. If you can use more than one of them in a single sentence, do so: *father-in-law, apparatus, commander-in-chief, sheaf, medium, phenomenon, berry, handful, datum.*

6.2 Possessive (Genitive) Case

Case refers to the form a noun or pronoun takes that shows its relationship to other words in the sentence. In English, nouns have only two case forms, the common form *(dog, book, John)* and the possessive, which is the common form plus an *s* or *z* sound *(dog's, book's, John's)* or a plural form with no additional sound *(dogs', books')*. An *of* phrase *(of the dog, of the book, of John)* can function as a possessive and is usually regarded as an alternate form.

Uses of the Possessive

The possessive case of nouns is most commonly used to show possession (a *student's* book, a mannerism *of the professor*). But it also shows other relationships:

1. **Description:** a *day's* work, a suit *of wool, yesterday's* paper.
2. **Doer of an act:** the *wind's* force, the *dean's* permission, the permission *of the dean.*
3. **Recipient of an act:** the *bill's* defeat, the execution *of a spy.*
4. **Subject of a gerund** (see page 61): the *doctor's* warning, the *play's* closing.

Forms of the Possessive

In speech, possessive and plural forms are identical, and we can distinguish between them only by the way they are used: the possessive is followed by another noun (The *boy's work* was finished), whereas the plural is not (The *boys worked* hard). It is impossible to distinguish between the singular and plural possessive except in the larger context of what is being said.

In writing, the apostrophe signals the possessive case, and the position of the apostrophe *(boy's, boys')* ordinarily tells us whether a possessive is singular or plural.

> Insert an apostrophe where it belongs in the word marked or take out the unnecessary apostrophe.

Position of the Apostrophe

Most singular nouns form the possessive by adding *'s*, as do the few plural nouns that do not end in *-s* (such as *men, women, children*):

6.2

Noun

> the **teacher's** remarks (the remarks *of the teacher*)
>
> a **day's** work (the work *of a day*)
>
> the **children's** playground (the playground *of the children*)

Plural nouns ending in *-s* form the possessive by adding an apostrophe alone:

> the **teachers'** meeting (the meeting *of teachers*)
>
> the **musicians'** union (the union *of musicians*)
>
> the **Joneses'** relatives (the relatives *of the Joneses*)

Singular nouns ending in *-s* usually form the possessive by adding an apostrophe alone, just as plural nouns do, or by adding *-s* if an extra syllable would be pronounced. Either is correct, but you should be consistent in whichever form you use.

> Mr. **Jones'** [or **Jones's**] business   the **hostess'** [or **hostess's**] gown
>
> **Delores'** [or **Delores's**] father   the **actress'** [or **actress's**] role

Group words.   With group words or compound nouns the *'s* is added to the last term:

> The **Queen of England's** duties   the **attorney general's** job
>
> her **mother-in-law's** address   **someone else's** responsibility

Nouns in series.   When two coordinate nouns (joined by *and, but,* or *nor*) are in the possessive, the apostrophe usually is added only to the last one if there is joint possession: *Barbara and Tom's* mother. But if there is individual possession, the apostrophe is used with both nouns: *Barbara's and Tom's* bicycles, *neither Barbara's nor Tom's* teacher.

Plural nouns as modifiers.   The apostrophe is not used in some expressions in which the plural noun is considered a modifier: *teachers* college, *Veterans* Administration, *United States* Post Office. Substitution of plural noun modifiers for the possessive is increasing today, so you should carefully note letterheads, signs, official publications, and the like to determine customary usage.

of Phrases and *'s* Forms

The *'s* form of the possessive is customarily used with living things (my *uncle's* house, a *cat's* paw, a *robin's* nest) and an *of* phrase with inanimate objects (the door *of the room,* an angle *of inclination,* the beginning *of the end*). But in many instances either form may be used, the choice depending largely upon the sound and intended emphasis of the expression (the *book's* cover, the cover *of the book*). Some idiomatic expressions are usually stated in one form only (a *week's* wages, a *moment's* hesitation, an embarrassment *of riches,* the wages *of sin*).

Awkward use of *'s* forms.   An *of* phrase is sometimes preferable to an *'s* form to avoid a clumsy or unidiomatic expression or a statement that may be ambiguous. When the modifying noun is separated from the word it refers to by a phrase or a clause, an *of* phrase should be used:

> The apartment **of the woman** who won the contest was ransacked last night. [not *The woman who won the contest's apartment* nor *The woman's apartment who won the contest*]

The *of* phrase is useful in distinguishing between the recipient and doer of an act, particularly if the meaning is unclear in context. *John's photographs* might mean either photographs *of* him or photographs *by* him, but *the photographs of John* would ordinarily mean that John was the subject of the pictures.

The double possessive.   In a few statements both the *of* and *'s* forms of the possessive are used, an idiom of long standing in English: that boy *of Henry's,* some friends *of my father's,* a remark *of the author's.*

• *Exercise*

Indicate which of the italicized nouns in these sentences are correctly written with *s* endings and which should have *'s* or *s'*.

1. The *energies* of our system will decay, the *suns* glory will dim, and the earth will no longer tolerate the race which has disturbed *its* peace.

2. One of Sir James *Barries* humorous characters said, "Facts were never pleasing to him. . . . He was never on *terms* with them until he stood them on their *heads.*"

3. As flies to wanton *boys,* are we to the *gods;* they kill us for their sport.

4. When the *childrens* laughter began to peal in the garden, the *Joneses* neighbors closeted themselves in the air-conditioned family room.

5. The king was "the *peoples* prayer . . . the young *mens* vision and the old *mens* dream."

6.3 Use of *A* and *An* with Nouns

The choice between *a* and *an* depends on the initial sound of the word that follows rather than the initial letter. *A* is used before words beginning with a consonant sound (long *u* has the sound of the consonant *y*):

> a car   a European country   a *D*   a used car

An is used before words beginning with a vowel sound:

> an ape   an *F*   an hour   an honor   an oar

6.4 Noun Modifiers

When an adjective is the customary form in an expression, it should be used in place of a clumsy or unidiomatic noun modifier:

> After graduating from St. Olaf, Karen took her **medical** [not *doctor*] training at Northwestern.

> After sparking his team to victory in the city championship Les went on to play with a **Canadian** [not *Canada*] team.

But for words that do not have exact adjective equivalents, the noun forms are freely used as modifiers: a *murder* mystery, *kitchen* utensils, *radio* reception, *prison* walls. In some expressions either the noun or adjective form may be used: *atom* bomb, *atomic* bomb.

Noun forms used as modifiers—particularly units of measurement—are ordinarily singular: a ten-*ton* truck, a six-*foot* jump. (Used as nouns, the forms would be plural: ten *tons* of coal, a jump of six *feet*.)

• *Exercises*

1. Noticing how nouns are used in what you read will help you familiarize yourself with their various uses and may help you learn to discriminate among various styles. For each of the kinds of reading listed below, count and classify the nouns that appear in four paragraphs according to these categories: plural nouns, concrete nouns, abstract nouns, possessive nouns, and total number of nouns.

   a. Article in a newsmagazine (*Time, Newsweek*, etc.)
   b. Article in an opinion magazine (*Harper's, Atlantic*, etc.)

   c. Article in a popular magazine (*Redbook, Sports Illustrated,* etc.)
   d. Article in a newspaper
   e. Editorial in a newspaper
   f. One of your textbooks

2. Read each sentence below and then select the noun form you consider appropriate. If the choice is optional, explain the context in which each form would be used. Consult your dictionary if necessary to find the standard plural form.

   a. Delicately the proud (man-of-wars, men-of-war) dipped their masts and fired (eight-gun, eight-guns) salutes.
   b. Their (enemies, enemys) stood towering on the crests of the hills and then stormed thunderously into the unprotected (valleys, vallies).
   c. The (atom, atomic) blast flowered evilly behind the desert dotted with pale (cactuses, cacti).
   d. (A, An) awful explosion set the (axis, axes) of the earth quivering like a slackening top.
   e. "The television (media, medium)," he said, "is responsible for our permissive attitude toward violence."

3. The sentences below contain various errors in noun forms. Read the sentences carefully, as if you were proofreading your own composition, and make the necessary corrections.

   a. The father's-in-laws mood got worse as each bottle of wine was dumped into the punch, and soured completely when wine was spilled on a bride's-maid dress.
   b. The kingdom of vertebrae includes ourselfs and all beasts, birds, reptiles, frogs, and fishes.
   c. The boy down the street's car was painted as brightly and strangely as a preening peacocks tail.
   d. With a team of great black oxes he broke the soil to plant his first crop.
   e. The doctor's last bill's effect upon the editor's-in-chief health was more than the medicine could cure.

7 Pronouns

The word *pronoun* means *for a noun*. A pronoun is a word similar to a noun in function, but it does not specifically name a person, place, thing, or idea. Usually it is used as a substitute for a previously stated noun, called its antecedent. A pronoun refers to its antecedent for its specific meaning, which is generally evident from its context:

7.1

Ref

> My uncle phoned last night. **He** is coming by plane.
>
> Men over forty are invited to join. **They** may apply by mail.
>
> My friend and I are invited to a party with her cousins. **We** are going to **it** with **them.**

Pronouns free you from the necessity of repeating nouns every time you wish to designate a person, place, thing, or idea. They also help bind statements together. When a pronoun in a sentence refers to a noun in the preceding sentence, there is a natural connection between the two sentences. Notice how the pronouns in the following passage help give it continuity:

> If the history of the earth's tides should one day be written by some observer of the universe, it would no doubt be said that **they** reached **their** greatest grandeur and power in the younger days of Earth, and that **they** slowly grew feebler and less imposing until one day **they** ceased to be. For the tides were not always as **they** are today, and as with all that is earthly, **their** days are numbered. — Rachel Carson, *The Sea Around Us*

Pronouns should be used more carefully in writing than they sometimes are in speaking. Readers need to see pronouns in the form that indicates their function, and they need to be able to follow a pronoun's reference to its antecedent without confusion. The following sections discuss the most common problems in using pronouns. The table on page 88 lists the various kinds of pronouns and their forms.

7.1 Reference of Pronouns

 Change the pronoun marked so that its reference will be exact and obvious; if necessary, substitute a noun for the pronoun or revise the sentence.

Pronouns Referring to a Definite Antecedent

The antecedent of a pronoun should be clearly stated, not merely implied, and the pronoun should refer specifically to this antecedent:

> INACCURATE: He had been vaccinated against typhoid, but **it** did not protect him. [No antecedent for *it*]
>
> ACCURATE: He had a typhoid **vaccination,** but **it** did not protect him. [*Vaccination* is the antecedent of *it*]

Instead of changing the antecedent, it is often better to substitute a noun for the inexact pronoun:

> INACCURATE: She couldn't understand how to make the cake until I wrote **it** out.
>
> ACCURATE: She couldn't understand how to make the cake until I wrote out **the recipe.**

A simple test for accurate reference is to see whether the antecedent could be substituted for the pronoun. If not, the sentence needs revision.

> INACCURATE: She talked a lot about the technique of horsemanship, although as a matter of fact she had never ridden **one** [horsemanship?] in her life.
>
> ACCURATE: She talked a lot about the technique of horsemanship, although as a matter of fact she had never ridden **a horse** in her life.

The antecedent of a pronoun should not be a noun used as a modifier or a noun in the possessive form:

> INACCURATE: To make an attractive tulip border, plant **them** close together. [*Tulip* is used as a modifier.]
>
> ACCURATE: To make an attractive border of **tulips,** plant **them** close together.
>
> INACCURATE: Bill provided a lot of excitement one afternoon when he was skipping rocks across the pond and hit a young **girl's** shoulder **who** was swimming under water. [A noun in the possessive functions as a modifier.]
>
> ACCURATE: Bill provided a lot of excitement one afternoon when he was skipping rocks across the pond and cut open the shoulder of a young **girl who** was swimming under water.

Ambiguous Reference

Sometimes the meaning of a pronoun is unclear because the pronoun could refer to two different antecedents. To eliminate such ambiguity, either substitute a noun for the pronoun or clarify the antecedent:

> CONFUSING: When Stanton visited the President in February, **he** did not know that **he** would be dead within two months.

CLEAR: When Stanton visited the President in February, **he** did not know that **Lincoln** would be dead within two months.

Sometimes ambiguous reference may be avoided by making one of the antecedents singular and the other plural:

AMBIGUOUS: In the nineteenth century many businessmen [plural] exploited the workers [plural] at every point, not caring whether **they** were making a decent living wage, but only whether **they** were getting a lot of money.

CLEAR: In the nineteenth century many businessmen [plural] exploited the worker [singular] at every point, not caring whether **he or she** was making a decent living wage, but only whether **they** were getting a lot of money.

7.1

Ref

Using the same pronoun for different implied antecedents is particularly annoying to a reader and should be avoided:

CONFUSING: We pulled out our spare, which was under the seat, and put **it** on. **It** dampened our spirits for a while, but we decided to go on with **it.** [The first *it* refers to the tire, the second to the mishap, the third to the trip.]

REVISED: We pulled out our spare, which was under the seat, and put the tire on. The flat dampened our spirits for a while, but we decided to go on with the trip.

Identifying the antecedent by repeating it after the pronouns is a makeshift practice that should be avoided:

CLUMSY: Boswell first met Johnson when **he** (Johnson) was fifty-four.

REVISED: Johnson was fifty-four when Boswell first met **him.**

Ambiguity sometimes results from a careless use of possessive pronouns:

AMBIGUOUS: Mrs. Hurst was a very popular woman and **her accusation** scandalized everyone in town. [Was Mrs. Hurst the accuser or the accused?]

REVISED: Mrs Hurst was a very popular woman and **the accusation she made** [or **the accusation made about her**] scandalized everyone in town.

Pronouns Referring to Ideas and Statements

This, that, which, and *it* are often used to refer to ideas or situations expressed in preceding statements:

Always do right. **This** will gratify some people and astonish the rest. — Mark Twain

Nor is the way in which a speech community rounds off its numbers haphazard; rather **it** is explainable as an interplay between language and culture. — Peter Farb, *Word Play*

Review: Kinds of Pronouns

- *Personal Pronouns:*

	Subject	Object	Possessive
First person			
Singular	I	me	my, mine
Plural	we	us	our, ours
Second person			
Singular and plural	you	you	your, yours
Third person			
Singular			
masculine	he	him	his
feminine	she	her	her, hers
neuter	it	it	its (of it)
Plural	they	them	their, theirs

- *Relative Pronouns:*

who	whom	whose
that	that	
which	which	whose, of which

- *Interrogative Pronouns:*

who	whom	whose
which	which	whose, of which
what	what	

- *Reflexive and Intensive Pronouns:*

myself, yourself, himself, herself, itself, oneself, ourselves, yourselves, themselves

- *Demonstrative Pronouns:*　　this, these, that, those

- *Indefinite Pronouns:*

all	both	everything	nobody	several
another	each	few	none	some
any	each one	many	no one	somebody
anybody	either	most	nothing	someone
anyone	everybody	much	one	something
anything	everyone	neither	other	such

- *Reciprocal Pronouns:*　　each other, one another

- *Numeral Pronouns:*

one, two, three . . . first, second, third . . .

> Perhaps the enjoyment of music is always suffused with past experience; for me, at least, **this** is true. — Ralph Ellison, "Living with Music"

In such constructions, the idea to which the pronoun refers should be obvious.

Use of *who, which, that*

Who refers to persons, *which* generally refers to things, and *that* refers to either persons or things.

> Students **who** [or *that*] plan to enter the university in the fall quarter should forward transcripts of their records to the registrar.
>
> In five minutes he solved a problem **that** [or *which*] I had struggled with for nearly five hours.
>
> This is a matter about **which** more information is needed.

That usually introduces restrictive clauses. *Who* and *which* are used both restrictively and nonrestrictively. See 11.4, Commas with Nonrestrictive Modifiers.

The use of *which* to refer to persons is not usually desirable. *Which* is often used, however, to refer to impersonal organizations of people like groups, clubs, companies, and so on:

> The state legislature, **which** [not *who*] passed the act despite the governor's protest, had its eye on politics.
>
> The Maryland Company, **which** manufactured farm implements, has gone into bankruptcy.

Use of *he* or *she*

The masculine pronoun *(he, him, his)* has customarily been used when referring to a noun or pronoun that includes persons of both sexes *(student, teacher, clerk, everyone, anyone, somebody)*:

> Each entering freshman is required to report promptly for **his** scheduled physical examination.
>
> Everyone who is eligible to vote should make certain that **he** has registered before the deadline.

There is no particular reason why the masculine pronoun should be used in such situations except that it is more convenient and less cumbersome to use a single pronoun than it is to use two pronouns to signify both sexes:

> Everyone who is eligible to vote should make certain that **he** or **she** has registered before the deadline.

It seems likely, however, that the use of both masculine and femi-

nine pronouns will become more common, or that plural constructions will be used more frequently:

> **Every student** who wishes to can get **his** or **her** textbooks at the Co-op
> immediately after registration.
>
> **All students** who wish to can get **their** textbooks at the Co-op immedi-
> ately after registration.

A third alternative is possible. The use of *they (their, them)* as a
common-gender singular is already widespread in spoken English,
and may in time occur more frequently in writing, especially when
the antecedent is an indefinite pronoun that includes both sexes:
Everyone who wishes to can get *their* textbooks at the Co-op.

• *Exercises*

1. Use pronouns to replace the repetitious nouns and make a single,
   smoother sentence.

   Example: John saw the sports car. John knew at once that he must
   own the sports car.

   Revision: John saw the sports car and he knew at once that he must
   own it.

   a. Christopher lit George's cigar. The cigar glowed brightly.
   b. "My goodness, yes," Susan's husband said, "Susan's husband will
      tell you about Susan. Susan has left town."
   c. The second baseman told the first baseman that the second base-
      man wanted to take the first baseman to dinner after the game.
      The first baseman said no.
   d. When the teacher gave the students the students' assignment, the
      students groaned. Then the students did the work.

2. Revise each of the following sentences in which the reference of
   pronouns is inexact, misleading, or otherwise faulty.

   Example: A general interest bookstore would probably do better in
   this town than an obscure one.

   Revised: A general interest bookstore would probably do better in
   this town than a bookstore that specializes in obscure
   books.

   a. After he had studied *kung fu* for three months, he began to boast
      that he was an expert one.
   b. An exercise room is available in the basement of the new physical
      education building which can be used by both students and fac-
      ulty.
   c. Tolliver's wild flower text is useful, but its descriptions of the
      high-plains ones are vague.
   d. Football is a more complex game now than in the past, with its
      play books and game movies, but many are still brutally rough.
   e. When the women were about to leave the exhibit of quarterhorses,
      they ran into their mates.

7.2 Agreement of Pronoun and Antecedent

agr **Make the pronoun marked agree in form with the word to which it is related.**

To be clear in meaning, a pronoun must agree in number with its antecedent—the noun to which it refers. When a pronoun serves as subject, the number of the verb is determined by the pronoun's antecedent. (See also 5, Agreement of Subject and Verb.)

7.2

agr

Personal Pronouns

Personal pronouns, like nouns, have both singular and plural forms, as listed in the table on page 88. A personal pronoun referring to a singular antecedent should be singular; one referring to a plural antecedent should be plural. Errors in agreement are most likely to occur when a pronoun is separated from its antecedent by some intervening element:

INACCURATE: Although the average **American** believes theoretically in justice for all, **they** sometimes fail to practice it. [*American* is singular; *they* is plural.]

ACCURATE: Although the average **American** believes theoretically in justice for all, **he or she** sometimes fails to practice it. [*American* and *he or she* are both singular, as are their verbs.]

INACCURATE: After reading his **arguments** in favor of abolishing property, I found that I was not convinced by **it**. [*Arguments* is plural; *it* is singular.]

ACCURATE: After reading his **arguments** in favor of abolishing property, I found that I was not convinced by **them**. [Both *arguments* and *them* are plural.]

When a pronoun's antecedent is a collective noun, the pronoun may be either singular or plural, depending on the meaning of the noun (see 5.2):

The **class** planned **its** next field trip.

The **class** had **their** pictures taken.

A pronoun referring to coordinate nouns joined by *and* is plural:

When **Linda and Gail** returned, **they** found the house empty.

Usually a singular pronoun is used to refer to nouns joined by *or* or *nor:*

Dick or **Stan** will lend you **his** car.

In general, the principles governing agreement between a pronoun and coordinate nouns are the same as those governing agreement between a compound subject and verb; see 5.1.

Relative Pronouns

When a relative pronoun is used as the subject of a dependent clause, the antecedent of the pronoun determines the number of the verb and of all reference words:

> George is one of those people who **have** trouble making up **their** minds. [The antecedent of *who* is the plural *people,* which requires the plural verb, *have; who* also requires the plural reference *their* for the same reason.]

> George is a person who **has** trouble making up **his mind.** [The antecedent of *who* is *person.*]

Indefinite Pronouns

A number of words that are indefinite often function as pronouns: *some, all, none, everybody, somebody, anybody, anyone.* Some of these words are considered singular; others may be singular or plural, depending on the meaning of the statement. In revising your papers be sure that verbs and reference words agree in number with indefinite pronouns.

Everyone, anybody, somebody. *Everyone, everybody, anyone, anybody, someone, somebody, no one, nobody* are singular forms and are used with singular verbs (Everyone *has* left; Somebody *was* here; Nobody ever *calls*).

All, some, none.   *All, any, some, most, more* are either singular or plural, depending upon the meaning of the statement:

> All of the turkey **has** been eaten.

> All of these questions **were** answered.

> Some of the dialog **is** witty.

> Some of the farmers **have** opposed price supports.

None may be either singular or plural, depending upon the context. In current usage it is commonly used with a plural verb, but formal usage still prefers a singular verb unless the meaning is clearly plural.

> None of our national parks **is** more scenic than Glacier.

> None of the charges **has** been proved.

> None of the new homes **are** as well constructed as the homes built twenty-five years ago. [The sentence clearly refers to all new homes.]

The emphatic *no one* is always singular:

> I looked at a dozen books on the subject, but no one **was** of any use to me.

Each. *Each* is a singular pronoun and usually takes a singular verb and singular reference words:

> **Each** of the players on the football team **has his** own idea about physical training.

Although the use of the plural form to refer to *each* is considered informal (*Each* of the children ran as fast as *their* legs could carry *them*), this construction is sometimes found in writing when the plural idea is uppermost:

> Each of these peoples undoubtedly modified Latin in accordance with **their** own speech habits. — Albert C. Baugh, *History of the English Language*

See also 9.3, Demonstrative Adjectives, for agreement of *this* and *that* (*this kind, that sort*).

• *Exercise*

Rewrite the following sentences, changing the words indicated. Make all other changes that would naturally occur, including those in pronoun, noun, and verb forms.

Example: Change *an athlete* to *athletes.* When an athlete gets out of shape, he is probably insuring the end of his career and the end of his team's winning record.

Rewritten: When *athletes* get out of shape, *they* are probably insuring the end of *their* careers and the end of *their* team's (or *teams'*) winning record (or *records*, if *teams'*).

a. Change *a person* to *people.* When a person weaves in and out of traffic lanes, he is endangering the lives of other motorists as well as his own.

b. Change *Another* to *Other.* Another grocery store also reports that its meat sales have fallen off.

c. Change *anyone* to *everyone.* My sister wanted to be able to help anyone who looked insecure or troubled, and to make him feel at ease, no matter who it happened to be.

d. Change *one* to *some.* One actor may interpret the role of Hamlet one way, another another way: if one decides that the role is pathetic, another may decide that his view — the tragic one — is correct.

e. Change *each* to *all.* Until the law determining the age of legal majority was changed, each student was expected to provide her home address so that her grades could be sent to her parents.

7.3 Case of Pronouns

Case   **Change the form of the pronoun marked to show how it functions in the sentence.**

Subject and Object Pronouns

Most personal pronouns and the relative or interrogative pronoun *who* have one form when they are used as subjects *(I, she, he, we, they, who)* and another when they are used as objects *(me, her, him, us, them, whom)*. A simple test may help you know which pronoun form to use. In a sentence like this, "He left the books for Sarah and (I, me)," omit *Sarah and*. Then it becomes clear that *me* is the form to use. Subject and object forms are listed in the table of pronoun forms on page 88.

After prepositions.   The object form of a personal pronoun is used after a preposition (a letter for *him;* among *us* three). When a pronoun immediately follows a preposition, there is seldom any question about the proper form, but when there are two pronouns, or when a noun is used with the pronoun, writers are sometimes tempted to use a subject form.

> INCORRECT: The work was divided between **she** and **I**.
> REVISED: The work was divided between **her** and **me**.
>
> INCORRECT: The same is no doubt true of what European and Asiatic nations have head about **we** Americans.
> REVISED: The same is no doubt true of what European and Asiatic nations have heard about **us** Americans.

After *than* in comparisons.   In written English, *than* is considered a conjunction, not a preposition, and is followed by the form of the pronoun that would be used in a complete clause, whether or not the verb appears in the construction:

> I am older than **she** [is].
>
> John dances better than **I** [do].
>
> I like him better than **she** [does].
>
> I like him better than [I like] **her**.

It is I, it's me.   Formal English prefers the subject form after the linking verb be:

> It is **I**.
>
> That is **he**.

But educated as well as uneducated people frequently say *"It's me"* or *"That's him." Me* is more natural in this expression because the pronoun stands in the object position, immediately after a verb. All authoritative grammars and dictionaries consider *it's me* acceptable general usage. Fortunately, this construction seldom occurs in writing, except in dialog, where "It is *I*" would sound stilted.

The notion that *I* is somehow more "correct" or polite than *me* sometimes leads people to use the subject form even when the pronoun is the object of a verb: Father took Jerry and *I* to the game. The object form should be used in such constructions: Father took Jerry and *me* to the game.

7.3

Case

Who, whom.   The distinction between *who* and *whom* has practically dropped from speech (the *Oxford English Dictionary* says *whom* is "no longer current in natural colloquial speech"), and it may eventually disappear in writing. For example, in this construction—*Who* are you taking to the concert?—most would agree that *who* seems natural, since it's in the subject position, although formal usage would require *whom,* as the direct object (You are taking *whom* to the concert?).

In most writing it is probably best to make the distinction between *who* and *whom: whom* is the standard form when it is the object of a preposition and comes immediately after the preposition (To *whom* were you speaking? He was a man in *whom* we placed great trust). In other objective constructions *whom* is also used; use *who* when it is the subject of a verb, even in subordinate clauses which may themselves be in the objective case:

> Taxes will go up no matter **whom** we elect [*whom* is the direct object of the verb *elect*].

> Taxes will go up no matter **who** is elected [*who* is the subject of the verb *is elected*].

The easiest way to check your usage is to arrange the elements in the clause in a subject–verb–object order (we elect *whom; who* is elected); *whom* serves as object, *who* as subject. Sometimes intervening words cause problems, but the principle stills holds:

> He made a list of all the writers **who** [subject of *were*] he thought were important in that century.

Possessive Pronouns

In writing, the chief problem in the use of possessive forms of pronouns is the apostrophe. Remember that an apostrophe is not used with the possessives of personal pronouns (a relative of *ours;*

the tree and *its* leaves), nor with the possessive of the relative pronoun *who* (a boy *whose* name was Tom).

Possessive of personal pronouns. Personal pronouns have two forms for the possessive (see p. 88): one is used as a modifier before a noun (*my* roommate, *her* favorite hat); the other is used (by itself or in a phrase) after a noun (That pencil is *mine;* a friend of *hers*). While either form may be used in many statements (*our* government, this government of *ours*), there are some constructions in which one form is obviously better than the other:

> CLUMSY: We decided to pool **their** and **our** resources.
> REVISED: We decided to pool their resources with **ours.**

Its, it's.   *Its* without the apostrophe is the possessive form of *it; it's* with the apostrophe is the contraction for *it is* or *it has:*

> Everything should be in **its** proper place.
> **It's** [it is] an ill wind that blows no good.
> **It's** [it has] been a long time.

One of the mistakes most frequently marked on student papers is using *it's* for *its.* If you tend to confuse these two forms you should check each instance of *its (it's)* when revising your papers: for example, if you've used *it's,* read the word as *it is* or *it has;* your meaning will reveal any errors.

Possessive of indefinite pronouns.   Several of the indefinite pronouns *(all, any, each, few, most, none, some)* are used only in *of* phrases for the possessive:

> They were both happy when things were going well, but adversity brought out the best side **of each.**

The apostrophe and *s* are used with the possessive forms of other indefinite pronouns, just as they are with nouns:

> **Anyone's** guess is as good as mine.
> One man's meat is **another's** poison.
> **Somebody's** books were left in the classroom.

When indefinite pronouns are used with *else,* the apostrophe and *s* are added to *else* and not to the preceding word:

> These notes are somebody **else's.**
> Anyone **else's** offer would have been accepted.

Possessive of *who* and *which*.   *Whose* is the possessive form of the relative pronoun *who. Who's,* the informal contraction for *who is* or *who has,* is not used in most writing.

Best known of American primitives is Grandma Moses, **whose** paintings are familiar to thousands.

It is the white-collar worker **who is** [informal: *who's*] least likely to be affected by seasonal unemployment.

Although *whose* usually refers to persons and *of which* to things, *whose* is regularly used to refer to inanimate things when *of which* would be awkward.

7.4

Pron

. . . we would cross a room in which no one ever sat, **whose** fire was never lighted, **whose** walls were picked out with gilded mouldings.— Marcel Proust, *Remembrance of Things Past*

• *Exercise*

Read the following sentences and correct any pronouns used incorrectly.

Example: She answered the phone, trying to sound very dignified, and said, "Would you like to leave a message with I?"
Revised: *I* should be *me*.

1. She divided what was left of the cake equally between Margaret and I.

2. A book in which a man and a woman collaborate should deal accurately with human nature, for between him and her they represent the two sexes.

3. Most of the other actors have had more experience than me and make fun of my stage fright.

4. Whom do you think is going to be chosen as editor?

5. A letter came for Paul and I inviting us to a committee meeting.

7.4 Reflexive and Intensive Pronouns

The reflexive form of a personal pronoun is used to refer back to the subject in an expression where the doer and recipient of an act are the same:

I had only **myself** to blame.

He hurt **himself** skiing.

The same pronoun form is sometimes used as an intensive to make another word more emphatic:

The award was presented by the governor **himself.**

Life **itself** is at stake.

In certain constructions *myself* is mistakenly considered by some people as more polite than *I* or *me* (My wife and *myself* accept with pleasure), but in standard English the reflexive form is not used as the subject or as a substitute for *me:*

> Another fellow and I [not *myself*] saw the whole thing.
>
> Sam invited John and **me** [not *myself*] to dinner.

Hisself and *theirselves* are not standard English forms.

7.5 Choice of Personal Pronoun Form

Personal pronouns indicate the person or persons speaking (first person: *I, we*), the person spoken to (second person: *you*), or the person or thing spoken of (third person: *he, she, it, one, they*). In writing, the choice of form may be a problem since the writer can refer to himself or herself as *I, one,* or *we*. Some questions that frequently arise in using these pronouns are considered here.

I, we.   There is no reason to avoid the pronoun *I* in any situation where it is needed. Some writers think that the use of *I* makes their writing too personal and subjective. But remember that every piece of writing is written by some *I;* it is often better for the *I* to be presented plainly and honestly, rather than to try to get around the natural use of *I* by devices that only call attention to themselves.

> AWKWARD: After exploring the subject, **the writer** finds that mass hysteria is a rather common occurrence.
> REVISED: After exploring the subject, **I** find that mass hysteria is a rather common occurrence.

We is useful for general reference (*We* are living in an atomic age), but as a substitute for *I,* the "editorial we" is out of place in most writing.

> AWKWARD: The conclusions in **our** paper are based upon information **we** obtained from the local police.
> REVISED: The conclusions in **my** paper are based upon information **I** obtained from the local police.

You.   Overuse of the generalizing *you* (meaning people in general) should be avoided. Its implied reference to the reader may sometimes be irritating:

> AWKWARD: When **you** begin reading *The Waste Land,* **you** are totally confused.
> REVISED: When **I** began reading *The Waste Land,* **I** was totally confused.

If it is not irritating, use of *you* is often inappropriate and inaccurate. In the sentence above, *you* directs attention to some particular second person, but attention should go either to the writer (as in the revision) or to all readers. Use of the generalized *you* should be confined to situations which genuinely apply to everyone:

> When **you** suddenly enter a dark room, it takes a while for **your** eyes to adjust.

7.6

Shift

You can be used successfully, as in a familiar essay, when the writer seeks to establish a close relationship with the reader.

One. One is used, particularly in formal writing, to refer either to people in general or to the writer:

> Watching the scene on television, **one** senses the drama of the situation.

But this use of *one* is impersonal, rather stiff, and often ungainly, especially when *one* is repeated several times. General English characteristically uses personal pronouns in such expressions:

> Watching the scene on television, **I** [or *you*] can sense the drama of the situation.

In current American usage, it is standard practice to refer to one (meaning the writer or anyone) by the third-person *he* and *his* or *she* and *her:*

> **One** should be cautious if **he** wants to avoid offending **his** friends.

7.6 Avoiding Shifts in Pronoun Form

Shift   **Make the words or constructions marked consistent in form. Pronouns should be consistent in person and number; verbs should be consistent in tense.**

In using pronouns for general reference, be consistent and do not make unnecessary shifts from singular to plural forms or from *we* to *you* or *one*.

> INCONSISTENT: After **one** has selected the boat **he** is going to learn in, it would be a good idea if **you** first learned the theory of sailing. Most of **us** have at least seen a sailing boat, but seeing one and sailing one are two different things. **One** might think that a boat can sail only with the breeze and not against it. Or **they** might think that a stiff breeze is necessary to sail a boat.

CONSISTENT: After **you** have selected the boat **you** are going to learn in, it would be a good idea if **you** first learned the theory of sailing. **You** have probably seen a sailing boat, but seeing one and sailing one are two different things. **You** may think that a boat can sail only with the breeze and not against it. Or **you** may think that a stiff breeze is necessary to sail a boat.

The pronoun *one* is more likely to lead to shifted constructions than are the other forms. Unless you intend to be impersonal and feel confident in your use of *one*, use *you, we, he, she,* or a noun substitute in these situations.

• *Exercise*

Revise the following sentences to correct the needless shifts in person or number.

Example: The modern car is very complex, and they are always breaking down.

Revised: The modern car is very complex, and *it is* always breaking down.

Or: Modern cars *are* very complex, and they are always breaking down.

1. Some writers think teachers use grammar as a means to block your creative abilities.

2. When a person has worked for a year in Washington, one is reluctant to return home to an ordinary job.

3. When a student has spent a lot of time on his compositions, they are apt to be disgruntled if all they get is grammatical criticisms. Anybody would feel the same way if you had a teacher like mine.

4. Although a pocket dictionary can give some help, they cannot replace a standard desk dictionary.

5. Nobody in the class seemed very sure of their ability to analyze style.

8   Verbs

Vb   **Change the verb form marked so that it conforms to standard usage.**

8.1

The emphasized words in these sentences are verbs:

> The hunter **shot** a deer.
>
> Our next speaker **will be introduced** by the chairperson.
>
> **Are** you ready?

Except in questions, verbs usually follow the subject. In meaning, they indicate action *(run, manufacture, write)*, condition *(am, feel, sleep)*, or process *(become, grow)*. In form, they may be one word *(do)* or a phrase *(should have done)*, and may add letters (prove*s*, prove*d*) or change internally (s*i*ng, s*a*ng, s*u*ng) to indicate person, number, tense, and voice. The table on page 111 lists the terms used to describe the principal characteristics of verbs.

    The following sections discuss some of the most common problems in the use of verb forms. See also 4, Verbals, and 5, Agreement of Subject and Verb.

8.1   Tense

    Make the tense of the verb marked conventional in form or consistent with others in the passage.

By means of the different tenses, writers set the time of the situation they are describing (as happening in the past, going on at present, or occurring in the future) and also show the continuity of the action or explanation. Consistent and conventional use of tense keeps the sequence of your writing in order and enables a reader to follow the sequence.

Tense Forms

The appropriate form of a verb should be used to indicate each of its tenses. Problems seldom arise with regular verbs, because they have only two forms: the infinitive or base form used for the present tense *(walk, imagine, sleep)* and a form ending in *-ed, -d,* or *-t* for the past tense and past participle *(walked, imagined, slept).* See 8.2 for the forms of irregular verbs.

Except for the simple present and past tenses, English verbs show distinctions of time by various phrase combinations *(have walked, had walked, will walk,* etc.), often supported by adverbs (for example, "he is about to go" as a future). The table on page 103 lists the most frequently used active tenses and the verb phrases most commonly associated with time distinctions.

Time and Tenses

The various tenses in English serve to indicate particular moments or periods in time:

PAST TIME: *Past tense* — **I cooked** meat pies yesterday. [indicates something that happened at a particular time in the past]

Past progressive tense — **I was cooking** meat pies when they came in. [indicates something going on during a period of time in the past]

Perfect tense — **I have cooked** meat pies many times. [indicates something that has happened at various times in the past]

Past perfect tense — **I had cooked** meat pies long before I found the recipe I use now. [indicates something that happened before some time in the past]

PRESENT TIME: *Present tense* — **I cook** meat pies. [indicates something that happens or can happen in the immediate present]

Present progressive — **I am cooking** meat pies. [indicates something that is going on at the present time]

FUTURE TIME: *Future tense* — **I will cook** meat pies for dinner tomorrow. [indicates something that can happen at some time in the future]

Future perfect tense — **I will have cooked** the meat pies before she gets home with the wine. [indicates something that will take place before some particular time in the future]

Notice how the tenses are used to indicate differences in time in these sentences:

He **has finished** supper [perfect] and **is looking** [present progressive] at television.

He **had finished** supper [past perfect] and **was looking** [past progressive] at television.

He **had finished** supper [past perfect] when I **arrived** [past].

He **finished** supper [past] when I **arrived** [past].

Review:

Most Frequently Used Verb Tenses

	I	he, she, it	we, you, they
• Present Tenses			
PRESENT (immediate present)	ask	asks	ask
PRESENT PROGRESSIVE (continuing present)	**am** asking	**is** asking	**are** asking
• Past Tenses			
PAST	asked	asked	asked
PAST PROGRESSIVE (continuing period in past)	**was** asking	**was** asking	**were** asking
PERFECT (past time extending to the present; past participle plus *have* or *has*)	**have** asked	**has** asked	**have** asked
PAST PERFECT (a time in the past before another past time; past participle plus *had*)	**had** asked	**had** asked	**had** asked
• Future Tenses			
FUTURE (future time extending from the present)	**will** ask **am** going to ask	**will** ask **is** going to ask	**will** ask **are** going to ask
FUTURE PERFECT (past time in some future time; future tense of *have* plus past participle)	**will have** asked	**will have** asked	**will have** asked

When the verb of a main clause is in the past or past perfect tense, the verb in a subordinate clause is also past or past perfect:

> They slowly **began** to appreciate what their teacher **had** [not *has*] **done** for them.

> Up to that time I **had** never **seen** Slim when he **hadn't** [or *didn't have;* not *hasn't*] a wad of tobacco in his mouth.

Exception: A present infinitive is usual after a past verb:

> I **would have liked** very much **to attend** [not *to have attended*] her wedding, but I was out of town.

Consistent Use of Tenses

Shift   **Make the words or constructions marked consistent in form. Verbs should be consistent in tense; pronouns should be consistent in person and number.**

Unnecessary shifts in tense (as from the present to the past, or the past to the future) confuse the sequence of your writing:

> UNNECESSARY SHIFTS: I **sit** down at my desk early with intentions of spending the next four hours studying. Before many minutes **passed,** I **heard** a great deal of noise down on the floor below me; a water fight **is** in progress. I **forgot** about studying for half an hour, for it **is** quite impossible to concentrate on Spanish in the midst of all this commotion. After things **quieted** down I **began** studying again, but **had** hardly **started** when a magazine salesman **comes** into my room. [mixture of present and past]

> CONSISTENT: I **sat** down at my desk early with intentions of spending the next four hours studying. Before many minutes **had passed,** I **heard** a great deal of noise down on the floor below me; a water fight **was** in progress. I **forgot** about studying for half an hour, for it **was** quite impossible to concentrate on Spanish in the midst of all that commotion. After things had **quieted** down I **began** studying again, but **had** hardly **started** when a magazine salesman **came** into my room. [past tense throughout]

In single sentences inconsistencies in verb tenses often occur when a writer shifts the form of two or more verbs that should be parallel:

> SHIFTED: For years I **have been attending** summer camp and **enjoyed** every minute of it.
> CONSISTENT: For years I **have been attending** summer camp and **enjoying** every minute of it.

8.2 Irregular Verbs and Auxiliaries

Some of the most commonly used verbs in English create problems in writing because of their irregular forms or optional uses.

Irregular Verb Forms

8.2

$\mathscr{U}_{b}$

Writers sometimes depart from the standards of edited American English when they form some tenses of the irregular ("strong") verbs. This is most likely to happen when a writer uses some dialect form or other unedited form (He *seen* the show last week) or when a writer confuses forms with similar spellings *(choose, chose)*. The following list shows the principal parts of irregular verbs that sometimes cause problems. The *past tense*, second column, is used in the simple past (She *wrote* a letter). The *past participle*, third column, is used with auxiliaries to form verb phrases (The bird *had flown* away; Soon this *will be forgotten;* The chimes *are being rung*). The past participle cannot be used alone as a full verb in the past tense.

When two forms are given, both are acceptable (He *lighted* a cigarette; He *lit* a cigarette). Verbs marked with an asterisk (*) are discussed in the sections following. For verbs not given here, consult a recent dictionary. Caution: If your dictionary labels a form in question *nonstandard, obsolete, archaic, dialect,* or *rare* it is not suitable for most general writing.

Infinitive	Past tense	Past participle
arise	arose	arisen
bear (carry)*	bore	borne
bear (give birth to)*	bore	borne, born
begin	began	begun
bite	bit	bitten, bit
blow	blew	blown
break	broke	broken
bring	brought	brought
burst	burst	burst
catch	caught	caught
choose	chose	chosen
come	came	come
dig	dug	dug
dive	dived, dove	dived, dove
do*	did	done
drag	dragged	dragged
draw	drew	drawn
dream	dreamed, dreamt	dreamed, dreamt
drink	drank	drunk

drive	drove	driven
eat	ate	eaten
fall	fell	fallen
fly	flew	flown
forget	forgot	forgotten
freeze	froze	frozen
get*	got	got, gotten
give	gave	given
go	went	gone
grow	grew	grown
hand (a person)	hanged, hung	hanged, hung
hang (an object)	hung	hung
know	knew	known
lay (place)*	laid	laid
lead	led	led
lend	lent	lent
lie (recline)*	lay	lain
light	lighted, lit	lighted, lit
lose	lost	lost
pay	paid	paid
prove	proved	proved, proven
ride	rode	ridden
ring	rang, rung	rung
rise	rose	risen
run	ran	run
see	saw	seen
set*	set	set
shake	shook	shaken
shine	shone, shined	shone, shined
show	showed	showed, shown
shrink	shrank, shrunk	shrunk
sing	sang, sung	sung
sink	sank, sunk	sunk, sunken
sit*	sat	sat
slide	slid	slid, slidden
speak	spoke	spoken
spring	sprang, sprung	sprung
stand	stood	stood
steal	stole	stolen
swim	swam, swum	swum
take	took	taken
tear	tore	torn
throw	threw	thrown
wake	waked, woke	waked, woke
wear	wore	worn
wring	wrung	wrung
write	wrote	written

Forms of the Verb *be*

The verb *be* has eight forms, three more than any other verb in English. In addition to the infinitive, there are three forms in the present tense, two in the past tense, the present participle, and the past participle:

	I	he, she, it	we, you, they
PRESENT TENSE:	am	is	are
PAST TENSE:	was	was	were
PRESENT PARTICIPLE:	being		
PAST PARTICIPLE:	been		

8.2

Vb

The forms of *be* are not troublesome in ordinary situations, at least not if you are reasonably well acquainted with edited American English. Some dialects do use *be* differently, for example, *she be singing*. These forms are usually not found in general written English, however.

Ain't. *Ain't* is an idiolect and dialect contraction; *aren't* and *isn't* are the standard forms. In questions with *I, am I not* is formal; *aren't I* is the form most often used. Since the forms are rarely needed in writing except in dialog, the form most natural to the speaker would be used.

• *Exercise*

Rewrite this paragraph, filling in the proper forms of the verbs indicated in parentheses, including any necessary auxiliary verbs.

As the action begins, it is clear that the old man (perfect of *rise*) and (perfect of *bid*) the young soldier enter. The audience is aware that the young soldier (perfect of *know*) for a long time that it was the old man who (past perfect of *slay*) his father. When the soldier (past perfect of *return*) from the war, his mother (past perfect of *forsake*) her deathbed to tell him how the old man (past perfect of *steal*) into the house, (past perfect of *find*) the loaded gun on the night table, and, even as the mother (past of *shrink*) into the corner of the room, (past perfect of *shoot*) her husband. Laden with this heavy sorrow, her heart (past perfect of *burst*). Within the next few moments of action the young soldier (future perfect of *bind*) the arms of the old man and (future perfect of *begin*) to lead him from the room.

Choice of *can* or *may*

In all levels of usage *can* is used for ability (This car *can* do better than 80 miles an hour; He *can* walk now with crutches), and *may* for possibility (That *may* be true; We *may* get there before dark).

To express permission, formal English and edited general English use *may* (*May* I go now? You *may* have any one you like).

Although general spoken English increasingly uses *can* in such expressions (*Can* I go now? You *can* have any one you like), in writing it is best to use *may*.

do — did — done

Some idiolects and dialects use *done* alone (He *done* his best to please her) when edited American English calls for standard forms. Particular care should be given to the past tense and the past participle:

PRESENT TENSE: I, we, you, they **do**; he, she, it **does**
PAST TENSE: I, you, he, she, it, we, they **did**
PAST PARTICIPLE: I, you, we, they have (had) **done**; he, she, it has (had) **done**

don't, doesn't.   *Don't* is the contraction for *do not* (I *do not,* I *don't*), *doesn't* is the contraction for *does not* (he *does not,* he *doesn't*). The substitution of one form for the other (*Don't* she look pretty?) is not consistent with edited forms of the language.

Idioms with *do*.   *Do* is used in many standard idioms (set expressions): *do* without, *do* away with, make *do:*

> When the Dean of Women arrived, she seemed **done in** [better: *exhausted*].
>
> They **did** [better: *cheated*] the government out of $50,000.

Consult a dictionary whenever you are unsure about the appropriateness of a particular expression with *do* or *done.*

born — borne

The past participle of *bear* in the sense of "carry" is spelled *borne:* a leaf *borne* by the wind, he had *borne* many hardships. In the sense of "give birth to," the spelling is *born* in the passive voice, *borne* in the active: *born* in Miami, a *born* loser, a child *born* to her (but, she had *borne* a child).

get — got — gotten

The principal parts of the verb *get* are *get, got,* and *gotten* or *got.* Both forms of the past participle are used in the United States:

> He could have **gotten** [or *got*] more for his money.
>
> Her efforts had **gotten** [or *got*] no results.

Used with *have* to show possession (see below), the form is always *got.* In other constructions, *gotten* is more common.

have got, have got to. *Have got* in the sense of possession (I *haven't got* a black tie) or obligation (We *have got to* finish this experiment today) is widely used in speech and is acceptable in most kinds of writing. Some writers of formal English avoid the expression, regarding *got* as redundant and preferring *have* alone (I *haven't* a black tie; We *have to* finish this experiment today). Although *have* alone carries the meaning, it is so frequently used as a mere auxiliary of tense that we do not often consider it as a verb of full meaning, and either *have* or *have got* is usually considered acceptable.

8.2

Vb

Idioms with *get*. In many common idioms *get* is standard usage for all levels of speaking and writing:

STANDARD:	get up	get along with (someone)
	get away from	get over (an illness)
	get ahead	get tired

Other expressions with *get* are considered informal, and you may want to avoid them in college writing:

INFORMAL: Long-winded discussions **get** on my nerves.
This modern music **gets** me.
Some people seem to **get** away with murder.
A stray bullet **got** him in the shoulder.

When you are in doubt about the standing of an idiom with *get*, consult a recent dictionary.

lie — lay

Lie, meaning to recline, does not take an object. Its principal parts are *lie, lay, lain:* You *lie* down for a rest, or *lie* down on the job; Yesterday he *lay* in bed all morning; The log had *lain* across the road for a week. The present participle of *lie* is *lying:* The log was *lying* in the road; I found him *lying* in bed.

    Lay, meaning to put or place, takes an object. Its principal parts are *lay, laid, laid:* He should *lay* down his cards; She *laid* her purse on the table; The cornerstone was *laid*. The present participle of *lay* is *laying:* He was *laying* the foundation. The same forms are used when *lay* means to produce an egg.

sit — set

The verb *sit* (as in a chair) does not take an object. Its principal parts are *sit, sat, sat:* I like to *sit* in a hotel lobby; He *sat* there an hour; I have *sat* in the same chair for three semesters.

    The verb *set,* meaning to put something down, takes an object.

Its principal parts are *set, set, set: Set* the soup on this pad; They *set* the trunk in the hall yesterday; She has *set* candles in the windows.

For correct uses of *set* in its many other meanings, consult the dictionary.

shall — will

In current American usage, *will* is generally used with all persons of the verb for the future tense (I *will* leave tomorrow. He *will* arrive at six. We *will* return later). To express determination or for emphasis, usage is divided about *will* and *shall* (I *will* not permit it. They *shall* pass). Some formal writers make the following distinctions between *shall* and *will:*

Simple future

FIRST PERSON:	I shall ask	we shall ask
SECOND PERSON:	you will ask	you will ask
THIRD PERSON:	he, she, it will ask	they will ask

Emphatic future

FIRST PERSON:	I will ask	we will ask
SECOND PERSON:	you shall ask	you shall ask
THIRD PERSON:	he, she, it shall ask	they shall ask

These distinctions are seldom made today except by the most conservative formal writers.

shall and **will** in questions.   In questions, *will* is used in all persons, but *shall* is often used, especially in formal English, if there is a notion of propriety or obligation:

Will I go? Where **will** we go next? What **will** you do now?
OBLIGATION: Shall I go? What **shall** she wear?

Some writers use *should* and avoid both *shall* and *will:*

Where **should** we go next? **Should** I go?

In the negative, *won't* is the regular form:

What **won't** they think of next?

Why **won't** you go?

Overuse of *shall*.   *Shall* should not be used in statements where *will* is the standard form:

Whether or not Congress **will** [not *shall*] pass the bill is not for me to guess.

Some people apparently think that *shall* is a more correct (or elegant) form than *will*. It isn't.

Review: Terms Used in Describing Verbs

VERB FORMS (8.1). English verbs have three principal parts:

INFINITIVE (the base form) PAST TENSE PAST PARTICIPLE
ask (to ask), go (to go)   asked, went asked, gone

REGULAR AND IRREGULAR VERBS (8.1 and 8.2). Regular verbs add -ed to form the past tense and past participle (ask, asked, asked). Irregular verbs change form in other ways (sing, sang, sung; go, went, gone).

TENSE (8.1). The "time" of a verb's action as expressed in the form of the verb:

PAST: I went   PRESENT: I go   FUTURE: I will go
(For other tenses, see the table on p. 103.)

TRANSITIVE AND INTRANSITIVE.
A verb is **transitive** when it has an object: The teacher *demanded*(v) *order*(o).
A verb is **intransitive** when it does not have an object: He *slept*(v) well.

ACTIVE AND PASSIVE VOICE (8.3). A **passive** verb is a form of *be* and a past participle: *is believed, was believed, had been believed, will be believed.* All other verbs are **active.**

MOOD (8.4). The manner in which a statement is expressed (an almost obsolete distinction now):
The **indicative mood** expresses a fact or a statement: I *am* thrifty.
The **subjunctive mood** is used in some conditions and in clauses like the following: It is necessary that he *be* twenty-one.

AUXILIARY VERB (8.2). A verb used in a verb phrase to show tense, voice, etc.: *am* going; *had* gone; *will* go; *should have been* done.

LINKING VERB OR COPULA (1.1). A verb that "links" its subject to a predicate noun or an adjective: She *is* a teacher. The days *became* warmer.

FINITE AND NONFINITE VERBS. A **finite verb** (from the Latin *finis*, meaning "end" or "limit") can be limited (5 and 8):
In **person** by a pronoun or subject (I *sing*, she *sings*)
In **time** by a tense form (she *sings*, she *sang*)
In **number**, singular or plural (he *sings*, they *sing*)
Finite verbs are full verbs in sentences and clauses: I *had gone* before he *came.*

THE NONFINITE VERB FORMS (participles, infinitives, gerunds) are not limited in person or number and are ordinarily used in phrases (4): Before *leaving* I thanked our host. She needed a hat *to wear* to the party.

8.2

Vb

should—would

Should and *would* are used in statements that carry a sense of doubt or uncertainty:

> It **should** be cooler by evening. [Contrast with the meaning of: It *will* be cooler by evening.]
>
> I wasn't ready as soon as I thought I **would** be.

Should, like *shall,* is often used to express the idea of propriety or obligation:

> You **should** wash your hands before meals.
>
> I **should** answer her letter this week.

In polite or unemphatic requests, both *would* and *should* are used for the first person and *would* for the second person:

> I **would** be much obliged if you could help me.
>
> I **should** be much obliged if you could help me.
>
> **Would** you please give this your earliest attention?
> I wish you **would** write more often.

In indirect discourse *would* and *should* serve as the past tenses of *will* and *shall.*

> DIRECT DISCOURSE: Mary said, "I will go."
> INDIRECT DISCOURSE: Mary said that she would go.
>
> DIRECT DISCOURSE: "Shall we adjourn?" the president asked.
> INDIRECT DISCOURSE: The president asked if they should adjourn.

Guideline for Review

Writers sometimes use *would* with another verb to suggest continuous or habitual action: The man *would* always be waiting at the corner. He *would* give me a quarter for candy. I *would* refuse it. It's generally better to depend on the accurate verb tense of the primary verb: The man *was* always *waiting* at the corner. Every time he saw me he *offered* me a quarter for candy. I always *refused* it.

• *Exercises*

1. Supply the proper form of the verbs in parentheses in each of these sentences. Some of the constructions may call for an infinitive, participle, or gerund (see 4).

   Example: Last night the wind (whip) the leaves so that they (spin) like the arms on a windmill.
   Answer: whipped, spun

a. Once she had (do) the exercises, she (do) her reading with much greater pleasure.
b. In the saloon, the dark-bearded cowboy pushed aside his beer and slowly (draw) his gun.
c. He could have (get) a higher grade if he had worked a little longer on the project.
d. Within a few minutes the care-(ride) sheriff (ride) up to investigate.
e. Before he called, she had (lie) down to rest a few minutes.
f. A low moan was (wring) from his lips.
g. He had (rid) the town of many criminals before.
h. At the hitching post the horse (shake) his mane and nervously (paw) the ground.

2. Write sentences following the instructions below.

a. a single sentence that uses both *can* and *may*
b. a sentence that uses the past tense of *sit*
c. a sentence that uses the past tense of *set*
d. a sentence that uses *should* to express an obligation
e. a sentence that uses *would* as the past tense of *will*
f. a sentence that uses *should* as the past tense of *shall*

8.3 Active and Passive Voice

We frequently have a choice of making a noun either the subject or object in a sentence, with a resulting difference in verb form:

> ACTIVE VERB: Jim's father **gave** him a car.
> PASSIVE VERB: Jim **was given** a car by his father.

The passive consists of a form of *be* plus the past participle *(is given, are chosen, was taken, have been corrected)*.

Appropriate Passives

The great majority of English sentences use active verbs, but sometimes the passive is appropriate. Passive constructions are natural if the actor is unknown or unimportant to the statement:

> The game **was postponed** because of rain.
>
> The expressway **will be completed** by spring.
>
> The entire fuel-handling operation **is conducted** by remote control, of course, and fresh fuel assemblies **can be delivered** to the storage rack or spent ones **removed** from it while the reactor is in operation. — T. R. Bump, "A Third Generation of Breeder Reactors." *Scientific American*

A passive verb may also be appropriate if the writer wants to emphasize the object or the act rather than the doer:

The fire **was discovered** by the night watchman.

The bill **is supported** by congressmen of both parties.

Inappropriate Passives

Pass **Change the passive verb or verbs to active.**

Passive constructions often are weak or awkward and should be changed to the more direct active form:

> WEAK PASSIVE: A distinction **is made** by sociologists between achieved and ascribed status.
> ACTIVE: Sociologists **make** a distinction between achieved and ascribed status.
> PASSIVE: All of the major Russian novelists **were studied** in my comparative literature course.
> ACTIVE: **I studied** all of the major Russian novelists in my comparative literature course.

It is sometimes awkward to combine an active and a passive verb in the same sentence:

> AWKWARD: The city **needs** more money to build new schools, and it **will** probably **be raised** through a bond issue.
> REVISED: The city **needs** more money to build new schools and **will** probably **raise** it through a bond issue.

• *Exercise*

Revise the sentences below so that they still mean the same thing, but are in the active voice.

Example: It has always been felt by me that the study of biology is boring.
Revised: I have always felt that studying biology is boring.

1. Biology is thought by students to be very time-consuming.

2. It is also felt that cutting up dead frogs is disgusting to some students.

3. Sometimes tests are given by biology professors which are thought to require too much memorizing.

4. Also, it is costly to some to pay the lab fees.

5. For these reasons, it is an opinion of mine that the abolishment of required biology should be considered by school authorities.

8.4 Use of the Subjunctive Mood

Certain instances of untypical verb forms are known as the subjunctive mood. The word *mood* is a variant of the word *mode* and indicates *manner*. A verb in the subjunctive mood, then, is a verb used in a particular manner, to express a future contingency or a condition contrary to fact. Use of the subjunctive forms in current English is quite limited and inconsistent, even in formal English. There is almost always an alternative construction, and writers seldom need to use the subjunctive.

8.4

Vb

In Conditions

The subjunctive is sometimes used, especially in formal English, to express contrary-to-fact, impossible, or improbable conditions:

> If I **were** in your position [I'm not], I wouldn't accept his offer.
> He said if he **were** President [he isn't], he would remove them.

In *that* Clauses

The subjunctive is used in many set expressions (usually in a formal, often legal, context) for recommendations, demands, and so on:

> FORMAL: It is required that the applicant be over twenty-one.
> STANDARD: The applicant must be over twenty-one.

> FORMAL: I ask that the interested citizen watch closely the movements of these troops.
> STANDARD: I ask the interested citizen to watch closely the movements of these troops.

In Formulas

The subjunctive is found in numerous formulas and set phrases, locutions surviving from a time when the subjunctive was used freely:

> If I were you   If only she were here   As it were
> Be that as it may   Come what may

• *Exercise*

Complete the following sentences using subjunctive verb forms.

1. If I . . . .

2. She said if she . . . .

3. Were he to . . . .

4. It is necessary that each student . . . .

5. What would you do if she . . . .

8.5 Idioms With Verbs

 Change the word or expression marked so that it will be idiomatic.

An idiom is a usage that has become established through custom. Verbs and verb phrases should be both idiomatically correct and appropriate to the general level of a writer's usage. The chart on page 117 lists some verb forms that should be avoided because they are clumsy or not in good edited form. Others are acceptable in informal or general usage but are sometimes frowned upon in formal English.

• *Exercise*

Correct any faulty verb forms that you find in the following sentences. Some of the constructions call for verbals (see 4).

Example: He often had came to the same bar.
Revised: He often *had come* to the same bar.

1. The students were not use to seeing the Chancellor in Duffy's Tavern, ordinarily a student hangout.

2. It was raining hard, and he had almost drownded before he come upon a place to find shelter.

3. He was wet through and through, and he said that his feet were nearly froze.

4. Having rode across the prairie all day, Lonesome Jim was thoroughly wore out and could not get his legs unbended.

5. Early in the day the TV stations broadcasted the news that the President was going to make a speech that night.

6. Having born a pack, a shovel, a canteen, a map case, and a notebook for thirty miles, Jim laid down and went to sleep immediately.

7. There don't seem to be any way to keep him from sleeping when he is tired.

8. His grandfather believed that the family had originally came from northern Georgia.

9. He sat the overdue books on the counter and waited to pay the fine.

10. They got up before dawn, drunk coffee and ate rolls, checked the map, and taken back roads west for the next stage of their journey.

Review: Troublesome Idioms with Verbs

ABLE TO: A clumsy and unidiomatic expression when used with a passive infinitive: "This shirt **can be** [not *is able to be*] washed without shrinkage."

AGGRAVATE, IRRITATE: In formal usage **aggravate** means to intensify or make worse; **irritate** means to vex or annoy: "The seriousness of his crime was **aggravated** by the prisoner's implication of innocent people." "Stop **irritating** me with those silly questions." Informally **aggravate** is used in the same sense as **irritate**: "I was never so **aggravated** in my life." The distinction between the two words should be observed in college writing.

BEING THAT: To introduce a dependent clause of reason or cause, **being that** is an unacceptable substitute for **because, since,** or **for**: "Randy decided to major in pharmacy **because** [not *being that*] his uncle was a successful pharmacist."

CONTACT: Many people dislike this verb as a substitute for "get in touch with someone," although it is widely used in business: "Will you **contact** our Mr. Hubble?" In general and formal writing "call" or "see" is ordinarily used.

ENTHUSE: Dictionaries label this verb colloquial and prefer **be enthusiastic about** or **show enthusiasm.** While **enthuse** is in fairly common use, it is generally better to use another form in college writing.

FIX. In general usage **fix** commonly means repair or prepare (fix a broken clock, fix lunch for three). It also means to make fast or establish (fix the tent to its pegs, fix tariff prices). **Fix** is informal in the sense of to **get even with** (I'll **fix** you for that).

LEAVE, LET: **Leave** means to depart or to abandon; **let** means to permit: "**Let** us **leave** this place." Using **leave** for **let** is inconsistent with edited forms of the language.

PREDOMINATE, PREDOMINANT: **Predominate** is a verb: "The captain's will **predominated** throughout the voyage." **Predominant** is an adjective: "His **predominant** characteristic is laziness."

SUSPECT, SUSPICION: **Suspect** is the verb meaning to distrust or imagine: "The police **suspected** foul play." **Suspicion** is a noun, and when used for **suspect** is a localism, inappropriate to college writing except in dialog.

TRY AND, TRY TO: Both are accepted idioms: **Try and** is the more common in general English (**Try and** get your work in on time); **try to** is the preferred form in formal English (**Try to** get your work in on time).

WANT, WANT TO, WANT THAT: In the sense of **ought** or **should, want** is informal: "You **should** [not *want to*] review your notes before the test." In statements of desire or intention, **want to** is the standard idiom: "I **want you to get** [not *for you to get* or *that you get*] all you can from this job." In such constructions **want that** and **want for** are not standard.

9 Adjectives and Adverbs

*Adj /
Adv* Use the appropriate form of the adjective or adverb marked.

Nouns and verbs can be used without adjectives and adverbs. Adjectives and adverbs are not usually used without nouns and verbs. That indicates the value and the function of adjectives and adverbs. They are secondary to nouns and verbs. What they contribute to sentences, however, is genuine and useful:

> The can on the shelf contains gas.
>
> The **red** can on the **lowest** shelf contains a **poisonous** gas.

By *expanding* the sentence, the adjectives *restrict* its meaning: the sentence is a statement about a particular can on a particular shelf containing a particular substance.

Adjectives and adverbs enable a writer to specify, to distinguish (not *shelf,* but *lowest shelf*). These modifiers may add descriptive details (a scene of *pleasant* memories; he laughed *loudly*), limit or make more definite the meaning of a key word (the *first* book; he left *immediately*), or qualify statements (*Perhaps* you've had enough).

In sentences we identify an adjective or an adverb by finding the word or word group to which it is related: it is an adjective if it modifies (relates to) a noun or pronoun, an adverb if it modifies (relates to) a verb, an adjective, another adverb, or the whole sentence.

> ADJECTIVE: a **cheerful** smile [modifies the noun *smile*]
> ADVERB: She smiled **cheerfully** as she raked in her winnings. [modifies the verb *smiled*]
>
> ADJECTIVE: The car is **fast.** [modifies the noun *car*]
> ADVERB: She drove **fast.** [modifies the verb *drove*]

Other examples of use are discussed in the sections that follow.

9.1 Position of Adjectives

Most writers have few problems with adjectives. The forms of adjectives are relatively simple, and they are usually easy to place in a sentence. The typical position of adjectives (and of participles and nouns used as adjectives) is immediately before the words they modify, though other positions are sometimes possible:

> Shaking off from my spirit what must have been a dream, I scanned more narrowly the **real** aspect of the building. Its **principal** feature seemed to be that of an **excessive** antiquity. The discoloration of ages had been great. **Minute** fungi overspread the **whole** exterior, hanging in **fine tangled** web-work from the eaves. — Edgar Allan Poe, "The Fall of the House of Usher"

9.2

adj.

> I can see the woods in their **autumn** dress, the oaks **purple,** the hickories **washed** with gold, the maples and the sumacs **luminous** with **crimson** fires, and I can hear the rustle made by the **fallen** leaves as we plowed through them. — Mark Twain, *Autobiography*

Two or more adjectives are often placed after the word they modify to gain emphasis or to avoid a clumsy expression:

> Except for a boy, **tall** and rather **gangly,** the room was deserted.

> . . . the sailors thronged the streets in flapping blues and spotless whites — **brown, tough,** and **clean.** — Thomas Wolfe, *Look Homeward, Angel*

If an adjective is modified by other words, it often comes after the noun:

> The old man, exceedingly **weary** from his trip, lay down to rest.

9.2 Predicate Adjectives

Predicate adjectives — adjectives that follow linking verbs — refer back to the subject (see 1.1). The common linking verbs are *be (am, is, are, was, were, has been), seem, appear, become, grow, prove,* and verbs describing sensations like *taste, feel, smell, look.*

Sometimes these verbs are followed and modified by adverbs (The weeds grew *rapidly*). To determine whether a predicate adjective or an adverb should be used, see whether the word modifies the subject or the verb. When it modifies or refers to the subject, use an adjective; when it modifies the verb, use an adverb:

> The children looked **unhappy.** [predicate adjective, describing *children*]

> As the rain continued to fall, the children looked **unhappily** out the window. [adverb, modifying *looked*]

> Overnight the weather turned **cold.** [predicate adjective, modifying *weather*]

> He turned **abruptly** when he heard his name called. [adverb, describing the way in which he *turned*]

good — well

Good is an adjective (a *good* time; This cake tastes *good*). *Well* is either an adjective (He was a *well* boy; Are you feeling *well?* All is *well*), or an adverb (He writes *well*). Either *good* or *well* may be used as a predicate adjective with the verb *feel,* but with different connotations:

> Don't you feel **well?** [referring to a state of health, not ill]

> It made him feel **good** to pack his own bag and get into the front seat and drive his own car. [referring to a general attitude or bodily sensation — comfort, happiness, well-being] — John Dos Passos, *The Big Money*

Do not use the adjective *good* in place of the adverb *well:*

> The team played **well** [not *good*] for five innings.

bad — badly

As an adjective, *bad* is the usual form after linking verbs:

> She feels **bad.** The milk tastes **bad.** The situation looks **bad** to me.

But *badly* is also used when the emphasis is on the verb: I feel *badly* [or *bad*] about your troubles. Many people object to such uses of *badly,* however, and it is just as well to avoid them in writing.

• *Exercises*

1. Write sentences following the directions given below.

   a. Write a sentence in which *good* is used as a predicate adjective.
   b. Write a sentence in which *bad* is used as a predicate adjective.
   c. Write a sentence in which *glad* is used as a predicate adjective.
   d. Write a sentence in which *good* is used as a predicate adjective and *well* is used as an adverb.

2. Copy ten magazine advertisements or television commercials that use sentences with predicate adjectives, such as *Carlton is lowest.*

9.3 Demonstrative Adjectives

This and *that* (called demonstrative adjectives) are the only adjectives with plural forms: *this* idea, *these* ideas; *that* project, *those* projects. *This* and *these* usually refer to something nearby, or something the writer is more closely associated with or more interested in. *That* and *those* usually refer to something farther away, or something the writer is less immediately interested in.

This car gets good mileage.

That car is a lemon.

These books are required for this course.

Those books are recommended for further reading.

This and *that* are often used with *kind* and *sort*, which are singular nouns and should be preceded by singular modifiers:

I like **this kind** of records best.

Jokes of **that sort** annoy me.

9.4

adv

9.4 Forms of Adverbs

A number of common adverbs *(now, quite, there, too)* have no distinctive forms, but the majority of adverbs are made by adding *-ly* to an adjective: *accidental-ly, particular-ly, real-ly, sincere-ly.* A few adjectives ending in *-ly (early, likely)* are also used as adverbs.

Although adverbs can be made by adding *-wise* to a noun *(lengthwise, sidewise)*, this practice has been greatly overused *(budget-wise, economy-wise)*. It is better to avoid such words.

Long and Short Forms of Adverbs

Some adverbs have two forms: one with an *-ly* ending (long form), the other without (short form): *slow — slowly, loud — loudly, tight — tightly.* Adverbs used with or without the *-ly* ending include:

bright	even	rough	straight
cheap	fair	second	tight
close	loose	sharp	wrong
deep	loud	slow	
direct	quick	smooth	

The long and short forms are often interchangeable:

Go **slow.** Go **slowly.**

Don't talk so **loud.** Don't talk so **loudly.**

The rope was drawn **tight.** The rope was drawn **tightly.**

But in some situations the long and short forms are not interchangeable. The long forms are used between *to* and the base form of a verb *(to wrongly accuse,* not *to wrong accuse)* and generally between the subject and verb (They *closely* watched). The short forms are used more with short words: *new* found friends, but *newly* acquired rank. Formal writers tend to use the long forms, other writers more of the short forms. But since comprehensive rules cannot be given, each writer has to choose between the forms largely on the basis of the tone and sound of the sentence.

Bobtailed Adverbs

When an adverb has only the *-ly* form, take care not to drop the ending. Some temptations are *considerably, seriously,* and *differently:*

> Twenty-five dollars is **considerably** more than I want to pay. [not *considerable*]
>
> People often told him that he should take things more **seriously.** [not *serious*]
>
> She worked **differently** from the others. [not *different*]

Dropping the *-ly* in such words is a characteristic of some dialects and of informal conversation. A dictionary will tell what the standard adverb form is.

The bobtailed adverbs most likely to be found in writing are *bad, real, sure.* In general or edited English these forms are adjectives only; the adverbs have *-ly:*

> He danced **badly.**
>
> It was a **really** outstanding performance.
>
> They were **surely** enjoying themselves.

most—almost

Almost is an adverb meaning "very nearly":

> I **almost** lost my mind. [adverb, modifying the verb *lost*]
>
> The train was **almost** always on time. [adverb, modifying the adverb *always*]

Most is an adjective meaning "the greatest number":

> **Most** fishermen are optimists. [adjective, modifying *fishermen.*]

You'll sometimes hear *most* used as an adverb in speech: This train is *most* always on time. When an adverb is needed in writing, use *almost.*

9.5 Position of Adverbs

Adverbs Modifying a Single Word

Unlike adjectives, adverbs can have various positions in the sentence. Try to place them in a position that clearly indicates your intended meaning and desired emphasis.

When an adverb modifies a single word, its typical position is immediately before that word:

> a **quite** late party [modifies *late*]
>
> They **never** finished the job. [modifies *finished*]

This often puts the modifier of a verb between an auxiliary and participle:

> He had **quietly** withdrawn.

9.5

mm

A modifier of a verb often follows the verb or comes after the verb and its object:

> He withdrew **quietly**.
>
>   v   o
> They finished the job **hurriedly**.

See also 4.2, p. 65, Split Infinitives.

Sentence Adverbs

A good many adverbial modifiers — single word adverbs, phrases, or clauses — cannot sensibly be related to another single word in a sentence. It is conventional to say that these adverbs "modify the whole sentence" and to call them *sentence adverbs*. Their position is variable:

> **Unfortunately** they had already left.
>
> They had already left, **unfortunately**.
>
> They had **unfortunately** already left.

This flexibility makes it possible to shift the position of many sentence adverbs for variety as well as for emphasis.

Misplaced Adverbial Modifiers

mm   **Revise the sentence so that the expression marked is clearly related to the word or statement it modifies.**

Be careful not to misplace a modifier so that the meaning of a statement becomes ambiguous or even ludicrous:

> AMBIGUOUS: Using several pen names, the two editors have almost written every article in the magazine. [*almost* seems to modify *written*]
>
> CLEAR: Using several pen names, the two editors have written **almost** every article in the magazine.

Modifiers are sometimes placed so that they could refer to either one of two elements; these are sometimes called "squinting modifiers":

> Although it was often said that the old boat would sink **somehow** it seemed blessed with unsinkability. [*Somehow* might modify the preceding verb *sink* or the following clause. Adding a comma after *sink* would clear up the ambiguity.]

In some constructions, misplacing the modifier may alter the intended meaning:

> The way I can stand in front of a store window and persuade myself that I need useless articles **even** surprises me. [intended meaning: *surprises even me*]

See also 4.3, Misrelated Modifiers, and 4.4, Dangling Modifiers, for a discussion of the placement of verbal modifiers.

Position of *only* and Similar Adverbs

In formal usage, limiting adverbs like *only, merely, hardly, just* are placed immediately before the element they modify:

> I need **only** six more to make a full hundred.

> The audience seemed **hardly** to breathe when the girl began speaking.

In spoken usage limiting adverbs usually stand immediately before the verb:

> I **only** need six more to make a full hundred.

> The audience **hardly** seemed to breathe when the girl began speaking.

This pattern, typical of spoken English, is usual in general writing, when no misunderstanding of the author's meaning will occur:

> When the brilliant lightweight boxer, Kid Lewis, stood for Parliament in his native borough, he **only** scored a hundred and twenty-five votes. — George Orwell, *The English People*

> He **only** remembers one verse of the song and he has been repeating it. — Eugene O'Neill, *A Moon for the Misbegotten*

• *Exercise*

Study the following sentences carefully and state where you would place the indicated modifier within each sentence. If more than one position is possible, explain what change of emphasis would result from shifting the modifier.

Example: Add *almost:* The fire had burned down to nothing.
With modifier: The fire had *almost* burned down to nothing.
Or: The fire had burned down to *almost* nothing.

1. Add *certainly:* The fields were carpeted with snow that had fallen in the night, for there had been none yesterday.

2. Add *scarcely:* Some had landed, oddly enough, on the back patio, where the wind was now blowing.

3. Add *almost:* Farther out in the yard, the doghouse was covered to the roof so that it looked like a small mound of cotton.

4. Add *even:* The garden walks were so obliterated by drifts that my father, who had laid out the garden, did not know where they were.

5. Add *more or less:* You could tell where one path went by following the clothesline, which had a ridge of snow that made it visible from the house.

6. Add *only:* Yesterday I had seen the yard with a few flowers growing.

7. Add *definitely:* "It's beautiful to look at," my father said, "but you'll have to shovel the walks because your mother will want to hang out the wash she did last night."

8. Add *better:* Picking up the old battered shovel, I went out into the bitter wind, knowing I would be able to get the job done before the snow hardened.

9. Add *hardly:* Although I walked on the white snow-blanket softly, I had taken a few steps when I fell in a position from which I could extricate myself.

10. Add *merely:* Because it was a moderate snowfall, I laughed and went on with my work.

9.6

Adv

9.6 Double Negatives

A statement in which a second negative needlessly repeats the meaning of the first negative is called a *double negative:* "The trip will *not* cost you *nothing.*" Such constructions do appear in other languages. In French, for example, two words (*ne* and *pas*) are needed to make a negative. In edited American English, however, one negative is sufficient: "The trip will cost you *nothing*" or "The trip will *not* cost you anything."

Obvious double negatives like *not* with *nothing* seldom cause problems. Watch for concealed double negatives, when *not* is combined with *but* or with adverbs of negative meaning such as *hardly, barely, scarcely.*

Can't hardly, couldn't scarcely. Such common expressions as "I can't hardly hear you" and "There wasn't scarcely enough money left to pay the taxes" are double negatives, because *hardly* and *scarcely* in this sense mean *almost not.* The standard idioms that should be used in writing are "I *can* hardly hear you" and "There *was* scarcely enough money left to pay the taxes."

Can't help but.   The construction *can't help but* (or *cannot help but*) is an established idiom. Many writers, however, avoid it, using instead one of the expressions in the following sentences:

> I **cannot but** feel sorry for him. [formal]
>
> I **can't help feeling** sorry for him. [general]

Irregardless.   *Regardless* is the standard usage. The suffix *-less* is a negative ending; the addition of the negative prefix *ir-* in *irregardless* creates a double negative.

9.7 Comparison of Adjectives and Adverbs

 Make the comparison of adjectives or adverbs more accurate or more appropriate.

Most adjectives and adverbs have three different forms to indicate degrees of the characteristic they name. The positive degree (or simple form of the modifier) expresses no comparison *(red, slow, seriously);* the comparative degree represents an increase or decrease of the positive form, or makes a specific comparison between two things *(redder, slower, more seriously,* or *less seriously);* the superlative indicates the greatest (or least) degree among three or more things (the *reddest* apple of all, the *slowest* runner on the team, the *most—* or *least—seriously* presented argument).

Forms of Comparison

Most adjectives and adverbs are compared in one of two ways: by adding *-er, -est* to the positive form, or by prefixing *more, most* (or *less, least*).

	Positive	**Comparative**	**Superlative**
ADJECTIVES:	hot	hotter	hottest
	brilliant	more brilliant	most brilliant
	expensive	less expensive	least expensive
ADVERBS:	near	nearer	nearest
	sincerely	more sincerely	most sincerely
	often	oftener, more often, less often	oftenest, most often, least often

In general, the *-er, -est* forms are used with words of one syllable *(longer, driest)*, and *more, most* with words of more than two syllables *(more interesting, most rapidly)*. With two-syllable words a writer often has a choice of either form *(abler, more able; easiest, most easy)*. The sound of the expression may determine which form is used:

> His step was **steadier** and **more elastic.** Even his bloodshot eyes looked **fresher,** and his hair and beard were **softer.** — Eyvind Johnson, *Return to Ithaca*

9.7

Comp

A few common modifiers form the comparative and superlative degrees irregularly:

bad	worse	worst
good, well	better	best
far	farther, further	farthest, furthest
little	less, lesser, littler	least, littlest
many, some, much	more	most

worse — worst.   *Worst* is the appropriate form for the superlative: That was the *worst* [not *worse*] show I have ever seen.

farther — further.   In formal English a distinction is sometimes made between *farther,* referring to physical distance (It was six miles *farther* to town), and *further,* referring to abstract degree (We will study these suggestions *further*). In general English, *further* is commonly used for both distance and degree.

Use of the Comparative Form

The comparative form of an adjective or adverb is ordinarily used when two things are compared:

> You're a **better** man than I am, Gunga Din!
>
> Blood is **thicker** than water.
>
> She works **more diligently** than her roommate.

But in some expressions the comparative form is used when no actual comparison is mentioned (higher education, the lower depths, Better Business Bureau). In others, the reader is left to supply the comparison (Look younger, liver longer . . . than what?). Writers of advertising copy are particularly fond of this use of the comparative because of the favorable inferences the reader may draw: Smoke a *milder* cigarette; More protection for *fewer* dollars; Sudso gets clothes *cleaner*. This construction is meaningless and should generally be avoided. If we don't know what Sudso is being compared to, then to say that Sudso get clothes *cleaner* doesn't tell us anything.

Use of the Superlative Form

The superlative form ordinarily indicates the greatest degree among three or more persons or things:

> He was voted the member of his class **most likely** to succeed.

> Many critics consider *King Lear* the **greatest** of Shakespeare's tragedies.

In spoken English the superlative is sometimes used for comparing two things (Put your *best* foot forward). The same construction is occasionally seen in writing, but it is usually better to keep the superlative for comparisons among three or more.

Superlative forms also occur in expressions in which no direct comparison is implied (*best* wishes, *deepest* sympathy, *highest* praise, *most* sincerely yours). The form with *most* is frequently used as an intensive to signify a high degree:

> For example, Herbert Spencer (1820–1903), a **most** influential English philosopher . . . .—Melvin Rader, *Ethics and Society*

The informal use of a heavily stressed superlative to indicate only general approval should be avoided in serious writing:

> Hasn't she the **sweetest** voice? (Better: Hasn't she a **sweet** voice?)

Comparison of *Unique* and Similar Words

Some people regard words such as *unique, perfect, dead, empty* as logically incapable of comparison or qualification because their positive forms express absolute states. Ordinarily, we wouldn't expect to say that something is *more unique, more perfect, deader,* or *emptier,* but in actual usage these terms are often qualified or modified by comparative forms, as in the following examples:

> We, the people of the United States, in order to form a **more perfect** union . . . .—Preamble to the Constitution of the United States

> . . . The **more unique** his nature, the more peculiarly his own will be the coloring of his language.—Otto Jespersen, *Mankind, Nation, and Individual from a Linguistic Point of View*

Whether words like *unique* should or should not be qualified is a matter that can be determined only by appropriateness. In college writing, they should ordinarily be used without qualification; invested with their full meaning, they are valuable words that say something precisely.

Qualifiers are acceptable in some instances. If you say that A is *more nearly unique* or *more nearly perfect* than B, you are not talking about absolute states that should not be qualified; you are saying that A is closer to being unique or perfect than B is.

9.8 Making Comparisons Idiomatic

 Change the expression marked so that it will be idiomatic.

In writing, expressions of comparison should be more carefully and more fully stated than they often are in speaking. Expressions that might pass unnoticed in conversation (such as *all the higher the ladder will reach* or *the slowest of any runner on the team*) are too slipshod to be used in careful writing (where the same ideas would be expressed: *as high as the ladder will reach* and *the slowest runner on the team*).

Comparing Comparable Things

When using comparisons in your writing, make certain that the things compared are of the same kind and actually comparable:

> TERMS NOT COMPARABLE: The rhinoceros has a hide almost as tough as an alligator. [*hide* and *alligator* are not comparable]
> COMPARABLE TERMS: The rhinoceros has a hide almost as tough as that of an alligator [*or* **as an alligator's**].

> TERMS NOT COMPARABLE: One reviewer compared these short stories to O. Henry.
> COMPARABLE TERMS: One reviewer compared these short stories to those written by O. Henry [*or* **to O. Henry's**].

Completing Comparisons

Statements involving comparisons should be written out in full, particularly if any misunderstanding might arise through shortening one of the terms:

> AMBIGUOUS: I owe him less than you.
> CLEARER: I owe him less than I owe you.
> *Or:* I owe him less than you do.

> AMBIGUOUS: He admires Eliot less than other modern poets.
> CLEARER: He admires Eliot less than other modern poets do.
> *Or:* He admires Eliot less than he does other modern poets.

Double comparisons with *as . . . as, if . . . than* should be filled out in writing.

> He is **as** tall **as, if** not taller **than,** his brother. [*not:* He is as tall if not taller than his brother.]
> The styles vary **as** much **as, if** not more **than,** the colors.

Since the *if . . . than* construction tends to interrupt sentence movement, it is usually preferable to complete the first comparison and then add the second, dropping *than:*

> He is as tall as his brother, if not taller.
>
> The styles vary as much as the colors, if not more.

Use of *other* in Comparisons

Other is used when the comparison involves things of the same class, but not when the things being compared belong to two different classes:

> She is a better dancer than the **other** girls.
>
> She dances better than any [not *any other*] boy in school.
>
> *Blithe Spirit* was more successful than the **other** plays we produced.
>
> I think movies are more entertaining than any [not *any other*] book.

Other is not used with superlative comparisons:

> Pavlova was the best of all the [not *all the other*] Russian ballerinas.
>
> The Egyptians had attained the highest skill in medicine that had up to that time been achieved by any [not *any other*] nation.

Use of *like* or *as* in Comparisons

To introduce a prepositional phrase of comparison, *like* is standard usage:

> They are **like** two peas in a pod.
>
> He looks **like** his father.
>
> Bicycle riding, **like** golf, can be enjoyed at almost any age.

Avoid substituting *as* for *like* or *such as* in prepositional phrases like this:

> Some writers **like** [not *as*] Faulkner and Caldwell take their material from a particular region.

To introduce a clause of comparison with a definite subject and verb, formal and general English both prefer *as, as if, as though* to *like:*

> He acted **as if** he didn't feel well.
>
> He wanted to be a doctor **as** his father had been.
>
> She took to skiing **as** a duck takes to water.

• *Exercises*

1. Some of the adjective and adverb forms and expressions of comparisons in these sentences would be inappropriate in most college writing. Revise each sentence to make it acceptable.

a. The ship lay in the harbor like it was a natural fixture.
b. It had been there so long that the weather had turned it more wharf-colored.
c. Many things would be needed to refurbish it, as caulking, paint, new masts, and glass for portholes.
d. All in all, it was the most 19th-century sight in the town.
e. The ship looked as much if not more pathetic than an old hound lying forgottenlike nearby a deserted farmhouse.
f. Still, the scene was real fine artwise, and camera enthusiasts were taking pictures most every clear day of the year.
g. Picturesque as the sight was, everyone agreed it was the saddest.
h. I thought wistfully of how trim and noble the ship must have been in her heyday, what with her tall masts and most every sail stretching out to catch the wind.
i. The reason for its being there was most unique; the owner had died of a sudden before he could make it into a museum.
j. A sailing ship is the most romantic, because it pits man against the elements more than any other motorized boat does.
k. To sit on the wharf and watch the old ship rot, that's what made me feel badly.
l. Much the most dreariest of sights is watching anything lose its former beauty.
m. I only wished I could have seen her in her prime, when she was shipshape.
n. Her prow was cut sharp back, so that she could cleave the waves like a knife through hot butter.
o. She was clearly the best of all the other ships I have ever seen, bar none.

9.8

fd

2. Fill in the modifiers called for in the paragraph below, choosing modifiers that will help create a consistent tone for the paragraph.

   Sometimes, late in the evening, when I have worked (adverb) and (adverb) at my desk, I stop and lean back in my (adjective) chair and hear night sounds (adjective) and (adjective) in the distance. Sometimes I hear a (adjective) car passing, or someone calling far away, or (adjective) music from some car radio, or a bird song, (adjective) and (adjective). Then I remember that there is a world outside my window (adjective) (adverb), and I go to the door and stand a moment, looking out (adverb).

Review: Parts of Speech

Nouns: A noun designates a person, place, thing, quality, action, or idea: *plumber, France, piano, anger, studying, truth.* Nouns function in sentences chiefly as subjects, objects, complements, and appositives. (See p. 78.)

Pronouns: A pronoun functions as a noun but does not name a specific person, place, thing, or idea: *I, you, it, who, which, himself, this, everyone.* A pronoun usually serves as a substitute for a previously stated noun. (See p. 85.)

Verbs: A verb indicates action, condition, or process: *walk, is, become.* (See p. 101.)

When forms of verbs are used in sentences as nouns or modifiers rather than as verbs, these verb forms are called *verbals.* (See p. 60.)

Verbals are classified by form and function as —

Infinitives (*to talk, to think*) which function either as nouns or modifiers;

Participles (*talking, talked; thinking, thought*) which function as adjectives;

Gerunds (*talking, thinking*) which function as nouns.

Adjectives: An adjective modifies a noun or a noun equivalent: *blue, glamorous. older.* (See p. 118.)

Adverbs: An adverb modifies a verb, an adjective, another adverb, or a whole statement: *soon, quietly, especially, incidentally.* (See pp. 118, 121.)

Prepositions: A preposition shows the relationship between a noun (or noun equivalent) and some other word in the sentence: *in, at, of, before.*

A preposition introduces a *prepositional phrase*, which consists of the preposition followed by a noun (or noun equivalent), plus any modifiers of the noun: *in the tree, at me, of great importance, before dinner.* Prepositional phrases usually function as modifiers. (See p. 32.)

Conjunctions: A conjunction links together words, phrases, or clauses: *and, but, since, because, either . . . or.* (See pp. 34, 36.)

Interjections: An interjection is an expression of emotion that either stands alone or is inserted into a sentence without being grammatically related to the sentence: *oh, wow, help, no.* (See p. 135.)

10 End Punctuation

Every complete sentence requires a mark of punctuation at the end, either a period, a question mark, or an exclamation mark. The great majority of sentences are statements, requiring a period (.). Direct questions are followed by a question mark (?), and emphatic or exclamatory statements are ended with an exclamation point, or mark (!).

10.1

Periods and question marks also have several conventional uses in addition to their function as end stops.

10.1 Periods

 Insert a period at the place marked.

Periods are the most common end stops; they mark the end of all sentences that are not direct questions or exclamations.

Periods After Statements

> Madagascar is an island off southeast Africa.
> "Where is he now?" she asked. "Tell me."
> "Oh."

Periods After Indirect Questions and Courtesy Questions

An indirect question is really a statement *about* a question, and is never followed by a question mark.

> He asked us where we got the money. (A direct question would be *Where did you get the money?*)
>
> They wanted to know what I had been doing since I graduated.
>
> Will you please return this copy as soon as possible. (This is a courtesy question, a polite request phrased as a direct question, but followed by a period.)
>
> May we hear from you at your earliest convenience.

Periods After Abbreviations

A period is conventionally used after most abbreviations:

Mr. H. L. Matthews	Oct.	Ph.D.
St. Paul, Minn.	D.D.S.	etc.

133

An abbreviation within a sentence may be followed by additional punctuation (After she gets her M.A., she might go on to get her Ph.D.), but at the end of a sentence no additional mark is needed unless the sentence is a question or exclamation. (Does he have a Ph.D.?)

Periods are sometimes omitted from abbreviations, especially if they are made from initial letters: UNESCO, GOP. Consult an up-to-date dictionary for the preferred form of particular abbreviations. If usage is divided (A.W.O.L., AWOL, or a.w.o.l.), follow a consistent style throughout your paper. (See 16.1, Abbreviations.)

Periods with Figures

A period (decimal point) is used before fractions expressed as decimals and between whole numbers and decimals, and to separate dollars and cents:

.05	4.6	3.14159	95.6%
$4.98	$.98	*but* 98 cents	*or* 98¢

See 14.2 for periods used as ellipses to mark the omission of words.

10.2 Question Marks

?
.

Punctuate this sentence or sentence element with a question mark.

After Direct Questions

A question mark is used after a sentence expressing a direct question:

> What can we do?
>
> Did Napoleon dislike Elba?
>
> Really?

When a sentence begins with a statement but ends with a question, the ending determines the punctuation:

> Perhaps this explanation is poor, but is there a better one?

After Questions Within a Sentence

A question mark stands immediately after a question that is included within a sentence:

Someone once remarked (wasn't it Mark Twain?) that old second-hand diamonds are better than no diamonds at all.

"Are you engaged?" he blurted.

When a question mark and quotation marks occur together, the question mark goes inside the quotation marks if the quotation is a question. The question mark goes outside the quotation marks if the whole sentence is a question:

10.3

He asked himself, "Is this the best of all possible worlds?"

Do you agree that this is "the best of all possible worlds"?

To Indicate a Doubtful Statement

A question mark is used, with or without parentheses, to show that a statement is approximate or questionable:

Geoffrey Chaucer, 1340(?)–1400

Geoffrey Chaucer, 1340?–1400

Sometimes writers place a question mark in parentheses to indicate humor or mild sarcasm:

She gave him an innocent (?) wink over her menu.

If humor or sarcasm requires a signal for the reader to recognize it, it would probably be better to revise the entire passage.

10.3 Exclamation Marks

Insert or remove exclamation mark at the place indicated.

An exclamation mark is used after an emphatic interjection (Oh! Ouch! Fire! Help! No, no, no!) and after statements that are genuinely exclamatory:

The building had disappeared overnight!

What torments they have endured!

There is seldom a need for exclamation marks unless you are writing dialog. Don't use an exclamation mark unless the statement is genuinely emphatic; it will not lend weight to a simple statement of fact, nor will the use of double and triple marks add anything.

• *Exercises*

1. Rewrite the following items, changing the end punctuation. Make any other changes you need in order to use different end signals.

a. My first job, as an elevator operator, was the most thrilling I've ever had! To me it was almost as if I was an actor, waiting my cue to speak and move!! My audience responded! How could they help it? They had to get off!!

b. What fear he must have felt while he swayed there!

c. He asked us where we got the money.

d. Win one of sixteen luxurious all-expense paid vacations at Disneyland!

e. How I hope we will win!

2. All end punctuation has been omitted from the passage below. Supply the marks that you think are needed.

It was quite a joke when the CBS Sports commentators mused on the air about how important the Super Bowl has become even though it started life as a quintessential non-event the reason it's become important, they didn't mention, is television, which has inflated it into an incredible Madison Avenue tribal rite talk about your turnovers this one has been a dilly

Commercial time on this year's telecast sold for a record $468,000 per minute, but there was only one one-minute spot on the show, the full-length version of Mean Joe Green's Coca-Cola commercial this ad was reprised with a 30-second version later in the show and, indeed, reinforced in the viewer's mind each time Green, who happened to be playing in the game for Pittsburgh, appeared on the screen—Tom Shales, "'Super Sell' Raked in Millions for CBS"

3. In the passage below, end punctuation has also been omitted. Supply the appropriate marks.

Dear Abby: I am writing about a problem that is perplexing to me my husband is absolutely perfect in every respect except for one habit that I cannot seem to break him of

Instead of throwing out food containers after he has emptied them, he puts them back in the refrigerator I can't begin to tell you how many empty cartons, bottles and cans I have found in the refrigerator

No amount of scolding, pleading or nagging seems to help

He offers no explanation for this screwball behavior I think he's too lazy to walk to the trash can on the other side of the kitchen

Can you, or your readers, offer any kind of solution so that I can have a perfect husband—*Frustrated*

Dear Frustrated: You're crying with a loaf of bread under each arm and an empty ketchup bottle in the refrigerator if a man must have but one flaw in an otherwise flawless character, I can think of none so harmless, inoffensive and easy to forgive as your husband's cherish this paragon of virtue he's a candidate for sainthood—Abigail Van Buren, "Dear Abby"

11 Commas

/ᶺ／ Insert a comma at the place indicated.

Commas mark a slight separation between grammatical units, similar to brief pauses in speech. They are highly important to the meaning of all kinds of writing, and they are important in determining the pace and tempo of writing. About two-thirds of all punctuation marks used are commas.

11.1

To use commas well, you must know not only when to use them but also when to omit them. The principal uses of the comma are described in the following sections and summarized in the table on page 140. The table also lists some constructions in which commas should *not* be used, as discussed in 11.9, Misused Commas.

/ᶺ／

11.1 Commas Between Coordinate Clauses

A comma is customarily used before the conjunction linking the coordinate clauses in a compound sentence, especially when the clauses are long or when it is desirable to emphasize their distinctness. Notice that the comma always comes *before* the coordinating conjunction, not after it:

> This town does not actually exist, but it might easily have a thousand counterparts in America or elsewhere in the world. — Rachel Carson, *Silent Spring*

> The village was to the scale of the town of Lilliput, and I could have straddled over Toad Hall. — Aubrey Menen, "Dazzled in Disneyland"

Short Clauses Joined by *and, or, nor*

The comma may be omitted before the conjunctions *and, or, nor* in compound sentences if the coordinate clauses are short and closely related in thought:

> Life is short [ ] and time is fleeting.

> He had to get home [ ] or his father would be furious.

> Nancy didn't like her [ ] nor did I.

137

General writing often omits the comma where formal writing would use one, as between the two independent clauses in this example:

> I remembered being taken for a haircut and scraping my knee on the footrest of the barber's chair and I remembered my father's face as he soothed my crying and applied the stinging iodine. —James Baldwin, "Notes of a Native Son"

Clauses Joined by *but, yet*

In both formal and general writing a comma is used between independent clauses joined by *but* or *yet* to emphasize the contrast:

> This was not the man they had known, but ten perilous and eventful years had passed since their last meeting.
>
> It is an imperfect system, yet it is better than none.

Clauses Joined by *for*

A comma is necessary between clauses joined by *for* used as a conjunction, so that it won't be confused with the preposition *for*:

> He was an easy target, for anyone could pull the wool over his eyes. [*for* as a conjunction]
>
> He was an easy target for anyone who wanted to take advantage of him. [*for* as a preposition]

11.2 Commas After Conjunctive Adverbs

When two independent or coordinate clauses are linked by a conjunctive adverb, use a semicolon before the adverb and a comma after it (see also 12.1):

> I'll go to the party if you think I should; **however,** I'd rather be pecked to death by a flock of turkeys.
>
> He tried it here but didn't like our ways; **consequently,** he's leaving for the back country.

11.3 Commas After Long Introductory Elements

Adverb clauses and long modifying phrases are usually set off by a comma when they precede the main clause. When these elements end a sentence, a comma may or may not be necessary.

Adverb Clauses

Adverb clauses (see 3.2) are often placed at the beginning of a sentence for variety or emphasis. In this position they are usually separated from the main clause by a comma:

> **When he said that we would be expected to write a theme** every day, I nearly collapsed.

> **Before penicillin and other antibiotics were developed,** pneumonia was often fatal.

The comma is frequently omitted when the introductory clause is short and closely related to the main clause, especially if both clauses have the same subject:

> **When I lived in New York** [ ] I went to the theater every month.

> **After he seized control** [ ] the situation changed drastically.

11.3

When an adverb clause *follows* the main clause, no comma is used if the subordinate clause is closely related to the meaning of the sentence:

> I nearly collapsed [ ] **when he said that we would be expected to write a theme every day.**

> Pneumonia was often fatal [ ] **before penicillin and other antibiotics were developed.**

If a following subordinate clause is only loosely related to the main clause and would be preceded by a distinct pause in speech, it is separated from the main clause by a comma:

> The new wing will be finished by spring, **unless, of course, unexpected delays occur.**

> I have known readers who find Huxley unreadable, **although they have found it impossible to explain why.**—Colin Wilson, "Existential Criticism"

Long Modifying Phrases

Long modifying phrases are generally punctuated in the same way as adverb clauses. When they come before the main clause, they are followed by a comma:

> **To understand fully the impact of Einstein's ideas,** one must be familiar with those of Newton. [infinitive phrase]

> **Leaning far out over the balcony,** he stared at the waves below. [participle phrase]

> **In such a situation,** speakers of the creole often deny their mother tongue. [prepositional phrase]—Peter Farb, *Word Play*

Review: Commas

- **Commas Are Used:**

1. Between coordinate clauses (11.1)
   a. When they are joined by *and, or, nor* if the clauses are long or not closely related
   b. When they are joined by *but* or *yet*
   c. When they are joined by *for*
2. After conjunctive adverbs that link coordinate clauses (11.2)
3. After long introductory elements (11.3)
   a. When an adverb clause precedes the main clause (usually optional if the introductory clause is short and closely related)
   b. When a long modifying phrase precedes the main clause (usually optional if the phrase is short and closely related)
4. With nonrestrictive modifiers (11.4)
   a. To set off subordinate clauses and phrases that do not limit or restrict the meaning of the term they modify
   b. To set off appositives
5. To set off interrupting and parenthetical elements (11.5)
6. To separate coordinate items in a series (11.6)
   a. In a series of words, phrases, or clauses not joined by conjunctions (optional before *and* joining the last item in a series)
   b. In a series of coordinate adjectives, all modifying the same noun
7. To separate constructions for clarity (11.7)
8. In certain conventional places (11.8)
   a. In numbers
   b. In dates
   c. In addresses
   d. With titles and degrees
   e. In correspondence
   f. With phrases identifying direct quotations

- **Commas Should Not Be Used: (11.9)**

1. Between main sentence elements
2. Between two words or phrases joined by *and*
3. Between main clauses without a connective
4. With restrictive modifiers
5. After the last item in a series

140

When the phrases are relatively short and closely related to the clauses they modify, the comma is often omitted:

In this context [ ] the meaning is entirely different.
To evade the draft [ ] he moved to Costa Rica.

When the modifying phrase *follows* the clause, commas are unnecessary if the thought seems to flow smoothly from one to the other:

One must be familiar with Newton's ideas [ ] **to understand fully the impact of Einstein's.**

Special treatment may be necessary [ ] **in cases of severe malnutrition.**

The local residents often saw Elgin [ ] **wandering among the ruins.**

But if the phrase is only loosely related to the clause or if it modifies some distant expression, a comma should be used to prevent confusion:

11.4

Wilson nervously watched the man, **alarmed by his silence.** [The phrase modifies *Wilson,* not *man.*]

• *Exercises*

1. Complete the sentences started below, punctuating wherever necessary.

   a. When she hit
   b. If I can
   c. Although he
   d. At this particular time and place

2. Read the following sentences carefully. In which of the places marked with brackets would you insert a comma? In which do you consider a comma optional? Not appropriate? Give specific reasons for your choice of punctuation.

   a. When a man assumes a public trust [1] he should consider himself as public property. — Thomas Jefferson
   b. Let us all be happy and live within our means [1] even if we have to borrow money to do it. — Artemus Ward
   c. Whenever punctuation problems arise [1] it is a good idea to consult the text [2] and determine the proper usage.
   d. Walk right in [1] and sit right down.

11.4 Commas with Nonrestrictive Modifiers

Rest If the modifier marked is nonrestrictive, set it off with a comma or commas; if it is restrictive, do not separate it from the term it modifies.

Subordinate Clauses and Phrases

A *nonrestrictive* modifier is a subordinate clause or a phrase that does not limit or define the term it modifies. In other words, it does not *restrict* the term's meaning; if it were omitted, the meaning of the sentence would not change much. Most problems occur with clauses introduced by *who, which,* or *that,* but nonrestrictive phrases may also cause difficulty. Nonrestrictive modifiers are set off by commas to indicate their subordinate function in the sentence:

> Last night's audience, **which contained a large number of college students,** applauded each number enthusiastically.
>
> The people of India, **who have lived in poverty for centuries,** desperately need financial and technical assistance.
>
> Vasari's history, **hovering between fact and fiction,** is not a reliable source of data.

Notice that the modifiers in the three preceding sentences are not essential to the terms they modify. Although some information would be lost if they were removed, the central meaning of each sentence would not change.

A *restrictive* modifier limits or defines the meaning of a term; without it, the sentence would take on a different meaning or become difficult to understand. Since it is essential to the sentence, it is *not* set off by commas:

> He is a man **who thinks for himself.**
>
> Ortiz discovered many temples **which were pre-Toltec in origin.**
>
> The questions **that he did not answer** were the most interesting ones.

Almost all clauses beginning with *that* are restrictive. All clauses in which the relative pronoun can be omitted are restrictive (the questions *he failed to answer,* the book *I read*).

In distinguishing between restrictive and nonrestrictive modifiers, consider the nature of the term modified and the context in which it occurs. If the term is fully defined in itself and cannot be confused with another, the modifier that follows is nonrestrictive. But if the term is vague or ambiguous without the modifier, the modifier is restrictive. Compare the function of the modifier in each of these passages:

> Children **who can't swim very well** should stay off the diving board.
>
> Children, **who can't swim very well,** should stay off the diving board.
>
> Last month I read a novel and a biography. The novel, **which especially appealed to me,** was written by Hawthorne.
>
> Last month I read several novels and a biography. The novel **which especially appealed to me** was written by Hawthorne.

While in Rome, I took photographs in the vicinity of St. Peter's. The square, **designed by Michelangelo,** is perfectly symmetrical.

While in Rome, I took photographs of squares designed by Michelangelo, Bernini, and Borromini. The square **designed by Michelangelo** is perfectly symmetrical.

A good test to apply in distinguishing between restrictive and nonrestrictive modifiers is to read the passage aloud. If your voice drops slightly in pitch and hesitates briefly before and after the modifier, the modifier is probably nonrestrictive and requires commas. If you read the passage smoothly without a pause, the modifier is probably restrictive and needs no commas.

Appositives

11.4

Appositives — nouns or noun equivalents that extend the meaning of a preceding expression — are usually nonrestrictive modifiers and are set off by commas:

Thomas Malthus, **author of the first serious study of population growth,** foresaw one of our greatest modern problems.

Lincoln delivered a famous address at Gettysburg, **site of a crucial Civil War battle.**

Notice that such appositives, like other nonrestrictive modifiers, must be set off by *two* commas when they occur in the middle of the sentence.

Restrictive appositives and those used as part of a person's name require no commas:

I thought the question referred to Lewis **the novelist** rather than to Lewis **the union leader.**

William **the Conqueror** invaded England from Normandy.

• *Exercise*

The following sentences contain both restrictive and nonrestrictive modifiers. Punctuate each sentence appropriately. If the sentence makes sense either way, explain the difference in meaning between the restrictive and the nonrestrictive modifier.

Example: The alligator which was often hunted for its hide is in danger of becoming extinct.
Correction: insert commas after *alligator* and *hide*

1. The wall that was built by Hadrian served its purpose for many years.

2. Abraham Lincoln sometimes called "The Great Emancipator" has become a symbol to many groups which crave independence.

3. Diamonds that are synthetically produced are more perfectly formed than natural diamonds which have serious flaws.

4. American movies that are exported abroad are popular in countries that have no native movie industry.

5. The French chef whose accomplishments are well known is eagerly sought by expensive restaurants and hotels.

6. Cockfighting outlawed by the Mexican authorities still takes place in areas where the police seldom turn up.

7. The oboe which is a woodwind instrument is played by means of a reed inserted in the mouthpiece.

8. The early settlers who were exposed to severe winters and who expected Indian attacks usually constructed forts many of which can still be found.

9. Drunk drivers who are responsible for many traffic fatalities obviously do not consider the value of human life.

10. The common belief that science can solve everything is another example of the naive optimism that most people are prey to.

11.5 Commas to Set Off Interrupting and Parenthetical Elements

A word, phrase, or clause that interrupts the movement of a sentence is usually set off by commas or other appropriate marks. Whether or not the degree of interruption is sufficient to require commas depends on tone and emphasis. Formal English uses commas more frequently than general English for this purpose:

> There are, **however,** few college subjects in the humanities and the social sciences in which forty-five hours of the teacher lecturing and the students listening can be useful. — Nathan Glazer, "The Wasted Classroom"

> The city, **after all,** is not just a collection of buildings and services. — Barbara Ward, "The City May Be as Lethal as the Bomb"

> **As I have said before,** I believe that now as in the days of the founding fathers, even the faintest possibility of achieving such an order depends upon the steadfast faith of this country. — Adlai Stevenson, Speech on United Nations Charter Day

To decide whether or not to set off short phrases with commas, read the passage aloud with the kind of emphasis you want to give it. If your voice drops and you pause slightly before and after the phrase, commas should be used. If the phrase seems to run naturally into the rest of the sentence, probably no commas are necessary:

> Machines are useful, **of course,** in doing complex calculations.
> Machines are **of course** incapable of what we call creative thought.

Adverbs that Compare or Contrast

Adverbs that compare or contrast some preceding idea *(however, therefore, consequently, too, also)* are generally set off by commas when they occur within a sentence:

> It was in Paris, **too,** that we felt the spirit of the American expatriots of the twenties.
>
> The largest single group of terms in the dictionary, **however,** is that in the general vocabulary, which belongs to all speakers of American English. — Patrick E. Kilburn, "Ruckus in the Reference Room"

11.5

When such words appear at the beginning of a sentence, they may or may not be followed by a comma, depending on the emphasis desired:

> **Thus** the way was cleared for further explorations.
>
> **Nevertheless,** work did not always proceed according to plan.

When a clause beginning with such an adverb is joined to a preceding clause, the *semicolon* must be used, since these words are weak connectives. They relate ideas to one another but do not join them grammatically (see 12.1, page 154, Semicolons Between Main Clauses Linked with a Conjunctive Adverb):

> Business recessions take place periodically; **however,** they are generally short-lived.
>
> The natives are incredibly poor; **moreover,** they have little hope of bettering their lot.

When adverbs that closely modify the verb or the entire sentence *(perhaps, so)* begin the sentence, they should not be followed by a comma. Similarly, conjunctions are part of the clauses they introduce and should not be set off from them:

> **Perhaps** a solution can still be found.
>
> **But** the average American cannot afford such luxuries.

Weak Exclamations

Weak exclamations *(well, oh, say)* and *yes* and *no* sometimes occur as modifiers, particularly at the beginning of a sentence. They are conventionally separated from the sentence they modify by commas:

Well, not much can be done about it now.

Yes, times have changed.

It is doubtful whether the ordinary city-dweller is more grasping than the French peasant, say, or even the sturdy New Englander. — Herbert Muller, *The Uses of the Past*

Names in Direct Address

Names which occur as interrupters in direct address are also set off by commas:

I firmly believe, **fellow citizens,** that justice will prevail.
It seems to me, **George,** that your attitude is poor.
Workers of the world, unite!

11.6 Commas to Separate Items in a Series

Words, Phrases, or Clauses in a Series

A comma is the mark ordinarily used to separate coordinate words, phrases, or clauses in a list or series:

He remembered these feelings as precisely as he remembered the clothes, the cars, the furniture, the songs, the slang. — Arthur Mizener, *The Far Side of Paradise*

We were taught how to sit gracefully, how to walk, how to converse politely.

Although usage is divided, most writers prefer to use a comma before a connective joining the last item in a series:

We had hot dogs, potato salad, soft drinks, and watermelon at the class picnic.

It was left to the House of Representatives to decide whether the Presidency should go to Jackson, Adams, or Crawford.

In some informal writing, especially in newspapers, the final comma is omitted if no misinterpretation is possible. However, because there is quite often the possibility of misreading, it's generally better to use a final comma:

At the rock concert we heard Blackberry Wine, Golden Gate Bridge, Red Eye and the Bull Dogs. [Is Red Eye and the Bull Dogs one group or two?]

If each of the items in a series is joined by a conjunction, commas are ordinarily omitted. The following sentence illustrates series with and without connectives:

> Scenes down on the farm **or** among raftsmen poling their flatboats **or** among the prairie schooners and Indians of the West were present in the canvasses of painters like George Caleb Bingham, William Sidney Mount, and Alfred Jacob Miller. — Holman Hamilton, "The American Renaissance"

See also 12.1, page 155, Semicolons to Separate Elements Containing Other Marks.

Coordinate Adjectives

Commas are used to separate adjectives in a series when they modify the same noun. Since each performs the same function, such adjectives are called *coordinate*. In a coordinate series each member could sensibly be joined by *and* instead of a comma, or the order of modifiers could be reversed:

11.6

$\land$
$,$

> He spoke of the **violent, exciting, challenging** era that followed the Civil War.

Commas are not used when the adjectives are arranged so that each one modifies the entire following expression. Such items cannot be joined by *and* or reversed in order:

> She made a **tasty** [] **Hungarian** goulash.
> He spoke longingly of the **good** [] **old** [] **prewar** days.

Notice that a comma is never used between the last adjective in a series and the noun it modifies.

• *Exercise*

In which of the places marked with brackets would you insert a comma? In which do you consider a comma optional? Not appropriate?

a. If a man can write a better book [1] preach a better sermon [2] or make a better mousetrap [3] than his neighbors [4] though he builds his house in the woods [5] the world will make a beaten path to his door. — Ralph Waldo Emerson
b. Put your trust in God [1] my boys [2] and keep your powder dry. — attributed to Oliver Cromwell
c. When I was a child [1] I spake as a child [2] I understood as a child [3] I thought as a child: but when I became a man [4] I put away childish things. — 1 Corinthians
d. Professor Tillman [1] author of several books [2] gave a series of lectures on the depression.

11.7 Commas to Separate for Clarity

Commas tend to keep distinct the constructions they separate and should be used wherever necessary to prevent misreading. They are useful in the following situations:

1. When the subject of a clause may be mistaken for the object of a verb or preposition that precedes it:

   As far as I can **see, the results** have not been promising.

   When the rains are **over, the fields** are plowed.

2. When a word has two possible functions, a comma can guide the reader in interpreting it properly. Words like *for, but,* and *however,* for example, may be used in several ways:

   The surgeon's face showed no emotion, **but** anxiety and a little nervousness must have been hiding behind that impassive mask. [. . . showed no emotion but anxiety . . .]

   Sharon was thoroughly embarrassed, **for** her parents treated her like a child. [. . . was thoroughly embarrassed for her parents . . .]

   However, I interpreted his remarks liberally and continued my work.

   However [ ] I interpreted his remarks, they made no sense.

3. A comma is sometimes necessary for clarity when one expression might be mistaken for another:

   After he broke his **hand, writing** was very difficult for him.

4. When the same word occurs consecutively, a comma may be used, although usage is divided on this:

   Whatever **is, is** right.

11.8 Commas in Conventional Places

Follow current practice in the use of commas in conventional places. Such commas help the reader quickly recognize distinct units of information.

Numbers.   Commas are conventionally used to group numbers into units of threes in separating thousands, millions, etc.:

   2,853   84,962   3,542,869

Commas are not generally used in round numbers of four figures, serial numbers, or street addresses:

There were about 2000 words in the article.
The serial number of my typewriter is 11-6445793.
He lives at 11085 Champagne Point Road.

Dates.   Commas are used to separate the day of the month and the year:

February 8, 1928   November 21, 1975

When only the month and year are given, a comma is not necessary, although it is frequently used:

October 1929 *or* October, 1929

The form favored in military usage — 16 March 1962 — is more common in British than in American writing.

11.8

Addresses.   Commas are used in addresses to separate towns, counties, states, and districts; they are not used between state and ZIP code, however.

⟨,⟩

Toledo, Ohio 43601
Hamilton, Madison County, New York
He was born in Washington, D.C., in 1937.

Titles.   Commas are used to separate proper names from titles and degrees:

Marshall Field, Jr.
Jerome Blum, M.A., Ph.D.
Gen. H. L. Matthews, U.S.M.C., Ret.

Notice that the final element in dates, addresses, and titles is followed by a comma if it falls within a sentence:

He was born on December 7, 1929, twelve years before we entered World War II.

She was born in Miami, Ohio, and lived there for seven years.

Sammy Davis, Jr., followed his father into show business.

Letters.   Commas are conventional after the salutation of informal letters (Dear Shirley, Dear Uncle Joe,) and after the complimentary close of most letters (Yours truly, Sincerely yours,). A colon is used after the salutation of a formal or business letter (Dear Mr. Miller:).

Quotations.   A comma is customarily used after expressions that introduce direct quotations:

Sherman said, "Only a fool would carry on like that."

If the phrase interrupts a sentence in the quotation, it is set off by two commas:

"Only a fool," Sherman said, "would carry on like that."

No comma is needed with very short quotations, exclamations, or phrases closely built into the structure of the sentence:

Father always said "Time is money."
She began to scream "Fire!" as soon as she saw the smoke.
One famous writer called slavery a "peculiar institution."

11.9 Misused Commas

No ⌃   Remove the superfluous comma at the place marked.

Students frequently use too many commas because of a mistaken notion that the more punctuation, the better. Remember that too many commas are as bad as too few, and be prepared to justify every comma you use. The most common errors in using commas are described below.

No Comma Between Main Sentence Elements

Since a comma is a mark of separation, it should not ordinarily be used between those elements of a sentence that naturally go together: subject and verb, verb and object (or complement), preposition and object. There should be no marks where the brackets stand in the following sentences:

SUBJECT AND VERB: Sometimes students who have attended expensive preparatory schools [ ] have trouble adjusting to large public universities.

VERB AND OBJECT: I have often noticed [ ] that a person's physical characteristics may influence his personality.

VERB AND COMPLEMENT: Whenever the dogs in the kennel appeared [ ] restless or hostile, the trainer took steps to pacify them.

PREPOSITION AND OBJECT: Nothing troubled her except [ ] that her friendship with Swift was causing gossip.

No Comma Between Two Words or Phrases Joined by *and*

Be careful to distinguish between coordinating conjunctions joining independent *clauses* and those joining other sentence elements, such as compound subjects or verbs. Except for coordinate clauses (11.1), two items joined by *and* or by one of the other coordinating conjunctions are not ordinarily separated by a comma. Commas would be out of place in the following compound constructions:

> Primitive agricultural tools [ ] and bits of clay pottery were found. [compound subject]

> He either talked too much [ ] or else said nothing at all. [compound predicate]

> In his senior year he was captain of the football team [ ] and secretary of his class. [compound complement]

> She wanted more time for study [ ] and contemplation. [compound object of preposition]

No Comma Between Main Clauses Without a Connective

11.9

No 5

A comma alone is an inadequate mark of separation between two main clauses. If the clauses are not joined by a coordinating conjunction, they must be separated by a semicolon or punctuated as individual sentences. See 2.2, Comma Faults.

No Comma with Restrictive Modifiers

A restrictive modifier is one that is essential to the meaning of the sentence (see 11.4); it should not be separated from the element it modifies by a comma. The boldface elements in the following example are restrictive and should stand as they are here, without commas:

> The conenose, or kissing bug, is an insect **whose painful bite can draw blood.**

> The book **that I left at home** is the one I really need for class.

No Comma After the Last Item in a Series

A comma is never used between the last adjective in a series and the noun it modifies:

> He imagined himself as a **rich, handsome, successful** [ ] man of the world.

A comma is not used after the last item in other kinds of lists or series:

> The work of such modern masters as Picasso, Matisse, van Gogh, and Gauguin [] shocked conservative critics when it was introduced at the famous New York Armory show in 1913.

• *Exercise*

Commas have been omitted from the following passages. Copy the paragraphs, punctuating with commas wherever you think appropriate; be prepared to account for the commas you insert. The first passage is from a version of "Rapunzel," the second from *Huckleberry Finn,* the third from a recent issue of *Glamour.*

1. There was once a man and his wife who had long wished in vain for a child and at last they had reason to hope that heaven would grant their wish. There was a little window at the back of their house which overlooked a beautiful garden full of lovely flowers and shrubs. It was however surrounded by a wall and nobody dared to enter because it belonged to a witch who was feared by everybody.

2. Mornings before daylight I slipped into cornfields and burrowed a watermelon or a mushmelon or a punkin or some new corn or things of that kind. Pap always said it warn't no harm to borrow things if you was meaning to pay them back sometime; but the widow said it warn't anything but a soft name for stealing and no decent body would do it.

3. If we really want to *get our act together* for the 80's to be sure we *maintain our space* and *stay well and truly centered the reality of it* is that it's time to admit that some of the language we are taking with us into this shiny new decade has lost its vigor. Idiom if it is used to salt and pepper what we say has to be fresh has to convey an immediate unexpected image. When *mellow* and *laid back* begin to sound more like candy bars than states of mind they aren't working any more.

    So we will if you will try very hard to prune the following out of our vocabularies:

    We will try never again to *set priorities*; we absolutely refuse to *prioritize.* We will try to avoid being *prepped out* or *California'd out* or *grossed out* or *burned out.* Prepositions have been carrying too heavy a burden — we will try to enjoy things without *getting into them* we will try to retreat with decorum before we become *out of it.* We will look for ways to convey understanding without having to assure anyone that *we know where he or she is coming from.*

12 Semicolons and Colons

Both semicolons and colons are strong marks of punctuation, but their functions are different and should not be confused; they cannot be used interchangeably. The constructions requiring each mark are well defined and relatively few, yet some students have trouble with them, particularly semicolons. The semicolon is a mark of separation: the colon, a mark of anticipation directing the reader's attention to what follows.

12.1 Semicolons

 Use a semicolon at the place marked to separate coordinate sentence elements.

As a mark of separation, the semicolon is much stronger than a comma and almost as definite as a period. If you read the following passage at a normal speaking rate, you will probably come to a complete stop after *crossroad* and after *tumble-down:*

> Our haunted house was not strictly in the best haunted-house tradition. It was not a ramshackle pile standing at a lonely crossroad; it was on a street inside the town and was surrounded by houses that were cheerfully inhabited. It was not tumble-down; it was a large, well-built mansion of brick, and it still stands, good as new. — Frank Sullivan, *The Night the Old Nostalgia Burned Down*

The few constructions in which a semicolon is required are listed below. Notice that in all its uses the semicolon marks a separation between *coordinate* elements — expressions of equal rank.

Semicolons Between Main Clauses Without an Expressed Connective

A semicolon must be used to separate main clauses that are not joined by one of the coordinating conjunctions *(and, but, for, or, nor, yet):*

> The penalty for not turning work in on time is a lowered grade; the penalty for not turning it in at all is failure.

These clauses are clearly separate in thought and structure and could be punctuated as separate sentences. A semicolon is used to combine such clauses when the writer considers them parts of one idea. Sometimes the second clause continues the thought of the first:

> Alfred Hitchcock was probably the first director to place *himself* at a slightly ironic distance from the action of his films; his own subtle mockery helped him confect high-gloss thrillers that serious people might enjoy without losing their sense of identity. — Jacob Brackman, "Onward and Upward with the Arts"

Sometimes the second clause presents a contrasting idea:

> But however immature they are, these lovers are not dull characters; on the contrary, they are hauntingly and embarrassingly real. — Arthur Mizener, *The Far Side of Paradise*

The use of a comma rather than a semicolon or period between main clauses without an expressed connective is considered a serious error in writing. (See 2.2, Comma Faults.)

Semicolons Between Main Clauses Linked with a Conjunctive Adverb

A semicolon is used before conjunctive adverbs like *however, therefore, consequently,* and *nevertheless* when they occur between clauses:

> On your income tax return you can deduct the cost of meals and lodging for business trips; **however,** you cannot deduct the cost of meals if you were not away over night.

> And, in fact, absence of intellectual content is the mark of the sentimental genre; **conversely,** it is because of her intellect that Jane Austen is never sentimental. — Brigid Brophy, "A Masterpiece, and Dreadful"

The use of heavy conjunctive adverbs between long clauses is probably more characteristic of a formal style, as the second example above may indicate. They do appear in other places, of course, as in the less formal first example above or in the following lines from Keats' "Ode on a Grecian Urn":

> Heard melodies are sweet, but those unheard
>   Are sweeter; **therefore,** ye soft pipes, play on;
> Not to the sensual ear, but, more endeared,
>   Pipe to the spirit ditties of no tone.

Many writers use these adverbs as transitions between sentences rather than as transitions between clauses:

> This is not the place to conduct a full evaluation of the biological family. **Nevertheless,** some of its important virtues are, nowadays, too often overlooked. — Leon R. Kass, "The New Biology"

It is no secret that organized crime in America takes in over forty billion dollars a year. This is quite a profitable sum, especially when one considers that the Mafia spends very little for office supplies. Reliable sources indicate that the Cosa Nostra laid out no more than six thousands dollars last year for personalized stationery, and even less for staples. **Furthermore,** they have one secretary who does all the typing, and only three small rooms for headquarters, which they share with the Fred Persky Dance Studio. — Woody Allen, *Getting Even*

Semicolons with Coordinating Conjunctions

A semicolon is sometimes used between main clauses connected by coordinating conjunctions if:

1. the clauses are unusually long,
2. the clauses are not closely related,
3. one or more of the clauses contain commas, or
4. the writer wishes to show an emphatic contrast between statements:

12.1

I have known many black men and women and black boys and girls who really believed that it was better to be white than black, whose lives were ruined or ended by this belief; **and** I myself carried the seeds of this destruction within me for a long time. — James Baldwin, "Unnameable Objects, Unspeakable Crimes"

In most cases these individualists are corporate executives, bankers, Wall Street lawyers; **but** they do not, as the economic determinists seem to believe, simply push the button of their economic power to affect fields remote from economics. — Robert Lubar, "The Prime Movers"

Semicolons to Separate Elements Containing Other Marks

Semicolons are often used in lists and series to separate elements that contain commas or other marks. In the following sentence, for example, the semicolons are necessary for clarity:

In response to a request for information from columnists Helen and Sue Bottel, the following changes were volunteered by young readers: "groovy" to "gravy baby"; "right on" to "right there" or "left arm"; "out of sight" to "out of state"; "scram" to "make like a banana and split." — Mario Pei, "The Language of the Election and Watergate Years."

Notice that here, just as with main clauses, the semicolon separates *coordinate* elements. It is never used between elements of unequal rank, such as phrases and clauses or main and subordinate clauses.

• *Exercise*

Commas and semicolons have been omitted from the sentences below. Insert the appropriate punctuation.

1. In the summer she visited Munich Heidelberg Frankfurt and Salzburg and in early fall she went on to Albania Greece and Egypt.

2. The weather was hot humid and miserable all day however a west wind cooled the air after dark.

3. Orchestra rehearsal begins at seven she will be there even though she needs to study.

4. The storm knocked out the electricity consequently we could not read or watch television.

5. She knew her parents were worried about her accordingly she called in to let them know she was all right.

12.2 Colons

 Insert a colon at the place marked, or change the misused colon.

A colon is a mark of anticipation, directing attention to what follows:

> Molecular biologists have now provided a fairly complete picture of how genes carry out their primary function: the specification of protein structure. — William B. Wood and R. S. Edgar, "Building a Bacterial Virus"

Students sometimes confuse colons and semicolons, but their functions are entirely different. The distinction is simple: a colon introduces or indicates what is to follow; a semicolon separates coordinate elements. The following passage illustrates the correct use of both marks (as does the sentence of the text immediately above):

> Smaller birds were less elusive: a pair of blue-winged warblers scolded us for coming so close to their nest, as the juncos had along the higher trail; a winter wren, reminiscent of the Long Trail in Vermont, lit up the woods with song; a kingfisher shot downstream with his loud rattle. — Paul Brooks, "The Great Smokies"

Anticipatory Use of Colons

A colon may be used after a main clause to indicate that a list, an illustration, or a summation is to follow:

Many standard food words mean money in nonstandard use: cabbage, kale, lettuce. — Stuart Berg Flexner, "American Slang"

Other gems of military gobbledegook are seemingly nondeliberate: *accidental delivery of ordnance equipment* to indicate shelling of our own or allied troops by mistake; *combat placement evacuator* for a shovel; *aerodynamic personnel accelerator* for a parachute. — Mario Pei, "The American Language in the Early '70's"

The colon is used as an anticipatory mark only after grammatically complete expressions. Do not use a colon between verbs and their objects or complements, or between prepositions and their objects:

COLON: He visited the following cities: Boston, Dallas, Chicago, Miami, and Seattle.

NO COLON: He visited Boston, Dallas, Chicago, Miami, and Seattle. [objects of verb]

COLON: The string section consists of four instruments: violin, viola, cello, and bass.

NO COLON: The four instruments in the string section are violin, viola, cello, and bass. [complements of verb]

12.2

Colons Between Main Clauses

A colon may be used between two main clauses when the second clause is an illustration, a restatement, or an amplification of the first:

Even the new jargon is disturbing: it hurts the spirit, somehow, to read the word *environments,* when the plural means that there are so many alternatives there to be sorted through, as in a market, and voted on. — Lewis Thomas, *Lives of a Cell*

I was impractical: I wanted to marry a poet. — Lillian Hellman, *Pentimento*

Colons Before Quotations

A colon is generally used between an introductory statement and a grammatically complete quotation, especially if the quotation is more than one sentence:

Here is a well-known verse from *Ecclesiastes*: "I returned and saw under the sun, that the race is not to the swift, nor the battle to the strong, neither yet bread to the wise, not yet riches to men of understanding, nor yet favour to men of skill; but time and chance happeneth to them all." — George Orwell, "Politics and the English Language"

Within the past two years, there have been an increasing number of references by Negro writers and speakers to the *Through the Looking*

Glass episode where Humpty Dumpty says: "When I use a word it means just what I choose it to mean — neither more nor less." — Haig A. Bosmajian, "The Language of White Racism."

When a short quotation is built closely into a sentence, it may be preceded either by a comma or by a colon, depending on how it is introduced:

As Alexander Pope said, "A little learning is a dangerous thing."

She reminded him of the words of Pope: "A little learning is a dangerous thing."

Colons in Conventional Places

A colon is customary in the following places:

1. After an expression introducing examples or a large body of material (as after *places* in the preceding sentence).
2. Between hours and minutes expressed in figures: 11:30 A.M.
3. In formal footnotes and bibliographies:

   Between volume and page: *The Nation,* 98:295
   Between chapter and verse of the Bible: Matthew 4:6
   Between the title and subtitle of a book: *China: A Modern Enigma*

4. After the formal salutation in a letter:

   Dear Sir: Dear Professor Jones:

See page 176 for use of capital letter after colons.

• *Exercise*

Either find and copy from your reading or write sentences according to the directions below:

1. a sentence with a colon preceding a list of information or examples

2. a sentence with a colon between two main clauses

3. a sentence with a colon before a quotation

13 Dashes, Parentheses, and Brackets

Dashes, parentheses, and brackets are all used to separate interrupting elements from the main thought of the sentence. Dashes are ordinarily used when the interruption is abrupt or emphatic; parentheses are used when the interruption is an aside or explanatory remark; and brackets are conventionally used when an editorial comment interrupts quoted material.

13.1

13.1 Dashes

/ -- /

/ -- /   **Use a dash or dashes to set off the expression marked.**

Dashes are used to set off added expressions and abrupt interruptions in thought. The dash is a useful mark of separation, but since it is a more emphatic way of setting off elements than either commas or parentheses, it should not be used to excess or in places where another mark (or none) would be more appropriate. On the typewriter a dash is made with two unspaced hyphens; there should likewise be no space on either side of the dash, between it and the words it separates.

Dashes are customarily used in the situations shown below.

1. To set off emphatic and abrupt interruptions:

   > In reality, the whole idea of a specifically feminine—**or, for the matter of that, masculine**—contribution to culture is a contradiction of culture.—Brigid Brophy, "Women Are Prisoners of Their Sex"

2. To mark sharp turns in thought:

   > He praised Ann's intelligence, her efficiency, her good taste—**and then proposed to her sister.**

   > He is a humble man—**with a lot to be humble about.**

3. To enclose added elements (usually to give greater emphasis to elements that could also be set off with commas):

   > Still we do condemn—**we must condemn**—the cruelties of slavery, fanaticism, and witch-burning.—Herbert Muller, *The Uses of the Past*

159

> With our love of record keeping — **doubtless a mark of our business society —** the origin of almost everything is known or easily discoverable. — Jacques Barzun and Henry Graff, *The Modern Researcher*

4. To set off an expression that summarizes or illustrates the preceding statement:

> He founded a university, and devoted one side of his complex genius to placing that university amid every circumstance which could stimulate the imagination — **beauty of buildings, of situation, and every other stimulation of equipment and organization.** — Alfred North Whitehead, "The Idea of a University"

5. To serve some special uses:
   a. To precede a credit line, as at the end of the quoted passages in this book.
   b. After introductory words that are to be repeated before each of the lines following:

> We pledge —
> To uphold the Constitution.
> To obey the laws of this state.

   c. To separate questions and answers in testimony:

> Q. — Did you see him?
> A. — No.

   d. To indicate interrupted dialog (usually *two* dashes separated by a space are used):

> "Well, I had always assumed that — —"
> "I don't care what you assumed," John snapped.

13.2 Parentheses

   Use parentheses to enclose the expression marked.

Parentheses are curved marks used chiefly to enclose incidental or explanatory remarks as shown below.

1. To enclose incidental remarks:

> He was adored (**I have spent some time looking for the right verb, and that's it**) by the members of the *Journal* staff, who greeted him each afternoon, in a sudden silence of typewriters, as if they hadn't seen him for a long time. — James Thurber, "Franklin Avenue, U.S.A."

2. To enclose details and examples:

> For seven long years **(1945–1952)** austerity was the key word in British economic life.

> The changes can be seen by comparing the profits made before 1929 **(upper diagram)** with those made after 1929 **(lower diagram).**

3. To enclose figures or letters used to enumerate points:

> The main questions asked about our way of life concern **(1)** the strength of our democracy, **(2)** our radical practices, **(3)** our concept of modern economy, and **(4)** the degree of materialism in our culture. — Vera Dean and J. B. Brebner, *How to Make Friends for the U.S.*

No punctuation marks are used before a parenthetical statement that occurs within a sentence. If a comma or period is needed after the parenthetical material, it is placed *outside* of the *closing* marks:

13.3

$\lceil / \rceil$

> There is talk with music (tapes and records), talk with film and tape (movies and television), talk with live public performance (demonstrations and "confrontations"). — William Jovanovich, "A Tumult of Talk"

When the parenthetical statement comes between sentences, the appropriate end punctuation is placed *inside* the closing mark:

> Fearing federal intervention, Vincent Columbraro, the Buttered Toast King, called for a truce. (Columbraro has such tight control over all buttered toast moving in and out of New Jersey that one word from him could ruin breakfast for two-thirds of the state.) — Woody Allen, *Getting Even*

13.3 Brackets

$\lceil / \rceil$ **Use brackets to set off any insertion in quoted material.**

Brackets are used to insert brief editorial comments and explanations in material quoted from other writers:

> Lest it be thought that I am exaggerating, listen to Mencken: "The impact of this flood **[of common-speech, non-fashionable Americanisms]** is naturally most apparent in Canada, whose geographical proximity and common interests completely obliterate the effects of English political and social dominance." — Eric Partridge, *Slang Today and Yesterday*

Comments or directions may be bracketed in conversation or in other quoted material to show that the speaker didn't actually say the enclosed words:

> For the first few minutes the practiced speaker, therefore, fills in time with his "Thank you" to the chairman introducing him. . . . Then come his formal salutations, "Mr. President, honored guests [**if there are any**], ladies and gentlemen." — *Amy Vanderbilt's Complete Book of Etiquette*

The Latin word *sic* (meaning *thus* or *so*) is sometimes inserted in brackets within quoted material to mark an error in spelling, usage, or fact that appeared in the original:

> The author's next letter was headed "Danbury, *Conneticut* [**sic**] Oct. 6, 1854."

Most current writers feel that the insertion of *sic* to mark the errors of others is more snobbish than scholarly, and the practice has declined.

In this book brackets are used with examples of writing to enclose words that might better be left out of a sentence, to suggest an improved expression, and to comment on a construction. These special uses are illustrated below:

> At the end of an hour and a half we arrived at [**the spot where**] the red flag [**was situated**].
>
> He looks **similar to** [**like**] his father.
>
> **Most** fishermen are optimists. [adjective, modifying *fishermen*]

Occasionally brackets are used for parenthetical material that falls within parentheses — thus ([ ]) — but such constructions are awkward and can usually be avoided. Consult the preceding section to be sure that you don't confuse the normal uses of parentheses and brackets; see 13.2, Parentheses.

• *Exercise*

In each numbered space in the following sentences, which mark of punctuation would you consider most appropriate: a comma, a semicolon, a colon, a dash, or a parenthesis? Is punctuation necessary in all cases? If more than one choice is possible, list the marks in order of your preference.

a. Let us begin by looking [1] at the two countries where population pressures are most severe [2] India and Pakistan.

b. The finalists in diving were [1] Wilkins [2] U.S.A. [3] and Oyama [4] Japan [5] no one else had qualified.

c. To Ahab the white whale became an obsession [1] even Starbuck [2] the first mate [3] could do nothing to shake him out of it.

d. Reisman divides behavior into two major classes [1] inner-directed [2]

directed toward pleasing the self [3] and other-directed [4] concerned
wih pleasing others [5].

e. The Edsel was [1] the most carefully planned and lavishly promoted
new car in automobile history [2] but it was a total failure.

f. Someone [1] was it Carlyle [2] ironically used a truss factory [3] as a
symbol [4] of modern [5] industrial progress.

g. Some industries have established good relations with their unions by
increasing benefits [1] vacations, insurance, pension plans [2] but
many manufacturers feel that there is only one permanent solution to
their chronic labor problems [3] increased automation.

h. The key word in the essay [1] *faction* [2] is carefully defined by
Madison at the beginning [3] then he goes on to explain [4] what
forms it may take.

i. An audience is basically one of three things [1] although various mix-
tures are also possible [2] friendly, hostile, or indifferent.

j. When Cadwallader quit talking [1] the chairman snorted [2] tugged at
his ear [3] and spoke [4] "If you ladies and gentlemen [5] there were
no ladies present [6] believe that I will support this recommendation
[7] then you have lost your minds."

k. All of these [1] black-eyed peas [2] turnips [3] sweet potatoes [4]
radishes [5] are growing now in our garden against the coming of
frost.

l. When our younger daughter was about six [1] it's a little hard to tell
since she was usually several things at once [2] and her brother was
about twelve [3] he taught her all about golf.

m. Their original home lies off the main route between Fort Worth and
Lubbock [1] Texas [2] about 225 miles from here [3] in a county
that in many years has the lowest per capita income in the state.

n. Sometimes [1] even at my age [2] I can't say curse words because
I'm afraid my mother [3] she has an ear that's accurate up to 1,000
miles [4] will hear and come get me.

13.3

[/]

14 Quotation Marks, Ellipses, and Italics

In general the more common punctuation marks—periods, question marks, commas, semicolons, and so on—indicate intonation and degrees of interruption that would occur if the material was read aloud. They show how the writer wants the words grouped together for meaning and emphasis.

The three marks discussed in this section—quotation marks, ellipses, and italics—are somewhat different in purpose. They are visual guides that tell the reader at a glance such things as whether the words are a writer's own and whether they are being used in a special way. Compare the following pairs of sentences:

> He said I was a fool. [He accused the *writer* of being a fool.]
> He said, "I was a fool." [He called *himself* a fool.]
>
> He spoke of Watson's moral decline. [the moral decline of Watson]
> He spoke of Watson's *Moral Decline.* [a book by Watson]

Although quotation marks, ellipses, and italics are used less often than other punctuation, it is important to know how to use them correctly. They are often necessary in writing that is likely to contain references to the writing of others.

14.1 Quotation Marks

 Make the quotation marks and accompanying punctuation conform to conventional usage.

Quotation marks are necessary to set off direct speech and material quoted from other sources. They are also used around some titles and around words used in special ways.

Usage varies, but double quotations (" ") are the usual marks in American publications. Use single marks (' ')—made on the typewriter with apostrophes—only for a quotation within a quotation (see p. 166). Whether double or single, quotation marks are always used in *pairs,* before and after the quoted material.

Quotation Marks to Enclose Direct Discourse

Statements representing actual speech or conversation are enclosed by quotation marks. The following passage illustrates typical punctuation for direct discourse. Notice not only the quotation marks but the punctuation used with them:

> When we got home, Cathy asked, "Did you win the game?"
> David said, "You'd better believe it. I got four hits, and we won 8 to 5."
> I hobbled to my chair.
> "And Daddy hit a triple," Mindy said. "You should have seen him run."

In dialog the words of each speaker are customarily indented like paragraphs, as in the example above. But when short speeches or statements are quoted to illustrate a point in exposition, they are usually included in the paragraph where they are relevant rather than being set off:

14.1

> Hoist is pronounced hist. I heard a tall story the other day about a man who was histed up on the end of a derrick boom while his companions accused him of making free with another man's wife. "Come on, confess!" they shouted. "Isn't it true you went with her all last year?" For a while he swung at the end of the boom and denied the charges. But he got tired finally. "You did, didn't you?" they persisted. "Well, once, boys," he replied. "Now hist me down." — E. B. White, "Maine Speech"

Only *direct discourse,* which represents the actual words of the speaker, is enclosed by quotation marks. *Indirect discourse,* which gives the substance of what the speaker said but not the exact words, is *not* enclosed in quotes:

DIRECT DISCOURSE: The coach said, "Get in there and fight."
INDIRECT DISCOURSE: The coach told us to get in there and fight.

DIRECT DISCOURSE: "At the present time," the senator replied, "I haven't made up my mind about the bill."
INDIRECT DISCOURSE: The senator replied that he had not yet made up his mind about the bill.

Quotation Marks Around Quoted Material

Words taken directly from another writer or speaker must be clearly set apart, either by quotation marks or by some other conventional typographic device such as setting them in reduced type. Whether you are quoting a phrase or several paragraphs, make certain that you follow the exact wording and punctuation of your source.

Short Quotations. Quotation marks are used around quoted phrases and statements that are included within the body of a paragraph. The quoted material may be worked into the structure of a sentence or may stand by itself:

Another immortal pun is Eugene Field's comment on the actor Creston Clarke that "he played the king as though he were in constant fear that somebody else was going to play the ace." — Max Eastman, *The Enjoyment of Laughter*

While Iago, for example, is gulling Roderigo, he scoffs at him with superb disdain: "I have rubb'd this young quat almost to the sense / And he grows angry" *(Othello,* 5.1.11 – 12). — Maurice Charney, *How to Read Shakespeare*

Long Quotations. When quoted material is relatively long — more than one full sentence from the original source or more than four lines in your paper — it is usually indented ten spaces (three more for the beginning of a new paragraph) but not enclosed in quotation marks:

A British member of Parliament, A. P. Herbert, also exasperated with bureaucratic jargon, translated Nelson's immortal phrase, "England expects every man to do his duty":

England anticipates that, as regards the current emergency, personnel will face up to the issues, and exercise appropriately the functions allocated to their respective occupational groups.

— Stuart Chase, *The Power of Words*

A Quotation Within a Quotation. Use single quotation marks around quoted material that appears within a quotation which is itself enclosed in double marks:

If they depended solely on economic theory to guide them, they would be in the position of the man John Williams mentions: "About the practical usefulness of the theory, I have often felt like the man who stammered and finally learned to say, 'Peter Piper picked a peck of pickled peppers,' but found it hard to work into conversation." — C. Hartley Grattan, "New Books"

In the rare instances when a third quotation occurs within a second, double and single marks are alternated, like this:

In the next passage he gives an example of Mill's uncontrolled temper: "Mill attacked Beaton with a poker after reading his comment that 'A work of genius is not, as Mr. Mill says, "a spontaneous outflowing of the soul"; it is the product of intellectual discipline, a quality Mr. Mill notably lacks.' "

Such a proliferation of quotation marks is confusing and can usually be avoided, either by indenting and single-spacing the main quotation or by paraphrasing some of the material:

In the next passage he gives an example of Mill's uncontrolled temper, telling how Mill attacked Beaton with a poker after reading his comment that "A work of genius is not, as Mr. Mill says, 'a sponta-neous overflowing of the soul'; it is the product of intellectual disci-pline, a quality Mr. Mill notably lacks."

Quoted Verse.   A phrase or portion of a line of verse may be built into a sentence and enclosed by quotation marks, as is this phrase from *Romeo and Juliet:*

> "A plague on both your houses" was the general attitude toward the parties in any conflict, no matter what the outcome.— Percy Finch, *Shanghai and Beyond*

If the quoted passage extends over several lines of the poem, it is best to line it off exactly as it appears in the original, and indent. Quotation marks are unnecessary:

14.1

> Milton opens *Paradise Lost* by announcing that he will write

> > Of Man's first disobedience, and the fruit
> > Of that forbidden tree whose mortal taste
> > Brought death into the World. . . .

If two or three lines of verse are incorporated into a paragraph, the passage is enclosed in quotation marks and the line breaks are indi-cated by diagonal lines (/):

> Milton opens *Paradise Lost* by announcing that he will write "Of Man's first disobedience, and the fruit / Of that forbidden tree whose moral taste / Brought death into the World."

Quotation Marks Around Titles

Quotation marks are used to set off the titles of short written works such as single poems, essays, short stories, and magazine articles. The titles of books and the names of newspapers and magazines are italicized:

> ***The Oxford Book of English Verse*** includes only two poems by Oliver Goldsmith: **"Women"** and **"Memory."**

> Judith Blake and Kingsley Davis have contributed an article titled **"Norms, Values, and Sanctions"** to ***The Handbook of Modern Sociology,*** edited by Robert E. L. Faris.

See 14.3, Italics, and 30, The Research Paper.

   A few titles are neither set off by quotation marks nor underlined for italics: the Bible, Old Testament, the Constitution of the Unit-ed States, Lincoln's Gettysburg Address, Montgomery Ward Cat-alog, the Denver Telephone Directory (or any other catalog or directory).

Quotation Marks to Set Off Words

Words used in some special way within a sentence are often set apart by quotation marks or by italics (underlining).

A Word Used as a Word.   A word used as a word or as an example rather than for its meaning in a passage is either italicized or enclosed by quotation marks. Use one or the other consistently:

> People often confuse the meanings of words that sound alike, such as **"allusion"** and **"illusion."**
>
> I have trouble typing *artificial* and *expectation.*

Apologetic Quotes for Slang and Colloquial Expressions.   In serious writing, an expression associated with unedited or colloquial forms of English is sometimes put in quotation marks to show that the writer knows it is not considered appropriate in formal usage:

> The disheartening outcome of recent international conferences has convinced some of our statesmen that certain nations consider us as little more than "fall guys."

The trouble with apologetic quotes is that they focus the readers' attention on the expression and make them wonder why the writer chose to use it. If you think a word or phrase is right for what you are saying, it's best to use it without apology.

When a real or imaginary person is frequently referred to by his or her nickname, it is not set off by quotation marks:

> Abe Lincoln   Huck Finn   Babe Ruth   Liz Taylor

In general writing there is seldom any need to use apologetic quotes around a word or expression. If the word is appropriate, use it without quotation marks. If it is not, use another.

Words Used Derisively.   Sometimes a writer may use quotation marks around a term to show derision or sarcasm.

> This remarkable piece of "art" consists of a large canvas covered with mud and old bus transfers.
>
> She was so "genteel" that she avoided any reference to the human body.

It's generally better to try to make the whole tone of the passage derisive rather than to rely on quotation marks as signposts.

Quotation Marks with Other Punctuation

The following conventions govern the use of other punctuation with quotation marks:

1. Commas and periods are always placed *inside* the closing quotation mark:

   "Yes," Roger agreed, "it's too late to worry about that now."

   Her watch case was described as "waterproof," but "moisture-resistant" would have been more accurate.

2. Semicolons and colons are placed *outside* the closing quotation mark:

   This critic's attitude seems to be "I don't like any movie"; on a few occasions, though, he has said kind words for a travelog or a documentary film.

   Fully a third of the railroad passengers were what trainmen call "deadheads": people who ride on passes and never tip.

3. Question marks, exclamation points, and dashes are placed inside *or* outside the final quotation mark, depending upon the situation. They come *inside* when they apply to the quotation only:

   Mother looked at me and asked, "Why do you say that?"

   He gave me a skeptical look which seemed to mean "Look who's talking!"

   Terrence interrupted, "No, listen to this —" and proceeded to recite a poem none of us had ever heard before.

14.1

They are placed *outside* the final quotation mark when they apply to the entire statement:

   Who was it who said that "good guys finish last"? [The whole sentence is a question.]

   And to top it all off, she refers to her automatic dishwasher as "essential equipment for gracious living"!

End punctuation marks are never doubled. If a quotation ends your sentence, the end punctuation within quotation marks also indicates the end of the sentence:

   Ever since I moved to Boston to conduct symphony concerts exclusively, one of the principal questions put to me in interviews is "How much do you miss opera?"—Erich Leinsdorf, "What Makes Opera Run"

Notice that no period is added after the final quotation mark, even though the sentence is a statement, not a question. Occasionally it is necessary to use double marks *within* a sentence to avoid a possible misreading, as in the sentence following the one quoted above, but such instances are rare:

   Mind you, not "Do you miss opera?", because the questioner takes it for granted that it is impossible for one who has conducted so much opera to live without it, but "How much?" — Erich Leinsdorf, "What Makes Opera Run"

• *Exercise*

Write sentences according to the directions below.

1. a sentence that includes the names of two poems.

2. a sentence that includes a short quotation from a book.

3. a sentence in which you identify a speaker and the speaker says something as direct discourse.

4. the sentence above converted to indirect discourse.

5. three sentences giving dialog between two speakers as direct discourse.

6. the three sentences above converted into indirect discourse.

14.2 Ellipses

/ ... /   Use an ellipsis to indicate any omission in quoted material.

A punctuation mark of three spaced periods, called an ellipsis (plural: *ellipses*), indicates that one or more words have been omitted from quoted material. If an ellipsis comes at the end of a sentence, the sentence period (or other end punctuation) is retained, and the three periods of the ellipsis follow it. There is no space between the last word and the end punctuation:

> Fourscore and seven years ago our fathers brought forth upon this continent a new nation . . . dedicated to the proposition that all men are created equal. Now we are engaged in a great civil war. . . . We are met on a great battlefield of that war. . . . — Abraham Lincoln, Gettysburg Address

> Does this sound harsh today? . . . Yes, but I cannot sell my liberty and my power, to save their sensibility. — Ralph Waldo Emerson, "Self-Reliance"

To indicate that an entire paragraph or more or an entire line or more of poetry has been omitted, a full line of ellipses is used:

> That's my last Duchess painted on the wall,
> Looking as if she were alive. . . . [two words are omitted here]
> . . . . [two lines omitted]
> Will't please you sit and look at her?
> 			— Robert Browning, "My Last Duchess"

Ellipses are sometimes used, especially in narrative, to indicate interruptions in thought, incompleted statements, or hesitation in speech, as in this description of the dying words of John Wilkes Booth, the assassin of Lincoln:

> Water was poured into his mouth. He blew it out feebly, opened his eyes and moved his lips to shape the words: "Tell . . . mother. . . ." Then he fainted again. When he came to, he finished his sentence: "Tell . . . mother . . . I . . . died . . . for . . . my country." — Eleanor Ruggles, *Prince of Players*

14.3 Italics

14.3

Ital **Underline the word or expressions marked to correspond to the conventions for using italic type.**

Ital

Words are set off or emphasized in most published works by printing them in slanting type called *italics*. In handwritten or typed papers, such words are underlined:

> The article first appeared in <u>Harper's Magazine</u> and was reprinted in <u>The Reader's Digest.</u>

Italics for Titles

The names of newspapers and magazines and the titles of books, plays, films, and other complete works published separately are conventionally italicized (or underlined):

Newsweek	*The Chicago Tribune* (or: the
The Great Gatsby	Chicago *Tribune*)
the novel *Huckleberry Finn*	*Hamlet*, Act III
Webster's Eighth New Collegiate	the movie *Ben Hur*
Dictionary	Dante's *Divine Comedy*

Titles of articles, short stories, poems, and other short pieces of writing that are part of a larger work are usually enclosed in quotation marks:

> "The Easy Chair" was a regular feature in *Harper's Magazine.*

See 14.1, page 167, Quotation Marks Around Titles, and 30, The Research Paper.

Italics for Words and Phrases Used as Examples

Words used as words or as examples rather than as parts of a sentence should be italicized or set off by quotation marks. (See also 14.1, Quotation Marks to Set Off Words.)

> Even on a sophisticated level there is some variation in word usage. For instance, what in other parts of the country is called a *sidewalk* was and may still be called in my native section of Maryland a *pavement,* and what is elsewhere called a *pavement* was in our usage the *street* if in town and the *road* if in the country. — Thomas Pyles, *Words and Ways of American English*

Italics for Foreign Words

Words from foreign languages that have not been absorbed into English should be italicized, not set off by quotation marks:

> In Antiquity every tree, every spring, every stream, every hill had its own *genius loci,* its guardian spirit. — Lynn White, Jr., "The Historical Roots of Our Ecological Crisis"

Sometime soon after he arrives in Hawaii, a sweet lassitude creeps over the *malihini* (newcomer). — *Time* magazine

Foreign expressions that would ordinarily be underlined for italics include terms like *coup d'état, Weltschmerz, deus ex machina, mañana.* In most books and formal writing, the accents and other marks are used.

Scientific names for plants, insects, and so forth are also italicized:

> The mistletoe *(Phoradendron flavescens)* is the state flower of Oklahoma.

Words from other languages that are now widely used in general English are not considered foreign terms and so are not underlined or otherwise set off:

bourgeois	debut	laissez-faire	sputnik
chalet	debutante	prima donna	status quo
chic	fiancee	slalom	vice versa

Although dictionaries usually designate words that are now anglicized (have become part of the English language) and those that are not, their usage tends to be conservative. If you are certain that an expression marked "foreign" is familiar to your readers, you need not underline it.

Abbreviations of the less common Latin words and phrases used mainly in reference works are sometimes italicized, but Latin abbreviations in general use are not:

> e.g.   et al.   etc.   ibid.   i.e.   vs.   viz.

Italics for Emphasis

Italics are used in printed material to indicate an emphatic word or stressed statement:

Since we cannot have our fill of existence by going on and on, we want to have *as much life as possible* in our short span. — Susanne K. Langer, "Man and Animal: The City and the Hive"

Italics should be used sparingly for emphasis. When used excessively or with words that do not deserve stress, this device may strike a reader as affected.

• *Exercises*

1. Write sentences following the directions below:

   a. a sentence in which you quote two lines of a poem.
   b. a sentence in which you use quotation marks to set off a single word.
   c. a sentence in which you quote something you have read with ellipses to indicate that you have omitted something.
   d. a sentence that includes a word or phrase italicized for emphasis.

2. All the quotation marks and indentions have been removed from the following passage from a short story. Rewrite the passage, using quotation marks and indentions to show dialog and changes in speaker.

   They do say, Mr. Adams said to Old Man Warner, who stood next to him, that over in the north village they're talking of giving up the lottery. Old Man Warner snorted. Pack of crazy fools, he said. Listening to the young folks, nothing's good enough for *them*. Next thing you know, they'll be wanting to go back to living in caves, nobody work any more, live *that* way for a while. Used to be a saying about Lottery in June, corn be heavy soon. First thing you know, we'd all be eating stewed chickweed and acorns. There's *always* been a lottery, he added petulantly. Bad enough to see young Joe Summers up there joking with everybody. Some places already quit lotteries, Mrs. Adams said. Nothing but trouble in *that,* Old Man Warner said stoutly. Pack of young fools.
   — Adapted from Shirley Jackson, "The Lottery"

3. Write passages as suggested below:

   a. a sentence in which you quote the opening line of a popular song or a poem.
   b. a short paragraph in which you quote the opening paragraph of an editorial from a local paper.
   c. a short passage in which you quote an entire stanza of a popular song or a poem.
   d. a single sentence in which you mention the name of a current magazine and the names of two articles it contains.
   e. a sentence in which you quote a question.

4. All of the quotation marks have been omitted from the following paragraph in a recent article. Rewrite the passage, using quotation marks where appropriate.

14.3

Ital

Sneer words are those adjectives that put some distance between the speaker and the subject by saying, I'm using this next word under protest. Examples of sneer words are self-proclaimed, self-styled, would-be, purported, and that Soviet favorite, so-called. — William Safire, "Sneer Words," *The New York Times Magazine,* January 13, 1980

5. Rewrite the passage above, omitting *by saying, I'm using this next word under protest.*

15 Capital Letters, Hyphens, and Apostrophes

Capital letters, hyphens, and apostrophes are convenient signals that writers are generally expected to use. These signals are not, however, just habits: writing in which capitals are improperly used may seem sloppy or affected to readers; words incorrectly hyphenated may be difficult to read, and can cause faulty modification; misuse of apostrophes often makes the writer seem careless.

15.1

15.1 Capital Letters

Cap

Cap Capitalize the word marked; be consistent in use of capital letters.

lc Write the word marked with a lowercase (small) letter.

Most uses of capital letters are standard conventions; writing in which capitals are used inconsistently or unconventionally may focus attention on the wrong words and interrupt the natural flow of thought.

The following sections describe the most frequent uses of capital letters. A complete listing of all forms is obviously impossible. Consult a recent dictionary or style manual if you are in doubt whether to capitalize a particular word.

Capitals to Mark Units of Expression

Capital letters are used to draw the reader's attention to the beginning of a statement or to individual words in titles.

First Word of a Sentence. Capitalize the first word of every sentence or expression punctuated with an end stop (period, question mark, or exclamation mark):

Has the change helped? Not much. The reason is obvious.

First Word of a Line of Poetry. In traditional verse style, the first word of each line is capitalized:

Full many a gem of purest ray serene,
The dark unfathomed waves of ocean bear;

175

> Full many a flower is born to blush unseen,
> And waste its sweetness on the desert air.
> —Thomas Gray, "Elegy Written in a Country Churchyard"

First Word of a Quotation.   The first word of a direct quotation that is in itself a complete sentence is capitalized:

> He said, "The future of mankind cannot be left to chance."
> "The crisis is here," she said. "We must act now."

But no capital is used when the quotation is fragmentary or built into the structure of the sentence, or when the second part of a quoted sentence is interrupted by an expression such as *he said:*

> According to the advertisement, it was the "most spectacular picture of the year."
> "The argument is based," he said, "upon a false premise."

In Parentheses.   A complete sentence enclosed in parentheses is always capitalized when it stands alone, but when enclosed *within* another sentence, it usually is not:

> The broadcast, sponsored by a local bank, was frequently interrupted by lengthy commercials. (Apparently the sponsor doesn't believe that silence is golden.)
> Fitzhugh was the member of a prominent family (his mother was the granddaughter of Sir Thomas Wyatt) and was received in the highest circles.

After a Colon.   A complete sentence standing after a colon is not usually capitalized when the connection with the preceding clause is close:

> Indeed, if Galileo had not been so expert an amateur theologian he would have got into far less trouble: the professionals resented his intrusion.—Lynn White, Jr., "The Historical Roots of Our Ecological Crisis."

The sentence after the colon is often capitalized when it is distinctly separate or when the writer wants to give it emphasis:

> Quite a few teachers in the departments of science would tell the student: We scientists deliver the laws of nature to the philosopher, who has to interpret them.—Philipp Frank, *Relativity: A Richer Truth*

In Titles of Written Material.   The first word, the last word, all important words (nouns, pronouns, verbs, adjectives, and adverbs), and all prepositions of more than five letters are capitalized in the titles of books, magazine articles, themes, and so forth:

"The Battle Hymn of the Republic"   *Of Mice and Men*
Pottery Through the Ages   *Tender Is the Night*

I and *O*.   The pronoun *I* and the exclamation *O* are always capitalized to prevent reading them as parts of other words:

> Give a man a girl he can love.
> As **I, O** my love, love thee. . . . —James Thomson, "Gifts"

The exclamation *oh* is not capitalized unless it stands first in a sentence.

Capitals for Proper Nouns and Their Derivatives

The names of specific people, places, and things, and the words derived from them are conventionally capitalized (Karl Marx — Marxism; Africa — African sculpture; Lent — Lenten menu). Examples of the most frequent types of proper nouns are given in the following sections.

15.1

Cap

In a few cases, words originally derived from proper nouns have dropped the capital in the course of frequent use (pasteurized milk, a jersey blouse, french fries). Usage differs about the capitalization of others (diesel, levis). Up-to-date dictionaries provide a guide in such matters, as do the practices of current publications.

Names and Titles of People.   A person's name or nickname is capitalized:

Franklin Delano Roosevelt	Eudora Welty	Hank Aaron
Shirley Chisholm	Mindy	Dizzy Gillespie

A title should be capitalized when it is used as part of a person's name, but not when it is used as a descriptive term. A few titles of high rank are usually capitalized whether or not the officeholder is named: the President (of the United States), the Pope, the Queen of England, the Chief Justice of the Supreme Court. Titles referring to a position or an office rather than to the specific person holding it are not capitalized:

Capitals	No capitals
Professor Townsend	Francis Townsend is a professor.
Sergeant David Moore	A sergeant maintains discipline.
Judge R. A. Snow	She was elected judge.
The President [of the U.S.] vetoed the bill.	The president of the company resigned.
The Queen addressed the opening session of Parliament.	England has had several queens.

Names of family relationships are usually capitalized when used with a person's name or when used as proper nouns standing for the name. They are not capitalized when used as common nouns or when preceded by a possessive:

Capitals	No capitals
Grandma Moses	She is a grandmother.
Aunt Sarah	My aunt's name is Sarah.
I showed Mother the card.	I showed my mother the card.
Whatever Father said, we did.	His father was demanding.

Names of Groups.   Names referring to racial, national, linguistic, political, or religious groups are capitalized:

Negro	Swede	Democrat	Catholic
English	Italian	Republican	Jew
French	Finn	Communist	Moslem

Names of social and economic groups are not capitalized (except occasionally for stylistic emphasis):

the middle class	the intelligentsia	the bourgeoisie

Names of Organizations.   Names and abbreviations of business associations, clubs, fraternities, and other voluntary organizations are capitalized:

National Association of Manufac- turers (NAM)	Boy Scouts
	League of Women Voters
Rotary International	United Auto Workers (UAW)
National Organization for Woman (NOW)	Phi Beta Kappa

The words *freshman, sophomore, junior, senior* are capitalized only when they refer to organized groups and their functions (the Freshman Class, the Junior Prom), not when they refer to an academic status (She is a sophomore; The seniors must write a thesis).

Names of Places.   Words that designate specific geographical divisions or particular places and areas are capitalized:

Asia	Ghana	Hyde Park
European	Texan	the Bowery
Latin America	Boston	Third Avenue

When the names of directions are used to identify geographic areas, they are generally capitalized. When they merely indicate direction, they are not:

Capitals	No capitals
the old West	west of Suez
a Southerner	a southern exposure
the Far East	eastern Tennessee

Names of Institutions.   The names of specific public and private institutions and their divisions and departments are capitalized. Names that apply to a whole class of institutions are not:

Capitals	No capitals
Chicago Public Library	a public library
U.S. Public Health Service	public health problems
Rock Falls High School	our high school

Specific high-school or college academic courses are capitalized; general subjects are not, except for language courses:

Capitals	No capitals
Modern French Literature	literature
Advanced Narrative Writing	composition
Chemistry 101	chemistry
Abnormal Psychology 410	psychology

15.1

Cap

Names of Specific Objects.   Names of specific objects, such as ships, planes, structures, famous documents and artifacts, and brand-name products are capitalized:

the S.S. *Independence*	the Golden Gate Bridge
the Super Chief	the Lincoln Memorial
a Gremlin	Magna Charta

Names of Units in Time.   Capitalize words designating specific periods, events, months, days, and holidays:

the Stone Age	the Norman Conquest	Thursday
the Renaissance	the Battle of Waterloo	Labor Day
the Civil War	January	

Names of seasons are not generally capitalized:

winter   summer   spring   fall   autumn

Sacred Names.   References to deities and to sacred texts are capitalized. Pronouns referring to the Christian Trinity are also usually capitalized:

God	Holy Ghost	Talmud
the Savior	Bible	Koran
Virgin Mary	New Testament	Buddha

Abstractions.   Abstractions like ideas, qualities, or conditions may be capitalized, especially in formal and sentimental writing, to show that they are being discussed in some ideal or absolute state. Sometimes abstractions are personified, particularly in poetry:

Throughout recorded history, Man has responded to the challenge of Nature.

The pursuit of the Good Life is a persistent human preoccupation.

In general writing, capitalized abstractions are seldom appropriate. College students should confine them to formal papers of critical analysis or philosophical theory and follow the practices found in readings assigned in the course for which the papers are written.

Distinguishing Proper and Common Forms.   Some words can be spelled either with or without capitals. These forms must be distinguished because they often have different meanings:

Capitals	No capitals
a Democrat (a member of the Democratic Party)	a democrat (one who believes in democracy)
a Republican principle (of the Republican Party)	a republican principle (of a republic)
Orthodox beliefs (of the Greek Orthodox Church)	orthodox beliefs (conventional)
Catholic sympathies (of or with the Catholic Church)	catholic sympathies (broad; universal)
Romantic poetry (of the Romantic Period)	romantic poetry (concerning romance or love)

• *Exercise*

In the sentences below, from *Time* magazine (April 11, 1977), all capital letters have been replaced by lower case letters. Supply capitals and any other necessary marks wherever you think they are appropriate.

1. added senate majority leader robert byrd: "this is no time to show weakness."

2. the town of belmonte, perched atop a rocky hilltop in northern portugal, is dominated by a giant stone cross, a ruined castle and the roman catholic church of the holy family.

3. french choreographer maurice bejart had a devil of a time casting his ballet rendition of goethe's faust.

4. life's little dilemmas department: the hilarious installment of the odd couple that you've always wanted to see is being rerun tonight on channel 11 at precisely the same time that channel 5 is featuring the latest episode of mary hartman, mary hartman.

15.2   Hyphens

Hyph   **Insert or remove hyphen between the words marked to conform to current usage.**

Hyphens are used to connect two or more words used as a single expression *(heavy-hearted, will-o'-the-wisp)* and to keep parts of other words distinct *(anti-inflation)*.

Hyphens are needed in some instances to prevent misreading *(un-ionized)* or to differentiate between the same words used in different ways (a *drive in* the evening, a *drive-in* theater). But generally they are used as a matter of convention *(brother-in-law, hocus-pocus)*.

In printed matter the use of hyphens varies considerably: newspapers and general English use relatively few hyphens; formal English uses more. The important thing to look for in proofreading is consistency. If an expression is hyphenated the first time it occurs, it should be hyphenated throughout.

This section lists the most common uses of hyphens. See also 22.2, Spelling and Word Division.

15.2

Hyph)

Hyphens in Compound Words

A hyphen is used between two or more words considered as a single unit in certain expressions, as discussed below.

Names for Family Relationships. Some compound names for family relationships are hyphenated; others are not:

> HYPHENATED: father-in-law, great-grandfather, sister-in-law
> ONE WORD: stepson, stepmother, grandfather
> TWO WORDS: half brother, second cousin

Compound Numbers. A hyphen is used in numbers from twenty-one to ninety-nine. Fractions are hyphenated except when the fraction already contains a hyphenated number:

> thirty-three   four-fifths of a box
> one hundred twenty-eight   one-half inch
> twenty-first birthday   one thirty-second of an inch

Compounds with *Self*. Most group words beginning with *self* are written with hyphens *(self-contained, self-pity, self-support, self-government);* some may be written with a hyphen or without *(self support, self government)*. A very few words beginning with self are written as one word: *selfsame, selfless, selfhood*. Consult a recent dictionary to find out which form is preferred.

Standard Compound Nouns. A number of compound nouns are regularly written with a hyphen: *bull's-eye, good-for-nothing, jack-o'-lantern, secretary-treasurer*. Other similar compounds are written as one word *(beeswax, newsprint, policyholder)* or as two words *(intelligence test, labor union, shipping point, water cooler)*.

Since practice is likely to vary with many of these forms, you often have the option of using or not using a hyphen. Where no confusion of terms is apt to arise, most writers would omit the hyphen. If you are in doubt whether a hyphen is necessary, consult a good recent dictionary.

Hyphens in Group Modifiers

When two or more words act as a closely linked modifier immediately before another word, they are often hyphenated to suggest the close relationship:

> **gray-green** eyes   a **nineteenth-century** poet
> a **well-kept** lawn   an **all-out** effort

A hyphen should always be used to prevent a possible misreading:

> a **slow-motion** picture   a **pitch-dark** room
> a **navy-blue** uniform   some **reclaimed-rubber** plants

When the first word of a group modifier is an adverb ending in *-ly*, no hyphen is used after it:

> richly deserved praise   openly antagonistic attitude

Compound modifiers formed with present or past participles are usually hyphenated when they precede a noun:

> a **good-looking** man   a **well-planned** attack

Such phrases are not usually hyphenated in other positions:

> Her father was good looking.   The attack was well planned.

Long phrases or clauses used as modifiers are hyphenated:

> . . . and he offers dramatic recitals about guerrillas (whom he didn't meet) and possible ambushes (which he didn't find), all of it pretty much in the **gosh-we-could-even-hear-the-guns-in-the-distance** school of war reporting. — G. Barrett, "Korean Scenario"

This type of construction is most likely to be found in informal writing. It is not effective if overused.

Hyphens with Prefixes

Hyphens are used between certain prefixes and the root word either as a matter of convention or to prevent ambiguity. Dictionaries list most of these forms.

1. Between a prefix and a proper name:

> pre-Renaissance   post-Civil War
> anti-Communist   un-American
> ex-President Truman   pro-German

2. Between some prefixes that end with a vowel and a root word beginning with a vowel, especially if the root word begins with the same vowel:

   re-elected   semi-independment   re-ink

When the parts have become merged in general use, no hyphen is necessary, though it is often still found:

   cooperation   coordinate   preexistent

3. To prevent possible confusion with a similar term or when the prefix is stressed:

   to **re-cover** a sofa (to *recover* from an illness)
   a **run-in** with the police (a *run in* her stocking)
   to **re-sort** buttons (a seaside *resort*)

15.2

Suspension Hyphens

The suspension hyphen is often used to carry the modifying expression from one word over to the next:

   Two-word forms first acquire the hyphen, later are printed as one word, and not infrequently the transition is from the **two-** to the **one-word** form, bypassing the hyphen stage. — *GPO Style Manual*

Unnecessary Hyphens

Don't hyphenate a term that is currently written as a single word or as two words. Even if your dictionary lists as alternatives such old-fashioned forms as *to-night* and *post-man,* use the first or preferred form. Here is a brief list of words that students are sometimes tempted to hyphenate:

One word	Separate words
anybody (pronoun)	all right
basketball, baseball, football	class president
bookkeeping	grade curve
footnotes	high school
himself, myself, ourselves	"How do you do?"
nevertheless	motion picture
outdoor	no one
outwit	press agent
overlooked	report card
percent (or per cent)	school days
roundabout	second in command
semicolon	six o'clock
taxpayer	tax rate
today, tomorrow	water pressure
throughout	
uphold	
whatever	

• *Exercise*

Indicate which of the following expressions should be written as separate words, which should be one word, and which should be hyphenated. The words in parentheses indicate the sense in which the expression is intended.

a lot (of work to do)	non communist
baseball	not with standing (a conjunction)
dark horse	over look (to slight or neglect)
every one (is present)	out and out (outright)
flame thrower	Ping Pong
gilt edged	re written
give and take	school board
hydro therapy	self satisfied
in so far as	semi colon
jet black	some body (is missing)
left overs (food)	space craft
man hunt	ten word (telegram)
man of war (a ship)	three quarters (of an inch)
may be (perhaps)	un American
never the less	where abouts (at what place)

15.3 Apostrophes

 Insert an apostrophe where it belongs in the word marked, or take out the unnecessary apostrophe.

An apostrophe (') is used in contractions, to mark the plural form of some expressions, and to indicate the possessive case of nouns. Although it is a minor mark that seldom affects the reader's interpretation of a statement, its omission or misuse is noticeable.

Apostrophes in Contractions

Contractions are an attempt to represent the rhythms of speech. They are appropriate in dialog, informal writing, and much general writing. They are used frequently in this book; we believe that they are appropriate in almost any kind of writing. You should remember, however, that many teachers, editors, and readers think that contractions are out of place in formal and academic writing.

When a contraction is appropriate in writing, an apostrophe is used to indicate the omission of one or more letters:

can't	I'll	it's (it is)	we're
don't	I'm	o'clock	won't

Notice that *till* (as in "from morning till midnight") is *not* a shortened form of *until* and no apostrophe is used with it.

An apostrophe is used with dates from which the first figures are omitted (the class of '59, the spirit of '76). In formal writing, dates should usually be written in full.

Apostrophes with Possessive Case Forms

An apostrophe is used with the singular and plural forms of nouns and indefinite pronouns to mark the genitive case:

John's car	children's games
New York's parks	your parents' permission
a stone's throw	anybody's guess

An apostrophe is *not* used with the possessive forms of the personal pronouns *his, hers, its, ours, yours, theirs:*

15.3

   the city and **its** suburbs   these seats are **ours**

See 6.2, Forms of the Possessive, and 7.3, Possessive Pronouns.

Apostrophes for Plurals of Letters and Figures

An apostrophe is generally used before an *s* to form the plurals of figures, letters of the alphabet; and words considered as words:

   the early 1900's [*or* 1900s]
   several size 16's [*or* 16s]
   a .44 pistol and two .22's [*or* .22s]
   There are four *s*'s four *i*'s, and two *p*'s in *Mississippi.*

Apostrophes for Letters Dropped in Representing Speech

An apostrophe is commonly used to indicate the omission of sounds in representing speech:

   "But J. C. he wouldn't let me be until I brought him over. Just kept on saying', Mamie I'm not a-goin' to move until I see where I'm goin'." — Ann Petry, *The Narrows*

It is not necessary in representing conversation to indicate all such omissions, and frequent apostrophes make for difficult reading.

• *Exercise*

In the two paragraphs below, capital letters, apostrophes, and hyphens have been omitted. Insert them where you think they are appropriate.

1. i arrived at eau clair in late april with my wife, who had joined me at the end of spring training. we rented a single room with a tiny kitchenette on the second floor of an old two family house. it disturbed me that, unlike most baseball wives, carol knew nothing

about the game to which i had devoted my life. she took her cues solely from my enthusiasms and despairs. whenever i pitched decently—a rarity—i had to tell her so, and then she would smile and say, "thats nice, dear." when i was knocked out of the box in the first inning and she saw my dejection, she commiserated with me: "well, its certainly not your fault. its hard to do good when you only play a little bit. . . . why doesnt your manager let you play as much as the other pitchers?"—Pat Jordan, *A False Spring*

2. "but sir, i dont think i really deserve it, it was mostly bull, really." this disclaimer from a student whose examination we have awarded a straight "a" is wondrously depressing. alfred north whitehead invented its only possible rejoinder: "yes sir, what you wrote is nonsense, utter nonsense. but ah! sir! its the right *kind* of nonsense."—William G. Perry, Jr., *Examining in Harvard College*

16 Abbreviations and Numbers

Abbreviations and numbers are useful and appropriate in technical, business, and legal documents, as well as in some specialized instances such as reference works and scholarly footnotes. In most general writing, however, words and figures are usually written out. This chapter discusses the conventions followed in using abbreviations and numbers in most general writing.

16.1 Abbreviations

  Write in full the abbreviation marked or, if an abbreviation is appropriate, change it to the correct form.

Dictionaries list most current abbreviations, either as regular entries or in a separate section, but they don't indicate when these forms should be used. The following sections discuss the kinds of abbreviations that are appropriate in formal and general writing as well as some forms that should not be used. If you are in doubt whether a particular abbreviation is appropriate, you will usually do better to avoid it.

Abbreviations for Titles, Degrees, and Given Names

The courtesy titles *Dr., Mr., Mrs.,* and *Mssrs.* are always abbreviated when used with proper names, as are *Jr.* and *Sr.: Mrs.* Lester H. Holt, *Mr.* Claude C. Sampson, *Jr.* The convenient *Ms.,* used as a courtesy title equivalent to *Mr.* in addressing a woman without regard for her marital status, must remain an abbreviation, since it was devised as an abbreviation and does not stand for any word. Academic degrees are also generally abbreviated: *M.A., Ph.D., LL.D., M.D., D.D.S.* If a degree of honorary title is added after a name, it is the only title used:

> William Carey, **M.D.,** *or* **Dr.** William Carey [not *Dr.* William Carey, *M.D.*]
>
> James T. Holloway, **Esq.,** *or* **Mr.** James T. Holloway [not *Mr.* James T. Holloway, *Esq.*]

In formal writing, titles like *Reverend, Professor, President, Sena-*

tor, Admiral are usually written out in full. In most other styles they may be abbreviated *if* the first name or initials of the person are used:

Standard forms	Forms to avoid
The Reverend James T. Shaw	The Rev. Shaw
The Reverend Mr. Shaw	Rev. Shaw
Rev. J. T. Shaw	The Reverend delivered a sermon.
Professor John Moore	Prof. Moore
Professor Moore	John Moore is an English Prof.
Prof. John R. Moore	
General Westmoreland	Gen. Westmoreland
Gen. William Westmoreland	The Gen. was given a new command.

Spell out given names (sometimes called Christian names) or use initials. Avoid such abbreviations as *Geo., Thos., Chas., Wm.:*

> George Harriman *or* G. F. Harriman [not *Geo.* F. Harriman]

Saint is almost always abbreviated when it is used with a name:

> **St.** Francis, **Ste.** Catherine, **SS.** Peter and Paul, Sault **Ste.** Marie

Abbreviations for Agencies and Organizations

If a government agency or other organization is known primarily by its initials (or by some other shortened name), the writer should generally use the familiar abbreviation rather than the full name:

FBI	TVA	AFL-CIO	NBC Network
CIA	GOP	SPCA	MGM Studios
FHA	ROTC	4-H Club	*GPO Style Manual*

Abbreviations that are pronounced as words (called *acronyms*) have become very common: UNESCO, CARE, VISTA, NATO, SEATO, Amvets.

See page 191 for discussions of the use of capitals and periods in abbreviations.

Abbreviations for Place Names and Dates

The names of countries, states, months, and days are usually written out except in journalistic writing and reference works:

United States	Ghent, Belgium	Wednesday, November 3
South America	Portland, Oregon	Christmas [not *Xmas*]

Words like *Street, Avenue,* and *Boulevard* should be written out in general writing, not abbreviated as they might be in addressing a letter.

A few unusually long place names are customarily abbreviated even in rather formal writing: the *USSR;* Barbados, *B.W.I.* (for British West Indies); Washington, *D.C.*

Abbreviations for Units of Measurement

In ordinary writing, most expressions for time, weight, and size are customarily written out:

in a minute	**rather than**	in a min.
hour		hr.
several pounds		several lbs.
four grams		4 gr.
weight		wt.
a half inch		½ in, or ½′
sixty centimeters		60 cm.

These units are abbreviated in directions, recipes, references, and technical writing when they are used with figures: ¼ lb. butter, 16 ft. 3 in. In technical writing, the period is usually omitted after an abbreviation unless the abbreviation spells a word:

3 ft *but* 3 in.

Abbreviations for Scientific and Technical Terms

Some scientific words, trade names, and other expressions are referred to by their abbreviations when they are familiar to readers and would be needlessly long if written out:

DDT (in place of **d**ichloro-**d**iphenyl-**t**richloro-ethane)
ACTH (in place of **a**dreno**c**orticotropic **h**ormone)
Rh factor (**Rh**esus factor)
DNA (**d**eoxyribo**n**ucleic **a**cid)
FM radio (**f**requency **m**odulation radio)

If an abbreviation is to be used repeatedly and may not be familiar to every reader, explain it the first time it is introduced:

The International Phonetic Alphabet, commonly known as the IPA, provides a more precise method of recording speech than does our conventional alphabet.

Measurements expressed in technical terms are abbreviated when they are used with figures:

Tests show the car's highest speeds to be 34 **mph** [miles per hour] in low gear, 58.7 **mph** in second, and 93.5 **mph** in third.

The turntable can be adjusted to play records at either 78, 45, or 33⅓ **rpm** [revolutions per minute].

Expressions of this kind are written with either three periods or

16.1

ab

none (m.p.h. or mph). They are not abbreviated when used without figures:

> The speed of a ship is usually given in knots rather than in **miles per hour.**

Other Standard Abbreviations

There are a few standard abbreviations that are used in all kinds of writing:

a.m., p.m.   The expressions a.m. (*ante meridiem,* "before noon") and p.m. (*post meridiem,* "after noon") are always abreviated: 6:00 a.m., 12:24 p.m. Current usage prefers small letters for these abbreviations, but they may be capitalized.

The abbreviations a.m. and p.m. are used only in referring to a specific time:

> STANDARD: He had an appointment at 3:00 p.m.
> NOT: He had an appointment in the p.m.

B.C., A.D.   These expressions are used to distinguish dates in history in reference to the birth of Christ; they are always abbreviated. **B.C.** means "before Christ," and follows the date; A.D. stands for *anno Domini,* "in the year of our Lord," and *precedes* the date.

> 836 B.C.   A.D. 76   A.D. 1984

Commonly Used Latin Expressions.   English has absorbed a number of Latin expressions that are conventionally abbreviated. The following are in common use and should not be italicized:

> cf.   *confer* — compare (with another source)
> e.g.   *exempli gratia* — for example
> etc.   *et cetera* — and so forth (never *and etc.*)
> i.e.   *id est* — that is

Many writers prefer the English equivalents for these and similar expressions. In college writing, the overworked catchall *etc.* should generally be avoided. Substitute *and so forth (and so on, and the like)* or rephrase the list, introducing it with *such as* or a similar qualifier. See also 30.8, pages 452–453, Abbreviations in Endnotes.

The Ampersand.   In college writing the ampersand (&) should not be used as a substitute for *and* unless it appears in an expression or title that you are copying: *U.S. News & World Report,* Doubleday & Company, Inc.

Capitals with Abbreviations

Abbreviations are capitalized when the words they stand for are capitalized or when the abbreviation represents a title:

> DAR (Daughters of the American Revolution)
> USAF (United States Air Force)
> Lt. Col. Edward Brown
> St. Matthew, St. Thomas Aquinas
> 100 degrees F. (Fahrenheit)

When an abbreviation stands for words that would not be capitalized if they were written out, no capitals are needed unless the abbreviation begins a sentence.

Periods with Abbreviations

16.2

Num

A period should be put after the abbreviation of a single word and usually between the letters of abbreviations for longer terms:

p.	doz.	N.Y.	c.o.d.
ch.	Lt.	B.A.	A.T.&T.
Nov.	hp.	e.g.	P.S.

Usage is divided about the punctuation of abbreviated names made of two or more letters written as a unit. Some publications prefer periods *(P.T.A., B.B.C.)*, but a growing number are using the solid form *(PTA, BBC)*, especially when the abbreviation is generally used instead of the full name. Some dictionaries list optional forms. It doesn't make much difference which form you use as long as you are consistent throughout your paper.

When an abbreviation falls at the end of a sentence, only one period is used: He owned a hundred shares of A.T.&T.

16.2 Numbers

Num **Follow conventional usage for words or figures for numbers; be consistent in the treatment of numbers.**

There are few firm rules about using figures or words for numbers occurring in most writing. In general, books and magazines write out all numbers through one hundred and also larger numbers that can be written in two words *(six thousand, three million)*. This style is usually appropriate for college papers and for most other kinds of general and formal writing. Newspapers and informal writing generally use figures for all numbers over ten, and some scientific and technical publications use figures exclusively.

GENERAL AND FORMAL: four, ten, fifteen, ninety-four, 114, 22,500, thirty thousand, five million [but usage varies]

INFORMAL: four, ten, 15, 94, 114, 22,500, 30,000, 5,000,000 (or 5 million)

There are a few special situations (described in the section following) in which figures are always customary. In other cases, use the form that is appropriate not only for your audience but for your material. In general, write out all simple one-digit and two-digit numbers and round numbers that can easily be read; use figures for numbers that cannot be written in two words and for series of numbers that are to be compared.

WORDS APPROPRIATE: He shot three quail and one rabbit.

FIGURES APPROPRIATE: The next ship unloaded 3500 pounds of king salmon, 947 pounds of chinook salmon, and 200 pounds of crab.

WORDS APPROPRIATE: Five votes were cast for the class president's proposal, twenty-one against it.

FIGURES APPROPRIATE: In Colorado 10,547 farmers voted for controls; in Indiana, 17,003; in Minnesota, 10,750. The nationwide total was 87.2 percent in favor.

WORDS APPROPRIATE: If I had ten dollars for every time I've broken one of my resolutions, I would have at least a thousand dollars by now.

FIGURES APPROPRIATE: Dresses in the $25–$35 range were selling well, those from $36–$50 fairly well, and those over $50 hardly at all.

Whichever form you use, be consistent. Don't change needlessly from words to figures or from figures to words in the same piece of writing:

INCONSISTENT: When I was 15, I thought anyone over thirty-five was old.

CONSISTENT: When I was fifteen, I thought anyone over thirty-five was old.

Conventional Uses of Figures

Figures are customarily used in all the following situations:

1. Dates are always written in figures except in formal social correspondence, such as wedding invitations. The forms *1st, 2nd, 3rd,* and so on are sometimes used in dates, but only when the year is omitted:

    October 10, 1976   Oct. 10, 1976   October 10   October 10th

2. Hours are written in figures before a.m. or p.m.; they are spelled out before *o'clock:*

7 a.m.	1800 hours (military usage)	twelve noon
11:35 p.m.	one o'clock	twelve midnight

3. Mathematical and technical numbers, including percentages:

3.14159	longitude 74°02′E.
99.8 percent, 99.8%	.410 gauge shotgun

Except in dates and street numbers, a comma is used to separate thousands, millions, etc., although it may be omitted in four-digit figures:

     1,365 (or 1365) pounds   8,393,624   17,016

4. Page numbers and similar references:

pp. 183–86	page 12
chapter iv	Genesis 39:12
Ch. 19	Act III, scene iv, line 28 (III, iv, 28)

5. Sums of money, except sums in round numbers or, in formal style, sums that can be written in two or three words:

Figures	**Words**
a bargain at $4.98	two thousand a year
The British pound was once	a dollar a pound
worth $4.85.	

6. Street numbers (with no commas between thousands):

     2027 Fairview North   Apartment 3C, 1788 Grand North

7. Statistics and series of more than two numbers, especially when the numbers are to be compared:

     The survey showed that the class contained 24 Democrats, 18 Republicans, and 3 Socialists.

Plurals of Figures. The plural of a figure is written either with *'s* or *s:*

     Six nines: six **9's**, six **9s**   By tens: by **10's**, by **10s**

Numbers at the Beginning of Sentences. These numbers are written out unless they are dates:

     Two to 3% of loading and up to 10% is common and 20 to 30% in specially surfaced papers. . . .—"Paper Manufacture," *Encyclopaedia Britannica*

     1960 was a year of devastating drought in China.

Arabic and Roman Numerals

Arabic numerals (1, 2, 17, 96) are used in almost all cases where numbers are expressed in figures. Roman numerals, either lowercase or capitals (i, ii, cxlvi; I, II, CXLVI), are occasionally used to number outlines, chapters, acts of a play, or formal inscriptions. They are almost always used to number the front matter of a book; a new pagination in Arabic numerals begins with the body of the book.

In Roman numerals a small number preceding a larger is to be subtracted from the larger (ix = 9, xc = 90). The following table shows the common Roman numerals (lowercase):

1	i	10	x	50	l	200	cc
2	ii	11	xi	60	lx	400	cd
3	iii	15	xv	70	lxx	500	d
4	iv	19	xix	80	lxxx	600	dc
5	v	20	xx	90	xc	900	cm
6	vi	21	xxi	99	xcix	1000	m
7	vii	30	xxx	100	c	1500	md
8	viii	40	xl	110	cx	1066	mlxvi
9	ix	49	xlix	199	cxcix	1979	mcmlxxix

Cardinal and Ordinal Numbers

Figures indicating number only are *cardinal numbers:* 1, 2, 3, 72, 135. The numbers indicating order *(first, second, seventeenth)* are *ordinal numbers.* Except in routine enumeration, ordinals should be spelled out rather than abbreviated to *1st, 2nd, 17th.*

Since the ordinals can be either adjectives or adverbs, the forms ending in *-ly (firstly)* are unnecessary and are now rarely used.

• *Exercise*

Read the following sentences carefully, keeping in mind the principles stated in the preceding section. Rewrite faulty sentences, making whatever changes are necessary. Since there are cases where there's a choice in usage, remember that one of the principles of using numbers and abbreviations is to be consistent.

1. When we arrived at the theater on 8th St., we found that the evening's performance would start an hr. late.

2. The University recently added 2 new members to its faculty—Jos. Blumenthal, MA, and Mary Persons, Doctor of Philosophy.

3. Six members of the OAS conferred recently with U.N. Representative Geo. H. Bush at his office in N.Y.

4. Fifty-five to 60% of U. of C. students approved the 2 o'clock curfew; about 30% were violently opposed.

5. His monument to St. Francis, a remarkable piece of sculpture, weighed over 2500 lbs. and rivaled his monument to Saint Peter.

6. P. 237 of the manual lists the home addresses of U.S. Senators & p. 298 lists their D.C. addresses.

7. On Dec. 23 CBS will dramatize the most celebrated Xmas story of recent times — "The Christmas Carol" by Chas. Dickens.

8. Dr. Roscoe Caries, D.D.S., reported that in an experiment involving two thousand and forty-four children, tooth decay was not significantly reduced.

9. Lee had 4 sisters (ranging in age from sixteen to 31 yrs.) and a widowed mother.

10. After 10 months the FBI agent finally tracked Groark to Ogden, Miss., where he found him suffering from d.t.'s in the barn of the Rev. John Gantry.

16.2

num

17 Spelling

This recommendation of steadiness and uniformity [in spelling] *does not proceed from an opinion that particular combinations of letters have much influence on human happiness; or that truth may not be successfully taught by modes of spelling fanciful and erroneous. . . . Language is only the instrument of science, and words are but the signs of ideas; I wish, however, that the instrument might be less apt to decay, and that signs might be permanent.* — Samuel Johnson

 Correct the spelling of the word marked.

For college writing, and for much of the other writing that you may do, I have been recommending *edited American English*. One purpose of editing is to make language consistent with itself, so that, for example, if a writer uses the word *theatre* seven times in an essay, it will always be spelled in the same way. Another purpose of editing is, if it does not interfere with some purpose of the writer, to eliminate errors and unconventional usages. One feature of language that often requires careful editing is spelling.

Sometimes people talk about spelling as if it were some monstrous and unnatural act. It isn't that, but it isn't always easy. Some people spell well; others don't. All of us occasionally misspell; some frequently misspell. Accurate spelling doesn't appear to have any direct connection with good writing. But good edited writing is characterized by accurate spelling. Out of regard for yourself and for your reader, you should make certain that whatever you write is as free from error as possible. You want your reader to see the same word that you intended to write, and your reader is entitled to expect that you will follow the conventions of spelling. Misspelled words seldom interfere with meaning, but they may distract your reader from what you are trying to say, or, worse, lead your reader to assume that if you don't care about your spelling you don't care about what you are saying.

17.1 Overcoming Spelling Problems

English spelling would be easier if each sound used in speaking were represented by a single letter or even by a combination of letters. But the way a word is pronounced and the way it is spelled do

196

not always match. The same letter or combination of letters may represent a variety of sounds, as does the *a* in *fare, hat, many, lay, far, war, human,* or the *ou* in *though, bough, enough, through.* And one sound may be represented in a variety of ways: b*ee,* bel*ie*ve, prec*e*de, s*ea,* mach*ine.* As a further complication, a number of English words are written with silent letters: lam*b, p*sychology, *k*nife, r*h*ythm, *w*rote. Others, called *homonyms,* sound alike but are spelled differently: *meat, meet, mete; sight, site, cite; write, right, rite; its, it's; peace, piece.*

Obviously, absolute correctness in spelling is not easy to achieve in English. Most mistakes can be avoided, however, if you are willing to take the time and effort necessary

1. to learn the spelling of difficult words,
2. to use the dictionary when you are in doubt, and
3. to proofread what you have written.

17.1

Sp

Eliminating Careless Mistakes

Carelessness undoubtedly accounts for many of the misspelled words in student papers. It may result from too rapid writing (as in papers written in class) or from failure to proofread the finished copy carefully. Typical examples of careless misspelling are *their* for *there, to* for *too, who's* for *whose, it's* for *its, fourty* for *forty* — basic words that you learned before entering high school. Most people make careless mistakes when writing rapidly, but conscientious writers eliminate them by proofreading.

Accurate proofreading requires careful word-by-word reading. If you have difficulty checking your own writing, try following each line with a pencil point, so that you have to look at every word separately. Some people find it helpful to read their papers aloud, pronouncing each word distinctly. Any method is useful if it makes it easier for you to see the way that the words have actually been put down on paper.

Using a Dictionary

If you are uncertain about the spelling of a word, consult your dictionary. The trial-and-error method of writing a word several ways until it "looks right" *(curiousity? couriousity? curosity?)* is unreliable.

For papers written outside class, it's probably best to check spelling in *revision.* If you stop to look up the spelling of every doubtful word while you are writing a first draft, you may lose the flow of thought or interrupt the sentence movement. Put a check in the margin or over the word as you are writing; then when you are ready to revise, look up each word you have marked.

Learning to Visualize Words

People who do a good deal of reading tend to be better spellers than those who read little, for seeing a word on the printed page tends to fix it in the mind. Sometimes, however, we learn to recognize a word in reading without really noticing how it is spelled. Very few Americans, for example, ever learned to spell the last name of Leonid Brezhnev, the Soviet premier, though they saw it in their newspapers every day for years. Many people have a similar problem with such common English words as *occasion, occurrence,* and *precede.* When you meet a new word—or when you have to look up a familiar word—look at it carefully, noticing each syllable, and try to fix it in your mind for future use.

Writing Practice

If you are willing to take the time, you can often get the spelling of troublesome words straight in your mind by writing them until you spell them right without hesitation. It sounds like a tedious process, but it's probably worth the time if it enables you to become comfortable with words so that you can use them. If you are uncertain about the spelling of *embarrass,* for example, write or type the word ten, twenty, or more times, in its various forms, until the spelling becomes automatic: *embarrass, embarrassed, embarrassment, embarrassing.*

Separate into syllables words that you find difficult to spell (consult your dictionary for the proper divisions). Stress those letters or combinations of letters that trouble you:

em baR Rass	par aL Lel
oC Ca sion al ly	preJ U dice
o MiT Ted	rep E ti tion
op tI mist	sep A rate

It helps to say the word as you write it, either aloud or to yourself. The combination of (1) seeing a word letter by letter, (2) writing it carefully, and (3) pronouncing it will overcome some spelling problems.

Learning New Words

Learn to spell new words correctly as you find them in your college courses. You can't use a new or unfamiliar expression in your writing until you can spell it with confidence. Make a note of the words you will probably have to write in reports or in examinations. Underline key words in textbooks and observe their spelling on the blackboard. Then write them out in syllables, pronouncing them as you do so:

ba cil lus	Gen ghis Khan
bi par tite	me tath e sis
car bon if er ous	pro pri e tar y
de men tia prae cox	u ni cel lu lar

When instructors in various courses complain that their students can't spell, they are usually referring either to very common words or to special words in the essential vocabulary of their subject.

Keeping a Spelling List

You can help yourself in proofreading if you will keep a list of words you have misspelled or that you have trouble spelling. The words should be spelled correctly and should be easy to find so that you can refer to them when proofreading your papers. The purpose of such a list is to prevent the same mistakes from occurring in one paper after another.

17.2

Sp

17.2 Common Spelling Errors

The following list contains one hundred words frequently misspelled in student papers. Each word is divided into syllables so that you can see the parts more clearly.

ac com mo date	de pend ent	in ci den tal ly
ac quaint ed	de scrip tion	in de pend ent
a cross	de vel op	in tel li gent
a gree ment	din ing room	ir re sist i ble
all right (two words)	dis ap pear ance	judg ment [*or* judge ment]
al read y	dis ap point	knowl edge
a nal y sis	dor mi to ry	lei sure
ap pear ance	em bar rass	li brar y
ar ti cle	en vi ron ment	lik a ble [*or* like able]
ath let ics	e quip ment	main te nance
at tend ance	ex ag ger ate	man u fac tur er
be lieve	ex ist ence	mis spelled
ben e fit ed	ex treme ly	mo not o nous
Brit ain	fa mil iar	mys te ri ous
bus i ness	fas ci nate	nec es sar y
change a ble	for eign	no tice a ble
choose	for mer ly	oc ca sion al ly
com par a tive	for ty	oc cur rence
con ceive	gram mar	o mit ted
con science	height	op por tu ni ty
con tin u ous	hin drance	par tic u lar ly
de ci sion	im ag i nar y	pas time
def i nite	im me di ate ly	per form

pre ced ing	rep e ti tion	tend en cy
prej u dice	re sem blance	there fore
priv i lege	sched ule	trag e dy
prob a bly	sec re tar y	tru ly
pro ce dure	seize	un doubt ed ly
pro nun ci a tion	sep a rate	un til
pro por tion	sim i lar	u su al ly
psy chol o gy	soph o more	val u a ble
quan ti ty	suc ceed	writ ing
re ceive	sym pa thize	
re fer ring	tem per a ment	

You may find this list useful in testing your spelling ability and in checking and correcting errors in your papers. A spelling list of your own, however, will be more profitable to study than lists made by others, because it will help you to concentrate on your individual problems.

Errors Caused by Faulty Pronunciation

Although faulty pronunciation is not a major cause of misspelling, it is responsible for some very common mistakes:

Correct spelling	Misspelling
ath let ics	ath aletics
priv i lege	privlege
en vi **ron** ment	enviroment
mis chie **vous**	mischievious
pre scribe	perscribe
dis gust	discust

Pronounce each syllable to yourself when writing longer words *(ac-com-pa-ny-ing, par-tic-u-lar-ly, stud-y-ing)*. Also notice that many longer words contain letters that are blurred or lost in speech: tem-per-*a*-men-tal, ac-ci-den-*tal*-ly, lab-*o*-ra-to-ry.

Omission of Final *-ed*

One of the most common spelling errors is the omission of *-ed* at the ends of words. This sometimes occurs because of analogy to speech, where the *-ed* sound often is lost in rapid conversation or is assimilated by the following sound. To catch such errors in writing, you will have to rely on your eye rather than your ear. There are three principal trouble areas:

In Verb Forms.   Regular verbs form their past tenses and past participles by adding *-ed*. Be careful not to drop these letters, especially before words beginning with *t*, like *to*. *Used to* and *supposed to* are commonly misspelled:

I **used to** [not *use to*] misspell words.
He is **supposed to** be [not *suppose to* be] an authority.

In Verbal Modifiers.   The past participle is often used as a modifier *(stewed prunes, raised platform)*. Here too the tendency in pronunciation is to drop the *-ed*, and many such shortened forms have become established: *grade school, oilcloth, cream cheese, roast chicken*. Others are sometimes found in print but are debatable: *bottle beer, whip cream, advance headquarters*. In college papers it is better to use only shortened forms that are generally accepted. In less formal writing, more latitude is allowed, but dictionaries, current written practice, and appropriateness to the paper should serve as guides.

17.2

In Modifiers from Nouns.   Adjectives are often formed by adding *-ed* to nouns: *long-haired, heart-shaped, two-faced*. When the *-ed* is dropped in such forms — a growing tendency in current English — the result is a noun modifier (see 6.4): *king-size bed, hard-surface road, high-heel shoes*. Established forms like these are appropriate in all writing. It's usually better, however, to keep the *-ed* (as in *advanced courses, middle-aged, old-fashioned*) unless you have seen the form in print without the *-ed*.

Confusion of Words That Sound Alike

Be careful not to confuse words of identical or similar sound. It is easy when writing rapidly to put down *their* for *there*, *its* for *it's*, *maybe* for *may be*, but conscientious writers will check their finished work closely for errors of this sort. Substituting one form for another may suggest an idea that the writer did not intend:

Psychiatric treatment changed Bobby from a withdrawn, unhappy child to a normal, happy boy **excepted** [should be *accepted*] by his group.

The following pairs of words are often confused in writing. See if you can distinguish between them.

accept – except	conscience – conscious	personal – personnel
advice – advise	coarse – course	principal – principle
affect – effect	credible – creditable	quiet – quite
aisle – isle	desert – dessert	stationary – stationery
allusion – illusion	its – it's	than – then
birth – berth	lead – led	their – there
capital – capitol	loose – lose	to – too
choose – chose	passed – past	weather – whether
cite – site	peace – piece	who's – whose

• *Exercise*

Make up sentences that will illustrate clearly the differences in meaning in the paired words on page 201.

Examples: Everyone *except* Sam *accepted* the invitation.
    It's difficult for the leopard to change *its* spots.

Separate Words and Combined Forms

Observe the distinctions between expressions that are written as one word and those written as two. These forms frequently need to be checked in revision:

> **all ready** [adjective phrase]: The girls were at last **all ready** to leave.
> **already** [adverb of time]: It was **already** dark when they arrived.
>
> **all right** [adjective phrase, conventionally written as two words]:
> The seats seemed **all right** to me. (The forms *alright* and *alrite* are not accepted in edited usage.)
>
> **all together** [adjective phrase]: We were **all together** at the depot.
> **altogether** [adverb, meaning wholly]: That's **altogether** another matter.
>
> **a while** [noun]: They talked for **a while.**
> **awhile** [adverb]: Can't you stay **awhile** longer?
>
> **may be** [verb phrase]: He **may be** the next mayor.
> **maybe** [adverb, short for *it may be*]: **Maybe** you'll have better luck next time.

Certain phrases may be mistakenly written as one word through analogy with other forms or because they are often run together in speech:

> The assignment was **a lot** more difficult than I expected. [not *alot*]
> The judge **threw out** his testimony. [not *throughout*]
> The puppy was always there at the owner's **beck and call.** [not *beckon call*]

17.3 Spelling Troublesome Plurals

Nouns Ending in *-y, -o,* or *-f*

Nouns ending in *-y* following a vowel form the plural regularly by adding *-s (toys, bays, joys, monkeys).* But nouns ending in *-y* preceded by a consonant change *y* to *i* and add *-es:*

apology, apologies	curiosity, curiosities	library, libraries
company, companies	ferry, ferries	study, studies

Exception: In forming the plural of proper names, the *-y* is retained and *-s* added: all the *Kellys,* both *Marys.*

Nouns ending in *-o* preceded by a vowel form the plural by adding *-s (folios, studios, tattoos).* If the final *-o* is preceded by a consonant, the plural is usually formed by adding *-es,* but a few nouns add *-s* only:

echoes	potatoes		pianos	sopranos
heroes	tomatoes	But:	solos	tobaccos
Negroes	vetoes		banjos	Eskimos

A few nouns ending in *-o* add either *-s* or *-es* to form the plural: *cargos, cargoes; hobos, hoboes; zeros, zeroes.* Because no rule can be given for adding *-s* or *-es,* a writer must either memorize the plurals or consult a dictionary.

Nouns ending in *-f* or *-fe* often form the plural regularly *(beliefs, chiefs, fifes, roofs).* But some common words ending in *-f* form their plurals by changing *-f* to *-ves:*

calf, calves	knife, knives	self, selves
half, halves	leaf, leaves	thief, thieves

The plural of a few nouns ending in *-f* may be either *-s* or *-ves: elfs, elves; hoofs, hooves; scarfs, scarves; wharfs, wharves.*

17.4

Sp

Group Words and Compound Nouns

Most compound words and group words form their plurals by adding *s* to the last word of the group, whether the expression is written as one word or two:

Singular	**Plural**
baby sitter	baby sitters
cross-examination	cross-examinations
major general	major generals

But when the significant word is the first term (as it often is in hyphened compounds), that word is the one made plural:

daughters-in-law	passers-by
men-of-war	presidents-elect

The plural of nouns ending in *-ful* is made by adding *-s* to the last part of the word: two *cupfuls,* three *tablespoonfuls.*

17.4 Some Principles of Spelling

Chaotic as spelling is in English, some principles are helpful for spelling common words. Listed below are guides to spelling that you have probably heard before. You may find more detailed information by consulting the spelling section in the front pages of your dictionary.

Final *-e*

Words ending in silent *-e* generally retain the *-e* before additions (called *suffixes*) beginning with a consonant (*-ment, -ly, -some, -ness*), but drop the *-e* before additions beginning with a vowel (*-ing, -able, -ous, -ary*).

-e Retained Before a Consonant:

arrange – arrangement	nine – ninety
awe – awesome	require – requirement
definite – definitely	shape – shapeless
hope – hopeless	spite – spiteful

Exceptions:
argument   awful   duly   ninth   truly

-e Dropped Before Another Vowel:

argue – arguing	imagine – imaginary
arrive – arrival	shape – shaping
conceive – conceivable	value – valuable
grieve – grievous	write – writing

Exceptions. In a few words silent *-e* is retained before a vowel to avoid confusion with other forms:

dye	dyeing	(compare *dying*)
singe	singeing	(compare *singing*)

Words ending in *-ce* or *-ge* retain the final *-e* before additions beginning with *a, o,* or *ou* (so that the final *-c* or *-g* will not suggest the "hard" sound):

changeable	noticeable	unmanageable
courageous	outrageous	vengeance

-ie- and *-ei-*

The familiar jingle learned by most schoolchildren is helpful in spelling *-ie-* and *-ei-* words: "Write *i* before *e* except after *c*, or when sounded as *a* as in *neighbor* and *weigh.*"

Words with *-ie-*.   Words with *-ie-* are more common than words *with -ei-*. The typical sound of *-ie-* is $\bar{e}$:

achieve	chief	grievous	niece
believe	field	hygiene	siege

Other *-ie-* words are *mischief, sieve,* and *view.*

Words with *-ei-*.   After *c*, and also to spell the sound $\bar{a}$, *-ei-* is generally used:

ceiling	perceive	eight	reign
conceive	receipt	freight	vein
deceive	receive	neighbor	weigh

The long $\bar{e}$ sound is spelled *-ei-* (rather than *-ie-*) in a few words: *either, leisure, neither, seize, weird.* Other sounds spelled *-ei-: counterfeit, foreign, height, heir.*

Doubling the Final Consonant

Double the final consonant before a suffix beginning with a vowel (*-able, -ed, -er, -ing*) with (1) words of one syllable ending in a single consonant after a single vowel *(brag, hit, sit)* and (2) with words of more than one syllable, ending the same way and accented on the last syllable *(commit, forget, prefer).*

17.4

Sp

One-syllable words			Words of more than one syllable		
bat	batter	batting	commit	committed	committing
grip	gripping	gripped	control	controllable	controlled
pin	pinned	pinning	occur	occurrence	occurred
spot	spotty	spotted	omit	omitted	omitting
wet	wetter	wettest	prefer	preferred	preferring

The consonant is *not* doubled (1) in words with two vowels before the final consonant *(daub, daubing; keep, keeper; spoil, spoiled),* or (2) in words ending with two consonants *(help, helped; peck, pecking; lurk, lurked),* or (3) when the accent of the lengthened word shifts to an earlier syllable *(infer', in' ference; prefer', pref'- erable; refer', ref' erence).*

Usage is divided about doubling the final consonant of some words not accented on the last syllable, but American spelling generally favors the single consonant.

bias – biased	quarrel – quarreling
counsel – counseled, counselor	travel – traveler, traveled
diagram – diagramed	worship – worshiped, worshiping
kidnap – kidnaping, kidnaper	

Final *-y*

A final *-y* preceded by a consonant regularly changes to *i* before all suffixes except those beginning with *i:*

body – bodies	happy – happiness
busy – business	lonely – loneliness
carry – carried, carrying	marry – marriage, marrying
duty – dutiful	mercy – merciful
easy – easily	study – studious, studying
envy – envious	Tory – Tories

Final -*y* preceded by a vowel remains unchanged when a suffix is added:

boy – boys, boyish   enjoy – enjoyable, enjoyment, enjoying
delay – delayed, delayer   play – playful, playing, played

See also 17.3, Spelling Troublesome Plurals.

-cede, -ceed, -sede

Only one word ends in -*sede: supersede.* Only three end in -*ceed: exceed, proceed, succeed.* All other words of this sort end in -*cede: precede, recede, intercede, secede,* etc.

-able, -ible, -ance, -ence

Words with these endings should be carefully checked for correct spelling. Words ending in -*able* (like *advisable, desirable, improbable, suitable*) are much more common than those ending in -*ible* (such as *audible, divisible, horrible, visible*). But since no rules govern the formation of these endings, consult a dictionary if you are in doubt.

A few words are spelled with either -*able* or -*ible* endings. Dictionaries indicate the more common or preferred spelling by putting it first *(collapsible, collapsable; preventable, preventible).*

The spelling of words ending in -*ance, -ant; -ence, -ent* must also be watched, since pronunciation does not distinguish them (attend-*ance,* confid*ence;* defend*ant,* exist*ent*).

17.5 Variant Spellings

When a word is currently spelled in two ways *(extol, extoll),* use the more common form.

Many words have secondary spellings, usually British or simplified forms generally labeled in dictionaries as *Brit., Variant, Archaic,* and so on, so that you can choose the form appropriate to your subject and style. Most people writing today, and certainly anyone who has difficulty with spelling, will ordinarily prefer:

1. The more modern of two equally reputable spellings: *draft, mold, plow* instead of *draught, mould, plough.*
2. The simpler form of a specialized word if it has attained currency among the people who use it most: *anesthetic, catalog, medieval, program, sulfur* rather than *anaesthetic, catalogue, mediaeval, programme, sulphur.*

Although it is possible to simplify the spelling of many common words (as *thoro* for *thorough, enuf* for *enough*), conventional spelling is expected in most kinds of writing.

3. American rather than British spellings: *center, labor, pajama* rather than *centre, labour, pyjama.*

For the spelling of proper names (the British *Labour* Party) and for direct quotation (the Prime Minister described it as "a *humourless* situation"), British spelling should be followed, but in other situations the American forms should be used.

• *Exercises*

1. This exercise should help to fix some of the general principles of spelling in your mind. Copy the words in each of the following groups, making the additions or changes indicated:

   17.5

   Sp

   a. Supply *-ei-* or *-ie-* as required for correct spelling:

all--d	fr--ght	s--ve
bel--ve	h--ght	s--ze
conc--ve	l--sure	th--r
counterf--t	n--ther	v--l
for--gn	p--ce	w--rd

   b. Add *-ed* to the following verbs to show whether the final consonant is doubled or not. If there is a choice for forms, indicate both of them:

bargain	droop	quarrel
bias	drop	question
chide	kidnap	refer
clot	list	travel
dine	play	whelp

   c. Add *-ing* to each of these words, making any necessary changes in the root form of the world:

become	endure	prove
control	hope	use
dine	hurry	write

   d. Change each of these words to an adjective ending *-ous:*

continue	dispute	mischief
courage	glory	outrage
courtesy	grieve	sanctimony

   e. Add *-able* or *-ible* to the following words, changing letters wherever necessary to conform with accepted spellings:

accept	digest	repair
advice	force	sense
contempt	justify	train

f. Add *-ance, -ant* or *-ence, -ent* to these words, making any other
    necessary changes:

ascend	dally	provide
compete	defend	revere
confide	maintain	vigil

2. Read the following paragraph, correcting the misspelled words. Feel
    free to consult a dictionary; you may want to see how many mistakes
    you can find and correct without a dictionary first, however.

The principal that every great man is a national calamity is easily defensable. It is difficult to concieve that strong men will not
irresistably impose upon their countrymen their own eccentricities
and prejadices. Napoleon, for example, beleived that he had a
definate destiny to succede, a mysterous "star" guiding him and
France to great heighths. He did not dream of any hinderance
from the other nations of Europe. His plans were to seperate them
one by one and to sieze all power and priveledge. Only Britian
refused to acommodate itself to his grandiose schemes. His tem-
perment was characteristic of his enviroment; massively fasinated
by Romantic psycology, he had an exagerated consciousness of
the independant existance of his charisma. Napoleon was tradgi-
cally dissappointed in his hopes, as were his spiritual forebears,
Alexander the Great, Caesar, Louis XIV, and his inheritors,
Hitler and Mussolini.

Part Two
Practices in Composition

COMPOSITION

18 DISCOVERING WHAT YOU HAVE TO SAY
19 OCCASIONS AND OPPORTUNITIES IN WRITING
20 ORGANIZING YOUR MATERIAL
21 WRITING THE FIRST DRAFT

DICTION

22 USING A DICTIONARY
23 THE MEANING OF WORDS
24 THE EFFECT OF WORDS

SENTENCES AND PARAGRAPHS

25 SENTENCE LENGTH AND ECONOMY
26 SENTENCE VARIETY, CONTROL, AND EMPHASIS
27 PARAGRAPHS

PRACTICAL WRITING TASKS

28 REVISING AND CORRECTING A PAPER
29 PRACTICAL AND VOCATIONAL WRITING
30 THE RESEARCH PAPER

18 Discovering What You Have to Say

If I put down something, that thing will help the next thing come, and I'm off. If I let the process go on, things will occur to me that were not at all in my mind when I started. These things, odd or trivial as they may be, are somehow connected. And if I let them string out, surprising things will happen. — William Stafford, "A Way of Writing"

All of us have things to say, although often we don't know it. What we have to say is not always at the front of our minds, fresh, compelling, ready to be said. More often than not we have to find what it is, learn to know it, and watch it take first one shape, then another. This means exploring the world we're in, testing our personal resources, weighing our judgments and our whimsy, and evaluating our information.

From the start, whether you are in a composition course or doing some work that requires writing, don't be surprised if you need to spend more time thinking and hunting than you do writing a complete draft of your paper. Of course there is no *requirement* that you think or hunt. It is possible to write without doing much exploratory thinking, but what often comes out then is a pale reflection of the thinking someone else has done.

"Bad writing" is often bad because it is anonymous writing; it has no character. It is a summary of conventional thoughts and phrases that do not *show* the writer's thinking; anyone might have written the same thing. Good writing begins when you learn to accept and trust yourself as a source of delight, information, and insight for others, when you accept the responsibility of knowing yourself and learning to say what it is that uniquely connects you with a subject. Good writing begins when you start taking over your experiences, learning all that they signify, and speaking out in words that you have made your own. Good writing begins when you make what you write *yours*. If what you are writing doesn't matter much to you, then it is likely to sprawl across the page, inert and dull even if it is mechanically correct, as unconvincing to readers as it is uninteresting to you.

18.1 Finding and Exploring What You Have to Say

Some years ago, C. Day Lewis commented on his own writing: "I do not sit down at my desk to put into verse something that is already clear in my mind. If it were clear in my mind, I should have no incentive or need to write about it, for I am an explorer, not a journalist, a propagandist, or a statistician." Later in the same passage he went on to say that "often I have gone some way with the poem before I am able to grasp the theme which lies hidden in the material that has accumulated." He is talking about writing poetry, but what he says gives a clue to most other forms of writing as well. There's no reason to expect that you already know everything you will say when you sit down to write. You'll have to hunt for it. And when you find it, it may be a chameleon: it may change color while you look at it.

Ancient rhetoricians called this process of searching *invention,* and it's a good word to use. It comes from a Latin verb, *invenire.* Meanings given to this verb include

18.1

Plan

1. to come upon, or find;
2. to fabricate mentally, to create or devise in the mind.

Both actions are important. *Invention* is a name for the processes by which you come upon, or *meet,* your own experiences, the things you know, and the things other people know; and you *make* something out of them in your mind by finding the way they mean something to you and the way they fit together. Invention doesn't end when you start to write. Every word may suggest new possibilities or eliminate earlier notions. This process of finding or making may continue through any revisions you make in the completed paper.

Examining a Situation for Possible Subjects

Often, of course, your situation will determine what subjects you will write about. If you are in business, you must answer your correspondence. If you are in a laboratory, you must report your findings. If you are in a history class that requires three book reports, you must turn in the papers. Topics for writing may develop out of discussions in your composition class, or your composition teacher may assign a specific topic for you to write about. But even if you are given a specific topic, your thinking hasn't been done for you.

Having a topic doesn't always make it possible for you to write, or give you a reason for writing. If you are assigned a topic such as

"My Last Summer Job," you still have to determine what you have to say and why it is worthwhile to say it. You have to learn what the subject calls for from you and what kinds of resources are available for treating the subject. You have to think about how the material can be most usefully presented to a particular audience, and about how you can be yourself, do justice to a subject, and meet an audience honestly.

If you're free to choose your own topic, there is still a lot of thinking and searching before you. Sometimes, given the freedom to choose their own topics, writers accept whatever ideas first come to mind, or use materials already available to them without thinking them through. Consider this essay, written in a freshman composition class:

My Theater Experience

I worked at a theater before coming to college. When my parents started managing the drive-in, they drafted me to do the odd jobs there.

While working in the cafeteria, box-office, and the projection booth, I met many new people. I found that people come to a movie for different reasons. One man said that he came to get away from his wife and kids. Many boys and girls came to have dates. A few people, however, actually came to watch the movie.

At the drive-in, I experienced different emotions due to the actions of my customers. One lady aroused my indignation when she claimed that her son, who was six feet in height, was under twelve years of age. A boy eleven years old does not have to pay admission; therefore her son was admitted free. I was amused when one boy tried to hide in the back floor of a car, under a quilt, while the driver drove into the theater. I am aware of such tricks, and the boy was caught. One girl caught her slacks on the barbed wire while climbing over the fence at the back of the theater. I helped her off the fence, and I sold her a ticket. She never came over the fence again.

I experienced new and enlightening experiences at the theater. At the drive-in, I found that real people are often more entertaining than people in the movies.

It's easy enough to see why a writer would decide to use this topic. Not everyone works in a drive-in theater; in fact, few do, so a writer can safely assume that writing about work in a drive-in theater from firsthand experience is a subject not too many other writers are going to use. But even if a topic seems obvious and ready-made, it still deserves some searching and investigating.

The author of this essay has made a start. He knows what his subject is, and he has put some things on paper. But he doesn't appear to have looked at his experiences very closely, nor has he shown the drive-in experience as it belongs uniquely to him. We're left wondering about what's *really* different about working in a drive-in, about who the "new people" are, about just exactly what makes people more entertaining than movies, about that girl hanging on the fence. We don't know what all of these things mean to the author: we don't know exactly how he sees them, or how they've entered his life. The author needs to spend more time remembering episodes and practices and reflecting on what they mean.

Whether a subject is given to you, or whether you can choose your own subject and you choose one that seems to be obvious, you still have exploratory work to do. Still more troublesome are those occasions when you are free to write on your own subjects, and none at all comes into your mind.

When that happens, you have the whole world before you, and there are so many possibilities that sometimes it's like having no possibilities at all. You're called upon to understand and write about your own private and unique view of some part of the world, and to combine multiple and varied impressions into a personal interpretation. What do you do? How do you get started?

Collecting Your Impressions

18.1

Plan

Keeping a Journal. One thing you can do that may help you with your writing requires daily attention over a long period of time. Some composition teachers may require you to *keep a daily journal;* if your teacher doesn't, you might try on your own. Commit yourself to make daily entries. The entries may be words, phrases, sentences, paragraphs, essays, poems, bits and pieces. The point is to record things that matter to you or puzzle you or cause you to wonder. Put down what you see and learn and feel and know. Copy into your journal things you have read or heard that move or entertain you. A journal can get you in the habit of expressing yourself on paper.

To make a journal work, you need to make daily entries: saving up for a week and writing a group of entries won't give you an account of what you were conscious of on *different* days. Don't be hesitant, and don't imagine that every entry should be something important. If a song you hear on the radio moves you, try to say why and how it moved you. If something goes sour in one of your classes, try to figure it out by recalling what different people said and did.

Making Abstractions Concrete. A second thing you can do requires some practice, and could be a part of your journal. Try writing concrete phrases and sentences about abstract ideas and impressions that come to you. The purpose in doing this is for you to

get in the habit of putting your ideas and impressions into quite
specific settings or terms, as in the following examples:

EASE AND RELAXATION: an unhurried visit to the Wagon Wheel Art
  Gallery in Colorado.
FEAR: the whir of a rattlesnake when you can't see it; the taste of brass
  in your mouth after an out-of-control car just misses you.
COMFORT: some good fresh pipe tobacco and some exciting books on
  a Friday evening with the weekend still ahead.
ANXIETY: a message to call home without any indication of what it's
  all about.

Creating particular scenes and terms to describe ideas and impressions may help you avoid falling back on standard phrasings and
clichés when you are trying to put yourself on paper. (See also
23.4, Concrete and Abstract Words.)

Neither the journal nor this practice in making knowledge concrete will guarantee that you always find good subjects to write
about. Both may help by letting you see which way your thoughts
and impressions are likely to run, which topics are likely to appear
and reappear in journal notes, and which kinds of topics seem to
matter to you most.

Seeing Patterns and Connections.   There are several other things
that may help you discover what you're going to write about or
help you think about subjects that are assigned. The questions and
observations that follow may help you see patterns and connections in your own ideas and impressions, and to relate these patterns to things around you.

1. Do you notice which things seem to recur in your experience?
   Actions, attitudes, emotional reactions, and other experiences
   may never be *exactly* repeated, but there are likely to be recognizable likenesses and patterns among your experiences. If
   there are, they may help you to find a subject, or to see an assigned subject in a new way.
2. How do you look at your experiences? What do you focus on?
   How and when does your focus change? When you first entered
   your composition class, did you see and hear individuals, or did
   you respond to the class as a whole? How do you look at it
   now? Shifting your focus from long range to close range, looking at one part, then at another, then at both in relation to each
   other enables you to see what's around you, and what happens
   when your focus shifts.
3. How do your experiences differ from the experiences of others?
   How varied is your experience? How do the things you are familiar with appear to other people? Answering questions like

these may help you understand your own ideas and impressions and learn what there is in them that has significance for you.

4. What can you learn about an idea, an event, or an experience by looking at it in three different ways? If you regard a subject as something fixed, you can examine its parts. If you regard your subject as changing and dynamic, you may see the relationships among the parts. Or, your subject may be part of a larger context, and you may want to see how it fits into this larger scene.

5. What is there in your experience that can be shared with another? Can you find a way of presenting your experience that will make it possible for another to share? How can you use the knowledge and values that others have so as to connect them with you and your subject?

Asking and answering these questions will not guarantee that you can always find good subjects. They may help you to think about what you know and feel and to discover what's there that has significance. Without extensive exploration, it is possible for you to write competently. It's likely, however, that *good* writing won't occur until something matters enough to you that you need to catch it on paper and, perhaps, to show it to someone else.

18.1

Limiting Your Subject

Plan

There is little danger that the subject you select will be too narrow. It is the large subjects like "American Foreign Policy," "The Aims of Higher Education," and "The Role of Women in Contemporary Society" that lead to difficulty. Most writers can only repeat commonplace judgments and empty generalities about such ambitious subjects, and after writing a paragraph or two, they find that they have nothing more to say.

Limit the subject you select so that you can develop it fully in the required number of words. Most college themes are short—a thousand-word theme would fill only one newspaper column. Because even ten thousand words would not be enough to cover most large subjects ("Justice," "Crime Prevention," "Forestry"), break down such subjects into topics you can handle. "Prime-Time Soap Operas," for example, might be limited to "The Effect of Prime-Time Soap Operas on Children." But since there are many children and several soap operas, you might write a more interesting paper and offer more interesting judgments by focusing specifically on your little brother and soap operas. The suggestions above about ways of looking for subjects are also ways of limiting your subject—the more specific your questions about a subject, the narrower your final topic is likely to be.

It's best to concentrate on a single, well-defined aspect of the subject rather than on the subject as a whole:

General subject	More specific topic
Voting as an obligation of citizenship	Arousing student interest in voting
Sportsmanship	How sportsmanship differs in tennis and baseball
Smog control	The effectiveness of smog control devices for cars

As you gather information, your topic may change slightly — and it may continue to change through all the preliminary stages of your thinking. The important thing to remember at first is to keep the topic specific and to avoid falling back on a general subject.

At this stage of thinking about your subject, jot down on paper every idea that occurs to you, whether you are sure you will use it or not. One idea often suggests another and better one, and may help you to reshape or clarify your thesis (see page 218). After a reasonable amount of reflection, you will usually have more than enough material to write a paper of the assigned length.

• *Exercise*

Here is a list of general subjects. For each one, narrow the subject to a well-defined aspect that could be a specific topic for a paper: *campus fashions, college architecture, prestige symbols, modern heroes, school discipline, current music.*

Some Ways of Thinking About Your Subject

There are some particular ways of thinking about subjects that may help you discover what is most interesting or useful or valuable in them. Asking some or all of the questions below may help you recall information that you already have about your subject, or call your attention to information that you need but do not possess; some may help you see some principle illustrated in your subject.

The first set of questions may be useful to you as you first begin thinking about your subject and also after you have developed a specific proposition or thesis and are seeking a way to explain it.

1. What can you learn by *definition?* To what class does your subject belong? How does it differ from other members of the same class? Can definition help you determine just what your main point is? If you have determined what your main point is, does definition give you a way of organizing your discussion?
2. Will *comparison* with something you know well help you understand your subject? Can you detect similarities in your subject

and one or more other things? Does detecting differences between your subject and a similar thing help you understand your subject? Does your subject differ in degree from similar things?

3. Studying *relationships* may tell you something about your subject and show you a way to organize your discussion. How is your subject connected with a cause? How and why did your subject come to be? Is your subject to be studied as an effect of some causes, or as a cause of later effects? What are the antecedents of your subject? What consequences are likely to follow from your subject? With what ideas or things is your subject incompatible? Are there ideas that are contradicted by your subject?

4. Is there expert *testimony* about your subject that you can call on? Are there laws, principles, precedents, or other kinds of testimony that will help you understand your subject and validate it to others?

Suppose, for example, that the general subject of *sportsmanship* interests you. Perhaps you're interested in athletics, or perhaps you've just seen an episode of bad sportsmanship, or perhaps you've simply wondered why people behave differently in games. The questions above may help you discover how to go about discussing sportsmanship or to find what needs most attention. If you set out to define sportsmanship, a first step is to determine what class of things it belongs to. Is sportsmanship a *virtue,* a *mark of civility,* a *quality,* a *social disguise for aggression?* The problem of defining sportsmanship, in other words, may get to be so important that you decide that this is your subject and you don't have to look further. Each of the sets of questions above may give you a specific way of talking about sportsmanship.

18.1

Plan

Another set of suggestions lies in seven relationships that give coherence to discussions. If we put these relationships in the form of questions, they may give you some more ways to inquire into your subject:

1. With what is your subject *coordinate?* What can be linked to your subject by *and?*

2. From what is your subject *observably different?* What can be linked to your subject by *but?*

3. What can be cited as a *cause* for your subject? What can be linked to your subject by *for?*

4. What can be cited as a *result* of your subject? To what conclusions does your subject lead? What can be linked to your subject by *so?*

5. What are the *alternatives* to your subject? What can be linked to your subject by *or?*

6. What does your subject *include?* What examples, narratives, episodes can be linked to your subject?
7. What *sequences* exist within your subject? Is your subject part of a larger sequence?

To see how these questions might work, go back to the sample subject that started off as "Prime-Time Soap Operas," then became "The Effect of Prime-Time Soap Operas on Children," and finally became "Prime-Time Soap Operas and My Little Brother." If you say, "My little brother watches all of the prime-time soap operas *and . . . ,*" when you finish the sentence in your own way you'll probably have to name some other things he does that are like watching the soap operas. If you say, "My little brother watches all of the prime-time soap operas *but . . . ,*" when you finish the sentence you'll probably find yourself talking about ways your little brother is different from other children who watch these programs. If you ask what sequences there are in your little brother's actions, that may lead you to discuss how he behaves after watching the programs, or the ritual he goes through to get ready to watch the programs.

These two sets of questions and suggestions can be used in two ways: first, as guides to thinking about your subject *before* you have settled on a central thesis you wish to develop, and second, as guides to developing and organizing your work *after* you have arrived at a central proposition.

Locating a Thesis

When you have thought and planned enough to select a specific topic, and you know pretty well your position toward it, it is often helpful (and sometimes necessary) to compose a *thesis statement.* This definite statement of the main point or central idea of your paper is useful for three reasons:

1. it will help you see just where you are going and why;
2. it will give you a single focus for the development of your paper;
3. it will help you select the material you will use in the paper.

Usually a single declarative statement, the thesis statement should normally be either a simple or complex sentence, though dependent modifiers can be added: if the thesis sentence has a *single* main clause (as in simple and complex sentences), then you're encouraged to keep one dominant idea at the center of attention in your paper.

The thesis sentence is not the topic of your paper or its title; it is a sentence that answers the question "What is the main idea that I

Review:

Finding a Subject and Locating Material

- *For Help in Finding a Subject*

1. Keep a journal and record ideas and information.
2. Practice making abstractions concrete.
3. Look for patterns and connections:
   a. What things recur in your experience?
   b. How do you look at things? When and why does your focus change?
   c. How does your experience differ from that of others?
   d. What do you learn when you look at an experience or possible subject as fixed? as changing and dynamic? and as part of a larger context?
   e. What can you share with someone else?

- *For Help in Thinking About a Subject*

1. What can you learn by definition?
2. Will comparison tell you something about the subject?
3. What kind of relationships does your subject have with other things?
4. Is there testimony available about your subject?
5. What can be linked to your subject by *and?*
6. What can be linked to your subject by *but?*
7. What can be linked to your subject by *for?*
8. What can be linked to your subject by *so?*
9. What can be linked to your subject by *or?*
10. What does your subject include?
11. What sequences occur in your subject?

18.1

am trying to present to the reader?" A statement of the central or controlling idea of a paper titled "The Honor System" might read "The honor system works only as well as the students want it to work" or "The honor system at this college is popular with the faculty but not with the students." In a paper explaining a process or activity, the thesis sentence might be "Learning to play the violin demands patience as well as talent" or "Performance is more important than appearance when you are buying a used car."

To write a thesis sentence, you must stop and think about the materials of your subject and decide what is important or interesting. The essay "My Theater Experience" (see p. 212) might have been given direction and focus by a good thesis sentence. The author might have written several essays about his theater experience. Consider some of the possibilities:

1. Since the writer indicates that he did many odd jobs around the theater, he could have developed an essay on the behind-the-scenes operation of a drive-in theater.
2. The writer remarks that he "met many new people" and that "people come to a movie for different reasons"; he might have developed an essay on the types of people who attend drive-in movies or on the reasons people have for attending or on the significance of drive-in movies in leisure living.
3. The writer "experienced different emotions"; he might have developed an essay on the range of emotional responses he experienced and how he adjusted to them.
4. The writer might have written an informal essay on amusing episodes at a drive-in theater.
5. The writer might have developed an essay on the erratic, often unseemly behavior of people at drive-in theaters.

Suppose that a little thought leads the writer to choose the fifth possibility. Perhaps the first is so familiar to the writer that it is no longer very interesting. The possibilities listed second above probably require some interviews and some attendance statistics that the writer can no longer gather. Perhaps the third and fourth possibilities don't seem important enough to tell about. But the fifth possibility is a good one, the writer thinks; here is a chance to write about the way people behave in the dark when they think no one is watching, at least no one they know ("People in the Dark," incidentally, wouldn't be a bad title). But just deciding on the fifth possibility doesn't give the writer a direction or focus. Writing a thesis sentence requires that the writer decide what the central thought is and say it in a single sentence. Consider some possible thesis sentences from the fifth suggestion above for a new essay on experience in a drive-in theater:

My experience working in a drive-in theater taught me that people behave differently in the dark, resorting to trickery, deceit, and foolishness.

I learned from my work in a drive-in theater that public manners and private manners are not the same.

Darkness seems to generate behavior in people that they would not dream of in the light.

At this point, a thesis sentence is still tentative, and further thinking and outlining may suggest changes. But each of these thesis statements suggests definite ways to get started on developing the paper. (See also 21.2, Controlling Direction.) Don't expect everything you read or write to have a clear thesis sentence. Thesis sentences are more likely to occur when you are writing to explain something or to argue a proposition. In some essays, for example, the effect is cumulative, and no single sentence establishes a central thesis.

• *Exercise*

Each of the following topics has a thesis statement that can lead to an interesting paper, but some of the points listed don't have any bearing on the controlling idea and should be changed or eliminated. Arrange the ideas in groups that belong together, eliminating or changing them as necessary.

18.1

Plan

1. *Salmon Fishing:* Salmon fishing is a thrilling and inexpensive sport.
   a. Requires skill
   b. Prizes offered for biggest fish
   c. Equipment need not be expensive
   d. Boats can be rented cheaply
   e. Salmon fight to the last breath
   f. Columbia River and Puget Sound two of the best areas
   g. Conservation efforts have paid off
   h. Baked salmon is a delectable dish
   i. How the Indians prepare salmon
   j. No thrill equals that first strike

2. *Regulating Children's TV Habits:* Although some TV programs are undesirable, parents should not regulate what children watch.
   a. There are some excellent educational programs
   b. Developing good judgment depends on practice in choosing
   c. TV often takes place of baby-sitter
   d. Children want to watch what playmates watch
   e. Some TV programs bad for immature minds
   f. Children resent too much discipline
   g. Outdoor exercise also important
   h. Free play of curiosity develops intellect
   i. Violence fascinates children
   j. Overprotection in youth produces distorted ideas of reality

Using Available Resources

Two kinds of resources — what we might call *private resources* and *public resources* — should be considered in developing a paper. Some subjects require one, some the other, some both.

Private Resources.   You already know enough about some subjects to treat them well. Your own experience will provide subjects and material for many college themes: what you have done in school and out, the jobs you have held, your hobbies, the people you know, the places you have visited, the courses you are taking in college. Consider this brief list of topics and see how many you could write on from your own experience:

Overcoming Self-Consciousness	Considerations in Buying a
A Job I Disliked	Car
Advice to a High-School Student	A Successful Amateur Play
About to Enter the University	Building a Record Collection
Living Within a Budget	

You need not feel that a paper based upon your personal experiences will be boring to others. Some beginning writers are afraid that their own experiences have been too limited, or that their opinions and attitudes are too commonplace to be of interest to anyone but themselves. But much published material is based upon incidents and attitudes that are in no way unique or sensational ("Making Your Hobby Pay," "The Most Unforgettable Character I Have Met," "Diary of a City-Bred Farmer"). If you are interested in what you have to say, your readers probably will be too. A fresh and lively account of the experiences of a baby-sitter is more readable than a dull description of a journey up the Amazon.

If you are far enough along in your thinking and planning to formulate a thesis, you will be able to tell whether or not your present knowledge, opinions, and attitudes are sufficient material. For papers based on personal experience, ask yourself as many questions as you can think of about the subject. If you are going to explain how a person should apply for a job, recall and analyze your own experiences in looking for work. How did you find out what jobs were available? How did you decide which jobs to apply for? Did you apply in person or by letter? If you were not hired, what were the probable reasons? What mistakes, if any, did you make either during an interview or in your letter of application? If you were going to apply for another job, would you go about it in the same way?

A similar analysis will help you gather material for papers presenting personal opinions or attitudes. If you decide to enumerate the qualities of a good teacher, think of two or three of your teachers who were outstanding and try to discover what qualities they had in common: a sound knowledge of their subject? a genuine interest in students? a willingness to help the slower students? fairness in grading? a sense of humor? You could extend your analysis by considering also one or two teachers who were definitely unsatisfactory, to see what qualities they lacked.

Public Resources.   Not all papers can be written entirely from personal opinion or experience. Many subjects call for information that must be gathered by reading, by observation, or through personal interviews. Some subjects will demand thorough research and formal presentation. Others may require only the addition of your casual reading as support. Still others — such as some of the interpretive essays you will be asked to do in English courses — may require that you gather additional information (for example, information about literary techniques), even though the paper is going to be an informal expression of your response to meaning in something you have read. It is perfectly permissible to use your reading casually for any subject that requires it — that is, not as in a formal report with documentation, but as the natural supplement to what you wish to say.

18.1

In using outside resources to develop material for a paper, read critically, and think about what you read. Be careful to distinguish between verifiable *facts* (the cost of living index in New York City and in Chicago) and *opinions* (the reasons why the Republican Party lost the 1976 election). On controversial subjects, read and weigh the opinions on all sides of the question before arriving at a firm opinion of your own.

Make the effort to understand and assimilate material from published sources before using it in a paper. Instead of copying an author's words, think about the ideas he is expressing. Do you agree or disagree with them? Why? Proper acknowledgment should always be made for borrowed material — in a footnote if the paper requires formal documentation, or informally if the situation seems to warrant, as for the quotations opening the sections of this handbook. (See 30.8, Documenting the Paper, for details on using materials from printed sources.)

• *Exercise*

See what possible subjects you can find in a daily newspaper. For each subject you find, make some rough notes on what you might be able to do with the subjects, and indicate what kinds of resources you might need to draw on. Try finding subjects in each of these features from the newspaper: *front-page stories, editorials, regular feature columns, and "fillers."*

18.2 The Meeting Place of Author, Subject, and Audience

Some kinds of writing you may do for your own sake—diaries, notes, and the like. Some kinds of writing you may do for the sake of the subject—laboratory reports, case histories, meditative explorations. Often, however, an audience of some kind is waiting, and you must find a just and happy balance among the material and arguments available on a subject, the interests, needs, and peculiarities of an audience, and your own character. You must be honest to yourself, do justice to a subject, and earn an audience.

The Writer's Position

If you imagine yourself, a subject, and an audience at the three points of a triangle, you'll be able to visualize some of the problems in determining where to stand. If you stand too close to your subject, you may forget to share it with an audience. If you stand too far from your subject, you may not see it clearly. If you stand too close to your audience, you may sound too chummy. If you stand too far from the audience, you may seem remote and aloof.

It is possible—even common—for a writer to be so busy trying to win the audience that the subject and even the writer are given scant service. Good writing requires honesty of the writer—an honest, serious approach to the subject and to the audience, and an honest critical understanding of his or her own capabilities. Since we simply cannot say all that there is to be said about a subject, it is unlikely that what we write can ever express all that we want to say or all that should be said at a given time. But that does not mean that our pieces of writing are by definition poor things. Any good writer is limited, but he or she can still declare honestly how the world looks from one viewpoint or think things through in the company of an audience.

Before you begin writing the first draft of a paper, and as you are writing, you need to know where you stand. Does the subject make any claim on you? Do you have anything at stake? Have you explored the subject enough to begin to know it well, at least in some ways, and perhaps to make it interesting to others? Do you know how important your subject is to you or to others? What have you learned? How have your own ideas developed and been clarified? Can you verify your beliefs by testing them against experience? Can you examine and evaluate your beliefs by testing them against experience and social conditions? Writing isn't trivial: it not only offers a way to speak to people in other times and places, but also makes it possible for you to know what you think and how you came to think it and to examine your thinking, testing it against experience.

Adjusting to the Audience

As you write, you need to decide how to approach your audience. Must you address the audience logically and impersonally? Does the subject justify a more emotional presentation? Should you concentrate instead on thinking the subject through for yourself and honestly revealing that process to an audience? Can you combine these possibilities in such a way that you and your audience will meet and share the information or ideas you are presenting?

Sometimes it is too easy to forget that you have an audience at all. An assignment does not often give you a purpose for writing or an audience for your writing, and unless you *discover* a purpose and relate it to an audience, even a dutiful fulfillment of the assignment may amount to little. If you ignore your audience, your work may be fruitless, no matter how correct.

Though it is difficult to think of an audience when you are writing alone at night, and it seems easiest to get the paper written without bothering about some real or imagined audience, remember that when you write something, somebody real reads it. Language can sometimes have an isolating effect; any one of us can get wrapped up in what we're saying and forget about others. To combat that tendency, think of an audience for your work: stop and say things so that others can understand. We sometimes keep each other at more than arm's length, never moving close enough to acknowledge each other as real people. A subject may never seem real to an audience unless *you* are real to them, a real person thinking real thoughts that matter to you.

18.2

A speaker has some advantages here over a writer. A speaker can see the audience, and the audience usually has some character that can be known. A writer can never know with certainty who the audience will be. Sometimes it is appropriate to write specifically for your class, or for people who read habitually, or for people like yourself, or for an ideal audience of readers who are willing to set aside their own views and learn what you have to say. In any of these settings, if you value yourself, your subject, and your audience, you must try to anticipate and meet the audience's expectations. It's discouraging to write something that is right and exciting, only to discover that no one paid any attention.

If your subject is controversial, and if your audience is likely to have intense feelings about the matter, you may have particular problems in finding the right approach to an audience. On matters where feelings and emotions are strong — politics, ethics, conservation and ecology, social, professional, or sexual relationships —

we have difficulty hearing each other, and we're not always likely to listen to logic. How can we meet an audience in such a situation? There is no easy way.

One thing you can do is to move over into the shoes of your audience. You can begin by looking at the issue at hand from your audience's point of view. You can, for example, try to describe something as another person might see it—some scene or object, say, that is displeasing to you but pleasing to another. Or you can try to impersonate another and write an explanation or argument as the other person would.

You can be yourself and still be open to others. You can acknowledge opposing views and work to understand them. If people disagree with us, it's usually because they see good in a different way, and we can try to see it as they do, without sacrificing our own views. It takes time and patience to search for the common ground where you and an audience can meet, but that is the grace we owe each other.

The following chapter will discuss in more depth some of the rhetorical approaches that may help you plan your writing so that your subject most effectively reaches your audience.

• *Exercise*

For this exercise, if possible, use a paper you have already written. The first two or three paragraphs will probably be enough to work with.

1. Rewrite the opening paragraphs as they might be if you were farther from the subject physically or remote from it emotionally.

2. Rewrite the opening paragraphs as they might be if you were physically much closer to your subject or emotionally closer to or more involved with it.

3. Rewrite the opening paragraphs as they might be if you were far from your audience.

4. Rewrite the opening paragraphs as they might be if you were close to your audience.

• *An Essay in Progress, 1: First Notes*

Here and at the end of Chapters 19, 20, 21, and 28, you'll find reproduced various stages of an essay in progress. The notes below are a student's first scattered attempts to determine what to write about. At the end of Chapter 19 you'll find some tentative development of these notes; at the end of Chapter 20, some false starts and a brief outline for the essay; and at the end of Chapter 21, the first draft of the essay, which, in fact, is what the student turned in as the completed essay. It is, as you'll see, the essay discussed earlier in this chapter, "My Theater Experience." Reproduced with the first draft are some of the instructor's comments about the essay. Finally, at the end of Chapter 28, you'll find a revision of the essay.

You'll see as you follow this essay in progress that writing *is* a process that can be carried on indefinitely. Even though you've made an outline, you don't stop thinking about what to say; even though you've written a first draft, that doesn't mean everything is at an end. Many writers—perhaps most—keep working on what they have written through several stages of revision. There is always more to be thought and said.

The class assignment for this essay was to explore the significance for you of some experience you have had that you think most other students haven't.

18.2

Plan

the time the parents fought at
a Little League baseball game
   -- what significance?
   -- seemed silly at the time
   -- kids didn't understand
   -- maybe something about
      competitiveness?
   -- maybe something about
      sports fans?

working at the drive-in theater
   -- interesting experiences
   -- many drive-ins have gone
      out of business, not many
      would have worked at one
   -- learned about human nature
   -- tricks to get in without paying

trips to Grand Canyon

watching my grandfather make sausage
   -- recipe
   -- how long it takes

The first rough notes stop here. The trip to Grand Canyon hasn't suggested any particulars to the student. Sausage-making hasn't suggested very much. The first two topics have suggested more, and it may be that, given the assignment, the key to the student's choice is the note following the second topic, "not many would have worked at one." Notice that at this point the student hasn't worked out any particular significance for this experience except the general notion, "learned about human nature."

19 Occasions and Opportunities in Writing

No writer has ever lived who did not at some time or other get stuck.
—Jacques Barzun, "Calamophobia, or Hints Toward a Writer's Discipline"

The preceding chapter suggested some ways to look for a subject and discover a subject's potential, and discussed some of the problems with and possibilities for looking at a subject and an audience. The chapter ended with an account of a kind of triangular relationship among a writer, audience, and subject. This chapter will take up where it left off.

Writers do get stuck sometimes. They can lose track of their subject, or become so wrapped up in the sound of their words that they forget the substance, or suffer any of a hundred different ailments. But one great blessing when you write is that you don't have to invent everything for yourself. Customary practices in different kinds of writing—indeed, the very existence of different kinds of writing—give you resources to draw upon. Other writers have written before you; their exploration and practice will often help to show you ways of doing things. The preceding chapter stressed *your* resources as means of discovering what you have to say. This chapter suggests that other writers, by their practices in different kinds of writing, also offer resources to you.

It is not easy to think about "different kinds of writing" and learn from them unless you have at least a reasonably satisfactory way of sorting them out. In one way or another, all writing is personal. Even a piece of writing that is intended for public use and that is supposed to be impersonal and objective begins with a person and a pencil. Thus, it may be that there are as many kinds of writing as there are examples of writing. Still, it seems likely that there are ways to group different pieces of writing—by similar techniques, for example, or by similar purposes. It doesn't seem unreasonable to suppose that there are identifiable kinds of writing, in which examples of each kind have some features in common.

The title of this chapter is meant to suggest a way of discriminating among kinds of writing. It suggests that there are *occasions* and *opportunities* in writing. We write at different times, in different places, under the burden of different needs, and with different possibilities. Occasions for writing change. Even when all the writing you do is for a class, the occasion isn't always the same: assignments change, and each occasion provides a different set of opportunities. What you do in one piece of writing may be impossible in another; but when you lose one set of opportunities, you gain another.

An example may help to clarify the distinction between *occasions* for writing and *opportunities* for writing. Suppose you are assigned to write a book review for your freshman English class. That provides the *occasion* for writing: given the *occasion* you know the time you'll have to write, where you'll write, whom you're writing for, the need to write, what kind of thing to write. You have an *occasion* for writing, and the occasion creates certain opportunities for writing – that is, it gives you a chance to do certain kinds of things. Since you're supposed to write a book review, you have some reason to say what the book is about, how it is organized, what viewpoint it reveals, how satisfactory it seems to be in handling the subject, what your reaction to it is. You have various opportunities *to explain* the book and your response and perhaps some opportunities *to argue* with the book or about its effectiveness. However, you don't have much opportunity *to narrate* or *to describe* or *to meditate privately*. If, instead, you were assigned to write a biographical essay about the author, you would have ample opportunity *to narrate,* fewer opportunities *to argue.* The nature of an *occasion* for writing gives you certain *opportunities* for writing.

In the pages that follow, we suggest several ways to sort kinds of writing, and we linger over one or two of them. When writing is classified, however, it's useful to remember that each kind occurs on a specific occasion and offers specific opportunities. Knowing about different kinds of writing is interesting in its own right, but valuable to you, as a writer, only if it helps you understand how others have used different occasions and opportunities so that you may find help in their examples. That will make it easier for you to be sure of what you're doing and why you're doing it.

Different kinds of writing (or speaking) are commonly confused. If a teacher asks for your personal reflections on a movie you've just seen, and you turn in an essay about the director of the movie, then you and the teacher are not working with the same kind of writing, the same occasion, or the same opportunities. If you want a political candidate to justify his voting record, and instead he or she gives you an opinion about a current issue, you and the candidate have confused kinds, occasions, and opportunities.

It's crucial that you understand the purpose of your writing and that you know what kinds of writing will let you do what you want

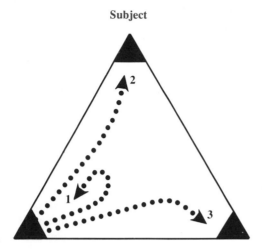

Subject

Author   Audience

or need to do. Seeing how other writers have worked with different opportunities on different occasions should help you to see what is possible.

19

Writ

One way to see the nature of different kinds of writing is to return to the triangular relationship mentioned earlier and start with a simple diagram representing chief elements in writing. (The following paragraphs depend on James Kinneavy's *A Theory of Discourse* for help in differentiating among kinds of nonfiction.) This triangle connects chief elements—writer, subject, audience. The dotted lines inside are meant to suggest something about the nature of different kinds of writing, as we'll see.

In many kinds of writing, the author is dominant; the writing is by the author and, in many ways, *for* the author. As line 1 in the diagram shows, this kind of writing leaves the author and returns to the author. It may be called *expressive writing,* for the author's need to express himself or herself is the primary motive in such writing.

You should note two things about *expressive writing.* First, there are many different kinds of *expressive writing.* Personal letters, diaries, and journals often seem intended chiefly as personal expression; some descriptive writing is the author's account of learning to see. Some expository and argumentative writing turns out to be *expressive writing* when the author, instead of seeking to explain or to persuade, that is, to reach an audience, uses the occasion for meditative purposes to work out personal thoughts about a subject. Second, expressive writing offers some opportunities and sets some limits that other kinds of writing don't. You are probably free, for example, to write more informally than you might other- wise and to use looser forms of organization. You are your own prime object of attention in this kind of writing; you must first of all be honest with yourself. In other kinds of writing the subject de- serves primary attention, and you must get out of the way. As line 2 indicates, some writing is focused on the subject, with the author and any possible audience fading into the background. Kinneavy calls this kind of writing *referential writing;* it refers to something outside the author. Many business letters are *referential writing,* as are most reports, including book reports, laboratory reports, and other class reports. Most answers on essay examinations and most writing about literature are forms of *referential writing.* You don't have the same kind of freedom in this kind of writing that you might with *expressive writing;* the subject must be dealt with, and that may require tighter organization, a more technical language, and a close control of your own opinions. But you need not think of *referential writing* as only limiting; sometimes it is a great ad- vantage to get outside yourself and plunge into the exploration of a subject.

In other kinds of writing, which Kinneavy classifies as *per- suasive writing,* the audience seems to be the proper target of at- tention. Many forms of writing are intended to move or to per- suade an audience. Sermons belong to this group, as do letters of recommendation, critiques, all forms of argument, and some kinds of public letters, like letters of protest. Writing in this class may make particular demands on you; it may require close, lucid rea- soning that an audience can easily follow, and sure, specific evi- dence that will support assertions. Most troublesome of all—it may require you to be believable to others in a way not demanded by *expressive writing* or *referential writing.*

The particular writing tasks you will face both in and out of school may each have special requirements, forms of expression, and styles. This general scheme of organization—*expressive writ- ing, referential writing,* and *persuasive writing*—is a reminder that the different pieces of writing you do may have different *aims,* ac- cording to the occasions on which they occur and the opportunities made possible. The language you use, the style you develop in sen- tences and paragraphs, the forms of organization you depend on, the relationship you establish among yourself, your subject, and your audience—all may vary according to what you intend to do. It makes a difference in the way we talk or write whether we are talk- ing about ourselves, some subject outside ourselves, or to an audi- ence. Speakers and writers sometimes go astray when they forget what they are supposed to be doing. We've all had teachers who have become so involved in their subject (referential discourse) that they have forgotten their audience of students (requiring persuasive discourse). We've all heard salesmen and politicians so intent on selling themselves to us (persuasive discourse) that they have forgotten to know very much about their subject (requiring referential discourse).

These terms — *expressive writing, referential writing,* and *persuasive writing* — are useful because they are a reminder that different occasions provide different opportunities and allow you to work toward different purposes. Each of these kinds of writing may require you to use different *methods,* different arrangements of *language;* but you'll find that *many* different methods and arrangements of language are possible in each of these kinds of writing.

In the following pages, we will use another set of terms to suggest different *modes* or *attitudes* in writing: *exposition, narration, description,* and *argumentation.* This set of terms is useful in at least two ways. First, these terms may be more familiar to you than the terms we've used above. Second, and more important, they interlock with the three terms used earlier and reinforce the idea that each *aim* of writing (expressive, referential, persuasive) can be served by different ways of writing:

19.1

1. **Expressive writing** may sometimes be explanatory or expository; it may use narration or description; it may be argumentative in the sense that you are wrestling with a subject to determine your own views.
2. **Referential writing** is probably most often expository, but you may need to use narration and description to explain something, or even argument when something about the subject is in doubt.
3. **Persuasive writing** is argumentative in attitude; it is designed to change an audience in some way; to do that, you may need to explain, to describe, to narrate.

Some other methods of classifying kinds of writing are discussed briefly at the end of this chapter. The point is that knowing what others have done with different kinds of writing — knowing what is possible — is a way to learn what you can do, what opportunities you have on different occasions.

19.1 Exposition

The purpose of exposition is to *inform* your readers, to increase their knowledge, to help them understand a situation or a process, to give them information about an idea or belief. It ranges from the explanation of small personal matters ("How to Select a College

Wardrobe") to complex scientific treatises ("The Effect of Ultraviolet Light on Steroids").

Skill in exposition is essential in all schoolwork. You will probably do more expository writing, in which you inform your reader or explain a point of view, than any other kind of writing. Most of the reading required in school, except in literature courses, is also expository. Increasing skill in expository writing, then, is a major aim of composition courses.

Gathering Information

Whatever your subject and whatever the length of your paper, you will have to exercise judgment in deciding what resources to use and in gearing your information to your particular audience and situation. (See 18.1, Using Available Resources, and 30, The Research Paper.) Some of the short expository papers you will be assigned in college can be based entirely on your own knowledge and experience. Other papers will require that you gather and evaluate information from various sources in order to develop your subject adequately.

Even when you base your paper on a personal experience, such as building a boat or working in a drive-in theater, you may find it useful to add to your information by reading in the library or by talking to people who have had similar experiences. It is a good idea in planning such a paper to make a list of points about which your memory is hazy or about which you lack adequate information. Then, to fill in the gaps, you can extend your observations or read what others have reported about the subject.

For typical information papers on subjects such as "The Electoral College" or "Devices for Controlling Air Pollution," you will usually need to consult a variety of printed sources—books, magazines, newspapers—to find information you cannot gather firsthand.

Relating Specialized Information to Your Reader

In gathering and selecting additional facts to use in an expository paper, be particularly careful to consider your audience. If you are writing a paper for a group of bridge fanciers, you probably need not define terms like *point count* and *slam* or explain how a *finesse* is made, since your readers would be familiar with such fundamentals. But if you are writing about bridge for an English class, you cannot expect the typical student to have this knowledge; to make sure that your audience understands, you must take the time to insert brief explanations. If you omit them, the whole paper may be puzzling or even incomprehensible to general readers. Remember that you are writing the paper to tell them something new, to add to their knowledge in an area where they do not have your background. Put yourself in their place: what words or ideas might be unfamiliar to them? How can you explain these things so that they will understand them?

The following passages show effective and ineffective ways of relating specialized information to general readers:

> INEFFECTIVE: There are various ways to bridge the gap from one solo to the next. The trumpeter may play a series of riffs accompanied only by the rhythm section. This is probably the most common method.
>
> EFFECTIVE: There are various ways to bridge the gap from one solo to the next. Probably the most common method is for the trumpeter to play a series of short, conventional jazz phrases, called "riffs," accompanied only by the rhythm section — piano, bass, and drums.
>
> INEFFECTIVE: If the bleeding becomes severe or there is a chance of infection, you may have to cauterize the wound.
>
> EFFECTIVE: If the bleeding becomes severe or there is a chance of infection, you may have to cauterize the wound by searing it with a piece of metal that has been held over a flame until it is red hot.

Documenting Your Information

19.1

Exp

When your own observations form the basis of the paper, be sure to tell the readers why you consider your statements to be fairly authoritative. Otherwise they may not be sure how much value to attach to them. Somewhere near the beginning of the paper, state the circumstances under which you gathered your facts:

> Since I was sixteen I have spent my summer vacations working in a local department store, first as a stock clerk and later as an assistant display manager. During that time, I have become familiar with the typical organization of a large retail store. . . .
>
> My home is only nine miles away from the Menominee Indian reservation, and I have had frequent opportunities to meet and talk to members of the Menominee tribe. . . .
>
> In gathering examples for this paper, I spent ten hours listening to radio programs featuring rock-and-roll records and copied down the lyrics of a dozen of the current favorites. . . .

When you incorporate published material into your paper, be sure to reproduce it accurately and to credit the sources, whether you quote them directly or not. It is not fair to present someone else's experiences or observations as if they were your own. In a research paper, credit is given formally by means of footnotes (30.8, Documenting the Paper), but in a general paper mention may be made informally. The following are some typical examples of how such acknowledgments can be handled:

> Franklin Soames, the author of *Zapotec Culture,* found that. . . .

> At a recent medical convention, H. L. Matthews, the noted urologist, was quoted as saying. . . .
>
> But according to Jean Lafontant, in a recent article in *Saturday Review*. . . .

Sources which have been used extensively may be given in a note at the beginning or at the end of a paper:

> Much of the material for this paper was taken from C. D. Darlington, *The Evolution of Man and Society* (New York: Simon & Schuster, 1969).

• *Exercise*

Look for several pieces of expository writing and bring them to class for discussion. Notice in particular how much detail different writers use, how writers convey specialized information, how much time they spend on different parts of their subject. Try to find selections that illustrate different relationships between the writer and the subject (involved? dispassionate? aloof? distant? close?). Explanations are likely to occur in many interesting places; look at the labels of jars and cans, the owner's manual that comes with some appliances or a car, a popular magazine for crafts and mechanics, textbooks, a book on how our language developed, the jacket commentary for a record album.

19.2 Narration

The purpose of narrative writing is to re-create an experience or event, usually without expository comment. Like description, narration depends upon particulars, but unlike description, it moves through a time period:

> The day we bought the farm, rain streaked the windshield so we could not see our way on the dirt roads. Going to the bank, we passed a deer feasting by the highway, and would have called it a good omen if we had been talking. Across a table we passed paper checks, receiving paper back; so often discussed, it seemed an empty gesture, an unchosen choice I had let mold my life. The day we bought the farm, the wet April grass hinted of the chill to come, while I tried to keep warm under a parka, waiting to take possession. In the evening, I wrote to keep from arguing — tallying in my head — a catalog of injuries. — Judith Beth Cohen, *Vermont Diary*

Point of View

The particulars of narrative writing are reported to an audience selectively through a given point of view. Ordinarily it is neither possible nor desirable to present every action in a sequence of events. Rather, you should focus on those aspects of an experience that, from your point of view, make it worth preserving.

Most of the narrative writing you do will be presented as the narrative of either a first-person observer or participant or of a third-person observer. Personal narratives and autobiographical sketches are ordinarily told in the first person, but it will depend on the story you tell whether you present yourself as participating or observing. In historical writing, reports, and case histories, you will ordinarily present the action in the third person, letting the events speak for themselves.

Whether you report an action as a participant or observer, try to focus attention directly on what went on. In the following passage the narrator draws attention to *himself* rather than to the event he is narrating:

> I was riding with a friend late one night, returning from a long weekend trip. I was extremely tired, and I am sure he was too, and as a result we weren't very observant about traffic lights. I did notice in the distance one very red blinker light, though. I also saw a car directly in front of ours, like a slow moving ship in a submarine's sights. I knew immediately that we were going too fast to stop, so my natural reaction was to brace myself for a crash. It seemed to me that I could hear the tires squealing for minutes before anything happened. I was surprised to find during those actually few short seconds that I was seeing a variety of vivid colors that I hadn't even noticed before. I was aware of the yellow dividing strip of the highway, and still off in the distance, the brilliant red flashes of the traffic signal. There were also the browns and grays and whites of the surrounding buildings, that I hadn't seen a few moments before, but now were things of sharp beauty.

19.2

Narr

This narrative could be tightened up, and the *I*'s made less conspicuous, by revising some of the sentences:

> Late one night I was riding with a friend. We were both extremely tired after a long weekend trip and not very watchful of the traffic lights. But I was dimly aware of one very red blinker light in the distance. Suddenly a car loomed up in front of us, like a slow moving ship seen through a submarine's sights. We were going too fast to stop, and instinctively I braced myself for the crash. Our tires squealed for what seemed minutes. Actually only a second or two passed, but in that brief instant, all the color of the scene jumped into view—the bright yellow dividing strip of the highway, the brilliant red flashes of the traffic light, the browns, grays, and whites of the nearby buildings. For one sharp moment everything took on a strange and fearful beauty.

A reader will understand your experience more clearly if you concentrate on the events as they happened instead of on your feelings about them.

Use of Tenses

In narrative writing events are typically written down in chronological order, with verbs and adverbs controlling the movement:

> . . . **After a long half hour,** the rain **eased** a bit and the clouds **rose.** I **relaxed** a little. I **was showing** them that a rookie **could get through. Just then,** the engine **stopped** cold. As a rule, **when** an engine **fails,** it **will give** some warning. The water temperature **will rise,** or the oil pressure **will drop,** or there **is a knocking or clanking.** Even if it **is only for a minute or two,** it **gives** the pilot a chance **to look around** and **head for** a field or open place. However, **when** the timing gear in a Liberty engine **failed, one second** it **was roaring along** even and strong, and **the next** there **was** a tremendous silence. I **quickly twisted** all the knobs and gadgets in the cockpit, but there **was** no response, and the engine **stayed** dead. **While** my hands **were trying to restart** the engine, my neck **was stretching** and my eyes **searching** for some sort of field to **land in.** I **was surrounded** by heavily forested, sharply rolling hills. To my left **was** a cuplike basin with a small clearing. It **was** downwind, but my gliding radius **didn't allow** much choice. I **went** for it. — Dean C. Smith, "Flying by Guess and by God"

Most narrative writing uses the past tense, but the present (or "historical present") is sometimes used to create a sense of events actually happening, as in this paragraph:

> Above me the clouds roll in, unfurling and smoking billows in malignant violet, dense as wool. Most of the sky is lidded over but the sun remains clear, halfway down the west, shining beneath the storm. Over my head the clouds thicken, then crack and split with a roar like that of cannonballs tumbling down a marble staircase; their bellies open — too late to run now! — and suddenly the rain comes down. — Edward Abbey, *Desert Solitaire*

Whether a narrative is written in the present or past, one tense should be kept throughout. This paragraph illustrates unnecessary and confusing tense shifts:

> As I **hop** [present tense] on the city transit that will take me to the University, I notice that as always the bus is filled past capacity. As I **turned** [past] around, I saw a blind man sitting directly behind me with a dog lying at his feet. I **watch** [present] the dog, sitting there perfectly still, looking through the glass doors. Suddenly the dog **got up** [past], nudged his master, who pulled the cord above his head and with no difficulty got off the bus and proceeded up the street. I **wondered** [past] how a dog could be trained to know when to get off the bus, when to cross the street, and when to wait for a signal. Dogs seem to have more sense than some humans.

Pacing a Narrative

Because it moves through a time sequence, narration presents some problems not found in other types of description. Foremost among these is the problem of pacing. Whether a series of events that you are narrating covers three years, three weeks, or three hours, you cannot reproduce the entire sequence — nor should you want to, for much of the time in any sequence of events is filled with action that has no particular bearing on the experience you are relating. The problem is to pace the telling of your story so that thorough attention goes to the significant actions and less attention to actions that have less immediate impact for your narrative.

If you study any example of effective narrative writing you will see, as Leo Rockas has noted, a balance of "remote" narration and "minute" narration. We *do* something just about all the time, but it may be that only a small portion of our doing is directed toward an end that is central to the experience we are trying to preserve in narrative. Still, if the significant actions that warrant narration are to have any context and continuity, they must be seen as part of a continuing stream of events. What you must do, then, is find a way to suggest a considerable amount of time in a relatively short space (remote narration) and so create a context for your slower, more detailed account of the significant actions (minute narration). If you are a reader of comic strips, you will remember that in a strip such as *Steve Canyon* or *Mary Worth* the cartoonist-narrator will occasionally use a picture or two to show the characters at their regular work; but when some dramatic episode nears its climax, he may use the full strip for several weeks to present a single, climactic action. In a detective novel, two weeks of routine work may pass in a sentence, while a brief fight lasts two pages.

19.2

Narr)

Including Adequate Details

If your narrative is to come alive for your reader, you must include enough details to make it interesting and understandable. Avoid any statement that might leave the reader wondering "What?" or "Why?" or "When?" or "Who?" In this paragraph, for example, the narrator fails to tell *what* his teacher said or *why* "the results of the contest were disappointing":

> On the night of the final judging, I was so nervous I could hardly move my fingers. As I waited backstage for my turn to appear, I was sure I had forgotten the opening notes of my number completely. I began thinking of ways to escape; maybe I could faint or pretend to be violently ill. But then at the last minute my piano teacher came by to wish me luck and **said something that suddenly changed everything.**

> When my turn came, I played with ease and confidence. **Although the results of the contest were disappointing,** I was pleased that I had conquered one of my major enemies — stage fright.

In selecting details, choose those that illuminate or enliven significant actions. A narrative should not be loaded down with minute and unimportant details. You can usually make your point and still keep the action moving by selecting two or three lively incidents, as in this example:

> Grandmother didn't need reasons for fussing at Grandpa. She told everyone that he wouldn't chop wood or carry water for her. If he did bring wood to her, she would throw it out the window, stick by stick, not caring where it landed. If he brought her water, carrying it from the spring, several hundred feet away, she would pour it out — over him, if possible. Then she would take the empty pail and her cane, and trudge painfully down the long slope to the spring and back again, though it might take her half the morning, the time depending upon her mood and strength. "If I want fresh water, I have to carry it myself, because George is walkin' to Marionville or sittin' on his behind somewhere," she would say to anyone she chanced to see. "And if I want wood, I have to get my boy Jake to come over and chop it for me." — Bertie Johnson, "The Never-Ending Time," *The New Yorker*

See also 27.3, Continuity in Narrative Paragraphs.

* *Exercise*

Look for several pieces of narrative writing and bring them to class for discussion. Who is doing the narration? Where is he or she in relation to the action? How do you know you can trust the writer to give you an accurate account of the action? When is the pace fast? When is it slow? Look at a variety of different kinds of narration: check the sports pages in your newspaper for accounts of different ball games and notice how the narrative of a headlined game differs from that of a game assumed to be less interesting or important. Look at a history text or at some good books on an area of history that interests you (notice, for example, how an account of the battle of Shiloh in a text on American history differs from an account in a book devoted entirely to the Civil War). Notice how a movie critic summarizes the action of a movie, or how *TV Guide* summarizes the action of a show.

19.3 Description

The purpose of descriptive writing is to enable a reader to see an object, person, or scene as you have seen or imagined it. This requires an eye for significant details as well as a knack for putting sense impressions into words. Description is often written for its own sake, as a form of artistic expression, and it may also be an important part of other kinds of writing, from long research papers to technical reports and case histories.

Seeing Your Subject Clearly

To make a description vivid to a reader, you must first of all know where you stand, physically and mentally, in relation to the thing you are writing about. How did you see your subject? From what angle? Under the weight of what mood? How can you define your subject, distinguishing it from similar things in the same class? What makes this particular sunset, for example, different from all others?

Descriptive writing succeeds only when you show your audience the specific, identifying details of object or scene. This requires that you see it clearly yourself, that you understand what you see, and that you say *precisely* what you see, as the writer has done in this passage:

> I know how a prize watermelon looks when it is sunning its fat rotundity among pumpkin vines and "simblins"; I know how to tell when it is ripe without "plugging" it. I know how inviting it looks when it is cooling itself in a tub of water under the bed, waiting; I know how it looks when it lies on the table in the sheltered great floorspace between house and kitchen, and the children gathered for the sacrifice and their mouths watering. I know the crackling sound it makes when the carving knife enters its end and I can see the split fly along in front of the blade as the knife cleaves its way to the other end; I can see its halves fall apart and display the rich red meat and the black seeds, and the heart standing up, a luxury fit for the elect.—Mark Twain, *Autobiography*

No two persons look at a scene in exactly the same way. What makes one writer's description more vivid than another's is the kind of details selected and the way they are arranged.

Selecting and Arranging Details

Good descriptive writing is precise. If in describing a person you write "I first noticed this lady because she was wearing a funny hat," your description won't mean much to the reader because there are many kinds of funny hats. State in specific terms what the hat looked like: perhaps it was a black velvet beret covered with seashells or perhaps it was a miniature merry-go-round.

Notice how lifeless the description is in this paraphrase, from which the specific expressions have been removed:

> After Lincoln became a lawyer, he started to pay more attention to his appearance. But even though he wore his hair in the accepted fashion of the time, he still wasn't well dressed. As a result, he acquired the

> reputation of being one of the most careless dressers in town, along with another local man, who was a judge, and who was equally careless about the way he looked.

By way of contrast, compare the description as it was written:

> And though Lincoln had begun wearing broadcloth and white shirts with a white collar and black silk cravat, and suggestions of sideburns coming down three-fourths the length of his ears, he was still known as one of the carelessly dressed men of Springfield, along with Stephen Logan, who wore unbleached cotton shirts and had sat two years as a circuit court judge wearing an unbleached cotton shirt with no cravat or stock. — Carl Sandburg, *Abraham Lincoln: The Prairie Years, I*

Being specific in descriptive writing doesn't mean that you should overload your sentences with adjectives and adverbs. While such words are used to "describe" or qualify other words, too many of them can be disastrous to any piece of descriptive writing. To refer to the Grand Canyon as *"absolutely* the *most marvelous* sight I have *ever* seen in my *entire* life" may give your readers some hint about your emotions, but it won't tell them much about the Canyon or help them re-create your impression of it.

The details you select for a descriptive passage should contribute to a central impression. (See 27.3, Continuity in Descriptive Paragraphs.) Often a few well-selected details will give a sharper picture than a large number of ill-assorted ones, as in this quick sketch of old houses:

> Houses are like sentinels in the plain, old keepers of the weather watch. There, in a very little while, wood takes on the appearance of great age. All colors wear soon away in the wind and rain, and then the wood is burned gray and the grain appears and the nails turn red with rust. The windowpanes are black and opaque; you imagine there is nothing within, and indeed there are many ghosts, bones given up to the land. They stand here and there against the sky, and you approach them for a longer time than you expect. They belong in the distance; it is their domain. — N. Scott Momaday, *The Way to Rainy Mountain*

To give focus to a description, you may find it useful to adopt one of the methods for developing material discussed in 21.2. For example, a spatial arrangement that takes you from left to right in picturing your subject, or from high to low, or from near to far, may help you create order in your description.

Often objects attract attention to themselves and deserve to become subjects for description because of some special impression they make. Thus, an interesting way to organize description is to focus attention on the dominant impression, subordinating all else. In the following passage the impression of quiet laziness, idleness, dominates the scene:

> After all these years I can picture that old time to myself now, just as it was then: the white town drowsing in the sunshine of a summer's morning; the streets empty, or pretty nearly so; one or two clerks sitting in front of the Water Street stores, with their splint-bottomed chairs tilted back against the walls, chins on breasts, hats slouched over their faces, asleep — with shingle-shavings enough around to show what broke them down; a sow and a litter of pigs loafing along the sidewalk, doing a good business in watermelon rinds and seeds; two or three lonely little freight piles scattered about the levee; a pile of skids on the slope of the stone-paved wharf, and the fragrant town drunkard asleep in the shadow of them. — Mark Twain, *Life on the Mississippi*

Good descriptive writing demands restraint and discrimination. It also takes practice to get the exact effect that you want. One way to get additional practice is to study published examples of descriptive writing that appeal to you, observing what kinds of details the writers use and how they present them.

19.4

arg

• *Exercise*

Look for several pieces of descriptive writing and bring them to class for discussion. Notice how many of the sentences contain specific sensory details and impressions. Notice the arrangement in each selection, and see if you can determine what the description is for. Where is the writer in relation to the subject? Check advertisements, stage directions in printed plays, passages in novels, fashion magazines, craft magazines, textbooks, merchandise catalogs.

19.4 Argumentation

Whereas the purpose of exposition is to *inform* your readers, the purpose of argumentation is to *convince* them. The two kinds of writing have much in common, and both are based on facts or impressions gathered from various sources. But expository writing simply *presents* information, while argumentative writing *uses* it to support or test a belief. A paper describing current fashions in clothing, the social habits of bees, or the history of the slave trade invites the readers to share the writer's knowledge of the subject; a paper attacking campus rules for dress, on the other hand, expresses an opinion and tries to convince the reader of its validity. Argumentative writing is designed to make an audience recognize, admit, or adopt something. It makes a claim on the audience's intellect and judgment. Like exposition, argumentative writing ranges widely, from matters close at hand ("Down with Large Classes") to those of major public concern ("Let's Get Rid of the Electoral College").

Locating the Argument

An argumentative paper *proposes* something. Whether it calls for action or simply asks for the recognition of a point of view, it centers on a proposition that the writer must be prepared to prove.

An argument from a proposition, as Edward P. J. Corbett has said in *Classical Rhetoric for the Modern Student,* is similar to a factual report in that it can ordinarily be judged as true or false; but a statement of fact is not in itself an occasion for argument, since presumably facts can be checked. An argument is also similar to a statement of opinion, in that it represents a judgment the writer has made; but an opinion is not an occasion for argument unless it is based on *facts* instead of mere preference, for only then can its validity be proved.

In planning a persuasive paper, you must take the time to formulate your proposition carefully. As your thesis statement, your proposition gives direction and unity to your argument. Ordinarily it needs to be simple—composed ideally of a single subject and a single predicate. If you argue, for example, that "County government must be put into new hands on election day and reformed to keep state and federal agencies from encroaching on local authority," you have, by using a double predicate, introduced two arguments, both of which must then be proved.

You should find the suggestions in 18.1, Locating a Thesis, helpful in formulating an arguable proposition.

Using Resources and Evidence

When we state our opinions in informal situations, we often give little or no evidence to support them: "John is a reckless driver"; "The cost of living is going up every day"; "Divorce is the main cause of juvenile delinquency." This does not mean that we have no good reasons for believing as we do, but simply that our reasons are usually known and accepted by our listeners. On occasions when our opinions are questioned, we may attempt to support them with facts drawn from our experience and reading: "John had two accidents last month, and he always drives too fast." "Steak is up sixty cents a pound, and a refrigerator costs almost twice as much today as it did six years ago." "Psychologists say that emotional stability depends on a secure family life." Such evidence is considered acceptable or even convincing in informal situations, usually because the listener's personal regard for the speaker lends some weight to the evidence.

In writing, however, the relationship with your audience is far more impersonal; authority must rest much more on the facts themselves. Readers who know neither John nor you will want to know what kind of accidents John had and who was at fault; they will wonder whether "too fast" means in excess of speed limits; they may suspect that "always" is an exaggeration. Before accepting your opinion in regard to the relation between divorce and delinquency, they may want to hear what psychologists say in their own words, to be sure you are not misinterpreting their remarks or ignoring opposed opinions.

The more facts supporting your opinion that you can gather from experience or from the written statement of others, the more reason you can give your readers to accept that opinion. You will not be able to present absolute *proof,* but the greater the weight of your evidence, the more probable it will seem to them that your belief is the best one.

Types of Arguments

19.4

arg

Some traditional kinds of argument may suggest certain ways of thinking about your material that will lead you to the evidence you need. One is the *argument from nature.* Not long ago on a college campus a young man who wished to call attention to inadequacies in the campus guidebook petitioned to have his name placed on the ballot in an election for homecoming queen. He maintained that he was eligible on the grounds that the guidebook stipulated only that candidates should be students under twenty-one; sex was not mentioned in the body of the rules. The young man's petition was denied through an argument from nature. Pointing out that the rules came under the heading "Eligibility requirements for homecoming queen," his opposition seized on the meaning of the word *queen*—by nature a female—to deny his eligibility. An argument from nature may be developed by a number of techniques: by defining the nature of a thing; by studying the meanings attached to the key words in a proposition; by classifying the subject in order to establish a frame of reference in terms of which it can be discussed.

People cannot always agree on the nature of things, of course, and for that reason they have often turned to other kinds of argument. The *argument from analogy* brings a subject and argument into a reader's knowledge by suggesting its similarity to something better known, as in the fairly common—but usually ineffective—analogy of government and business. The evidence you bring to this kind of argument must show that the comparison is both significant and accurate.

The *argument from consequence* enforces a proposition by examining cause and effect, antecedent and consequence. This is a useful kind of argument, but it is limited by the fact that human affairs are not ordered by certain laws of causality. Poverty *sometimes* breeds crime; prolonged tyranny *frequently* leads to revolution; honesty is *occasionally* rewarded. Before expressing an opinion about the outcome of some course of action, or about the cause of some event, make sure that the weight of evidence lends probability to your statement.

The *argument from authority* depends upon the testimony of respected persons, the authority of institutions, the weight of important documents. This is probably the least popular of the traditional kinds of argument, for most audiences prefer to feel that the truth is *discovered* in the course of an argument, rather than that it has been *pronounced* by authority.

Taking the Argument to Your Audience

Whatever kind of argument you use, and those above are only samples, remember that your readers have some confidence in their own intelligence and judgment and are likely to resent a writer who attempts to make up their minds for them. (See the discussion of author-audience relationships in 18.2.) State your facts as specifically as possible — so that your readers can check them for themselves if they want to — and give your reasons for whatever conclusions you draw. Compare the following statements for effectiveness:

> VAGUE: A few years ago, the president of a large corporation said that taxes were too high.
>
> SPECIFIC: In a speech to the Toledo Chamber of Commerce on April 14, 1974, Oscar Winslow, president of the Winslow Steel Corporation, said, "Corporation taxes today are so high that they are destroying business incentive."
>
> VAGUE: In many of his newspaper articles, H. L. Mencken made slighting references to democracy. Anyone can see that he despised it.
>
> SPECIFIC: In his articles for the Baltimore *Sun,* H. L. Mencken frequently referred to democracy in terms such as these: "the domination of unreflective and timorous men, moved in vast herds by mob emotions" (July 26, 1920); "it may be clumsy, it may be swinish, it may be unutterably incompetent and dishonest, but it is never dismal" (July 14, 1924).

In trying to persuade readers to accept your opinion, you will naturally want to gather facts that will support your position. It is not fair to your readers, however, to suggest that *all* evidence reinforces your belief. They may be familiar with contrary evidence; even if they are not, its absence may make them suspect that you are stacking the deck in your favor. In a court of law, an attorney who deliberately suppresses evidence damaging to his or her case may be disbarred from future practice. The consequences to writers are usually not so serious, but they may also lose the case.

When you come across facts that do *not* support your opinion, give them as careful consideration as you do those that do. Is their source authoritative and relatively free of bias? Do they offer serious and relevant reasons to question your present opinion? Do they outnumber the facts you can find to support it? It may be that you will want to alter or modify your proposition after taking opposing facts into account. You may decide that your original opinion was wrong; many writers are unaware of the flimsy basis of their beliefs until they begin trying to substantiate them.

Even if the facts you gather do not change your opinion, it is unfair to simply discard those that fail to support it. In fact, it will strengthen your position in the readers' eyes if you frankly admit unfavorable evidence along with your reasons for being unpersuaded by it. Remember that the readers are your jury. If you have arrived at an opinion by weighing opposing evidence sensibly, they should be able to do the same.

19.4

Testing the Argument

arg

One way to test your argument, or to examine the argument of another writer or speaker, is to scrutinize it for flaws in reasoning and in the use of evidence. Probably the most common flaws are these:

Hasty Generalization. In informal situations, we often overgeneralize from the facts: "She's *never* on time"; "Advertising is *only* a pack of lies." A little consideration shows us that in reality all-or-none, black-or-white situations are rare; reality is more accurately described in terms of finer shadings and degrees. Most readers are aware of this, and although they will accept and make statements like the above uncritically enough in conversations, they are suspicious of them in writing.

Be especially cautious in using terms like *all, always, everybody, nobody, never, none, only,* and *most.* Before making such all-inclusive statements, make sure that they are justified. If there are any exceptions to some assertion you make, nodify your language to make it more accurate. Don't say that *all* young people want a home and family: *some* or *many* might be more accurate. Before you say that *most* early marriages end in divorce, ascertain from some reliable source whether more than 50 percent actually do; otherwise you are not justified in using *most.* Keep in mind that the English vocabulary provides you with a wealth of qualifying terms (*some, few, often,* to name only a few) and choose those that most accurately describe the number, extent, and frequency of the facts you are asserting.

Compare these two statements for precision of expression. Both are based on the same facts (of the delinquents in the State Training School, 75 percent come from low-income families, 45 percent have used narcotics at some time, and 20 percent have IQ scores over 100):

> OVERGENERALIZATION: **Almost all** delinquents in the State Training School come from homes **on the verge of starvation. Most** of them are **dope addicts,** and **very few** are **brilliant.**
>
> ACCURATE STATEMENT: **Three out of four** delinquents in the State Training School come from **low-income homes. Almost half** of them have **at least experimented** with narcotics. **A significant minority** are **above average mentally.**

False Analogy.   Comparison and analogy are effective means of arguing, but only if there is really a basic similarity between the compared terms. If, for example, a university administrator sets out to argue for new rules and economies in his or her school on the basis that it should be run like a business, we should probably reject that argument on the grounds that the analogy is not valid, for similarities between a business and a university seem only incidental, not essential.

Post Hoc, Ergo Propter Hoc.   This fallacy (literally, "after this, therefore because of this") is the fairly common one of assuming that two events or things are causally related simply because they are related in time. The young man who gets a raise a week after using a new deodorant probably owes his success to something else.

Non Sequitur.   The label *non sequitur* ("it does not follow") applies to errors of reasoning in which the conclusion does not follow from the evidence presented. Sometimes a step in reasoning has been omitted, and the fallacy can be corrected by supplying the missing link. But sometimes the conclusion is drawn from evidence that has no bearing on the issue: that Mary Starr uses a particular toothpaste has nothing to do with its quality; that a man does not beat his wife has nothing to do with whether he is a good husband; that the army teaches useful skills has nothing to do with the wisdom of sending troops to other countries.

Begging the Question.   This term applies to an argument that assumes the truth of what needs to be proved. A politician who argues "Our feeble county government, desperately in need of reform, must be placed in new hands on election day" is begging the question unless he *proves* that the present government is feeble and in need of reform.

Ignoring the Question. This is a broad term that applies to all arguments that are irrelevant, as when a governor argues that his administration is not corrupt because the state budget is balanced. Another way he might ignore the issue would be to resort to an *argumentum ad hominem* ("argument against the man"), attacking the integrity of his opponents rather than the charge of his own corruption. Or he might use *glittering generalities* such as "my devotion and dedication to the fine people of this great state" to draw his audience into acquiescence by the weight of good words. All arguments that use emotional means to persuade an audience to arrive at a judgment without examining the evidence are ways of ignoring the question.

When you have finished the first draft of an argumentative paper, examine it carefully for flaws. Have you weighed the available evidence? Are your generalizations supported by fact? Are your inferences valid? Make sure that your argument is both honest and sound.

19.5

Writ

• *Exercise*

Look for several pieces of argumentation and bring them to class for discussion. In each, try to determine just what the central topic of debate is and what kind of evidence the writer uses. Notice what kind of relationship the writer tries to establish with the audience. Test the argument against your own judgment and common sense and against the fallacies listed above. You may find it helpful to look at newspaper editorials, letters to editors, advertisements, television commercials, graffiti, bumper stickers, political and social commentary in magazines.

19.5 Other Ways to Study Writing

The purpose of this chapter is to show that the work of other writers may help you in your own writing by showing you how they have used different approaches to suit different occasions. The chapter has discussed *expressing, referring,* or *persuading* by using *expository, narrative, descriptive,* or *argumentative* methods.

Obviously, there are other ways of thinking about different kinds of writing that may help you to understand your own aims better and find appropriate alternatives in different situations.

1. Some writers propose that *all* kinds of writing are persuasive. If you are writing description, for example, presumably you want an audience to see something as you saw it. If you are writing exposition, presumably you want an audience to understand something as you understand it. If you think of all writing as persuasive, then you may have to find another way to distinguish between different kinds of writing. Perhaps you could begin by saying that there is objective persuasion and subjective persuasion. Then you could explore how modes like description, narration, and exposition can be useful in these two kinds of writing.

2. Some forms of writing are *static*. In description and definition, for example, change and passing time are relatively unimportant. Static forms focus on something as it is at a given time. That makes it possible to linger over details, images, and clarifications. Other forms are *temporal*. In narration and process, for example, change and passing time are particularly important. Temporal forms focus on something that is happening, which allows the writer to concentrate on pacing, tempo, and change. Other forms are *mimetic*. They imitate the actions and words of people. In drama and dialogue, for example, the focus is on the sound and interaction of human voices as the writer tries to imitate reality. Still other forms are *mental*. In personal reverie or in public persuasion, for example, the focus is on clarification of the writer's own state of mind, either for its own sake or for the sake of influencing others.[1]

3. Writing can be classified according to writers' attitudes toward their subjects and audiences. Attitude influences the choices of methods that carry messages to audiences. Nine kinds of writing are classified according to attitude: confident, judicious, quiet, imperative, impassioned, compassionate, critical, angry, and absurd writing.[2]

4. Writing can be classified according to the distance in time and space between the speaker and the listener. Reflection is communication with oneself. Conversation, between two people within vocal range. Correspondence, between remote individuals or small groups with some knowledge of each other. And publication is impersonal communication to a large anonymous group extended over space and/or time.[3]

5. Writing can be classified according to purpose. The four basic purposes for writing are (1) to clarify what the subject is; (2) to substantiate a thesis; (3) to evaluate the subject; and (4) to recommend that something be done about the subject.[4]

Clearly, there are different ways of thinking about different kinds of writing. For your own purposes, watch other writers and learn *what* they do with their opportunities on different occasions. Learn what they have found it *possible* to do. Learn what you need or want to do, and take help where you can get it.

[1]Leo Rockas, *Modes of Rhetoric* (New York: St. Martin's Press, Inc., 1964).

[2]Winston Weathers and Otis Winchester, *The Attitudes of Rhetoric* (Englewood Cliffs, NJ: Prentice-Hall, Inc., 1970).

[3]James Moffet, *Teaching the Universe of Discourse* (Boston: Houghton Mifflin Co., 1968).

[4]Caroline Eckhardt and David Stewart, "Towards a Functional Taxonomy of Composition," *College Composition* (December 1979).

• *An Essay in Progress, 2: First Efforts at Development*

```
        Most drive-in movies used to be out at the edge of town, where
the sounds and sights don't interfere with things going on in
town.  Now, you may find them almost anywhere in town.  I guess so many
people have air conditioning in their cars and houses that they are
closed up and can't be disturbed by the noise.  Most of the time, the
back of the screen forms the front of the theater.  Some of them are
decorated with paintings or lights. . . .
        I first learned that I was going to work at the drive-in during
the summer right after my parents took over management of the place in
February.  After they had some time to look the place over, they saw
that an odd-job person was needed.  I knew I was going to be needing a
job for the summer anyway. . . .
        Strange experiences—boy under a quilt
                        girl caught on barbed wire
                        lying about age
```

19.5

Writ

By this time the student had obviously chosen to write about working in a drive-in theater; these are some trial runs at getting started. The first paragraph above suggests that the essay will be largely descriptive. The second seems to be the opening of a narrative. Either might have turned out well; the student may have rejected both because the assignment said "explore the significance," which seems to call for explanation. (See end of Chapters 18, 20, 21, and 28.)

20 Organizing Your Material

> . . . a writer has to lay words and sentences end to end; that is what writing is. He has to lay them in some kind of order, according to some plan or other — familiar or new, symmetrical or bizarre. Different plans have different uses. . . . — Robert Gorrell, "Toward a Linear Rhetoric of the Essay," *College Composition and Communication,* May 1971

Before you begin to write, spend some time thinking through the order in which you intend to present your material. With some subjects the material itself will determine organization. For example, narratives and papers that describe personal experiences usually follow the order of events, and an explanation of a process follows a step-by-step pattern of presentation. In descriptive writing ("A Trip Through the Carlsbad Caverns") the normal order may be from one point to another (entering the Caverns, going to the first level, arriving at the Big Room) or from a general impression to the specific details that give rise to it, arranged more or less in the order of prominence.

The order of presentation may require more thought with other topics such as "A Criticism of Olivier's *Hamlet*" or "Repression and Rationalization as Defense Mechanisms." Whether you select the subject or your instructor assigns one, in most instances you will have to examine the material carefully to find the best order for your special purpose. (See 21.2, Developing Your Material, for suggestions about choosing a pattern of development.) Outlining your material is one good way to determine its best organization.

20.1 The Outline in Relation to the Paper

The usefulness of an outline depends on the material in it. No matter how correct the form — in numbering, punctuation, and structure — if the outline doesn't help you write your paper, it serves no purpose. You can make a pretty outline *after* you've written the paper if you just want to have an outline to turn in. Of course, that's a waste of your time. Outlines are useless unless you take them seriously. Outlines in themselves are no great matter. What matters about outlines is that they represent a writer's care about the subject and possible readers. Taken seriously, they represent a writer's effort to think a subject through and get information and ideas together in the best relationship.

You can learn a number of things from a good outline. From the main divisions in a good outline you can estimate the number and relative length of the paragraphs in your paper, although usually the paragraphs will not correspond exactly to the headings. You can frequently construct topic sentences for these paragraphs by rephrasing or expanding the outline headings. The divisions will show where transitions are needed and suggest the kind of development that will be possible: contrast, comparison, illustration, or others. (See 27.2, Patterns of Paragraph Development, and 21.2, Developing Your Material.)

An outline should be long enough to suit your purpose, and no longer. It should be no more complex than the material demands. The number of main headings for most papers ranges from three to five. A larger number of main headings for a thousand-word paper, for example, suggests that the division is haphazard or that the organization is faulty. The same principle applies to subheadings. Outlines that run from A through J or K need revision, for no single topic ordinarily needs such minute subdivision. And except for very complex material, there is seldom any need to go beyond the third-level subheading.

20.1

Org

When you are asked to submit an outline with your paper, it should represent the plan that you actually followed. Your outline serves then as the table of contents. You may find it necessary in writing the paper to depart occasionally from your original plan; if so, make the corresponding changes in the final outline before handing it in.

Outlines are probably most useful for papers — such as research papers or technical reports — that you have thought through carefully before you ever attempt a first draft. In such instances, an outline is a commitment you make after you've gathered evidence and information, sorted it, thought, and planned. Then you deliberately commit yourself to a single plan with the outline. Ordinarily, anything that doesn't fit the plan is irrelevant, and doesn't belong in the paper. If a traditional outline is to work well for you, you have to accept it as a guide, and therefore do only what the outline calls for you to do. A traditional outline — the kind discussed in later sections of this chapter — is really a plan that is already complete.

If you think for a moment about what traditional outlines look like, you will see that their form indicates, in at least two ways, that most of the thinking for your paper is already done. First, a traditional outline indicates that you have already decided that some things are more important than others. By the time you've finished a traditional outline, you know that some things are primary (and so are listed under Roman numerals) while other things are secondary (and so are listed under capital letters), while still other things are merely illustrations or details (and so are listed under

Arabic numerals). Second, to make a traditional outline, you have to be far enough along in your thinking to be sure about how many parts your paper has; a traditional outline focuses attention upon the separate parts of your paper.

For these reasons, traditional outlines don't always serve your purpose (though if an outline is part of your assignment, be sure to provide it). Sometimes, though, a less formal plan, one that you may develop partly as you write, will work better. As you write you may discover ways of thinking or seeing you hadn't found before, and you may decide to try them. In other words, a plan may only be a series of moves that you make to achieve some purpose; an informal plan, instead of specifying every step you'll take, may simply identify the direction of your work and indicate how each step you take contributes to your purpose.

Remember that an outline, whether detailed and formal or loose and informal, is first of all meant to help you write. A plan can help show you where to go, and can also give you check points along the way: Where is the right starting place? Where do I want to be when I'm finished? What does the reader need to know? What do I want the reader to think or believe or feel? How can I get a reader to accept or respect my position? What steps must I take? How should those steps be connected?

20.2 Types of Outlines

Four kinds of outlines are widely used: the scratch outline, the thesis-sentence outline, the topic outline, and the sentence outline. Sometimes your instructor will tell you which form to use. When you have no specific instructions, select the form that best suits your method of working and the kind of paper you are writing. In planning a long paper, especially one involving research, you will probably want to make a topic or sentence outline. For short papers and extemporaneous writing, informal notes or a scratch outline will generally serve the purpose. Even for long papers, you may find it useful to work informally for some time before committing yourself to a final, detailed plan. It is not uncommon, for example, for writers at work on long projects to draft key passages — an opening paragraph, a closing paragraph, a passage developing the central idea — and then to fit these bits of writing into a more formal plan, along with jotted notes, sentences, and other scraps of ideas. Whatever techniques you use, the important thing is to develop a plan that will guide you in writing your paper.

Scratch Outlines

A scratch outline is a series of notes — single words or phrases — jotted down to refresh your memory as you write. An outline of this sort is useful when time is limited, as when you are writing examinations or brief papers in class. The following is a sample scratch outline for a theme on the subject "The Value of Summer Jobs":

> Earning money for clothes and school
> Sense of responsibility
> Learning to budget own time and money
> Opportunity to learn about different kinds of jobs
> Develop good work habits and maybe learn practical skills

The exact form of a scratch outline is not particularly important, since ordinarily you will be the only one who sees it. If the list is longer than five or six items, you may need to arrange the entries in some logical order (or number them) before beginning to write.

Thesis-Sentence Outlines

20.2

Org

If you have developed a thesis sentence (page 218), you may be able to use its parts as the terms of your outline. This can be especially helpful for short papers and essay examinations. Suppose, for example, that upon arriving in class you are given an assignment to write a short theme during the class period, and that one of the possible topics is "Campus Fashions." Suppose further that your experience and observation enable you within a few moments to jot down the following ideas on this general subject:

> Down-home country style dress is common
> Standard fraternity-sorority dress is just as common
> There are some variations, like camp style and freaky new fashions
> Most people dress pretty much alike
> It's getting harder to tell the two styles apart

It is possible to arrange these notes as a scratch outline, as suggested above. Another moment's reflection, however, might enable you to exercise tighter control over your theme by formulating a thesis sentence such as this:

> While there are some interesting variations in fashion here and there on campus, including camp and freaky fashions, the dominant modified country and standard fraternity dress, which draw closer together every day, give our campus a near-homogeneous appearance.

If you can get this far quickly, you can use the thesis sentence as your outline. The sentence above, for example, could forecast a fairly brief, six-paragraph theme, each paragraph developing in sequence the structural units of the thesis sentence:

PARAGRAPH 1: a brief introduction that ends with the thesis sentence
PARAGRAPH 2: the interesting variations in fashion (this, judging from the form of the thesis, is an interesting but minor part of the theme)
PARAGRAPH 3: the modified country style
PARAGRAPH 4: the standard fraternity style
PARAGRAPH 5: recent illustrations that show the two coming together
PARAGRAPH 6: a conclusion on the homogeneity of style on your campus

One particular advantage of this method of organizing is that you can plan the shape and emphasis of your theme by planning the shape and emphasis of your thesis sentence. Your observation might lead you to revise the thesis sentence above in this way:

While the dominant modified country and standard fraternity dress (which draw closer every day) give our campus a near-homogeneous appearance, some very interesting variations have appeared here this year.

A short theme developed from this sentence would have a totally different emphasis from the one suggested above.

Topic Outlines

The topic outline, the most frequently used kind of formal outline, is helpful in organizing papers of more than five hundred words. It consists of brief phrases or single words (not sentences) that are numbered or lettered to show the order and relative importance of the ideas.

The first thing to do is to get all your ideas down on paper. On the subject "The Army as a Career for College Men and Women," your preliminary thinking might produce this rough, unsorted list of ideas:

Security
Promotion slow but steady
Many different branches appeal to different interests
Low pay
Commissioned ranks open to men and women graduates
Can't be fired
Cost of uniforms
Discipline often annoying
Frequent moves hard on soldier's family
See interesting places and people
Social life restricted to small circle
Good retirement benefits
Annual vacation with pay
Military job training useful in civilian careers

Determining the Central Idea.   A quick glance at the list above reveals that some points stress the advantages of an army career; others, the disadvantages. The next step then is to divide the notes into two columns:

Advantages	Disadvantages
Security	Low pay
Promotion slow but steady	Cost of uniforms
Many different branches appeal to different interests	Discipline often annoying
Can't be fired	Frequent moves hard on soldier's family
See interesting places and people	Social life restricted to small circle
Good retirement benefits	
Annual vacation with pay	
Commissioned ranks open to men and women graduates	
Military job training useful in civilian careers	

In this form the relationship between the various ideas is not shown (What is the relationship between "Promotion slow but steady" and "Many different branches appeal to different interests"?) and there is no clear balance between the two columns (Is "Security" supposed to balance "Low pay"?). In analyzing the columns, however, you can see that there are two main ideas in each—the financial aspect of an army career and the living conditions that go with army life. You might then balance the notes in this way:

20.2

Org

    I. Financial aspect
       A. Disadvantages
          1. Low pay
          2. Cost of uniforms
       B. Advantages
          1. Security
          2. Promotion slow but steady
          3. Commissioned ranks open to men and women graduates
          4. Can't be fired
          5. Good retirement benefits
          6. Annual vacation with pay
          7. Military job training useful in civilian careers
   II. Social aspect
       A. Disadvantages
          1. Discipline often annoying
          2. Frequent moves hard on soldier's family
          3. Social life restricted to small circle
       B. Advantages
          1. Many different branches appeal to different interests
          2. See interesting places and people

When the notes are arranged in some system, decide on a main point you want to make in your paper. "The Army as a Career for College Men and Women" doesn't tell what you are going to say about the subject; it is a title, not a central idea.

At this stage you can see that there is more and stronger material on the financial advantages of a military career than on its disadvantages. On the other hand, the disadvantages of living conditions seem to outweigh the advantages. But assuming that you want to treat the subject fully and in a favorable light, you could frame a tentative statement of purpose: "Although there are definite disadvantages to an army career, the advantages outweigh them." This statement will now govern the reworking of the outline. At this stage it is still tentative and can be changed as the purpose becomes clearer in your mind.

Revising the Outline.   With the central idea as your guide, arrange the outline so that every part of it contributes directly to the purpose of the paper. Examine each heading to see if it needs to be strengthened or elaborated upon, if it repeats or overlaps another heading, or if it is unrelated to the central idea.

In the first part of the outline "Cost of uniforms" seems to be a weak point. Aren't officers given allowances for their uniforms? Possibly "Expense of frequent entertaining" is a stronger point, so substitute it for "Cost of uniforms."

The financial advantages of an army career seem to stand out, but looking at these entries closely, you will see that some overlap or are actually minor parts of other points. The heading "Security" obviously covers "Slow but steady promotion," "Commissioned ranks open to men and women graduates," and "Can't be fired." Closer examination reveals that "Annual vacation with pay" is an aspect of living conditions rather than of finances; it should therefore be shifted to the second main heading.

Under "Advantages" in the second main heading, the first entry, "Many different branches appeal to different interests," seems out of place or else incorrectly phrased. Perhaps the point is that military people may be able to find jobs they like or are best fitted for.

As the plan now stands, the first part seems stronger. To make the argument more convincing, it would be a good idea to reverse the present order: begin with "Living conditions," and then end the paper on an emphatic note—the training that the army affords for success in other fields. After these changes have been made, and after some headings have been reworded to make them parallel in form, the final outline might be:

Thesis sentence: Although from the standpoint of finances and living conditions, there are some disadvantages to an army career for men and women, the advantages outweigh them.

  I. Living conditions
    A. Disadvantages
      1. Discipline often annoying
      2. Frequent moves hard on family
      3. Social life restricted to a small circle
    B. Advantages
      1. Opportunity to find the job one is suited for
      2. Annual leaves with pay
      3. Chance to travel, to see new places, and to meet new people
 II. Financial considerations
    A. Disadvantages
      1. Low pay
      2. Frequent entertaining expensive
    B. Advantages
      1. Security
        a. Slow but steady promotion, including commissions for men and women graduates
        b. Permanent employment
        c. Good retirement benefits
      2. Preparation for success in civilian careers after retirement

20.2

Org

The outline now can be the basis for an orderly paper that makes a definite point.

Sentence Outlines

A sentence outline is developed in the same way as a topic outline, but the ideas are more fully expressed. Each heading is expressed as a complete sentence, usually consisting of just one main clause:

Thesis sentence: Although from the standpoint of finances and living conditions, there are some disadvantages to an army career for college men and women, the advantages outweigh them.

  I. Living conditions are a major consideration in choosing a career.
    A. Army life has several shortcomings in this respect.
      1. The strict discipling imposed is often annoying.
      2. Frequent moves are hard on an officer's family.
      3. Social life is usually restricted to a small circle of army families.
    B. On the other hand, there are certain advantages to life in the army.
      1. The military, with its wide range of occupations, gives one an opportunity to find the job he or she is best suited for.
      2. There are generous annual leaves with pay.
      3. Wide travel opportunities can introduce one to new places and people.

II. Financial considerations are also of major importance.
A. Two disadvantages are apparent.
    1. Army pay is low compared to that in many civilian jobs.
    2. Officers are burdened with the cost of frequent entertaining.
B. The advantages, however, are more striking.
    1. The army offers a high degree of job security.
        a. Promotions are slow but steady, with commissions open to men and women graduates.
        b. There is almost no danger of dismissal.
        c. Retirement benefits are good.
    2. An army career is an excellent preparation for success in civilian careers after retirement.

Each heading is a complete sentence, and only one sentence — not two or three. Each sentence is also in the form of a statement, not a question. And all the sentences are in the same tense.

The chief advantage of a sentence outline is that the ideas will have to be clear and fully thought out before they can be stated in complete sentences. For that reason it is sometimes assigned for training in writing long formal reports such as the reference paper.

• *Exercises*

1. Choose three of the following general subjects, narrow them to a topic specific enough for a 500-word theme, and write a scratch outline for each: *population growth, study abroad, student summer work, television standards, automobile safety standards, automation, popular myths.*

2. Write a scratch outline on any one of the following topics that appeals to you, or choose your own. When you have jotted down all your notes, frame a thesis sentence and put the notes in the form of a topic outline:

Why People Watch Excavations	Speaking in Public
Should Physical Education Be Required in College?	Unusual Place Names
	Forecasting Election Results
Income Is Not the Primary Goal of Education	I Prefer Bach
	Our Local Parking Problem

20.3 Standard Outline Form

Numbering, indention, punctuation, and other physical aspects of outlines follow certain conventions, particularly when the outlines are to be read by someone other than the writer. When you are required to turn in an outline with your paper, use the type of outline your instructor specifies and put it in standard form.

Numbering and Indention

Make the numbering of your headings consistent throughout. This is the typical method for numbering and indenting a topic or sentence outline:

Thesis sentence: _____

_____	(Sentence statement)
I. _____	(Roman numeral for main head)
A. _____	(Capital letter for subhead)
1. _____	(Arabic numeral for second sub-
2. _____	head)
a. _____	(Lowercase letter for third sub-
b. _____	head)
B. _____	
II. _____	

The main heads (I, II, III . . .) are set flush with the left-hand margin. The subheads are indented four or five spaces in typed copy and about three quarters of an inch in longhand, or they may be indented so that they are directly under the first word of the preceding heading, as shown in this book.

When a heading runs over one line, the second line is indented as far as the first word of the preceding line:

20.3

Org

> I. The photoelectric cell, known as the "electric eye," has been put to a variety of practical uses.
>   A. It is used in elevator floors to enable the elevator to stop at exactly the right level.

When you make an outline, avoid overelaborate and confusing systems. There is rarely any need to go farther than the third subhead (a, b, c . . .). Two levels of headings are often enough for a short paper.

Punctuation and Capitalization

In a topic outline, capitalize only the first letter of the word beginning the heading (and all proper nouns), and do not put any punctuation at the end of the entry, because these headings are not complete sentences.

> I. Present need for physicists
>   A. In private industry
>   B. In government projects
>   C. In colleges and universities

Punctuate every heading in a sentence outline just as you would punctuate the sentences in your paper: begin with a capital letter and end with a period. Except for proper nouns, other words in the heading are not capitalized (a heading is not a title).

I. The advantages of specialization in college are numerous.
   A. Students can set goals for themselves.
   B. They can obtain more knowledge about their subjects.

Content of Headings

Each heading in an outline should be specific and meaningful:

Vague and useless	Specific
The Profession I Want to Follow	The Profession I Want to Follow
I. Introduction	I. Lifelong interest in veterinarian's work
II. Why I prefer this work	A. Grew up with animals
III. What the opportunities would be	B. Saw importance of veterinarian's work
IV. The chances for success	C. Worked with a veterinarian last two summers
V. Conclusion	II. Many opportunities in veterinary work today
	A. In rural areas
	B. In cities
	III. Worthwhile and well-paid profession

Headings like "Introduction," "Body," and "Conclusion" aren't useful unless you indicate what material belongs in the sections. Instead of using general labels such as "Causes" and "Results," indicate what the causes or results are; it will save time later.

Putting headings in the form of questions or in statements that will have to be filled in later is not an efficient practice. The necessary information will have to be supplied when you write, so you might as well supply it in the planning stage.

Indefinite	Definite
I. The Wars of the Roses	I. The Wars of the Roses
A. When they began	A. Started 1455
B. Why?	B. Caused by rivalry between Houses of Lancaster and York

Dividing the Material

Generally, if a heading is to be divided at all, it should be divided into more than one part. When there is only one heading under a topic, it usually repeats what is in the topic and should therefore be included with it:

Unnecessary division	Accurate division
The Smithsonian Institution	The Smithsonian Institution
I. Established by an Englishman	I. Established by James Smithson, an Englishman, in 1846
A. James Smithson	
1. In 1846	

The heads of an outline should represent equally important divisions of the subject as a whole, and should be parallel in grammatical form and tense. In a topic outline, if *I* is a noun, *II* and *III* are also nouns; if *I* is a prepositional phrase, so are *II* and *III*. The same principle applies to subdivisions. A sentence outline should use complete sentences throughout and not lapse into topic headings.

Unequal headings	**Equal headings**
Growing Roses	Growing Roses
I. Preparing the soil	I. Preparing the soil
II. Planting	II. Planting
III. Growing the plant	III. Watering
IV. Mildew	IV. Fertilizing
V. Insect pests	V. Spraying
VI. Using a spray gun	

The subdivisions should also designate equally important and parallel divisions of one phase of the main divisions:

20.3

Org

Unequal subheads	**Equal subheads**
I. Job opportunities in Wisconsin	I. Job opportunities in
A. Raising crops	Wisconsin
B. White-collar work	A. Agriculture
C. Dairy farms	B. Business
D. Factory jobs	C. Industry
E. Breweries	

Headings of equal rank should not overlap: what is in *II* should exclude what is covered in *I*; *B* should be clearly distinct from *A*.

Overlapping	**Accurate**
Ways of transporting freight	Ways of transporting freight
I. Water	I. Ship
A. Ships	A. Passenger ships
B. Freighters	B. Freighters
II. On the ground	II. Truck
A. Trucks	III. Railroad
B. "Piggyback" in trucks	A. Loaded into cars
III. Railroads	B. "Piggyback" in trucks
IV. In the air	IV. Airplane

Whatever form of planning you do or design you use, take it seriously. Use your plan as an opportunity to see your subject and its parts, and as an opportunity to try different arrangements. Remember that any outline is tentative; you may learn a better way of planning as you go.

• *Exercise*

Check the following outlines from the standpoint of effective and useful planning. Then state specifically what you consider to be the unsatisfactory aspects of each one, in form and content. Revise the outlines accordingly.

1. Types of American schools

   I. Schools open to everyone
     A. Elementary schools
     B. There are many colleges and universities
     C. Secondary or high
     D. Providing technical instruction
     E. Private schools

2. Why everyone should be able to swim.

   I. Everyone should learn to swim.
     A. As early as possible.
       1. Children have been taught as young as three years

   II. The ability to swim may save your life.
     1. never swim alone
     2. don't show off in the water
     3. Many schools require students to pass swimming tests.
       a. my experiences
       b. Red Cross lifesaving test

3. Increasing automation in industry presents many problems.

   I. Unemployment
     A. Permanent layoffs
     B. Shorter working hours
     C. Decreases job opportunities

   II. What is automation?
     A. Definition
     B. Uses
       1. Where it cannot be used
     C. There are many advantages to automation

   III. Increased leisure time
     A. Recreation
       1. Hobbies
       2. Traveling
       3. Adult education classes

   IV. New skills are required.
     A. Trained technicians
     B. The unskilled workers are laid off.
       1. Providing government benefits
       2. Providing added training

   V. Is automation here to stay?

• An Essay in Progress, 3: First Efforts at Organization

First scratch outline: meet new people

           reasons people go

            -dates

            -see movie

            -get away

           experience different emotions

           lying about age

           boy under quilt

           girl on fence

           people more entertaining than movie

Second version: Introduction

          -where I worked

          -why I worked there

    1. Met new people -they go to movie for

        different reasons

          -get away

          -dates

          -see movie

    2. Experience different emotions

        -indignant at lying

        -amusement at boy under quilt

           girl caught on fence

    Conclusion: people more entertaining than movie.

20.3

Org

By this time the student had chosen to write a kind of expository essay about his experiences at a drive-in theater. The simple outline suggests that the student intends to explain his experience by citing examples and particular episodes.

Notice that the writer has begun to put his experiences in some order and that he has listed some episodes to include. The outline is brief. It might be enough, though item 2 doesn't have much in it. The conclusion predicts some comment about the significance of this experience.

(See end of Chapters 18, 19, 21, and 28.)

21 Writing the First Draft

. . . The great thing is to last and get your work done and see and hear and learn and understand; and write when there is something that you know; and not before; and not too damned much after.—Ernest Hemingway, DEATH IN THE AFTERNOON

To get started, I will accept anything that occurs to me. . . . So, receptive, careless of failure, I spin out things on the page. And a wonderful freedom comes. If something occurs to me, it is all right to accept it. It has one justification: it occurs to me. No one else can guide me. I must follow my own weak, wandering, diffident impulses.—William Stafford, "A Way of Writing"

When you are reasonably satisfied with your preparations and your plans for organizing your material, it's time to begin the actual writing. You probably shouldn't expect to be completely satisfied with your preparation and planning. Even with long and careful preliminary work, you won't always have a good sense of all that you are going to say until you do the writing itself. Sometimes, when you have studied a subject and thought it out, you'll be able to lay out a plan for a piece of writing that has in it everything you wish to say in the order you wish to say it, and your own attitude toward your subject matter will already be clear. If that happens, the actual writing may be easier than usual: you may have little to do but complete your outline or plan by adding illustrations and transitions.

Often, however, even when you have thought your subject through and have a good, thorough, workable plan, you still won't have a good sense of all that's to be said—you still won't know exactly which illustrative material you may need to use to fill out parts of your plan, and your own attitudes toward the material may not be clear until you have found the words for them. It has often been remarked that we do not always know what we think until we hear what we say. Thinking and planning are not always over when you've developed a plan for your writing.

For this reason, when you are composing papers outside the classroom, it is usually best to write them out in rough draft first. Revising and copying can come later. No matter how certain you are about the material and the order of presentation, a complete first draft is important if the final paper is to represent your best work.

Up to this point you have been dealing with ideas in abbreviated

266

or shorthand forms as notes or outline headings, though you may have written bits and pieces in complete form. Now you are ready to put it all down in full sentences and paragraphs, to see the whole paper as your reader will, and to make whatever changes may be necessary for continuity and effectiveness.

21.1 Getting Started

Begin writing the first draft as soon as you have decided on the content and organization of the paper. Don't wait for "inspiration" or the proper mood — write while the ideas and information are still in your mind; an outline that you put away for three hours or three days can look cold and unfamiliar if your mind isn't still turning in the same way. For almost everyone writing is work, and you must often begin writing when you would much prefer to do something else. If you wait until the last minute, your first draft may have to serve as your final paper, and the cracks and loose screws in it will show.

21.1

Draft

The beginning of a paper is often the most difficult part to word effectively. If you can't think of a good opening sentence, begin with some other part; if the wording of a good first paragraph doesn't come to you at once, start with a part that comes more easily. You shouldn't waste time trying to get an ideal opening; as you work, a good start will often occur to you. Many beginnings are written last. (See 21.4, Opening Paragraphs.)

Once you have broken the ice by writing two or three sentences, you'll often find it easier to go on, even without that elusive "inspiration." Writing, like many other activities, calls for a warm-up, and you may have to do a few laps and some wind sprints before you're ready to go.

As a rule, write the first draft as rapidly as you can. Your paper will have more life if you put your ideas down one after the other without pausing to worry about correctness. At this stage you should concentrate on getting down the gist of what you have in mind. You are the only one who will see your first draft, and matters of spelling, punctuation, and wording can be taken care of in revision. (See 28.1, Revising a Draft.)

Plan to write your rough draft uninterrupted, if possible. When you are working on a paper that is too long to be written in one sitting, it sometimes helps to stop in the middle of a paragraph or a passage that is going easily and well, perhaps even in the middle of a sentence. This ordinarily makes it easier to get started again when you come back to your work. Take time to read over what you have already written before you begin writing again.

Leave plenty of space in the first draft for making corrections and changes. There should be ample margins on both sides of the page and space between lines for insertions and corrections.

21.2 Developing Your Material

Make the first draft as complete as possible. Write down more than you will probably use in your final paper; be generous with explanations and illustrative examples. It is much easier to cut out material in revision than it is to look for more to satisfy the requirements of length or completeness of presentation. Papers that are heavy with material added at the last moment always seem disjointed. Those that have been pruned down from, say, fourteen hundred to a thousand words are likely to be more compact and to the point.

Put in any good ideas that occur to you when you are writing the first draft, even though they may not have appeared in the original plan. In this stage you do not need to follow the outline down to the last minor subdivision. Frequently a sentence written on paper will bring to mind an aspect of the topic that you overlooked when your material was in note form. If the new idea turns out to be irrelevant, it can be omitted in revision; but if it is important, you can alter your outline to include it.

Kinds of Development

As the paper grows from the organization plan you have decided on, it should follow the form of development that best suits the topic and that will be clearest to the reader. If you have made an unusually complete plan for your paper, the plan itself may tell you how to develop and amplify each part. Often, however, an outline or some other kind of plan will tell you what is to be in each part of your paper, not what to do with it, or how to write it out. The patterns of development discussed in the section on paragraphs (27.2) may be useful to you in developing whole papers, though adequate development of a whole paper may require a combination of different kinds of paragraphs. Which kind predominates is determined by the needs of the paper. These are some of the most commonly used types of order:

1. **Time and sequence:** describing events in the order of their occurrence. This is appropriate in narrative writing (a report of an athletic contest, an account of an incident in history) or in de-

scribing a process (the construction of a log cabin, stages in the development of a frog).

2. **Space:** describing objects as they exist within a certain area, often used in descriptive or expository writing (a description of a city from outskirts to center, of a mural from left to right).

3. **Increasing complexity:** beginning with the simple or familiar and proceeding to the more complex or unfamiliar (discussing wind instruments beginning with the toy whistle, continuing to simple recorders, and ending with orchestral instruments like the flute and oboe).

4. **Comparison and contrast:** discussing all the features of one idea or situation, then all the features of another, and ending by drawing a conclusion about the two ("Television and Newspapers As Sources of News," "Public Schools and Private Schools"). If such a plan seems to make the paper break in the middle, present a sequence of comparisons and contrasts on each major point — not all the features of public schools and then of private schools, but some order like this: 1. Cost of attendance, 2. Curriculum, 3. Facilities.

5. **Support:** beginning with a general statement or impression and then supporting it with specific examples, details, reasons. This method is often useful in argumentation and for such topics as "The Value of Studying Foreign Languages," "The Problems of Increasing Automation," "Freshman Composition Courses Should Be Abolished."

6. **Climax:** beginning with a specific fact or situation and unfolding the subject until it stands completed at the end. A paper about the development of the polio vaccine might begin with the need for the vaccine, then take up the problems facing researchers, go on to explain how solutions were found, and end with the production of an effective vaccine.

7. **Cause to effect or effect to cause:** beginning with an analysis of causes, culminating in a statement of effect, or stating the effect first, then moving to the analysis of cause. The subject should determine which pattern is better: if you are writing about your city's traffic mess, for example, you might want to describe that problem briefly at the beginning as an effect already known, then proceed to an analysis of the causes, which are probably less well known.

21.2

Draft

The working outline should represent the kind of development most appropriate to your subject. Often two kinds of development are used in combination: a narrative could follow both the order of time and that of climax; the method of support might be used effectively with comparison or climax. The essential thing is that you present your material in some sensible order.

Controlling Direction

One way to get into your draft and develop your meaning—especially if you are having trouble starting your paper or a particular section of it—is to use a sentence to direct the development. In your opening, for example, you can use your thesis sentence to forecast the development of your theme as a whole. (See 21.2.) And in the body of your paper, you can similarly work with sentences to direct the development of each section.

Suppose that you have developed this topic outline as the basis for a paper:

The Profession I Want to Follow

Thesis sentence: I want to become a veterinarian because of my lifelong interest in veterinary work, because of the many opportunities it offers, and because it is a worthwhile and well-paid profession.

I. Lifelong interest in veterinarian's work
   A. Grew up with animals on a farm
   B. Saw importance of veterinarian's work
   C. Worked with a veterinarian last two summers
II. Many opportunities in veterinary work today
   A. In rural areas
   B. In urban areas
III. Worthwhile and well-paid profession

The thesis sentence is a guide, directing the development of the outline and the theme. It could be used, for example, to predict a climactic development that places increasing stress on the series of three factors.

The separate sections of the theme could also be directed by opening sentences. For example, we can assume that Section I will require at least three paragraphs. To control the relationships among them, the writer could introduce the section like this:

Although I grew up with animals on a farm and saw the importance of the veterinarian's work, I didn't really understand all that a veterinarian does until I worked with one the last two summers.

This sentence, which might be used to open the first paragraph of the first section or might be used alone as an introduction, shows how the ideas in Section I are related and gives the writer a direction: there is a time sequence which suggests that the three paragraphs might be narrative; the last paragraph should probably get the dominant stress.

The first section closes with the idea that the writer is aware of the value of the veterinary profession. Section II, then, might open with a sentence like this:

The needs for veterinary work are great in the country and surprisingly varied in the city.

This sentence, which makes the rural and urban needs coordinate, could forecast a balanced treatment by the method of comparison. The section would probably be developed in two paragraphs. Section III might then be directed in this way:

> Because the needs for veterinary medicine are great, the work is worthwhile; because the work is needed, the pay is good.

This balanced introductory sentence could lead the writer into a balanced, judicious paragraph stating an effect — the causes having been analyzed in Sections I and II.

Sometimes a writer can also use particular patterns of paragraph development (27.2) to determine a means of expanding the material; this can be especially helpful in writing short themes. Suppose you arrive in your composition class some Monday morning to find an assignment on the blackboard for an in-class theme. One of the suggested subjects invites your response to the idea of an honor system. If you are familiar with the patterns of paragraph development, you might be able very quickly to settle on a design, a means of developing your paper. Not everyone has participated in an honor system; not everyone knows what it is. You might therefore decide that the purpose of your paper would be to explain what an honor system is. Knowing the pattern of definition, you could develop your explanation like this:

21.2

Draft

> PARAGRAPH 1: entirely **illustration,** describing an honor system in action
>
> PARAGRAPH 2: **comparison** of honor system with similar things, such as codes of behavior in clubs
>
> PARAGRAPH 3: **contrast,** an account of how honor system is unlike other codes

The sequence of three paragraphs forms a definition: the first by illustration identifies the *term;* the second by comparison puts the term in a *class;* the third by contrast shows how it *differs* from other members of the same class. With this three-paragraph definition, you might then be able to write a fourth, concluding paragraph of evaluation.

● *Exercise*

For each of the three topics listed below, write out five sentences to show how you would develop the topic according to the suggested pattern of development, as shown in the example.

Example: topic: New artists change our musical tastes. *pattern:* time

a. In the mid-1950's, Elvis Presley changed the direction of pop music with "Blue Suede Shoes" and other hits.
b. By the early 1960's, folk musicians like Bob Dylan and the Kingston Trio brought different sounds to the attention of the nation.

c. The Beatles took the spotlight in the later '60's, and spawned an entirely "new" sound, which many other groups imitated.
d. The early 1970's found a new and "slicked-up" country sound which brought country music onto the popular music charts in a big way.
e. Many singers and groups have come and gone in the past twenty years, but it is interesting that some artists have not only been able to change with the times, but they have also helped shape and change our musical tastes, making way for new styles, including acid rock, punk rock, and other new forms of music.

1. *topic:* Building a new shopping center downtown. *pattern:* space

2. *topic:* Opinion is divided on the harmfulness of marijuana. *pattern:* comparison and contrast

3. *topic:* The discovery that the world is round changed both science and everyday life. *pattern:* cause to effect

---

21.3 Relating Paragraphs in Sequence

As you write your first draft, remember that you are going to have to take a reader with you. Your individual paragraphs should represent a progressive development of the subject. If there is too wide a gap in ideas between the end of one paragraph and the beginning of the next, the reader may not be able to follow your line of thought.

Showing the Connection Between Paragraphs

Link paragraphs by connecting the topic of a new paragraph with the topic of the preceding one. This is not as hard as it may sound; usually it's easy — and natural — to phrase the opening statement of a paragraph so that it grows out of what you have just said. In the paragraphs below, linking words are in boldface type:

> What about the Indians? There are no Indians in the Arches country now; they all left seven hundred years ago and won't be back for a long time. But here as elsewhere in the canyonlands they left a **record** of their passage. Near springs and under overhanging cliffs, good camping spots, you may find chipping grounds scattered with hundreds of fragments of flint or chert where the Anasazi hunters worked their arrowpoints. You may find shards of pottery. At other places you will see their writing on the canyon walls — the **petroglyphs** and **pictographs.**
>
> **Petroglyphs** are carved in the rock; **pictographs** are painted on the rock. Whether in one form or the other **they** consist of representations of birds, snakes, deer and many other animals, of human, semihuman and superhuman figures, and of designs purely abstract or symbolic. In some places you find only **petroglyphs,** in other places only **picto-**

graphs, in some places **both.** The explicitly representational often comes side by side with the highly abstract.

In style the **inscriptions** and **paintings** range from the crude and simple to the elegant, sophisticated and subtle. **They** seem to include the work of different cultures and a great extent of time. . . . — Edward Abbey, *Desert Solitaire*

Connections from paragraph to paragraph are established here by repeating key words *(petroglyphs* and *pictographs,* linked with *records),* by pronoun references to key words *(both, they),* and by synonyms of key words *(inscriptions* and *paintings).*

Showing the Relation to the Topic of the Paper

Whenever possible, show the relation between the paragraph and the topic or thesis of the paper. This is a good way to keep your paragraphs going in the same direction. For example, in this discussion of the games played by primitive peoples, the author begins each paragraph by introducing a different kind of sport:

> PARAGRAPH 1: Wrestling is probably universal. [four sentences follow]
>
> PARAGRAPH 2: Races· are far more common. [three sentences follow]
>
> PARAGRAPH 3: Ball games are also widespread, but vary greatly in type. [six sentences follow]
>
> PARAGRAPH 4: Frequently the ball games are played in a more elaborate way. [fourteen sentences follow]
>
> PARAGRAPH 5: In the Plains and Southwest of our country the "hoop and pole" game enjoyed great popularity. [six sentences follow]
>
> PARAGRAPH 6: Compared with such sports ropeskipping seems simple, but the Australian Euahlayi make an art of it. [two sentences follow]
>
> PARAGRAPH 7: Polynesians lead in aquatic sports. [four sentences follow]
>
> PARAGRAPH 8: Maori stilt-walkers raced one another across streams, and also tried to upset one another's balance. [two sentences follow] — Robert H. Lowie, *An Introduction to Cultural Anthropology*

21.3

Draft

Transition Paragraphs

For major transitions, such as from one main section of a long paper to another, a brief paragraph (sometimes just one sentence) will often serve to prepare readers for what is coming next. Notice the middle paragraph below:

> But nothing in that end of town was as good as the dumpground that scattered along a little runoff coulee dipping down toward the river from the south bench. Through a historical process that went back, probably, to the roots of community sanitation and distaste for eye-

sores, but that in law dated from the Unincorporated Towns Ordinance of the territorial government, passed in 1888, the dump was one of the very first community enterprises, almost our town's first institution.

More than that, it contained relics of every individual who had ever lived there, and of every phase of the town's history.

The bedsprings on which the town's first child was begotten might be there; the skeleton of a boy's pet colt; two or three volumes of Shakespeare bought in haste and error from a peddler. . . . — Wallace Stegner, *Wolf Willow*

Ordinarily the subject matter of successive paragraphs is so closely related that separate transition paragraphs are not needed, and in short papers they are usually out of place.

21.4 Opening Paragraphs

The first paragraph of a paper usually has two functions: to introduce the subject and to catch the reader's interest. Plan your paper so that you can get into your subject as quickly as possible. The shorter the paper, the more direct your beginning should be.

If, after finishing your first draft, you find that you have written an obviously weak beginning, see if the second or third sentence, or even the second paragraph, may not provide a better starting point. Often the first few lines of writing are simply a warm-up, and the paper actually begins a few sentences later.

Effective Openings

No matter what you are writing about, the beginning of your paper should catch the readers' interest and get them into the subject. Some of the ways to accomplish this are discussed below.

A Statement of Purpose or Point of View. This should not be a mechanical statement ("In this paper I am going to give you my reasons for majoring in political science.") or a flat rewording of the assignment, but a natural lead into the topic:

> When I decided to enter the university, like most freshmen I had only the vaguest notion of what subject I intended to major in. But now after two quarters of haphazardly chosen course work, and after a good deal of self-analysis, I have decided that **there are at least four good reasons why I should major in political science.**

If your purpose is to discuss one aspect of some general subject, the first paragraph can make the limits of your paper clear:

The Great Lakes are one of the major lake systems of the world. Through the centuries many large cities have grown up along their perimeter as people recognized their value for inland navigation, water supply, and recreation. Pollution of their waters by industrial wastes has also inevitably increased through the years, until now it presents a serious threat. **The pollution problems in Chicago are typical of those of the Great Lakes area as a whole.**

A Definition. If your paper deals with some subject which has a variety of meanings for different readers, it is good to make your definition clear at the outset. There is no need to start with a flat and stereotyped statement like "According to Webster, a hobby is 'an engrossing topic, occupation, or plan, etc., to which one habitually returns.'" Give a definition that fits your own approach to the subject:

A hobby, as I see it, is an activity that takes up most of your spare time and all of your spare money. At least that has been my experience since I became interested in photography. . . .

An Important Fact. One of the quickest and clearest ways to open a paper is with the statement of an important fact that will lead to the general topic. This is a natural opening for a narrative and can also be good for a discussion of ideas:

There have been two downright attempts by government to curb freedom of the press in America since Plymouth Rock. The first took place when John Peter Zenger, a New York publisher, was jailed in 1735 for criticizing the British colonial governor, but through a brilliant defense by Andrew Hamilton, a salty old Philadelphia lawyer, was acquitted. In the second instance, 63 years later under our own young Constitution, the accused was less fortunate. — Alvin Harlow, "Martyr for a Free Press," *American Heritage*

Publishers estimate that there are approximately 800 books-only bookstores in the entire United States. This is the rough equivalent of the number of bookstores in the city of London alone. — Marya Mannes, "Empty Bookstores Equal Empty Minds," *Fort Worth Star Telegram*

A Reference to Personal Experience. If your subject is one with which you have had some personal experience, a reference to your connection with it provides an appropriate beginning. In an essay on the complex problems of leading a university, for example, the author, a university president, begins in this way:

Before Clark Kerr went through the revolving presidential door at Berkeley, he defined the modern multiversity president's job. It was, he said, to provide "sex for the students, football for the alumni, and parking for the faculty." Eight years later, after my own maiden year

21.4

Draft

as president of the University of Cincinnati—whose 36,104 students make it the largest urban multiversity in the country after New York City's—I can report: The parking problem is worse. College football is being energetically chased by man-eating tigers (in our case the Bengals). Sex is so taken for granted as to rate no priority.—Warren Bennis, "The University Leader," *The Saturday Review*

A Lively Detail or Illustration.   A good way to arouse the reader's interest and curiosity is to begin with a lively detail—perhaps with an anecdote, an apt quotation, or an allusion to some current topic. Such material should of course be related to the subject of the paper, as is this beginning of an article on the conservation of natural resources:

> Millions of years ago, a volcano built a mountain on the floor of the Atlantic. In eruption after eruption, it pushed up a great pile of volcanic rock, until it had accumulated a mass a hundred miles across at its base, reaching upward toward the surface of the sea. Finally its cone emerged as an island with an area of about 200 square miles. Thousands of years passed, and thousands of thousands. Eventually the waves of the Atlantic cut down the cone and reduced it to a shoal—all of it, that is, but a small fragment which remained above water. This fragment we know as Bermuda.
>
> With variation, the life story of Bermuda has been repeated by almost every one of the islands that interrupt the watery expanses of the oceans. . . .—Rachel Carson, *The Sea Around Us*

Openings to Avoid

The opening paragraph should mark the actual beginning of the paper and be clearly related to the subject. If it does not create interest in the subject or get it under way, it probably does not belong in the paper. These common mistakes make poor beginnings:

Beginning Too Far Back.   If you are discussing the organization of the United Nations, there is no need to begin with the reasons for the failure of the League of Nations, nor is there any reason to begin a paper on Lincoln as President with an account of his legislative career. The shorter your paper, the more direct should be your beginning. A statement of your purpose or a rewording of your central idea is the simplest way to begin a paper written in class.

An Apology or a Complaint.   A statement such as this is discouraging to most readers: "Being a mere freshman, I'm afraid that what I have to say on this topic won't be of much value. . . ." Complaints are also better left unwritten: "Before I started to write this theme, I thought I could find some interesting material on it in the library, but there wasn't any. . . ." Remember that readers are interested only in the ideas that you present, not in the difficulties or disappointments you may have had while writing the paper.

Too Broad a Generalization. "Science in the last fifty years has made more progress than any other branch of knowledge" is a generalization far too sweeping to explain or prove in a five-hundred-word or even a five-thousand-word paper. Statements such as this are likely to be more impressive to the writer than they are to the reader. Wherever possible, begin with a specific statement: "Though smaller than your thumb, an electronic device called the transistor has had a tremendous effect on radio and television sets."

A Self-Evident Statement. Avoid starting a paper with a remark so obvious that it need not be mentioned: "America has a great number of resorts and parks situated in many scenic localities." And resist the temptation—it's good exercise, anyway, once in a while—to open your paper with some commonplace observation that gives no hint of your subject: "It has been said that the only thing constant in life is change." If you have started your paper with a self-evident remark, see if the sentence immediately following is a good beginning for your paper.

21.4

Draft

• *Exercise*

Revise the following opening statements so that they at least tell readers what the paper is about. Try also to make the statement lively enough to catch the readers' interest.

Example: In your modern world of today, personal hygiene has become very important for success in the modern complex world of business.

Good opening: These days, if you want to get ahead, it probably helps to look good and smell good.

Better: Each year, Americans spend billions on creams, deodorants, aftershaves, soaps, and other products designed to make them look and smell good. It is a sad reality that one's success in the world is probably determined as much by grooming as it is by talent.

1. There are many topics of importance in the news these days. One of the many important topics is how we are going to control inflation.

2. I have always liked certain kinds of hobbies. One of the most interesting hobbies I enjoy writing about is training guinea pigs, which is a very interesting hobby.

3. The abolishment of capital punishment and the reasons why I favor it is the subject of this paper.

4. The morning was dark and gray. A fog enshrouded the dormitory, and reflected my mood as I approached the delicate topic of required physical education.

5. "There are two sides to every question," says the proverb. This is not so in the case of the controversy over whether or not to register handguns. Only one opinion can be substantiated with facts. According to my dictionary, a handgun is a "gun which can be held in one hand easily, usually a pistol."

21.5 Closing Paragraphs

The beginning and ending of your paper — the point at which you meet your readers and the place at which you leave them — should be among the most interesting and forceful parts of your paper. Make the ending definite and emphatic, if possible — unless, of course, you are writing a paper that specifically calls for another tone, such as reverie or whimsy. Otherwise, plan your paper so that it won't trail off or leave your reader up in the air. The final paragraph should round out your discussion in such a way that the reader will know you have said all you intended to say and that you have not stopped because you were tired of writing or because time ran out. Remember that the total effect of your paper may depend largely upon the way you end it.

Effective Conclusions

Your final paragraph should tie together the ideas you have been developing and emphasize the main point of the paper. Some suggestions for effective conclusions follow:

A Climax.   Make your final paragraph the culmination of the ideas you have been developing, or save the most important idea for the last. The concluding paragraph thus becomes the climax of the paper. A student paper of about a thousand words, which has described in detail the operation of a large used-car lot, brings all the details to a focus in this conclusion:

> This used-car lot was sponsored by an organization which sells over a million cars a year, so it was by no means a fly-by-night affair. Although no sloppy repairs were done, and no highly crooked deals were tolerated, there was just a slight suspicion that the company was getting the best of every customer on every deal. This company, however good or bad, is representative of many similar organizations in the United States.

A Suggestion for Action.   If you have been criticizing some situation (parking on the campus, the price of textbooks, daylight saving time), end your paper with a positive suggestion for action, or at least a clear call for action, as in this paragraph:

> At the end of her freshman year in college a girl I know wrote home to her mother, "Hooray! Hooray! Just think—I never have to take English any more!" But this girl had always been an excellent English student, had always loved books, writing, ideas. It seems unnecessary and foolish and wrong that English teachers should so often take what should be the most flexible, exciting, and creative of all school courses and make it into something that most children can hardly wait to see the last of. Let's hope that we can and soon will begin to do much better.— John Holt, "How Teachers Make Children Hate Reading," *Redbook*

A Summary Statement.   Longer and more formal papers are sometimes concluded by restating the main points of the discussion. But for most papers written in composition courses, it is seldom necessary or advisable to summarize what has been said. The result is often a weak and mechanical ending.

21.5

Tying the Ending to the Beginning

Draft

The final paragraph may repeat, in different wording, the opening idea. This method is useful in longer papers, both to remind the reader what the main subject is and to give it final emphasis. It is also helpful, if not overdone, in shorter papers, where the repetition of key ideas, key words, or key figures may give the reader a sense of a circle neatly closing. The two paragraphs below are the opening and closing of an essay in which the author reminisces about his instructor in writing:

> When I was a freshman, *Gulliver's Travels* taught me more about writing than any other book. Other freshmen might find little to learn from it, but that is because they do not have Craig LaDriere for a teacher. . . .
>
> Freshman English is not supposed to be a source of innocent merriment. Its object all sublime is to make thought yield to words. Nobody quite learns how, but I went farther with Jonathan Swift and Craig LaDriere than ever before or since.— Francis G. Townsend, "A Freshman in Lilliput," *College Composition and Communication*

Endings to Avoid

Avoid unemphatic, inconclusive, or contradictory endings. Here are some typical pitfalls to avoid in your closing paragraphs:

An Apology.   Ending a paper with an apology for its shortcomings only serves to emphasize them:

> I am sorry this paper is so short, but I always have a difficult time putting my ideas on paper.

If you carefully work out your ideas before writing and then present them as effectively as you can, you will not need to apologize for your efforts.

A Qualifying Remark.   If the last sentence of a paper is an exception or a qualifying remark, it weakens everything that has been said before:

> Although I haven't answered why some people refuse to face facts, I have come to the conclusion that not facing facts may be a natural part of human nature. Of course this can be carried to extremes.

There may be two sides to every subject, but when the purpose or scope of your paper is limited to the arguments for one side only, don't suddenly shift to the other side in your conclusion. If, for example, you have been presenting every argument you can think of in favor of price controls or strict ecological legislation, don't end like this: "Of course, there is much to be said for the other side also." If you feel such a qualifying statement is necessary, make it earlier in the paper.

Minor Details or Afterthoughts.   A paper describing the role of the pitcher in baseball shouldn't end with a remark about other aspects of the game:

> Baseball is one of America's favorite sports, and to spend an afternoon at Wrigley Field watching two great pitchers battling for a victory is an exciting experience. What I have said about pitching gives you an idea what a pitcher must keep in his mind while out there on the mound, or as a substitute on the bench. **There are eight other players on the team besides the pitcher and the same can be written about each individual player and his position.**

Some concluding statements make a reader wonder whether the writer actually finished his paper or abandoned it in the middle of an idea:

> I could go on for pages describing the other interesting people I met on the ship, but the length of this paper doesn't permit it.

Instead of putting a sentence such as this at the end of your paper, round out the description fully, or if the topic is already developed sufficiently, see if the next to the last sentence wouldn't make a respectable conclusion.

21.6 Writing a Title

Word the title of your paper so that it gives a definite and accurate idea of the subject matter in as few words as possible. A title need not mystify or startle the readers, although it may perhaps arouse their curiosity or appeal to their sense of humor. Interesting titles are always appreciated, but one that is brief, simple, and exact will serve the purpose.

A title should not suggest more than the paper actually covers. If you are discussing your tastes in music, avoid such sweeping titles as "Modern Jazz" or "Music of Today"; use instead "Music I Like" or "Why I Prefer Billy Joel." A report on the experiences of a baby-sitter scarcely deserves the title "Child Psychology" or "The Care of Infants"; "Experiences of a Baby-Sitter" will be good enough if you cannot think of a better title.

Unnecessarily long titles are not satisfactory, especially those that merely repeat the assignment: "An Experience in Childhood That Left a Lasting Impression on Me." The thesis sentence of your paper is not intended to serve as a title. Instead of writing "Reading Taught by Sound Should Replace Sight Reading," name the subject: "Reading by Sound."

The title is not part of the paper, and it should not be referred to by a pronoun in the first sentence. If you want to mention the title in your opening, rephrase it slightly.

21.6

Draft

Unsatisfactory	Satisfactory
Becoming a Citizen	Becoming a Citizen
This is not a difficult process in the United States. . . .	It is not difficult for an immigrant to become a citizen of the United States. . . .

• *Exercise*

Below are five sample beginnings and endings from student papers. For each one, write two or three sentences criticizing the writing, including the title, if necessary. (Point out effective writing, too.) Then, pick two from the five and rewrite them yourself.

Example: Beginning paragraph from a paper called "Good Neighbors or Bad"

Since I myself have never been outside of the United States, it may be foolish of me to think I can make any useful suggestions about our Latin American policy. However, I have read about recent events in the Caribbean and South America with great interest, and, if you will bear with me, I would like to comment at some length on our present policy.

Critique: (1) Writer doesn't really complete his thesis statement until the last two words of the paragraph. (2) Writer needlessly emphasizes his own weaknesses, which turns off the reader. (3) The title might be too general.

Rewrite: Recent events in the Caribbean and South America have stirred up a great deal of interest in the press about our neighbors to the south. It seems to me that we should take this opportunity to reexamine our country's role in these events, and perhaps our entire Latin American policy.

1. *Beginning paragraph from a paper called "The Utility of Cats"*
   When the California Gold Rush was at its height, grain supplies were so devastated by rats that prospectors eagerly paid $100 and up for cats. One enterprising merchant is said to have made a fortune by bringing a shipload of stray cats from New York to San Francisco via Cape Horn. Although the cat has not always been so highly prized, its usefulness to human beings has been recognized since the days of Pharaohs. Its continuing popularity in the United States is certainly due to its utilitarian as well as to its decorative qualities.

2. *Beginning paragraph from a paper called "Modern Chicken Farming"*
   The world today is not what it was fifty years ago. Just think of all the amazing technological changes that have taken place. The automobile has replaced the horse and buggy; radio and television have revolutionized communications; modern medicine has conquered disease. And in 1945 the atomic age was born. Chicken farming, too, has changed drastically from what it was in 1920. I would like to describe some of those changes in the pages that follow.

3. *Closing paragraph from a paper called "What a Liberal Education Means to Me"*
   But the greatest value of a liberal education is a personal one; it goes beyond politics and economics. Besides helping the individual to live in his world, it helps him to live with himself. Liberal studies stimulate a love of reason and a flexible, inquiring attitude toward the great questions of mankind. They keep the mind strong and alert and stimulate a well-rounded intellectual development which is as essential to a full life as physical development. A liberal education, in the deepest sense, is an education for life.

4. *Closing paragraph from a paper called "The Population Explosion"*
   All the statistics indicate that the future is bleak for the human race if the population explosion is not checked. Food, water, and other essential resources are even now inadequate. Living space is dwindling fast. Of course the picture may not be as dark as it looks. Maybe science will find a solution before long, or maybe the explosion will just taper off.

5. *Closing paragraph from a paper called "Population Pressures"*
   An architect recently suggested that cities could be built in the sea to house the extra millions. They would consist of concrete buildings like silos attached to pontoon islands, and could extend as far

below the water as they do above. People who lived on the lower levels could then watch the fascinating underwater world through their living-room windows! People have never even begun to exploit the sea and know very little of its hidden wonders.

• *An Essay in Progress, 4: The First Draft*

My Theater Experience

21.6

Draft

I worked at a theater before coming to college. When my parents started managing the drive-in, they drafted me to do the odd jobs there.

While working in the cafeteria, box-office, and the projection booth, I met many new people. I found that people come to a movie for different reasons. One man said that he came to get away from his wife and kids. Many boys and girls came to have dates. A few people, however, actually came to watch the movie.

At the drive-in, I experienced different emotions due to the actions of my customers. One lady aroused my indignation when she claimed that her son, who was six feet in height, was under twelve years of age. A boy eleven years old does not have to pay admission; therefore her son was admitted free. I was amused when one boy tried to hide in the back floor of a car, under a quilt, while the driver drove into the theater. I am aware of such tricks, and the boy was caught. One girl caught her slacks on the barbed wire while climbing over the fence at the back of the theater. I helped her off the fence, and I sold her a ticket. She never came over the fence again.

I experienced new and enlightening experiences at the theater. At the drive-in, I found that real people are often more entertaining than people in the movies.

The student turned in this short essay, which also appears on p. 212. The instructor wrote these questions and observations on the student's paper:

1. Have you shown what's really different about working in a drive-in movie? Are these experiences different from those of someone working in, say, an amusement park?

2. You say you met m<u>an</u>y new people, but you don't show us very many.

3. You say you experienced different emotions, but you mention only indignation and amusement. And have you shown us why the girl caught on the fence is amusing?

4. Are there other experiences and episodes you could tell about?

5. You spend only two sentences in the last paragraph showing what significance this experience had for you. Is that all?

6. Have you focused on what is most significant?

   — perhaps the range of emotional experiences and how you adjusted to them
   — perhaps the way you learned about the erratic behavior of people when they think no one will see them

(See end of Chapters 18, 19, 20, and 28.)

22　Using a Dictionary

There was a time when the meaning of language presented no problem, when it was a simple matter, upon being challenged as to meaning, to call to witness the dictionary. But in our age of universal skepticism, we have come to know that dictionaries are not depositories of eternal meanings of language. Dictionaries are made by ordinary human beings, who have collected data from — of all people — you and me, the general users of the language. —James E. Miller, Jr., WORD, SELF, REALITY

While it probably is more reliable than any single one of us, a dictionary is not a supreme authority that can be quoted to settle all arguments about words and their meanings. Rather, it is a record of the ways in which language is actually used, and any dictionary is an incomplete record. The pioneer lexicographer Samuel Johnson concluded long ago that it was foolish for a man to attempt to "embalm his language." But the notion still persists that a dictionary is — or should be — a code of law for language use.

For this reason there has been considerable debate, and some heated argument, about whether a dictionary should *prescribe* or *describe* language use. Some people want a dictionary to tell us which pronunciation is right, which meaning is proper, which use of a word is legitimate.

Other people, including the editors of many dictionaries, declare that dictionaries are not intended to rule our use of language. Almost any rule that a dictionary could offer to govern pronunciation or definition would have originated in observation of how people at some time in the past actually pronounced and defined words. If a dictionary, then, sets out to be a system of law, the editors would be converting the *habits* of some past time into *rules* for the present.

The editors of most recently published dictionaries want to *register* how the language is used. To that end, many offer a variety of acceptable pronunciations for many words, with no effort to dictate what is "best." Some editors, too, omit usage labels (which declare that some words are *colloquial* or *vulgar* or *erroneous*) on the ground that the correctness or appropriateness of a word can seldom be determined out of context.

Contexts change, and language changes. The changes are not always good, and it's understandable that we might sometimes wish for an authority to stop changes that are not good, such as

22

Dict

those in which a unique or precise meaning of a word is lost. But changes often *are* good: our language has for centuries, for example, been enriched and enlarged by the addition of words from other languages.

Since language changes — sometimes for the worse, probably more often for the better — a dictionary cannot control, but simply record the way it is actually used. The standards for determining what good language is rest in other hands (see Introduction).

22.1 Selecting a Dictionary

A good dictionary, though not a final authority, is an indispensable reference tool for every college student. Dictionaries answer questions about the meanings, spellings, origins, and pronunciations of words. They also give information about the forms of words (plurals, past tenses) and idiomatic constructions (what preposition, for example, is commonly used with a particular noun or verb). One of the most valuable habits a writer can acquire is the regular use of a dictionary.

Dictionaries differ in size and purpose, but certain criteria apply in evaluating any dictionary for general use. First of all, it should be up to date. New words and expressions are continually coming into the language *(acrylic, ambience, apartheid, brainstorming, détente, psychedelic)* and old words are always being used in new senses (a *crash* program, an advertising *flyer*, a publicity *handout*). Even spelling and pronunciation can change with time *(catalog, catalogue; ab′ də men, ab dō′ men)*. In addition, most dictionaries are somewhat encyclopedic, including information about prominent people and places. There are always new names to be added *(Waldheim, Zimbabwe)* and new facts to be recorded.

In an effort to keep their entries up to date, most dictionaries make limited changes every year or so. Check the copyright dates before you buy a dictionary to find out when it was last revised. You might also want to look up some words that have recently come into use to see if they are included.

In evaluating a dictionary you should also consider the quality of its editing. A good dictionary of current English is not simply an updating of earlier word books; it reflects the research and judgment of a large staff of experts who record and analyze hundreds of thousands of examples of words in actual use. It is the responsibility of the lexicographer to make certain that the language has been sampled adequately and that all the most common uses of even uncommon words have been found. Then all these raw materials must be carefully gone through, some discarded and some re-worked. Eventually the result should be a concise yet accurate description of the words that constitute the great bulk of our language. Whatever "authority" a dictionary has, then, depends on the scholarship, discrimination, and judgment of its editors.

Dictionaries for General Use

The most complete descriptions of contemporary English are to be found in the various unabridged dictionaries. Though not practical for desk use, these large dictionaries are invaluable for reference, and at least one of them is available in every college and public library:

> *The Oxford English Dictionary*
> *The Random House Dictionary of the English Language*
> *Webster's Third New International Dictionary.* The most complete record now available.
> *World Book Dictionary*

Two older dictionaries continue to be very useful:

> *The Century Dictionary and Cyclopedia.* Although this ten-volume work, the most comprehensive dictionary ever published in the United States, has not been reprinted since before World War I, it contains much information not available in more recent dictionaries. *The New Century Dictionary* is basically an abridgment of this work.

> *Webster's New International Dictionary of the English Language.* The second edition of the unabridged Webster, first published in 1934, is no longer in print but remains available in most libraries.

22.1

Dict

For everyday use, the most practical dictionary for a student to own is one of the shorter "college" dictionaries listed below. Each of these dictionaries has its own special strengths, but all are well edited and adequate for general use:

> *American Heritage Dictionary*
> *Random House Dictionary,* College Edition
> *Webster's New World Dictionary of the American Language*
> *Webster's New Collegiate Dictionary*

Sample entries from one of these dictionaries, labeled to show some of the features of a dictionary, are reproduced on page 290.

Special Dictionaries

The general dictionaries — abridged and unabridged — are supplemented by a number of specialized dictionaries that you may need to consult for material not to be found in general works.

Historical Dictionaries. Good dictionaries for general use are based in part upon scholarly dictionaries made over long periods of time. *The Oxford English Dictionary* (twelve volumes and a *Supplement,* 1888–1928) is a historical dictionary of the words and idiomatic phrases of the English language. It traces the various forms and meanings of each word, giving the date of its first appearance in recorded English and illustrative quotations from writers to show its typical use at various times in its history (a dozen or more columns are sometimes devoted to a single word). In many kinds of study it is a basic source for research. *The Shorter Oxford English Dictionary* (two volumes) is an abridgment of the larger work and somewhat easier to use; recently the entire work has, by virtue of miniaturized print, been published in two volumes that come with a magnifying glass.

   The Dictionary of American English (four volumes), made on the same plan as the *Oxford,* gives the history of words as they have been used by American writers from 1620 to 1900. *A Dictionary of Americanisms* (two volumes) gives the history of words that originated in the United States and brings the record of American English down to 1944.

Dictionaries in Special Subjects. Dictionaries of slang, usage, and other specialized language uses are available, and most special fields have dictionaries of their specialized vocabularies. It is a good idea to know the titles of those in any fields you are going to work in. The following list merely suggests the range of such books. Most of them are revised from time to time.

   Ballentine, J. A., *Law Dictionary*
   Chambers's Technical Dictionary
   Clark, D. T., and B. A. Gottfried, *Dictionary of Business and Finance*
   Dorland, W. A. N., *American Illustrated Medical Dictionary*
   English, H. B., *A Student's Dictionary of Psychological Terms*
   Good, C. V., *Dictionary of Education*
   Hackh, I. W. D., *Chemical Dictionary*
   Rice, C. M., *Dictionary of Geological Terms*

22.2 Learning to Use Your Dictionary

Dictionaries differ not only in the information they include but in the way they present it, and the best dictionary in the world will be of little value to you unless you know how to read and interpret the information it provides. Before using a new dictionary, read the front matter carefully. It will explain the organization of entries,

the method of indicating pronunciation, the use of restrictive labels, and the meaning of abbreviations and symbols used in the
definitions and etymologies. Then look carefully at a page of entries to see how words and phrases are handled. Test your understanding of the pronunciation guide by using it to pronounce some
familiar words. Look through the table of contents to see what sections of information your dictionary provides in addition to the
main alphabetical list of words. You may find a short grammar of
the English language, a discussion of punctuation, a table of signs
and symbols, a list of colleges and universities in the United
States, and a guide to the preparation of manuscript copy.

A little time spent in learning to use your dictionary can make it
immensely useful to you. The following sections describe the kinds
of information found in most dictionaries; the sample entries on
page 290 show how one dictionary presents this information, but
most dictionaries are similar.

• *Exercise*

To help you familiarize yourself with your dictionary, write out the following information about it, for discussion in class or to be handed in.

1. The title, the name of the publisher, and the most recent copyright
   date. This date may be found on the back of the title page.

2. A list of the sections following the introduction and preceding the dictionary entries (such as "How to Use the Dictionary," "A Guide to
   Pronunciation," "Usage levels").

3. A list of the material in the appendix (if any), such as "Signs and
   Symbols," "Biographical Names," "Colleges and Universities in the
   United States."

4. Do the words appear in one alphabetical list or in separate lists (for
   biographical names, geographical names, abbreviations, etc.)?

5. Are derived forms (*cynical* and *cynicism* from *cynic,* for example) listed separately as main entries in the alphabetical list, or are they listed
   under the base word?

6. Do the etymologies come at the beginning or at the end of an entry?

7. The order of the definitions of the words. Does the older meaning or
   the current meaning come first in such words as *bibulous, cute, ghastly,
   shrewd, liquidate, souse* (noun). *recession, fulsome?*

22.2

Dict

Spelling and Word Division

Develop the habit of using your dictionary to check the spelling in
your papers. If you are unable to find a word because you are uncertain of one of the beginning letters, try to think of other possible

entry and word division —— **mo‑ment** \'mō‑mənt\ *n* [ME, fr. MF, fr. L *momentum* movement,

etymology —— particle sufficient to turn the scales, moment, fr. *movēre* to move]

definition, with examples —— **1 :** a minute portion or point of time : INSTANT **2 a :** present

    showing use of the word time ⟨at the ~ he is working on a novel⟩ **b :** a time of excellence

    in context or conspicuousness ⟨he has his ~s⟩ **3 :** importance in influence or

usage label —— effect : notable or conspicuous consequence **4** [*obs*] **:** a cause or

motive of action **5 a :** a stage in historical or logical development

6 a : tendency or measure of tendency to produce motion esp.

about a point or axis **b :** the product of quantity (as a force) and

the distance to a particular axis or point **7 a :** the mean of the

*n*th powers of the deviations of the observed values in a set of sta‑

tistical data from a fixed value **b :** the expected value of a power

of the deviation of a random variable from a fixed value *syn* see

IMPORTANCE

part‑of‑speech labels —— **mo‑men‑tar‑i‑ly** \ˌmō‑mən‑'ter‑ə‑lē\ *adv* **1 :** for a moment **2**

: INSTANTLY **3 :** at any moment

synonyms and antonyms —— **mo‑men‑tary** \'mō‑mən‑ˌter‑ē\ *adj* **1 a :** continuing only a mo‑

ment : TRANSITORY **b :** having a very brief life : EPHEMERAL **2**

: operative or recurring at every moment *syn* see TRANSIENT *ant*

agelong **— mo‑men‑tar‑i‑ness** *n*

entry of variant spelling —— **mo‑ment‑ly** \'mō‑mənt‑lē\ *adv* **1 :** from moment to moment **2**

: at any moment **3 :** for a moment

mo‑men‑to \mə‑'ment‑(ˌ)ō\ *var of* MEMENTO

moment of inertia : the ratio of the torque applied to a rigid body

free to rotate about a given axis to the angular acceleration thus

produced about that axis

moment of truth 1 : the final sword thrust in a bullfight **2 :** a

pronunciation guide —— moment of crisis on whose outcome much or everything depends

"run‑on" entries, words —— **mo‑men‑tous** \mō‑'ment‑əs, mə‑'ment‑\ *adj* **:** IMPORTANT, CONSE‑

    whose meaning is clear QUENTIAL **— mo‑men‑tous‑ly** *adv* **— mo‑men‑tous‑ness** *n*

    from main entry **mo‑men‑tum** \mō‑'ment‑əm, mə‑'ment‑\ *n, pl* **mo‑men‑ta** \‑'ment‑

ə\ *or* **momentums** [NL, fr. L, movement] **:** a property of a mov‑

ing body that determines the length of time required to bring it to

rest when under the action of a constant force or moment; *broadly*

: IMPETUS

cross reference —— **mom‑ma** \'mäm‑ə, 'mɔm‑\ *var of* MAMMA

Mo‑mus \'mō‑məs\ *n* [L, fr. Gk *Mōmos*] **:** the Greek god of blame

and mockery

¹mon \'män\ *dial chiefly Brit var of* MAN

abbreviation —— **²mon** *abbr* **1** monastery **2** monetary

¹Mon \'mōn\ *n, pl* **Mon** *or* **Mons 1 :** a member of the dominant

native people of Pegu in Burma **2 :** the Mon‑Khmer language of

the Mon people

homographs, entries spelled —— **²Mon** *abbr* **1** Monaghan **2** Monday **3** Monmouthshire

    alike but different in **mon‑** *or* **mono‑** *under stress the (1st)* "o" *is sometimes* ō *although not*

    meaning, derivation, *shown at individual entries*\ *comb form* [ME, fr. MF & L; MF, fr. L,

    or pronunciation fr. Gk, fr. *monos* alone, single — more at MONK] **1 :** one : single

: alone ⟨*mono*plane⟩ ⟨*mono*drama⟩ ⟨*mono*phobia⟩ **2 a :** contain‑

ing one (usu. specified) atom, radical, or group ⟨*mono*hydrate⟩

prefix entry —— ⟨*mono*xide⟩ **b :** monomolecular ⟨*mono*film⟩ ⟨*mono*layer⟩

ə **abut**	⁎ **kitten**	ər **further**	a **back**	ā **bake**	ä **cot, cart**
aú **out**	ch **chin**	e **less**	ē **easy**	g **gift**	i **trip** i **life**
j **joke**	ŋ **sing**	ō **flow**	ȯ **flaw**	ȯi **coin**	th **thin** t̲h̲ **this**

pronunciation key —— | ü **loot** | u̇ **foot** | y **yet** | yü **few** | yu̇ **furious** | zh **vision** |

spellings for the same sound. (Is it *gibe* or *jibe?*) Remember that dictionaries give the spelling not only of the base form of a word but also of distinctive forms—the principal parts of verbs, the plurals of nouns, the comparative and superlative forms of adjectives and adverbs—that are in any way irregular.

Your dictionary may give two spellings for a word when usage is divided *(hemoglobin—haemoglobin; although—altho)*. Use the spelling that the editors have indicated is the more common one. (The method of listing variants will be explained in the front matter.) Avoid spellings labeled British (such as *colour, gaol*) in favor of the usual American spelling.

Dictionaries divide words into units (usually corresponding to spoken syllables) by means of small dots or spaces: *de·mar·ca·tion, de light ful*. This device will enable you to see each part of the word clearly and to notice if you have omitted or transposed any letters. In writing, divide a word at the end of a line only where your dictionary shows a division. The word *reorganization,* for example, might be divided at the end of a line in any one of five places: *re·or·ga·ni·za·tion.* Not all dictionaries divide every word in exactly the same way, but by following the practice of any good dictionary you will avoid such careless blunders as dividing *bedraggled* into *bed-* and *raggled.* See also 17, Spelling, and 28.2, Manuscript Form.

• *Exercise*

What information do you find in your dictionary on the spelling of these pairs of words? Are the spellings interchangeable? If so, which form would you use and why?

aesthetic—esthetic   favor—favour
carat—karat   gaol—jail
catalog—catalogue   licorice—liquorice
catsup—catchup   sac—sack
draft—draught   traveling—travelling

22.2

Dict

Pronunciation

Because English spelling is not consistently phonetic (there are over 250 ways to spell the forty-odd sounds in English), dictionaries use a system of special symbols to show how words are pronounced. The word *bamboozle,* for example, might be respelled this way after the entry word: băm bōō′ zəl. The pronunciation key at the bottom of the page will illustrate, with familiar words, the sounds represented by the symbols, ă, ōō, and ə. Since the consonants *b, m, z,* and *l* have no special marks over them, you may assume that they are pronounced in the usual way. The accented syllable in *băm bōo' zəl* is indicated by a heavy stress mark. Phonetic spellings also indicate secondary stress, when appropriate, usually by a lighter mark (') but sometimes by a different symbol. Since the system for showing pronunciation varies somewhat from dictionary to dictionary, you should study carefully the explanatory notes in the front of your own book before attempting to use its pronunciation key.

Dictionaries often list two or more pronunciations for a word when usage is divided. Although the first pronunciation is usually the more common one, it is not necessarily "preferred," and you should use whichever pronunciation is customary in your own community.

• *Exercises*

To familiarize yourself with the pronunciation key in your dictionary, write out the following exercises:

1. What pronunciations does your dictionary list for each of these words? Is the first pronunciation given the one you hear most frequently? If not, tell how it differs, including the stress (accent):

address	creek	greasy	pianist
adult	decadent	herb	poinsettia
Celtic	drama	impotent	research
coupon	gibberish	leisure	Oedipus

2. How is each of these words pronounced when used as a noun? As a verb?

confine	escort	impact	misuse
conflict	exploit	import	refuse
consort	ferment		

Meaning

Dictionaries are perhaps most important for what they tell us about the meanings of words. To a reader, a dictionary is useful for finding the meanings not only of unfamiliar words but also of familiar words used in new senses. To a writer, dictionary definitions are most useful for checking the meanings of words there may be some doubt about.

Dictionaries begin each definition, or group of definitions, with an abbreviation showing whether the word is being defined as a noun *(n.)*, adjective *(adj.)*, verb *(vb.)*, transitive verb *(v.t.)*, intransitive verb *(v.i.)*, or other part of speech. This information is important, for words usually have different meanings in different grammatical contexts. Sometimes the meanings are closely related (for example, the meanings of *advance* as a verb, a noun, or an adjective) but sometimes they are completely different (the meanings of *fly, plant,* and *court* as verbs or as nouns).

In looking for the meaning of a word in context, therefore, you must ordinarily isolate the right group of definitions before you can find the particular meaning you are looking for. Then you should look over all of the definitions included in that group. Some dictionaries give the oldest meaning first and other dictionaries the most common one. Often you will want neither of these but a more specialized meaning that comes late in the entry. At the end of the entry, or at the end of a group of definitions for one part of speech, you may also find one or more idioms listed.

In using dictionary definitions, you should keep two general principles in mind:

1. A dictionary does not *require* or *forbid* a particular meaning or use of a word; it merely *records* the most common ways in which a word has actually been used. Therefore you must exercise judgment in deciding whether a particular word will be appropriate in a particular context.
2. A dictionary definition is for the most part a record of the *denotation,* or specific meaning, of a word; at best, it can only suggest the *connotation,* or suggestive qualities, which varies with context and with use. (See 23.1.) In general, it is better not to use a word until you have heard it or read it and know at least some of its connotations.

22.2

Dict

• *Exercises*

1. Answer the following questions by referring to the definitions given in your dictionary:

   a. In what kind of writing would it be appropriate to use the word *gimmick?*
   b. In what profession would the word *dolmen* most likely be used?
   c. Where would you be most likely to hear the word *legato?*
   d. When a woman *rests on her laurels,* what is she doing?
   e. Which of the following expressions would be underlined in a paper to indicate they belong to a foreign language?
      Realpolitik   de facto   sarong   savoir-faire   toccata   vice versa

2. Consult your dictionary and choose the best definition for the italicized word in each of these sentences:

   a. At ten he became a printer's *devil.*
   b. His *fellowship* expired at the end of the year.
   c. Luther objected to the sale of *indulgences.*
   d. The entrance fee was *fixed* at twenty dollars.
   e. She has extremely *catholic* reading tastes.
   f. They soon discovered that the resort was a *white elephant.*

Areas of Usage and Special Labels

Some words (or particular meanings for some words) are labeled in a dictionary as *dialectal, obsolete, archaic, foreign, colloquial, slang, British, United States,* or are identified with some particular activity or field — *medicine, law, astronomy, music, sports, manufacturing, electricity.* One of the college dictionaries *(American Heritage)* even includes a separate section on usage. Words unlabeled in a dictionary are considered part of the general vocabulary.

Usage labels can serve as rough guides, but you should bring your own observation to bear on individual words. Certainly you would ordinarily avoid words marked *obsolete* or *archaic,* but many words that carry no label *(albeit, perforce)* would be equally out of place in most college writing. On the other hand, many words marked *Dial.* or *Colloq.* (such as *highbrow*) might fit perfectly well into both informal and general English. The label *colloquial,* which many people mistake to mean nonstandard, simply suggests that a particular usage is more characteristic of speech than it is of writing. The label *U.S.* means that the usage is found in the United States but not in other parts of the English-speaking world.

Most dictionaries of the English language include frequently used words and expressions from foreign languages. Some dictionaries indicate that such terms are generally considered foreign by listing the language in parentheses: *(It.), (Fr.).* Some also use an identifying mark, such as a dagger or an asterisk, before all foreign-word entries. Such labels are useful because they help distinguish between foreign words that are now considered part of the English vocabulary *(chalet, aria, mesa)* and those that are still considered distinctly foreign *(dolce far niente, Weltanschauung, enceinte)* and must be underlined in a paper. (See 14.3 Italics for Foreign Words.)

• *Exercise*

Answer the following questions by consulting the *grammatical information* given in the dictionary entry for each word:

1. What is the past participle of *shear?*

2. What is the past tense of *bear* in the sense of *carry?*

3. What does *feign* mean when it is used intransitively?

4. What does *gull* mean when followed by a direct object?

5. What is the plural of *ghetto?*

6. What is the plural of *stratum?*

Synonyms and Antonyms

Most dictionaries list words of similar meaning *(synonyms)* with the basic or most comprehensive word of a group and explain how these various related words differ slightly in meaning, especially in connotation. Sometimes the entry for a word will also list an *antonym*, a word of opposite meaning, as *cowardly* would be an antonym for *courageous*.

There are several specialized books containing lists of related words: *Webster's Dictionary of Synonyms*, Fernald's *Standard Handbook of Synonyms, Antonyms, and Prepositions*, Soule's *A Dictionary of English Synonyms*, *Webster's Collegiate Thesaurus*, and Roget's *Thesaurus*. The *Thesaurus* is probably the most widely used book of synonyms, but since it does not give definitions, its chief use is to remind writers of words they recognize but do not use regularly. If you find words that appear to be appropriate but you are not completely sure, check their definitions in a dictionary.

Etymology

A dictionary not only tells how a word is used and pronounced but also gives its origin, or *etymology*. Sometimes the etymology is merely a notation of the language from which the word was borrowed (as *decor* is from French and *Gestalt* is from German) or a statement of how it was coined. But often the etymology is fairly complicated; the development of the word *advance*, for example, can be traced back through Middle English to Old French and finally to Latin. The explanatory notes at the front of your dictionary include a discussion of etymology and a key to the abbreviations and symbols used on tracing a word's origin.

Knowing how a word originated will often help you understand and remember it. Knowing that *philanthropy*, for example, comes from the Greek words *philein* (to love) and *anthropos* (man) may help fix its meaning in your mind. It may also help you figure out other words by analogy *(philology, anthropocentric)*.

Etymologies often illustrate how word meanings have changed from their original to their present use and are interesting as records of human thought and experience.

22.2

Dict

• *Exercises*

1. Consult the *etymologies* in your dictionary to answer the following questions:

   a. What is the origin of these words?

sandwich	assassin	lecture
robot	okra	semester
farm	radish	geology

b. Which of the following words have retained most or all of their original meanings? Which have retained some? Which none?

bigot	fiasco	pilot
curfew	miscegenation	silly
fecund	pedigree	tragedy

2. The following questions can be answered by finding the special information they require in the dictionary. In some cases it is attached to the regular word entry; in others special sections at the back or front of the dictionary must be consulted.

a. Write sentences using the words shown below. Be sure your sentences distinguish among the similar words put together as sets:

deviate — digress — diverge — swerve
slim — thin — slender — skinny
fictitious — legendary — mythical
giggle — titter — snicker — chuckle
latent — potential — dormant

b. Give antonyms for the following words: *authentic, chaste, devout, futile, venial.*
c. Who was John Huss? When did he live?
d. Where are the Carpathian Mountains?
e. How large is a lemming?
f. Is Mexico City smaller or larger than Paris in population?
g. Where is Miami University?
h. How long is a furlong?
i. What does the symbol B/L mean in business and commerce?
j. What does the sign ∴ mean in mathematics?

23 The Meaning of Words

Respect for the word—to employ it with scrupulous care and incorruptible heartful love of truth—is essential if there is to be any growth in society or in the human race.—Dag Hammarskjöld, MARKINGS

*A word is dead
When it is said,
Some say.
I say it just
Begins to live
That day.—Emily Dickinson*

We usually take for granted that we know the meanings of the words we use, except when there is a question of accuracy *(infer* or *imply?)* or of appropriateness *(boss* or *supervisor?).* But if you are to use the words that will best convey your meaning, you need to do more than simply accept and use the first words that come to mind. You need to take an active interest in words as words. What gives a particular word its special meanings in different situations? In what different ways can a word be used? How will others take the words you use? Words have many possible meanings. If you are to choose those that best serve your purpose, you need to know first what the choices are.

23.1

Mng

23.1 Words in Context and Situation

Words do not actually have "meaning" until they are used in speaking or writing. Then their meaning derives partly from the *context,* or the words around them, and partly from the *situation* in which they are used, which involves the attitudes and purposes of either a speaker and listener or a writer and reader.

It is easy to see how the context limits the meaning of a word. A word like *deck, run, fly,* or *match* can be used in several senses, but usually in a particular sentence it can have only one meaning:

> Tomorrow we'll take a **run** up to the lake.
> You will have to **run** to catch the train.
> Frowning, she noticed the **run** in her stocking.
> Aaron scored the third **run** after there were two out in the seventh.

He did a **run** of scales and decided that was enough practice.
When the store opened on the morning of the sale, there was a **run** on piece goods.

The situation in which a word is used also helps clarify its meaning. The word *bill* in "The bill is too large" would mean one thing if the speaker were trying to identify a bird and another if he were discussing family finances. A writing situation includes at least a topic of discussion, a writer, and the potential audiences. The writer must use words that are not only appropriate to the topic but that will help the reader know the writer and see the writer's world.

• *Exercise*

The meaning of a word often depends on the context in which it is used. Write two sentences using each of the following words to show how the meaning of the words can change as they move from one context to another: *realize, studio, elevation, pitching, cup, book, stack, feedback.*

Denotation: The Core of a Word's Meaning

When we think first about the meaning of words, we usually think of their *denotation,* what they have come to represent as a result of the ways they have been used. This is the meaning that dictionaries record and try to describe for us. The thing that a word refers to or suggests is called its *referent.*

Some kinds of words have more definite denotations than others because their referents are more limited or more exact. Depending on their definiteness, words may be classified into three groups:

1. **Concrete words,** words that name specific people, places, or objects, are the most exact in meaning: *Walt Whitman, Lake Erie, my bicycle, the library, reindeer, a Boy Scout knife.*
2. **Relative words,** words that describe qualities, are less definite than concrete words and frequently depend for their meanings on the situation or on the writer's past experience with a term: *hot, pretty, honest, angry, silly, impossible.* In New York City, a *tall* building might mean any structure over twenty stories, but in a city with no skyscrapers, *tall* might refer to any building higher than five stories.
3. **Abstract words,** words that refer to general concepts — acts, situations, relationships, conditions — are the least definite: *reasoning, citizenship, education, intelligence, culture, objectives, art.* Since these words have a range of reference (think of all the activities that may be included in *education,* for example), rather than a specific referent, they are more difficult to use exactly than concrete words. (See also 23.4, Concrete and Abstract Words.)

Connotation: The Power to Suggest Meaning

Most words have been used by so many different people in such different circumstances for such different purposes that they have acquired associations and suggestions that go beyond their denotation. The word *twilight,* for example, has been used so often in association with melancholy or romance that we sometimes don't think of it as a time of day. And someone has suggested that the word *nightingale* would lose all its suggestion of beauty and be merely the name of a bird only to a tone-deaf ornithologist. These qualities that words have acquired from their expanded use are called *connotation.*

Very often the chief difference between words of closely related denotation is in their connotation. Both *inexpensive* and *cheap* refer to low price, but *cheap* may also connote poor quality; *average* and *mediocre* both refer to the middle of a range, but *mediocre* suggests dispraise; *belief, faith, creed, dogma* all refer to ideas held, but they differ widely in suggesting how they are held. It is easy to see why some students of language say that there are no true synonyms.

Dictionaries try to suggest the shades of meaning that words may have, but the best way to find the exact connotations of a word is to observe how it is actually used in current writing and speech. The connotative value of a word often changes over time. *Sly,* for example, once meant *skillful,* but as it is generally used now it would fit into the same context as *devious* or *tricky;* it may even suggest *criminal* or, sometimes, *lecherous.* Words like *genteel* and *bucolic* have lost their favorable connotation as the values they represent have lost much of their appeal. Certain words, usually those whose referents arouse widely ranging responses, are extremely variable in connotation: *pop art, radical, socialism, jazz.* When you use such words, be cautious, making sure that your attitude is clear to your reader and that you are being fair to your subject. Words with high connotative value, like words that are associated with prickly controversies, may create special problems for you. The art of the whittler who sat in the town square may be useful to you here.

The whittler, a man widely known for his uncannily realistic carvings of birds, when asked how he managed to achieve such realism in his carvings, said, "Well, I just whittle off all the wood that don't look like a bird." When you use words that have high suggestive power, you may have to whittle off all of the meanings that you do not want to express. This may mean taking the time to define, to set limits to what you are trying to say, to establish clearly how you want to use the words. Any potential readers you have are real people, too, and they are at liberty to take your words in

23.1

Mng

any way they wish unless you have shown them the limits of meaning that you have in mind. If you refer to a coeducational dormitory, for example, some people will hear a reference to free sex and a scandalous decline in moral character, *unless* you take pains to declare the nature of a coeducational dormitory as you wish them to see it.

• *Exercise*

The connotative value of words is very important in determining their use: for example, you might say "I am *plump;* you are *heavy;* he is *fat*"; three different pictures emerge. Arrange the following groups of words into columns, according to their connotation: favorable, neutral, or unfavorable.

1. student, scholar, bookworm

2. stubborn, firm, pigheaded

3. counterfeit, replica, copy

4. racy, obscene, blue

5. unusual, bizarre, unique

6. tolerant, flexible, wishy-washy

7. caustic, penetrating, sharp

8. reserved, aristocratic, snobbish

9. buffoon, wit, comic

10. officer, policeman, fuzz

11. svelte, skinny, thin

12. literary artist, hack, writer

23.2 Fair Words and Slanted Words

Your readers don't always see things as you see them, or know them as you know them, just as you don't see and know things as they do. If you want your readers to see and know things as you do, at least for a moment, you have to show them where you are, how you have positioned yourself. Words chosen carefully for their connotative value can help you show your readers what your attitude is toward your subject. An honest and fair representation of the position you have taken toward your subject is entirely proper and fitting. Sometimes, however, writers assault their audience — intentionally or accidentally — by using words weighted in their favor. Such writing is often called *slanted writing.*

Words Used Fairly for Effect

It is not possible to speak or write in completely neutral, objective language about anything that has fully engaged our interest. To write well about a subject, we must care about it enough to take a position or make a judgment concerning it.

In factual as well as in imaginative writing, interest, liveliness, and effectiveness depend greatly on the successful use of connotation. Our awareness of all the values that words have enables us to represent our subject precisely, to address our audience with a varied and appealing language, and to show where we stand in relation to our material. Honestly used, words with high connotative value give *shape* and *texture* — as opposed to *slant* — to what we say.

Fair use of the power of suggestion occurs in this passage, especially in the first sentence:

> Earth-dwellers now have the choice of making their world into a neighborhood or a crematorium. Language is one of the factors in that option. The right words may not automatically produce the right actions but they are an essential part of the process. — Norman Cousins, "The Environment of Language," *Saturday Review*

The passage occurs in an essay pleading for ethical uses of language, and the author clearly wants to sway us. The word *earth-dwellers* cancels differences arising from sex, race, creed, or nationality, and reminds us instead of our common character and interdependence. The word *neighborhood* suggests security and companionship, weighting the argument in favor of that choice, while the word *crematorium* conjures up the unspeakable horrors of genocide. Slanting here appears to be fair: it is plain that we are getting the author's opinion and that we are not being deceived.

23.2

Slant

Slanted Words

The story is told of a harvester of enormous appetite who shortened the legs of the dining table on the side where he sat so that the food would slide toward him for instant availability. By exploiting the suggestive power of words, writers can similarly tilt arguments and meanings in their favor.

Sometimes slanting occurs only because writers, in their enthusiasm, allow words that are too intense to intrude in statements presented as fact. To say "All television programs are designed for the twelve-year-old mind" is allowing a personal distaste for television programing to make the writer careless. Often *all* or *most* should be *many,* or a superlative should be reduced to a less extreme word, or *only* or *nothing but* should be changed to allow for other possibilities.

Much unfair slanting occurs in statements of opinion where a writer, knowingly or not, assumes that he or she is the only reliable resource. There is nothing slanted in a simple statement of one's likes or dislikes ("I can't stand these people with their long hair"). But the same opinion stated as a general fact in slanted wording ("Long, stringy hair and freaky clothes are signs of decadence") implies that the writer expects the reader to share that opinion without thinking about it.

Just as writers who unfailingly trust themselves as the only reliable resource are likely to slant their writing, so are writers who, in their enthusiasm for their own position, fail to consider more than one possibility. The following passage is from an essay in which the author argues that destroying the wilderness and its resources is a perfectly natural and appropriate human activity:

> The trumpeting voice of the wilderness lover is heard at great distances these days. He is apt to be a perfectly decent person, if hysterical. And the causes which excite him so are generally worthy. Who can really find a harsh word for him as he strives to save Lake Erie from the sewers of Cleveland, save the redwoods from the California highway engineers, save the giant rhinoceros from the Somali tribesmen who kill those noble beasts to powder their horns into what they fondly imagine is a wonder-working aphrodisiac?
>
> Worthy causes, indeed, but why do those who espouse them have to be so shrill and intolerant and sanctimonious? What right do they have to insinuate that anyone who does not share their passion for the whooping crane is a Philistine and a slob? From the gibberish they talk, you would think the only way to save the bald eagle is to dethrone human reason. — Robert Wernick, "Let's Spoil the Wilderness"

Unexamined assumptions (wilderness lovers are hysterical) and unsubstantiated assertions (they speak gibberish) are the source of much slanting. For this reason, many of the most serious instances of slanting come in writing on social or political problems, especially when the words reflect prejudice. This type of slanted writing can be objected to on at least four grounds:

1. it doesn't accurately represent the situation being discussed;
2. it suggests that the writer is at the very least careless of what he or she says and more probably willing to distort the facts for his or her own purposes;
3. it stands in the way of an intelligent and constructive approach to problems that affect the public interest; and
4. it is likely to antagonize the readers (unless they are similarly prejudiced) and so prevent clear communication.

Not all slanted writing uses obviously weighted words. The disapproval that emerges in the following passage comes not so much from emotion-carrying words (there are relatively few) as from the use of mostly plain but much overused words in sports broadcasting:

> We know by heart all the lines of the script, starting with the traditional opening speeches by the game announcers, who function as the Chorus. Both teams are up today. They have come to play. They have the will to win. They are sky-high. There is no tomorrow. — Russell Baker, "End Zone," *The New York Times Magazine*

Slanted writing is often clever and sometimes funny. But remember that you have a responsibility to deal fairly with both your subject and your audience.

• *Exercise*

Practice shifting the values expressed in writing by rewriting the opening three paragraphs in two newspaper articles so as to slant the account one way or another. Bring to class for discussion some items you find in magazines or newspapers that seem slanted to you.

23.3 Choosing the Right Word

2f 2f Replace the wrong word marked with one that accurately conveys your intended meaning.

23.3

2f 2f

In most factual prose, words should be used in their established forms and senses; if they are not, the reader may be mislead or confused. An expression such as "The scene *provoked* his imagination" (in which *provoked,* commonly meaning "angered," is inaccurately used instead of *stimulated*) interferes with communication. In revising your papers, check any words that you are unsure of, especially those that are not part of your regular vocabulary. Be particularly alert to words that are easily confused.

Distinguishing Words of Similar Spelling

In English there are many pairs of words that closely resemble each other in sound or spelling but have quite different meanings: *moral* and *morale, personal* and *personnel, historic* and *histrionic.* When writing hastily, you may accidentally substitute one word for another, but you can easily eliminate such errors by proofreading your work and by referring to a dictionary when necessary. When words of identical pronunciation, called *homonyms,* are confused in writing, the mistake may be called a spelling error (*bear* for *bare; there* for *their*). But your instructor is likely to label it **WW** (wrong word) if he or she suspects that you may not know the difference in meaning (*principal* for *principle; affect* for *effect*).

The following words are frequently confused in college papers. If you are not sure of the distinction between them, remember your dictionary, or see the glossary of usage on page 483:

accept – except	detract – distract
adapt – adopt	formally – formerly
affect – effect	human – humane
allusion – illusion	imply – infer
censor – censure	persecute – prosecute
cite – site	precede – proceed
complement – compliment	principal – principle
conscientious – conscious	respectful – respective
credible – creditable – credulous	stationary – stationery

• *Exercise*

Write sentences using the words listed above. Be sure that your sentences show clearly the differences in meaning.

Distinguishing Words of Similar Meaning

Word errors frequently occur because the writer has failed to distinguish between words of similar meaning. A synonym is a word of *nearly* the same meaning as another:

angry – annoyed – indignant
frank – candid – blunt
multitude – throng – crowd – mob
strange – peculiar – quaint – bizarre

A few words have identical meanings and are therefore interchangeable (*flammable – inflammable; ravel – unravel; toward – towards*). But most synonyms, while they refer to the same idea or object, differ somewhat in denotation or connotation and thus cannot be substituted for each other without affecting the sense or tone of the statement. One term may be more formal than another (*coiffure – hair-do*); more concrete (*tango – dance*); more exact (*charitable – kind*); or more personal (*dad – father*).

Usually it is not the more subtle distinctions between closely related words that cause trouble (*necessary – indispensable; intrinsic – inherent*), but the failure to distinguish between common words in different contexts:

The mysteries of the unknown arouse curiosity that must be **fulfilled.**
[for *satisfied*]

We may expect food consumption to increase everywhere because of the **growth in people.** [*increase in population*]

The only way to avoid such errors is to notice how words of similar meaning are used in various contexts. Connotation as well as
denotation should be considered. Notice, for example, how unexpected the last word in this statement is:

> In the 1870's, Dodge City was a lawless gathering place for gun-toting
> cowboys, professional bad men and killers, and other **scamps.**

Scamps might be quite appropriate in referring to mischievous
children, but the term is conspicuously out of place in this company of desperadoes. Some synonyms are too heavy or too flippant
for the context:

> The water was rougher past the next bend, and we had **difficulty cir-
> cumventing** the rapids. [too formal: had *trouble getting around* would
> be more appropriate]

> I enjoyed studying Plato, because among other things **I got the low-
> down on** what is meant by a Platonic friendship. [too informal: *learned*
> would be better]

But remember the principle of appropriateness. There are special
situations in which such incongruities might be useful. Mark Twain
and Will Rogers, for example, could sometimes, by mixing different kinds of language, get comic effect from the incongruity.

Writers sometimes use strings of fanciful synonyms to avoid
repeating the same expression for an idea or object *(cats, felines,
furry beasts, tabbies, nine-lived creatures)*. Such "elegant variations" are pretentious and are usually more annoying than simple
repetition. Readers expect key words to be repeated when they
cannot be replaced by pronouns *(cats . . . they)*. Factual synonyms *(these animals)* are also unobtrusive and will seldom strike
the reader as repetitious.

23.3

Distinguishing Words of Opposite Meaning

Some words that have contrasting or wholly opposite meanings are
frequently confused, probably because the writer associates them
mentally but has reversed their meanings. Among the most common antonyms or near antonyms are the following. Make sure that
you know their meanings.

concave — convex	inductive — deductive
condemn — condone	physiological — psychological
explicit — implicit	prescribe — proscribe
famous — notorious	subjective — objective
former — latter	temerity — timidity

Confusing such pairs may result in your saying the very opposite of what you intend. Half-knowing a word is often more dangerous than not knowing it at all.

• *Exercise*

Write sentences using the words listed above. Make sure that your sentences show clearly the difference in meaning.

Learning New Words

Although many word errors are caused by confusion or carelessness, it's easy to use the wrong word (or settle for the almost-right word) simply because you do not know another one. College papers are likely to deal with complex ideas and precise distinctions that may demand a larger vocabulary than you have needed in the past.

It has been estimated that children enter first grade knowing about 25,000 words and add 5000 every year, so that they leave high school with a vocabulary of perhaps as many as 90,000 words. The average vocabulary for college graduates is approximately twice this size. These figures are for *recognition* vocabulary, the words that we understand when we read or hear them. Our *active* vocabulary, the words we actually use in writing or speaking, is considerably smaller.

Most people use only about a third as many words as they recognize. Thus, an obvious way for you to enlarge your working vocabulary is through conscious exercise. In making an effort to say precisely what you mean you should search not only among the words in your active vocabulary, but also among those you have learned to recognize. Frequently we find new words in reading (*cybernetics, rhetoric, apartheid*) and learn their meanings from the context or from a dictionary. Using these words in writing or speaking helps to make them more readily available for future use.

It is sometimes possible to guess the meaning of a word by knowing its parts. Many scientific words, for example, are formed with suffixes and roots from Greek or Latin:

mono- (one)	-graph (writing, written)	poly- (many)
bi- (two)	bio- (life)	macro- (large)
tele- (at a distance)	photo- (light)	micro- (small)

Since the combined meanings of the parts may only approximate the meaning of the whole, however, it is usually safer to use a dictionary and learn the entire word.

Ordinarily we learn and remember words not for their own sake but for the meanings they represent. We have a good stock of words in the fields that interest us because facts and ideas are retained in verbal form. Thus, anything that extends the range of your ideas or experiences will help to enlarge your vocabulary. The typical college course, for example, adds to a student's vocabulary several hundred new words and new meanings for familiar words.

When you meet a new word that is likely to be useful, learn it accurately at the start — its spelling and pronunciation as well as its usual meaning. Students often have trouble in their college courses because they only half know the specialized words essential to a subject. Using these words in conversation, when they are appropriate, or in reviewing course work with another student will fix them in your mind so that you can use them easily and accurately in examinations, papers, and class discussions.

• *Exercises*

1. The first word that comes to mind is not necessarily the best one, even if it means *approximately* what you intend. Read each of the following sentences carefully and choose the word in parentheses that most *exactly* expresses the intended meaning.

   a. The latest statistics (dispute, refute, rebuke) his claim that the economy is expanding.
   b. In time Einstein (convinced, persuaded, showed) most physicists that his theory was correct.
   c. Most states have laws that (stop, deter, prohibit) gambling.
   d. We stopped in our stroll on lower Main Street to (give, donate, contribute) some money to a blind man.
   e. The remarks at the end of his speech (implied, inferred, insinuated) that he had some financial support for his plan.

23.3

2. Examine the diction in the following sentences to determine whether some words are misused. If so, rewrite the faulty sentences, supplying more exact or more appropriate words. Be prepared to explain why you made each change.

   a. Within the next few days the assassin gained considerable renown.
   b. I do not like to be around him, for his perpetual pessimism aggravates me.
   c. A student who is writing a research paper should compulsively read through the leading works devoted to his subject.
   d. If we adopt the plan, how will the changes in procedure effect the goals?
   e. I found this poem extremely obtuse, and even after struggling over it for hours with a dictionary and an encyclopedia I could not decipher many of its illusions.

23.4 Concrete and Abstract Words

Words can be classified according to the nature of their referents as *abstract* or *concrete* (page 298). Abstract (general) words refer to ideas, qualities, acts, or relationships. Concrete (specific) words refer to definite persons, places, objects, and acts. This list demonstrates the differences between the two kinds of words:

Abstract (general)	Concrete (specific)
institution	Austin College
labor	running a ditching machine
men's organization	Lions Club
a politician	the senator from Kentucky
food	cheesecake
an educator	my history teacher
creed	Westminster Confession

Often a word cannot be labeled as abstract or concrete until it is read in context:

> ABSTRACT: Honest labor never killed anyone. [a generalization about all labor]
>
> CONCRETE: In the GM contract dispute, labor seeks a five-cent per hour wage increase. [in the context, a specific reference to the United Automobile Workers]

Effective Uses of Concrete and Abstract Words

Concrete words are essential in discussing situations, incidents, and processes that are based upon personal experience or direct observation: impressions of people or places, discussions of plans for the future, explanations of the writer's attitudes or interests.

Abstract words, on the other hand, are usually necessary in discussing general ideas ("The Intangible Values of Education"), for summarizing facts or stating opinions, or for analyzing theoretical problems ("Is Specialization in Education Undesirable?").

Abstract words are more characteristic of formal than of general or informal English and are best used by writers with a good deal of experience in handling ideas. In this passage, for example, the writer uses very few concrete words, yet the meaning is clear to anyone who is interested in jazz:

> Some of the most brilliant of jazzmen made no records; their names appeared in print only in announcements of some local dance or remote "battles of music" against equally uncelebrated bands. Being devoted to an art which traditionally thrives on improvisation, these

unrecorded artists very often have their most original ideas enter the public domain almost as rapidly as they are conceived to be quickly absorbed into the thought and technique of their fellows. Thus the riffs which swung the dancers and the band on some transcendent evening, and which inspired others to competitive flights of invention, became all too swiftly a part of the general style, leaving the originator as anonymous as the creators of the architecture called Gothic. — Ralph Ellison, "The Charlie Christian Story"

But broad ideas can also be discussed in concrete terms. For example, the passage below occurs on the opening page of an essay on morality, an abstract idea:

> At midnight last night, on the road in from Las Vegas to Death Valley Junction, a car hit a shoulder and turned over. The driver, very young and apparently drunk, was killed instantly. His girl was found alive but bleeding internally, deep in shock. I talked this afternoon to the nurse who had driven the girl to the nearest doctor, 185 miles across the floor of the Valley and three ranges of lethal mountain road. The nurse explained that her husband, a talc miner, had stayed on the highway with the boy's body until the coroner could get over the mountains from Bishop, at dawn today. "You can't just leave a body on the highway," she said. "It's immoral." — Joan Didion, "On Morality"

When Shakespeare in Sonnet 73 wrote about the sad longing associated with the loss of what we love, he didn't use abstract words, but rather presented images of autumn, twilight, and a dying fire, concrete images that suggest ending, loss, and longing. When Keats told of his excitement when he discovered Homer's works, he didn't write about *excitement, stimulation, amazement, discovery,* or other abstractions; instead he pictured specific situations where such excitement would occur:

23.4

abst

> Then felt I like some watcher of the skies
>   When a new planet swims into his ken;
> Or like stout Cortez when with eagle eyes
>   He star'd at the Pacific — and all his men
> Look'd at each other with a wild surmise —
>   Silent, upon a peak in Darien.
>
>   — "On First Looking into Chapman's Homer"

Generalization is appropriate — even necessary — when a writer must summarize a large body of facts. This is frequently done in short papers on general subjects, where the writer's primary concern is to survey briefly the available facts and explain their significance. The important thing in such cases is to choose general words that *accurately* summarize the specific details examined, without distortion or unnecessary vagueness. A student writing a paper on conservation, for example, might run across this passage:

> In the seven years from 1883 to 1890 the New South Wales Government was forced to spend not less than £1,543,000 in its attempt to control the scourge, and today rabbit control both in Australia and in New Zealand is a financial load upon every community. Many methods of eradicating this pest have been attempted. In Western Australia more than 2000 miles of fencing was erected at a cost of almost £500,000, but after it was all up it was found that some rabbits were already on the other side of the fence! Unfortunately, incidental to the compulsory use of poison for rabbits, there has been a very great destruction of wildlife as well as livestock, and phosphorus poisoning, employed for rabbit control, has been one of the principal causes of death among the marsupials and native birds. — Fairfield Osborn, *Our Plundered Planet*

In writing the paper, the student might effectively generalize from these facts as follows:

> Attempts to limit the rabbit population in Australia and New Zealand have been costly and destructive of other animal life.

It is perfectly proper to use abstract words when the material calls for them, if they can be used accurately and clearly. But writing on almost any subject gains force through the use of specific words. It is usually more convincing to generalize at the beginning or end of a paper, on the basis of a number of specific facts, than it is to pile up generalities throughout.

Excessive Use of Abstract Words

Abst   **Replace the abstract expression marked with one that is more specific.**

A common fault in the wording of many student papers is the use of abstract terms where concrete words would be more meaningful and certainly more interesting. Even if an assigned topic is so worded that it seems difficult to discuss in specific terms ("The Importance of Education," "What Democracy Means"), a paper can be reasonably factual, concrete, and convincing if it is written in words that represent the writer's own experiences and beliefs.

Some students make the mistake of believing that the more general the expression, the more convincing and impressive it is. Others mistake the use of abstract words for intellectual discipline. The use of a general or indefinite expression where a concrete one would fit is annoying to readers:

> I began to participate in all of the different aspects of college pleasure.

We don't know if the writer began to drink. to study, to play bridge, to attend concerts, to sleep late, or to do all or none of these.

The excessive use of abstract words can become an unfortunate habit in writing. Some students never take *physics, history, economics,* or *French;* instead, they encounter *various interesting courses of study;* rather than going to a specific college, they attend *an institution of higher learning;* they do not play *golf, bridge, tennis,* or *baseball,* but *participate in various recreational activities.* Few traits of style are less convincing than the unnecessary use of vague, abstract terms for ideas that could better be expressed concretely.

• *Exercises*

1. The sentences below are general statements, and they may be somewhat vague. Rewrite each of them so that they use more concrete words and name more specific things. Don't worry about the length of your sentences — think instead about making them as specific as you can.

   a. City noises are sometimes raucous and distracting.
   b. Individuals who live in an urban metropolis can engage in more leisure activities.
   c. Fuel conservation will require some changes in our way of living.
   d. More people now are interested in keeping fit.

2. Sometimes you may need to generalize without citing specific information. Keep track of the information in each of the items listed below and then write out your generalization from each.

   a. one week's daily weather reports in a local newspaper
   b. one episode of a soap opera
   c. any three hours of listening to the same disk jockey on a radio station you are familiar with
   d. the letters to the editor in any three days' issues of a local newspaper

23.4

abst

24 The Effect of Words

Words constitute the ultimate texture and stuff of our moral being, since they are the most refined and delicate and detailed, as well as the most universally used and understood, of the symbolisms whereby we express ourselves into existence. We became spiritual animals when we became verbal animals. The fundamental *distinctions can only be made in words. Words are spirit. Of course eloquence is no guarantee of goodness, and an inarticulate man can be virtuous. But the quality of a civilization depends upon its ability to discern and reveal truth, and this depends upon the scope and purity of its language.*—Iris Murdoch, *"Salvation by Words,"* NEW YORK REVIEW OF BOOKS

Words occur in sentences, and sentences occur in paragraphs and compositions. If they are to yield to a reader the meaning that you want, words must be used accurately in context. They should be appropriate to the purpose and tone of the composition: the individual words should fit the subject, they should sound like the writer, and they should reach the intended reader.

Because you can't judge the effect of words out of context, you must rely on your own judgment in choosing words that will tell your meaning and reveal your attitude toward your subject. A dictionary is a useful guide to meaning, but it is of little help when it comes to putting proper words in proper places.

In the absence of specific guidelines, there are three things you can do to help make your word choice more effective. First, you can choose thoughtfully from the range of your present vocabulary the words that best suit your purpose. A good part of the time when we are writing or speaking, many of us just accept and use the first words that come along. Often we already own words that would be more precise and appropriate than the first ones we think of. Second, you can sharpen your judgment by paying closer attention to the language around you—the language of your classmates, your instructors, your parents, the people you hear speak on television and radio—and noticing the differences in usage that you hear and read. Third, you can read widely to familiarize yourself with the range and variety of writing. All written English is a bank you might draw on.

24.1 Formal Words

We may call a piece of *writing* formal, even if its vocabulary is largely from the range of general English, when its sentences are unusually complex, its organizational patterns tight and demanding. We call *vocabulary* formal if it ranges much beyond the characteristic spoken vocabulary, from words slightly more characteristic of writing than of speaking to such specialized words as *moribund, educand, genotype,* and *ailurophobe.*

Appropriate Use of Formal Words

In using formal language, you run the risk of sounding remote from your subject and from your reader. Unless you are at ease with formal words, you also run the risk of seeming affected. But some situations demand and deserve the precision of good formal usage. Some things cannot be said easily, or at all, otherwise. If the nature of your subject requires a formal vocabulary, as the following passages do, use it:

> Semantic aphasia is that numbness of ear, mind and heart—that tone deafness to the very meaning of language—which results from the habitual and prolonged abuse of words. . . . Semantic aphasia is also the near-pathological blitheness that permits three different advertisers in the same women's magazine to call a wig and two dress lines "liberated."—Melvin Maddocks, "The Limitation of Language," *Time*

> Through the centuries (if not millennia) during which, in their retelling, fairy tales became ever more refined, they came to convey at the same time overt and covert meanings—came to speak simultaneously to all levels of the human personality, communicating in a manner which reaches the uneducated mind of the child as well as that of the sophisticated adult. Applying the psychoanalytic model of the human personality, fairy tales carry important messages to the conscious, the preconscious, and the unconscious mind, on whatever level each is functioning at the time.—Bruno Bettelheim, *The Uses of Enchantment*

24.1

Big It

Formal words are appropriate to writers and speakers who use them easily and naturally and to situations that require them for precision. Increase the number of formal words in your vocabulary whenever you can, but use them only when they are necessary, not to translate ordinary matters into "big words."

"Big Words"—Stilted Language

Big It Replace the stilted word or words marked with words from the general vocabulary.

In *Modern English Usage* H. W. Fowler remarks that sometimes "We tell our thoughts, like our children, to put on their hats and coats before they go out." Noting that "the less of such change there is the better," he adds, "there is nothing to be ashamed of in *buy* or *see* that they should need translating into *purchase* and *observe*; where they give the sense equally well they are fit for any company and need not be shut up at home."

"Big words," as the term is used here, are any and all expressions that are too heavy or too formal for the situation. Such words sound stilted, whether they are short or long, common or uncommon. A typical fault of inexperienced writers is the use of big words in a misguided effort to sound profound:

> It is difficult to filter out one specific cause for a social problem. Most often there are many minute factors interrelated and closely correlated. Our conception of a social problem today possesses more magnitude than that of two or three decades ago. We now consider the world as a unit rather than an aggregation of component entities.

Ideas are easier to understand and are more convincing if the wording is natural. It should be exact, not inflated beyond the requirements of the subject or the expectations of the reader. The language of the sentences just cited, for example, might be simplified as follows:

> A social problem can seldom be traced to a single, specific cause. Today we are much more aware of the complexity of social problems than we were twenty or thirty years ago, for we have come to see that all societies are interrelated.

Writers are most likely to use stilted language when they aren't certain what attitude they should take toward their material or toward their readers. They may use inflated diction because they wrongly believe that certain papers should be as formal and impersonal as possible, or that big words will impress the reader, or that inflated diction is humorous ("a fair damsel garbed in the mode of the moment" instead of "a fashionably dressed young woman").

An extreme use of big words is sometimes called *gobbledygook* —inflated diction that seems to have lost all contact with the matter being discussed. Writing full of such jargon is often found in print today, especially in specialized journals and government publications, but this does not make it good English. Here is what James Thurber had to say of such language:

> Great big blocky words and phrases bumble off our tongues and presses every day. In four weeks of purposeful listening to the radio and reading the newspapers I have come up with a staggering list, full of sound and fury, dignifying nothing: "automation," "roadability," "hummature," "motivational cognition" (this baby turned up in a series of travel lectures and was never defined), "fractionalization," "varietism," "redesegregation," "additive," "concertization" (this means giving a concert in a hall, and is not to be confused with cine-

matization or televisionization). . . . Ization is here to stay. It appeals to bureaucrats and congressmen because of its portentous polysyllabification. Politicians love it the way they love such expressions as "legislativewise." Lord Conesford, stout defender of the Queen's English, recently paraphrased Churchill's "Give us the tools and we will finish the job" by Washingtonizing it like this: "Supply us with the implements and we will finalize the solution of the matter." —James Thurber, *Alarms and Diversions*

The remedy for too many big words is simple: Read aloud what you have written, preferably some time after you have written it; if you find the language markedly different from what you would use in conversation, look at the words carefully to see whether you can find simpler substitutes.

The trouble with gobbledygook is that people who talk and write that way get to thinking that way. When that happens, they lose connection with the world where humans live, a language machine spins on and on, and the sound of human voices fades.

Technical Words

In writing intended for a general audience, unfamiliar terms not made clear by the context should be defined or explained. Technical terms or unfamiliar expressions that often need explaining include

1. Scientific terms *(isotope, lobotomy, gneiss)* and other expressions restricted to a specialized activity *(a cappella, heroic hexameter, escrow, chiaroscuro, farinaceous, binary)*.
2. Words used in special senses rather than in the usual way (the *spine* of a book, to *justify* a line of type, the *recorder* as a wind instrument, a *frog* as a fastener for a jacket).
3. Foreign words and phrases not customarily used by most people *(lex talionis, pourboire, eisteddfod, Walpurgisnacht)*.

24.1

Big It

You should not use an inexact or wordy expression in place of a necessary technical term. If, for instance, the subject of a paper is "Mountain Climbing," it is better to define and use a word like *piton* than to say "those little metal gadgets that ropes are tied to." Do not use unfamiliar words just to show off, but use and explain those that are essential to your subject.

Often a simple definition or explanation can be worked into the sentence where the technical term is introduced, as in the following examples:

> The ability of the heart to function depends primarily on the state of the heart muscle, or myocardium, as it is technically known.

> In the study of rhetoric we are first to consider *inventio,* or what we now refer to as the problems of pre-writing.

> In cold weather the Eskimos wear mukluks (fur boots) and parkas (short fur coats with fur hoods).

As a rule, do not simply quote a dictionary definition, which may be too narrow, but compose one that fits the style and scale of your own paper. Compare a dictionary definition of *oligarchy* with this description of the term:

> I mean by "oligarchy" any system in which ultimate power is confined to a section of the community: the rich to the exclusion of the poor, Protestants to the exclusion of Catholics, aristocrats to the exclusion of plebeians, white men to the exclusion of colored men, males to the exclusion of females, or members of one political party to the exclusion of the rest. A system may be more or less oligarchic according to the percentage of the population that is excluded; absolute monarchy is the extreme of oligarchy. — Bertrand Russell, *The Impact of Science on Society*

The crucial thing in defining a term is to give an adequate description of the way *you* are using it, with details and concrete illustrations to clarify the meaning.

• *Exercise*

Rewrite the following passages in clear and effective English.

1. *From a student composition:* Our high school was eminently well equipped for various recreational pursuits. For those of sportive inclinations, there was the capacious gymnasium, which resounded to multitudinous roars whenever our champions engaged a challenging contingent.

2. *From a professional journal for teachers:* This film demonstrates the progress of an idealized date, from the ideational impetus to the request, acceptance, the dating experience itself, and the final leavetaking, in the process raising some significant questions regarding dating and suggesting partial answers as discussional guides.

3. *From a letter to the editor:* Is the love of monetary remuneration such that it acerbates all else into obliviousness? Can we not conjure into our configurations and substratums of consciousness some other destination than the all-mighty dollar?

24.2 Informal Words

Informal words include those marked *colloquial* in dictionaries and most of those marked *slang*. They are part of general English but may not be appropriate to all kinds of writing.

Appropriate Use of Informal Words

Informal words are often appropriate in discussions of informal or humorous situations, and activities such as sports. They are also sometimes fitting in discussions of more important topics, where the language is typically general English. You will find such words used, without apology or quotation marks, in many reputable publications. Note the boldface words and phrases in the passages below:

> Even so, these two bits of intellectualistic slang are preferable to certain other clichés so commonly heard as to be allowed to befoul the language almost unnoticed. No study is **worth its salt** unless it is *in depth;* no memorandum can be taken seriously unless it is a *position paper;* and everyone is **at sea** until he is *orientated.* — Russell Lynes, "Dirty Words," *Harper's*

> It is about 40 years since the pioneer feminists **raised such a rumpus by rattling the cage bars** that society was at last obliged to pay attention. — Brigid Brophy, "Women Are Prisoners of Their Sex," *Saturday Evening Post*

If you are tempted to apologize for informal words by putting them in quotation marks, ask yourself whether they are genuinely appropriate. If they are, use them without apology, but if not, replace them with words from the general vocabulary.

Inappropriate Use of Informal Words

 Change the informal expression to one that is more general.

24.2

It is disconcerting to a reader to encounter an informal expression in relatively formal writing:

> The displaced persons in Europe experienced many **tough breaks** after the end of the war. [more appropriate: *hardships*]

> The natives believe that they can expiate certain offenses against tribal customs by **throwing a feast.** [better: *giving a feast*]

In formal writing, informal words not only indicate a shift in variety of usage but may also suggest that you've grown careless toward your subject:

> When Desdemona failed to produce the handkerchief, Othello began to suspect that she **wasn't on the level.**

Be particularly careful about certain expressions so widely used that you may not realize (until the slip is called to your attention) that they are considered informal rather than general usage:

> Plays of this sort are seldom seen **in our neck of the woods.**
>
> Faulkner had **a funny habit** of writing long, rather complicated sentences.

• *Exercise*

Listen to the conversations of people around you and take note of occasions when you and they fall back on inappropriate or inaccurate informal words in place of more precise words. Record such instances on paper for discussion in class.

24.3 Live Words and Death Masks

Good writing, whether factual or fictional, captures a reader's interest and holds attention; other writing, concerned with similar facts or ideas, may strike a reader as lifeless and boring. In either instance the wording may be correct enough, but in the more enjoyable and memorable reading, the words are fresh and direct:

> Then a tremendous flash of light cut across the sky. Mr. Tanimoto has a distinct recollection that it travelled from east to west, from the city toward the hills. It seemed a sheet of sun. —John Hersey, *Hiroshima*
>
> Supper was a young squirrel who had nevertheless achieved an elder's stringiness, roasted in foil on the embers, and a potato baked in the same way. —John Graves, *Goodbye to a River*

The search for fresh and direct expression does not require that you should strain obviously for effect, by searching for unusual expressions or words, any more than it requires that you should use eccentric punctuation or unconventional sentence structure. It does mean that you should take an interest in the freshness of your expression and that you should take sufficient time and thought to put aside *death masks* in favor of live words.

We have used the expression *death masks* as a general name for several kinds of words and expressions, including worn-out terms, euphemisms, incongruous figures of speech, or currently overworked expressions. A *death mask* is a casting made of someone's face just after death—and that seems to have little to do with words. But two ideas are brought together in the term that describes the effect of some words: they are dead—they lack vitality and freshness; they hide or mask meaning. A euphemism, for example, is lifeless language, and it hides the writer's meaning, masking it as something else. Several varieties of death masks are discussed in the following sections.

Vogue Words

We naturally use words that are in current use. All of us from time to time resort too easily to "vogue words," words that our society has currently adopted as signals of value. *Meaningful* is such a word; *dialogue* is another, and *ambience* is a third. These words and others like them come into popular use in a number of ways, and then suddenly they are everywhere. The problem is that when we start using words and phrases such as "the bottom line," or "relevant," or "scenario," then the vogue words begin to take the place of thinking, and we use them automatically.

Other vogue words can be listed: *game plan, flat out, lib* (short form of *liberation*), words with *-in* (*work-in, love-in, sit-in*), *participatory democracy, pick up on, get it together*, words with *-wise* (*profitwise, timewise*). A useful activity would be for you to note the vogue words in your own community.

Trite Expressions

Trite   **Replace the trite expression with one that is fresher or more direct.**

Trite expressions, or clichés, are pat phrases so familiar that, given the first words, we can usually finish the expression without thinking:

> This is going to hurt me more _____
> He is down but not _____
> Gone but _____
> It isn't the heat but _____

24.3

Trite

Try to avoid the following overworked expressions that occur with relentless frequency in student papers:

Cliché	Comment
according to Webster	Did Webster write the dictionary you are using?
history tells us	A dubious personification, one that often leads to empty generalizations.
the finer things of life	Name two or three. No matter what they are — a good pipe, a Beethoven quartet, a cheesecake — they'll be more convincing to the reader than this nebulous phrase.
last but not least	Is the last item or fact *never* of least importance?

The problem with trite expressions is that you can use them without thinking. They are there in the air, and you can fill a gap on your page by plucking one. They are part of a community language; using them easily becomes habitual. But when you use trite expressions, they replace your own words and thoughts, and so they mask your own meaning.

Figurative language (24.4) adds interest to writing when it is fresh and appropriate, but stale comparisons and personifications only serve to bore the reader. It will not make anything seem cooler, hotter, or neater if you describe it as *cool as a cucumber, hot as a two-dollar pistol,* or *neat as a pin.* Here is a short list of trite figures of speech; you can probably think of many similar expressions:

quick as a wink	at the drop of a hat
lost in thought	a watery grave
sly as a fox	run like a deer
rotten to the core	like a shot from a cannon
white as snow	brave as a lion
in a nutshell	Mother Nature
darkness overtakes us	spreading like wildfire
commune with nature	bull in a china shop
the rat race	the crack of dawn

Similarly, many quotations have lost their vividness through overuse:

a sadder but wiser man	all the world's a stage
stone walls do not a prison make	water, water, everywhere

There are many fresh, vivid, less-quoted lines, if you wish to enliven your writing with quotations.

When you find yourself using overworked expressions, look at them closely to see if they actually mean anything to you; usually you will decide that they really mean very little, and you will make your point another way.

Euphemisms

A euphemism is a polite and often affected expression used in place of a more common term which the user fears might be offensive. Euphemisms are often used in conversation out of consideration for the listener's feelings: a teacher might tell parents that their child is *slow* or *exceptional* rather than *dull* or *stupid*; a salesperson is more likely to tell a customer that he has a *problem figure* than that he is *overweight* or *fat.* But although euphemisms are often necessary in social situations, they ordinarily sound evasive or affected when they are used in writing.

Euphemistic expression	Direct expression
a reconditioned automobile	a used car
underprivileged, disadvantaged	poor
senior citizens	old people
halitosis	bad breath
unmentionables	underwear
expecting	pregnant
pass away	die
lay to rest	bury
our statement apparently has escaped your attention	you haven't paid your bill
preferred customers	customers who pay their bills regularly

• *Exercise*

The sentences below contain clichés and trite expressions. Rewrite them in more direct language or, if you can, fresh figurative language.

1. If he wins the election—and he may—we are all up the creek without a paddle.

2. Silence reigned supreme among us as the principal gave us a piece of his mind.

3. When he got to the campus post office and found his failure notice, it was a bitter pill to swallow.

4. Armed to the teeth with notes and coffee, he started to work on his research paper.

5. The chairman nipped the squabble in the bud and got the discussion down to brass tacks.

6. Each and every man should take out life insurance so that his loved ones will be well provided for when he goes to his eternal reward.

7. I told him straight from the shoulder that his work was no longer acceptable.

8. If it didn't mean showing my hand too soon, I would tell the newspapers that I intend to throw my hat in the ring.

9. A teacher is called upon to render services beyond the call of duty time and time again. His unselfish devotion to the youth of America goes a long way toward making this a better world to live in.

10. The investigators didn't leave a stone unturned in their relentless search for the fugitive from justice.

24.4

Fig

24.4 Figures of Speech

Figures of speech are expressions of comparison, personification, or association that are used to intensify statements or to make

Review: Types of Figurative Language

HYPERBOLE: Deliberate exaggeration for interest and emphasis.

It was a day **to end all days.**
He's the **greatest** second baseman **in the world.**

IRONY: Use of a word or phrase to signify the reverse of its literal meaning.

For Brutus is an **honourable man.** . . . Shakespeare, *Julius Caesar*
That's just **great.** [expression often signifying disgust]

LITOTES: Deliberate understatement.

Hemingway was **not a bad writer.**
Golly, what a **gully!** [said of the Grand Canyon]

METAPHOR: Implied comparison between two unlike things, often used to show some unexpected likeness between the two.

. . . . Out, out, **brief candle!**
Life's but a walking shadow, a poor player
That struts and frets his hour upon the stage
And then is heard no more. . . . Shakespeare, *Macbeth*

METONYMY: Substitution of an associated word for what is actually meant.

Suited to the **plow,** he sought to live by the **pen.**

ONOMATOPOEIA: Use of words to create a sound appropriate to the sense.

It was a hot day in late July when I sat with Uncle Miles at Belting beside the **strippling ream.** The deliberate Spoonerism was Uncle

them more expressive and vivid, usually by shifting from the ordinary uses and meanings of words. This is a literal, nonfigurative statement:

The fewer words a person uses, the more quickly his or her meaning will be understood.

The same idea can be expressed in a more memorable way by a well-chosen figure of speech:

. . . meaning is an arrow that reaches its mark when least encumbered with feathers. — Herbert Read, *English Prose Style*

Notice how the use of well-chosen figures of speech enlivens this description of a summer morning in New York:

Miles's, and it did seem to express something about the stream that rippled beside us as we sat on the spongy grass. —Julian Symons, *The Belting Inheritance*

OXYMORON: Coupling contradictory terms.

At age eleven she **enjoyed the fright** of reading *Dracula*.

PERIPHRASIS: Substitution of a descriptive phrase for a name, sometimes of a name for a descriptive phrase.

Be true to the **red, white, and blue.**
From the baseball stories of my youth, I remember the **Splendid Sprinter** and the **Yankee Clipper.**

PERSONIFICATION: Attribution of human qualities to nonhuman or abstract things.

They turned and waved, and then the jungle **swallowed** them.

SIMILE: Stated comparison between two unlike things (see *Metaphor*).

My mistress' bosom **is as white as the snow, and as cold.** —Joseph Addison, *The Spectator*

SYNECDOCHE: Naming a part when the whole is meant, or naming a whole when a part is meant.

The poor man had twelve **mouths** to feed.
Wisconsin meets **Oregon** in the Rose Bowl.

24.4

Fig

Heat has an effect on sound, intensifying it. On a scorching morning, at breakfast in a cafe, one's china cup explodes against its saucer with a fierce report. The great climaxes of sound in New York are achieved in side streets, as in West 44th Street, beneath our window, where occasionally an intestinal stoppage takes place, the entire block laden with undischarged vehicles, the pangs of congestion increasing till every horn is going — a united, delirious scream of hate, every decibel charged with a tiny drop of poison. —E. B. White, *The Second Tree from the Corner*

The use of figurative language is not limited to purely descriptive passages or to "literary" subjects. You will find figures of speech used freely and effectively in such diverse material as financial articles, literary criticism, advertising copy, sports writing, and political discussions. The chart above defines some of the more common types of figurative expressions.

Effective Figures of Speech

 Change the figure of speech marked to an expression that is more appropriate to your subject and your style; avoid inconsistent figures.

Although figures of speech, if they are fresh and perceptive, clearly have an appeal, they are *not* mere ornaments. Indeed, when they seem to be ornaments, we can usually conclude that they are used unnaturally and ostentatiously. If they are vivid and natural, they make writing attractive, but they can accomplish much more than this.

Each kind of figurative language has its special uses. Metaphor and simile, for example, can enlarge our perception and under-standing of a subject, and can say much in little space. If a writer says, "The old cowpuncher's parenthetical legs were covered by worn brown chaps," we gain from the metaphor a pretty clear pic-ture of the cowboy's shape; some notion of his age and the amount of time he has spent on a horse; and some insight into his character and the writer's attitude toward him (the choice of metaphor sug-gests a familiar, even comic treatment). We can learn something about a subject in one area by the light cast on it from language of another area, much as we do in reading parables and allegories, which in a sense can be considered extended metaphors.

For these reasons, figurative expressions should be in keeping with your subject and your style, and they should be accurate enough to contribute to the meaning. Expressions that are too strong or that strive too hard to be picturesque only confuse or irri-tate the reader:

> As fall comes in with its gentle coolness, Mother Nature **launches her chemical warfare,** changing the leaves into their many pretty colors.
>
> My grandfather's barn was **like a medieval fortress shrouded in legend.**

Straining for unusual expressions seldom results in effective writ-ing. The figures to use are those that actually come to mind when you are trying to give an exact account of the subject. They should be fresh, if possible, but, even more important, they should fit their context and sound natural.

Consistent Figures of Speech

A figure of speech should not begin with one kind of picture and switch to another wholly unrelated one. These *mixed metaphors,* as they are usually referred to, often present a ludicrous picture instead of the fresh insight the writer intends:

The nineteenth century **became a door** opened by some of the braver authors, through which many of the earlier ideas of writing for children, which had been **crushed or discarded, again sprang to blossom,** and spread into the many branches of children's literature that we have today.

If you can look at your own writing with some degree of objectivity, you can usually determine whether a figure is consistent or not. Sometimes an expression that seemed very vivid at the moment of writing proves, upon rereading, to be confusing or even ridiculous.

• *Exercise*

The critic I. A. Richards has speculated that we use figurative language more than we are aware. He maintains that we can barely get through three sentences without it. Try checking out this claim in any magazine you have handy. Go through an article or two, copying the figurative language that you find. Try classifying it according to the types of figures listed in the chart on pages 322 – 323.

Example: There were nine *hands* on the ranch (synecdoche) who tended the cattle and also the fields of wheat that *rippled like waves* (simile) in the wind.

24.4

Fig

25 Sentence Length and Economy

It is as important for the purpose of thought to keep language efficient as it is in surgery to keep tetanus bacilli out of one's bandages.—Ezra Pound, LITERARY ESSAYS

Good sentences are sometimes leisurely, unfolding slowly and gradually rounding out an idea; sometimes they are direct and emphatic. They may be balanced, or curt, or loose. They may be accumulating, piling up facts or ideas or observations to achieve a meaning, or they may be discriminating, distinguishing grammatically among facts and ideas and observations to state a meaning. In other words, they are as different as people.

The stylistic qualities of sentences are matters of choice rather than of rule. You can write short, grammatically correct sentences almost indefinitely, but if you wish to say what cannot be said in that way—to expand your meaning or to vary it—then you must choose from among the various correct grammatical constructions the forms that will be effective for your situation. Remember that reading first-draft sentences critically and revising them can be extremely important to you in developing a good style.

This chapter is about the stylistic features of sentence *length*, including economy of wording. Chapter 26 considers the variety of forms, or *patterns*, that sentences may take to communicate meaning.

25.1 Sentence Length as a Matter of Style

Written sentences may vary in length according to your purpose, the way in which you typically express your ideas, and the type of material you are presenting. Longer sentences generally occur in rather formal discussions of complex ideas, shorter ones in rapid narrative, easy exposition, and other general writing.

Sentence length varies somewhat according to the fashion of the times. Early nineteenth-century writers built their ideas into sentences that often averaged thirty to forty words. Current writing uses somewhat shorter sentences, averaging between twenty and thirty words. These figures are only averages, of course; individual sentences may vary greatly in length.

326

There is no special virtue in either long sentences or short ones. More important is the total effect of a passage in which the sentences are characteristically long or short. In the following paragraph by a well-known writer, the sentences are noticeably shorter than the average for professional writers. Average length is just over fifteen words, and six of the thirteen sentences have fewer than fifteen words. Yet the form seems appropriate enough for its time and place.

> July 3, 1943
> We received a letter from the Writers' War Board the other day asking for a statement on "The Meaning of Democracy." It presumably is our duty to comply with such a request, and it is certainly our pleasure.
> Surely the Board knows what democracy is. It is the line that forms to the right. It is the don't in don't shove. It is the hole in the stuffed shirt through which the sawdust slowly trickles; it is the dent in the high hat. Democracy is the recurrent suspicion that more than half of the people are right more than half of the time. It is the feeling of privacy in the voting booths, the feeling of communion in the libraries, the feeling of vitality everywhere. Democracy is a letter to the editor. Democracy is the score at the beginning of the ninth. It is an idea that hasn't been disproved yet, a song the words of which haven't gone bad. It's the mustard on the hot dog and the cream in the rationed coffee. Democracy is a request from a War Board, in the middle of a morning in the middle of a war, wanting to know what democracy is.—E. B. White, "Democracy." From *The Wild Flag* (Houghton–Mifflin); © 1943 E. B. White. Originally in *The New Yorker*. Reprinted by permission.

But in another essay, White uses somewhat longer sentences (average length, twenty-two words) with a more leisurely tempo:

> I would rather train a striped zebra to balance an Indian club than induce a dachshund to heed my slightest command. For a number of years I have been agreeably encumbered by a very large and dissolute dachshund named Fred. Of all the dogs whom I have served I've never known one who understood so much of what I say or held it in such deep contempt. When I address Fred I never have to raise either my voice or my hopes. He even disobeys me when I instruct him in something that he wants to do. And when I answer his peremptory scratch at the door and hold the door open for him to walk through, he stops in the middle and lights a cigarette, just to hold me up.—E. B. White, "Dog Training," *One Man's Meat*

25.1

SL

Length alone is seldom as important as variety and appropriateness, and your ability to use the form, long or short, that best suits your purpose and your material will give variety and liveliness to your writing.

Sometimes, especially when you first start writing in college, you may be tempted to keep sentences short. It's safe: punctuation errors and other troubles may be less likely to show up in short sentences. The world around you may sometimes seem to show you evidence that short statements are the characteristic form of human utterance. The opening lines of newspaper stories are often filled with short sentences. Radio disc jockeys often speak a staccato rhythm of short sentences. Television commercials and magazine ads and billboards depend almost exclusively on short, presumably punchy statements.

Don't be too cautious, and don't be too quickly convinced by the apparent evidence for short statements. There are some things that you can't say briefly. There are some times when a leisurely accumulation of insight and observation in a sentence will let you be more thorough, more honest. John Erskine, the novelist, remarked some time ago that "When you write, you make a point, not by subtracting as though you sharpened a pencil, but by adding." As you add to sentences, more often than not they become more specific. Start with a base sentence, for example:

> The girl sat in the chair.

The statement is generalized. The girl is given no identity, nor is the chair; the manner of sitting is not specified. But consider what happens when we add to the statement:

> 1. The small girl sat in the big chair.
>
> 2. Quiet and thoughtful, the small girl sat curled in the big, brown, high-backed chair.
>
> 3. Quiet and thoughtful, the small girl sat curled in the big, brown, high-backed chair, her legs tucked under her, a book in one hand, a cup of coffee in the other.
>
> 4. Quiet and thoughtful, lost in what she was reading, the small girl sat curled in the big, brown, high-backed chair by the record player, her legs tucked under her, a book in one hand, a cup of coffee in the other.

With each addition, the scene is more clearly specified.

Here an interesting paradox occurs: *by adding you take away.* If you write the sentence *The girl sat in the chair,* since you give no identity or distinguishing marks to the scene, readers are at liberty to see the girl and the chair according to *their own* experiences. As you add specifying details to the sentence, making it more clearly a scene from *your* experience, you gradually subtract from your readers' visualization of the scene and make it possible for them to see it as you do. With each addition, the texture of detail in the sentence becomes richer. Many ways of adding to your basic sentences are open to you:

1. you can make the subject, the verb, or the complement compound;
2. you can insert appositives into the subject-verb-complement structure;
3. you can use verbals or verbal phrases;
4. you can use noun clauses for the subject or the complement;
5. you can use adjective clauses to modify the subject or the complement;
6. you can use adverb clauses to modify the verb;
7. you can add adjectives, adverbs, or prepositional phrases.

With each addition — and there are others that you can devise by reviewing the section on the grammar of sentences — it is also possible to begin rearranging the sentence.

- *Exercise*

Five short sentences appear below. Rewrite each one of them in two different ways, adding constructions as suggested below:

Example: The singer looked surprised.

Revision 1: The singer, a woman no longer young, looked surprised.
Revision 2: The singer, looking surprised, turned toward the orchestra behind her.
Revision 3: The singer, tall and stately, looked surprised.
Revision 4: The singer, who is best known for her recordings of Schubert, looked surprised.
Revision 5: The singer looked surprised when the bassoonist called out to her.

1. The third baseman hit a double.
2. Mrs. Merriwether took the job.
3. The book is interesting.
4. The class inspired her.
5. Joe fell.

25.2

25.2 Sentence Length and Meaning

 Rewrite the passage marked to eliminate choppy or stringy sentences and to show the relationship of ideas.

Appropriate sentence length is determined less by the number of words in a sentence than by what a sentence contributes to the total meaning of a paragraph. Self-evident or extremely obvious statements contribute nothing to writing:

> These scientific theories came into being only after definite steps had
> been taken.

Of course definite steps were taken. This statement is so general
that one could substitute for *scientific theories* almost anything
that comes to mind — the Brooklyn Bridge, the United Nations, a
college dance, or a term paper.

Choppy (Too Short) Sentences

Some sentences say too little because a simple idea has been broken up unnecessarily into two or more statements, as in this example:

> I took my first course in mathematics at Riverdale High School. This
> was first-year or elementary algebra.

Most readers will not feel any need to invest their time in these individual sentences, which might better be combined:

> I took my first course in mathematics, elementary algebra, at River-
> dale High School.

A succession of very short sentences tends to give a piece of writing a halting, jerky effect. Such sentences also impede the flow of
thought, for they fail to show how ideas are related:

> We arrived at the induction center that afternoon. We were divided
> up. We were sent to barracks. They were reserved for draftees. The
> barracks were old. The floors were scrubbed almost white. Vague
> scars of cigarette burns marked them. I wondered how many wars had
> brought draftees here.

The choppy movement of this passage gives an effect the writer
did not intend. The passage could be made smoother by combining
related statements:

> When we arrived at the induction center that afternoon, we were di-
> vided up and sent to the old barracks reserved for draftees. The floors
> were scrubbed almost white, but the vague scars of cigarette burns
> marking them made me wonder how many wars had brought draftees
> here.

Short sentences are useful in various writing situations — in dialog,
for emphasis, for creating a feeling of rapid action or of tension —
but you must exercise judgment if you are to use them successfully. In the following passage, for example, the writer's intention was
probably to convey a feeling of excitement, but the breathless style
defeats this purpose because it is continued too long, with no break
in sentence pattern:

> It was my senior year in high school. Our basketball team had won the
> trophy the year before. This year the team was considered even

stronger. Nearly every member of the pep club was seated. It was the final game. We had come all the way through the tournament without a defeat. This game would determine which team would be the champion. I looked toward the end of the gym. The referees were talking. They, too, were excited. Would that starting gun never go off! My hands were clammy. My cheeks burned.

Examine closely any passage in your own writing that contains a noticeable number of consecutive sentences under eighteen words. Try reading the passage aloud to see whether it conveys the effect you intended or whether the writing is simply hasty.

Stringy Sentences

Avoid stringing together (with *and, but, so, and then*) statements that should be written as separate sentences or as subordinate elements. Sentences carelessly tacked together in this manner are not only monotonous to read but lose all their emphasis because every idea seems to be of equal importance:

About fifty feet away I saw a buck deer running for safety **and so** I kneeled on my right knee **and then** I brought the rifle to my right shoulder. He was still running, **so** I fired one shot at him, **but** I missed, **but** he stopped and looked at me, **and then** I had a much better target to shoot at.

Reading such sentences aloud should reveal their weaknesses and help you to revise them for better organization:

About fifty feet away I saw a buck deer running for safety. Kneeling on my right knee and bringing the rifle to my shoulder, I fired once, but missed. He stopped to look at me, providing a much better target.

Stringy sentences often result from linking too many main clauses together *(Most people know that our productive system is the world's best* and *they have grown to expect great things from this system,* and *they should).* The cure lies in cutting down the number of coordinating conjunctions *(and, but, so)* and in subordinating ideas of lesser importance.

25.2

SL

Relating Ideas Clearly

Avoid combining unrelated ideas in the same sentence. If there is a relationship between the ideas, so that they can reasonably be combined, show what it is. Don't leave it to your reader to puzzle out:

As Byron is the poet of youth, it is appropriate that the new and completely reset edition of his poems should be published on March 1. [What is the relation between *youth* and the date of publication?]

> Nassau has a delightful climate that attracts hundreds of tourists every year, and some historians think that Columbus landed in this area in 1492. [If there is any relationship between Nassau's climate and Columbus, it should be stated.]

Sentences that are haphazard or contain contradictions can be improved by clarifying the intended relationship:

> HAPHAZARD: There is no evidence to support the fact that her marriage to another writer may have had some influence on her style.
> REVISED: Although her marriage to another writer may have had some influence on her style, there is not evidence to support this.
> HAPHAZARD: I consider *The Old Man and the Sea* one of the literary masterpieces of our time, but many people have disliked Hemingway's other novels.
> REVISED: Even those who have disliked Hemingway's other novels are likely to enjoy *The Old Man and the Sea,* which I consider one of the literary masterpieces of our time.

A sentence should be constructed so that the most important idea receives greatest emphasis; the relationship of other ideas can usually be shown in subordinate constructions. See also 26.2, Subordination to Control and to Clarify Meaning, and 26.4, Sentence Emphasis.

• *Exercise*

Rewrite the following passage, paying special attention to clarify the meaning and to eliminate ambiguities and contradictions.

1. My high-school days are over and I realize I cannot turn back time, so I must now make the best of my future. Now that I am continuing my education, I am also trying to improve on the mistakes I made in high school. One by one I am ironing out the deep wrinkled problems and solving them.

2. There is a lot of evidence that great scientific discoveries do not happen by chance, but usually involve thinking on the part of the scientist.

3. There are two major factors that help a person mature, heredity and environment. Although my heredity was good, my environment was a different matter. The friends I had were by no means juveniles, nor were they scholars. Since I spent most of my spare time with my buddies, I adopted the same habits they had concerning studying. We did not excel or fail in school, but we could have done a lot better.

4. As time passes, many complexities in our environment result from scientific and technological advancements which create new branches in every field of activity, thus causing the youth of today to seek out a more thorough education.

5. The body goes through certain changes between youth and old age, whether a person realizes it or not.

25.3 Avoiding Wordiness

Wdy **Make the sentence or passage marked less wordy and more direct.**

Sentence economy means wording statements so that their meaning can be grasped by the reader without unnecessary effort. No one likes to listen to a speaker who talks too much and says too little, and no reader likes to cut a path through a tangle of useless words or constructions to get at a relatively simple idea. Phrases, clauses, or other constructions that use many words to say what can be said more directly are called *circumlocutions.*

Practicing sentence economy doesn't mean that you should strip your sentences down to the bare minimum, as you might in composing a telegram or writing a classified ad. The shortest words and simplest constructions are not always the most economical, for they may fail to convey your exact or complete meaning. Economy of expression requires rather that you state your ideas in the most accurate and direct way possible.

Often it is possible to make a statement more direct by reducing a sentence or a clause to a phrase or a single word:

> **The snow lay like a blanket.** It covered the countryside. [two sentences]
>
> The snow, **which lay like a blanket,** covered the countryside. [one sentence contains the other reduced to a clause]
>
> The snow covered the countryside **like a blanket.** [one sentence contains the other reduced to a phrase]
>
> The snow **blanketed** the countryside. [one contains the other reduced to a single word]

One way to tighten sentence form is to eliminate unnecessary and ineffective verbs and their modifiers:

> WORDY: He crawled slowly over the river bank, looking for the flint chips which would mean that he had found a campsite.
>
> REDUCED: He crawled slowly over the river bank, looking for flint chips marking a possible campsite.

The two verbs that can most frequently be eliminated without any loss of meaning are *be* in its various forms and *have:*

> WORDY: **He is a native of the plains** and knows the value of water conservation.
>
> MORE ECONOMICAL: **A native of the plains,** he knows the value of water conservation.
>
> WORDY: A few of the fellows **who were less serious** would go into a bar **where they would have** a steak dinner and a few glasses of beer.

25.3

Wdy

MORE ECONOMICAL: A few of the **less serious** fellows would go into a bar **for** a steak dinner and a few glasses of beer.

WORDY: **There is** only one excuse **that is acceptable,** and **that is** "I have a class this hour."
MORE ECONOMICAL: **Only one excuse is acceptable:** "I have a class this hour."

If a large number of your sentences begin with *There,* see if some of them couldn't just as well start with another word:

WORDY: **There are two plays in our anthology,** and I like them both.
MORE DIRECT: I like both plays in our anthology.

WORDY: **There is a suggestion box** in almost all big business houses where employees may put ideas.
MORE DIRECT: Most big business houses provide suggestion boxes for their employees.

While a writer's style and the general movement of his or her sentences determine to a large degree whether shorter or longer constructions are more appropriate, the careless habit of consistently using two or more statements where one would be just as effective should be avoided in all styles of writing.

• *Exercise*

Rewrite the following paragraph, tightening it wherever possible by substituting words and phrases for clauses; eliminate all unnecessary words.

There were so many things to do and the summer was so short. We could go and chase rats in the barn, which was a dangerous and slightly sickening enterprise; we could teach a kitten how to play circus. We could climb to the roof of the corridor where we could watch the ducks file out to the pond, and crack dry mirthless jokes to one and another. We could help with the cider press, where all the apples with a rotten spot, those that had been claimed and contended for by the yellow jackets, disappeared into the hopper and gushed out the sides in a seethe of liquor that was brown and bubbly. There were so many things to do and the summer was so short.

25.4 Removing Deadwood

Dead Revise the sentence or passage marked to eliminate deadwood.

Deadwood is a term for a particular kind of wordiness: lazy words and phrases that clutter up a statement without adding anything to its meaning.

> Anyone acquainted with violin construction knows that the longer the wood is seasoned, the better **the result will be as far as** the tone of the instrument **is concerned.**

Empty expression like those in boldface above are excess baggage and do nothing to further communication. They often find their way into first drafts because they come so handily to use, but you should take care to prune them out in revision. Eliminating deadwood will make a statement neater and more direct without changing its meaning in the least, as these examples illustrate (deadwood in brackets):

> Every thinking person these days seems to agree [with the conception] that the world has gone mad.
>
> Because [of the fact that] she had been ill, she missed the first two weeks of classes.
>
> After a delay of forty-five minutes, the audience [got to the point that it] became restless and noisy.

The wordy formulas that serve as fillers in casual conversation are more noticeable and annoying in writing than they are in speech. Roundabout expressions should be replaced in revision by terms that say the same thing more directly:

get in touch with	*means*	**call** or **see**
due to the fact that	*means*	**because** or **since**
in this day and age	*means*	**now** or **today**
at the same time that	*means*	**while**

Certain words, generally in stereotyped phrase combinations, account for much of the deadwood found in student writing. This list, while not exhaustive, illustrates phrases built upon the most common of these words:

Word	As Deadwood	Deadwood Eliminated
case	**In many cases** students profit from the research paper.	Many students profit from the research paper.
character	Her gossip was **of a sordid and ugly character.**	Her gossip was sordid and ugly.
exist	The crime conditions **that existed** in Chicago became intolerable.	The crime conditions in Chicago became intolerable.
fact	In spite of **the fact that** he is lazy, I like him.	In spite of his laziness, I like him.
factor	Speed is also **an important factor.**	Speed is also important.
field	Anyone interested in **the field of** American history should take his course.	Anyone interested in American history should take his course.

25.4

Dead

instance	In many instances, students write their papers just before the deadline.	Often students write their papers just before the deadline.
line	He always thought he would be successful along agricultural lines.	He always thought he would be successful in agriculture.
manner	He glanced at her in a suspicious manner.	He glanced at her suspiciously.
nature	She seldom talks on any subject of a controversial nature.	She seldom talks on any controversial subject.
seems	It seems that we have not lost a daughter, but gained another icebox-raider.	We have not lost a daughter, but gained another icebox-raider.
tendency	When I am supposed to be working, I have a tendency to clean my pipes and dawdle.	When I am supposed to be working, I clean my pipes and dawdle.
type	His father had an executive type of position.	His father had an executive position.

These words have definite meanings in some expressions (a *case* of measles, a minor *character* in the play, a *field* of clover, and so forth), but as used here, they are meaningless and unnecessary deadwood.

• *Exercise*

Read the following sentences carefully, looking for roundabout expressions and deadwood. Then rewrite them into direct and economical statements.

1. In college one must put away the childish thoughts of her girlhood and begin thinking of the future that lies ahead with adult ideas and responsibilities.

2. Throughout my previous school days I have been the type of person who hasn't had to study a great deal to get grades above those obtained by the average student.

3. One of my bigger excuses was the fact that I claimed there were too many social activities currently in progress.

4. The method used to detect the approach of other ships is radar.

5. One lady aroused my indignation when she claimed that her son, who was six feet in height, was under twelve years of age.

6. Habits can be classified into two distinct types: one is the useful, progressive, uplifting kind while the other is of the nature that deteriorates character and often damages the physical body.

7. My scholastic averages show, in my opinion, a rather distorted picture of my true knowledge.

8. I have chosen this road of higher education to reach my goal, which is that of teaching children.

9. To reach this goal I must be well educated and have a thorough understanding of my subject.

10. The income from the tourist business is an important source of revenue for people who own businesses in Florida.

25.5 Avoiding Careless Repetition

 Eliminate the ineffective repetition of words, meaning, or sound.

Unless repeated for a definite reason, a word or a phrase should not be made conspicuous by too frequent use in the same passage.

Effective Repetition

Sometimes repetition is essential for meaning or for sentence structure:

> For three thousand years, poets have been enchanted and moved and perplexed by the power of their own **imagination.** In a short and summary essay I can hope at most to lift one small corner of that mystery; and yet it is a critical corner. I shall ask, What goes on in the mind when we **imagine?** You will hear from me that one answer to this question is fairly specific: which is to say, that we can describe the working of the **imagination.** And when we describe it as I shall do, it becomes plain that **imagination** is a specifically *human* gift. To **imagine** is the characteristic act, not of the poet's mind, or the painter's, or the scientist's, but of the mind of man. —Jacob Bronowski, "The Reach of Imagination," *American Scholar*

Intentional repetition may also be effective for emphasis:

> There is no way of becoming **inaccurate** by industry, and if you deliberately try to be **inaccurate** you fail. **Inaccuracy** is perhaps the most **spontaneous** and the **freest** of **gifts** offered by the Spirit to the wit of man. It is even more **spontaneous** and more **free** than the **gift** of writing good **verse,** or that rarer **gift** which I have also written of here—the **gift** of writing abominably **bad verse;** exceptionally **bad verse;** criminally **bad verse;** execrable **verse.** —Hilaire Belloc, *On*

Some kinds of words must of course be used over and over again:

25.5

Rep

articles *(a, an, the)*, conjunctions *(and, but, or)*, prepositions *(of, in, at)*, and pronouns *(it, that, my, which)*. Because their purpose is strictly functional, these words are usually not noticed.

Useless Repetition

Unintentional, unnecessary, and ineffective repetition of words is illustrated in this passage:

> When I was in high school, I would take a book home once or twice a week and maybe read it two or three hours at a **time**. **Most of the time** I would read **most** of my homework just in **time** to have it ready before class began. It was very easy **most of the time** to read the assignment and have it prepared when my **time** came to be called upon for recitation.

Repetition of this kind is weak and ineffective, for it focuses attention on words rather than on ideas. It also suggests that the writer may be careless and unconcerned with what he or she is saying.

Repetition of words.   Repeat words in a passage only when you have good reason for doing so. Key words (such as the subject) may sometimes be repeated for clarity or emphasis, but less important terms should not be used more often than necessary.

> CARELESS REPETITION: The **problem** of feeding its ever-increasing population is one of India's most acute **problems.**
> REVISED: Feeding its ever-increasing population is one of India's most acute problems.

> CARELESS REPETITION: Many people think **that** if a **product** is endorsed by a prominent person **that** it is a good **product** to buy.
> REVISED: Many people think that a product endorsed by a prominent person is a good one to buy.

Especially to be avoided is repetition of the same word in two different meanings:

> If I **run**, I'll get a **run** in my stockings.
> If I run, I'll **tear** my stockings.

> Astrology is so popular in Hollywood that many movie **stars** won't sign a contract unless the **stars** are favorable.
> Astrology is so popular in Hollywood that many of the movie stars won't sign a contract unless their **horoscopes** are favorable.

Repetition of Meaning.   Adding an expression that repeats the meaning of another (called *tautology*) is one of the most common forms of unprofitable repetition. The bracketed expressions in the following sentences are a form of deadwood (25.4). They should be omitted because they merely repeat ideas that are sufficiently expressed in other words in the sentences:

> In the modern world [of today], time has a meaning different than it had when transportation was slower.

> It is believed that the age of the earth is about two billion years [old].

> She decided to trim the family room in bright red, but the [resultant] effect was not what she had anticipated.

Words like *color, size,* and *shape* often needlessly repeat a meaning that is already clear:

UNSATISFACTORY: His hair was brick red **in color.**
REVISED: His hair was brick red.

UNSATISFACTORY: **The length** of the locks is about two thirds of a mile **long.**
REVISED: The locks are about two thirds of a mile long.

UNSATISFACTORY: Behind the house was an enclosed court which was rectangular **in shape.**
REVISED: Behind the house was an enclosed rectangular court.

The abbreviation *etc. (et cetera)* means "and so forth." To write *"and* etc." is equivalent to saying "and and so forth." Avoid this nonstandard expression.

Repetition of Sounds.   A sound should not be made conspicuous by careless repetition. The cumulative effect of certain suffixes like *-ly, -ment,* and *-tion* may be unfortunate:

> The concept of such sanctuary immunity unquestionably predominantly influenced the enemy to enter into the conflict.

> Written permission of the administration is required for reregistration of those students who are on probation.

Alliteration — the repetition of the same sound at the beginning of words in a series — is out of place when it attracts attention to the words at the expense of the ideas:

> I am looking for a shop that still has pleated pants for poor and paunchy professors.

> He then made himself comfortable in a rather rickety rattan rocker.

Even though your papers are not usually written to be read aloud, you should try to avoid unintentional sound patterns that may be momentarily irritating or distracting to a reader who has a well-tuned ear:

> The enemy was reported to have seized this important port, and reinforcements were hurrying up in support.

• *Exercise*

Revise the following sentences to eliminate careless or ineffective repetition of words, meaning, or sounds. If the repetition in any statement seems intentional and effective, explain what purpose it serves.

1. The hazy figures in the background are vague and indefinite, and they add a sinister note to the painting.

2. The advantage of getting a broader perspective through travel is only one of the advantages of spending a summer traveling through the United States.

3. Many people live so compulsively by the clock that they have a fixed time for eating, a fixed time for bathing, and a fixed time for everything but enjoying life.

4. An application of lotion to the area of inflammation should relieve the pain.

5. Concrete and steel have both been used successfully in skyscraper construction, but buildings of concrete must have much thicker walls at the lower levels than those of steel. On the other hand, concrete has a far greater decorative potential than steel.

26 Sentence Variety, Control, and Emphasis

There is a natural emphasis in his style, like a man's tread, and a breathing space between the sentences.—Henry David Thoreau, WALDEN

You can write just by putting down the words, phrases, and sentences that come to mind most easily, but most of us can't write *well* that way. Good writers don't always accept the first words that occur to them, or the first sentences that take shape on their papers. The construction of sentences can be arranged and rearranged, and you can gain some control over the sentences you write and emphasize your meaning to help ensure your reader's understanding.

26.1 Sentence Variety

Var) **Vary the sentence patterns in the passage marked to avoid monotony or to make your meaning clearer or more emphatic.**

Often when we are reading good writing, we don't notice the sentences and we are unaware of their patterns. But if the patterns become monotonous, either in length or in arrangement, then we are likely to notice and react unfavorably, even irritably. An easy variety and flexibility customarily pleases us more and lets us move without vexation from sentence to sentence, as in this passage:

> Hearing that Russia emphasizes foreign language, we have suddenly increased our own offerings. But too seldom have our schools analyzed our needs. One school has re-established Latin; another has introduced conversational French for infants. Seldom have they asked whether Latin and French are as imperative as knowledge of Moslem customs or religion, or what languages are needed and for what ends.—Lou LaBrant, "The Dynamics of Education"

This paragraph is readable and understandable at least partly because the movement is easy and natural, with variety in sentence structure. The four sentences begin, in order, with a verbal, a conjunction, a subject, and an adverb; length ranges from nine words

26.1

Var)

341

to twenty-seven words. The first sentence is an observation from experience; the second, opening with the conversational conjunction, states a critical reaction, which is amplified by illustration in the third. The last affirms the criticism and forecasts a proposal.

Varying Sentence Beginnings

When several consecutive sentences begin the same way — with a noun subject, for example — the passage is likely to be monotonous and to lack impact:

> **Meterology** has made many advances in recent years. **Weather observation balloons** have been developed to gather data from the upper stratosphere. **Time-lapse photography** has improved the study of cloud formations and patterns. **Barometric instruments** of greater sensitivity are widely used. **Radar** is useful in detecting the approach of storms and precipitation.

Sentence beginnings can be varied and made more interesting by occasionally starting with a modifier — a word, phrase, or clause — as in this passage from an essay on the Grand Canyon:

> **We** have almost come full circle. **Once** those who had seen the Canyon thought of it as useless. **Then came** those who thought it might be useful because of the river which flowed through it. **They** were in turn followed by men like Theodore Roosevelt, who saw the Canyon as a precious heritage of wonder and beauty. **Now, today,** it is threatened again by men interested only in exploitation, men who unfortunately have the means to destroy what no age before ours was "technologically advanced" enough to transform and mar.
>
> **"Human needs come first"** is the all too specious slogan of those for whom the words of Theodore Roosevelt carry no weight. **They** do not like to admit that those primary needs in which they happen to be interested are the "human needs" of temporary economic advantage. **That the Grand Canyon, the sublime "great unknown" of John Wesley Powell,** might fall victim to the manipulations of sloganeers should be unthinkable; that it is not unthinkable should be our shame.
>
> —Joseph Wood Krutch, "The Eye of the Beholder"

To begin sentence after sentence with the same kind of modifier is no less monotonous, of course, than to begin every sentence with the subject. Deliberately inserting or shifting modifiers to gain variety is a makeshift or affected practice, hence an ineffective one. The emphasis you wish to make and the general movement of the passage should determine your sentence beginnings.

Varying S — V — O Order

A less common means of varying sentence patterns is changing the usual order of subject-verb-object or subject-verb-complement in declarative statements. This is called *inversion:*

> Supplementing the guitars and drums are a solo cello, a ragtime piano, an Indian sitar, sound effects of barnyard animals, and a complete symphony orchestra. — Peter Schrag, "Facing the Music"

But except in questions and requests, inversion should ordinarily be used only when the words put first really deserve special emphasis by withholding the subject. Inversion used solely for variety may have painful results, as in this reversal:

> A garden city, with one of the most delightful climates in the world, is Victoria.

Loose and Periodic Sentences

Sentence patterns may also be varied if you use both loose and periodic sentences.

Loose sentences. In a loose sentence the main statement comes first, followed by subordinate elements that explain or amplify or alter its meaning. This pattern is the one most commonly used both in speech and in writing, for we characteristically make our points by adding on meanings. Notice especially the first, third, and last sentences in this passage:

> We caught two bass, hauling them in briskly as though they were mackerel, pulling them over the side of the boat in a businesslike manner without any landing net, and stunning them with a blow on the back of the head. When we got back for a swim before lunch, the lake was exactly where we had left it, the same number of inches from the dock, and there was only the merest suggestion of a breeze. This seemed an utterly enchanted sea, this lake you could leave to its own devices for a few hours and come back to, and find that it had not stirred, this constant and trustworthy body of water. In the shallows, the dark, water-soaked sticks and twigs, smooth and old, were undulating in clusters on the bottom against the clean ribbed sand, and the track of the mussel was plain. A school of minnows swam by, each minnow with its small individual shadow, doubling the attendance, so clear and sharp in the sunlight. — E. B. White, "Once More to the Lake"

One particular kind of loose construction, called *prolepsis* in early rhetoric texts, can be useful. *Prolepsis* is the expression of a general statement, which is then followed by amplifying details:

> Once on the mound, he was a most unlikely looking pitcher, slouching, tangle-footed, absent, with the aspect of a lost goose.

> Modern homes have lost a tempo they once had — urban activities speed them up, television governs some hours, and separation from relatives and neighbors leaves them alone.

26.1

Var

Such a construction can set the subject for a paragraph or short essay, determine its content, and act as an outline. The second sentence above, for example, could be amplified in an essay that had three key parts, each fully illustrating one of the three factors listed.

Loose, or *accumulating,* sentences are an interesting reflection of the writer. As you add to a sentence, amplifying and specifying your meaning, you show yourself in the *process of thinking.*

Periodic sentences.   A periodic sentence, however, is more often than not the statement of *completed thought.* Much less common both in speech and in writing, a periodic sentence is one in which the main statement is not completed until the end or near the end of the sentence:

> And around the sunken sanctuary of the river valley, stretching out in all directions from the benches to become coextensive with the disc of the world, went the uninterrupted prairie. — Wallace Stegner, "Quiet Earth, Big Sky"

Although periodic sentences occurred frequently in writing before this century, they are now much less common than loose sentences. They require planning beforehand and are more typical of a formal than of a general style. The very fact that periodic sentences are not widely used, however, gives the pattern all the more value as a means of achieving emphasis.

When you are framing a periodic sentence, make certain that the suspension is not awkward or unnatural, as it is in this example:

> The reader will probably agree after reading this essay **that Pearl Buck's example** of the woman who, after being married for a number of years and raising a family, gradually loses interest in most of her former outside activities, **is true.**

Varying Kinds of Sentences

If you discover in scrutinizing your first draft that you have written an essay in which most of the sentences have the same kind of clause structure, you should consider combining, dividing, or reshaping your sentences. Quite aside from the question of variety, different kinds of sentences — simple, compound, complex — are ordinarily necessary for meaning and for emphasis.

Sometimes a question or directive makes an effective variation from the usual declarative sentence:

> **What does it take to be a good American?** Suddenly there are demands for Italian power and Polish power and Ukrainian power. In Cleveland the Poles demand a seat on the school board, and get it. . . . — Peter Schrag, "The Forgotten American," *Harper's Magazine*

They need a total image of what it means to be a man. And Mr. Hefner's *Playboy* has no hesitation in telling them.

Why should such a need arise? David Riesman has argued that the responsibility for character formation in our society has shifted from the family to the peer group and to the mass-media peer-group surrogates. — Harvey Cox, *The Secular City*

Questions and commands can be effective if they serve a legitimate purpose, but like other sentence patterns they should not be used solely for the sake of variety. Unless the answer is self-evident ("Who would trade freedom for tyranny?"), don't raise a question without answering it. Never conclude a paper with a pointless, blunt question such as "What do *you* think?"

• *Exercises*

1. Make loose sentences by adding to the five simple sentences or independent clauses below. Try to add at least three additional units to each, as in the example.

   Example: It was a depressing day.
   Loose sentence: It was a depressing day, with black clouds obscuring the sun, a cold wind whipping through the trees, and even the birds hiding from the weather.

   a. This house is your dream house.

   b. The eastern third of China is the core of the nation.

   c. Oil played an important part in building America.

   d. The student council listened attentively.

   e. "Liberation" can mean a lot of different things.

2. Make periodic sentences by completing the sentences started below, as in the example.

   Example: After he found the candlestick on the rug,
   Periodic sentence: After he found the candlestick on the rug, and after he learned that the fingerprints were not those of the dead woman, and after he found the scratches on the lock, the inspector became convinced that this was a case of murder.

   a. When the sun went down

   b. After finals were over for the seniors

   c. Although regular class attendance is important

   d. While others might need lots of money

   e. If you have followed the map carefully up to this point

26.1

Var

26.2 Subordination to Control
and Clarify Meaning

Sub   Show the intended relationship between ideas by using
         appropriate subordination, or correct the faulty subor-
         dination.

By bringing related ideas together, you give continuity to your
writing and signal the direction of your thinking to your reader. But
even when ideas are so closely related that they belong in the same
sentence, they do not necessarily deserve equal weight. You must
decide, in every case, how contributing ideas can best be arranged
around a major idea, or how minor points can best accumulate to
help make a major point. This means that every sentence should be
composed.

An indiscriminate clustering of ideas in a sentence or paragraph
is a disservice to the writer, to the subject, and to the reader. Ideas
are *not* all the same: some are antecedents to others, some are
conditions of others, some are less important than others. If you
fail to show the relationship of one idea to another — whether in a
single sentence or in a series of sentences — you may be informing
your readers, in effect, that all your ideas are equally important or
that you are too lazy to bother making your meaning clear:

> FAILURE TO SUBORDINATE: I worked hard and I turned out a first-rate
> manuscript, and I missed my deadline and my publisher was angry.
> IDEAS EFFECTIVELY RELATED: Although I worked hard and turned
> out a first-rate manuscript, my publisher was angry because I missed
> my deadline.

In the first version, four sentences are presented, and all are
treated equally. In the revised version, the writer shows how the
four are related. One of the statements was chosen as dominant
("my publisher was angry"). One was reduced and rewritten as a
cause ("because I missed my deadline"), and the other two are
presented as contrary conditions.

Subordination serves writers in several ways. You can put minor ideas into grammatically dependent constructions in order to
stress your major point in an independent construction. And at the
same time, if you are judicious, you can precisely relate the major
and minor ideas. The key statements in the following passage occur at the first of each sentence. Because the author does not move
slowly toward his main points but chooses typically to announce
them directly at the start of each sentence, the sentences have a
kind of incessant beat, the key point coming first, to be followed by
contributing but subordinate statements. The sentences shaped in

this way make a rhythm appropriate to this account of the defeat and desolation of a people:

> The last of the Sioux war chiefs now became a reservation Indian, disarmed, dismounted, with no authority over his people, a prisoner of the Army, which had never defeated him in battle. Yet he was still a hero to the young men, and their adulation caused jealousies to arise among the older agency chiefs. Crazy Horse remained aloof, he and his followers living only for the day when Three Stars would make good his promise of a reservation for them in the Powder River country. Late in the summer, Crazy Horse heard that Three Stars wanted him to go to Washington for a council with the Great Father. Crazy Horse refused to go. He could see no point in talking about the promised reservation. He had seen what happened to chiefs who went to the Great Father's house in Washington. . . . —Dee Brown, *Bury My Heart at Wounded Knee*

Notice especially the first, third, fourth, and seventh sentences, where the initial key point focuses on the Indians, while the subordinate elements insert white men into the narrative.

Thoughtful subordination also allows you to move easily from sentence to sentence, using dependent constructions as transitions. Notice, for example, the subordinate clause introducing the last sentence of this passage:

> When you write, you make a point, not by subtracting as though you sharpened a pencil, but by adding. When you put one word after another, your statement should be more precise the more you add. **If the result is otherwise,** you have added the wrong thing, or you have added more than was needed. —John Erskine, "A Note on the Writer's Craft"

Because grammatical constructions are important signals of meanings, you should make certain in checking your first draft that you have not put major ideas into minor constructions, or minor ideas into major constructions—a fault known as inverted or "upside-down" subordination. See also 3, Subordinate Clauses and Connectives, especially 3.5, Faulty Subordination.

26.3

Paral
(//)

26.3 Parallelism

Paral
(//) **Make the sentence elements marked parallel in form.**

Ideas of equal value in a statement can be made parallel—that is, they can be expressed in the same grammatical form. Putting coordinate ideas in parallel constructions shows the reader that you regard two or more things as related and equal in importance; the *appearance* of parallel passages is a signal that they are closely related. Parallelism also helps the reader see in which direction the statement is going and makes for smoother writing, since it helps prevent unnecessary shifts in person and number and in the tense and mood of verbs.

Elements in Series

Words, phrases, and clauses in series are best stated in parallel form. The boldface words in the following sentence are parallel because each is the object of the preposition *with:*

> His mind was filled with artistic **projects, schemes** for outwitting his creditors, and vague **ideas** about social reform.

The compound predicates in this sentence are also parallel:

> His dramatic attempt to take over the conduct of his own case **alienated** him from his counsel, almost **broke up** the trial, and probably **helped** to cost him his life. —Joseph Kinsey Howard, *Strange Empire*

When coordinate ideas are not stated in parallel form, the statement is likely to seem awkward and unpolished:

> NOT PARALLEL: We were told **to write** in ink, **that we should** use but one side of the paper, and **we should** endorse our papers in the proper manner. [an infinitive phrase and two clauses]
> PARALLEL: We were told **to write** in ink, **to use** but one side of the paper, and **to endorse** our papers in the proper manner. [three infinitive phrases]

A preposition or other connectives should be repeated between the items of a series when necessary for clarity:

> PREPOSITION NOT REPEATED: These problems are currently of great concern **to** the school system, teachers, and many parents.
>
> CLEARER: These problems are currently of great concern **to** the school system, **to** teachers, and **to** many parents.
>
> CONNECTIVE NOT REPEATED: The opposing citizens argued **that** the increased tax rates were exorbitant and the commissioners should find some other way to raise the money.
>
> CLEARER: The opposing citizens argued **that** the increased tax rates were exorbitant and **that** the commissioners should find some other way to raise money.

Elements Being Compared or Contrasted

Elements that are compared or contrasted through the use of pairs of conjunctions such as *either . . . or, neither . . . nor, not only . . . but* (or *but also*) are usually clearer and more emphatic when they are stated in parallel constructions:

> This is the life of a musician in which are recorded **not only the events** of his life, **but also details** of all his works, which are analyzed and described fully. — Lionel McColvin, *The Wonderful World of Books*

Since readers expect similar constructions to follow pairs of conjunctions, they may be momentarily confused or sidetracked if the pattern is shifted:

> SHIFTED: You may go to the ski jump either by special train or a chartered bus may be taken.
>
> PARALLEL: You may go to the ski jump either by special train or by chartered bus.
>
> SHIFTED: He admired the senator not for his integrity, but because of his political cunning.
>
> PARALLEL: . . . cunning.

Making related ideas parallel is one of the jobs of revision. Similar forms for similar ideas help hold a sentence together.

Balanced and Antithetical Sentences

When parallel constructions, especially clauses, are noticeably equal in length and similar in movement, the sentence is called *balanced*. Balance is useful for emphatic statements, for comparing and contrasting ideas:

> Abbé Dimnet, in *The Art of Thinking,* was teaching the American how to think in a few easy lessons, just as ten years later Mortimer J. Adler was to teach him how to read in a few somewhat harder ones. — Leo Gurko, *The Angry Decade*

> The best model of the grand style simple is Homer; perhaps the best model of the grand style severe is Milton. — Matthew Arnold, *On Translating Homer*

26.3

Paral

(11)

When contrasting clauses occur in parallel constructions in a single sentence, the sentence is called *antithetical*. Such a construction fittingly emphasizes a striking or important contrast:

> You may eat without danger our canned food, fresh and hot, from your own campfire, but you will drink in peril the dirty water, polluted and foul, from the nearby stream.

Antithetical sentences can easily be overused, but they are occasionally effective to mark turning points in an essay — the first half of the sentence pulling together what precedes, the contrasting second half forecasting what follows.

• *Exercise*

Rewrite the following sentences, eliminating unnecessary words and making related elements parallel in form.

1. I wrote because it amused me, and I enjoyed correcting the work, too.

2. The town turned out to be hard to reach, a bore, and very chilly in the evening.

3. The squirrel in our front yard is a playful sort, and who mocks us from his tree.

4. He trudged his way through his homework, and finished off his notes, then turning on the TV.

5. The house was charming and a real buy, but it was not near enough public transportation nor quite large enough for our family.

6. People who haven't been to Alaska ask questions about the prices, how cold it gets in winter, and what is worth seeing.

7. I am tall and bald and have an ungainly gait.

8. This report is exceptionally complete and a fine example of concise writing.

26.4 Sentence Emphasis

Emph   **Rewrite the passage marked so that the position and expression of the ideas will show their relative importance.**

In composing your sentences you should help your reader to see your ideas in the same relative importance as you do—to distinguish among the most important, the less important, the incidental. Although the emphasis given to particular ideas depends in large part upon the way the whole paper is put together, from the beginning to the final paragraph, individual sentences can weaken or strengthen this effect. The sentences in the following paragraph, for example, are unemphatic because they are haphazardly constructed. They are wordy, the beginnings are weak, and the endings are unemphatic:

> There are some interesting points about contemporary American life in "The Mobile Society" by Herman Matthews. Some of the things he notes are the paradoxes in it. The way a person often reduces his independence by relying more on mechanical devices is one example the author gives. A man may actually become the machine's slave instead of its master, as he thinks he is.

To make the statements more forceful and concise, the writer might have revised the sentence structure in this way:

> In his essay "The Mobile Society," Herman Matthews points out some of the paradoxes in contemporary American life. He notes, for example, that increasing reliance on mechanical devices often reduces a person's independence. Thinking he is the machine's master, he may actually become its slave.

Emphasis by Position in the Sentence

Important ideas can be stressed by putting them in emphatic positions in the sentence. In longer statements the most emphatic position is usually at the end, the next most emphatic position at the beginning:

> If it was the workings of our democracy that were inadequate in the past, **let us say so.** Whoever thinks the future is going to be easier than the past **is certainly mad.** And the system under which we are going to have to conduct foreign policy is, I hope and pray, **the system of democracy.** — George F. Kennan, *American Diplomacy, 1900 – 1950*

Sentences — particularly those that introduce or sum up the main points of a topic — should end strongly. Statements that are qualified by a phrase or a word at the end are usually weak:

> UNEMPHATIC: The work at the mill was hard and often dangerous, but the mill hands didn't complain, or at least very seldom.
>
> IMPROVED: The work at the mill was hard and dangerous, but the mill hands seldom complained.
>
> UNEMPHATIC: These songs are dull and unoriginal, with few exceptions.
>
> IMPROVED: With few exceptions, these songs are dull and unoriginal.

Because the main statement is not completed until the end, periodic sentences are frequently more emphatic than loose sentences:

26.4

Emph

> LOOSE: Sociology 101 should interest every thoughtful student with its discussion of the theoretical as well as the practical aspects of human behavior.
>
> PERIODIC: Sociology 101, with its discussion of the theoretical as well as the practical aspects of human behavior, should interest every thoughtful student.

A particular kind of periodic sentence, the *climax* sentence, directs the reader through phrases and clauses arranged in ascending order to the most important element at the end:

> We shall fight on the beaches, we shall fight on the landing-grounds, we shall fight in the fields and in the streets, we shall fight in the hills; we shall never surrender. — Winston Churchill, Speech following Dunkirk, 1940

Sentences that begin with *There is* or *There are* tend to be unemphatic as well as wordy; frequent use of these constructions will make your writing seem flat and uninteresting.

> FLAT: There were several people who objected to the commission's plan.
> IMPROVED: Several people objected to the commission's plan.

Emphasis by Separation

Ideas can be emphasized by setting them off from other parts of the sentence with strong internal punctuation — semicolons, colons, or dashes (12 and 13):

> It is one thing to read *Time;* it is another to pronounce the words correctly. — E. B. White, *Quo Vadimus?*

> The northern Maine wilds were cloaked by a thick haze on my arrival, and when I flew out a week later there was a mountain-hugging fog. Within that span there was rain, more fog — and a bear called Lonesome George. — Lew Dietz, "The Myth of the Boss Bear," *True*

When the ideas warrant it, the most emphatic separation is into individual sentences:

> Adolescence is a kind of emotional seasickness. Both are funny, but only in retrospect. — Arthur Koestler, *Arrow in the Blue*

Emphasis by Repeating Key Words

Statements can be made emphatic by repeating important words or phrases:

> These and kindred questions **need** discussion, and **need** it urgently, in the few years left to us before somebody presses the button and the rockets begin to fly. — George Orwell, *The Orwell Reader*

> His highest hope is to **think** first what is about to be **thought,** to **say** what is about to be **said,** and to **feel** what is about to be **felt.** — Bertrand Russell, *Unpopular Essays*

In your reading you will sometimes see a word or phrase repeated deliberately for effect at the beginning of consecutive clauses or sentences:

> I believe this government cannot endure permanently half slave and half free. **I do not expect** the Union to be dissolved — **I do not expect** the house to fall — but **I do expect** it will cease to be divided. — Abraham Lincoln, "House Divided" speech, 1858

The Declaration of Independence illustrates this same kind of repetition. Occasionally you will also see a word or phrase repeated at the end of consecutive clauses, as in Psalm 136, where each verse concludes "for his mercy endureth forever." In the hands of a skilled writer, these techniques can be highly effective, but they should be used very sparingly, and only when a serious subject can be honestly and appropriately conveyed in the deliberate manner they suggest.

Effective (and intentional) repetition should be distinguished from careless repetition, as discussed in 25.5.

Emphasis by Mechanical Devices

The least effective way to emphasize ideas is by underlining or capitalizing words, by setting them off in quotation marks, or by using emphatic punctuation marks (!!!). Certain kinds of advertising rely heavily on such devices:

> "Oh, of course," you may reply, "it's just a matter of calories." But IS it? Suppose you had to choose between a larger glass of orange juice and half a sirloin steak? You would probably reach for the orange juice. Actually, *the steak would give you 15 times as many EN-ERGY-stimulating calories. Yet the total number* of calories in each is roughly the same! So, you see, it ISN'T "just a matter of calories." It's the KIND of calories that makes the big difference.

In college writing, mechanical devices for emphasis should ordinarily be avoided; the wording of the statement or its position in the sentence should give it the emphasis it deserves.

• *Exercise*

A. Rewrite the following sentences so that the important points are correctly emphasized.

1. Television programs today are very adolescent in content, at least most of them.

2. There were two magnificent volcano peaks which towered over the valley.

3. Theoretically, the plan seemed flawless; its results, however, were disastrous.

4. Students on the campus were completely unaware that under the abandoned stands of Stagg Field scientists had produced, through concentrated day-and-night effort under rigid security precautions, the first controlled atomic chain reaction.

5. There is something the average voter doesn't realize—that his ONE vote really *can make a difference;* in fact, it can change the outcome of the WHOLE ELECTION!

6. Thumbing frantically through his catalog and clutching his registration cards in his sweaty hands while he stands in line is the typical freshman.

7. Sculpture is an excellent hobby, although it can be expensive and not everyone has the skill to pursue it.

26.4

Emph

8. Outside his office there were several customers waiting and they insisted there were other matters they had to attend to.

9. The recent civil defense drill—like all the preceding ones—showed that public apathy toward survival methods is immense.

10. Many juvenile delinquents (you'd be surprised *how* many) have parents who refuse to try to *understand* them.

B. This chapter explores ways to arrange sentences so that they have the effect you want them to have. For additional work in composing sentences, practice some of the special arrangements below, either by composing your own sentences or by copying sentences that illustrate the arrangements from your reading.

1. A sentence with three parallel units
   Example: He was disappointed with his car, mad at the salesman, and disgusted with himself.

2. An antithesis, in which contrasting or opposite terms occur in successive clauses
   Example: I admire your courage, but I question your judgment.

3. A sentence in which the normal order (S−V−O) is inverted
   Example: One poll does not an election make.

4. A sentence in which conjunctions occur between each of the elements in a series
   Example: A loaf of bread and a jug of wine and thou may be all right with him, but I want a loaf of bread and a jug of wine and thou and air conditioning.

5. A group of sentences with repeated openings or a sentence with repetition at the beginning of successive clauses
   Example: ". . . We shall fight on the beaches, we shall fight on the landing grounds, we shall fight in the fields and in the streets, we shall fight in the hills. . . ."—Winston Churchill

6. A group of sentences with repeated endings or a sentence with repetition at the end of successive clauses
   Example: "The world will little note, nor long remember, what we say here, but it can never forget what they did here."—Abraham Lincoln

7. A sentence that begins and ends with the same words or phrases
   Example: A garden without onions and black-eyed peas may have abundant squash and other weeds, but it isn't a garden.

8. A group of sentences in which the last word in one sentence is the first word in the next
   Example: Excellence is our standard. Standard, we think, is sub-standard. Sub-standard is not permitted.

9. A sentence in which the words in the first clause are reversed in the second clause
   Example: ". . . Ask not what your country can do for you; ask what you can do for your country."—J. F. Kennedy

27 Paragraphs

. . . most paragraphs (except extremely short or transitional paragraphs) disclose or represent an action that took place within the writer's mind. — Richard L. Larson, "Sentences in Action: A Technique for Analyzing Paragraphs"

A paragraph can be taken as a form of punctuation. The indention of the first line of a paragraph tells your reader that you're taking a new step, shifting attitude, turning to a new feature of your subject, looking at some part of your subject in a different way. If a piece of writing shows a mind at work, then paragraph indentions are the signs that let a reader follow the mind's movement. But at the same time that it separates units of thought for reading ease, a good paragraph is clearly and smoothly related to the paper as a whole and sometimes serves the paper additionally by providing transition or by emphasizing key points. These features of paragraphs are explored in Chapter 21, Writing the First Draft, which discusses the use of paragraphs to control the direction of a paper, techniques for relating paragraphs in sequence, and the special character of paragraphs that open or conclude a paper. This section is concerned with the general problems of paragraph development and paragraph continuity.

27.1 Paragraph Development and Length

¶ dev The paragraph marked is not adequately developed. Add enough explanation or illustration to make the central idea clear and complete.

¶ dev

Some ideas can be fully expressed in a few simple statements; others may require from a hundred to two hundred words or more of explanation or illustration in order to be complete.

Underdeveloped Paragraphs

The effect of underdeveloped paragraphs is illustrated by the following student narration of a trip:

Two years ago I took my first trip to Alaska. On this particular voyage there were only forty-five passengers. I learned from the steward that the usual number of weekly passengers ranged from seventy-five to two hundred.

The fruit basket in each cabin was filled daily with apples, oranges, and other kinds of fruit. Since meals were included in the price of the ticket, we could choose anything we wanted from the menu without worrying about the price.

We arrived at our first port, Sitka, on a rainy day. We were told that the ship would be there for about four hours unloading cargo and that we could go ashore if we so desired. After taking a good look at the town, I decided that I would very much prefer to be on board ship.

These paragraphs don't work well because they raise questions that the writer fails to answer: Why were there so few passengers on this trip? (This should be explained in the first paragraph or else not mentioned.) What is the point of the second paragraph, which jumps so abruptly from the introductory statements? the abundance of food? how cheap it was? how much the writer enjoyed it? Some statement is needed at the beginning of this paragraph to link it with the preceding one and to express the main idea ("Because there were so few passengers, we were offered more food than we could eat. . . ."). The third paragraph leaves the reader wondering what Sitka looked like, what unpleasant things the writer saw that made him prefer to stay on his ship. Three or four explanatory sentences would have cleared up this point and would have made the paragraph more interesting.

The following paragraph is similarly underdeveloped. It is too brief to convey adequately the writer's ideas:

People have been faced lately with many different ideas and systems of government. Each has tried to win the majority to its side, frequently by force or by unscrupulous propaganda. Each person thinks of himself or herself as being representative of the majority.

This paragraph could be improved by listing some specific examples after the second sentence (Communism in Angola? monarchy in Spain?) and by using a separate paragraph to explain the third sentence.

A good way to avoid underdeveloped paragraphs is to explore all your ideas fully in the first writing, putting down everything that occurs to you. If the paragraph turns out to be too long or to contain irrelevancies, it is easy enough to trim it in revision. To do the reverse — to fill out an underdeveloped paragraph with details and explanations — takes much more time. (See 21, Writing the First Draft.)

Typical Content of Paragraphs

No rule exists that says a paragraph *must* do this, or that, or the other. Paragraphs may have one sentence or many. One paragraph may state a point and amplify it with explanation and illustration. Another paragraph may be nothing but illustration of a point made in a preceding paragraph. A whole series of paragraphs may contain only episodes and illustrations to explain an earlier point.

Still, it is probably reasonable to say that *most* fully developed paragraphs are composed of three kinds of statements:

1. **General statements** in a paragraph may range from attitudes and opinions (This is the better plan; You are wrong) to large generalizations (Everyone needs some form of artistic expression; College curricula are in desperate need of reform). General statements may also appear as *restatements,* where a general statement is put into different words for clarification; *summary statements,* where ideas already introduced are brought together, and *conclusions,* where material previously presented leads to a new judgment.

2. **Specific statements** are generally subtopics of a general statement. In a paragraph opening with the general statement "This is the better plan," the specific statement that follows might be something like "It has three particular advantages." Specific statements may often be used for one of the following purposes:

   to expand, where a sentence amplifies and explains a general idea already expressed;

   to define, where a sentence gives the meaning of a word or words in another sentence;

   to qualify, where a sentence restricts the meaning of a general statement already made;

   to concede, where a sentence acknowledges facts or ideas contrary to a statement already made;

   to refute, where a sentence introduces some kind of evidence contrary to a statement already made;

   to evaluate, where a sentence makes some judgment about a statement already made;

   to identify a cause or result, where a sentence states what produced the event described in a previous sentence, or what resulted from it.

(In this and in what follows, we are indebted to Richard L. Larson's study of paragraphing.)

3. **Details** are particular observations and facts (He is eleven years old; This violet is a Blue Akey; In two years the city's popula-

27.1

¶ dev

tion increased by 11,460) and summaries of facts (All day the planes had been running late). Details may be offered for several purposes:

> **to particularize,** where sentences give the specific facts or details implied in a more general statement;
>
> **to exemplify,** where sentences illustrate what is meant by a previous statement;
>
> **to describe,** where sentences give details to help the reader visualize an object, person, or scene;
>
> **to narrate,** where sentences show actions or events in series, in order to particularize a previous statement;
>
> **to support,** where sentences offer evidence for a previous statement;
>
> **to compare or contrast,** where sentences explain something already said by comparing it or contrasting it with something else.

Generalizations and statements of opinion are most convincing when supported by details, because details can usually be checked for accuracy. Much effective writing, in fact, is made up largely of *details,* with occasional *general statements* to hold them together and show their meaning, and with occasional *specific statements* to direct the reader's attention. The following short paragraph contains all three of these elements:

> [General statement:] There are not many good critics for an art, but there have been almost none for the modern theatre. [Specific statement to expand:] The intellectuals among them know little about an operating theatre and the middlebrows look at plays as if they were at a race track for the morning line-up. [General statement:] It is a mixed-up picture in many ways. [Detail to support:] One critic who wrote that *The Little Foxes* was a febrile play later called it an American classic without explaining why he changed his mind. — Lillian Hellman, "Theatre," *Pentimento*

Whatever the purpose of a paragraph is, its full development often depends on adequate use of both details and general statements. An *expository* paragraph, for example, is a unit of facts (details) and ideas (general statements) that serves *to explain.* This is the way a doctor begins an explanation of coronary thrombosis, a term unfamiliar to many readers:

> The diagnosis of "heart disease" is feared by all of us, and not without reason. As long as the heart beats there is hope, but we all realize that if the heart stops beating we will die.
>
> The ability of the heart to function depends primarily on the state of the heart muscle or myocardium, as it is technically known. Our existence, therefore, depends largely on the state of the blood vessels that bring nourishment to the myocardium — the coronary arteries. The

heart can, of course, be damaged by other disease processes. For instance, the heart may fail because it is irreparably damaged by an infection as in rheumatic disease, or by poisons, or toxins, as in diphtheria. — William A. R. Thompson, M.D., "Coronary Thrombosis," *Today's Health*

The first paragraph makes contact with the reader's common knowledge and concern. The second begins the actual exposition, explaining the meaning of the technical word *myocardium* and rapidly adding other facts that expand the reader's understanding of coronary thrombosis.

An *argumentative* paragraph is a unit of facts (details) and ideas (general statements) that serves *to persuade.* The paragraphs below occur early in an essay discussing the status of women and urging revision of the attitudes that cause woman to be treated as not-quite-human. The first paragraph opens with a general statement. The second sentence repeats the point in a more specific statement. Then the last three sentences (a general statement and two amplifying statements) offer a contrary view. The short second paragraph reiterates with supporting general statements the view given at the end of the first paragraph. The last paragraph is made up chiefly of details illustrating the view already announced:

> The first thing that strikes the careless observer is that women are unlike men. They are "the opposite sex" — (though why "opposite" I do not know; what is the "neighbouring sex"?). But the fundamental thing is that women are more like men than anything else in the world. They are human beings. *Vir* is male and *Femina* is female: but *Homo* is male and female.
>
> This is the equality claimed and the fact that is persistently evaded and denied. No matter what arguments are used, the discussion is vitiated from the start, because Man is always dealt with as both *Homo* and *Vir,* but Woman only as *Femina.*
>
> I have seen it solemnly stated in a newspaper that the seats on the near side of a bus are always filled before those on the off side, because, "men find them more comfortable on account of the camber of the road, and women find they get a better view of the shop windows." As though the camber of the road did not affect male and female bodies equally. Men, you observe, are given a *Homo* reason, but Women, a *Femina* reason, because they are not fully human. — Dorothy Sayers, "The Human-Not-Quite-Human"

27.1

¶ dev

Developing paragraphs by full use of details removes a frequent worry of beginning writers — "getting the required length." The bulk of the space in most papers should be taken up with specific details, which illustrate or support the general, interpretative, or summarizing statements.

● *Exercise*

Select one paragraph from each of three articles in a magazine, or from different magazines. Copy the paragraphs, numbering each sentence as you do so. Then determine what each sentence in each paragraph does and how it is related to the rest of the paragraph. Write down your observations in a phrase or two, numbering them to correspond to the sentences.

Topic Sentences

Both the clarity and completeness of a paragraph can often be enhanced by stating its main idea in what is called a *topic sentence:* a key sentence to which the other statements in the paragraph are related. The topic sentence sometimes comes at the start of the paragraph, as in this example:

> **A faith is not acquired by reasoning.** One does not fall in love with a woman, or enter the womb of a church, as a result of logical persuasion. Reason may defend an act of faith — but only after the act has been committed, and the man committed to the act. Persuasion may play a part in a man's conversion; but only the part of bringing to its full and conscious climax a process which has been maturing in regions where no persuasion can penetrate. A faith is not acquired; it grows like a tree. Its crown points to the sky; its roots grow downward into the past and are nourished by the dark sap of the ancestral humus. — Arthur Koestler, *The God That Failed*

Another method is to work *toward* the topic sentence, using it as a summary or a conclusion for the details in the paragraph, as in this passage from the New Testament:

> Behold the fowls of the air: for they sow not, neither do they reap, nor gather into barns; yet your heavenly Father feedeth them. Are ye not much better than they?/Which of you by taking thought can add one cubit unto his stature?/And why take ye thought for raiment? Consider the lilies of the field, how they grow; they toil not, neither do they spin:/ And yet I say unto you, That even Solomon in all his glory was not arrayed like one of these./**Wherefore, if God so clothe the grass of the field, which to day is, and to morrow is cast into the oven, *shall he* not much more *clothe* you, O ye of little faith?** — Matthew 6:26 – 30

There is no rule requiring topic sentences to be either first or last. They may appear in the middle of a paragraph, and they may appear both first *and* last, as when a writer returns at the end to his or her main point.

The purpose of a topic sentence is twofold:

1. to help the writer focus ideas on one central thought to which every statement in the paragraph is directly related, and

2. to make it easier for the reader to see what the paragraph is about, by specifically stating its controlling idea.

Topic sentences are most typically found in expository and argumentative writing, but often even in descriptive paragraphs a single sentence will state a dominant impression that is borne out by the remaining sentences. (See also 27.2, Inductive and Deductive Development.)

• *Exercise*

In the sample below, the first sentence is a topic sentence, and each following sentence in some way refers to it. Study the example, and then write similar paragraphs from the topic sentences provided.

Example: One popular linguistic myth is that people living in technologically unsophisticated cultures speak primitive languages./But the languages of native American Indians such as the Hopi, the Navajo, or the Washoe of Nevada are as complex in syntax and phonology as English or German./The many languages of Africa, also, are just as rich and complicated as any language in the Indo-European family./Even the Ainu — one of the most primitive people discovered thus far — prove to have a language that is capable of expressing the most subtle thoughts and needs of the speakers./If there is such a thing as a "primitive" human language in existence anywhere on earth, the burden of proof now rests with those who glibly equate mechanization with linguistic superiority.

1. I can think of five reasons why I should be elected President.

2. A car is still a necessity in our society.

3. What do students want from a college education?

Appropriate Paragraph Length

Remember that a paragraph indention is a mark of separation, indicating to the reader that one stage in the development of the topic has been completed and that another is about to begin.

27.1

A paragraph that attempts to cover more than one stage of the topic should be divided:

¶ dev

> About three years ago when I started my junior year in high school, a neighbor who was the captain of the local National Guard unit paid me a visit. He started talking about the wonderful possibilities the Guard had to offer — training in radio, electronics, and other technical subjects. Evidently he must have been a good recruiting officer, for after he talked for an hour, I fell for his argument and joined, thinking I might learn something. I did. [**Next sentence starts a new stage of the topic.**] After attending a few drills, I was able to draw some conclusions about this outfit and my place in it. All the fancy talk I had heard was just propaganda, for as soon as I got my uniform, they hustled me

> down to the anti-aircraft installation. From then on, for two and a half years, I spent most of my weekly drills wiping the guns while the NCO's stood around talking baseball and women to each other. Occasionally they would look busy when they saw an officer coming, but most of the time they loafed while I worked.

Since the discussion of recruiting clearly stops with "I did," the next sentence should begin a new paragraph.

Perhaps a more common fault of inexperienced writers is breaking up related statements into too many paragraphs. This distracts the reader and gives the writing a choppy effect:

> The day of the game finally arrives and the first thing you do is look out the window to check on the weather.
>
> As the paper predicted, it is a beautiful sunny morning with very little wind—real football weather. You try to pass the morning by reading about the game, while you are counting the hours and the minutes until the game starts.
>
> Finally you start for the game, only to find the nearest parking lot over a mile from the stadium. You begin the long walk across the campus, joining the thousands of people all as eager as you are, all hurrying in the same direction.
>
> As you pass the impressive Gothic buildings, memories of your college days come back to you, and you wish for a moment at least that you were back in school again.

The first two paragraphs concern the morning of the game and should be written as one; the last two paragraphs also deal with one topic—the trip to the stadium—and should similarly be combined.

To get an idea of how your paragraphs compare in length with those of experienced writers, examine some articles in several recent publications. Beginning writers generally write paragraphs averaging from forty to seventy-five words, but as they learn to develop their ideas more fully their paragraphs approximate those in books and magazines—seventy-five to a hundred words. Paragraphs in newspapers are usually considerably shorter, but they are deliberately abbreviated for fast reading and are not typical of general writing. Ordinarily if there are more than two or three indentions on a single page of one of your papers, you should look at your writing carefully to determine whether or not you have separated things that belong together in the same paragraph.

This does not mean that a short paragraph is automatically a poor one: even a one-sentence paragraph can sometimes be used to good effect. In the following passage, for example, a single short sentence conveys a dramatic moment and hence deserves to stand alone as the second paragraph:

And it was wild. The wind, whistling out of the south at 25 knots, the most that *Tinkerbelle* could stand up under reefed main, built up menacing seas that threatened to bowl her over on her beam ends. She had to be swerved around periodically to meet the biggest of the cross waves almost head-on or she'd have gotten into serious trouble. Yet on we swooshed like the proverbial scalded cat, reeling off a fraction less than two nautical miles every fifteen minutes.

"England, here we come!" I yelled at the stars.

But it was no time for exuberance; we were perched too precariously on the thin line between maximum speed and minimum safety. To remain on that perch demanded senses tuned to their greatest receptivity. It called for unwavering alertness, instant detection of the slightest change in conditions, and swift, appropriate responses. A moment's inattention could be disastrous. — Robert Manry, "Crossing the Atlantic in a 13-foot Sailboat," *Harper's Magazine*

In the next example, so much is packed into a single long sentence that it too fully deserves to stand as a paragraph:

. . . In the midst of a mighty struggle to rid our nation of racial and economic injustice, I have heard so many ministers say, "Those are social issues with which the Gospel has no real concern," and I have watched so many churches commit themselves to a completely otherworldly religion which made a strange distinction between body and soul, the sacred and the secular.

So here we are moving toward the exit of the twentieth century with a religious community largely adjusted to the status quo, standing as a tail light behind other community agencies rather than a headlight leading men to higher levels of justice.

I have travelled the length and breadth of Alabama, Mississippi, and all the other Southern states. . . . — Martin Luther King, Jr., "Letter from Birmingham Jail"

Single-sentence paragraphs that serve as transitions between one part of the discussion and another are fairly common in papers that have several main divisions. The one-sentence paragraph below is used to shift from the discussion of a technological development to a judgment of the development:

27.1

¶ dev

. . . There are already cryptic advertisements in the Personal columns of literary magazines, urging the purchase of electronic headsets for the training and regulation of one's own brain waves, according to one's taste.

You can have it.

Not to downgrade it. It is extremely important, I know, and one ought to feel elated by the prospect of taking personal charge, calling the shots, running one's cells around like toy trains. . . . — Lewis Thomas, *The Lives of a Cell*

The real test of paragraph length is not the number of words or lines but rather the answer to these questions: Why was indention necessary? Should any one of the paragraphs be written as two, for clarity and emphasis? Are two so closely related that they should be combined? Appropriate paragraph length follows almost automatically from effective paragraph development.

• *Exercise*

Take a good sampling of the length of paragraphs in your textbooks and in two or three magazines that you read. Take special note of paragraphs that are unusually long or short; how do you account for the atypical length?

27.2 Patterns of Paragraph Development

Much of the labor of writing consists of managing general statements and details, arranging them in sequences that move toward a point, or support a point, or move toward a transition, or achieve some other effect.

Inductive and Deductive Development

Two basic patterns for developing the main idea in a paragraph are *deductive development,* supporting a main point made at the beginning of the paragraph, and *inductive development,* moving toward a main point at the end. Deductive and inductive development are often referred to as the methods of *support* and *climax.* A deductive or support paragraph will, as you can see, often have its topic sentence at or near the beginning. An inductive or climax paragraph will often have its topic sentence at or near the end.

In the following inductive paragraph, the early sentences provide the data on which the conclusion—the last sentence—is based:

> The cottonwood means water but not, necessarily, surface water. Although water is present it may be too far underground, during the day, to be of any use. If you have what is called a survival problem and try to dig for this water during the heat of the day the effort may cost you more in sweat than you will find to drink, for it is difficult to satisfy your thirst with moist sand. I have tried it. Better to wait for nightfall when the cottonwood trees and other plants along the wash seem to release some of the water which they have taken in during the day and a potable trickle may rise to the surface of the sand. If it does not you are then welcome to march onward until sooner or later you should find a spring or at least a seep on the canyon wall. On the other hand, you might not. The desert is a land of surprises, some of which

are terrible. Terrible as derived from terror. **When out for a walk bring
your own water — not less than a gallon a day.** — Edward Abbey, *Desert
Solitaire*

The more common deductive pattern, illustrated in the following
paragraph, has the primary assertion or main point first, followed
by supporting details:

> **It is a town not wholly without traditions.** Residents will point out the
> two-hundred-year-old Manor house, now a minor museum; and in
> the autumn they line the streets on a scheduled evening to watch the
> volunteer firemen parade. That is a fine occasion, with so many heads
> of households marching in their red blouses and white gloves, some
> with flaming helmets, some swinging lanterns, most of them genially
> out of step. There is a bigger parade on Memorial Day, with more
> marchers than watchers and with the Catholic priest, the rabbi, and
> the Protestant ministers each delivering a short prayer when the pa-
> raders gather near the war memorial. On the whole, however, outside
> of contributing generously to the Community Chest, Manorites are
> not addicted to municipal get-togethers. — Phyllis McGinley, "Subur-
> bia, of Thee I Sing"

Notice that the central thought in both of these paragraphs is focused in a topic sentence, its position depending on the pattern the
writer has used to develop his main idea.

Other Patterns of Development

Some texts spell out a number of specific "methods" for developing paragraphs. The catalog of methods usually includes deduction
(support) and induction (climax) as well as these patterns:

1. **Illustration,** ordinarily another name for the overall method of
   elaborating a general statement by illustrative details
2. **Definition** (frequent in exposition and argument), the explanation of a term by logical definition, that is, by assigning the term
   to an appropriate species or class and then distinguishing it
   from other members of the class
3. **Comparison** and **analogy,** the explanation of a particular subject
   by pointing out its similarities to another subject, usually one
   that is better known or more easily understood
4. **Contrast,** the explanation of a particular subject by pointing out
   how it differs from another subject
5. **Cause-effect,** the arrangement of a paragraph according to
   cause-effect sequence, such as beginning a paragraph with a
   general statement giving a cause and filling out the paragraph
   with specific effects, or beginning a paragraph with a series of
   specific statements naming separate causes and concluding with
   a general statement that gives the effect

27.2

¶ dev

6. **Classification,** the explanation of a subject either by putting it into the class it belongs to and then examining the characteristics of the class, or by dividing the subject in order to consider its individual parts

7. **Chronological order** (characteristic of narrative writing and of expository writing concerned with explaining a process), the arrangement of events in temporal order

8. **Spatial order** (probably most characteristic of descriptive writing), the arrangement of objects in some systematic spatial sequence, as near to far, far to near, high to low

It is possible to write good paragraphs by deliberate use of any one of these patterns, and you can probably find examples of each in the magazines you read. The pattern of development in the following paragraphs is indicated in brackets:

DEVELOPMENT BY DEFINITION: Ibsen's *When We Dead Awaken* [term to be defined] is a play [the subject is classified as a play] about the use that the male artist and thinker — in the process of creating culture as we know it — has made of women, in his life, and in his work; and about a woman's slow struggling awakening to the use to which her life has been put. [This play is distinguished from other plays.] Bernard Shaw wrote in 1900 of this play: "[Ibsen] shows us that no degradation ever devized or permitted is as disastrous as this degradation; that through it women can die into luxuries for men and yet can kill them; that men and women are becoming conscious of this, and that what remains to be seen as perhaps the most interesting of all imminent social developments is what will happen 'when we dead awaken.'" [An authority is quoted to assist in the characterization of the play.] — Adrienne Rich, "When We Dead Awaken: Writing as Re-Vision"

CAUSE-EFFECT DEVELOPMENT: Overpopulation would drive wildlife to the wall [single cause stated: overpopulation]; the eagle and the elk would become memories [effect number 1]; the smell of pine already is synthesized and marketed in pressurized cans for use in deodorizing our apartments and — who knows — perhaps some day our cities [effect number 2]. Many would eat fish-flour [effect number 3], but few would know the taste of brook trout or fresh-caught salmon [effect number 4]. — Stewart L. Udall, "Our Perilous Population Implosion," *The Saturday Review*

All of these methods or patterns of development are good, but they are really nothing more than characteristic ways of thinking, operations we go through as we mull things over and work them out.

Combining Patterns of Development

You should notice too as you read that the various methods or patterns of development often converge in a single paragraph. The following short paragraph illustrates three patterns of development: By *defining* a conventional internal combustion engine in the first sentence, the writer is then able to *contrast* the diesel engine with it. The explanation of the diesel engine is then further developed by telling in *chronological order* how it works:

> The conventional gasoline engine functions by drawing a vaporized mixture of gasoline and air into itself, compressing the mixture, igniting it and using the resulting explosion to push a piston down a cylinder. In the cycle of the diesel, only air is drawn in; the air is then very highly compressed so that it heats up naturally. In the next stage, a very accurately timed and measured quantity of fuel is injected into the cylinder, and because of the heat of the air, the mixture explodes spontaneously, which is why the diesel is sometimes referred to as a compression-ignition engine. — Tony Hogg, "That Old-time Ignition," *Esquire*

A paragraph, like a full paper, should follow the form of development that best suits the subject and that will be clearest to the reader. See also 21.2, Developing Your Material.

• *Exercise*

Choose a topic from the sentences below, and write two different paragraphs from the one sentence. Choose two of the patterns discussed above.

1. Much of the flavor of a nation comes from its quaint customs.

2. Many people never pay much attention to the history and geography of the place they live.

3. Movies are worse than ever.

4. Suppose the telephone had never been invented.

27.3

27.3 Paragraph Continuity

A con

A con Rewrite the paragraph marked to make the relationships between ideas clear.

A paragraph represents a chain of thought: it is a series of statements that are associated in your mind and that you want the reader to see in the same relationship. The elements in most paragraphs should be related as closely as the elements in a sentence, where presumably the parts fit each other to make a whole. In the paragraph below, the relationships between successive statements are shown in brackets:

Have you got termites? In your house, I mean. It is the newest and most fashionable house disease. [Three sentences presenting the subject.] It used to be called "ants" and no one was interested [contrast]. Also sinus used to be called catarrh. But "sinus" made the old disease under another name popular [comparison]. Last summer in the fashionable country places the talk was all about termites. [Repetition of idea in third sentence.] How so and so suddenly stepped on her floor and went right through [example of the "talk"]. And, my dear, they had to call an exterminator and it cost hundreds and hundreds of dollars to get rid of the things: the whole house was almost torn apart and they had to treat the floors with the most awful smelling stuff! [Example continued.] If you hadn't had termites, you just weren't in Society. [Repetition of idea in third sentence.] — Roy Chapman Andrews, *This Amazing Planet*

It is not so important to be able to name the relationships as it is to make sure that they will be clear to your readers. They should not have to "read between the lines" to supply missing connections.

Methods of Showing Continuity

The most common ways of showing continuity between statements are

1. **repetition** of an important word from a previous sentence;
2. **use of a synonym,** a different word of much the same meaning as one already used;
3. **use of a pronoun** referring to a word or idea in the preceding sentence;
4. **use of a connecting word,** an adverb or a conjunction that points out the thought relationship.

These signs of the relationship between statements are emphasized and labeled in brackets in the following paragraph:

An instructive example of the failure of a people to take advantage of available materials is afforded by the Onas of South America. **In this respect** [synonym: failure to take advantage of available materials] **they** [pronoun: the Onas] may be contrasted with the Eskimos. **Here** [adverb: connecting with preceding two sentences] are **two peoples** [synonym: the Onas and the Eskimos] living in cold environments, the one to the north, the other to the south. **The Eskimos** [repetition] have made a most satisfactory adjustment to their environment. **They** [pronoun: the Eskimos] have good houses and a complete wardrobe. **Indeed** [adverb: connects and emphasizes], **the latter** [pronoun: a complete wardrobe] surpasses that of most civilized peoples of the past. **The Onas** [repetition], **on the other hand** [connective: shows contrast with preceding statements], go practically naked, and lacking adequate shelter, seek unsuccessfully to keep warm before an open fire. **Yet** [connective: contrast] **the Onas** [repetition] hunt the guanaco, the skin of which is suitable for clothing. In trying to account for the backwardness of **these people** [synonym: the Onas], **then** [connective: result], geographic conditions are not to be emphasized. — William F. Ogburn and Meyer F. Nimkoff, *Sociology*

The thought of this paragraph is a unit, and each statement follows the other clearly. You cannot start reading it after the first sentence without realizing that something has gone before. (The sentence "The Eskimos have made a most satisfactory adjustment to their environment" could start a paragraph, but if it did, the paragraph would be about Eskimos, not about Eskimos and Onas.)

We are inclined to overlook the absences of guides to the reader in our own writing, because the relationship of ideas is already clear to us, but we notice immediately when other writers forget to show the connection between ideas. Consider how the following unconnected paragraph is improved by showing the relationship between the statements:

UNCONNECTED VERSION: Many people today believe that objectionable movies should be censored by federal or local agencies. The recent emphasis in American films on immorality and violence is outrageous. They are undermining our nation's morals and our prestige abroad, according to many people. There may be some truth here. I agree with the diagnosis, but I cannot accept the cure. Censorship poses a greater threat to a democracy, in my opinion.

RELATIONSHIPS SHOWN: Many people today believe that objectionable movies should be censored by federal or local agencies. **These critics** have been outraged by the recent emphasis in American films on immorality and violence. **Such films,** according to **them,** are undermining our nation's morals and our prestige abroad. **This** may be true. **However,** although I agree with **their** diagnosis, I cannot accept **their** cure. It seems to me that censorship poses a greater threat to a democracy **than objectionable entertainment.**

27.3

- *Exercise*

In the sample paragraph below, each sentence picks up a word, phrase, or idea from the preceding sentence. Using the topic sentences provided, write paragraphs following this model.

¶ con

Example: Lots of Americans talk about "getting in shape," but few do much about it. By "getting in shape" I don't mean taking a walk now and then or wearing a girdle. There is only one way to get in shape, and that is with regular exercise. And regular exercise means setting aside some time of the day, every day, for strenuous physical activities. Among the useful activities are jogging, push-ups, and sit-ups.

1. The road to riches is usually a muddy path, not a freeway.

2. The registration system at this college is incredibly complicated.

3. Without the "missing link," evolution remains a theory.

Eliminating Irrelevant Ideas

Paragraph continuity is damaged by the introduction of irrelevant and unrelated ideas. These break the chain of thought and make a paragraph seem ragged:

> Among the oddities of the plant world, Venus's-flytrap is one of the most interesting. **Venus is the mythological goddess of love.** It is a carnivorous plant that catches and devours insects and occasionally even small birds. This is done by means of paired lobes that resemble the halves of an oyster or clam, **scientifically known as bivalves.** When the lobes are open, they expose a colorful interior that attracts insects in search of nectar. Once it is disturbed, the powerful lobes snap shut, and strong digestive juices go to work to break down and assimilate the body. **Some people have successfully grown these plants in their homes.**

The boldface statements in this example are not directly related to the subject of the paragraph, and in revision they should be omitted or transferred to another paragraph. The last sentence above, for example, might be appropriate in a paragraph telling how to grow Venus's-flytrap, but it is out of place in a description of the plant's physical qualities.

Continuity in Descriptive Paragraphs

The details in a descriptive paragraph should give the reader a clear, unified impression. Descriptive writing is more than simple enumeration. You need to choose the most effective details and arrange them so that the more important ones stand out. The following paragraph illustrates a lack of selection and focus. Some of the sentences focus on size, direction, and appearance. Others focus on busy activity. Too much attention is given to minor details, and as a result no single impression emerges:

> We entered the Roundup Room through a curtained entrance just past the check room on a right turn. The Roundup Room was a long ell-shaped affair with the end of the ell angling off to the left. It was about two-hundred feet long and probably fifty feet wide. Along the wall on the left ran a long bar made of dark wood. Behind the bar five bartenders were busily filling orders and giving them to a dozen or so waitresses ranging in age from about twenty to forty-five. Above the bar mirror on the wall were paintings of western scenes and cartoons, like those I described on the outside of the building. Down the aisle in front of us there seemed to be a beehive of activity, with couples coming and going to the small dance floor. I say "small" because it couldn't have been more than twenty-five feet square. On our right were small tables, all filled with customers, and on the right wall, farther down, were a number of small booths. We threaded our way through the smoky haze to an empty table.

If the writer intended to emphasize the overcrowding and confusion in this room, he should have concentrated on those features and omitted or briefly summarized such unnecessary details as the shape and dimensions of the room, the paintings above the mirror, the age of the waitresses, and so on.

When you are writing a descriptive paragraph, try to include only the material, facts, or images that will contribute to a single central impression. In the paragraph below, notice that everything is excluded except what contributes to the scene of grim austerity:

> The little crowd of mourners—all men and boys, no women—threaded their way across the market-place between the piles of pomegranates and the taxis and the camels, wailing a short chant over and over again. What really appeals to the flies is that the corpses here are never put into a coffin, they are merely wrapped in a piece of rag and carried on a rough wooden bier on the shoulders of four friends. When the friends get to the burying-ground they hack an oblong hole a foot or two deep, dump the body in it and fling over it a little of the dried-up, lumpy earth, which is like broken brick. No gravestone, no name, no identifying mark of any kind. The burying-ground is merely a huge waste of hummocky earth, like a derelict building-lot. After a month or two no one can even be certain where his own relatives are buried.—George Orwell, "Marrakech"

Continuity in Narrative Paragraphs

When you are relating an experience, describing an incident, or summarizing the plot of a story or play, keep the action moving in one direction and avoid unnecessary interruptions. The boldface sentences in the following paragraph destroy the continuity of the narrative because they stop the action:

> It was the seventh of August, 1976. My friend and I were hitchhiking from a small town in the northern part of the state. Unlike most adventurers I did not notice the sky nor did I feel the impending danger. **I guess I don't make a very good hero. Now I must get back to my story.** After waiting by the side of the road for some time, we were picked up by two men in an old Chevy.

27.3

¶ con

Later events in this narrative should show whether or not the writer is "a very good hero." This unnecessary remark not only slows down the story, but also suggests the outcome of the incident before it is unfolded.

The connection between statements in a narrative paragraph is usually simple, since it is controlled by time. Events follow each other as they happened in time or as they are imagined to have happened. The verbs usually carry this movement, and the continuity is made stronger by the repetition of the same grammatical subject from one sentence to another. Time may be emphasized and made more obvious by adverbs — *then, next, before, soon, later, presently* — or by adverbial phrases or clauses: *When he got to the corner* . . . , *After the last dance.* . . . The boldface verb forms and adverbs of time in this passage show how large a part words of action and time play in giving continuity to a narrative paragraph:

> They **ran** for three hours. **Finally, avoiding** hummocks and **seeking** low ground, they **intercepted** the rain squall. **For ten minutes** they **ran** beneath the squall, **raising** their arms and, **for the first time, shouting** and **capering. Then** the wind **died** and the rain squall **held** steady. They **were studying** the ground. **Suddenly** one of them **shouted, ran** a few feet, **bent forward** and **put** his mouth to the ground. He **had found** a depression with rain water in it. He **bent down,** a black cranelike figure, and **put** his mouth to the ground. — Eugene Burdick, "The Invisible Aborigine," *Harper's Magazine*

To maintain continuity in narrative paragraphs, keep the tense of verbs consistent. If you start with one tense — the past or the present — don't shift without reason to another. See also 19.2, Narration.

• *Exercise*

Each of the following three paragraphs lacks continuity. Rewrite them, making whatever rearrangements, additions, or omissions are needed to make the continuity clear.

1. My grandparents still follow many of their national customs. They have lived in the United States for almost forty years. The traditional ceremony of the eggs begins on the night before Easter, when my grandmother prepares a dozen elaborately decorated eggs. Despite her age, she still has a very firm hand. The eggs are passed from hand to hand around the table, where the whole family has gathered. My grandfather chants a prayer meanwhile. The eggs are taken outside and buried in the garden, and everyone goes to bed for the night. Then everyone takes the candle he has left lighted in his window and returns to the garden. As dawn is breaking, the eggs are dug up and placed in a basket decorated with flowers. There is a sumptuous breakfast to celebrate the successful recovery, and humanity's redemption by Christ has been acted out.

2. By 1937 Americans began to grow aware of the menace of fascism. The United States government extended the Neutrality Act to cover the war in Spain. This prevented the republicans from getting American guns and supplies. Up until 1937 Americans had paid more attention to domestic than to foreign problems because they had not been dramatized. But tensions were mounting in Europe, and the Spanish Civil War attracted a great deal of interest. A Gallup poll taken in 1937 showed that 65 percent sided with the republican forces against

the fascist Franco. It was 75 percent in 1938. Of course Hitler represented fascism at its worst, as we all know.

3. When I got about thirty feet out into the lake, I saw that the water was rougher than I had thought. Several large breakers hit me full in the face, and I took in too much water for comfort. There are techniques good swimmers use to avoid getting swamped by breakers, but I had never learned them because I didn't think it was important at the time. I decided to head back toward the rocks, but I couldn't see the flat shelf where I had entered. In desperation, I headed toward a jagged group of rocks nearby. Just as I got close to it and was groping for a foothold, a large breaker threw me against a sharp edge and knocked me breathless. Being thrown against rocks in rough waters is a danger many inexperienced swimmers overlook.

27.3

¶ con

Do not be afraid to seize whatever you have written and cut it to rib-bons; it can always be restored to its original condition in the morning, if that course seems best. Remember, it is no sign of weakness or defeat that your manuscript ends up in need of major surgery. This is a com-mon occurrence in all writing, and among the best writers.—E. B. White, ELEMENTS OF STYLE

When you have finished the first draft of a paper, try putting it aside for a while before you think about it any more, or check it over, or revise it. Most people find it difficult to look at their own writing carefully and critically while the ideas they have tried to express are still running about in their minds. For this reason, it's helpful to write a first draft as early as possible, so that you can wait a day or two (or at least several hours) before examining it. If the assignment gives you time to write a draft and put it aside for a week or two, you may be astonished to discover how perceptive a critic you are when you return to it for revision.

The purpose of revision is to *re-see* or to *re-scrutinize* what you have written so that you may add to it, subtract from it, rearrange it, improve the organization, alter the tone, shift the intention, as well as check the general form, spelling, grammar, and conventions of your writing. You will probably save time and improve the quality of your writing by going over your draft slowly and systematically. A hit-or-miss approach to revision is likely to be a waste of time, since you may catch only glaring faults or problems that just happen to attract your notice. The chart on pages 376 and 377 may help you keep some major points in mind as you revise.

28.1 Revising a Draft

No one else knows what you are trying to get said when you write. An experienced teacher can sometimes read your first efforts, ask some leading questions, and thus help you to understand what you want to say, but no one knows exactly all that is milling around in your mind. You have to be the first judge of what you are writing. Your first draft may be all right, even good, if you care about the subject, if you have a lot at stake in the writing, and if you have thought a long time about how to work your way through the writing. Most of the time, however, most of us find that even a good first draft isn't enough, isn't quite exact. Most of us have to keep working on what we write.

No one can predict exactly what you may have to do in order to revise your paper most usefully. Sometimes your work may need to be expanded so as to hold more—more details, more examples, more long sentences to slow the pace, more short sentences to speed the pace. Sometimes your work may need to be compressed where you have taken too long to say something, or where something needs to move more quickly. Sometimes you may need to change the tone—from angry to thoughtful, from heavy and ponderous to quiet and meditative, from aggressive to ironic. Sometimes you may need to rearrange the structure, moving a paragraph from here to there, shifting two sentences so that they end a paragraph. And sometimes you may need to spend considerable time tidying up, checking for punctuation, spelling, construction, trying to guarantee the intelligibility of what you have written.

Consider the example below. It is the second paragraph of a student's first draft about a boat trip to Alaska. A longer passage from the same first draft appears on p. 356 in the chapter on paragraphs, where you'll find some comments and recommendations. In the first draft the introductory paragraph is brief; it tells only when the student took the trip and how many other passengers went along. The second paragraph is:

> The fruit basket in each cabin was filled daily with apples, oranges, and other kinds of fruit. Since meals were included in the price of the ticket, we could choose anything we wanted from the menu without worrying about the price.

This scarcely seems satisfactory. The author gives us two sentences which are not related to each other in any special way. Though each mentions food, the two together have no particular effect—the paragraph merely reports some items of information in a perfunctory way.

In the process of revision the author made what turned out to be some false starts. First, he decided to re-write the essay concentrating on what he saw. With that in mind, he reduced the significance of his first sentences. Here, he treats food as just one of many distractions and he reduces the two sentences to subordinate parts of a sentence that focuses on something else.

28.1

Draft

> Although there were distractions everywhere—games, entertainment, baskets of fresh fruit provided in my room every day, and meals at which I could choose anything I wanted from the menu—I was still impatient to reach our first port, Sitka, and to see Alaska.

Review: A Checklist for Revising

But that didn't work. As the student acknowledged in a conference, although he enjoyed seeing parts of Alaska, that hadn't left the greatest impression on him. His greatest pleasure, it turned out, was in the voyage itself and the accommodations offered on the ship. Next he made another false start:

> The service on board ship was prompt and efficient. Every day a steward delivered a basket of fresh fruit to my room—apples, oranges, and other kinds of fruit. The meals were particularly fine. The waiters were careful and quick. The food was beautifully displayed, and it was delicious.

Although that wasn't it, either, it turned out that with this revision the student was closer to what fascinated him most about the trip. The student said that this was the only vacation his family had ever taken. His father and mother had begun planning the trip before they were married, and it had been a goal ever since. Gradually he began to remember more and more details and more and more of his feelings about the trip. Eventually, he realized that what had delighted him most about the trip was that for a few days he could enjoy luxury. Once the student came to that understanding of the experience, his tone changed. He re-wrote the essay, focusing on the things that had seemed particularly luxurious to him, and in re-writing this paragraph he focused on food:

28.1

Draft

> By the second day I felt like a bad Roman emperor, reveling in daily banquets. They fed us food as if they had never heard of fat and we had never heard of cholesterol and heart attacks. Every day a steward delivered a basket of fresh fruit to our room. There were apples and oranges and sometimes peaches and tangerines and a slice of fresh pineapple. Once in a while a lush purple plum or two were hidden among the other fruit. The meals were beyond believing. For the first

few minutes of the first meal I felt guilty, but then I realized I was in paradise. The cost of the meals was included in the price of the ticket; I could choose anything I wanted from the menu without worrying about the price. There were huge roasts of beef or thick slabs of ham, shrimp, fried fish, baked fish, grilled fish. There were fruit salads, green salads, shrimp salads, and trays of sliced carrots, cauliflower, and piled olives and pickles. There were more vegetables than I could recognize. And then there was the dessert table — rich cakes, fat pies, ice cream, puddings, and a whole section of the table reserved for different varieties of chocolate dessert. It was probably my only chance to feel rich and decadent, and I loved every minute of it. I scarcely knew it when we reached Sitka, our first landing, and after that I ate my way from port to port.

Sometimes it takes a while to get your memory and your mind working. As you can see, the author of this passage didn't just change a few words or add a few commas in revising, but actually continued thinking and talking about what he wanted to say and how he wanted to sound. Revising needn't be just a matter of making the paper look neat, though that counts, too. The "Notes on an essay in progress" at the ends of Chapters 18, 19, 20, and 21 and this chapter may help you to see more about revising.

28.2 Manuscript Form

m̶ ✄   **Be sure the manuscript is in the form specified.**

Make a neat and accurate copy of your revised paper to submit to your instructor. Follow the directions he or she gives you for the form: the size and the kind of paper; margins and spacing; numbering of pages; endorsement. Typical manuscript form is described in the following pages.

Typed Papers

If you have a typewriter and know how to use it, it is a good practice to type all papers written outside class. Typed manuscript is easier to read than most handwriting.

In typing your final draft, use unlined white 8½-by-11 inch paper, but not onionskin that lets the type show through.

Use double spacing throughout except for triple spacing before and after long (more than four lines) quotations.

Follow standard conventions in typing. For the figure 1 use lower case l (not capital I). For a dash use two hyphens with no space between the words and the dash:

```
The book--a first edition--was missing.
```

Check your work carefully for typographical errors. Uncorrected typing mistakes are usually considered to be errors.

Handwritten Papers

If you cannot type, you need not worry. With reasonable care, handwritten papers can be made just as acceptable as those that are well typed.

Use lined white paper 8½ by 11 inches, with lines at least one half inch apart. Writing done on closely lined paper is hard to read and difficult to correct. Do not use pages torn from spiral-bound notebooks, because their rough edges stick together. Use black or dark blue ink.

Handwritten papers should be easy to read. If a word looks misspelled or is difficult to decipher, it may be marked as an error. Handwriting that is too small puts an unnecessary strain on the eyes of the reader; handwriting that is excessively large is no less difficult to read. Try to strike a happy medium in size. If you have developed what you consider to be an individual style of penmanship, make certain that it will be as legible and attractive to others as it is to you.

Margins and Spacing

Leave ample margins on both sides of the page. An inch and a half on the left and an inch on the right are customary margins in hand-written and typed papers. Leave at least an inch and a half at the top and an inch at the bottom of every page.

Indent paragraphs uniformly. Five spaces from the left-hand margin is an acceptable indention for typed papers, and about an inch for those written in longhand. Don't indent any line that is not the beginning of a paragraph, even though it is the first line on a page. The last line on a page should not be left partly blank unless it is the end of a paragraph.

Don't crowd your writing at the bottom of a page. Start a new page, even if it will contain only a line or two.

Division of Words

28.2

Div   **Divide the word marked according to the syllabication given in a reliable dictionary.**

ms

If you leave plenty of room at the right-hand side of your page, you will not have to divide many words at the ends of the lines. It is a good idea to divide words only if writing them out or putting them on the next line would make the lines conspicuously uneven.

Words of one syllable should not be divided at all: *through, played, bright.* Also avoid breaking a word if a single letter will be left at the beginning or end of a line. There is no point in dividing a word like *a-lone;* the single letter at the end of the line is less attractive than the space left by carrying the whole word over to the next line. See 22.2, Spelling and Word Division.

Words spelled with a hyphen *(mother-in-law, self-confidence)* should be divided only at the hyphen.

Form of the Title

The title appears on the first page of your paper. On unlined paper, place it in the center about two inches from the top of the page or double-spaced from your name, course title, etc. (as instructed by your teacher); on lined paper, write the title on the top line. Leave a blank line between the title and the first line of the text.

Capitalize the first and last words in your title and all others except short words like *and, the, a, an,* and prepositions of fewer than six letters.

Breaking and Training a Horse	How Not to Become Overweight
The Art of Making Friends	Strength Through Community

No period should be put after a title. However, if the title is expressed as a question or as an exclamation, it should be followed by the proper end punctuation.

Why not ERA?   Man Overboard!

Titles are not enclosed in quotation marks. Even when familiar quotations are used as titles, no marks are needed:

Blood, Sweat, and Tears   The Home of the Brave

Numbering Pages

The first page of a manuscript is not numbered. Begin with the second page, using Arabic numerals (2, 3, 4 . . .) for paging. Numbers are customarily put at the top of the page in the right-hand corner or in the center. Make certain that the pages of your paper are in the right order before you turn the paper in.

Long tables, diagrams, charts, and other material supplementary to the text itself are usually put on separate pages, placed near the part that refers to them, and numbered consecutively with the other pages.

It is not necessary to write "more" at the bottom of each page or to put "Finis" or "The End" at the conclusion.

Endorsing the Paper

Sign your papers as you are expected to. Include all the information that is asked for, and put it in the right order. Clear and uniform endorsement is a real convenience to the teacher who must handle the papers.

Ask your instructor how the papers should be submitted, whether folded, flat, or otherwise and how they should be held together. Use binders only for longer papers.

Proofreading

When you finish your final draft, put it aside for a while and then proofread it carefully before handing it in. No matter how perfect the finished product may appear, it will pay to give it one final check. Errors somehow creep into even the most careful writing. To find them, you will have to get away from the paper for a time so that you can look at it with a fresh eye.

Look for slips of the pen or typing errors, for the omission of words and marks of punctuation. And look particularly for the kind of mistakes that have been marked on your previous papers.

Making Corrections in the Final Copy

Changes and corrections should be kept to a minimum, particularly on important papers. When you have to make major changes in the final copy (rewording sentences, revising paragraphs), do the page over. For minor changes (spelling, punctuation, adding or striking out a word), make the corrections neatly and according to standard practices.

To add a word, use a caret (∧) and write the missing word directly above it:

```
                     be
Manuscript should easy to read.
                  ∧
```

To strike out a word, draw a straight line through it (don't use parentheses or brackets):

```
Final copy should be as ~~as~~ accurate as possible.
```

28.2

ms

To indicate the beginning of a new paragraph where you have failed to indent, write the symbol ¶ immediately before the first word of the new paragraph:

```
                                      ¶
So ended my first day away from home. The second day. . . .
```

To correct a misspelled word, draw a line through it and write the correct form directly above. This makes a neater and more legible correction than an erasure:

Quality is more important than ~~quanity.~~ *quantity*

To indicate in typed copy that two letters should be reversed in order (transposed), use a curved line:

be~~tw~~een   rec~~ie~~ve   Smith~~s~~ novel

Submitting Manuscript for Publication

If you are going to submit a manuscript for publication, you should type it (or have it typed) and follow the suggestions already given. Many publications have their own preferences about the form in which manuscripts should be submitted, and many will send guide sheets or samples to writers who want to submit work.

Be sure that your name is on the manuscript. One way to identify your work is to put your complete name and address in the upper left-hand corner of the first page. It's also a good idea to put at least your last name on each page. A simple way to do this is to put it adjacent to the page number (for example: Jones, 2).

Enclose a stamped, self-addressed envelope with any manuscript you submit. Most publications will not take responsibility for returning manuscripts unless you do.

If you are serious about submitting a manuscript for publication, it's a good idea to study a reference such as *Writer's Market*. A new edition with a new date is published each year. The current volume includes about twenty pages of general advice for writers and about seven hundred pages of information about various categories of magazine and book publication.

28.3 Revising a Corrected Paper

In composition, as in other areas of experience, you often learn by making mistakes. No matter how conscientiously you have applied yourself to a written assignment, you may find that the instructor has marked a number of corrections to be made on the returned paper. To improve your writing skills, you must give serious attention to these corrections. Many instructors require their students to revise all corrected papers and resubmit them. But even if the instructor does not ask for revisions, it is worth your time to make a careful analysis of all correction marks and to revise or rewrite the paper accordingly. A cursory glance down the margins is not enough — if errors and weaknesses are not studied and corrected they will no doubt recur in other papers.

Some papers, of course, may contain only minor errors, requiring the change of a few words or punctuation marks on the original. Often, though, a satisfactory revision means sentences or even whole paragraphs must be rewritten or rearranged. For passages that require extensive changes, experiment with different versions. Then read the revisions through several times to determine which is the best one.

In correcting a paper, it is important to understand *why* the corrections are necessary. If the instructor's mark is not immediately clear to you, consult the correction symbol key at the front of this handbook and then read the relevant section in the text, noting the examples and comparing them with the passage marked.

Compare the original and corrected versions of the student paper reprinted on pages 384 – 387. This paper exhibits a variety of faults. (The most serious fault is pointed out in the instructor's overall comment: "Your general approach is vague and unrealistic. What do you actually *do* when you are studying your best?") Study the instructor's marks on the original version and determine their meaning. Then examine the changes (underlined) made in the corrected paper.

Whenever you write a paper, your *last* paper is a valuable resource. If your teacher has marked it thoroughly, his or her marks and suggestions may let you see what kinds of mistakes you are likely to make, where your attention is likely to wander, what you are likely to omit, what you are likely to include unnecessarily. The author of the paper shown on the next four pages should probably be particularly concerned about the instructor's general comment on the importance of dealing directly and realistically with the subject matter. Even the corrected version of this paper, although it eliminates most of the specific faults in the original version, is still pretty conventional and not very interesting.

In correcting this paper, the writer might also have observed that there are two large categories of weaknesses in his or her writing: faulty diction and awkward sentence construction. The instructor has called the student's attention to poor word use in five instances: the inaccurate *consists of;* the poor connective *and;* the vague and inappropriate *a good mood;* the inflated *fatigued and stupefied by a plethora of chaotic data;* and the colloquial *call him a square.* In addition, the passages marked for sentence economy (Wdy) and awkwardness (Awk) are marred by poor word choice as well as faulty sentence construction. The author shows little skill

28.3

Cor

ms

Good Study Habits

It is important for every college student to develop good study
habits. A lucky few have already developed them in high school, but
for the majority of students the greater demands of college work <u>requires</u>　*agr*
some adjustment. Good study habits <u>consist</u> primarily of two things: a
mature mental attitude and appropriate physical techniques.

Going to college is a demanding full-time job, <u>and</u> students　*Dic*
should be prepared to spend about forty-five or more hours a week on
it. Like any other job, it requires effort and concentration. Some
students are indifferent toward required courses, <u>which they feel are
uninteresting or cannot see how they are related to their chosen course
of study</u>. Students should remember that if colleges require certain
courses, usually of a general nature, this means that <u>they</u> present ba-　*Ref*
sic knowledge that every educated person is expected to acquire while in
college. If <u>you</u> are indifferent to such courses, <u>you</u> are condemning　*Shift*
<u>yourself</u> to a lopsided intellectual development, which <u>you</u> will prob-
ably regret later on in life.

<u>Whether attending class or studying at home,</u> full concentration
is essential. Students sometimes complain that they do poorly in
courses even though they spend many hours studying <u>everyday</u>. "Studying" means inattentively running their eyes over a page between frequent
distractions <u>from the radio, conversing with their roommates, and day-
dreams</u>. Five hours of this kind of studying is worth less than an hour
of uninterrupted concentration on the material. A student who goes to a
lecture without having done the assigned reading and without having reviewed his notes from the last lecture is not really in a <u>good mood</u> to
acquire new information and relate it to what he already knows.

An erratic and undisciplined approach to study is usually <u>disas-
terous</u>. Many students ignore course assignments until just before an
examination. Then they frantically do all the required reading in one
or two nights, try to decipher sloppy, disorganized notes, and stay up

Good Study Habits

It is important for every college student to develop good study habits. A lucky few have already developed them in high school, but for the majority of students the greater demands of college work require some adjustment. Good study habits are based on two things: a mature mental attitude and appropriate physical techniques.

Going to college is a demanding full-time job, so students should be prepared to spend about forty-five or more hours a week at it. Like any other job, it requires effort and concentration. Some students are indifferent toward required courses because they consider them uninteresting or unrelated to their chosen field. They should remember that such courses are required because they provide general knowledge expected of every college graduate. Students who neglect these courses are limiting their intellectual growth and usually regret it later.

Full concentration is essential both in the classroom and in the study room. Students sometimes complain that they do poorly in courses even though they spend many hours studying every day. But to many of them "studying" means inattentively running their eyes over a page between frequent distractions from the radio, conversations with their roommates, or daydreams. Five hours of this kind of studying is worth less than an hour of uninterrupted concentration. The same principle applies to class attendance. A student who goes to a lecture without having done the assigned reading and without having reviewed his or her notes from the last lecture is not concentrating on acquiring new information and relating it to what he or she already knows.

An erratic and undisciplined approach to study is usually disastrous. Students with poor study habits ignore course assignments until just before an examination. Then they frantically do all the required reading in a day or two, try to decipher their sloppy, disorganized

28.3

Cor

awk

Shift

Big It

Pass

all night over black coffee cramming hundreds of facts into their heads. The result is usually that he comes to the examination fatigued and stupefied by a plethora of chaotic data. All of this could have been avoided if the student had kept up with his assignments and had gotten into the habit of taking neat, orderly notes which were reviewed by him regularly. Studying for an examination should involve only glancing over his notes and readings and planning how to organize related facts to answer the questions most likely to be asked.

Inf

Log

A student should not be afraid that his room mates and friends will call him a square if he sets aside regular times for daily study and refuses to be interrupted. On the contrary, most good students are respected by their fellow students and popular because they devote more time to social activities than students with poor study habits.

Correction Symbols Used in Sample Paper

MS   Do not enclose titles of papers in quotes. Set them off from the body of the paper by extra space.

Agr   Avoid blind agreement. Despite intervening words, subject and verb must agree: *demands* (**S**) *require* (**V**).

WW   Choose words for their exact meaning.

Dic   Use a more exact connective (than *and*) to show the relationship of ideas.

//   Constructions joined by coordinating conjunctions should be equivalent in rank and meaning.

Wdy   Express ideas as directly and economically as possible.

Ref   Pronouns should refer clearly to a definite antecedent. The pronoun *they* might seem to refer to *colleges* or *students* as well as to *courses*.

Shift   Avoid shifts in person (*they* to *you* in the second paragraph, *they* to *he* in the fourth).

notes, and stay up all night over black coffee cramming hundreds of facts into <u>their</u> heads. The result usually is that they come to the examination <u>not only</u> <u>exhausted</u> <u>but</u> <u>also</u> <u>confused</u> <u>by</u> <u>a</u> <u>mass</u> <u>of</u> <u>unrelated</u> <u>facts.</u> <u>They</u> <u>could</u> <u>have</u> <u>avoided</u> <u>all</u> <u>this</u> <u>by</u> <u>keeping</u> <u>up</u> <u>with</u> <u>their</u> <u>as-</u> <u>signments,</u> <u>making</u> <u>orderly</u> <u>notes,</u> <u>and</u> <u>reviewing</u> <u>their</u> <u>notes</u> <u>regularly.</u> Studying for an examination <u>then</u> <u>would</u> <u>involve</u> <u>no</u> <u>more</u> <u>than</u> <u>glancing</u> <u>over</u> <u>the</u> <u>material</u> <u>and</u> <u>mentally</u> <u>organizing</u> <u>it</u> <u>in</u> <u>terms</u> <u>of</u> <u>the</u> <u>questions</u> <u>most</u> <u>likely</u> <u>to</u> <u>be</u> <u>asked.</u>

Students should not be afraid that their <u>roommates</u> and friends will <u>make</u> <u>fun</u> <u>of</u> <u>them</u> if they set aside regular times for daily study and refuse to be interrupted. On the contrary, <u>good</u> <u>students</u> <u>are</u> <u>usu-</u> <u>ally</u> <u>respected</u> <u>for</u> <u>their</u> <u>scholastic</u> <u>achievements</u> <u>and,</u> <u>because</u> <u>they</u> <u>use</u> <u>their</u> <u>time</u> <u>more</u> <u>efficiently,</u> <u>are</u> <u>usually</u> <u>freer</u> <u>to</u> <u>participate</u> <u>in</u> <u>social</u> <u>activities</u> <u>than</u> <u>are</u> <u>students</u> <u>with</u> <u>poor</u> <u>study</u> <u>habits.</u>

DM	The sentence should include the word to which the modifier refers.
¶ **con**	Make sure the relationships among ideas in a paragraph are clear to the reader.
No,	Do not separate subject and verb by a comma: *A student* (S) *is* (V).
AWK	Smooth out awkward passages when revising a first draft.
Big W	Stilted, unnecessarily heavy language is out of place in all kinds of writing.
Pass	Avoid the awkward use of the passive voice, especially an unnecessary shift from passive to active.
Inf	Writers should be consistent in their level of usage. The informal *call him a square* is out of place in this relatively formal paper.
Log	Make sure the the logic of a statement is clear to the reader. Devoting a large amount of time to social activities does not necessarily make a student popular; neither do good study habits. The writer's intended meaning is made clear in the revision.

28.3

Cor

at selecting accurate, appropriate, and forceful language to express his or her ideas. To avoid word errors the writer will have to become more alert to other writers' use of words, consult the dictionary frequently, and study his or her own first drafts critically to eliminate wordiness and pretentiousness.

The instructor has also marked several passages for sentence and paragraph weaknesses. The second paragraph concludes with two long, clumsy sentences (Wdy). The third paragraph lacks continuity (con), because the student has omitted certain words and expressions necessary to indicate connections and transitions between ideas. The fourth paragraph contains two jumbled, awkward sentences (Awk). In the corrected version, the student has made each of these passages more clear and direct, and has gained valuable practice in expressing the ideas economically. To avoid weak sentences in future papers, he or she should read the sentences and paragraphs aloud to see whether they are difficult to follow, repetitious, or ambiguous. And to assure continuing improvement, the student should become more alert to sentence patterns used by other writers, particularly in published material.

Even so, writers who analyze their errors and revise their papers as carefully as the writer of the sample paper did will soon find that even their original drafts are improving.

• *Exercises*

1. Mark up the following student essay as if you were the instructor, write a helpful comment at the end, and assign the paper a grade. Compare your suggestions and evaluations with others in the class.

"The Farmers and Food Prices"

When people complain about high food prices, the blame always ends up in the farmer's lap. "Those farmers are making a fortune and we're almost starving!" I hear people say. Well, I can tell you that the farmers do not make a fortune, and that compared to any other workers, farmers are overworked, underpaid, and have jobs with the most risk and least security.

Labor unions have decreed that laborers can work no more than forty hours a week without being paid overtime, which is time-and-a-half. And if you ask a laborer to work on Sundays or holidays, they get double-time. But the farmers have to work every day, often from sunup to sundown (which in the summer is over fourteen hours). Cows must be milked everyday, Sundays and holidays included. And when the crops are ripe, the farmer's must work to harvest them seven days a week until all are in. There is no forty-hour week, no overtime, no double-time, for farmers.

Laborers have unions which negotiate wage contracts for them. Members of the most powerful unions get longevety and cost-of-living raises yearly. But farmers get paid what the food processors feel like paying them. They cannot strike for higher wages. The only thing they can do is withhold their crops from the market until prices rise to where they think they should be. But if they do that, people think their just being greedy, when really their only doing what laborers are doing, trying to get a living wage.

If you asked a laborer to work at a job where all the products he works on, through no fault of his own, can disintegrate over night and where he will get no pay if this happens, he will just laugh at you. But farmers do just that. They must work to get out a product which may or may not materialize, depending on purely outside influences, particularly inclement weather. If there is a too-wet spring, they cannot plant in time. If there is a too-wet fall, the harvest is delayed or sometimes even ruined. If there are shortages of gasoline or fertilizer, farm work will be held up. The farmers are at the mercy of the elements and the various chemical shortages that can happen at any time.

So, its not the farmers who make a killing while your food bill goes up. Any money they make can never fully pay them for the risk they take and the hard work they do day in the day out, year after year.

2. Rewrite one of your own recent papers, paying particular attention to the comments of your instructor.

• *An Essay in Progress, 5: A Revised Version*

```
                    My Theater Experience


    My parents took over the management of a drive-in theater in Feb-
ruary of my senior year in high school.  When they did, they learned
that someone was needed to do odd jobs.  I was drafted.  I worked there
two or three nights a week during the spring, and when school was out I
worked six nights a week until it was time to get ready to go to col-
lege.  I worked in the snack bar, in the box office, in the projection
booth, and I did whatever else needed doing.

    Often, people I knew came to the drive-in, but I also met many
new people.  Sometimes I talked to them, and sometimes, like when I
worked in the snack bar, I heard them talking to each other.  I guess
people go to drive-in movies for a lot of reasons.  One man said that
he came to get away from his wife and kids.  I guess it was quiet when
he sat alone in his car. Many boys and girls came on dates.  Some peo-
ple came to watch the movie.

    The behavior of the customers provided interesting experiences
and aroused different emotions.  I was pretty indignant at one lady
when she claimed that her son, who must have been six feet tall, was
```

28.3

under twelve. I admitted him free, but I didn't believe her. I was
angry when one boy tried to hide in the back floor of the car under a
quilt while the driver drove in, but the other 339 variations on that
trick were amusing. One girl caught her slacks on the barbed wire while
climbing over the fence at the back of the theater. I helped her off
the fence, and I sold her a ticket. I like to think she might still be
there if it weren't for me.

The summer was full of new and enlightening experiences. People
sometimes do strange things at a drive-in, and behave in ways they
wouldn't anywhere else. Maybe it's because it's always dark there, and
they think no one will notice. Anyway, real people were often more
entertaining than the people in the movies.

Since the summer I've wondered about whether working there meant
anything except that I earned a little money. Sometimes I get a little
sad. Drive-in theaters are interesting, but I guess they are just
about obsolete. The first ones opened in the 1930s, but they were most
popular during the 1940s and early 1950s. That was right after most
people got cars and before most people had television or air conditioning. Now drive-ins are mostly a part of history. I feel kind of like
a dinosaur.

After some time had passed and after considerable consulta-
tion, the student turned in this revised version of the essay. Notice
what the writer has done in this version. In the first paragraph he
kept most of his original first paragraph (see end of Chapter 21),
but added more information about when he worked and what he
did. He also went back to one of his first efforts at developing an
idea (see end of Chapter 19) and borrowed a few words from
that to show more clearly when he worked and how he came to be
working.

The second paragraph hasn't changed much from the first draft,
except in two ways: the writer inserted a sentence (the second in
the paragraph) to account for his meeting many new people and he
became more tentative ("I *guess* people go to drive-in movies for a
lot of reasons. . . ."), indicating that he understands he doesn't
know all their reasons.

The third paragraph hasn't changed much either, though a couple of brief additions ("339 variations" and the last sentence) add
some color. In the fourth paragraph the writer has picked up an
idea from the teacher's critical suggestions (see end of Chapter 21)
and written more about people's erratic behavior.

The most noticeable change in this revision is the final paragraph, which is completely new. The writer has gone back to one of his first efforts (see end of Chapter 19) and developed a bit of drive-in theater history. This has enabled him to get to his last three sentences, which make a good ending.

The essay is still not perfect. It's not the best freshman essay ever written. But this revision is appreciably better than in the first draft. Revision has helped. It's not always easy to see, but the writer must have known in his last paragraph that he was doing something a lot better than he had done the first time, and that's a feeling worth working for. (See end of Chapters 18, 19, 20, and 21.)

28.3

Cor

Practical and Vocational Writing

Though often letters, speeches, and reports must be written in a hurry and, because of the countless considerations that clear writing involves, are bound in some way to fall short of the full intended meaning, conscientious people will always regret this necessity and arrange their affairs as far as possible to avoid it. — *Robert Graves and Alan Hodge,* THE READER OVER YOUR SHOULDER

I keep cautioning my students and anyone who will listen to me not to use the jargon of trades, not to use scientific language, because they're going to be out of date the day after tomorrow. — *Katherine Anne Porter,* WRITERS AT WORK

Sometimes we hear woeful tales of the nonhuman language used in business and professional writing and in specialized writing assignments in school. Sometimes the stories are true:

> The parent of a Houston high school pupil received a message from the school principal concerning a special meeting on a proposed new educational program.
>
> The message read:
>
> "Our school's cross-graded, multi-ethnic, individualized learning program is designed to enhance the concept of an open-ended learning program with emphasis on a continuum of multi-ethnic, academically enriched learning using the identified intellectually gifted child as the agent or director of his own learning. Major emphasis is on cross-graded, multi-ethnic learning with the main objective being to learn respect for the uniqueness of a person."
>
> The parent wrote the principal:
>
> "I have a college degree, speak two foreign languages and four Indian dialects, have been to a number of county fairs and three goat ropings, but I haven't the faintest idea as to what the hell you are talking about. Do you?" — *Fort Worth Star Telegram,* January 26, 1977

Often in specialized assignments and in writing associated with business and professional work, writers depend upon ritual phrases and standardized patterns of organization. Some businesses and professions, indeed, expect writers to conform to standard practices long established and widely used in vocational writing. And to be sure, if a writer has to answer 122 letters inquiring about the same market item, it is clearly more convenient and economical to use a form letter.

Still, whatever can be recommended for writing in general can also be recommended for particular forms of practical and professional writing. The vocabulary should be accurate, and the spelling should be orthodox. Even if you are going to use organizational patterns developed by someone else (as in some report writing or business correspondence), you don't have to quit thinking. Your language should be fresh and precise, untroubled by specialized jargon, euphemisms, clichés, and mystifying gobbledygook. Your sentences should be clear, direct, and economical. Your tone should be natural and unstilted.

The papers that you write in school are not so different from the practical, business, or technical writing that you may do outside of school. A letter of recommendation, for example, is both informative and persuasive, just as many school papers are. It offers information about a person's past (usually narrative) and about that person's present (often descriptive) in order to make an argument for his or her future. A letter in which you apply for a job is a kind of specialized personal essay, not entirely different from some personal writing that you will do in a composition class except that in the letter of application you may pay closer attention to your audience.

Practical and vocational forms of writing are different from school writing, however, in at least one major respect. In a sense, such writing is not your own. Ordinarily the occasion and the purpose are determined by some institutional need, not by your own choice. Even essay examinations in school may be expected to conform to a kind of established, non-personal form. They are, at any rate, not occasions for free-swinging experiments in writing. In most forms of practical and vocational writing, your writing is a medium serving a company, an institution, or something other than your own personal preferences. You can still be yourself, but you may also need to fulfill the expectations of others.

The following pages discuss some of what is expected in various forms of practical and vocational writing.

29.1 Essay Examination Answers

Answering an examination question in essay form is similar to writing a short expository or argumentative paper. In studying for the course, you have become familiar with a fairly wide range of information; to answer a specific question, you must recall the relevant material, organize it, and present it in essay form.

Reading the Questions

Because most examinations have a time limit, students often begin writing feverishly after no more than a glance at the questions. The results of such frantic haste are usually disappointing. You can use the allotted time far more profitably if you take a few minutes at the start to read all the questions and directions. If a choice is offered, decide which questions you are best prepared to answer and cross out the others. If the questions have different values, plan the amount of time to spend on each: a question worth 10 percent, for example, should not take up 30 percent of your time. Try to save a few minutes at the end to check your answers.

Before beginning to write, be sure to read the question thoroughly. Many answers are unsatisfactory simply because students misinterpret or forget the question in their hurry to fill the paper with words. Examine each question carefully and decide what kind of answer it requires. Don't misread or overlook key words. Notice in the following questions how a change in one word would affect the whole question:

> Explain the effect [causes] of the Spanish-American War.
> Describe the reproduction [digestion; development] of the frog.
> Discuss the structure [sources; significance] of *Moby Dick*.

Since the verb often determines the nature of the answer, take particular care to interpret it properly. Here are some of the verbs instructors commonly use in essay questions.

analyze: give main divisions or elements, emphasizing essentials
classify: arrange into main classes or divisions
compare: point out likenesses (and sometimes differences, as well)
contrast: point out differences
criticize: give your opinion as to good and bad features
define: explain the meaning, distinguish from similar terms
describe: name the features in chronological or spatial order
discuss: examine in detail
evaluate: give your opinion of the value or validity
explain: make clear, give reasons for
illustrate: give one or more examples of
interpret: give the meaning or significance
justify: defend, show to be right
review: examine on a broad scale
summarize: briefly go over the essentials

Writing the Answers

Before beginning to write an answer to a question, remember that the instructor expects you to demonstrate *specific* knowledge on the subject. A succession of vague generalities will not be acceptable. Even if you are discussing a fairly broad general topic, support whatever generalizations you make with specific illustrations. Do not omit essential particulars because you assume the *instructor* is familiar with them already; the main purpose of the examination is to find out what knowledge *you* have acquired.

A scratch outline (see 20.2) of the main points you plan to develop in your answer may be useful as a guide in writing. But whether you make an outline or not, make a concentrated effort to set your thoughts down in some logical order: all the sentences should relate to the question asked, and each should lead to the next in an orderly fashion. Many essay answers are unsuccessful because students, although well-informed, present information in a haphazard, unrelated fashion, giving the impression that they are thoroughly confused on the subject. It is often useful to repeat the key terms of the questions and the main points you'll be making about the terms in a thesis statement at the beginning of your answer. This can serve as an organizational guide for your writing.

Remember that the *length* of the answer is not the criterion of its worth: choosing the right facts and organizing them sensibly will impress the reader far more. Avoid throwing in unrelated material just to demonstrate your knowledge or to disguise your ignorance of more pertinent information. Since the time you have to write your answer is limited, you should confine yourself strictly to what you know about the specific question asked. Your instructor is not likely to give you much credit for a short essay on the wrong subject, no matter how good it may be.

Examination answers should be written in acceptable general English. Although instructors do not expect an essay written in class to be as fully developed and as polished in style as one written at home, they do expect it to be adequate in grammar, usage, and the mechanics of writing. Even if a paper is otherwise accurate, frequent misspellings do much to lower the reader's opinion of it. Take particular care to spell and use correctly any technical terms or names that have been used in the course: *myosis, mercantile, assize, neurosis, imagery, Lamarck, Malthus, Schopenhauer.* Instructors are understandably disturbed if they think you have paid scant attention to terms you have heard in class and read in the text numerous times. Careful proofreading of the answers may help you eliminate any careless errors you may have made and will also give you a chance to fill in gaps in information.

29.1

Exam

Examples of Essay Answers

Printed below are essay answers in biology, history, and American literature. Read each question carefully, decide what sort of answer is required, and compare the two student answers. Then read the criticisms that follow. The sentences in the answers are numbered to facilitate discussion.

QUESTION: Define *dominant* as it is used in genetics.

ANSWER A: (1) In genetics, dominant is the opposite of recessive. (2) Different characteristics are inherited by the individual by means of genes acquired from the male and female parents. (3) These genes are arranged, or carried, on chromosomes, and are paired, one from each parent. (4) A good deal is still unknown about the behavior of genes, although the science of genetics is making rapid progress. (5) Gregor Mendel, a monk, made discoveries in heredity by doing experiments with sweet peas. (6) He found that certain traits are stronger (dominant) and others are weaker (recessive). (7) Therefore, if two genes carry the same characteristic, one will be dominant over the other. (8) Examples of this are dark eyes, normal color vision, etc.

ANSWER B: (1) The term *dominant* as used in genetics refers to that situation in which one gene in a pair takes precedence over another in determining a given characteristic in the individual. (2) For example, if a child inherits a gene for blue eyes from one parent and for brown eyes from the other, he will have brown eyes. (3) This is because the brown-eyed gene is *dominant;* the blue is *recessive.* (4) He still carries both genes and may transmit either to his offspring, but one has masked the effect of the other in his physical appearance. (5) Clear dominance does not occur in all pairings, however. (6) Sometimes *mixed dominance* occurs, as in the case of sweet peas, where a cross between a red and a white parent produces pink offspring. (7) Some cases of dominance are *sex-linked;* the gene for color blindness in humans, for instance, is dominant in the male and recessive in the female.

CRITICISM: Answer A contains irrelevant general information (sentences 2–5) and does not give a clear definition of *dominant.* You cannot explain the meaning of a word simply by naming its opposite (sentence 1). "Stronger" and "weaker" (sentence 6) are poor synonyms because they have such a variety of meanings. The answer also misleads by oversimplification: sentence 7 implies that complete dominance occurs in *all* pairings of genes. It is also not clear to what species of life the two examples in the last sentence (dark eyes and normal color vision) refer.

Answer B is satisfactory. The term is clearly defined in the first sentence. Sentences 2–4 give an example of its use, distinguish it from its opposite, and add an important qualification. Sentences 5–7 note two important variants in the meaning of the term. There is no irrelevant material.

QUESTION: Compare and contrast English and Spanish colonial methods in the New World.

ANSWER A: (1) The Plymouth colony suffered many hardships in the early years of its existence. (2) This was also true of the Roanoke colony, but it eventually failed and did not survive. (3) The climate was more promising there, but it seemed as if the kind of people it included, like gentlemen unused to work, adventurers, and renegades, did not have the patience and religious fervor of the New England settlers. (4) The same was true of the Spanish colonies in Florida and elsewhere — the climate was good, but the men were selfish and had no direction. (5) The Spanish were more cruel toward the Indians than the English, and there was nothing constructive in their aims.

ANSWER B: (1) The Spanish generally thought of the New World as a reservoir of riches to be tapped. (2) The great Spanish conquerors, like Cortez and Pizarro, were explorer-adventurers whose main aim was to subjugate the native population and wrench from them whatever riches and power they possessed. (3) The Spanish method was usually to impose a military dictatorship upon a restive populace; the domination depended on military force. (4) The English, on the other hand, thought of the New World colonies as a *permanent* extension of English civilization. (5) Their methods were not to immediately extract native riches, but to plant the seeds of English life in the new continent. (6) Unlike the Spaniards, the English generally emigrated in family units, placated rather than subdued the native inhabitants, invested labor and capital in the New World soil, and awaited long-term fruits. (7) Settlement was their aim rather than exploitation.

CRITICISM: More than half of answer A (sentences 1 – 3) contrasts *two English colonies* rather than *English and Spanish colonial methods.* Mention of climate in sentences 3 and 4 is also irrelevant to a question dealing with methods. "Selfish" and "had no direction" need further explanation, as do "cruel toward the Indians" and "nothing constructive."

Answer B is much more satisfactory than A. The basic differences in aim and the consequent differences in method are fairly well stated. The first section of the answer (sentences 1 – 3) describes Spanish methods; the second (sentences 4 – 7) presents the significant differences in English aim and method.

QUESTION: Explain the significance of Walt Whitman's *Leaves of Grass* in the development of American literature.

ANSWER A: (1) *Leaves of Grass,* by Walt Whitman, was published in 1851, more than a hundred years ago. (2) It was a long personal poem in free verse. (3) At first it did not get a very favorable reaction, although some critics liked it, but today it is widely praised. (4) It was important because
　　1) free verse
　　2) celebrated America
　　3) democratic
　　4) realism
(5) Carl Sandburg, in poems like "Chicago," (1920?) writes in the tradition established in *Leaves of Grass.* (6) Among Sandburg's contemporaries were Vachel Lindsay and William Vaughn Moody and Hart Crane. (7) *Leaves of Grass* brought new freedom to

29.1

Exam

American poetry because it broke from many of the old traditions in poetry like that of Longfellow and Whittier. (8) Therefore, it is truly significant.

ANSWER B: (1) Although Whitman's *Leaves of Grass* has many characteristics of nineteenth-century Romantic literature, it is an important landmark in American literature. (2) At a time when American poetry was rigidly conventional in meter and rhyme, Whitman boldly experimented with varying line lengths and free verse. (3) In subject matter, too, *Leaves of Grass* explored new frontiers. (4) A disciple of democracy and modern technology, Whitman made frequent reference to common trades and people, machinery and the less savory details of urban life, all considered "low" subjects unfit for poetry by such traditionalists as Longfellow and Whittier. (5) In his choice of such subjects and in the frankness with which he discussed human behavior, Whitman was preparing the way for the Realistic movement which was to emerge toward the close of the century. (6) Twentieth-century celebrants of industrial America like Sandburg and Hart Crane were poetic descendants of Whitman; even today, poets like Allen Ginsberg are indebted to Whitman in style and attitude.

CRITICISM: In answer A, sentences 1–3 and 6 do not specifically relate to the question. The heart of the answer seems to be sentence 4, but the unexplained list of headings conveys nothing. If these points are important, each should be developed in a separate sentence or two. Sentences 5 and 7 also seem to be relevant but are vague. *What* tradition did *Leaves of Grass* establish? *What* old tradition did it break? Was "Chicago" written in 1920 or not?

In answer B, the points merely listed in A are developed and made specific. The relation of the poem to both earlier and later poetic traditions is explained. All sentences are relevant and are well related to each other.

29.2 Writing About Literature

In college English courses students are often asked to write about literature — to examine, interpret, and discuss fiction, poetry, drama. Literary analysis and interpretation are not radically different from the close reading and interpretive writing you might do in history, philosophy, and sociology courses or from your critical response to an editorial, magazine article, sermon, or letter to the editor. In much the same manner, we can examine a piece of literature critically and sort out our thoughts about it in order to understand it more fully.

Still, writing about literature is sometimes troublesome. You may sometimes find yourself thinking that "It's all a bunch of symbols and hidden meanings." You may sometimes feel that writing about literature requires a more specialized language and more advanced knowledge than you have. If an assignment calls for you to write an interpretive essay on a poem or story or play, and if you feel hopeless, or if you feel that "tearing a story or poem apart to analyze it spoils the story or poem," it may help if you remember some simple things.

First, a story or a poem or a play is someone's words, and they've been waiting, perhaps for generations, for you, an audience. Someone from out there in time and space is speaking to you. He or she may be hard to understand or say something you can't respond to easily; he or she may say something you can't accept. But you *can* understand, and the speaker who is sending his or her words to you deserves some of your time.

Second, curiosity may be a better guide to literary analysis than having a double handful of literary terms memorized. But you do have to learn to trust your curiosity when you look at a poem, for example, and be willing to ask questions: Why these words instead of others that would have served? Why doesn't the poem speak to me directly? Why do things occur in the order in which they occur? Exactly who is speaking to me? Am I meant to be the audience, or am I overhearing a speaker speak to someone in the poem? Why this? And why that? If you trust your curiosity, you can begin to find your way into a poem, for only the poem will provide answers to questions about the poem.

Third, when your assignment is to write an analytical essay about a piece of writing, unless your instructor has given a very specific assignment, it's all right to seize an interesting point—a puzzling line, a peculiar phrase, a strange incident—and use it as a focal point for your essay. Unless your instructor has specifically called for a particular kind of discussion, you should feel under no obligation to talk about everything in a poem or a play or a story. If something in the work strikes you, set out to learn what you can about it, to figure it out.

In answering the questions that come up, or in discussing the points that interest you, use the poem or play or story that has been assigned, not your own experience. It's easy, sometimes, to treat the assigned work as a starting place for talking about similar experiences you've had, similar feelings you have enjoyed or suffered. The text of the work is the proper source of evidence and material. You should also avoid trying to paraphrase the assigned work, converting it to your own language. This may be something you need to do to aid in your own understanding, but don't think of paraphrasing as an end point. When you paraphrase a poem, for example, you're writing translation, not commentary. It's helpful

29.2

Lit

to remember that most human things — including stories, poems, plays, yourself, and your acquaintances — are too complex to be reduced to a simple generalization or maxim or to a "moral of the story." A story or a play, for example, can be read in several ways (remember that different people see you in different ways, too); there's not likely to be a single "right" way to talk about a piece of literature.

Some Questions to Start With

Some features of literature provide good questions that may help you get started in exploring a piece of writing. Attempting to answer any one of the questions about these features may get you sufficiently involved in the writing to be able to see more questions and to understand more of what is going on.

1. **Genre.** Does the *kind* of writing that you are studying give the author a perspective that he or she wouldn't have otherwise? Does it create limitations for the author, or does it offer special advantages? What can a writer do in a poem that can't be done in a short story? What can be done in a play that can't be done in a poem?

2. **Speaker.** Who controls what we learn from the literary work? Who is telling the story? Who is speaking in the poem? Is the author speaking, or is it someone else? What difference does it make? Why does the author choose to tell the story, present the poem, or show the drama in that particular way? What distance is there between the author and us, or between the author and the speaker? Whose version of events are we reading?

3. **Setting.** What is the setting? Is it localized and shown in specific detail? If it isn't, why isn't it? What kind of environment do the characters live in? What effect does it have on them?

4. **Character.** How do we learn about the characters? If a poem is at issue and no characters appear except the speaker, how do we learn about him or her? Are the characters revealed by their words, by their actions, by both? What difference does it make? Are they identifiable as individuals, or do they seem to be representative types?

5. **Style and tone.** How does the author speak to us? What does the author reveal about himself by the way he speaks? If characters speak, do they have distinguishable styles? What do they reveal about themselves? What will the vocabulary tell us about the speaker or speakers? Does the style of the sentences tell anything about the speaker or about the work? What images and figures of speech occur? How do they determine the tone of the work?

6. **Structure and rhythm.** Why is the work arranged as it is? What part of the structure gets primary attention? What part seems to get the least attention? How is the tempo of the work controlled? When does the author slow down the pace of the work? When is the pace speeded up?

Some Suggestions for Writing and Literary Study

If you have plenty of time for your writing, and if your instructor is willing for you to support and possibly amplify your own critical commentary with material gathered in research, the following classification of types of literary study may help you to focus on a subject when you are planning a paper about a work of literature. This classification is based largely on a list of areas for literary research compiled by B. Bernard Cohen in his *Writing About Literature*.

1. **Textual analysis.** One kind of literary criticism is devoted to a close examination of the text itself — preparation and publication, revisions, errors or misprintings, various editions, and so forth. Part of the meaning of Book III of *Gulliver's Travels* was clarified, for example, with the discovery — some 175 years after initial publication — of a short passage that had been printed in the first edition but had been deleted thereafter. It is unlikely that you will do highly specialized textual research for the papers you are assigned in undergraduate courses, but you can often find a subject in existing textual problems (such as the effect on the meaning of Keats' "Ode on a Grecian Urn" of the punctuation of the last two lines).
2. **Relationships among the author's works.** It is sometimes useful to examine the work at hand by considering it in the light of the author's other works. For example, it may be possible to understand the manner of *Gulliver's Travels* better by considering it along with "A Modest Proposal" and some of Swift's other satires.
3. **Relevance to biography.** Some papers on literary subjects can profitably examine the particular circumstances in the author's life that helped give shape to the work.
4. **Study of the creative process.** If primary sources such as letters and diaries are available, it is possible sometimes to study a given work for what it reveals about the creative process. Why did Swift write the four books of *Gulliver's Travels* in an order other than that in which they are printed?
5. **Relation of the work to literary theory.** It is also possible to develop fruitful explorations of a work by examining it in the light of theories about art and literature current when the work was written.

29.2

Lit

6. **Impact of the times on the work.** Sometimes it is interesting to approach a work as an artifact, to determine how it records and reflects the ideas and events of its own time.

7. **Relationship of the work to literary tradition.** A work of literature can be studied in terms of the literary habits, assumptions, and techniques the author has inherited from other writers. You might examine *Gulliver's Travels,* for example, to see how Swift adopted, rejected, or refined the techniques of satire that were already in use.

8. **Relationship of the work to a particular subject area.** Sometimes you can find a worthwhile subject for a paper by looking at a literary work for what it reveals about a particular field of interest or idea. You could, for example, increase your understanding of *Gulliver's Travels* and write something of interest about it by focusing on what it says about English politics.

9. **Reception of the work.** You can often learn a great deal about a work by discovering how it was received in its own day or at any later time.

29.3 Public Letters

Although letter-writing is not ordinarily taught in composition courses, it is one of the most important forms of written expression. In many situations, letters are the only means you have to make yourself heard. They deserve your best effort.

What you say in a letter and the way you say it will depend upon your purpose, the person you are writing to, and, above all, upon the way you customarily express yourself. Courtesy and reasonableness, even in a letter of complaint, are always best in business correspondence. Beyond that, you should be familiar with the conventions of correspondence, so that the form and appearance of your letters will make the intended impression. The form established for business letters is standard for most kinds of formal correspondence.

Neatness, clarity, and directness are the chief virtues of a business letter. It should include all relevant information (such as dates, prices, description of merchandise) and should be as brief as possible and still be clear. The tone should be courteous, even if you are complaining about an error.

The sample letter of application on page 411 illustrates the form and tone of a typical business letter. Notice the position and punctuation of the heading, inside address, greeting (salutation), and close.

General Appearance

Select stationery of appropriate size and good quality, with envelopes to match. For business letters the standard sheet is 8½ by 11 inches, the same size as ordinary typing paper.

Typed letters are expected in business correspondence, and they are increasingly popular for personal correspondence. In typing your letter, leave generous margins and center the body of the letter so that the page will look well balanced. Space paragraphs distinctly, using either block or indented form. Block paragraphs are set flush with the left margin of the letter; they are separated by a line of space, as shown in the sample on page 411. For indented paragraphs, begin five spaces from the left-hand margin. Be consistent in form. If a letter runs to more than one page, use a separate sheet of paper for each page and number the pages at the top.

The Heading. A heading should be typed in the upper right-hand corner, giving the writer's complete address and the date. The standard form is the block pattern, with end punctuation omitted. The name of the city, the state, and the month are generally written out in full:

```
902 Luther Place
Duluth, Minnesota 55804
January 5, 1980
```

If you use a letterhead which includes the address, type the date below it, flush with the right-hand margin or centered, depending on the design of the letterhead.

Inside Address and Greeting. The inside address of a business letter gives the full name and address of the person or firm to whom it is directed. It appears flush with the left-hand margin, at least one line below the last line of the heading. No punctuation is used at the ends of the lines. If you wish to mention the person's title or position in the firm, put the designation immediately below the name in the inside address:

```
Ms. Linda Peterson
Personnel Director
Allen, Swift and Company
4863 Commercial Street
Dallas, Texas 75222
```

29.3

Let

The greeting, or *salutation,* appears below the inside address, separated from it by a line of space. In business letters it is followed by a colon. If the letter is addressed to a particular individual in a firm, you may use either the name or an impersonal greeting:

```
Dear Mr. Keiser: [or Dear Sir:]    Dear Miss Jenkins: [or Dear Madam:]
```

Until recently it was customary to use the masculine form of address *(Gentlemen: Dear Sir:)* if the letter was addressed to the firm as a whole or to an individual whose name was unknown. Since the recipient is just as likely to be a woman as a man, however, alternative salutations are becoming more widely used. One acceptable salutation is simply the name of the company or, if appropriate, the title of the individual or department:

```
Dear Sir or Madam:    Dear Editor:    Dear Matthews Camera Company:
```

Close and Signature.   A conventional expression called the *complimentary close* is used at the end of the letter. Only the first word of the close is capitalized and a comma customarily follows. The general tone of the letter will suggest how formal the close should be:

Formal	Less formal
Yours truly,	Sincerely yours,
Yours very truly,	Sincerely,
Respectfully yours,	Yours sincerely,

The close can be either flush with the left-hand margin or in the middle of the page.

The signature is always written in longhand below the close. For clarity, however, you should type your name below your signature. A woman may indicate her marital status in parentheses if she wishes, but this practice is dying out among businesswomen.

Addressing the Envelope.   Both the address of the person to whom you are writing and your own address should be clear and complete on the front of the envelope. A block style—with the left-hand margin even—is the standard form for both addresses.

No punctuation is used at the end of the lines in this form. A comma is used between the name of a city and the state if they are put on the same line, but not between the state and the ZIP code: Chicago, Illinois 60611.

When you abbreviate street designations, use the standard forms *(St.* for *Street, Ave.* for *Avenue, Blvd.* for *Boulevard).* For names of states, use only those abbreviations given in your dictionary *(Penn., Okla.)* or the ZIP code directory.

Use an envelope that matches your stationery and fold the letter to fit. With long business envelopes, a standard sheet (8½ by 11 inches) is folded horizontally into three sections. With short business envelopes, it is folded once across the middle and then twice in the other direction.

Some Criteria for Public Letters

Private letters are likely to be extended, long-distance forms of private conversation, though some may in the course of time come to have public uses and be publicly displayed. *Public* letters are a part of public discourse; they are typically not written forms of private or intimate conversation. They are written, usually, where there is work to be done, where public decisions are to be made and registered, where records must be kept. But that doesn't mean that public letters must, as a consequence, be impersonal, cold, or nonhuman.

Many public letters—letters of recommendation, job applications, information letters, and others—are stylized, ritualized performances. Their authors sometimes fall into the habit of using a stiff, impersonal style that is remote and official-sounding, or they lapse into the jargon of a particular trade or profession, or they fall into the strange world where bureaucratic dialects are accepted as good English, where simple things become complex and complex things become impossible.

It's not uncommon, for example, to find business, professional, technical, and semi-technical letters depending excessively on current fad words—*parameter,* for example, and *viable* and *dialogue.* It's easy enough to fall into the habit of overusing some words and phrases, such as these:

> *After a dialogue with* for *after talking with*
> *Implementing a decision* for *deciding*
> *Making a survey in depth* for *studying*
> *Causative factor* for *cause*
> *Optimum* for *most* or *best*

The list might go on and on.

29.3

There are at least three reasons why we all sometimes use such stylized, pompous, trite, or unnecessary words and phrases. In the first place, we see enough of such language—in income tax instructions, federal prose, legal documents, sales agreements, and elsewhere—that it's natural for us to conclude that there is an "official" kind of language. What's needed, however, is clear and direct language.

In the second place, many people who write business, professional, and technical letters have to write *many* such letters. If a person has to write, let's say, thirty or forty letters in a single day, it's certainly understandable if he or she relies on certain phrasings and words, repeating them again and again. It's understandable, but it's not desirable: when a writer depends upon certain habits of phrasing, then those habits of language become binding, and govern what a writer can say.

Third, we often depend upon standardized forms when we write public letters. If you have to write twelve letters in one afternoon requesting payment for a bill, it's likely that you will use the same or nearly the same form in each letter. Many companies, in fact, have some standardized forms that can be used in writing the various company letters that go out from the company. If we often depend upon standardized forms, then we may often depend also upon standardized, "official-sounding" language.

Public Letters Should Be in a Natural Style.   A public letter does not have to be written in an "official" language. Even when you are writing as a representative of a company, for example, you can still sound like yourself. That doesn't mean that you should write public letters that are cute or highly personal or full of folksy, back-slapping chatter.

The letter below was written in response to a customer's letter of complaint about gas mileage in a new car recently purchased from an automobile manufacturer's sales dealer. The customer's letter was mailed directly to the manufacturer's public representative in Detroit. The representative sent the letter back to a local company agent who replied to the customer's original letter (the names have been changed to protect the innocent and the guilty):

```
Mr. Patrick C. Wayne
7313 Arena Drive
Madrigal, Missouri 65543


Dear Mr. Wayne:


This will acknowledge your letter to Detroit which has been re-
ferred to this office for handling.


We have been unable to contact you by phone during normal working
hours; however, we have reviewed your gas consumption problem
with the Service Manager at Westside Reo Motor Company, Mr. Ted
```

```
Warsaw. We suggest you call him for an appointment that can be
arranged when our Service Development Manager will be at the
dealership in order that he may assist in checking out your
vehicle.

We do thank you for writing.

Very truly yours,
```

B. M. Bell

```
B. M. Bell
Customer Relations Manager
```

Now this is not a "bad" letter. But it was written by a human being to be read by a human being, and such a letter might as well *sound* human. The first sentence, for example, might just as easily read as follows:

```
I have the letter you sent to our Detroit office.
```
or
```
Our Detroit office has sent me your letter.
```

In the original opening sentence the customer has been turned over to "this office" for "handling," which sounds altogether impersonal. Nowhere does the original letter acknowledge that the customer is a thinking person who *might* be right in his complaints about the car. A new second sentence or an addition to the first might be helpful:

```
    I have the letter you sent to our Detroit office, and I am
sorry to learn of the problems you have had with your new Reo.
```
or
```
    Our Detroit office has sent me your letter. I hope we can
work out the problems you have had with your new Reo.
```

In the second paragraph, the original letter gets better. There is, however, no good reason for the writer to use *we; I* would do as well. *Vehicle* in the last sentence is too vague. *Car* is more specific. The customer, seeing the word *car,* might believe that the letter writer actually knew which kind of vehicle was under discussion.

A human being ought to show up even in the most public letters. Impersonal language is not more accurate or official than natural, human language.

29.3

Let

Public Letters Should Be Accurate.   Information should be complete and correct. Judgments should be stated clearly as judgments, and opinions and interpretations should be clearly identified. Consider some simple examples, all letters to the editor, from *Time* (June 27, 1977). The first three were all written in response to an earlier article on jogging.

```
    I am happy to see that the American people are finally awakening

to the benefits and joys of running.  I am a long-distance runner, and

I intend to run forever.
```

This complete letter contains only the three short, relatively simple assertions. The first is a statement of attitude, the second of fact not easily open to question, and the third another of attitude. We know where the author stands, and we know that he is making no demands on our credibility. The letter is accurate.

The second letter is also short:

```
    Joggers make me sick.  There are plenty of them around

here.  They run past me with supercilious smirks on their red

faces.  What are they trying to prove?  I hope they all drown in their

own sweat.

    I'm 100 lbs. overweight and love it. I eat and drink what I

please.  To hell with the physical-fitness fanatics.
```

This letter also is accurate. We know what we are reading, an expression of opinion, and we can assume it is reliable. We are not being asked to accept opinions as facts. The third letter is similar:

```
    I see that jogging is now a full-blown fad. Good! If we are to

judge from other fads, that means it will blow over in a few months, or

at most a year or so.  Like, for instance, Hula Hoops.

    As an old Army man, I can tell you what jogging really

is.  Jogging is double time. And I say, the hell with it!
```

We get reliable signals from this letter, too. The first sentence is clearly a report on the author's perception ("I see . . ."). The second is a single word, and the exclamation point following it testifies that this is the author's enthusiastic judgment. The third sentence avoids making an unsupportable statement by acknowledging the conditions ("If we are to judge from other fads, . . ."). The author's use of hula hoops as an example in the fourth sentence seems accurate enough; it can easily be tested by our own knowledge or quick research.

The three letters above are accurate. They make no false claims. We are not asked to accept questionable data.

The fourth letter is different. It was written in response to an earlier article in *Time* about the nation's defense:

```
    I want to commend you for your in-depth cover story analyzing the
state of the nation's defenses.
    One small part of the article is of deep concern to me, however.
It perpetuates the myth about the cost of the volunteer force.  In fact,
the active-duty military personnel share of the Defense Department budget
has gone down from 31% to 27% since the end of the draft. Retirement,
civilian personnel costs and other nonvolunteer force-related costs have
gone up, but these increases are not tied to the end of the draft.
```

We can't be quite sure of this letter's accuracy. The author opposes "the myth about the cost of the volunteer force," and to that end cites a budget reduction. This information is, if not inaccurate, not full enough to be significant to us. Unless we know how much money and how many volunteers are involved, the percentage figures don't mean much. The military force may very well be costing more than it did when the draft ended.

Public letters need to be accurate (and that entails providing full and open information) for at least three reasons. In the first place, accuracy is a goal and an obligation for anyone. Second, in many of the public transactions that are conducted through letters, your reader will not know as much as you know, which makes it particularly important to be accurate. Finally, even when your reader knows most or all of what you know, it is important and valuable for readers to know how you use information, how you organize data, how you make decisions and judgments.

Public Letters Should Provide a Track for Readers to Follow. Readers should know the context in which a letter is written. They should know why a letter is written, its origins, or what the letter is responding to. They need to be able to see your connections and follow the sequence of your thoughts. If they can't, then your letter is likely to seem either abrupt and rude or tyrannical, expecting readers to agree with your assertions simply because they are yours.

Consider a typical good example. This letter is from a college student to an attorney; the writer is asking the reader to participate in a survey:

29.3

Let

Dear Mr. Abernathy:

You and several other prominent local lawyers were recently quoted in The Daily News in a discussion of current problems in education, especially problems in language use. The discussion and your comments so interested me that I decided to write my term paper in Political Science 1053 on "The Legal Profession's View of Today's Pre-law Education."

I hope you will be willing to complete the enclosed questionnaire. All you will need to do is to check yes or no in response to each of the questions. Your answers will be kept confidential. If you wish, I will send you a summary of the results based on my survey of fifty lawyers in this area.

Your answers, of course, will be useful to me in writing my paper. More than that, I believe they will be useful in discussions of changes in education. I hope you will check the answers and return the questionnaire in the enclosed, self-addressed envelope.

Sincerely yours,

The letter provides the information necessary for the reader to understand the context. The first sentence tells how the writer, a stranger, came to be writing, and the second sentence establishes the occasion. The second paragraph makes a specific request and states the terms the writer offers. The last paragraph tells the potential uses of the information that the writer is seeking. Throughout the letter the writer has explained his mission clearly, making it possible for the recipient to respond easily and conveniently.

Whether you are writing to an institution or to a person, to a stranger or to an acquaintance, be sure that you tell readers enough for them to follow the sequence of your thoughts. The sample letters that follow show you what other people characteristically do when they write certain kinds of public letters; both the content and the tone may help you in your own letter writing.

Letters of Application

Letters of application are important enough to warrant special attention. Most prospective employers now prefer to receive a short letter of application accompanied by a resumé. Although the letter should be brief, it's often helpful to tell why you want to work for a particular company or what you feel you can offer the company.

Review: Sample Letters

- *Letter of application*

Heading

856 East Oceanside Drive

Los Angeles, California 90016

October 5, 1980

Inside address

Dr. Robert Gruen

Director of Research

Bloch-Peterson Foundation

780 West Augusta Boulevard

Los Angeles, California 90004

Salutation

Dear Dr. Gruen:

Body

Your classified notice in the current Journal of Pathology indicates that there is an opening for a bacteriologist on your staff. I would like to apply for the position.

I feel that my experience in bacteriological research would suit me very well for the type of research Bloch-Peterson specializes in. My resume, which is enclosed, gives the details of my academic and professional background.

If I can provide any other information, I shall be glad to do so. I can be available for an interview at your convenience.

Close

Sincerely yours,

Joanne Trestrail

Joanne Trestrail

Resume

Joanne Trestrail

856 East Oceanside Drive

Los Angeles, California   90016

(213) 267-1927

Objective   Applied research, especially in some area of disease
                     control and prevention.

Experience   June 1979-present
                     Los Angeles Board of Health
                     Assist Dr. Lucille Lesiak in epidemological studies,
                     concentrating on communicable diseases among Los
                     Angeles elementary school children.   Do analytical
                     laboratory when required.

                     Summer 1978
                     Froude Institute, Chicago, Illinois
                     Helped Dr. Joseph Roth prepare the statistical ta-
                     bles for his recently published <u>Tropical</u> <u>Diseases</u>

                     Summer 1976
                     Laboratory Assistant, Department of Bacteriology
                     Midwestern University, Green Bay, Wisconsin

                     References available on request
Education   1978-1980
                     University of Southern California, Los Angeles
                     Master of Science in Bacteriology

                     1974-1978
                     Midwestern University, Green Bay, Wisconsin
                     Bachelor of Science in Biology

                     Summer 1977
                     University of Chicago
                     Seminar in microbiology and statistical techniques

Clubs and   League of Women Voters
Organizations   Apollo Music Club
                     Los Angeles Cyclists

Director of Customer Complaints
Bolton's Stores Inc.
107 Townley Blvd.
Chicago, Illinois 60690

Dear Sir or Madam:

I want to compliment you on your prompt service in delivering the FX-31
pocket calculator that I ordered through your 24-hour phone service. I
was pleased to find that you carried the specific model that I needed.

However, I"m sorry to say that the calculator has not produced the results that were advertised. Instead of showing eight digits, this machine has five. The independent memory bank also does not record more
than one entry.

I am sure that this particular instrument is not representative of your
products and that you will see that the enclosed FX-31 is properly re-
paired or replaced.

As a regular customer of Bolton's, I am generally pleased with your
merchandise and hope to continue shopping at your store.

Sincerely,

John Neal

John Neal

Teacher Placement Bureau

Homer Hall, 108

Central University

Central, Alabama

To whom it may concern:

I am writing at the request of Mr. Bob Boyd so that this letter may be
added to the dossier which you are compiling.

Mr. Boyd and I first became acquainted in 1970 when he was enrolled in
my freshman design class. He was an alert and able student, and during
the several years of his stay here, and his subsequent careers at Western University and Northern State University, my opinion of him as a
student and friend continued to strengthen even more. He belongs to
that small group of former students that all of us know, whom we can
recommend to any possible employer without reservation.

Yours truly,

Rachel Wade

Rachel Wade

Associate Professor of Art

The letter should follow standard business-letter format (see page 411).

A resumé is a one-page summary of pertinent information about yourself, including personal data, educational background, and employment record. The form shown on page 412 would usually be considered acceptable, although it is not always necessary to define your objectives. It is a good idea to indicate the nature of the work you did at your places of employment, along with any specific accomplishments. You should also list any awards or honors and publications, if appropriate. If you wish to name references or people who would be willing to recommend you, a list can be inserted at the end of the resumé.

Always ask the permission of people you list as references. Give their complete addresses and correct titles (Professor, Dr., Mrs.). *Mr., Mrs., Ms.,* and *Dr.* are the only titles that are abbreviated. All others are written in full.

If you are asked to include documents (such as photographs, transcripts of academic records, or photostats), use a crush-proof envelope. If you want the enclosures returned to you, include a self-addressed, stamped envelope.

29.4 Reports

Some Criteria for Reports

Three particular qualities of reports are worth special notice. You may remember discussions in various places throughout this book of basic differences among kinds of writing. Some kinds of writing are personal or expressive; they give authors the opportunity to make themselves known. Some kinds are active or persuasive. Some kinds are referential; they explain or account for things without necessarily attempting to persuade readers.

Reports Should Be Referential. In a report, the author may be deeply involved with the subject, and he or she is surely responsible for the report. But although an author may appear in a report as a spokesperson or as an investigator (even using the first-person), the author is not part of the subject.

29.4

Rept

Reports Should Examine Some Subject Outside the Author. A report is not meant to be an occasion for self-expression. Neither is it usually meant to be persuasive, though some reports end with recommendations. More often than not, a report simply examines or discusses a subject; decisions or action are made by the readers.

For example, in a business, one department—say market re-search—may report to another—product development—on the habits and preferences of a certain segment of the market, without recommending how a certain kind of product be developed. A re-search report that you are likely to write in college may suggest various courses of action to resolve an issue and what you think the results might be, but you wouldn't necessarily have to recom-mend which course should be followed.

In the report on pages 417–419, notice that the author seems to be chiefly concerned with conveying information. Paragraph 2 pro-vides some immediate background—figures on women's employ-ment during the past ten years. Paragraph 3 connects the report with other contemporary issues, including traditional conceptions of sex roles and arguments associated with women's liberation. Paragraph 5 provides further background, an account of the tradi-tional reasons cited for employment of women. But by paragraph 6, the writer is dealing with the new features of women's employ-ment, seen against the quick background he has sketched.

Reports Are Often Based on Research.   Reports are *referential*. They *convey* information and opinion. These two qualities help account for a third distinctive quality of reports: *they are charac-teristically based on investigation,* not meditation or personal opinion. Reports may have to be documented—that is, you may need to show the sources of your information through notes and attach a list of references.

Methods of Writing Reports

Remember that you needn't reinvent the wheel every time you write something new; that is, remember that other writers have probably used forms and organization similar to those you will need. You should make use of these models whenever you can.

If you must write reports for your work, you might examine ear-lier reports in your company's files. If your college course work requires you to write reports, your instructors may suggest partic-ular plans or formats for the work, or show you examples of other reports. In either instance—at work or at college—remember that almost any library, regardless of size, will have books on business and professional writing that will usually include guides to report writing. Other people have written reports; you don't have to start from scratch.

The occasions on which reports must be written are so diverse and the kinds of reports that may be called for are so many that no single guide can show you how to write every kind of report. How-

Review: Sample Report

• *Money Need, Social Change Combine to Cut Apron Strings*

(1) Sometime this year, probably within the next month or so, the percentage of American women who hold jobs or are looking for work is expected to reach 50. According to figures released last week, in April, 49.7 percent of all women — a new high — were in the labor force, an increase from March's 49.3 percent and a signal of a continuing upward swing.

(2) In the last decade, the Labor Department says, 14 million new jobs have been filled in this country and women have filled 10 million of them. Last year, in large part because of the rapid entry of women into the labor market, the number of jobseekers grew just about as rapidly as the number of jobs. That is one reason why the unemployment rate stayed so high last year — the average, 7 percent, give or take a tenth of a point — despite the fact that employment rose at a record rate, by 4.1 million jobs.

(3) Some economists and politicians discuss the phenomenon in a faintly accusatory manner. Though the suggestion is never directly put, it is there: If only women would stay in their traditional homemaker's role, instead of seeking liberation through a different lifestyle, the nation's unemployment troubles would be solved. Or, such commentators recommend, unemployment should be redefined, so that "nontraditional" workers such as women be properly weighted. But such scapegoat thinking, other experts contend, only obscures fundamental economic reasons for the trend.

(4) Undoubtedly, social factors play a role in the growing flood of women into the work force. "But the fact is more and more women are working out of necessity," says Alexis M. Herman, director of the Women's Bureau of the Labor Department. "Women don't have the option of working inside the home or outside the home any more," she adds. "Economic needs require that they go out and find a job."

(5) Miss Herman has estimated that 60 to 65 percent of women who hold jobs do so for purely economic reasons. Many of them must work because they are the only source of economic support for themselves and their families. A Women's Bureau study published in mid-1976 showed that over 23 percent of working women have never been married. Another 19 percent of women workers were widowed, divorced or separated from their husbands, and because of social and cultural trends, the number of women living without husbands is increasing. In 1960, for exam-

ple, 28 percent of women aged 22 to 24 were single; by 1976 the number had risen to 46 percent. For most of them, there is little alternative to work other than welfare or unemployment compensation. As Geraldine Coleman, a 27-year-old mother of three who works as an auto mechanic for Sears Roebuck and Co., puts it, a job is not simply a matter of lifestyle: "I work because it is a matter of survival. A single parent like me needs a job and needs one at a male salary."

(6) More than half of all working women, however, are married, some of them to men who are unable to work, and still more have husbands who are unemployed for one reason or another. These women, too, must work as the sole support of their families and themselves. Of working women with working husbands, close to half had husbands who earned $10,000 a year or less when the data for the 1976 women's bureau study was collected. "Often," Miss Herman explains, "a second income means the difference between poverty and an adequate standard of living."

(7) But it is not just the wives of low-wage earners who are taking jobs to supplement their husband's income, and help keep the family budget solvent in the face of inflation. Women in middle-income families are taking jobs in response to the economic squeeze. In part, such women are going to work to maintain the standard of living to which they have become accustomed. But increasingly, a second income is being sought to achieve traditional goals, such as college education for their children or for a one-family home.

(8) Sandra Hall, whose husband is a Secret Service agent, recently went to work as a computer repair specialist. "I work first of all for the money," she said. "One income wasn't sufficient. We want to maintain a middle-class lifestyle — meaning for us a townhouse in Reston [Va.] and braces on the boy's teeth. Also they are continually raising utility rates and other things are going up all the time. Of course I've always wanted to work anyway. I've been working all my adult life."

(9) "I'm working at this job for one reason — to make enough money to put my kids through college," said a woman with a civil service job in Washington whose $26,000 a year salary is only marginally below her husband's. When both children are in college at the same time all of her after-tax salary, working costs deducted, would go for tuition and school expenses.

(10) The cost of that other American dream, the suburban home, is also rising so fast that it is fading beyond the reach of many one-income families that could, in past generations, have afforded one. In fact, the cherished notion of the American family, in which the father goes out to earn daily bread and the mother stays at home in a cottage, with or without a rose garden, to take care of the children, is now more myth than reality.

(11) Two years ago, the Urban Institute extrapolated from Bureau of Labor Statistics data that only 19 percent of all Americans were members of families in which the father worked and the mother stayed at home, with one or more children. Ralph Smith, an economist with the institute, said that the number of these supposedly archetypical family groups will continue to shrink.

(12) Changes in the structure of the economy have also contributed to the rapid growth of the percentage of women in the labor force, says Julius Shiskin, director of the Bureau of Labor Statistics. While employment has been declining or stagnant in manufacturing and construction industries, which are dominated by men, it has been rising fairly rapidly in clerical and service industries. Few working women now have jobs such as Mrs. Coleman's: Being an auto mechanic is generally considered man's work. Women are concentrated chiefly into 20 of the 480 job categories listed by the Labor Department, most of them clerical, such as secretarial or bookkeeping, or service, such as sales clerks, nurses aides and waitresses. But with women pouring into the workplace at an accelerated rate, most economists predict that more of them will be moving away from such traditional women's work. — Philip Shabecoff

29.4

Rept

ever, there is a basic organizational pattern common to many reports:

> Introduction:
>> a statement of the problem
>> the occasion or need for exploring the problem
>> anticipated or proposed method for exploring the problem
>
> Middle:
>> an account of the procedure followed in exploring the problem
>> an account of the information resulting from the investigation —
>>> tests, samplings, interviews, questionnaires, statistical investigations, library research of any kind
>
> End:
>> a presentation of the final findings, last suggestions, or proposals; a display of results, conclusions, and sometimes recommendations

Not all reports, of course, will have all of these parts, and not all reports will follow this order. Many reports do follow a pattern much like this, but some have special requirements:

1. **A memorandum,** for example, may present only the *end* of a chain of thought or an investigation.
2. **A progress report** may present the *middle* steps suggested above. A progress report is an account of what has been done so far in a given investigation or procedure.
3. **A briefing report** is meant, usually, to anticipate what is going to happen, to anticipate what should be known or done first, last, and in between, to anticipate problems. A *briefing* is intended to prepare someone or some group for what is to come.
4. **A critique or evaluation** looks at an enterprise or a piece of work after it is over. The pattern sketched above can be useful: one way to write a *critique* is to look back at the beginning to see if the work was begun at the best place and at the middle to see if everything was done that should be done, in order to look at the conclusion to see if it can be validated.

Whatever form you follow, remember that within your writing you can call upon most of the methods used in other kinds of writing. Reports depend upon description, narration, exposition, and argumentation, and each of the other chapters of this book is relevant to report writing. You may want to review especially Chapter 19 and the account there of various methods for developing and exploring material — definition, illustration, comparison, contrast, classification, cause-and-effect analysis, and the others.

Finally, as you prepare your own reports or as you study the reports of others, keep these questions in mind:

1. Is the language clear and direct, free of jargon?
2. How does the author show up in the work?

3. How is a context established for the work?
4. In what sense is the work referential? Does the subject dominate the work, or do other factors interfere?
5. Is the subject clearly examined? Are questions left unasked and unanswered?
6. What kind of investigation supports the work?
7. How is the work organized?
8. What methods of development are used?

29.4

Rept

30   The Research Paper

. . . not to know what has been transacted in former times is to continue always a child. If no use is made of the labours of past ages, the world must remain always in the infancy of knowledge.—Samuel Johnson

Anything you write *may* require some research. Whole libraries, as well as other resources, are available to you whenever you write anything. One of the decisions you make in thinking out any paper is whether or not you know enough already to handle the subject. If you don't know enough, if the subject requires treatment that you can't give, then any assignment may become a research assignment.

Often the planning and writing of a research paper (also called a library paper, a reference paper, or a term paper) is a separate and special part of freshman composition and other college courses. The preparation of a research paper has much in common with other writing assignments, but in addition it provides:

1. Practice in exploring the possibilities of a subject and limiting it so that it can be treated adequately in a paper longer than those you will customarily write; research papers may often range from 1500 to 4000 words.
2. An introduction to the resources of the library and training in the most efficient ways of locating information.
3. Practice in using source material intelligently—choosing between what is useful and what is not, evaluating the ideas of others, organizing and interpreting the information.
4. Acquaintance with documentation and manuscript form typically expected in academic work and in reports and papers prepared for publication.
5. An opportunity to learn something new about a subject and to gain specialized, thorough knowledge of it.

Because the reference paper is longer and more complex than most other compositions you may be asked to write, we discuss it here in successive steps:

1. choosing a topic (30.1);
2. locating appropriate source materials (30.2);
3. preparing the working bibliography (30.3);

4. evaluating your material (30.4);
5. taking notes (30.5);
6. planning the paper (30.6);
7. writing the first draft (30.7);
8. documenting the paper (30.8);
9. assembling the completed paper (30.9).

The actual task of preparing a reference paper, however, can seldom be divided into such neat categories. The steps overlap and certain operations must be repeated as work progresses. For example, as you get into your reading you may decide that your topic needs to be modified; and as you write your paper you may discover gaps in your information that must be filled in by further research. The best advice, perhaps, is to start on the assignment early and to take particular care in choosing and defining your topic so that both your research and your writing will have a clear focus.

30.1 Choosing a Topic

One important prerequisite for writing a good reference paper is that you have a genuine interest in the subject you are going to investigate. In some courses, the subject field may be limited by the general assignment (perhaps to various aspects of the United Nations, or to the history of a specific geographic area, or to an author or work of literature you have studied); but often the choice of a subject will be left up to you.

In either instance, you should be reasonably certain that the specific topic you select will be one that you will like to read about, to think about, and then to write about. Since a reference paper may take as much as five or six weeks to prepare, it can easily become a chore – and be largely a waste of time – unless you feel that what you are doing is of some interest and importance. The suggestions in 18.1, Finding and Exploring What You Have to Say, are as relevant to the reference paper as they are to other kinds of writing.

Choosing a Subject Area

Before making a definite decision on your topic, consider your various interests in and out of school. These general subjects may suggest particular topics that you might want to investigate:

1. A subject related to one of the courses that you are now taking or that you intend to take. For example, if you are going to major in business administration and you intend to take American

30.1

Topic

economic history next year, you might investigate early child labor laws or life insurance companies in the United States.

2. A subject related to your reading interests (biography, history, science fiction, detective stories) or one related to your favorite hobby or sport (music, dress design, mountain climbing, baseball).

3. A subject about which you now have an opinion but little actual information. Does capital punishment help prevent crime? Are children with high IQ's generally successful in later life? Do rapid readers retain more than slow readers?

4. A subject that has aroused your curiosity but that you have never had time or opportunity to investigate. In what ways are computers used in education today? Do sunspots actually affect the weather? How has the popularity of television affected book sales?

It is easier to remember that your paper has a purpose if you select a topic that ties in with one of your current interests.

Limiting the Topic

As soon as you know what general subject area you would like to concentrate on, think about finding a specific topic within that area that can be treated adequately and profitably in a paper of the assigned length. Keep these considerations in mind when you are narrowing your topic:

1. **Length of the reference paper.** An undergraduate reference paper is not expected to be the last word on a topic, but it must be more than a disconnected listing of commonplace facts or a superficial summary of a complex topic. Limit your topic enough so that your treatment of it can be reasonably thorough. The danger of selecting a topic that is too narrow is smaller than the danger of choosing one that is too broad and lacks focus. (See 18.1, Examining a Situation for Possible Subjects.)

2. **Availability of source material.** Before you begin to read and take notes, find out whether the more important books and periodicals that you will need are available in your college library. Since half a dozen or more sources are usually required for a reference paper, you should be certain that enough material is available before you begin your research.

3. **Complexity of the source material.** For some subjects (chemical structures of synthetic rubber, for example), the available material may be too technical for a general reader to understand — and perhaps too complicated for you to interpret without a good deal of study. You will probably be better off, even in a technical area, with a topic of current general interest.

Here are some steps to take to help you determine your approach to your topic:

1. **Do some preliminary reading.** Spend a few hours reading background material in one or more general or special encyclopedias, in some magazine articles, and perhaps in newspaper articles, if your subject is of current interest and likely to be covered by the daily press.
2. **Check reference sources.** Look through the library card catalog and the guides to periodical literature to see how the general subject you have chosen may be broken down into smaller units. A broad subject like *aviation* might first be limited to *commercial aviation,* then to the *functions of the CAB,* and then still further to *recent safety measures enacted by the CAB.*
3. **Define your idea as precisely as possible.** Even though you probably still will not be able to make a final statement of the central or controlling idea of your paper, your preliminary reading should have given you a reasonably accurate idea of the focus of your paper. This will help give direction to your research, so that you won't later have to discard much material as useless.

30.2 Locating Appropriate Source Materials

One purpose of the research paper is to acquaint you with the resources of your library so that you can locate the information you need quickly and efficiently. On most subjects, the material in the library is so extensive and so varied in form (books, periodicals, encyclopedias, newspapers, pamphlets, microfilm) that to keep from being hopelessly lost you need to know something about the essential works in your subject, the methods used to index and catalog material, and the quickest way to obtain this information.

This section deals with library facilities and the various aids that will help you find the material for a reference paper. Librarians are always willing to help students with their research problems, but every student should also be willing to help the librarians, too, by showing some knowledge of the standard sources of reference.

30.2

Lib

The Library Card Catalog

The card catalog is an alphabetical card index of the items in the library. The cards, filed in drawers or trays, are located in the main reading room or other central spot. Most card catalogs, in addition to listing all books in the library, give the titles of periodicals (and indicate what copies the library has), encyclopedias, government publications, and other works.

Almost all books are listed alphabetically in three places in the card catalog of most libraries: by author, by subject, and by title. The cards issued by the Library of Congress, like those reproduced on page 427 for *The Family* by William J. Goode, are almost universally used for cataloging.

You can save yourself many hours of thumbing through books that are not relevant to your subject by learning to interpret and evaluate the information given in the card catalog. The subject card includes the following information (keyed to the circled numbers on the card):

1. **Subject.** The subject heading on the catalog card tells in general what the book is about. Here the general subject is marriage. Also listed on the card (in item 7) are the other subject headings under which the book is cataloged.
2. **Call number.** The call number in the upper left-hand corner tells where the book is located in the library. In most libraries, borrowers obtain books by filling out a slip with the call number, author, title, and the borrower's name and address. If you have access to the stacks, the call number will enable you to locate the book you are looking for.
3. **Author's name.** If you are already familiar with the subject you are investigating, the author's name may tell you whether the book is likely to be authoritative.
4. **Title and facts of publication.** The date of publication is sometimes an important clue to the usefulness of a book. For example, if you are looking for contemporary facts on marriage, you will not waste time examining this book.
5. **Number of pages, illustrations, height.** The number of pages in the book suggests how extensive its coverage is. This book is rather short — 118 pages of text. Notice, however, that it contains illustrations that may be useful. (The indication of height — 24 cm. — is for librarians.)
6. **Special information.** The catalog card indicates that the book contains a bibliography that might prove helpful in directing you to other sources. None of the books listed, however, would be later than 1964, the year in which this particular book was published.
7. **Other subject headings.** The list of other subject headings under which the book is cataloged may give you ideas of other subject areas to look under for more material on your topic, as well as provide a further clue to the contents of the book listed.
8. **Facts for librarians.** The information at the bottom of the catalog card — such as the Library of Congress card number (64-17074) — is generally for the use of librarians.

Review: Sample Library Catalog Cards

• Subject Card

      (1) MARRIAGE

(2) 301.42
   G647f **Goode, William Josiah.** (3)
      (4) The family [by] William J. Goode. Englewood Cliffs, N.J.,
      Prentice-Hall [1964]
      (5) viii, 120 p. illus. 24 cm. (Foundations of modern sociology series)
      (6) Bibliography: p. 118.

      (7) 1. Family. 2. Marriage. 3. Social change. I. Title.

                 301.42   64-17074
                                  MARC

      (8) Library of Congress

• Author Card

301.42
G647f **Goode, William Josiah.**
      The family [by] William J. Goode. Englewood Cliffs, N.J.,
      Prentice-Hall [1964]
      viii, 120 p. illus. 24 cm. (Foundations of modern sociology series)
      Bibliography: p. 118.

      1. Family. 2. Marriage. 3. Social change. I. Title.

                301.42   64-17074
                                  MARC

      Library of Congress

• Title Card

        The family.
301.42
G647f **Goode, William Josiah.**
      The family [by] William J. Goode. Englewood Cliffs, N.J.,
      Prentice-Hall [1964]
      viii, 120 p. illus. 24 cm. (Foundations of modern sociology series)
      Bibliography: p. 118.

      1. Family. 2. Marriage. 3. Social change. I. Title.

                301.42   64-17074
                                  MARC

      Library of Congress

30.2

Lib

See 30.3, page 432, Preparing the Working Bibliography, to see what information from the library catalog card should be included on your own bibliography card.

Some libraries have replaced traditional card catalogs with a file of microfiche transparencies, which can be used with simple machines that enlarge the material and display it on a screen. Microfiche entries will usually not give you as much information as a library catalog card, but you can still usually expect to find sources listed in three different ways, by author, by title, and by subject.

Trade Bibliographies

The bibliographies published for booksellers and librarians should be consulted to locate books that are not listed in the card catalog of your library or to learn if a book is still in print. The most important trade bibliographies are these:

> **Books in Print.** A listing by author and by title of books included in *Publishers' Trade List Annual,* which lists — by publisher — all books currently in print.
>
> **Cumulative Book Index.** Gives complete publication data on all books published in the English language, listing them by author and by title. Published monthly, with cumulative volumes issued periodically.
>
> **Paperbound Books in Print.** Especially useful since some important books are available *only* in paperback. Published monthly, with cumulative volumes issued three times a year.
>
> **Subject Guide to Books in Print.** An invaluable index to the titles listed in *Books in Print.*

Periodical Indexes

A great deal of essential material, particularly on current topics, is available only in periodicals, which may range from popular magazines and newspapers to technical journals and learned publications. This material is cataloged in various guides and indexes, some of them published monthly, others annually. Knowing how to use periodical indexes will not only simplify the task of research but will also enable you to make your reference paper more authoritative and up-to-date. Most libraries have lists of the periodicals they have which tell also where the periodicals are indexed.

Readers' Guide.   The most generally useful of all periodical guides is the *Readers' Guide to Periodical Literature,* which indexes the articles in more than 120 magazines of general interest. It is published monthly in paperbound volumes which are afterwards gathered in large cumulative volumes covering a year or more.

The entries in the *Readers' Guide* are listed alphabetically both by subject and by author. The abbreviations used in the listings —

Review: Sample Entries from the *Readers' Guide*

(1) **POWELL, Joseph L. Jr**
    Not-so-cool Jody Powell. C. Mohr. il pors N Y
    Times Mag p20-1+ My 15 '77 *

(2) **POWER resources**
    Energy (cont) Sci N 111:249 Ap 16 '77
    Nightmare life without fuel; Time essay. I.
    Asimov. Time 109:33 Ap 25 '77
    Permanent energy shortage. Progressive 41:5-6
    Ap '77
      See also
    Coal supply
    Energy policy

Conferences
    Opening the debate; Time Inc's energy con-
    ference. il Time 109:27-8+ Ap 25 '77

Conservation
    Adventures in alternate energy;
        Michael Hackleman: electric truck is wind-
        powered, too. E. Moran. il Pop Sci 210:
        78-9 Ap '77
    At the grass roots, a rush to save fuel. il
        U.S. News 82:17 My 2 '77
    Close to home. A. J. Mayer. il Newsweek 89:
        25-6 My 2 '77
    Energy management: a crisis in industry. H. L.
        Breckenridge. bibl f Intellect 105:352-4 Ap '77
    Job for energy misers. M. E. Marty. Chr Cent
        94:463 My 11 '77
    Moral equivalents and other bugle calls; Time
        essay. S. Kanfer. Time 109:25 My 2 '77
    Plugging the leaks. Sci Am 236:57-8 Ap '77
    Tale of two suburbs: near Chicago and outside
        Cologne. P. Delaney; B. Seaman. il Time 109:
        23-4 My 2 '77
      See also
    Energy policy

Economic aspects
    Economic impact; energy policy. M. Ruby and
        others. il Newsweek 89:20-2+ My 2 '77
    For some firms, there's a bonanza ahead. il
        U.S. News 82:30 My 9 '77
    Getting more energy. D. Pauly and others. il
        Newsweek 89:27-8 My 2 '77
    $1 trillion—the cost of meeting U.S. energy
        needs. il U.S. News 82:19-20 My 2 '77
    Will energy conservation throttle economic
        growth? with interview with J. R. Schlesinger.
        il Bus W p66-72+ Ap 25 '77

(3) **POWERS, Stefanie**
    Problems and pleasures of living together; in-
    terview. ed by I. Silden. pors Harp Baz 110:
    114-15+ My '77

• *Explanation*

Entry **1** is a *subject entry*. An article about Joseph L. (Jody) Powell, titled "Not-so-cool Jody Powell," written by C. Mohr and
illustrated with portraits, appears on pages 20–21 and is continued elsewhere in *The New York Times Magazine*, May 15,
1977.

Entry **2** is also a *subject entry*, followed by a list of titles on power
resources. This entry is subdivided into more specific topics,
and cross references to related subjects are also listed.

Entry **3** is an *author entry*, but because the article is an interview
with the "author," an editor's name is also listed.

30.2

Lib

for the titles of periodicals, the month of publication, and various facts about the article itself — are explained on the first page of each volume. On page 429 is a reproduction and explanation of three consecutive main entries from a monthly issue.

Other Periodical Indexes.   In locating sources for a reference paper you may find it useful to refer to one of the specialized periodical indexes listed below. Most of them appear annually; the year after the title shows when publication began. The indexes are listed alphabetically.

Applied Science and Technology Index (1913). Subject index to periodicals on science, technology, and related subjects.

Art Index (1929). Author and subject index for fine-arts periodicals and museum bulletins.

Bibliographic Index: A Cumulative Bibliography of Bibliographies (1938).

Biography Index: A Cumulative Index to Biographical Material in Books and Magazines (1946/47).

Book Review Digest (1905). Author, subject, and title index to published book reviews; gives extracts and exact references to sources.

Business Periodicals Index (1958). Subject index to periodicals on all phases of business, including particular industries and trades.

Catholic Periodical Index: A Guide to Catholic Magazines (1930).

Dramatic Index (1909 – 1949). Index to articles and illustrations concerning the American and English theater.

The Education Index (1929 – 1964). Author and subject index for educational periodicals, books, and pamphlets.

Humanities Index (1974). Author and subject index to periodicals from various countries; devoted to articles in the humanities; valuable supplement to the *Readers' Guide.*

Poole's Index to Periodical Literature (1802 – 1881). Subject index to American and English periodicals, many of which are no longer published but are still important; precedes coverage of *Readers' Guide.*

Public Affairs Information Service (1915). Subject index to books, periodicals, pamphlets, and other material on economics, government, and other public affairs.

Social Sciences and Humanities Index (1907 – 1974). Author and subject index to periodicals from various countries; devoted chiefly to the humanities and social sciences; formerly titled *International Index to Periodicals;* now superseded by two separate indexes.

Social Sciences Index (1974). Author and subject index to periodicals focusing on the social sciences; supplements *Readers' Guide.*

United States Government Publications Monthly Catalog (1895). Lists various publications of the government in all fields.

Special Indexes

The New York Times Index. Monthly index to articles apppearing in *The New York Times,* with annual volumes. Since it gives the dates of events, speeches, and important documents, this index is helpful for finding articles of general interest in local papers, as well.

Ulrich's International Periodical Directory. Classifies American and foreign periodicals by subject area and tells which periodical index covers them.

Vertical File Index: A Subject and Title Index to Selected Pamphlet Material. Describes each pamphlet listed, tells how to purchase it, and lists the price.

Encyclopedias

The following general encyclopedias are authoritative and include many bibliographies and cross-references. All are regularly revised; several are supplemented annually with yearbooks.

Chamber's Encyclopaedia
Collier's Encyclopedia
Columbia Encyclopedia
Encyclopaedia Britannica
Encyclopedia Americana

Many subject areas, from art to science, are covered by reference works that go into more detail than general encyclopedias, and their coverage is more specialized. You should be able to find most of these by browsing in the reference room of your library. The librarian will also be able to tell you what reference works exist for your area of interest.

Yearbooks and Annuals

The following annuals provide up-to-date facts and figures on a wide variety of subjects, particularly those of current interest.

Information Please Almanac.

Social Work Year Book. Soçial work and related fields.

The Statesman's Year-Book: Statistical and Historical Annual of the States of the World, 1864 — . Historical and statistical events throughout the world.

The World Almanac and Book of Facts. This is one general reference that any student can afford to own, and one that anyone with a serious interest in current affairs can hardly afford to be without. The index is in the front of each volume.

Yearbook of the United Nations. Activities of the United Nations.

30.2

Lib

Guides to Reference Materials

Many other specialized reference works can be found by consulting the following guides:

Barton, Mary N., comp. *Reference Books: A Brief Guide for Students and Other Users of the Library.*

Murphey, Robert W. *How and Where to Look It Up.*
The Reader's Adviser: A Layman's Guide to Literature.
Shores, Louis. *Basic Reference Sources: An Introduction to Materials and Methods.*

Walford, Arthur J., ed. *Guide to Reference Material.*

Winchell, Constance M. *Guide to Reference Books.*

30.3 Preparing the Working Bibliography

A working bibliography is a list of the books, magazine articles, and other published works that you intend to consult when gathering material for your reference paper. The number of references you should collect will depend on the nature of the assignment, but it is always best to begin with more than you will probably need. If your working bibliography includes only a bare minimum of sources, you will probably have to take time later to find more: a book you want from the library may already be out on loan; one article on your list may prove to be too technical; another may merely repeat material you have already collected.

Whether your initial bibliography contains many sources or relatively few, you will probably want to add others as you get into your research and find new avenues you want to explore.

Some instructors may recommend a special system for maintaining a working bibliography and for taking notes. The system recommended below is widely used, and it is convenient.

Each entry in your working bibliography should be written on a separate card, either a 3-by-5 inch or 4-by-6 inch. With only one reference on each, cards can be rearranged quickly for alphabetizing; new ones can be inserted in the proper places and useless ones discarded. You may want to use 3-by-5 cards for the working bibliography and 4-by-6 cards for taking notes, since the larger cards will obviously hold more data and will also be readily distinguishable from your bibliography cards.

Bibliography cards for different types of references are illustrated on page 434. Each card should include all the facts you will need to identify the reference and obtain it from the library. It should also have all the information you will need in preparing the final bibliography. The punctuation suggested here is a standard form for bibliographies (see page 454):

1. **Author's name,** with the last name first, followed by a period. If the book is edited, use the editor's name, followed by a comma, followed by *ed.* If the article or pamphlet is unsigned, write the title first on the card.

2. **Title of the book,** underlined and followed by a period, or title of the article, in quotation marks and followed by a period.

3. **Facts of publication:**

   a) **For a book:** the city of publication, followed by a colon; the name of the publisher, followed by a comma; and the date, followed by a period. Former practice often left out the publisher's name, and usage is still divided. However, unless you are told otherwise, it's always safe to include it.

   b) **For a magazine article:** the name of the magazine, underlined and followed by a comma; the date of the issue, followed by a comma; and the pages covered by the article, preceded by *pp.* and followed by a period.

   c) **For a journal article:** the name of the journal, underlined and followed by a comma; the volume number in Arabic numbers; the date, in parentheses, followed by a comma; the page numbers, without *p.* or *pp.,* followed by a period.

   d) **For a newspaper article:** the name of the newspaper, underlined and followed by a comma; the date, followed by a comma; the section number, followed by a comma; the page on which the story appeared, followed by a comma; the column number, followed by a period.

4. **Library call number,** or the location of a reference work in the library. This information, placed in the upper left-hand corner, should be written just as it appears in the card catalog, so that you can relocate the reference if the need arises. See also 30.8, page 453, The Bibliography.

5. **Index number,** a number or code that you assign to the work, should be placed in the upper right-hand corner of the card. This same number should be used on any note cards you make that refer to this source.

The difference between a magazine and a journal is usually apparent from their content and format. Magazines generally have a wide public appeal and are published weekly or monthly, with dates corresponding to the issue. Each issue begins with page 1. Journals are usually of more limited appeal (e.g., *Journal of Physics*); they are often published less frequently than magazines (many are published quarterly), and the date does not always correspond to the actual date of issue ("Autumn" could be issued

30.3

Res

Review: Sample Bibliography Cards

- **For Book by One Author**

  785.09
  E 94

  1

  Ewen, David. *Orchestral Music: Its Story Told Through the Lives and Works of Its Foremost Composers*.

  New York : Franklin Watts, Inc. 1973.

- **For a Book, Edited**

  301.451
  L 616

  2

  Lerner, Gerda, ed. *Black Women in White America: A Documentary History*.

  New York: Random House. Pantheon Books, 1972.

- **For a Signed Article in an Encyclopedia**

  Reference
  Room
  Shelf 12

  3

  S [tout], G [eorge] L. "Conservation of Paintings." *Encyclopedia Brittanica*. Chicago : Encyclopedia Brittanica, Inc., 1967. Vol. 17, 75–79.

- **For a Magazine Article**

  051
  For
  v. 90

  4

  McQuade, Walter. "Management Problems Enter the Picture at Art Museums." *Fortune*, July 1974, pp 100–103, 169, 173.

- **For a Journal Article**

  Periodical
  desk

  5

  Pearsall, Robert Brainerd. "The Presiding Tropes of Emily Brontë." *College English*, 27 (January 1966), 266–273.

- **For an Unsigned Newspaper Article**

  Periodical
  desk

  6

  "Excerpts from Watergate — related evidence." *Chicago Sun Times*, July 12, 1974, p. 8, Col. 1.

434

between September and November). Therefore the volume and issue number are more important, especially since pagination is usually continuous throughout an entire volume (e.g., Volume 1, number 2, might begin on page 233).

30.4 Evaluating Your Material

Since writing a reference paper is in part an exercise in critical judgment, it is important that you learn to evaluate the sources you use. Try to find and use the most informative books and the most authoritative material available to you.

Facts to Consider in Evaluating

Writers engaged in writing their first reference papers on unfamiliar subjects are not expected to know offhand that a work by author A is wholly worthless or that author B is considered the foremost authority on the subject. They can, however, arrive at a fairly accurate estimate of their sources by considering these facts:

1. **Date of publication.** If your subject is one for which recent facts are important, see that the sources are up to date. The most recent edition of a book or an encyclopedia will generally be more useful and authoritative than an earlier one.
2. **Completeness.** With magazine articles, it is better to read the original article as it was printed in full instead of a condensation or reprint of it. Similarly, books are often more thorough than articles, although you will want to be sure that the book's author is reputable. Check the bibliographies in the books you look at for sources often referred to. Encyclopedias should usually be used only as a place to start your search for information.
3. **Facts and opinions.** Distinguish carefully between an author's facts and opinions. Label the opinions "So-and-so thinks that. . . ." In general, pay more attention to *facts* (unless your paper is about various opinions), since you will need facts to support your own opinions.
4. **Objectivity of the source.** A book or an article based in large part upon an author's opinions or biases — particularly when the subject is controversial — should not be used as your sole authority on the matter. Read material that is diverse before reaching a conclusion.

30.4

Res

When you are in doubt about the reliability of a source, a librarian or your instructor may be able to give you advice. Reviews in the more specialized journals evaluate books in their own fields. *Book*

Review Digest may also prove helpful. Taking the time to read reviews of books may help you judge their reliability. And, of course, after you have worked a while on your subject, you will be in a better position to evaluate the material yourself.

30.5 Taking Notes

Accurate and full notes are essential for writing a good reference paper. You can save time when taking notes if you approach the problem efficiently. Don't try to take down everything you read; instead, spend a little time looking over the book, the article, or the pamphlet to see if it contains the information you want. If you have given enough thought to formulating and narrowing your topic, you will have a pretty clear idea of what you are looking for.

When examining a book, look first at the index and the table of contents to see in what sections your subject is treated. See also if there are any tables, graphs, bibliographies, or further references that might be useful. Skim each chapter to find out what it covers. Then go over it again carefully, taking the notes you will need.

Notes should be taken on either 3-by-5 inch or 4-by-6 inch cards so that you can later arrange the material according to the plan of your paper. It is usually a waste of effort to try to take notes in numbered outline form since you probably won't know the final plan of your paper until you have finished your research. What is important is to make each note card accurate, clearly written, and clearly labeled. Each note card should contain these essential parts, as illustrated by the sample cards shown on page 438.

1. The **heading** at the top of the card, showing what material it contains.
2. The **index number** to identify the source and **page number,** accurately noted.
3. The **content,** facts or opinions (summarized in your own words or directly quoted) accurately recorded.

Notes that cannot be readily interpreted a week or a month after they have been written are obviously of little use; so too are incomplete or carelessly written notes. You can avoid a good deal of tedious, unnecessary work, including rereading and rechecking, by following these simple rules:

1. Use *one side* of each card only. Your material will then be easier to classify and arrange, and you won't run the risk of overlooking a statement on the back of a card.

2. Include only *one major point* or a few closely related facts from the same source on a single card. If the information is too extensive to write on one side of a card, use two or three cards and number them in sequence.
3. Get all the information *accurately* the first time you consult a source so that you won't have to make extra trips to the library.
4. Put all *direct quotations* in quotation marks. This includes all statements, single sentences, and phrases that you copy word for word from any source. If you omit a word or words in a direct quotation use ellipsis periods (. . .) to indicate the omission (14.2). If you are paraphrasing the source, state the idea in your own language. (See 30.8, page 446, Plagiarism.)
5. Write your notes in ink (penciled notes may become blurred with frequent handling) so that you won't have to recopy them. When you use abbreviations, be sure that you will know later on what they mean.

It isn't necessary to write out all your notes in complete sentences; practical shortcuts such as the omission of *a, the, was,* and other such words are good for summarizing material. If the method you use for taking notes in lecture courses or on your textbooks has proved successful, use it also for your reference paper.

Accurate notes are one of the chief tools of scholarship. Early and careful practice in taking them is excellent training that may be useful in later work.

30.6 Planning the Paper

The central or controlling purpose of a reference paper should be clear in your mind long before you have finished investigating all your resources. You know, for instance, whether you are trying to reach a conclusion about two opposing viewpoints or whether you are trying to explain an event or situation. When you have gathered a sufficient amount of material to put your topic in focus, it is time to formulate a thesis sentence (18.1, page 218) that will state your controlling purpose and to outline the order in which you will develop your material.

30.6

Examining and Arranging Your Notes

First read through all your notes to refresh your memory and determine the general order in which you will arrange your material. Then arrange the notes in piles, grouping together all the notes on a particular aspect of your subject. The headings at the top of each

Review: Sample Note Cards

- **Direct Quote**

  1

  Origins of Parliament   *Maurois*

  Hist. of Eng., 146

  "The convoking of the different 'Estates' of a Kingdom (military, priestly and plebian), in order to obtain their consent to taxation, was not peculiar to England in the fourteenth century."

- **Summarized Material**

  2

  Incidence of neurosis among the poor

  Harrington
  Other Amer., 119

  Though there is a myth that the richer you are the more neurotic you are likely to be, the truth is just the opposite: poor people suffer from mental illness more often than people in any other social class.

- **Statistical Data**

  3

  Enrollment in institutions of higher education (1000's)   *Stat. Abstract*
  1979   136

	1950	1960	1970	1975	1977
Total	2659	3216	7136	9023	9589
Public	1355	1832	5112	6838	7275
Private	1304	1384	2024	2185	2314

Review: An Original Source and Sample Notes

Our present chronological techniques make it possible to determine, directly or indirectly, the real age of many rocks and fossils. The ancient dream of natural scientists, especially of geologists and paleontologists, has been fulfilled: when they dig up a saurian, they can now say how many millions of years ago the animal walked the earth. When they find a fossil in coal, they can tell when that particular seam was laid down.

In 1650, Archbishop James Usher reckoned that the creation of the world had taken place at the stroke of nine o'clock on Sunday morning, October 23, in the year 4004 B.C. The scientists of the nineteenth century, a good deal more realistic, estimated the age of the earth, on the basis of the fossil record, as about 100 million years. Modern researchers have assigned an age of more than 4 billion years to some samples of rock.

For the scientist who knows how to read them, the strata of the earth's crust and the fossils locked within them represent an inexhaustible potential source of information. In deserts, the forces of weathering have exposed hundreds of layers, among them deep-lying and very ancient ones that date back to the early days of the earth's evolution. Normally, such strata lie many thousands of feet beneath the surface. Thus the desert affords special opportunities for learning about the evolution of our planet. But before we can understand the earth's past and future we must take up the question of how this planet, its atmosphere, and the life upon it came into being in the first place. — Uwe George, *In the Deserts of This Earth*.

• *Notes Taken for a Paper on Methods of Dating Fossils*

For such a paper, quick notes on various efforts at dating might be sufficient:

Dating at various times

George
~~*In the Deserts*~~ ...

present methods – can determine real age of
rocks and fossils
1,650 – Archbishop Usher dated creation – 9 a.m.,
– Sunday, Oct. 23, 4004 B.C.
19th century – earth about 100 million years
old now – more than 4 billion years

30.6

Plan

For such a paper, an actual quotation might be useful:

Deserts, as source of
information

George
In the Deserts...

p. 39 "In deserts, the forces of weathering
have exposed hundreds of layers, among
them deep-lying and very ancient ones
that date back to the early days of the
earth's evolution.... Thus the desert
affords special opportunities for learning
about the evolution of our planet."

card will be useful in helping you sort and arrange your material. At this stage you should note any gaps in your material that will have to be filled in with further reading before you start your first draft.

If any of the notes you have taken no longer seem relevant to your purpose in writing, put them aside in a tentative discard pile. Almost anyone engaged in research finds that a good deal of carefully recorded material has to be discarded. Don't succumb to the temptation to include material that has no bearing on your thesis simply because it is interesting or because you worked hard to find it.

Making a Preliminary Outline

When you have arranged your note cards to your satisfaction, state the central idea of your paper in a thesis sentence (not in two or more sentences nor in the form of a question). Then make a rough outline showing the order in which you intend to present your material. Each point in the outline should contribute in some way to the development of your central idea or thesis. Often your instructor will want to see your working outline before you go much further with the work. To crystallize your plan and to make it possible for your instructor to examine it and make suggestions, you should follow standard outline form. At this stage a topic outline is generally sufficient; if necessary, you can later expand the entries into complete sentences. (See 20, Organizing Your Material, for a discussion of outlining and outline form.)

Neither your preliminary outline nor your thesis sentence needs to be considered as final. It is better, in fact, to make a reasonably flexible outline so that you can make whatever changes seem desirable as you write and revise your first draft.

30.7 Writing the First Draft

A reference paper should represent your writing at its best – in organization, sentence structure, wording, and emphasis. The most convincing proof that you have actually learned something new from your research is the way you have evaluated, organized, and expressed your material. Instructions concerning the proper form of endnotes and bibliography (30.8) should be followed to the letter. The paper should be as neat as you can possibly make it, with each part in its proper order and no errors in spelling or punctuation.

30.7

Draft

Make certain that you are thoroughly familiar with your material before you begin to write. You should have the information on your note cards so well in mind that you can write rapidly and with confidence once you start. For this reason, it is a good idea to review your notes once more just before you begin writing.

This draft should be written in the same way you would write the first draft of any other important assignment (as discussed in 21, Writing the First Draft). Keep a running documentation on a separate page, as a first draft of your endnotes.

If a passage seems to need more facts or further documentation, don't interrupt your writing to do the necessary additional research. Put a question mark or some other notation in the margin, continue with your writing, and look up the material after you have finished the first draft.

Most reference papers are written in a rather formal, impersonal style. Usually there's no need to refer to yourself at all, but if you do, the reference should be brief. (It's also better to say "I" than to use "the writer" or other third-person references.) Remember, however, that impersonal writing does not have to be flat or lifeless. The information itself will provide the interest if you express it clearly and directly.

30.8 Documenting the Paper

Any paper based on the writing of others should acknowledge each and every source from which an idea or statement is taken. In a reference paper the acknowledgments are made by endnotes — notes on a separate page at the end of the paper (numbered in the way numbers appear in the text) that show exactly where the information was obtained. The method of documentation recommended by most instructors in English and the humanities is described on pages 448–455 and illustrated in the student papers beginning on page 458. (Your instructor will tell you where to put your notes, but if you are in doubt, a separate page at the end is always correct.)

Where Documentation Is Needed

When drawing on the work of another writer or researcher, you owe him or her the courtesy of giving credit where credit is due. You also owe your *readers* the courtesy of providing the sources of your information so that they can judge them for themselves and find additional information, if more is desired. Failure to document borrowed information is at best carelessness; at worst, it is plagiarism, which means offering material written by someone else as your own work (see page 446). Documentation is essential in two situations:

1. **After direct quotations.** Each statement taken word for word from a printed source should have a reference number at the end of the quotation and be properly identified in an endnote. The only exceptions to this rule are well-known expressions, such as familiar Biblical quotations ("Blessed are the poor"), famous lines from literature ("Something is rotten in the state of Denmark"), and proverbs ("A bird in the hand is worth two in the bush").

2. **After all important statements of fact or opinion taken from written sources and expressed in your own words.** Facts include figures, dates, scientific data, and descriptions of events and situations about which you have no firsthand knowledge, such as what happened at a session of the United Nations, how coffee is cultivated in Brazil, or the role of Madagascar in World War II. Opinions and interpretations that are not actually your own would include statements such as one writer's reasons for the popularity of baseball in the United States, or an opinion on foreign policy from a newspaper editorial.

In some publications, notes are also used for comments or additional information that the writer does not wish to include in the text. In freshman research papers, however, this practice should be kept to a minimum; if a statement is worth making, it usually belongs in the text.

Documentation is *not* needed for statements that would pass without question. These include obvious facts ("Certain chemicals cannot be used in the preservation of foods in the United States"), matters of common knowledge ("Hiroshima was devastated by an atomic bomb in August 1945"), general statements, and expressions of the writer's own opinion ("The medical and biological sciences have made unbelievable progress in the last twenty years").

If you have a full page in your draft without any references, you should probably check it again to see if any documentation is needed. A great many endnotes for a single page may indicate that some of the material could better be combined or rephrased to eliminate unnecessary references.

30.8

Doc

The following sections discuss some things to consider in integrating documented material into the text of your paper.

Using Direct Quotations

In incorporating material from sources into your research paper, you will often have to decide whether to quote directly or to restate the material in your own words. In general, direct quotations are preferable only in these situations:

1. **Important statements of information, opinion, or policy.** Whenever the *exact* wording of a statement is crucial in its interpretation, it should be quoted in full:

> President Kennedy told Khrushchev that Russia could not expect to spread Communism abroad without opposition: "What your government believes is its own business; what it does in the world is the world's business."[2]

2. **Interpretations of literary works.** When a statement or opinion in your paper is based on a passage in a poem, essay, short story, novel, or play, quote from the passage so that the reader can see the basis for your interpretation:

> The closing passages of *Moby Dick* also suggest that the whale represents some omnipotent force hostile to man. Ishmael says that Moby Dick rushed at the ship with a "predestinating head," and that "retribution, swift vengeance, external malice were in his aspect . . . in spite of all mortal man could do."[1]

When you are writing a paper that requires frequent references to a literary work, however, you need to note the edition of the text you are using only once, the first time you use a quotation. Thereafter, you may identify quotations by giving (immediately after the quotation, in parentheses) the page numbers for fiction; the line numbers for poetry; the act and scene for drama (followed by the line numbers if the play is in verse):

> Man, who once stood at the center of the universe, confident that he was the end of Creation and could claim kinship with the angels, is now—to use the playwright's favorite figure—shrouded in a "mist" that isolates him from God and shuts off all his questioning about the problems of ultimate order. As Webster has Bosola say of the Cardinal in *The Duchess of Malfi,*
>
>> Thou, which stood'st like a huge pyramid
>> Begun upon a large and ample base,
>> Shalt end in a little point, a kind of nothing. (V.v.76–78)

3. **Distinctive phrasing.** If your source states some idea or opinion in a particularly forceful or original way that would be weakened by paraphrasing, quote the exact words:

> Russell does not believe that our age lacks great ideas because religion has declined: "We are suffering not from the decay of theological beliefs but from the loss of solitude."[13]

A quotation should be smoothly integrated into the text of your paper. Even though its source is given in an endnote, it should be preceded by some brief introductory remark like "one leading educator recently said that . . ."; "as Edmund Wilson points out . . ."; "an editorial in the *Chicago Tribune* argued that. . . ." The best way to learn about integrating quotations in your own work is to observe how professional writers use quotations, as in the examples below.

> Mario Pei, one of our most distinguished students of the misuse of language, has also noted the trend toward non-language. Dr. Pei has given us a new coinage for obfuscation by government: he calls this form of non-language "true weasel words," and he states, in an article titled "The American Language in the Early '70's," "The four prime areas for weasel words are, as usual, the military, government, politics, and commercial advertising." Pei's insight is precise: "The real military contribution to language," he says,
>
>> comes from the higher echelons. Here we find not only those reprehensible and often deplored terms, *kill ratio* and *body count.* . . . — Robert F. Drinan, "The Rhetoric of Peace," *College Composition and Communication*
>
> In two essays included in his much-acclaimed recent book, *Language and Silence,* George Steiner describes several ways in which, in his view, "A language shows that it has in it the germ of dissolution.":
>
>> Actions of the mind that were once spontaneous become mechanical, frozen habits (dead metaphors, stock similes, slogans). Words grow longer and more ambiguous. . . . — Ronald Gross, "On Language Pollution," *Etc.*

See 14.1, Quotation Marks Around Quoted Material, for a discussion of ways to set up long and short quotations from both prose and poetry.

Paraphrasing

Although a reference paper relies heavily on the writings of others, it should not consist simply of a long string of word-for-word quotations from sources. Like any other paper, it should represent your own characteristic style. Except in the situations described in the preceding section, information from a source should ordinarily be *paraphrased*—restated or summarized in your own words. Otherwise your paper will have a jumbled, patchwork effect that may distract or confuse the reader. Compare the two following passages for effectiveness:

30.8

Doc

> TOO MANY DIRECT QUOTATIONS: Authorities disagree about the dating of these pyramids. Professor Sheldon Muncie says, "The preponderance of evidence collected by investigators in recent years points to a date no earlier than 1300 A.D. for the construction of the lowest level"[1] Professor William Price basically agrees with him:

"Bricks of this type were not used in the surrounding areas until the late fourteenth century."[2] But Robert McCall found that "The radiocarbon readings are completely out of line with the standard textbook dates; the original substructure is at least 700 years older than Muncie's earliest estimate."[3]

PARAPHRASE: Authorities disagree about the dating of the pyramids. Professors Sheldon Muncie and William Price concluded, on the basis of the type of brick used and other evidence, that they were begun no earlier than the fourteenth century.[1] But Robert McCall's radiocarbon readings indicate a date earlier than 600 A.D.[2]

The best way to write a smooth paraphrase is to absorb the content of the source passage and then, without looking at it, to write its information down in your own words. When you have finished, you should check it for accuracy and any unconscious borrowing of phrases and sentences. Remember that even though the words are your own, the information or ideas are not; you will still have to acknowledge the source.

Plagiarism

Most writers know that copying another's work word for word without giving the author credit is considered plagiarism. But they often assume that this practice is frowned on only when long passages are involved—whole pages or paragraphs. Consequently, they feel free to copy phrases and sentences without using quotation marks or acknowledgments. Actually, *any uncredited use* of another's information or ideas is plagiarism whether the wording is changed or not. Under the mistaken notion that uncredited paraphrasing is acceptable, students often reproduce sources almost exactly, changing only a word here and there. An honest paraphrase, however, is one in which the *ideas* of the source are stated in the writer's *own words,* and it is still necessary to credit the source. The following examples show the difference between genuine paraphrase and plagiarism of source material:

ORIGINAL SOURCE (from Alexis de Tocqueville, *Democracy in America,* 1, 248–249): No political form has hitherto been discovered that is equally favorable to the prosperity and the development of all the classes into which society is divided. These classes continue to form, as it were, so many distinct communities in the same nation; and experience has shown that it is not less dangerous to place the fate of these classes exclusively in the hands of any one of them than it is to make one people the arbiter of the destiny of another. When the rich alone govern, the interest of the poor is always endangered; and when the poor make the laws, that of the rich incurs very serious risks. The advantage of democracy does not consist, therefore, as has sometimes been asserted, in favoring the prosperity of all, but simply in contributing to the well-being of the greatest number.

STUDENT VERSION A: Hitherto no one has found a political form that favors equally the prosperity and development of all the different classes of society. Experience has shown that it is just as dangerous to place the fate of these classes in the hands of one class as to let one nation dictate the destiny of another. Government by the rich endangers the poor; and the poor make laws that often harm the interests of the rich. Therefore, the advantage of democracy does not consist in raising general prosperity, but simply in adding to the well-being of the majority.

Plagiarism. By omitting any reference to De Tocqueville, the writer implies that these ideas are his or her own. In organization the paragraph follows the source very closely — same order of ideas, same number and structure of sentences. Many of the words and phrases are lifted bodily from the source without quotation marks to indicate that they are not the writer's. In other cases, word order has been simply rearranged and synonyms substituted (*found* for *discovered, nation* for *one people, adding* for *contributing, majority* for *greatest number*).

VERSION B: De Tocqueville says that no form of government in history has been uniformly beneficial to all classes of society. He maintains that both the rich and the poor, when in control of the government, pass laws favorable to their class and repressive toward the other. According to him, the virtue of a democracy is that it benefits the majority, not that it benefits the whole.[1]

Paraphrase. The writer admits, both in the text and in a footnote, that the ideas in the paragraph are De Tocqueville's. He states them in his or her own words and does not slavishly follow the source. Quotation marks are unnecessary, since none of the phrases are De Tocqueville's.

ORIGINAL SOURCE (from Lionel Trilling, "F. Scott Fitzgerald," *The Liberal Imagination,* p. 42): Thus, *The Great Gatsby* has its interest as a record of contemporary manners, but this might only have served to date it, did not Fitzgerald take the given moment of history as something more than a mere circumstance, did he not, in the manner of the great French novelists of nineteenth century, seize the given moment as a moral fact. . . . For Gatsby, divided between power and dream, comes inevitably to stand for America itself.

30.8

Doc

VERSION A: Of course the one thing that makes *The Great Gatsby* interesting is its picture of the life of the twenties, but if it were only this it would by now be out of date. Instead, like the great French novelists, Fitzgerald made the particular moment a moral symbol. Gatsby, the main character, divided between power and dream, represents the American dilemma.

Plagiarism. This version does not reproduce the source as closely as Version A of the De Tocqueville passage; it more subtly plagiarizes the original. Again, the writer gives no indication that the ideas expressed are not his or her own. The wording, except for "divided between power and dream," is largely original. The comparison between Fitzgerald and the great French novelists is not original, and implies a critical breadth suspiciously beyond the range of most undergraduate writers.

VERSION B: As Lionel Trilling points out, *The Great Gatsby* is much more than a record of the manners of the twenties. In miniature, Gatsby represents America, "divided between power and dream."[1]

Paraphrase. The writer credits Trilling as the originator of the ideas he presents. He also puts quotation marks around the one phrase he uses verbatim.

Endnote Substance

Generally, each endnote should contain at least four essential facts (the information a reader would need to locate the source): the author's name, the title of the work, the facts of publication (publisher, place, and date), and the specific page or pages of the source used.

Endnote Form

Practices in note form vary, chiefly in punctuation and kinds of abbreviations. This section follows the form recommended by the *MLA Handbook* of the Modern Language Association, the form most often used in academic writing in the humanities. Alternative systems are frequently used in scientific papers (see p. 453). Follow carefully any changes your instructor may want you to make in the form described here.

In the text of the paper, the endnote number is placed *at the end of the quotation or statement* for which the source is being given; it is never placed before the borrowed material. The number is raised slightly above the line and is placed outside the end punctuation of the statement to which it refers: ". . . nearly 400,000 in 1953."[13] Endnote numbers are generally consecutive throughout the paper in Arabic numerals beginning with 1.

The notes themselves should appear at the end of the paper on a separate page entitled *Notes*. (Some instructors may prefer footnotes.) Indent the first line of each note and begin with its number, raised, followed by a space before the first word of the note. Double space within and between notes. You may number the first page of notes and you must number any subsequent pages. See the endnotes of the sample papers on pp. 465 and 479.

Sample Endnotes

Books

First reference. Study the sample notes below, noting the order of the information and the punctuation used between the elements. The first time you refer to a book in a note, include as much of the information as is relevant in each case. However, if the author's full name has been given in the text, it need not be repeated in the endnote. This is sometimes called a *split note.*

One author:

¹ Walter Gellhorn, <u>American Rights: The Constitution in Action</u> (New York: Macmillan, 1960), p. 178.

Two or three authors:

² Giles W. Gray and Claude M. Wise, <u>The Bases of Speech</u>, 3rd ed. (New York: Harper, 1959), p. 322.

More than three authors:

³ Walter Blair and others, <u>The Literature of the United States</u>, 3rd ed. (Glenview, Ill.: Scott, Foresman, 1966), I, 80.

[The Latin abbreviation *et al.* may be used instead of *and others.*]

An edited book:

⁴ <u>Letters of Noah Webster</u>, ed. Harry R. Warfel (New York: Library Publishers, 1954), p. 352.

[If the editor's name is more relevant to the citation than the author's, put that name at the beginning of the footnote: Harry R. Warfel, ed., *Letters of Noah Webster.*]

An article in an edited book of selections written by various authors:

⁵ Harry Levin, "Literature as an Institution," in <u>Literary Opinion in America</u>, ed. Morton Dauwen Zabel (New York: Harper, 1951), pp. 658–59.

A translated book:

⁶ Paul Valery, <u>Monsieur Teste</u>, trans. Jackson Mathews (New York: Knopf, 1947), p. 47.

A book for which no author is given:

⁷ <u>A Manual of Style</u>, 12th ed. (Chicago: Univ. of Chicago Press, 1969), p. 27.

A revised edition:

⁸ James C. Coleman, <u>Abnormal Psychology and Modern Life</u>, 5th ed. (Glenview, Ill.: Scott, Foresman, 1976), pp. 254–55.

30.8

Notes

A multi-volume work, all volumes published in the same year:

⁹ Walter Blair and others, The Literature of the United States,
3rd ed. (Glenview, Ill.: Scott, Foresman, 1966), I, 80.

[Note that if the note includes a volume number, the abbreviation *p.* or
pp. is omitted.]

A multi-volume work, the volumes published in different years:

¹⁰ Harold Child, "Jane Austen," in The Cambridge History of English Literature, ed. A. W. Ward and A. T. Waller, XII (London:
Cambridge Univ. Press, 1914), 231–33.

[The volume number here precedes the facts of publication.]

A book that is part of a series:

¹¹ David Fowler, Piers the Plowman, Univ. of Washington Publications in Lang. and Lit., 16 (Seattle: Univ. of Washington Press,
1961), p. 23.

Subsequent references. For subsequent references to the same
work that do not immediately follow the original reference, a short
form should be used: the author's last name only, if not more than
one work by the same author is being cited, and the page number:

¹² Gellhorn, p. 150.

If two sources by the same author have been previously cited,
the short form must also include the title, to make clear which
work the note re-refers to. A shortened form of the title may be
used:

¹³ Gellhorn, American Rights. p. 150.

If the book has no author, the title should be used:

¹⁴ A Manual of Style, p. 92.

Magazine, Journal, and Newspaper Articles

Endnotes for magazine and newspaper articles are handled in
much the same way. The volume number is used in noting an
article from a scholarly journal. The complete date is used for
newspapers and weekly or monthly magazines.

Signed article in a magazine:

¹⁵ Reed Whittemore, "The Newspeak Generation," Harper's, Feb.
1977, p. 20.

Unsigned article in a magazine:

¹⁶ "How to Save Energy," Newsweek, 18 April 1977, p. 72.

Article in a scholarly journal:

  17 Stewart Justman, "Mass Communication and Tautology," College English, 38 (1977), 635.

[The month is omitted for journals paged continuously throughout the volume. The abbreviation *p.* or *pp.* is omitted if the volume number is given.]

Signed article in a newspaper:

  18 Edward Cowan, "Mapping Out a National Energy Policy," New York Times, 10 April 1977, Sec. 3, p. 1.

[The edition of the newspaper is sometimes given. Locate newspaper articles by column, if possible. Unsigned articles are handled in the same way as those in magazines.]

  Subsequent references to articles in periodicals may be shortened in the same way as those for books (see p. 450).

Other Sources

These sample entries will help you arrive at a form for various other source material you may use.

Encyclopedia articles:

  19 Donald Culross Peattie, "Trees of North America," Encyclopedia Americana, 1973 ed., XXVII, 36.

[If the article is unsigned, begin with the title. Notice that the volume number is given in Roman numerals, and that the abbreviation *p.* or *pp.* is omitted.]

Biblical citations:

  20 Matt. 6:26-30.

[The abbreviation is suitable in notes, but not in the text. Often the identification is given in parentheses immediately following the quotation, rather than in an endnote, and very familiar quotations, such as "Thou shalt not steal," are not noted.]

Material at second hand:

  21 Ronald Bryden, "Pseudo-Event," New Statesman, 4 Oct. 1963, p. 460, in The Deputy Reader: Studies in Moral Responsibility, ed, D. B. Schmidt and E. R. Schmidt (Glenview, Ill.: Scott, Foresman, 1965), p. 78.

[Both the original source and the source from which the material was taken are given.]

Bulletins and pamphlets:

  22 U.S. Department of Labor, Occupational Outlook Handbook, 1974–75 Edition, Bulletin 1985 (Washington, D.C.: GPO, 1974), p. 40.

30.8

Notes

Unpublished dissertations and theses:

    23 Wallace Joseph Smith, "The Fur Trade in Colonial Pennsylvania," Diss. Univ. of Washington 1950, p. 19.

[Titles of unpublished works are enclosed in quotation marks.]

Interview:

    24 Personal interview with John X. Sawyer, Mayor, Santa Fe, New Mexico, 1 April 1980.

Abbreviations in Endnotes

Standard abbreviations such as those for states *(Menasha, Wis.; Norwood, Mass.)* are commonly used in notes (but *New York* rather than *N.Y.* in reference to the city). The following abbreviations may also be used to save space. Follow the recommendation of your instructor about whether to underline those from Latin.

anon.	anonymous
ca. or c. *(circa)*	about a given date *(ca.* 1490)
ch., chs.	chapter, chapters
col., cols.	column, columns
diss.	dissertation
ed.	edited by or edition (2nd ed.)
et al. *(et alii)*	and others (used with four or more authors); you may also simply write "and others"
e.g. *(exempli gratia)*	for example (preceded and followed by a comma)
i.e. *(id est)*	that is (preceded and followed by a comma)
l., ll.	line, lines (in typewritten copy it is better to write these out, to avoid confusion with the figures 1 and 11)
MS., MSS.	manuscript, manuscripts
n.d.	no date of publication given
n.p.	no place of publication given
p., pp.	page, pages (the word *page* is never written out in footnotes)
rev.	revised edition or revised by
sic	thus (placed in brackets after an error in quoted material to show that you are aware of the error; seldom used by contemporary writers)
trans. or tr.	translated by
vol., vols.	volume, volumes

The use of "ibid.," "op. cit.," and "loc. cit." is now considered not very helpful. It is just as simple, and clearer, to use a shortened reference to author and title (as illustrated on page 450).

Alternative Forms for Notes

Research papers in the sciences and social sciences often use systems of reference quite different from the system generally used in the humanities. The references have the same purpose—to give the author, title, and facts of publication of articles and books used, to acknowledge the source of materials, and to make it possible for a reader to go directly to a source for further information. The details of form vary considerably among the different scientific and technical fields and often among the books and journals within a field. If you are writing a paper for a course in the sciences, you will need to follow the system specified by your instructor or the form of a particular journal or style manual. Whatever system you follow, do not shift from one to another in your paper: consistency is essential in the use of notes.

Any description of notes makes their use seem much harder than it really is. If you have taken good notes with the exact sources clearly recorded, it is relatively simple to prepare documentation and place endnotes in the proper form in your final paper.

The Bibliography

The finished research paper concludes with a bibliography, on a new page, of the sources used in the paper. If the list includes only those books, articles, and other sources that have been documented in the endnotes, the bibliography is titled "Works Cited." If the list also includes references that you have explored in depth but have not cited directly, the bibliography is titled "Works Consulted." Your instructor will tell you which form you should use.

Your bibliography cards (30.3) should contain all the information you need to compile the final bibliography. The form for a bibliography differs somewhat from endnote form:

30.8

Biblio

Endnote entry:

[1] Walter Gellhorn, <u>American Rights: The Constitution in Action</u> (New York: Macmillan, 1960), p. 128.

Bibliography entry:

Gellhorn, Walter. <u>American Rights: The Constitution in Action</u>. New
    York: Macmillan, 1960.

Follow these general guidelines and the examples that follow for an acceptable bibliography form:

1. List all entries in alphabetical order, by the author's *last name,* or, if the author is unknown, by the first significant word of the title (disregard *A* or *The*). When two or more works by the same author are listed, use a line of twelve dashes, followed by a period, instead of the author's name for all but the first work.
2. Do not give the page numbers for books, but do list the inclusive pages for articles in periodicals and newspapers.
3. Do not separate the list according to kinds of publications. Since the bibliography for most student papers is short, all sources should appear in the same list.
4. Do not number the entries.

Double space within and between entries. Punctuation varies in different bibliographic styles, mainly in the use of commas, colons, and parentheses. The form shown in the examples illustrates one widely used style, but be sure to note carefully any different practices your instructor may want you to follow.

Sample Bibliographic Entries

Books

One author:

Coleman, James C. Abnormal Psychology and Modern Life. 5th ed. Glen-
    view, Ill.: Scott, Foresman, 1976.

Two or three authors:

Gray, Giles W., and Claude M. Wise. The Bases of Speech. 3rd ed. New
    York: Harper & Row, 1959.

[Notice that only the first author's name is listed last name first.]

More than three authors:

Blair, Walter, et al. The Literature of the United States. 3rd ed. 3
    vols. Glenview, Ill.: Scott, Foresman, 1969.

Two books by the same author:

Rush, Myron. How Communist States Change Their Rulers. Ithaca, N.Y.:
    Cornell Univ. Press, 1974.

————————————. Political Succession in the U.S.S.R. New York:
    Columbia Univ. Press, 1965.

[These may be arranged alphabetically by title or chronologically by date of publication.]

An edited book, especially one of another writer's work:

Shakespeare, William. The Complete Works of Shakespeare. Rev. ed.
    Hardin Craig and David Bevington, eds. Glenview, Ill.: Scott,
    Foresman, 1973.

An edited collection, date of publication unknown:

Reed, William L. and Eric Smith, eds. Treasury of Vocal Music. 6 vols.
    Boston: Branden Press, n.d.

A translation:

Pasternak, Boris. My Sister, Life. Trans. Olga A. Carlisle. New
    York: Harcourt, 1976.

An encyclopedia article:

Peattie, Donald Culross. "Trees of North America." Encyclopedia Ameri-
    cana. 1973 ed., XXVII.

Reprint:

Dexter, Walter. The London of Dickens. 1923; rpt. Philadelphia:
    Richard West, 1973.

Periodicals

Signed article in a magazine:

Whittemore, Reed. "The Newspeak Generation." Harper's, Feb. 1977,
    pp. 17–21.

Unsigned article in a magazine:

"How to Save Energy." Newsweek, 18 April 1977, pp. 70–80.

Article in a scholarly journal:

Tinder, Glenn. "Community: The Tragic Ideal." The Yale Review, 65
    (1976), 550–64.

Daily newspaper article:

Gowan, Edward. "Mapping Out a National Energy Policy." New York
    Times, 10 April 1977, sec. 3, p. 1.

Other Sources

30.8

Biblio

Unpublished dissertation:

Smith, Wallace Joseph. "The Fur Trade in Colonial Pennsylvania." Diss.
    Univ. of Washington, 1950.

Interview:

Sawyer, John X. Personal interview. 1 April 1980.

30.9 Assembling the Completed Paper

In preparing the final copy of your research paper, refer to the suggestions given in 28.2, Manuscript Form. You will also find it useful to study the sample student papers on pages 458–482. Proofread your final copy before turning it in. A well-researched paper can be seriously marred by careless errors and inconsistencies.

Final Order of Contents

The research paper, usually secured by a paper clip and in a manila folder, should contain all the parts in the order your instructor has assigned. Typically, the completed paper has the following units. Make sure that you include any other material (such as your first outline or first draft) that your instructor asks for.

1. **Outline.** Some instructors will expect you to turn in your final outline (topic or sentence outline) and the thesis sentence. The revised outline should correspond to the organization of the final paper.
2. **First page.** The title, author's name, instructor's name, course number, date, and so forth should appear on the first page of the paper, unless your instructor gives you different instructions. See sample papers which follow.
3. **Text of the paper.** The text is the final copy of the paper, complete with charts and diagrams, wherever needed. The numbering of the text usually begins on the second page, with Arabic numerals at the top right-hand corner.
4. **Endnotes.** The endnotes should follow the last page of text, starting on a separate page entitled "Notes."
5. **Bibliography.** The final bibliography should follow the last page of endnotes, starting on a separate page.

Each unit of the final paper is numbered separately, with the first page number usually omitted.

This extended explanation may suggest to you that writing a research paper is an impossible task to accomplish in a mere five or six weeks of work. It isn't. Done carefully, with due attention to each of the stages outlined in this section, it may be accomplished with no more effort than you would use for your other courses. And if your research paper represents your best work, you will find the assignment a satisfying one and good training for later work.

The following pages present two student papers, one complete with outline, text, endnotes, and bibliography, the other without outline.

• *A Note on the Sample Papers*

The following research papers were both written by students. Neither paper is perfect, as the two authors would acknowledge. They are reproduced here to illustrate what research papers look like in their final form. We're using two papers to show you more than one writer at work and as much variety as possible in both writing and documentation. You may understand all of the suggestions and forms given in Section 30 better when you see how research papers are put together: how spacing is handled, how endnotes and bibiliographies are displayed, how everything finally looks on the page. Although we are not suggesting that you imitate these papers, their formats are reasonably consistent with the standards suggested in this section. Unless your instructor specifies a different method, your paper should be displayed on the pages much as these are.

Examine the content of the two papers carefully. You may be able to see, for example, that further evidence and documentation might have strengthened a paper or that the authors rely too much on some sources.

In the first paper, for example, the author fails to support a crucial generalization with evidence from research. Referring to public behavior during a gasoline shortage, he cites two men he interviewed who believed that "the panic was caused by the news media's constantly keeping the gasoline shortage issue in front of the public" (page 6). Then he says, "before the news media picked up the gasoline shortage story, people were buying gasoline in their regular buying patterns. But after a week of seeing, hearing, and reading about the shortage, people panicked and long lines formed." Notice that this generalization is based solely on an interview with two men in the gasoline business. Interviews are useful, but not as a basis for telling us that the public had "a week of seeing, hearing, and reading about the shortage." A review of the newspapers published during the crucial week, for example, would have shown exactly how much space was given to the gasoline shortage. A research paper is not the place to *assert* that something is true; it is the place to try to *show* with evidence that something is true.

30.9

Outline

I.   Introduction

      A. Introduction of the concept of agenda setting

      B. Definition of agenda setting

II.   Examinations of the concept of agenda setting

      A. The McCombs-Shaw study

      B. The McLeod, Becker, Byrnes study

      C. The Benton-Frazier study

      D. The Miller study

      E. Other studies

III. Agenda setting in action

      A. The gasoline shortage of spring, 1979

      B. The gasoline shortage of fall, 1979

IV.   Conclusion

Douglas Jumper

English 101D

Ms. B. Norman

December 17, 1979

The Agenda Setting Function

of the News Media

in the Gas Crisis of Spring and Fall, 1979

The mass media are a part of our daily lives. There are few people in the United States today who do not see television, hear radio,
or read newspapers. Sociologists, journalists, educators, and others
have been trying to discover how the mass media affect our lives. One
of the recent theories being investigated is the supposition that the
mass media have an agenda setting function.

The hypothesis of agenda setting was stated by Bernard Cohen
when he noted that the press "may not be successful much of the
time in telling people what to think, but it is stunningly successful in telling its readers what to think about."[1] Cohen, writing
in 1963, was apparently the first to use the term _agenda setting_ as
applied to the press.[2] He was interested only in the relationship
between Washington correspondents and their foreign policy news
source.[3] The theory did not come under wider critical consideration
until 1968.

Maxwell E. McCombs and Donald L. Shaw investigated the agenda setting function of the press during the 1968 presidential campaign in Chapel Hill, North Carolina.[4] They looked at the relationship between what Chapel Hill voters said were the key issues of the campaign and the actual content of the mass media used by the voters during the campaign. They found a high correlation between what the media said was important and what the voters felt was important.

It was highly improbable, their study concluded, that the correlation was the result of the media's matching their message to the audience's interest "since numerous studies indicate a sharp divergence between the news value of the professional journalist and his audience."[5] Given the correlation they found, their study revealed that the "evidence is in line with the condition that must exist if agenda setting by the mass media does occur."[6]

The McCombs and Shaw study prompted a closer look at what the agenda setting function of the press is.

In 1974 a new examination appeared, a study of the effects of newspaper agenda setting on voters in Madison, Wisconsin, in the 1972 presidential election.[7] The study found that while the media gave heavy coverage to stories about honesty in government, the sample readers rated that as only average in importance. On the other hand, the sample readers rated the issues of defense spending and the tax burden as being more important than the amount of attention given by the media would have suggested. The study proposed that "legitimacy as well as exposure may be necessary for the public to perceive an issue as important."[8] The authors further suggested that the high salience

4

of defense spending and the tax burden, despite the very low media coverage, may reflect a "latent personal concern for economic problems."[9]
They found only limited support of the agenda setting theory, and that
was from among the people who considered the newspaper their main source
of political news. In their conclusion, the authors stressed a strong
warning against the "unrestricted acceptance of the agenda setting
function of the press as a broad, unqualified media effect."[10]

In 1977, Marc Benton and Jean Frazier took the agenda setting
theory a step further. Their study attempted to expand the theory and
to determine how agenda setting works at various levels of information
holding. They divided issues into three levels: general news issues,
subdivisions of problems with causes and proposed solutions, and specific information about the pros and cons for proposed solutions. They
found a low correlation between television agendas and the public agenda, but a strong correlation between newspaper-oriented respondents and
the newspapers' agendas. They found that agenda setting held at all
three of the levels.[11] It is important to note that the Benton and
Frazier study dealt with economic issues and therefore fits McCombs'
assumption that for the agenda setting function to work, the issue must
have legitimacy for the public as well as exposure by the media.

In a 1977 article, Bruce Westley discussed the agenda setting
function of the press in what he calls "the total social matrix within
which it occurs."[12] Westley contended that important forces are acting
upon the media agenda and that these forces are action groups. These
are typically loosely knit confederations that are organized around a
single agenda issue. These groups create events that the media cover

even though they know the events are created for that purpose.[13] This
aspect must be taken into account when one is studying the effects of
the agenda setting function of the press.

In her 1978 study of the relationships between the members of
Congress and reporters on Capitol Hill, Susan Miller found a symbiotic
instead of an adversary relationship between the two. The media representatives were often forced to rely upon the staff of Congressional
members to get their stories, even though in the process they were being used to give publicity to officials.[14] As Washington Post reporter
Tom Wilkinson put it, "We get used all the time. We try not to, but we
can't help it." He added that it would be impossible to put out a
newspaper if journalists never wrote anything that could be used by
public officials to enhance their reputations.[15]

Miller also found that the media brought topics to the attention
of Congressional committees and that news reporters sometimes increased
the significance of an issue and made it easier for the chairmen or
committee staffs to get members to agree to the need for Congressional
action.[16]

In other studies, it has been determined that newspapers are the
predominant force in setting the agenda for local issues.[17] There is
continuing disagreement, however, about whether the agenda setting
function works over extended periods of time. Kaid, Hale, and Williams
found in 1977 that agenda setting did not carry beyond a specific
event, such as what the President stressed in a particular speech, but
McCombs and Shaw suggested that the process continues over a period of
months.[18]

6

During the late spring and early summer of 1979, the Dallas-Fort Worth area in Texas (along with other parts of the United States) experienced a serious gasoline shortage. There was no advance warning of the shortage, and early morning gas lines seemed to appear suddenly.

During the shortage, area service stations affiliated with the major oil companies received only 70% to 78% of their usual monthly allotment of gasoline.[19] Suddenly, the buying public panicked and started lining up at the pumps, even if only for a few gallons to keep their tanks full.[20] According to Martin Zanotti, Executive Vice-President for Gulf Oil, and Jack Swaim, owner of a chain of "Dunlop-Swaim" Texaco service stations throughout Texas, the panic was caused by the news media's constantly keeping the gasoline shortage issue in front of the public. Before the news media picked up the gasoline shortage story, people were buying gasoline in their regular buying patterns. But after a week of seeing, hearing, and reading about the shortage, people panicked and long lines formed.

In the fall in the same area there occurred another gasoline shortage. Area retailers again received only 78% or less of their monthly allotment.[21] But the striking difference between the shortage in the spring and the shortage in the fall was that in the fall the public did not panic, and the long lines did not form at service stations. Zanotti and Swaim agree that the panic did not occur again because in the fall there was no media coverage.[22]

The agenda setting function appears to be very real in certain situations. It seems to be real, however, only in those situations where the media give exposure to some issue over some extended period of time. In those situations where there is not exposure over an extended period of time, the agenda setting function does seem to play a major role. During the gasoline crises in the spring and fall in the Dallas-Fort Worth area, the media appeared to play a major role in setting the public agenda. In the spring, with ample media exposure, the public soon learned to form long lines at the service stations. In the fall, with the same short supply but with no media exposure, no lines formed.

Notes

[1] Bernard C. Cohen, The Press and Foreign Policy (Princeton: Princeton Univ. Press, 1963), p. 13.

[2] Jack M. McLeod, Lee B. Becker, and James S. Byrnes, "Another Look at the Agenda Setting Function of the Press," Communication Research, 1 (1974), 134.

[3] L. John Martin, "Recent Theory on Mass Media Potential in Political Campaigns," Annals of the American Academy of Political and Social Science, 427 (Sept. 1976), 115.

[4] Maxwell E. McCombs and Donald L. Shaw, "The Agenda Setting Function of Mass Media," Public Opinion Quarterly, 36 (Summer 1972), 176-187.

[5] McCombs and Shaw, p. 185.

[6] McCombs and Shaw, p. 185.

[7] McLeod, Becker, and Byrnes, pp. 131-163.

[8] McLeod, Becker, and Byrnes, p. 160.

[9] McLeod, Becker, and Byrnes, p. 160.

[10] McLeod, Becker, and Byrnes, p. 159.

[11] Marc Benton and Jean P. Frazier, "The Agenda Setting Theory of the Mass Media at Three Levels of Information Holding," Communication Research, 3 (1976), 261-274.

[12] Bruce Westley, "Setting the Political Agenda/What Makes It Change?" Journal of Communication, 26 (Spring 1976), 43-47.

9

[13] Westley, p. 46.

[14] Susan Heilman Miller, "Reporters and Congressmen: Living in Symbiosis," Journalism Monographs, 53 (Jan. 1978), 1-25.

[15] Miller, p. 4.

[16] Miller, p. 3.

[17] Philip Palmgreen and Peter Clark, "Agenda Setting with Local and National Issues," Communication Research, 4 (1977), 435.

[18] Lynda Lee Kaid, Kathy Hale, and Jo Ann Williams, "Media Agenda Setting of a Specific Political Event," Journalism Quarterly, 54 (1977), 584-587.

[19] Personal interview with Martin Zanotti and Jack Swaim, 12 Nov. 1979.

[20] Zanotti and Swaim.

[21] Zanotti and Swaim.

[22] Zanotti and Swaim.

Works Cited

Benton, Marc, and Jean P. Frazier. "The Agenda Setting Theory of the
    Mass Media at Three Levels of Information Holding." Communication
    Research, 3 (1976), 261-274.

Cohen, Bernard. The Press and Foreign Policy. Princeton: Princeton
    Univ. Press, 1963.

Kaid, Lynda Lee, Kathy Hale, and Jo Ann Williams. "Media Agenda Set-
    ting of a Specific Political Event." Journalism Quarterly, 54
    (1977), 584-587.

Martin, L. John. "Recent Theory on Mass Media Potential in Political
    Campaigns." Annals of the American Academy of Political and So-
    cial Science, 427 (Sept. 1976), 125-134.

McCombs, Maxwell E., and Donald L. Shaw. "The Agenda Setting Function
    of the Press." Public Opinion Quarterly, 36 (Summer 1972), 176-187.

McLeod, Jack M., Lee B. Becker, and James S. Byrnes. "Another Look at
    the Agenda Setting Function of the Press." Communication Re-
    search, 1 (1974), 131-166.

Miller, Susan Heilman. "Reporters and Congressmen: Living in Symbio-
    sis." Journalism Monographs, 53 (Jan. 1978), 1-25.

Palmgreen, Philip, and Peter Clark. "Agenda Setting with Local and
    National Issues." Communication Research, 4 (1977), 435-452.

Westley, Bruce. "Setting the Political Agenda/What Makes It Change?"
    Journal of Communication, 26 (Spring 1976), 43-47.

Zanotti, Martin, and Jack Swaim. Personal interview. 12 Nov. 1979.

The following paper was written in answer to the same assignment. You may find it helpful to compare the two papers in content and format.

Nancylee Novell

English 101D

Ms. B. Norman

December 11, 1979

The ABCs of Public Television

Public Television was born in 1952. The Federal Communications
Commission (FCC) set aside that year "a number of TV channels and radio
frequencies to serve vaguely specified 'educational needs of the community.'"[1] Noncommercial broadcasting grew slowly, and at first only several universities, school districts, communities, and foundations took
advantage of those reserved channels and frequencies. The government
provided limited funds and support.

In 1966, the Carnegie Corporation set up a commission to study
the educational broadcasting system. Chaired by James Killian, Jr.,
the committee released the Carnegie Report in 1967 on the state of
public television with proposals and promises for the future. The same
year, Congress, under President Johnson, passed legislation to establish a non-governmental corporation to guide and advise public broadcasting. For better or worse, the infant public television was strid-
ing into the future. It had substance and some sustenance. Unfortu-
nately, it also had problems.

The public broadcasting system has been plagued by disunity and
inefficient channels of change and progress. These problems, coupled

2

with obscure and ambiguous language in both FCC regulations and the
first Carnegie report, have left public broadcasting without any clearly defined shape or format. Slightly more than 25 years later, public
broadcasting is reexamining itself and its role in the mass media.

There has been phenomenal growth in noncommercial educational
broadcasting, from only 95 stations at its conception to more than
1,200 FM radio and television stations today.[2] (Public broadcasting
includes both television and radio, but further discussion will deal
only with public television.) Public television has a great wealth of
budding and untapped potential. From 1970 through 1974, audience view-
ing of evening public television programs increased by almost 50 percent.[3] Recent reports show that more than 40 percent of all families
in the United States now watch public television at least once a
week.[4] Yet few Americans know anything about public television aside
from the fact that it presents excellent cultural events and children's
programs--all without commercials.

Public television is not a fourth network. The individual stations which make up these reserved channels are, for the most part,
privately, singly owned. They are governed and regulated by large com-
missions and establishments; however, they are not part of a larger
franchise like the three major networks and their subsidiary stations.
Stations can generally be classfied according to whether they are
owned by a university, community, state, or school. Each type of
station's procedures, formats, and goals are colored by the owning es-
tablishment.

All stations, public and commercial, come under the authority of

3

the FCC. The FCC issues all licenses and regulations.

The non-governmental corporation set up under the Public Broadcasting Act of 1967 is known as the Corporation for Public Broadcasting
(CPB). The CPB's function is to dispense Congressional funds to stations and to develop programming sources for the noncommercial licensees.[5] Board members are appointed by the President, with Senate approval. The CPB resembles our early American government under the Articles of the Confederation--and has the same inherent weaknesses. The
desire for local autonomy and programming gives the CPB very little
operating authority.

The Public Broadcasting Service (PBS) was established by the CPB
to aid in program distribution and interconnection for the local stations.[6] It has acquired much more power over the years and presently
acts as a separate trade association and spokesperson for public
television.

A third agency, created in 1973, is the Station Programming Cooperative (SPC). The SPC serves to consolidate scheduling. It "gives
every station a voice--measured by its ability to pay--in selecting almost half the PBS schedule (the other half is underwritten by foundations, corporations, and donations)."[7]

Public television is founded on several basic principles. The
Carnegie Report proposed several standards to build upon, as well as
stressing those inherent in the FCC regulations. Public television was
to be a nonprofit, noncommercial venture serving the educational needs
of the community and the cultural and entertainment needs not met by
the existing networks. Furthermore, the system would be insulated from

4

government, based on localism, and maintained by diverse and relatively disinterested financial support.[8]

   Public broadcasting as it exists now suffers from many ailments and growing pains. The principles upon which the system was founded, the legislation which created it, and the stations themselves have contributed to the problems which continue to hinder development and progress.

   The very term "public television" brings several problems to mind. "In terms of citizen involvement, it (public television) can barely claim the right to be a public institution at all. The vision and the clout of a dedicated few brought it into being, and its existence still depends in a large degree on support that is neither majoritarian nor deeply rooted in popular appeal."[9] Board meetings are usually closed, and a relatively elite group of financial backers determines many of the policies and practices.[10]

   Indeed, "'public' can mean a system funded out of public funds or a system funded by public subscription. What currently passes for public broadcasting is a hybridization of these two different ideas."[11] Last year, even though 2.7 million families gave $50 million to public television, the government contributed $1 for every $2.50 raised from private individuals, firms, and foundations.[12] And government funding is supposed to contribute a larger share over the next few years.

   The vagueness about the meaning of "public" extends to the definition of "noncommercial." Certainly public television stations may not operate at a profit or broadcast advertising for consumer goods. Commercial powers such as Exxon or Mobil, however, largely con-

trol much of public television programming by their ability to make
grants. Individual producers are frustrated and stifled by these huge
firms' efforts.[13] This kind of commercial support represents less than
10 percent of the total, but the programming so provided, such as Mas-
terpiece Theatre, includes some of the most prestigious on the
air. Public television officials would like to increase commercial
support in order to upgrade their programming; however, it is difficult
to know at what point commercial support would begin to destroy the
noncommercial principle of the system. Although public opinion on the
matter is split, the prevailing opinion would tend to limit heavy corporate involvement, however beneficial it might be to programming.

The uncertainty about what constitutes noncommercial operation
extends also to solicitation of funds by public television stations.
Public television stations are allowed to use only limited time for
on-the-air solicitation. The most common form of fund raising is
the annual auction of donated goods and services. FCC regulations were
amended to allow for the advertising of consumer goods that inevitably
occurs in this context. The auctions, however, tend to increase the
influence individual backers can have over programming. The stations
are faced with the choice of catering to the wishes of the contributing public or trying to fill the unexpressed needs of the noncon-
tributing public.

This issue leads directly to another basic problem that stems
from a lack of definition. Public television was created to serve the
educational needs of the community and provide alternative programming
to fill the needs not met by the existing networks. No one has ever

6

clearly defined either educational or alternative programming. The FCC
has preferred not to "specify programming content. It is easier to
classify types of licensees, and, once they qualify, let them make
their own decisions."[14] The industry has been left free to find its
own direction in programming and this has resulted in half-hearted,
widely diffused, and often unproductive efforts. Indeed, recent reports seem to suggest that "educational" and "public" television cannot
be one and the same.[15]

One of the early tenets of public broadcasting was localism.
Today less than 10 percent of a typical station's programming is
produced locally, and this percentage is shrinking due to economic in-
feasibility.[16] The lack of unity in the system tends to hinder progress. Stations are owned by diverse groups who differ with each other
on aims and issues. Some pursue large audiences, while others maintain
a purely educational bent. There is a great deal of debate regarding
centralism versus localism.[17]

The financial aspects of localism must also be considered. Although total hours of public television broadcasting have increased
over the years, local programming hours have decreased. Funding is the
main factor in this trend. A study in 1972 by Schramm and Nelson
showed that local programming is 2.3 times more expensive than national
programming because of the multiplier effect of duplicated efforts at
the local level.[18] Since other recent studies have also shown that
viewers prefer national programming to locally produced shows, stations
find it increasingly difficult to justify the additional expense of
local programming.

7

Another common complaint about programming is that expansion in
the field of major programs is very slow--three quarters of the PBS programs are reruns. Much of public television's programming depends on
British productions. "PBS president Lawrence K. Grossman acknowledged
this when he quipped, 'Where would American public television be if the
British didn't speak English?'"[19] Individual stations participate in
the Station Program Cooperative, which "votes" for the programs to be
carried on PBS. Currently proven, popular shows are almost always chosen over new ideas.

Many of public television's problems result entirely or in part
from the lack of funding. Funding is an ever-present problem. The
legislation that created public television is also responsible for the
system's most crippling defect. "The 1967 act was passed without providing for a permanent and dependable means of support for noncommercial television."[20] Presently, each dollar of federal appropriations
must be matched by $2.50 from nongovernmental sources. The result is
usually a frenzied period of local pledge weeks.[21] This dependence on
private individuals quite understandably gives a few people a great
deal of influence on programming, as noted previously. Insufficient
funds and the dependence on individual contributions hinder public
television's progress and restrict programming.

Several plans have been proposed to help ease the financial
crunch. Additional funds from non-interfering sources would tend to
take the pressure off the public television industry and allow for increased programming and progress along the lines of the original principles of the Carnegie Report.

8

The Carnegie Commission originally proposed that funding come from an excise tax on TV sets, but this suggestion was deemed politically infeasible.[22] An alternative suggestion is for commercial broadcasters to be taxed to support public broadcasters. The rationale for this subsidization is that if public stations were to be replaced by commercial stations, the existing commercial stations would suffer a great loss of revenue as program prices rose and advertising rates fell with the loss of commercial monopolistic control. This is an unlikely occurrence because public broadcasters would never unite to threaten the commercial networks with this alternative. Commercial networks also have great political strength and could oppose any taxes of this sort.

Many public broadcasting officials contend that there is nothing wrong with the present system that adequate funding from politically insulated sources can't cure.[23] Under the present system of funding, a great deal of programming control resides with Congress and the Appropriations Committee. The mere threat of fiscal cutbacks can be enough to remove programs that the Administration doesn't like from the season line-ups. The Nixon Administration attempted to prevent public TV from presenting controversial public affairs programs, for example.[24]

There have been several proposals for increased development of the system. One proposal calls for a network providing quality general programming without commercial interruptions, operated independently of the system. The remaining public channels would be expanded to full-time separate programming services, i.e., a public affairs channel, a science channel, a children's channel, and a cultural affairs chan-

nel.[25] This would allow for greater attention to quality programming
and greater diversification.

There is great potential in the present system of public television, but "public broadcasting needs redirection in its priorities, a
structural reorganization, and greater insulation from political interference."[26] A second study of the PBS by the Carnegie Commission, on
the future of public broadcasting, was undertaken in an effort to determine the direction public broadcasting should take. The commission,
known as Carnegie II, released its report in February of this year,
citing the system's weaknesses and offering recommendations. But industry and government officials were less than inspired by the report.
Time described the report as "excessively timid, short on vision and
long on words--particularly long on words."[27]

Carnegie II included among the weaknesses of public broadcasting
sparse resources, excessive federal influence, and organizational over-
growth. While making several excellent recommendations for future improvements, Carnegie II failed to consider how these improvements would
be implemented. The recommendations include:

*Substantially increasing the budget for public broadcasting to
$1.2 billion annually by 1985. About half of that sum would be
raised by local stations from a variety of non-federal sources.
*Reducing the impact of the increased federal contribution by
collecting "spectrum fees" of about $200 million from various
commercial users of the public airwaves.
*Replacing the CPB with a new Public Telecommunications Trust to
provide better insulation from political interference.

10

*Assuring more creative and more independent programming by es-

tablishing a $190 million annual Program Endowment.

It remains to be seen whether these recommendations will be put into

use, but the chances seem slim.[28]

Many of public broadcasting's present problems stem from the

original Carnegie Report, which dealt primarily with local stations--

their goals, needs, and wants. The presidential appointments to the

CPB board over the years have not strengthened the industry's posi-

tion. Also, interference by the Nixon Administration undermined the

board's effectiveness and helped to decentralize the industry.[29]

Public broadcasting has advanced tediously, and often not at all, over

the years. In her article, "A Crisis of Identity: Reflections on the

Future of Public Broadcasting," Anne W. Branscomb said:

> In short, much of the present dilemma of public broad-
>
> casting is the result of a too "benign neglect" by fed-
>
> eral agencies, coupled with a schizophrenia of the
>
> public broadcasting entities as to their proper roles,
>
> a myopia concerning their potential for development,
>
> and a certain lack of self-confidence in their survival
>
> quotient.[30]

If public broadcasting is to advance it must face up to its pres-

ent problems and solve them as efficiently as possible. Funding will

alleviate many of the concerns, and carefully planned self-direction

will facilitate progress. Public television is an excellent concept

which should be utilized to its fullest capacity.

Notes

[1] Douglass Cater, "Introduction: The Haphazard Business of Institution Building," in The Future of Public Broadcasting, ed. Douglass Cater (New York: Praeger, 1976), p. 1.

[2] Stuart A. Shorenstein, "Pulling the Plug on Instructional TV," Change, Nov. 1978, p. 36.

[3] Shorenstein, p. 37.

[4] "Recasting the Public System," Time, 12 Feb. 1979, p. 93.

[5] Anne W. Branscomb, "A Crisis of Identity: Reflections on the Future of Public Broadcasting," in The Future of Public Broadcasting, ed. Douglass Cater (New York: Praeger, 1976), p. 27.

[6] Branscomb, p. 27.

[7] Harry F. Waters, Ann Ray Martin, and Lucy Howard, "Public TV Comes of Age," Newsweek, 8 Mar. 1976, p. 72.

[8] Branscomb, pp. 9-10.

[9] Cater, p. 5.

[10] Les Brown, "Public Television at the Crossroads," Change, June-July 1978, p. 58.

[11] Branscomb, p. 35.

[12] "Public and Private Television," Change, Mar. 1979, p. 10.

[13] Brown, p. 58.

[14] Branscomb, p. 31.

12

[15] "Public and Private Television," p. 11.

[16] Brown, p. 59.

[17] Brown, p. 59.

[18] R. Bruce McKay, "Financing: A Problem or Symptom?" in The Future of Public Broadcasting, ed. Douglass Cater (New York: Praeger, 1976), p. 156.

[19] Brown, p. 58.

[20] Brown, p. 59.

[21] Brown, P. 59.

[22] Brown, p. 59.

[23] Brown, p. 59.

[24] Harry F. Waters and Lucy Howard, "A Boost for Public TV," Newsweek, 17 Oct. 1977, p. 106.

[25] Branscomb, p. 35.

[26] Brown, p. 58.

[27] "Recasting the Public System," p. 93.

[28] "Public and Private Television," p. 11.

[29] Brown, p. 59.

[30] Branscomb, p. 8.

Works Consulted

Brown, Les. "Public Television at the Crossroads." Change, June-July
        1978, pp. 58-60.

Carnegie Commission on Educational Television. Public Television: A
        Program for Action. New York: Bantam Books, 1967.

Carpenter, Iris. "Media Now--and Forever." American Education, Apr.
        1978, pp. 29-33.

Cater, Douglass, ed. The Future of Public Broadcasting. New York:
        Praeger, 1976.

Chapman, Stephen. "Down with Public Television." Harper's, Aug. 1979,
        pp. 77-84.

DeMott, Benjamin. "The Trouble with Public Television." The Atlantic
        Monthly, Feb. 1979, pp. 42-47.

Kitman, Marvin. "Time for Carnegie III." The New Leader, 26 Feb. 1979,
        pp. 21-22.

Macy, John W., Jr. To Irrigate a Wasteland. Los Angeles: University
        of California Press, 1974.

"Public and Private Television." Change, Mar. 1979, pp. 10-11.

"Public Television Tries to Break into the 'Big Time.'" U.S. News &
        World Report, 23 Aug. 1976, pp. 45-46.

"Recasting the Public System." Time, 12 Feb. 1979, p. 93.

Robinson, Paul. "TV Can't Educate." The New Republic, 5 Aug. 1978,
        pp. 13-15.

Shorenstein, Stuart A. "Pulling the Plug on Instructional TV." Change,
    Nov. 1978, pp. 36-39.

Waters, Harry F., and Lucy Howard. "A Boost for Public TV." Newsweek,
    17 Oct. 1977, p. 106.

Waters, Harry F., Ann Ray Martin, and Lucy Howard. "Public TV Comes of
    Age." Newsweek, 8 Mar. 1976, pp. 72-73.

"What's Ahead for Public Television." U.S. News & World Report, 30 Jan.
    1978, pp. 55-56.

Glossary of Usage

This glossary lists words and constructions that often cause confusion in writing; it is not, however, a replacement for a good dictionary. Many of these entries are discussed in more detail in the chapter of the *Handbook* in which they occur, for example, *lay, lie* in chapter 8, Verbs, and *who, whom* in chapter 7, Pronouns. The index lists the usage entries that appear within the *Handbook*.

a, an. The choice of *a* or *an* depends on the initial sound of the following word rather than the initial letter. Use *a* before words beginning with a consonant sound, *an* before words beginning with a vowel sound: *a* boat, *a* used boat, *a* European country, *an* alligator, *an* F, *an* hour.

accept, except. *Accept* means "receive" or "approve of"; *except* means "exclude" or "with the exclusion of":

Everyone has **accepted** the invitation **except** Sam.

advice, advise. *Advice* is a noun meaning "counsel" or "recommendation"; *advise* is a verb meaning "give advice" or "make a recommendation":

I **advise** you to follow your instructor's **advice**.

affect, effect. *Affect* is a verb meaning "influence" or "assume the appearance of"; *effect* is a noun meaning "result":

The weather **affected** our tempers.

The frightened child **affected** a defiant look.

The **effects** of radiation aren't completely known.

Affect is also a noun, a technical term used in psychology meaning "emotion," and *effect* is a formal verb meaning "to bring about."

aggravate, irritate. In formal English, *aggravate* means "make worse" and *irritate* means "annoy": *aggravate* the condition; an *irritating* habit. In general and informal usage, *aggravate* and *irritate* both mean "to annoy": his voice *aggravated* me; the mosquitoes were *irritating*. But since using *aggravate* to mean "annoy" might irritate some readers, it is useful to maintain the formal distinction.

Glos

ain't. A colloquial contraction meaning "aren't" or "isn't." *Ain't* is not considered appropriate in most writing.

all ready, already. *All ready* is an adjective phrase meaning that everything or everyone is prepared; *already* is an adverb meaning "previously":

> Finally the car was loaded and we were **all ready** to leave.
>
> The train had **already** left when we got to the station.

all right. The only correct spelling.

all the farther. A colloquial expression considered inappropriate in writing. "As far as" is the standard written form:

> This is **as far as** I am going.

all together, altogether. *All together* is an adjective phrase meaning "in a group"; *altogether* is an adverb meaning "wholly":

> The sale items were **all together** on one table.
>
> That's **altogether** another matter.

allude, refer. To *allude* is to make indirect mention of something; to *refer* is to state directly:

> I knew that his remark about trees **alluded** to the unfortunate incident at the picnic.
>
> He **referred** to the second chapter in order to make his point.

allusion, illusion. An *allusion* is a brief, indirect reference to a person, event, literary work, or the like. An *illusion* is a misleading appearance.

> She made an **allusion** to Yeats' "Second Coming."
>
> The little boy's smile created an **illusion** of innocence.

almost, most. *Almost* is an adverb meaning "very nearly"; *most* is an adjective meaning "the greater part of."

> He **almost** wrecked the car.
>
> **Most** drivers try to be careful.

Although in speech *most* is sometimes used to mean *almost,* the two words are not interchangeable.

a lot. Always two words.

a.m., p.m. (or A.M., P.M.) The abbreviations should always be used with numbers to refer to a specific time:

> The train leaves at 5:56 **p.m.**

Do not use the word "o'clock" with *a.m.* or *p.m.* Do not use *a.m.* or *p.m.* without a specific time.

among, between. *Among* usually refers to more than two; *between* refers to two only. However, *between* is sometimes used in informal English for more than two. *Between* is always used when the reference is to individual items, even though an "item" might consist of more than one unit:

> We had to choose **between coffee and cake** [as one item] **and punch and cookies.**

Do not use *or* between the items: *between him and her.*

amount, number. In general and formal usage, *amount* is used to refer to something as a mass: a large *amount* of black dirt; a certain *amount* of money. *Number* is used to refer to individual items: a large *number* of plants, a *number* of cars.

and etc. The use of *and* with *etc.* is redundant because *etc. (et cetera)* means "and so forth."

and which, but which. The use of *and* or *but* with a relative pronoun *(who, which, that)* in an adjective clause is superfluous and defeats the subordination; only the pronoun should be used:

> The sea anemone is a fascinating creature **which** looks more like a plant than an animal.

anyone, any one. These words are not interchangeable. *Any one* refers to one of a certain number of items or people; *anyone* is a singular, indefinite pronoun and refers only to a person:

> You may choose **any one** of those books to read.
>
> **Anyone** who pays the entrance fee may enter the race.

Everyone, every one, and *someone, some one* are similar types of words.

apt, likely, liable. See *likely, liable, apt.*

as. When used as a conjunction to introduce adverb clauses, *as* is often less exact than other adverbs such as *while, when, since,* or *because:*

> *While* we were eating, we talked about the election.
>
> We stopped to rest under a tree *because* the sun was so hot.

as, like. See *like, as.*

awhile, a while. *Awhile* is an adverb meaning "for a certain period of time." *A while* is a noun with an article:

> Can you stay **awhile?** [adverb modifying *stay*]
>
> Can you stay for **a while?** [noun, object of the preposition *for*]

bad, badly. *Bad* is the adjective, *badly* the adverb. Although *bad* is the preferred form following a linking verb (I feel *bad;* the situation looks *bad*), *badly* is sometimes used, especially after *feel* (she feels *badly* about hurting you). Many people object to such uses of *badly,* however, and it's just as well to avoid them in writing. But do use *badly* when it is called for: The day started off *badly* and got worse.

because. See *reason is because.*

being that. To introduce a dependent clause of reason or cause, *being that* is an unacceptable substitute for *because, since,* or *for:*

> **Because** I was so tired, I decided not to go to the party.

beside, besides. *Beside* means "at the side of"; *besides* means "in addition to."

> **Besides** attending the concert we lingered **beside** the monument.

between, among. See *among, between.*

bring, take. *Bring* suggests motion toward the writer: *Bring* me my slippers, please. *Take* suggests motion away from the writer: *Take* my slippers to the closet, please.

but that, but what. Even though *but that* and *but what* are used informally in dependent clauses, *that* is preferable in most writing: I don't doubt *that* he'll be there.

but which. See *and which.*

can be, able to be. *Able to be* is an awkward expression when used with a passive infinitive: Canoes are *able to be* carried easily by two people. *Can be* is preferable: Canoes *can be* carried easily by two people.

can, may. In written edited English, *can* is used to express ability, *may* to express permission:

> **Can** you dance? **May** I have this dance?

Can is frequently used informally in the sense of permission (*Can* I go too?), but it's best to avoid this use in writing.

can't hardly. Such common expressions as *can't hardly* and *couldn't scarcely* are double negatives, because *hardly* and *scarcely* mean "almost not." Use *can hardly* instead: I *can hardly* hear you.

can't help but. This is an established idiom, but many writers avoid it, using instead *cannot but* (formal) or *can't help:*

> I **cannot but** feel sorry for him.

> I **can't help** feeling sorry for him.

capital, capitol. The *capitol* is the building which houses the state or national legislative bodies. For all other meanings, use *capital.*

censor, censure. *Censor* means "repress" or "remove"; *censure* means "condemn" or "disapprove," often in an official sense:

> Chicago would like to **censor** X-rated movies.

> The senator whose entire family was on the payroll was **censured** by Congress.

center around. Although this is a commonly used expression, it is considered illogical by many. Use *center on* or *revolve around* instead.

cite, site. *Cite* is a verb, most often used in the sense of "quote" or "refer to"; *site* is a noun meaning "location," or a verb meaning "place in a certain location":

> Dictionaries often **cite** the way a word has been used by different writers.

> We've found the perfect **site** for a picnic.

complement, compliment. *Complement* is a noun or verb referring to completion or fitting together; *compliment* is a noun or verb suggesting praise:

> She saw a hat that would be the perfect **complement** for her suit.

> Nancy **complimented** Theodore on having the sense to come out of the rain.

connote, denote. A word's meaning is *denoted;* a word's suggestion is *connoted.*

conscientious, conscious. *Conscientious* is an adjective meaning "scrupulous" or "upright"; *conscious* is an adjective meaning "awake" or "aware":

> Pamela was **conscientious** about every responsibility she took on.

> Stephen was **conscious** of the noise in the background.

considerable, considerably. *Considerable* is the adjective, *considerably* the adverb. Using *considerable* as an adverb is non-standard:

> It was a **considerable** amount of money.
>
> The price was **considerably** higher today.

contact. Many people dislike *contact* in the sense of "get in touch with" (I'll *contact* you soon); in general or formal edited English a more precise word is ordinarily used: *see, call,* or *write.*

continual, continuous. Although the distinction has largely disappeared, *continual* refers to an action that occurs repeatedly over a period of time, *continuous* to an action that is in uninterrupted flow:

> The **continual** ringing of the phone began to annoy Joe.
>
> Many old people live with a **continuous** fear of being robbed.

could of, would of. These are mistaken expressions based on the spoken contractions *could've* and *would've.* Use *could have* and *would have* in writing.

credible, creditable, credulous. *Credible* means "capable of being believed" (a lie can be credible); *creditable* means "worthy of being believed" (a lie should not be creditable); but *credulous* means "willing to believe on the slimmest evidence."

data. Although *data* is used in general and informal usage for both the singular and plural, *datum* is used as the singular in formal writing.

detract, distract. *Detract* means "take away from"; *distract* means "to turn aside" or "divert the attention."

> The litter on the ground **detracted** from the beauty of the park.
>
> The wailing sirens **distracted** us from our conversation.

different from. This is the general idiom, but *different than* can be used to avoid an awkward sentence:

> Life in a small town is **different from** life in a large city.
> Living on a farm means a **different** life-style **than** living in a city does.
>
> *or:* Living on a farm means a life-style **different from** the life-style in a city.

disinterested, uninterested. Even though both words are commonly used to mean *uninterested,* a distinction should be maintained. Use *disinterested* to mean "impartial": *Disinterested* judges are better than *uninterested* ones.

done, don't. All varieties of standard English call for *did* in the past tense in all persons: I, you, he, she, it *did*. The past participle in all persons is *have* or *had done*. *Don't* is the contraction for *do not; doesn't* is the contraction for *does not:* I, you *don't;* he, she, it *doesn't.*

effect, affect. See *affect, effect.*

either . . . or. Singular subjects joined by *either . . . or* or *neither . . . nor* are generally considered singular, and take a singular verb:

> Either the bicycle or the moped is the transportation of the future.

If both subjects are plural, the verb is plural:

> Either bicycles or mopeds are the transportation of the future.

eminent, imminent. *Eminent* is an adjective meaning "noteworthy" or "famous": an *eminent* ambassador. *Imminent* is an adjective meaning "about to happen": The storm is *imminent.*

enthuse. This verb is a back formation from *be enthusiastic about* or *show enthusiasm.* While *enthuse* is fairly common in speech, it is generally better to use another form in writing.

equally as. Redundant. Use the one appropriate word: "He was *equally* unwilling a month ago" or "He was *as* unwilling as his brother."

etc. The abbreviation for *et cetera,* "and so forth." Do not use *and etc.*

every one, everyone. See *any one, anyone.*

except, accept. See *accept, except.*

expect. Colloquial in the sense of "suppose," "presume," or "think."

farther, further. In formal English *farther* is used to refer to physical distance: How much *farther* must we walk? *Further* refers to abstract degree: We will study these suggestions *further.* Although the distinction is not as strictly adhered to in general writing, it is better to maintain it.

fewer, less. *Fewer* is used to refer to countable items, *less* to something considered as a mass:

> If there are **fewer** people, it means **less** work for the clean-up crew.

flaunt, flout. Although frequently confused, these words are not synonyms: *flaunt* is to make a show of, or display something ostentatiously; *flout* is to disregard, or treat with scorn:

> Everyone was tired of the way he **flaunted** his inheritance.
>
> Some people always **flout** the traffic laws.

former, latter. Used to refer to the first or last of two items only. If more than two items, use *first, last.*

get, got, gotten. Both *got* and *gotten* are acceptable forms of the past participle of *get:*

> He could have **gotten** [or **got**] more for his money.

Many idioms with *get* are standard in all levels of writing: *get up, get away from, get ahead.* But some expressions are considered informal and should be avoided in college writing: *get on one's nerves, get away with murder, gets me* (for "annoy"), *get* in the sense of "hit" or "struck."

good, well. *Good* is an adjective: a *good* time; this cake tastes *good. Well* is either an adjective, in the sense of one's health, or, more usually, an adverb: The team plays *well* together. Since *good* is an adjective, it shouldn't be used in place of the adverb *well:* The car is running *well* since it was tuned up.

half. Both *a half* and *half a* are standard; the choice usually depends on sound and idiom: He ate *half a* pie; He ate *a half* serving. *A half a* is redundant.

The number of the verb is determined by the noun accompanying *half:*

> Half the children **are** . . . .
>
> Half the pie **is** . . . .

hang. People are *hanged,* pictures and other objects are *hung.* The distinction isn't strictly maintained as far as people are concerned, but objects are never hanged.

hardly. Since *hardly* is a negative meaning "almost not," don't use another negative with it. See *can't hardly.*

he or she. Although *he* has traditionally been used as the pronoun when both sexes are meant, more writers are using *he or she (him or her, his or her).* If constant repetition of *he or she* sounds awkward, try rewriting the passage into the plural *(they).*

hisself. Nonstandard for *himself.*

illusion, allusion. See *allusion, illusion.*

imminent, eminent. See *eminent, imminent.*

imply, infer. *Imply* means "suggest"; *infer* means "assume" or "draw a conclusion" from a suggestion or implication:

> Even though she didn't say anything, her expression **implied** that she thought her friend was acting foolishly.

> We **inferred** from the manager's remarks that we would not be getting raises this year.

Because *infer* is sometimes used to mean *imply,* it's helpful if your context also makes your meaning clear. In any case, maintain the distinction between the two words.

in, into. *In* generally refers to a location within, *into* to the action of going toward the location:

> She decided to sit **in** the chair that she had bumped **into** in the dark.

incredible, incredulous. *Incredible* means "very hard to believe"; *incredulous* means "not believing, skeptical":

> The gymnast showed **incredible** control on the balance beam.

> John was **incredulous** at the story the little green men were telling.

irregardless. Nonstandard for *regardless.* Since both *ir-* and *-less* are negative affixes, *ir-* is redundant.

irritate, aggravate. See *aggravate, irritate.*

is when, is where. Often incorrectly used to introduce an adverb clause as a definition:

> INCORRECT: Theater-in-the-round **is when** the audience surrounds the stage.

> CORRECT: A theater-in-the-round is one in which the audience surrounds the stage.

its, it's. These two words are often carelessly confused. *Its* is the possessive form of the pronoun *it:* everything in *its* place. *It's* is the contraction for *it is* or *it has: it's* raining; *it's* begun.

kind, sort. *Kind* and *sort* are singular when used with *this* or *that* and should be used with a singular noun and verb: *this kind* of book is my favorite, *that sort* of person annoys me. If the idea is plural, use *these* and *those: these kinds* of books are . . . , *those sorts* of people. . . .

kind of a, sort of a. Although frequently occurring in speech, *kind of a* is considered informal in writing. Write: We'll never see that *kind of* day again.

last, latest. *Last* refers to the final item in a series of something that is completed: the *last* chapter, *last* inning. *Latest* refers to the most recent in an ongoing series: the *latest* book I read (I'll read others), the team's *latest* defeat (we hope it's the last).

later, latter. *Later,* a comparative adjective, refers to time: the *later* the hour, the longer the shadows. *Latter,* an adjective or a noun, refers to the second of two items named. See also *former, latter.*

lay, lie. *Lay* is a verb meaning "to put or place"; it takes an object: *lay* the books on the desk. *Lie* is a verb meaning "to recline"; it does not take an object: *lie* down for a nap. The principal parts of *lay* are *lay, laid, laid:* He *laid* the books on the desk. The principal parts of *lie* are *lie, lay, lain:* She *lay* down for a nap.

learn, teach. The student *learns,* the instructor *teaches.* Using *learn* for *teach* is considered nonstandard.

leave, let. *Leave* means "depart or abandon"; *let* means "permit": *Let* us *leave* this place. Using *leave* for *let* is considered nonstandard.

less, fewer. See *fewer, less.*

let's us. Since *let's* is a contraction for "let us," *let's us* is redundant.

lie, lay. See *lay, lie.*

like, as. To introduce a prepositional phrase of comparison, use *like:*

> He looks **like** his father.
>
> Some people **like** the Joneses try to keep up with their neighbors.

To introduce a clause of comparison (with a subject and verb), use *as, as if,* or *as though:*

> It looks **as if** his father is not coming.
>
> She wanted to be a lawyer **as** her mother had been.

The use of *like* as a conjunction has become more widespread recently, but it is ordinarily better to use the preferred forms *as, as if,* and *as though.*

likely, liable, apt. Both *likely* and *liable* suggest that something will occur, but in formal usage *liable* is restricted to an unpleasant or disastrous occurrence:

> The tornado is **liable** to damage a large part of town.
>
> The tornado is **likely** to veer away from town.

The use of *apt* to suggest an occurrence is colloquial. Use *apt* only in the sense of aptitude: She is very *apt* at needlepoint.

loose, lose. The spelling of these words is sometimes confused. *Loose* is an adjective meaning "not tight" (*loose* sleeves), or a verb meaning "release" (*loosen* the rope). *Lose* is a verb meaning "misplace" (don't *lose* it).

may, can. See *can, may.*

may be, maybe. *May be* is a verb phrase suggesting possibility; *maybe* is an adverb meaning "perhaps":

> He **may be** the next mayor.
>
> **Maybe** it will rain this afternoon.

moral, morale. The adjective *moral* means "ethical" (a *moral* code of conduct); the noun *moral* refers to the ethical significance or practical lesson (the *moral* of a story). The noun *morale* means "state of mind": If all the workers do their share, the *morale* of the group will be good.

most, almost. See *almost, most.*

myself. A reflexive or intensive pronoun, used to refer back to *I* in the same sentence:

> I hurt **myself. I, myself,** am the only one to blame.

It is not more elegant or correct to substitute *myself* for *I*.

nohow, nowheres. *Nohow* is nonstandard for "not at all"; *nowheres* is nonstandard for "nowhere."

not . . . no. Constructions such as "I don't have no money," or "The tickets will not cost you nothing" are called double negatives, because the second negative needlessly repeats the meaning of the first one. They are common in some dialects, but are not appropriate to written forms of edited English.

number, amount. See *amount, number.*

of, have. Do not use *of* for *have* in expressions such as *could have* and *would have*. See *could of.*

of which, whose. *Whose* is the possessive form of the pronoun *who;* it's generally used to refer to persons; *of which* is the possessive form most often used for inanimate objects:

> One of the most interesting colonial Americans was Thomas Jefferson, **whose** ideas still sound very modern.
>
> It was a huge house, the rooms **of which** were dank and mildewed.

Often, however, *of which* is awkward; *whose* is generally used in such cases: ". . . the room *whose* walls were painted orange."

off of. A colloquial expression that means no more than *off:* He jumped *off* the cliff.

party. Colloquial in the sense of "person." Use *person:* Are you the *person* who wanted to see me?

piece, peace. Do not confuse the spelling of these homonyms: *piece* means "portion"; *peace* means "absence of hostility."

phenomena. The plural of *phenomenon,* a fact or event. If you use *phenomena,* be sure to use a plural verb.

plenty. As an adverb, *plenty* is colloquial: Use *very, quite,* or a more precise word in your writing. This coffee is *very* hot. In the sense of "more than sufficient," use *plenty of:* We have *plenty of* time.

plus. *Plus* is a preposition meaning "with the addition of"; its use as a conjunction (John *plus* Mary are . . . .) is disapproved of by many. A phrase using *plus* should not affect the number of the verb:

> The old apartment complex, **plus** the new townhouse section, contains a total of 225 units.

Plus is also used as a noun (The new lights are a *plus* for the city), but many consider such use journalese or jargon.

practicable, practical. The two words are not interchangeable. *Practicable* means "feasible or usable, but not necessarily proved successful." *Practical,* on the other hand, implies success in its application to living. An electric car may be part of a *practicable* solution to urban pollution problems; putting on the spare tire is the *practical* method of dealing with a flat tire.

precede, proceed. *Precede* means "to go before": *proceed* means "to continue," "to move along."

> The mayor's car **preceded** the governor's in the parade.
>
> Let's **proceed** with the meeting.

principal, principle. *Principal,* both as an adjective and a noun, means "chief": the *principal* of a school, the *principal* reason. A *principle* is a rule of conduct or action: the *principle* governing the operation of a windmill, *principles* for living.

raise, rise. *Raise* is a transitive verb, taking an object, meaning to cause (something) to move up; *rise* is an intransitive verb meaning to go up:

> Every morning when I get up I **raise** the window shade.
>
> Yeast causes bread dough to **rise**.

real, really. *Real* is an adjective, *really* an adverb, although in speech *real* is often used as an adverb. In writing, though, you should distinguish between the two:

> Their disagreement was **real**.
>
> You did a **really** fine job.

reason is because. A redundant phrase since *because* means "the reason that." The preferred phrase is "the reason is that."

> The **reason** we are late **is that** an accident tied up traffic.

refer, allude. See *allude, refer.*

respectful, respective. *Respectful* is an adjective meaning "considerate of" or "honoring"; *respective* is an adjective meaning "particular" or "in a certain order":

> He is very **respectful** of his instructors.
>
> Each application was placed in its **respective** file.

shall, will. In current American usage, *will* is generally used with all persons in the verb for the future tense. In formal usage, however, *shall* is used in the first person for the simple future (I *shall ask*), *will* in the second and third persons (she *will ask*). For the emphatic future, the use is reversed: *will* is used in the first person (I *will win*), *shall* in the second and third (they *shall leave*). *Shall* is not a more elegant term than *will*.

sic. *Sic* is Latin word meaning "thus" or "so." It is generally used only in quoted material, inserted in brackets, to indicate that an error was made in the original, not the copy. Its use has declined considerably in current writing.

site, cite. See *cite, site.*

sit, set. The verb *sit* (as in a chair) is intransitive, not taking an object: *Sit* down. The verb *set*, meaning to put something down, does take an object: *Set* the plants on the balcony.

some. *Some* used as an adverb (I was *some* tired) is colloquial; edited English would use *somewhat* or a more precise descriptive word. *Some* used as an adjective (That was *some* concert) is informal, and better avoided in writing.

someone, some one. See *anyone, any one.*

sort. See *kind.*

somewheres. Nonstandard for *somewhere.*

stationary, stationery. *Stationary* is an adjective meaning "fixed in position," "immobile." *Stationery* is a noun referring to writing materials. One way to remember the difference is to recall that both *stationery* and *letter* contain *er.*

supposed to, used to. Because in speech the *-d* ending of *supposed* and the *t-* of *to* are not distinguished, the *-d* is sometimes left off in writing phrases such as *supposed to* and *used to.* Remember that they are regular verbs in the past tense, and thus require the final *-ed.*

sure, surely. In conversion the adjective *sure* is often used in place of the adverb *surely. Surely* is the only adverb form:

> We **surely** enjoyed the new exhibit at the museum.

suspect, suspicion. *Suspect* is a verb meaning "distrust" or "imagine": The police *suspected* foul play. *Suspicion* is a noun, and when used for *suspect* is a localism, inappropriate in writing.

teach, learn. See *learn, teach.*

than, then. Do not confuse the conjunction *than,* usually used in comparisons, with the adverb *then:*

> I would rather get up early **than** sleep late.
> **Then** I have more time to do all the things I want to do.

their, there. Confusion of these two words is usually a spelling error: *their* is the possessive form of *they: their* house, *their* problem. *There* is used most often as an adverb or an anticipating subject: over *there; there* are five horses in the corral.

themselves, theirselves. *Themselves* is a plural reflexive or intensive pronoun: they hurt *themselves. Theirselves* is not a standard English form.

that kind. See *kind, sort.*

till, until. Interchangeable as prepositions or conjunctions: Wait *till* [or *until*] I get there. Notice that *till* is not a shortened form of *until,* and should not be spelled with an apostrophe. The form *'til* is occasionally seen, especially in "poetic" writing.

to, too. Confusion of these forms in writing is generally a careless spelling error. The preposition *to* is far more common than the adverb *too,* which means "also," "besides," or "very."

try and, try to. Both are accepted idioms: *try and* is common in general English: *Try and* get your work done. *Try to* is the preferred form in formal English: *Try to* get your work done.

uninterested, disinterested. See *disinterested, uninterested.*

used to. See *supposed to.*

used to could. Colloquial for *used to be able to:* I *used to be able to* swim quite well. Use *used to be able to, was able to,* or *could* in writing.

wait on. Common in some dialects in the sense of *wait for,* but in writing should be used only in the sense of "serving a customer."

want, want to, want that. In the sense of "ought" or "should," *want* is informal: You *should* [rather than *want to*] review your notes before the test. In statements of desire or intention, *want to* is the standard idiom: *I want you to get* all you can from this year's work. In such constructions *want that* and *want for* are not standard.

was, were. *Was* is the past tense of *be (is)* in the first and third person singular: I, he, she, it *was.* *Were* is the past tense for second person singular (you *were*) and first, second, and third person plural: we, you, they *were.* Use of "we was" or "you was" is not standard.

we, I. *We* (the "editorial we") should not be used when you mean *I:* I base *my* conclusions on information I received from several hotel managers.

well, good. See *good, well.*

who, whom. Although the distinction between *who* and *whom* is disappearing in many contexts, this is the general guideline: use *who* when it is the subject of a verb, even in subordinate clauses; use *whom* in all object positions (object of the preposition, direct object):

Who is going to the play?

Whom are you taking to the play? (You are taking whom?)

He is a man **who** never compromises his principles.

He is a man of **whom** it's been said, "He never compromises his principles."

whose. See *of which, whose.*

would of. An error for *would have.* See *could of, would of.*

Index

Page references in **boldface** type refer to the most important discussion of a topic.

A, an, 83, 483
Abbreviations, **187–91**
  in endnotes, 452–53
  periods after, 133
Able to, 117
Absolute modifiers, **67–68**
Abstractions, making concrete, 213–14
Abstract words, 298, **308–11**
  capitalization of, 179
Accent, in dictionary, 291–92
accept, except, 483
Accusative case. *See* Objects.
Acknowledgment of sources. *See* Bibliographies, Footnotes.
Acronyms, 188
Active voice, 111, **113–14**
  of verbals, 62
A.D., 190
Addresses,
  commas in, 149
  in letters, 403, 404
Adjective clauses, **50–51**
  as sentence fragments, 42
  restrictive and nonrestrictive, **141–44**
  See also Subordinate clauses.
Adjectives, 29, **118–21,** 132
  comparison of, **126–30**
  compound, 182
  coordinate, 147
  demonstrative, 120–21
  and double negatives, **125–26**
  in description, 242
  position of, **118–19**
  predicate, 119–20
  See also Modifiers.
Adverb clauses, **51–52**
  as sentence fragments, 42–43
  commas after, 139
  See also Subordinate clauses.
Adverbs, 29, 118, **121–25,** 132
  as interrupting elements, 145
  comparison of, **126–30**
  conjunctive, 36
  and double negatives, **125–26**
  forms of, 121–22
  hyphenation of, 182

  misplaced, 123–24
  position of, 122–25
  punctuation with, 145
  relative, 51
advice, advise, 201, 483
affect, effect, 201, 483
Agencies, abbreviations for names of, 188
aggravate, irritate, 117, 483
Agreement,
  blind, **74–77**
  pronoun-antecedent, **91–93**
  subject-verb, **69–77**
ain't, 107, 484
all, 92
all ready, already, 202, 484
all right, 202, 484
all the farther, 484
all together, altogether, 202, 484
Alliteration, 339
allude, refer, 484
allusion, illusion, 201, 484
almost, most, 484
a lot, 484
also, as conjunctive adverb, 36
a.m., p.m., 190, 484
Ambiguity,
  of reference of pronouns, 86–87
  punctuation to avoid, 148
among, between, 484
amount, number, 485
Ampersand (&), 190
Analogy,
  argument from, 245
  false, 248
  for paragraph development, 365
-ance, -ence, 206
and,
  ampersand (&) as substitute for, 190
  clauses joined by, 137–38
  and comma use, 150–51
  to form compound subjects, 69
  used needlessly, 51
and etc., 485
and which, but which, 485
Annuals, 431
anon., 452

Answers, omission of verb in, 39
Answers, for essay examinations, 393–98
Antecedents,
  agreement of pronouns with, **91–93**
  definite reference of, 86
Anticipating subject, 28
Antithethical sentences, 349
Antonyms, 295
anybody, 92
anyone, any one, 92, 485
Apologetic quotes, 168
Apostrophes, **184–85**
  misuse of, 81
  for possessive case, 81
Appositives, 31
  gerunds as, 62
  noun clauses as, 52
  punctuation of, 143
Appropriate language, 16–21
Arabic numerals, 194
Argumentation, **243–49**
  and audience, 246–47
  flaws in, 247–49
  and paragraph development, 359
  types of, 245–46
  using resources, 244–45
Argumentum ad hominem, 249
Articles *(a, an, the),*
  capitalization of in titles, 176–77
  choice of *a* or *an,* 83, 483
  repetition of, 338
  the to introduce gerund phrase, 64–65
as, 485
  in comparisons, 130
  and subordination, 56
as . . . as, 129
as, as if, as though, 130
as well as, subjects followed by, 71
Audience,
  and appropriate language, 18–20
  and argumentation, 246–47
  and writer, 225–26
Auxiliary verbs, 111
Author name,
  in bibliography, 433
  in card catalog, 426
  in endnotes, 448–52
awhile, a while, 202, 486

Awkward constructions,
  brackets within parentheses, 162
  choppy or stringy sentences, **330–31**
  inverted subordination, **58–59**
  noun clauses as complements, 53
  of which, 494
  passive verbs, 114
  possessive forms, 82
  tandem subordination, 58
  wordy sentences, **333–34**

Bad, badly, 120, 486
Balanced sentences, 349
barely, 125
B.C., A.D., 190
be,
  as linking verb, 27, 107
  case of pronoun after, 94–95
  complement after, 119–20
  forms of, 107
  in passive verbs, 111, 113
because, 495
  for exact subordination, 34, 43, 57
  introducing adverb clauses, 52
  to correct comma fault, 46–47
before, introducing adverb clauses, 52
Begging the question, 248–49
Beginnings of papers, 267, 270–71
  relation of to endings, 279
  thesis sentence in, 270
Beginnings of sentences,
  numbers at, 193
  variation in, 342
being that, 117, 486
beside, besides, 486
Biblical citations, 451
Bibliographies, 158, **453–55**
  cards for preparing, 433–35
  sample of, 453–55
  working version, **432–35**
Big words, 313–14
Blind agreement, 74–77
Bobtailed adverbs, 122
Books,
  bibliography cards for, 434
  bibliography form for, 454–55
  endnote form for, 449–50

born, borne, 108
both . . . and, 36
Brackets, **161–62**
bring, take, 486
British usage, 206–207, 291
Business letters. *See* Public
    letters.
but,
    as coordinating conjunction, 36
    comma with, 138
    in double negative, 125–26
    misuse of, 51
    semicolon with, 153
but that, but what, 486
but which, 51

C. or *ca.,* 452
Call numbers, library, 426, 433
can be, able to be, 486
can, may, 107–108, 486
can't hardly, couldn't scarcely,
    125–26, 487
can't help but, 126, 487
capital, capitol, 487
Capitalization, **175–80**
    at close of letters, 404
    for emphasis, 353
    in outlines, 261–62
    of abbreviations, 191
Card catalogs, **425–28**
Cardinal numbers, 194
Caret, 381
Case forms. *See* Objects,
    Possessive case, Subjects.
case, as deadwood, 335
Catalog, library, **425–28**
Cause-effect, 269
    for paragraph development, 365
-cede, -ceed, -sede, 206
censor, censure, 304, 487
center around, 487
cf., 190
ch., chs., 452
character, as deadwood, 335
Charts and tables, placement of,
    380
choose, chose, 201
Choppy sentences, **330–31**
Christian names, abbreviations of,
    187
Chronological order,
    for paragraph development, 366
    in narration, 238
Circumlocutions, 333

Citations, form of,
    in bibliographies, 453–55
    in endnotes, 448–53
cite, site, 201, 304, 487
Clarity, 10–11
    commas used for, 148
    in business letters, 402,
        408–409
    in good English, 18
    in sentences, 331–32, 346–47
    in topic sentences, 360
    parallelism for, 348
Classification, for paragraph
    development, 366
Clauses, 32, **34–35**
    adjective, **50–51**
    adverb, **51–52**
    coordinate, 137–38
    incorrectly joined, 44–48
    misused as sentences, 41–44
    noun, 52–54
    punctuation of, 137–44
    and sentence type, 35–38
    See also Main clauses,
        Subordinate clauses.
Clichés, 319–20
Climax, 269
    for closing paragraphs, 278
    sentences, 351
Close, in letters, 404
"Close" punctuation, 12
Closing of papers, **278–80**
coarse, course, 201
Coherence. *See* Clarity,
    Continuity.
col., cols., 452
Collective nouns, **72–74**
Colloquialisms, 168. *See also*
    Informal English.
Colons, **156–58**
    capitalization after, 176
    in letters, 403–404
    and quotation marks, 169
Comma faults, **44–48**
Commands (imperative sentences),
    38, 39
Commas, **137–52**
    appositives set off by, 143
    conventional uses of, 148–50
    distinguished from dash, 159
    distinguished from semicolon,
        153–56
    for clarity, 148
    in numbers, 193
    in series, 146–47

misused, 150–52
with conjunctive adverbs, 138
with coordinate clauses,
137–38
with interrupting elements,
144–46
with introductory elements,
138–39, 141
with nonrestrictive modifiers,
141–44
with parenthetical elements,
144–46
with quotation marks, 169
Common nouns, 79
capitalization of, 180
plurals of, 78, 80
preceding a gerund, 61, 63
Comparative form, 127
Comparison and contrast, 269
for paragraph development, 365
Comparison of adjectives and
adverbs, **126–30**
Comparisons,
construction of, 126–28
figurative comparisons, 321–25
for paragraph development, 365
idiomatic, 129–30
and parallelism, 348–49
use of *like* or *as,* 130
use of *other,* 130
See also Analogy.
complement, compliment, 487
Complements, 27, 30
agreement of verb with, 75–76
blind agreement, **74–77**
noun clauses as, 53
with verbals, 60
Complete subjects, 25
Complex sentences, 36–37
Complimentary close, 404
Composition. *See* Research
papers, Writing.
Compound adjectives, 182
Compound-complex sentences,
37
Compound nouns, 79
and spelling errors, 203
with hyphen, 181–82
Compound numbers, 181
Compound object, 35
Compound sentences, 36–37
punctuation of, 137–41,
153–55
Compound subjects, 35
agreement of verb with, 69–71

Compound words, 181
possessive form of, 81
Conclusions of papers, **278–80**
Concrete words, 298, **308–11**
Conjugation. *See* Verbs.
Conjunctions, 132
coordinating, 36, 46, 69
correlative, 36, 69–71
for paragraph continuity, 368
repetition of, 338
subordinating, 34, 46, 52,
55–56
Conjunctive adverbs, 36, 138
and comma faults, 46
and semicolons, 154
Connectives, 36, 52
for adverb clauses, 52
for continuity, 368
for exactness, 55–56
misused, 58
repetition of, 338
and subordinate clauses, 50–59
semicolon substituted for,
153–54
to correct comma faults, 46
using exact, 55–56
See also Conjunctions, Relative
adverbs, Relative pronouns.
Connotation, 293, **299–300**
connote, denote, 487
conscientious, conscious, 487
consequently, 36, 46, 154
considerable, considerably, 488
Consistency,
in abbreviations, 191
in figures of speech, 324–25
in footnote form, 453
in parallelism, 348–49
in tense, 104
in use of figures, 191–92
in use of hyphens, 181
Consonants, doubling of final, 205
contact, 117, 488
Context, and meaning of words,
297–300
continual, continuous, 488
Continuity
between paragraphs, 272–74
within paragraphs, 367–72
and sentence length, 329–32
Contractions, 184–85
Contrast, for paragraph
development, 365
Conversations. *See* Dialog,
Speech.

Coordinate adjectives, 147
Coordinate clauses, 36
    overuse of, 58, 331
    punctuation of, 137–38
Coordinate elements,
    commas between, 147, 153
    coordinate adjectives, 147
    semicolon with, 153
Coordinate ideas, parallel
    structure for, 347–50
Coordinating conjunctions, 36
    comma faults corrected by, 46
    joining clauses, 36, 46, 53,
        137–38
    overuse of, 331
    punctuation with, 153–54, 155
Copula, 111
Correcting a paper, 381–82. *See
    also* Revision.
Correctness, 19
Correlative conjunctions, 36
    agreement of subject and verb
        joined by, 69–71
    parallel constructions with,
        348–49
could of, would of, 488
Count nouns, 79
Countries, abbreviations for, 188
Courses (academic), capitalization
    of names of, 179
Courtesy questions, 133
credible, creditable, credulous,
    488
Criticism, writing, **398–402**
Current English, 3

Dangling modifiers, **66–67.** *See
    also* Misrelated modifiers.
Dashes, **159–60**
    with quotation marks, 169
data, 488
    agreement with, 174
Dates,
    abbreviations of, 188
    apostrophe with, 185
    commas in, 149
    figures in, 192
Deadwood, elimination of,
    334–36. *See also* Wordiness.
Death masks, **318–19**
Decimals, 134
Declarative sentences. *See*
    Statements.
Deduction, for paragraph
    development, 364–65

Definition,
    for openings of paragraphs, 275
    for paragraph development, 365
    and subject of paper, 216
Definitions, in dictionaries,
    294–95
Degree, of adjectives and adverbs,
    126
Degrees (academic), 187
Deity, capitalization of, 179
Demonstrative adjectives, 120–21
Demonstrative pronouns, 88
Denotation, 293, 298
Dependent clauses. *See*
    Subordinate clauses.
Description, **240–43, 370–71**
    modifiers in, 118, 242
    spatial order in, 242, 269
    verbless sentences in, 39
Descriptive approach to language,
    5
desert, dessert, 201
Details, 40
    as beginning of paper, 276
    in description, 241–43
    in narration, 239–40
    in paragraphs, 357–58
    parentheses enclosing, 161
    selecting and arranging, 241–42
    See also Facts.
detract, distract, 304, 488
Diagrams, placement of, 380
Dialects, 6–9, 15
    as dictionary label, 294
Dialog,
    punctuation of, 160, 165
    short sentences for, 39, 330
Diction,
    abstract and concrete words,
        298, **308–11**
    clichés, 319–20
    connotation, **299–300**
    context, **297–300**
    deadwood, **334–36**
    denotation, 298
    economy of expression, 333–34
    euphemisms, 320–21
    figures of speech, 321–25
    foreign words, 315
    formal words, **312–16**
    informal words, **316–18**
    meaning of words, 292–93,
        297–98
    repetition, 337–39
    slang, 11, 294, 316

slanted words, **300–303**
stilted language, 313–14
technical words, **315–16**
trite expressions, **319–20**
wordiness, **333–34**
See also Words, Usage.
Dictionaries, 197, **285–96**
college, 287
definitions in, 292–93
etymology in, 295
foreign words in, 294
grammatical information in,
292–93
historical, 288
labels in, 294
pronunciation in, 291–92
sample entries, 290
selection of, 286–88
synonyms and antonyms in, 295
unabridged, 287
usage in, 294
word division, 289, 291
different from, 488
Direct address, 146
Direct discourse, 164–65
Direct objects, 26, 30. *See also*
Objects.
Direct questions, 134
Direct quotations. *See* Quotations.
disinterested, uninterested, 488
Dissertations,
bibliography form for, 455
endnote form for, 452
distract, detract, 304, 388
Division of words, 289, 291,
379–80
do, idioms with, 108
do, did, done, 108
Documentation, in research
papers, **235–36.**
See also Bibliographies,
Endnotes.
done, don't, 489
don't, doesn't, 108
Double comparisons, 129
Double negatives, 125–26
Double possessives, 82
Drama, 398
Draft, of a paper, revising,
374–78

-e, and spelling errors, 204
each, 93

Economy of expression, 333–34
ed., 452
-ed,
doubling of consonant before,
212
ending for verbs, 101–102
spelling errors, 200
Edited American English, 3,
12–14, 16
effect, affect, 201, 304, 483
e.g., 190
-ei- or *-ie-,* 204
either . . . or, 348, 489
Ellipses, 170–71
eminent, imminent, 489
Emphasis, **350–53**
exclamatory sentences, 135–36
italics for, 172–73
mechanical devices, 353
periodic sentences, 351
punctuation, 133–36, 159–60,
161–62
reflexive pronouns, 97
repetition, 352
shall and *will,* 110
short sentences, 330–31
subordination, 36–37, 346–47
word order, 28, 118–19,
122–23, 342–43
-ence, -ance, 206
Encyclopedias, 431
Encyclopedia articles,
bibliography cards for, 434
bibliography form for, 455
endnote form for, 451
Endings of papers, **278–80**
Endnotes, **448–53**
abbreviations in, 452
alternative forms, 453
form of, 448
in first draft, 442
numbering of, 448
punctuation in, 158
samples of, 449–51
spacing of, 448
split, 449
Endorsing a paper, 381
End punctuation, **133–36**
with quotation marks, 169
English. *See* Edited American
English, Formal English,
Informal English, Standard
English, Usage.
enthuse, 117, 489
Envelopes, 404–405

equally as, 489
Essay examination answers,
  393–98
et al., 452
etc., 190, 489
Etymology, 295
Euphemisms, 320–21
everybody, 88
  agreement with, 92
  masculine or feminine pronoun
    with, 89–90
  possessive of, 96
every one, everyone, 92, 489
Examinations, essay answers for,
  393–98
Examples,
  colon to set off, 158
  in parentheses, 161
  italicized, 171–72
  See also Details, Facts.
Exclamation marks, **135–36**
  and quotation marks, 169
Exclamations, 38, 39
  inverted order in, 28
  omission of verb in, 39
  punctuation of weak, 145–46
exist, 335
expect, 489
Explanatory phrases, 42
  in brackets, 161
  in parentheses, 161
Expletives, 28
Exposition, **233–36**
  and paragraph development,
    358–59
Expressive writing, 231, 232

-f, and spelling errors, 202–203
fact, 335
factor, 335
Facts, in opening paragraphs, 275.
  See also Details, Examples.
Fallacies in reasoning, **247–49**
False analogy, 248
Family names, hyphens in, 181
farther, further, 127, 489
Faulty subordination, **57–59**
feel, 27
Feminine nouns, 79
Feminine pronouns, **89–90**
fewer, less, 489
field, 335
Figurative language, 320, **321–25**
  consistent, 324–25

effective use of, 324
  types of, 322–23
Figures, **191–94**
  conventional use of, 192–93
  in parentheses, 161
  periods with, 134
  plurals of, 185
  See also Numbers.
Finite verbs, 111
First drafts of a paper, **266–84,**
  441–42
  beginning and ending
    paragraphs, 260, 270–71,
    274–78
  development of thesis, 267–68
  of research papers, 441–42
  and outline, 252–65
  paragraph sequences, 272–74
  selecting a title, 281
  See also Writing.
First person pronoun, 88
  appropriateness of, in writing,
    98, 236–37
  I or *me,* 94–95, 97–98
  possessive of, 95–96
  reflexive and intensive forms of,
    97–98
fix, 117
flaunt, flout, 490
Footnotes. *See* Endnotes.
for, 36, 138
Foreign words, 294
  appropriateness of, 315–16
  italics for, 172
Formal English, 12–13, 15, 20
  conventions of, 144, 154, 179,
    181, 184, 187
  word choice in, 312–16
formally, formerly, 304
former, latter, 490
Fractions, 181
Fragments, **41–44**
  revising, 43
further, farther, 127, 489
Fused sentences, **48–49**
Future tenses, 103

Gender,
  of nouns, 79
  of pronouns, **89–90**
General English, 9–10
  conventions of, 138, 144, 179,
    181, 184, 187
  word choice in, 316–18

Generalizations, hasty, 277
Genitive case. *See* Possessive
    case.
Geographic areas, names of,
    abbreviations for, 188
    capitalization of, 178
Gerunds, 61, 62
    idiomatic use of, 64–65
    subjects with, 61, 63
get, got, gotten, 108, 109, 491
Gobbledygook, 314
good, well, 120, 490
Grammar, **24–40**
    agreement, **69–77, 91–93**
    clauses, 32, 34
    common sentence errors, **41–49**
    complements, 27
    main sentence elements, **25–29**
    modifiers, 29, 31, 33
    objects, 26
    phrases, 32, 34
    predicates, 26
    secondary sentence elements,
        29–32
    sentence types, **35–38, 341–45**
    unorthodox sentences, **38–40**
    verbs, **25–26**
    word order, **28–29**
Greek roots, of words, 306
Groups, capitalization of names
    of, 178
Group words, and spelling errors,
    203

Half, 490
Handwritten papers, 379
hang, 490
hardly, 124, 125, 490
Hasty generalization, 247–48
have got, have got to, 109
he or *she*, 490
    reference of, 89–90
Headings,
    in letters, 403
    in outlines, 262, 263
himself, herself, 88
hisself, 490
historic, histrionic, 303
Homonyms, 197, 303–304
however, 138
    as interrupter, 144
    between main clauses, 36, 46,
        154
Hyperbole, 322

Hyphens, 180–84
    for word division, 289, 379–80

I, me, 94–95, 97–98
I, we, 98, 177
ibid., 453
-ible, -able, 206
-ics, 73–74
Idiolects, 5–6, 15
Idioms,
    in comparisons, 129–30
    in dictionary, 293
    infinitives and gerunds, 64–65
    verbs and verb phrases, 116
    with *do*, 108
    with *get*, 108, 109
i.e., 190, 452
-ie- and *-ei-*, 204
if, 34, 43, 46
if . . . then, 129
Ignoring the question, 249
Illogical arguments, 247–49
Illustration, for opening
    paragraphs, 276
Imagery. *See* Figurative language.
Imperative sentences. *See*
    Commands.
imply, infer, 304, 491
in, into, 491
in addition to, 71
incredible, incredulous, 491
Indefinite pronouns, 88
    agreement with, 92–93
    masculine or feminine pronoun
        with, 89–90
    possessive of, 96
Indentation,
    for quotations, 165
    in letters, 403
    in outlines, 261
    in papers, 379
    with dialog, 165
Independent clauses. *See* Main
    clauses.
Indexes, of periodicals, **428–31**
Indicative mood, 111
Indirect discourse, 112, 165
Indirect objects, 26, 30. *See also*
    Objects.
Indirect questions, 133
Induction, for paragraph
    development, 364–65
infer, imply, 304, 491

Infinitives, 60, 62
  as absolute modifiers, **67–68**
  as misrelated modifiers, **65–66,**
    139
  idiomatic use of, 64–65
  infinitive phrases, 32
  split, 65
inflammable, flammable, 304
Inflected language, 2–3
Inflection. *See* Case, Number,
    Tense.
Informal English, 12, 15
  contractions in, 184
  subjectless sentences, 39
  word choice, 316–18
Institutions, capitalization of
    names of, 179
Intensive pronouns, 88, **97–98**
Interjections, 132
Internal punctuation. *See* Colons,
    Commas, Dashes,
    Parentheses, Semicolons.
Interrogative pronouns, 88
Interrupters, **144–46**
Interviews,
  bibliography form for, 455
  endnote form for, 452
Intransitive verbs, 111
Introductions. *See* Beginnings of
    papers.
Introductory elements, 138–39,
    141
Inverted subordination, 58–59
Inverted word order, 28, 76,
    342–43
Irony, 322
irregardless, 126, 491
Irregular verbs, **105–13**
irritate, aggravate, 117
is when, is where, 491
it, 87
Italics, 167, 168, **171–73**
it is I, 94–95
its, it's, 96, 491
it's me, 94–95
itself, 88, 97

Jargon, 314
Journal, keeping a, 213
Journal articles,
  bibliography cards for, 434
  bibliography form for, 455
  endnote form for, 450–51
just, 124

Key words, for emphasis, 352
kind, sort, 491
kind of a, sort of a, 492

l., ll., 452
Language, **2–21**
  appropriateness of, 16–21
  clarity, 10–11
  edited American English,
    12–14, 16
  elements of, 2–4
  formal, 12–13, 15, 20
  "good," 14–21
  informal, 12, 15
last, latest, 492
later, latter, 492
Latin,
  abbreviations for, 190
  roots of words, 306
lay, lie, 492
learn, teach, 492
leave, let, 117, 492
let's us, 492
Letters, public, **402–15**
  of application, 410–15
  commas in, 149
  criteria for, 405–10
  form for, 403–405
Letters (of the alphabet),
  omission of, 185
  in parentheses, 161
  plurals of, 185
Library card catalog, **425–28**
lie, lay, 109
like, in comparisons, 130
like, as, 492
likely, liable, apt, 493
Linking verbs, 27, 111, 119
Lists (series),
  parallelism in, 348
  possessive case in, 81
  punctuation of, 146–47, 151
Literature, writing about, **398–402**
Litotes, 322
Localisms, 11
Logic,
  errors in, **247–49**
  induction and deduction,
    364–65
  kinds of argument, **245–46**
loose, lose, 493
Loose sentences, 343
Lower case. *See* Capitalization.
-ly, 121, 122

Magazine articles,
　bibliography cards for, 434
　bibliography form for, 455
　endnote form for, 450–51
Main (independent) clauses, 34
　connectives to join, 36, 46,
　　154–55
　incorrectly joined, **44–48**
　inverted subordination, **58–59**
　modified by adverb clauses,
　　51–52
　punctuation between, 157
　stringy sentences, 331
　See also Subordinate clauses.
Manuscript form, **378–82**
　bibliographies, **453–55**
　corrections in, 381–82
　division of words, 289, 379–80
　endnotes, **448–53**
　handwritten papers, 379
　margins and spacing, 379
　outlines, **260–63**
　proofreading, 381
　sample papers, 457–82
　title, 380
　typed papers, 378–79
Masculine pronouns, **89–90**
may, 107–108, 486
may be, maybe, 493
Measurement (units of),
　abbreviations for, 189
　agreement with, 72–73
　noun forms designating, 83
Mental writing, 250
merely, 124
Metaphor, 322
Metonymy, 322
Mimetic writing, 250
Misplaced modifiers, **123–24**
Misrelated modifiers, **65–66**
Miss, Mrs., Ms., 403, 404
Misspelling. *See* Spelling.
Mixed constructions, 49
Mixed metaphors, **324–25**
Modifiers, 29, 31, 33
　absolute, **67–68**
　adjectives and adverbs, 29,
　　118–25, 131
　appositives, 31, 143
　commas misused after, 151
　compound, **182–83**
　dangling, 66–67
　group, 182
　kinds of, 33
　misplaced, **123–24**

misrelated, **65–66**
　nonrestrictive, **141–44**
　nouns as, 83
　position of, **118–19, 122–25**
　predicate adjectives, **119–20**
　prepositional phrases, 31, 32
　restrictive, **141–44**
　spelling problems with, 201
　squinting, 66
　subordinate clauses, 50–52
　verbal phrases, 61, 63
Money, figures used for, 193
Months, forms for names of, 179,
　188
Mood, of verbs, 111
　subjunctive, **115–16**
moral, morale, 493
most, almost, 122
Mrs., Ms., Miss, 403, 404
my, mine, 96
myself, 493

Namely, 42
Names,
　abbreviations for, 187
　capitalization of, 177–78
Narration, **236–40**
　paragraph continuity in, 371–72
n.d., 452
neither . . . nor, 36
　agreement with elements joined
　　by, 70
　parallelism with, 348
nevertheless, 36, 154
Newspaper articles,
　bibliography cards for, 434
　bibliography form for, 455
　endnotes for, 450–51
nohow, nowheres, 493
Nominative case. *See* Subject.
none, 92
Nonfinite verbs, 111
Nonrestrictive modifiers, **141–44**
non sequitur, 248
Nonstandard English, 11, 15
nor, 36
　agreement with elements joined
　　by, 70
　comma with, 137
not . . . no, 493
not only . . . but, 36, 348–49
Note-taking, **436–37, 438–40**
Noun clauses, 52–54
Noun modifiers, 83

Nouns, **78–84,** 131
  a or *an* with, 83
  as modifiers, 83
  classes of, 79
  collective, **72–74**
  compound, **181–82**
  forms and functions of, 79
  gender of, 79
  plurals of, 78, 80
  possessive of, **80–82**
  predicate nouns, 27
  proper, 79, 177
  reference of pronouns to, **85–90**
  used attributively, 29
n.p., 452
number, amount, 485
number, agreement with, 73
Number,
  of collective nouns, 72–74
  of compound subjects, 69–71
  of indefinite pronouns, 92–93
  shifts in, 99–100
  See also Agreement.
Numbering,
  in outlines, 261
  of footnotes, 448
  of letter pages, 403
  of manuscript pages, 380
Numbers, **191–94**
  abbreviations with, 189
  agreement with, 72–73
  commas in, 148
  compound, 181
  parentheses around, 161
  plurals of, 185, 193
  See also Figures.
Numeral pronouns, 88

-o, and spelling errors, 202–203
Objective case,
  of pronouns, 88, 94–95
  with infinitives, 60, 61
Objects, 26, 30
  compound, 35
  direct, 26, 30
  gerunds as, 62
  indirect, 26, 30
  infinitives as, 62
  modifiers of, 33
  noun clauses as, 52
  of prepositions, 94
  of verbals, 60, 61
  position of, 28, 29
  pronouns as, 88

Obsolete words, 294
Occupational dialects, 8. *See also*
  Shoptalk.
o'clock, 484
of,
  in gerund phrases, 64
  phrases, 82
of, have, 493
of which, whose, 494
off of, 494
Omissions,
  apostrophe to indicate, 184
  ellipses to indicate, 170–71
one, 99
one of those who, 74
only, 124
Onomatopoeia, 322
Opening paragraphs, **274–78**
or,
  agreement with elements joined
    by, 70
  comma with, 137–38
Ordinal numbers, 194
Organization of a paper. *See*
  Outlines.
Organizations, names of,
  abbreviations for, 188
  capitalization of, 178
other, in comparisons, 130
Outlines, **252–64**
  preliminary, 441
  revising, 258–59
  scratch, 255
  sentence, 259–60
  standard form for, 260–63
  thesis sentence, 255–56
  topic, 256–58
Oxymoron, 323

p., pp., 452
Page numbers,
  Arabic vs. Roman, 193
  in bibliography, 454
  in endnotes, 448, 449–52
  of manuscript, 380
Pamphlets, cited in endnotes, 451
Papers, **374–91**
  correcting final copy, 381–82
  correction symbols in, 386–87
  examples of, 384–87, 389–90
  manuscript form for, 378–82
  revising and correcting, 374–91
  See also Research papers,
    Subjects of a paper.

Paragraphs, **355–73**
  argumentative, 359
  closing, **278–80**
  continuity between, **272–74**
  continuity within, **367–72**
  deductive, 364–65
  descriptive, 370–71
  details in, 357–58
  development of, 365–67
  expository, 358–59
  general statements in, 357
  inductive, 364–65
  length, 361–64
  narrative, 371–72
  opening, **274–78**
  sequences, 272–74
  topic sentences in, 360–61
  typical contents of, 357–60
  underdeveloped, 355–56
Parallelism,
  in outlines, 262–63
  in sentences, **347–50**
Paraphrasing, **445–46**
Parentheses, **160–61**
  brackets distinguished from, 162
  capitals within, 176
Parenthetical elements,
  capitals in, 176
  in brackets, 162
  in parentheses, 160–61
  with commas, 144–46
  with dashes, 159
part, 76
Participles, 60, 62
  as absolute modifiers, **67–68**
  forms and typical uses, 62
  misused as sentences, 43
  position and reference of,
    65–67
  weak, 58–59
Parts of speech. *See* Adjectives,
  Adverbs, Conjunctions,
  Interjections, Nouns,
  Prepositions, Pronouns,
  Verbs.
party, 494
Passive voice, 28, 111, **113–14**
  of verbals, 62
  word order with, 28
Past tenses, 103
  in narrative, 238
  of irregular verbs, 105–107
  of regular verbs, 101–104
  of verbals, 62
  spelling errors with, 200

Percentages, use of figures for,
  193
Periodic sentences, **344**
Periodicals,
  bibliography form for, 434, 455
  endnote form for, 450–51
  indexes of, 428–31
Periods, **133–34**
  with abbreviations, 191
  with parentheses, 161
  with quotation marks, 169
Periphrasis, 323
personal, personnel, 201, 303
Personal experience, for opening
  paragraphs, 275–76
Personal pronouns, 88
  agreement with, 91–92
  avoiding shifts in, 99–100
  choice of, 98–99
  intensive form, 97–98
  possessive form, 96
  reflexive form, 97–98
  subject or object form, 94–95
  with verbals, 63
Personification, 323
Persuasive writing, 232, 233. *See
  also* Argumentation.
phenomena, 494
Phrases, 32, 34
  absolute, **67–68**
  as fragments, 42
  dangling or misplaced, **66–67**
  deadwood, **334–36**
  introductory, 138–39
  of comparison, 130
  parallel form for, **347–50**
  prepositional, 31
  restrictive and nonrestrictive,
    141–44
  verbal, 31, **61–64**
piece, peace, 494
Place names,
  abbreviations for, 188
  capitalization of, 178
Plagiarism, **446–48**
Plays, 398
plenty, 494
Plural nouns, 78, 80
  and agreement, 74
  as modifiers, 81
  collective nouns, **72–74**
  compound nouns, **181–82**
  possessive form of, 82
  spelling problems with,
    202–203

Plurals,
  apostrophe with, 81, 185
  forming, 78, 80
  of figures, 185, 193
  of letters, 185
  and spelling errors, 202–203
plus, 494
p.m., a.m., 190
Poetry, quoting, 167, 175
Point of view, 236–37
portion, 76
Positive degree, of adjectives and
  adverbs, 126
Possessive (genitive) case, **80–82**
  apostrophe with, 185
  double possessive, 82
  of nouns, 80–82
  subjects of gerund phrases, 61,
  63
Possessive pronouns, **95–97**
Post Hoc, Ergo Propter Hoc, 248
practicable, practical, 494
precede, proceed, 494
Predicate, 26, 30. *See also*
  Complement, Objects, Verbs.
Predicate adjectives, 27, 119–20
Predicate nouns, 27
predominate, predominant, 117
Prefixes, hyphen with, 182–83
Prepositional phrases, 31, 32
Prepositions, 132
  case of pronouns after, 94
  for parallelism, 347–50
Prescriptive approach to language,
  4–5
Present tenses, 103
principal, principle, 201, 303, 495
proceed, precede, 494
Progressive forms of verbs, 103
Prolepsis, 343
Pronouns, **85–100,** 132
  agreement of, **91–93**
  case of, **94–97**
  choice of, 98–99
  for paragraph continuity, 368
  indefinite, 88, 92–93, 96
  intensive, 88, **97–98**
  kinds of, 88
  masculine or feminine, **89–90**
  number of, **91–93**
  personal, 91–93
  possessive, **95–97**
  reference of, **85–90**
  reflexive, 97–98
  repetition of, 338
  shifts in person or number of,
  99–100
  subject or object form, 94–95
Pronunciation,
  in dictionaries, 291–92
  in regional dialects, 6, 7
  of homonyms, 303–304
  and spelling errors, 200
Proofreading, 381
Proper nouns, 79
  capitalization of, 177
public, agreement with, 73
Publication, submitting manuscript
  for, 382
Publication facts,
  on bibliography cards, 433, 434
  in card catalog, 426, 427
Public dialects, 8–9
Public letters, **402–15**
Punctuation,
  ambiguity corrected by, 148
  apostrophes, 184–85
  brackets, **161–62**
  "close," 12
  colons, **156–58**
  commas, **137–52**
  dashes, **159–60**
  ellipses, **170–71**
  end, **133–36**
  exclamation marks, **135–36**
  hyphens, **180–84**
  in addresses and letters,
  402–405, 411–14
  in bibliographies, 453–55
  in endnotes, 448–52
  in outlines, 261–62
  italics, **171–73**
  need for, 10–11
  of abbreviations, 191
  parentheses, **160–61**
  periods, **133–34**
  question marks, **134–35**
  quotation marks, **164–70**
  semicolons, **153–56**
  sentence mistakes corrected by,
  44–48

Qualifiers. *See* Modifiers.
Question marks, 134–35
  with quotation marks, 169
Questions, 38
  answers to, 39
  interrogative pronouns, 88
  inverted word order in, 28–29

on examinations, 393–94
punctuation with, 133, 134–35
shall and *will* in, 110
Quotation marks, **164–70**
other punctuation marks with,
168–70
Quotations,
acknowledgment of, 443–44
brackets in, 161
capitalization of, 176
colons before, 157–58
commas in, 149–50
ellipses in, 170–71
in note taking, 437, 438
punctuation of, 165–67
trite, 319–20
sic in, 162
See also Dialog, Direct
quotations, Endnotes.

Raise, rise, 495
*Readers' Guide to Periodical
Literature,* 428–29
real, really, 495
reason is because, 495
Reciprocal pronouns, 88
Redundancy. *See* Wordiness.
refer, allude, 484
Reference materials. *See* Source
materials.
Reference of pronouns, **85–90**
Reference papers. *See* Research
papers.
Referential writing, 232
Reflexive pronouns, 88, **97–98**
regardless, irregardless, 126, 491
Regional dialects, 7, 11
Regular verbs, **101–104**
Relative adverbs, 51
Relative pronouns, 34, 88
agreement with, 92
and or *but* before, 51
possessive of, **95–97**
sentence faults corrected by,
42–43
who or *whom,* 96–97, 497–98
who, which, or *that,* 89
Relatives, names of, 181
Relative words, 298
Religious names, capitalization of,
179
Repetition,
careless, **337–39**

for continuity, 368
for emphasis, 352–53
Reports, 415–21
Requests,
no subject in, 39
should and *would* in, 112
Research papers, **422–82**
assembling completed, 456
bibliography, **453–55**
choosing a subject for, 423–25
documentation for, **442–48**
endnotes, **448–53**
evaluating your material,
435–36
first draft, 441–42
note taking for, **436–37, 438–40**
planning, 437–41
preliminary outline for, 441
sample papers, 457–82
source materials, **425–32**
working bibliographies, **432–35**
See also Manuscript form,
Papers, Writing.
Resources, using, 222–23,
244–45. *See also* Source
materials.
respectful, respective, 495
Restrictive modifiers, 142
comma with, 151
introduced by *that,* 142
Resumés, 410, 412
rev., 452
Reverend, The Reverend, Rev.,
187
Revision,
of a corrected paper, 382–88
of outlines, 258–59
Roman numerals, 194
Run-on sentences. *See* Comma
faults.

-'s, to form possessive, 80
-s, -es, to form plurals, 78, 80
Sacred names, capitalization of,
179
Salutations, in letters, 158
scarcely, 125
Scientific terms, abbreviations for,
189
Scratch outlines, 255
Secondary sentence elements,
29–32
misused as sentences, **44–48**
See also Modifiers, Phrases,

Subordinate clauses.
-sede,-cede,-ceed, 206
seem, as deadwood, 336
self-, in compounds, 181
Semicolons, 145, **153–56**
  between main clauses, 153–55
  distinguished from colon, 156
  for emphasis, 352
  and other punctuation, 155, 169
  to correct comma fault, 46
Sentence elements, **25–29,** 30. *See also* Clauses, Phrases, Objects, Subjects.
Sentence fragments, **41–44**
Sentence length, **326–39**
  choppy sentences, 330–31
  and deadwood, 334–36
  and meaning, 329–32
  and repetition, 337–39
  stringy sentences, 331
  and style, **326–29**
  and wordiness, 333–34
Sentence outlines, 259–60
Sentences,
  antithetical, 349
  balanced, 349
  beginnings of, 342
  capitalization in, 175
  choppy, **330–31**
  classified by purpose, 38
  classified by structure, **35–38**
  coherence, 54–55
  comma faults, **44–48**
  commands, 38, 39
  complex, **36–37**
  compound, **35–36**
  compound-complex, 37
  deadwood in, **334–36**
  declarative, 38
  economy in, 333–34
  emphasis in, **350–53**
  end punctuation, **133–36**
  errors, **41–49**
  exclamatory, 38
  fragmentary, **41–44**
  fused, **48–49**
  grammar of, **24–40**
  imperative, 38, 39
  interrogative, 38
  length of, **326–39**
  loose, **343–44**
  main elements of, **25–29**
  mixed constructions, 49
  parallelism in, **347–50**
  periodic, 344

questions, 38
  repetition in, 337–39
  run-on, 48
  secondary elements of, **29–32**
  simple, 35
  stringy, 331
  subjectless, 39
  subordination to clarify meaning of, **54–59, 346–47**
  topic, 360–61
  types of, **341–45**
  unorthodox, **38–40**
  variety in, **341–45**
  verbless, 39
  wordiness in, 333–34
  word order in, **28–29**
Sequence, of paragraphs, 272–74
series, 76
Series,
  parallelism in, 348
  possessive case in, 84
  punctuation of, **146–47,** 151
set, sit, 109–10, 495
shall, will, 110, 495
she, 89–90
Shoptalk, 8
should, would, 112
sic, 162, 495
Signature, in letters, 404
Simile, 323
Simple sentences, 35
Simple subjects, 25
since,
  to correct comma fault, 46–47
  introducing subordinate clause, 34, 57
  misuse of other words for, 56, 117, 335
Singular nouns,
  noun modifiers, 83
  possessive of, 80–82
sit, set, 109–10, 495
site, cite, 201, 304, 487
Slang, 11
  as dictionary label, 294
  in quotation marks, 168
Slanted words, **300–303.** *See also* Connotation.
so, 56, 57
so that, 52
some, 92, 496
somebody, 92
someone, some one, 496
somewheres, 496
sort, 491

Sounds, repetition of, 339
Source materials, **425–32**
　annuals, 431
　card catalogs, **425–28**
　evaluating, 435–36
　periodical indexes, **428–31**
　trade bibliographies, 428
　yearbooks, 431
Spacing, in papers, 379
Spatial order, for paragraph
　development, 366
Speech,
　apostrophes in representing, 185
　vs. written language, 3
　See also Dialog.
Spelling, **196–208**
　common errors in, 199–202
　dictionary as guide to, 289, 291
　overcoming problems with,
　　196–99
　plural forms, 202–203
　possessive forms, 80–82
　principles of, **203–206**
　variant spellings, **206–207**
　words with similar spelling,
　　303–304
Split footnote, 449
Split infinitives, 65
Squinting modifiers, 66
Statement of purpose, 274
Statements, 38
Static writing, 250
Stationery, for letters, 403
stationary, stationery, 201, 496
Statistics,
　taking notes on, 438
　use of figures for, 193
Stilted language, 313–14
Street numbers, 193
Stringy sentences, 331
Style,
　figurative language, 320,
　　321–25
　paragraph development, 365–67
　sentence length, 326–29
　sentence variety, 341–45
　word choice, 297–311
　See also Formal English,
　　Informal English.
Subject of a gerund, 61, 63
Subject of an infinitive, 61
Subject of a sentence, 25, 28, 30
　agreement with verb, 69–77
　complement linked to, 119–20
　compound, 69–71

noun clause as, 53
Subjectless sentences, 39
Subject of a paper, **210–28,**
　423–25
　choosing, 423–25
　finding a subject, 211–23
　keeping a journal, 213
　limiting the subject, 215–16
　literary analysis, **398–402**
　locating a thesis, 218, 220–21
　making abstractions concrete,
　　213–14
　patterns and connections,
　　214–15
　thinking about the subject,
　　216–18
　using resources, 222–23, 234
　and writer and audience,
　　224–28
Subjunctive mood, **115–16**
Subordinate (independent) clauses,
　34, **50–59**
　adjective clauses, **50–51**
　adverb clauses, **51–52**
　and or *but* before, 51
　and comma use, 142–43
　as fragments, 42–43
　as modifiers, 31
　for exact statement, **54–57**
　in comparisons, 130
　noun clauses, 52–54
　restrictive and nonrestrictive,
　　142–43
　See also Subordination.
Subordinating conjunction, 34
Subordination, 32–35, **50–57,**
　346–47
　faulty, 57–59
　for exact statement, 54–57
　inverted, 58–59
　sentence errors corrected by,
　　41–49
　stringy sentences corrected by,
　　331
　tandem, 58
　See also Subordinate clauses.
such as, 42
Summaries, in closing paragraphs,
　279
Summary statement, 279
Superlative degree, 128
Support, for paragraph
　development, 269
supposed to, used to, 496
sure, surely, 496

suspect, suspicion, 117, 496
Suspension hyphens, 183
Syllables,
    accented, 291–92
    as aid in spelling, 198
    for word division, 289–91
    number of and comparison, 127
Synedoche, 323
Synonyms, 295, 304–305
    for paragraph continuity, 368
Syntax, 3. *See also* Sentence
    elements.

Tables and charts, placement of,
    380
Tandem subordination, 58
Tautology, 338–39
Technical words, **315–16**
    abbreviations for, 189
Temporal dialects, 7–8
Temporal writing, 250
Tense, **101–104, 105–13**
    consistent use of, 103–104,
        371–72
    forms of, 103
    in narration, 238
    of irregular verbs, 105–13
    of verbals, 62
Term papers. *See* Research
    papers.
Tests. *See* Essay examination
    answers.
Textual analysis, 401
than, then, 94, 201, 496
that, as relative pronoun, 34,
    42–43, 89
    introducing adjective clauses,
        50–51
    introducing noun clauses, 52, 53
    introducing restrictive clauses,
        142
    reference of, 89
that, as demonstrative adjective,
    120–21
that, clauses, 115
that is, 42
that kind, 496
their, there, 201, 496
themselves, theirselves, 88, 496
then, 36
there, 28
there is, there are, 75
therefore,
    as conjunctive adverb, 36

    as interrupter, 145
    punctuation with, 36, 46
these, those, 120–21
Theses. *See* Dissertations.
Thesis (of a paper), 218, 220–21.
    See also Subject of a paper.
Thesis-sentence outlines, **255–56**
Thesis statements, 218, 220, 244,
    270
they, reference of, 90
this, 87
    as demonstrative adjective, 87
    as demonstrative pronoun,
        120–21
those, 120–21
though, 51
thus, punctuation with, 145
till, until, 497
Time,
    adverbs used to emphasize, 238,
        371–72
    chronological pattern of
        development, 366
    shown by adverb clauses,
        51–52
    shown by tense, 101–102
Time, units of,
    abbreviations of, 188, 190
    capitalization of, 179
    figures or words for, 193
    punctuation of, 158
Title (of a paper), 281, 380
Title (of a written work),
    bibliography form for, 433
    capitalization of, 176–77
    endnote form for, 449–50
    in card catalogs, 426
    italics for, 171
    quotation marks with, 167
Titles (personal),
    abbreviations for, 187
    capitalization of, 177–78
    in business letters, 403
    punctuation of, 149
to, with infinitives, 65
to, too, 201, 497
Topics of papers. *See* Subject of
    a paper.
Topic outlines, **256–58**
Topic sentences, **360–61**
trans., tr., 452
Transition paragraphs, **273–74.**
    See also Continuity.
Transitive verbs, 111
Translations,

bibliography form for, 455
endnote form for, 449
Trite expressions, **319–20**
try and, try to, 117, 497
type, 336
Typed papers, **378–79**. *See also*
  Manuscript form.

Underlining. *See* Italics.
Units of measurement,
  abbreviations for, 189
  agreement with, 72–73
  noun forms designating, 83
unless, 52
Unpublished material, form for
  citing, 452, 455
Upper case. *See* Capitalization.
Usage, 1–22
  appropriate language, 16–21
  dialects, 6–9
  edited American English,
    12–14
  elements of language, 2–4
  idiolects, 5–6
  nonstandard English, 11
  varieties of, 4–14
  See also Diction, Words.
used to could, 497

Verbals and verb phrases, 31, 32,
  60–68
  absolute modifiers, **67–68**
  dangling modifiers, **66–67**
  misrelated modifiers, **65–66**
  using, 61, 63
Verbless sentences, 39
Verbs, 25, 30, **110–17**, 132
  active voice, **113–14**
  agreement with subject, 69–77
  auxiliary, 111
  be, forms of, 27, 107
  forms of, 103, 111
  idioms with, 116
  irregular, **105–13**
  linking, 119–20
  modifiers of, 29, 51–52
  mood of, **115–16**
  objects of, 26–27
  omission of, 39
  passive voice, **113–14**
  principal parts of, 111
  regular, **101–104**
  spelling errors with, 200–201

subjects of, 26–27
subjunctive mood, **115–16**
tenses of, **101–104**
voice of, **113–14**
See also Verbals.
Verse, quoted, 167
Vocabulary, methods for
  increasing, 306–307
Vogue words, 319
Voice, active and passive, 113–14

Wait on, 497
want, want to, want that, 117, 497
was, were, 497
we, I, 98, 497
we, us, 94
well, 120, 490
what, 52
when,
  as exact connective, 55
  introducing adjective clauses,
    50–51
  introducing adverb clauses, 52
  introducing noun clauses, 52
where,
  introducing adjective clauses, 51
  introducing adverb clauses,
    51–52
whether, introducing noun clauses,
    52, 53
which, 34, 42–43, 89
  and or *but* misused before, 51
  introducing adjective clauses,
    50–51
  introducing nonrestrictive
    clauses, 142
  possessive of, 96–97
  reference of, 89
while,
  as exact connective, 55
  introducing adverb clauses, 52
who, 34, 42–43, 89
  and or *but* misused before, 51
  introducing adjective clauses,
    50–51
  introducing nonrestrictive
    clauses, 142
  introducing noun clauses, 52
  possessive of, 96–97
  reference of, 89
who, whom, 95, 497–98
why,
  introducing adjective clauses, 51
  introducing noun clauses, 52

will, shall, 110, 495
Word division, **379–80**
    dictionary as guide for, 289, 291
Word forms, 2–3
Wordiness, **333–34**. *See also*
    Deadwood, Repetition.
Word order, **28–29**
Words, **297–311**
    abstract, **308–11**
    concrete, **308–11**
    connotation, **299–300**
    death masks, **318–19**
    denotation, **298**
    euphemisms, 320–21
    fair words, **300–303**
    figures of speech, **321–25**
    formal, **312–16**
    in context, **297–300**
    in quotation marks, 168
    informal, **316–18**
    learning new, 306–307
    repetition of, 338
    slanted, **300–303**
    trite expressions, **319–20**
    vogue words, 319
    with opposite meanings,
        305–306
    with similar meaning, 304–305
    with similar spelling, 303–304
    See also Diction, Usage.
worse, worst, 127
would, should, 112
would of, 498
Writer,

    attitudes of, 250
    and audience, 225–26
    position of, 224–25
Writing,
    argumentation, **243–49**
    closing paragraphs, **278–80**
    controlling direction, 270–71
    description, **240–43**
    developing material, **268–70**
    exposition, **233–36**
    expressive, 231, 232, 233
    the first draft, **266–84**
    getting started, 267–68
    narration, **236–40**
    occasions for, 229–30
    opening paragraphs, 274–78
    and organization, **252–65**
    other ways to study, 249–50
    persuasion, 232, 233
    referential, 232, 233
    relating paragraphs, **272–74**
    titles, 281
    See also Papers, Subject of a
        paper.

-y, and spelling problems,
    202–203, 205–206
Yearbooks, 431
yet, 138
you, 98–99
your, yours, 88

Zip codes, 404, 405